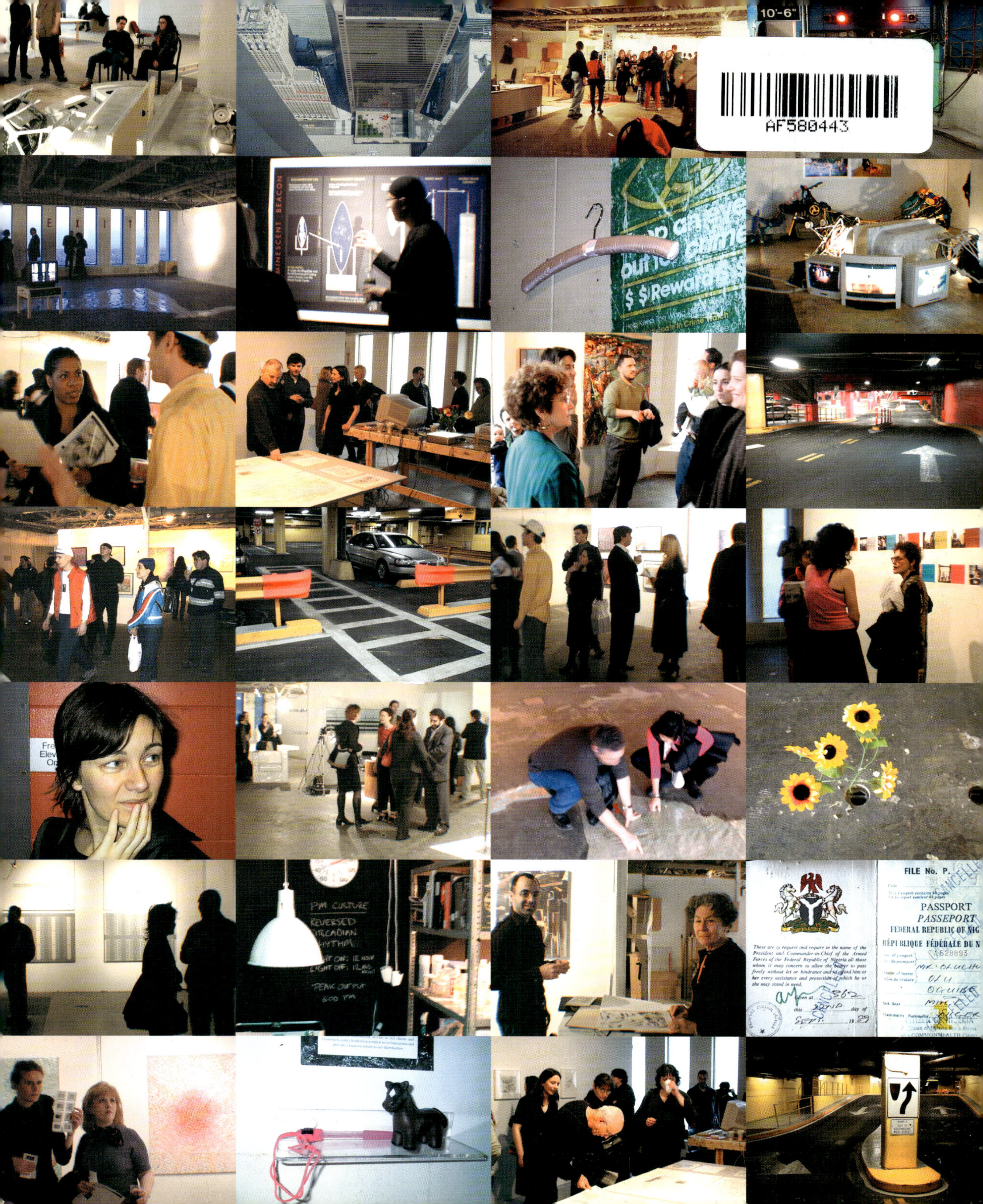
10'-6"
AF580443
$ $Rewards
PM CULTURE
REVERSED
RHYTHM
PEAK OUTPUT
6:00 PM
FILE No. P.
PASSPORT
PASSPORT
FEDERAL REPUBLIC OF NIG
RÉPUBLIQUE FÉDÉRALE DU N

DEDICATED TO

Michael Richards

1963–2001

Site Matters chronicles the celebrated artists residency program in the World Trade Center sponsored by the Lower Manhattan Cultural Council (LMCC). From 1997 to 2001, more than 130 artists worked high above New York City in the upper reaches of Tower One, each responding in a unique way to the spectacular views and potent socio-political context of this landmark site. Brought together here for the first time, these exciting and, now, historic works range widely—from panoramic cityscapes to new-media performance.

The WTC complex was much more than an international center of commerce, and for four years the LMCC artists-in-residence strove to unearth a fuller, more sustained portrait of the towers' inner life. They explored the hallways, elevators, basement and retail spaces, and worked together with tenants and building staff on complex site-specific projects. During the life of the program, these works raised compelling questions about the aesthetic, psychological and political aspects of the World Trade Center. Looking back, and looking forward, they fuel an important dialogue as the Twin Towers' legacy is debated.

Site

Essays by

Erin Donnelly

Moukhtar Kocache

Olu Oguibe

Liz Thompson

Anthony Vidler

Matters

The Lower Manhattan Cultural Council's
World Trade Center Artists Residency, 1997–2001

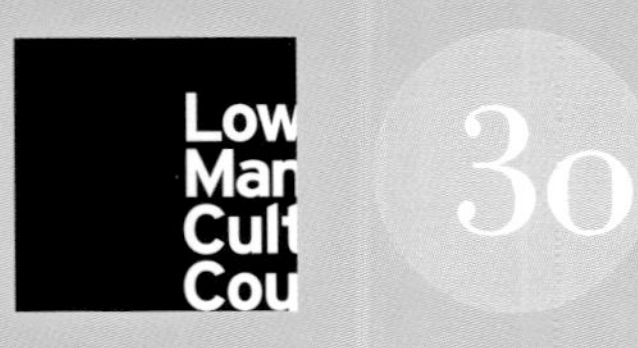

Published on the occasion of LMCC's 30th Anniversary

One Wall Street Court, 2nd Floor
New York, N.Y. 10005
www.lmcc.net

ISBN: 0-9726973-1-4
Library of Congress Control Number: 003116881

Editors: Moukhtar Kocache and Erin Shirreff
Design: Russell Hassell and Dolly Meieran
Printed in China by Oceanic Graphic Printing

Photo Credits
Cover image: Moukhtar Kocache
Pages 2–3: Christian Nguyen
Page 11: Christian Nguyen
Pages 48–49: Moukhtar Kocache
Pages 51, 89, 117, 185, 221, 267: Christian Nguyen
Pages 318–319: Patty Chang, Kelly Hashimoto and Kimberly SaRee Tomes, *Angel Falls,* 1999, Video still

Available through:
D.A.P. Distributed Art Publishers, Inc.
155 Sixth Avenue, 2nd Floor
New York, N.Y. 10013
Tel: 212-627-1999
Fax: 212-627-9484

Contents

LMCC Staff as of June 2004

Tom Healy, *President*
Tricia Mire, *Managing Director*

Wayne Ashley, *Curator of New Media*
Nolini Barretto, *Director of Marketing and Communication*
Lidy Chu, *Director of Development*
Deborah Dewees, *Director of Arts Services*
Erin Donnelly, *Curator of Visual Arts and Residency Program Director*
Kevin Gay, *Database Manager*
Douglas J. Ottomanelli, *Director of Finance and Operations*
Brian Padilla, *Systems Manager*
Narisara Vanichanan, *Associate Director of Community Arts and Planning*
Mark Vevle, *Marketing Manager*

Program Support

The World Trade Center artist residencies, from 1997 to 2001, were supported by the Port Authority of New York and New Jersey, American Express Company, the Jerome Foundation, the Lily Auchincloss Foundation, the Milton and Sally Avery Arts Foundation, the New York Mercantile Exchange Charitable Foundation and, in part, with public funds from the New York City Department of Cultural Affairs. The Nonprofit Finance Fund, the Pollock-Krasner World Trade Center Emergency Grant Program, netomat and many caring individuals from around the world helped artists who were in residence on September 11, 2001, replace materials and create new work.

LMCC is grateful for in-kind support for the World Trade Center artist residencies from Borders Books & Music, Harvestworks Digital Media Center, Philip Morris Companies Inc. (Altria), the School of Visual Arts MFA Computer Arts Department and Film/Video Arts.

The Lower Manhattan Cultural Council thanks our 30th Anniversary Circle Members for bringing us into the next thirty years of supporting artists and the community.

This publications was made possible, in part, through their generous support.

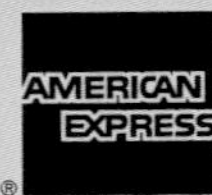

CB Richard Ellis

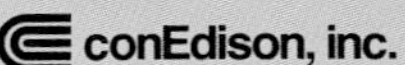

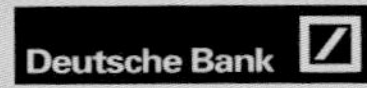

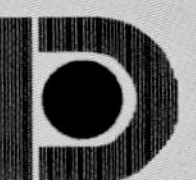

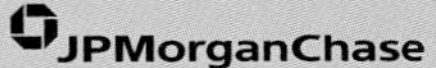

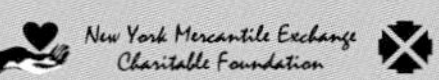

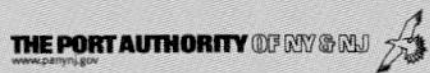

Site Matters was also made possible by grants from the Andy Warhol Foundation for the Visual Arts, the Elizabeth Firestone Graham Foundation and the National Endowment for the Arts.

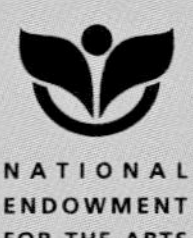

Acknowledgments

The *World Views* residency program blossomed as a labor of love through the dedication and work of an amazing community of people. We would like to acknowledge the following individuals for their contributions.

Cherrie Nanninga, Jenny Dixon, Carl Weisbrod, Lisa Frigand and Carl Scorza provided the original leadership and vision to bring artists into the World Trade Center. Liz Thompson, Moukhtar Kocache and Tricia Mire helped expand and grow support for the program from 1998 to 2001.

The management of the program on a daily basis would have been impossible without the dedicated team at the Port Authority of New York and New Jersey. They helped oversee administrative, legal and security matters, and helped us to better understand the World Trade Center. We give our most sincere thanks and appreciation to Bob Benacchio, Joe Cantelmo, Van Carney, Davella May, John Picone, Alan Reiss, Peggy Reynolds, Nancy Seliga and the many others who gave so generously of their time, and to Bob Lynch, who lost his life on September 11th.

LMCC's team of staff, interns, consultants and volunteers worked tirelessly to provide support to the artists and organize public events and open studios. Special thanks to Kathy Brew and Jen Charron for all they did to shape the program and support the artists. Many thanks to Oceola Bragg, Nicholas Constantakis, Dorothy Désir, Bruce Fagin, Fabiola Karimipour, Reynard Loki, Natasha Masumi, Jessica Mero, Brian Padilla, Sara Reisman, Charles Santos, Shayna Silverstein, Keith Spencer, Narisara Vanichanan and Kenny Wharton.

Countless colleagues in the art world lent their expertise, advice and intellectual support to the program and the artists. Many thanks to Paulo Herkenhoff, Regine Basha, Alun Williams, Willard Boepple, John Haworth, Cindy Gehrig of the Jerome Foundation and all of the jurors: Dan Cameron, Lawrence Chua, Lynn Cooke, Amada Cruz, Kevin Duggan, Tom Finkelpearl, Bruce Ferguson, Zhang Ga, Rachel Gugelberger, Christian Haye, Perry Hoberman, Barbara Hunt, Hitomi Iwasaki, Jennie C. Jones, Karen Jones, Raina Lampkins-Fielder, Rita McBride, Kevin McCoy, Antonio Muntadas, Warren Neidich, Graham Nickson, Carol Parkinson, Paul Pfeiffer, John Pilson, Jenelle Porter, Lorna Simpson, Franklin Sirmans, Carol Stakenas, Sara Tucker and Bruce Wands.

Others have our gratitude for the compassion, generosity and help they provided to the program and the artists in the aftermath of the attacks. Christel Sorin of France Telecom immediately offered LMCC temporary office space for our staff; Maciej Wisniewski of Netomat gave the artists temporary studio space; the New Museum of Contemporary Art staff, especially Dan Cameron, Lisa Phillips and Anne Ellegood, welcomed the Open Studios Exhibition to Soho; Maxwell Anderson and Raina Lampkins-Fielder gave LMCC and the artists an invaluable opportunity to reconnect with friends, loved ones and the arts community at the Whitney Museum of American Art in October 2001; Victoria Noorthoorn provided the artists with a safe place to meet at the Drawing Center; and Lowery Stokes Sims, Thelma Golden, Christine Y. Kim and Sandra D. Jackson of the Studio Museum in Harlem welcomed the arts community into their home for a memorial service for Michael Richards. We are deeply grateful to people in the funding community who reached out on a personal level to provide support to LMCC and the artists and to the many individuals and organizations around the world who sent donations to LMCC and the artists. And many thanks to Karen Kitchen and Debra Simon of the World Financial Center Arts and Events Program, Michael Counts and Michelle Stern of GAle GAtes et al. and Jed Walentas of Two Trees Management for helping us establish transitional residencies in Lower Manhattan and DUMBO, Brooklyn.

This publication would not have been possible without the diligent work of Erin Shirreff, Erin Donnelly, Teri T. Chan, Rebecca Guber, Russell Hassell, Moukhtar Kocache, Tricia Mire and Lidy Chu. Thanks also go to Kathy Brew for her editorial eye in looking over the final texts before going to print.

We dedicate this book to the memory of all those who lost their lives and to those who have suffered as a result of September 11, 2001. We hope that this publication of the *World Views* residency program will serve not only as a *memento mori* of a site that no longer exists, but also as an important historical record of the art that was created within it, and in response to it, on the cusp of a new century, a new millennium. *Arts longa, vita brevis.*

Foreword

Congratulations to the Lower Manhattan Cultural Council, the talented artists whose stellar work is featured in these pages, and all those whose efforts helped realize the publication of *Site Matters.*

The LMCC's artists residency program provided an impressive group with free studio space and career-building opportunities in unoccupied office spaces on the ninety-first and ninety-second floors of World Trade Center Tower One. It is only fitting that this book is dedicated to Michael Richards, the one LMCC artist-in-residence who tragically lost his life with so many others on September 11, 2001. The LMCC artists residency program lost only one of its artists on that terrible day, but the tragedy reverberated throughout each artist's life, just as it affected so many New Yorkers, Americans and people around the world.

A unique partnership between the LMCC, the City of New York and the Port Authority of New York and New Jersey made the LMCC residency program possible. As a result, hundreds of New York City artists, working in all disciplines, came downtown to share their work with countless New Yorkers and visitors. Creating art that was influenced by the site as well as art unrelated to it, the artists-in-residence established a pocket of artistic imagination in the midst of corporate space that allowed for a productive interchange of ideas among the many diverse people who worked in and visited the building.

The LMCC artists residency program continues today in a temporary home. In its innovative collaboration among cultural organizations, local businesses and government agencies, the program is a perfect example of the dynamic creativity that characterizes the best our great City has to offer. Over the past two years, the City and State have worked with the Lower Manhattan Development Corporation to build on the proud cultural legacy that the LMCC established at the World Trade Center. Today, as we continue to rebuild Lower Manhattan, artists and creative venues are central to the plans for the World Trade Center site.

Site Matters honors the thousands of people who were part of the World Trade Center community and whose presence helped inspire the work created there. I thank the LMCC for its ongoing work in creating an environment for the arts and for this book, which symbolizes the enduring spirit of downtown New York and all New Yorkers, past, present and future.

Michael R. Bloomberg
Mayor, City of New York

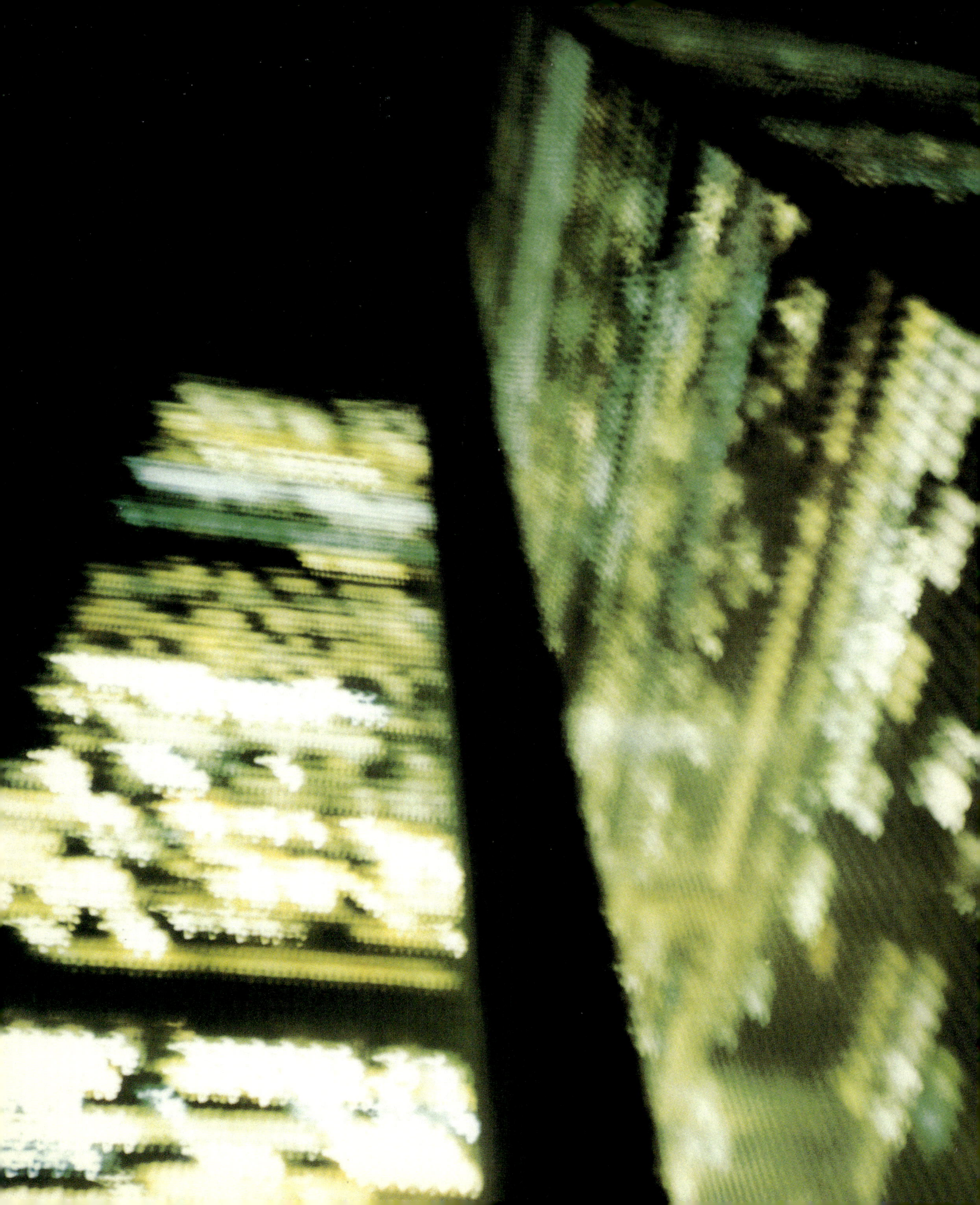

Introduction

"Studio" is the Latin brother of "study." Imagine a quiet, sunlit vault of solitude and contemplation, the artist alone with images and ideas.

But the kissing cousin of "studio" is "atelier," until recently the far more common name for an artist's workspace. Get out the dictionary and you'll find a Latin origin for "atelier" too—but this time from the word for a splinter of wood—evidence of a workshop, a place of sweat and activity, often a room full of people.

Andy Warhol worked in the silver-covered walls of The Factory, a crazy hive of talent, oddity and streams of gossip. A very different artistic animal was the Dutch artist Gerard Dou, equally famous and rich in his time, which was the very time New Amsterdam became New York. People gossiped about Dou because of how softly he stepped into his monk's cell of an alcove. This friend of Rembrandt and Vermeer would tiptoe into his silent studio day after day—in a period of great upheaval in Europe—and sit still for a long time, barely breathing, literally waiting for all the dust to settle before beginning to paint.

The dust has not settled at ground zero. The ground there is not still, because consensus was reached that those who lost their lives on September 11th, 2001, are well honored by rebuilding, keeping faith with the industry of the people who were in the buildings that morning because they had gone to work.

And yet, not enough people know that among the stockbrokers and kitchen workers, security guards and lawyers, consultants and checkout clerks, tourists and everyone else who rode the elevators every day in the World Trade Center, there was another kind of tenant. In one of the world's great commercial centers, there were people who weren't thinking about commerce. They were going to the office space on the upper floors of Tower One tiptoeing or barreling through their dreams and distractions into their studios. They went to work to make the wonderfully useless and necessary things and ideas we call art. One of those artists, Michael Richards, died because he was doing this, doing what he had to do.

This book has been made to record and honor four remarkable years of art that was conceived and created in the studios of Lower Manhattan Cultural Council's artists residency program at the World Trade Center.

LMCC is dedicated to nurturing the creative spirit, providing support, studio space and exhibition and performance opportunities, often in places where you would least expect them. After 9/11, LMCC went homeless for a time, and we lost much of our recorded past. It is a tribute to the resourcefulness and hard work of LMCC's residency artists and staff that such a beautiful book was even possible. We hope it inspires you.

May the dust never settle downtown—because artists will be kicking up a storm!

Tom Healy
President, LMCC

The Lower Manhattan Cultural Council was formed in 1973 by business, cultural and civic leaders with the simple mission of improving the quality of life in the Financial District of New York City. Now, thirty years later, LMCC continues to bring local, national and international artists downtown and has evolved to support hundreds of local artists throughout the diverse communities of New York City.

LMCC has played a significant role in reshaping the exchange among the artists, businesses and residents of Lower Manhattan through its unorthodox cultural programming. From small-scale street performances to fully staged presentations of internationally recognized artists and dance companies, from temporary site-specific art exhibitions to permanent public sculpture, our programs run from the traditional to the avant-garde. Our enduring aim is to reach out to workers, residents and visitors with free public events, while creating opportunities for emerging and established artists to produce and exhibit new work.

LMCC's offices were located in the World Trade Center, and many of our programs occurred in the complex's buildings and plazas. We were, and remain, an arts organization with fertile relationships with civic agencies, law firms and banks. In fact, a strong and fruitful partnership with the Port Authority of New York and New Jersey helped us realize many of our most successful programs, including Evening Stars, the popular performing arts series that brought world-class dancers and musicians to the World Trade Center plaza; the *Festival of Creative Communities,* which celebrated emerging performers from throughout the boroughs; and, of course, *World Views,* the World Trade Center artists residencies.

Published on the occasion of LMCC's thirtieth anniversary, *Site Matters* chronicles a unique moment in the history of LMCC and concretely demonstrates our organization's guiding principles. From 1997 to 2001, the Port Authority made it possible for LMCC to bring more than 130 artists from around the world into temporarily vacant office spaces. The exciting, diverse and now historically significant works that emerged from this unusual studio environment—a small fraction of which are illustrated here—stand as testimony to the influence of these iconic buildings on the hearts, minds and imaginations of everyone who worked there.

LMCC continues to initiate innovative projects that address artists' complex needs for funds, audience development and workspace, and that activate cultural spaces within our communities. By embracing the changing forces in our city and the art world, we will continue to invent new ways of contributing to the cultural life of New York.

Liz Thompson
Executive Director, 1997–2003

Up in the Air

Moukhtar Kocache

Ritual

Imagine yourself arriving via subterranean transportation. The muffled loudspeakers announce the destination, doors open, you step over the gap and land on a platform. Crowds hurry past in all directions. You navigate a maze of tunnels, stairs, corridors and escalators, skeptical as to whether you are heading in the right direction. Soon you emerge into a vast environment that looks like a transportation terminal but feels like a mall: the artificial lighting, dizzying array of signage and the hard floors and walls make the space feel strangely and utterly insulated, protected from the natural elements.

It is morning rush hour. An overwhelming hum reverberates throughout the passageways; the clamor of thousands of hurried footsteps, distinctly herdlike. You need to move quickly or you will literally be swept away. As you navigate the shop-lined space, littered with vendors and services, you notice more ephemeral elements: someone's perfume, a haunting glance, the Muzak that blasts throughout the space, the homey smell of coffee and cinnamon. The sensations are visceral, inescapable and all-encompassing. You head toward Tower One. The mirrored architecture that leads to each tower makes the journey confusing, even for a longtime adept. Ahead, the bank of revolving doors squeak rhythmically. You feel the strong draft as it hollers past their airtight openings, sunlight bouncing off glass and metal as you swiftly enter, and find yourself ejected into a massive lobby. The ambiance is retro, dreamlike. The low, suspended ceiling gives way to a disproportionately gigantic space, carrying your gaze toward a balcony above. The building begins to emerge. Flags representing the nations of the world hang from a mezzanine into the lobby. Utopian internationalism. We are the world.

So far your journey has been horizontal, but you are only halfway there. The lobby is bustling with people, but a sense of authoritarian order permeates the space. Electronic bells repeatedly signal the arrival and departure of elevators. Perfunctory security procedures ensue: wait in line at the desk for a pass or head straight to the elevator banks and use your WTC ID card. An elevator arrives. You and a group of strangers pack in and begin your vertical ascent. The initial acceleration triggers nausea; the pull continues, strong and determined. The chamber rattles and shakes, and you hear the sound of wind again. Before you know it, the elevator has

Sign in World Trade Center concourse
Photo: Christian Nguyen

WELCOME TO THE
WORLD TRADE CENTER

Tower One lobby
Photo: Christian Nguyen

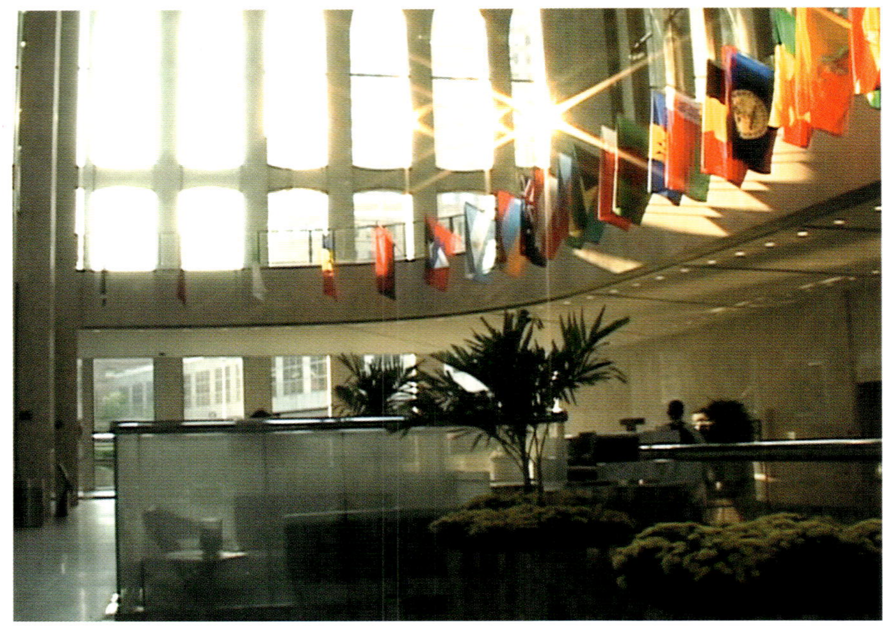

slowed down, regaining a sense of gravity. Doors open and you crowd into the Sky Lobby, a transitional area on the seventy-eighth floor with another set of elevator banks that will deliver each of you to your final destination.

A cacophony of electronic rings fills the space. You press the button; its groove resembles the arch of the building's windows. You wait. The lobby is flanked by a row of windows, benches and circular metal planters with colorful flowers. It is sunny and the Sky Lobby is so drenched with light that you have difficulty opening your eyes. But it is a short ride. When the doors open you are in a typical office building: long, narrow, carpeted hallways; drop ceilings with fluorescent lights. Doors lead to unexpectedly open spaces divided into cubicles. Windows surround the room on all sides—the only separation from sky, air and clouds. You get as close as you can to the pane and with trepidation take in the astounding panorama—the landscape beyond and the metropolis that lies beneath. Welcome to the World Trade Center.

Profile

From the beginning the World Trade Center was laden with controversy and politics. The seeds for its construction were planted in the postwar era of the late 1940s, when the victorious country began to prepare for unprecedented economic growth. In 1946, the New York Legislature created a World Trade Corporation to explore the viability of a trade center in Manhattan. In the mid 1950s, David Rockefeller created the Downtown–Lower Manhattan Association, which subsequently hired the firm Skidmore, Owings & Merrill to develop a plan for a new Lower Manhattan. Heavily involved in the development of Rockefeller Center, the United Nations and Lincoln Center, Rockefeller became increasingly intrigued with the idea of a world trade center. Along with his brother, Nelson, who was then governor of New York, Rockefeller began discussions with the CEO of the Port Authority who, in 1961, issued a proposal for a complex of buildings and facilities, initially conceived for the East River shore. Following government consolidations, state amendments and federal interventions with respect to transportation and bureaucracy between New York and New Jersey, the project was reenvisaged for the West Side and the Hudson River. Heralded by Austin Tobin, the Port Authority director, the initiative picked up steam, and in 1964, Seattle-born architect Minoru Yamasaki unveiled construction plans for the Twin Towers, estimated then at $525 million. Despite severe opposition by city planners, business owners, community groups and politicians, on March 25, 1966, demolition began, displacing, among many others, Radio Row, twenty six buildings that housed a concentration of electronics shops.[1] Two quintessential New York populations, small businesses and immigrants, were displaced as merchants and store owners had to relocate or go out of business, and immigrants from the eastern Mediterranean (who had made their home on Manhattan's Lower West Side, or Little Syria, since the late 1800s) were moved to Brooklyn and New Jersey to give way to the "new" city.

Groundbreaking for construction of this highly controversial and politicized project began in August 1966, with steel construction starting two years later. In late 1970, tenants moved into the northern tower, Tower One, and in January 1972, Tower Two. The official ribbon-cutting ceremony was held on April 4, 1973, while the complex and towers were still under construction. When completed the buildings, each at 110 stories, stood at 1353 feet (412 meters) tall. They contained ten million square feet of office space to be occupied by fifty thousand people. Each floor enclosed almost an acre of column-free space. Using a unique engineering technique, in which the supporting structure was also the skeleton of the building, the custom-made steel grid of the building contained windows that were designed to be the shoulder width of an average human, thus limiting the sensation of vertigo. The site was sixteen acres, with buildings grouped around a five-acre central plaza.

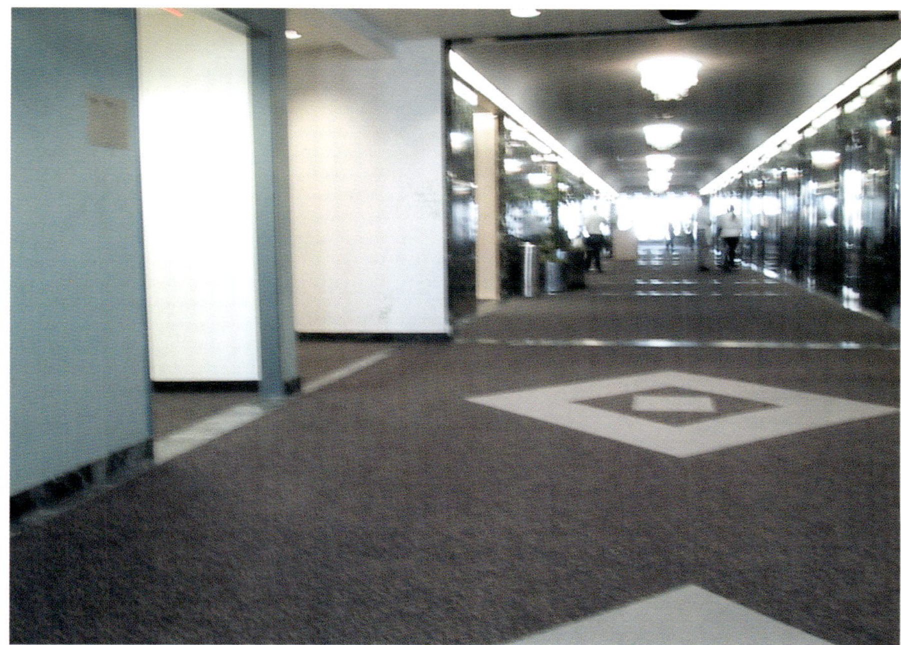

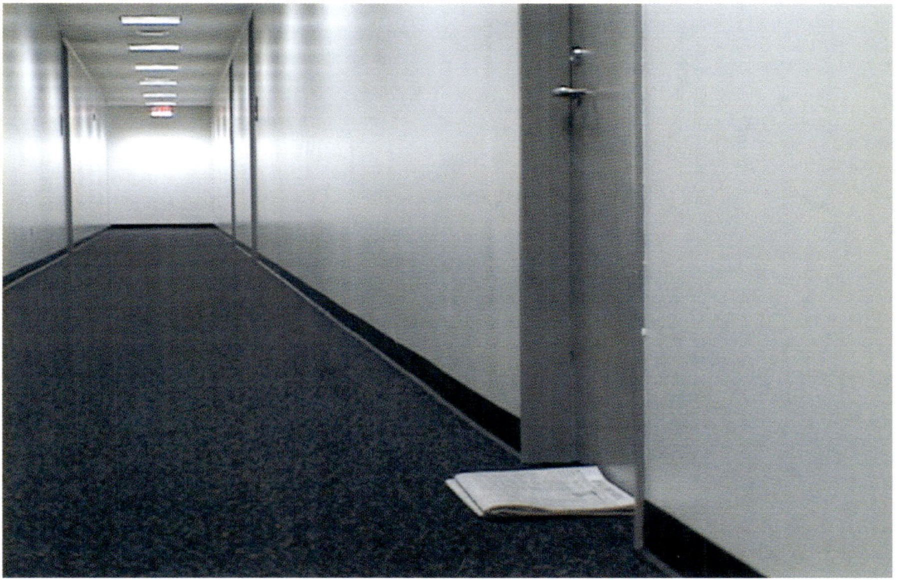

Tower One Sky Lobby
Photo: Jeff Konigsberg

Corridors, Tower One, 91st Floor
Photo: Christian Nguyen

Tower One Sky Lobby
Photo: Jeff Konigsberg

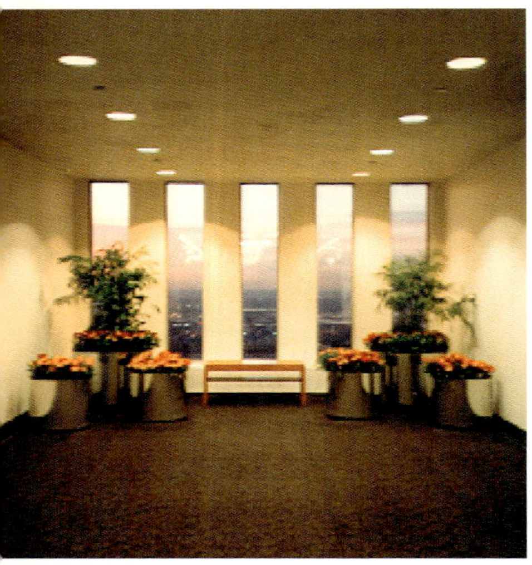

Each tower contained two Sky Lobbies, which were served by high-speed elevators on the forty-fourth and seventy-eighth floors. The center included seven underground levels filled with equipment, machinery, storage, parking and other facilities, and housed governmental services, shopping, subway stations and a PATH train station. Tower One accommodated the restaurant, Windows on the World, on its 107th floor and in Tower Two, on the same floor, was the observation deck, which, with guided audio tours, simulation rides and concessions, served as a major tourist destination.

Over the years, the World Trade Center struggled for financial viability. Many of its spaces remained vacant, and shoppers and city dwellers found its concourse level unattractive. Slowly the neighborhood began to change as more financial institutions moved to Lower Manhattan and services for workers and commuters began to be available. In the late 1980s, the neighborhood's residential population began to mushroom. And with the completion of the World Financial Center and Battery Park City on Manhattan's West Side, many conversions of office buildings into condos in the district's canyons, and the gentrification of Tribeca, a dynamic, culturally and economically well-rounded neighborhood began to emerge.

The World Trade Center underwent several facelifts. In the 1990s, a major effort was made to render its spaces and functions more corporate, and to turn its lazy terminal-like concourse into a first-class shopping mall. Occupancy rates at the towers, aside from normal global market fluctuations, increased and the Center entered a prosperous phase. Owned and operated by the Port Authority of New York and New Jersey, the towers were leased in the spring of 2001 to Real Estate developer Larry Silverstein. At that time a new future appeared to be destined for both the World Trade Center and the neighborhood.

Studios in the Sky

The *World Views* program was launched by the Lower Manhattan Cultural Council (LMCC) in partnership with the Port Authority of New York and New Jersey as a temporary project in 1997. Following the vision of artist Carl Scorza, who was seeking a window pitched high above New York to paint the city below, Jenny Dixon, then LMCC's executive director and Cherrie Nanninga, head of real estate at the Port Authority, asked the dean of the New York Studio School, Graham Nixon, to invite "perceptual" painters to work with some of the most inspiring views in the city. The artists were provided unrestricted access to temporarily vacant, raw space in both towers and at various elevations, on the 24th, 36th, 48th, 81st and 91st floors.

In the summer of 1998, I joined LMCC and along with Liz Thompson, LMCC's new director, and my colleague, Tricia Mire, and others in the field, began to imagine this project in a new light. Amazed and baffled by the site and its many unique sociopolitical layers, we recognized that it would be a fertile environment for artists wanting to pursue issues related to institutional critique, architecture, modernity, supermodernity, globalization, urbanism and popular culture. In November 1998, the residency program welcomed a group of emerging and mid-career artists with diverse backgrounds

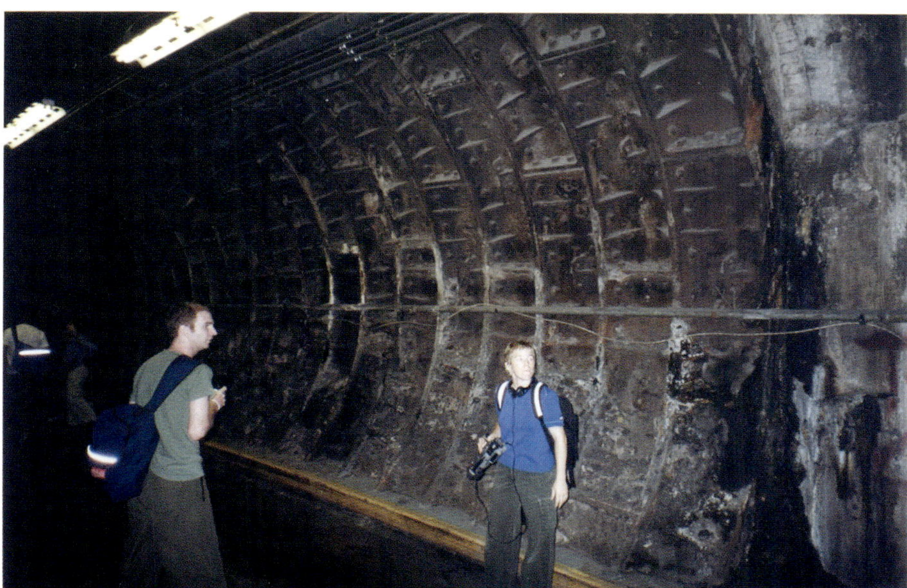

Basement tour, through an old subway tunnel
Photo: Yigal Nizri

and interests, working in a variety of media. In addition to perception and the views, the program's emphasis had now evolved to encompass the artists' experience of the environment and the aesthetic dynamics created by the site. The program was conceived as an artists colony: participants shared communal raw space with limited dividing walls on the ninety-first floor of Tower One and were allowed access to different spaces throughout the building for special projects. Isolation, contemplation, dialogue, exchange and collaboration were encouraged. In the summer of 1999, with the assistance of Kathy Brew (who at the time was director of Thundergulch, LMCC's new-media arts initiative), the residency expanded once again to include artists working with new media and technology.

Applicants from around the world described projects they wanted to pursue at the World Trade Center, and a jury of art professionals, critics, artists and curators selected approximately fifteen artists for each six-month cycle. Selection was based on the quality of the work, the actual proposals and the applicant's need for this opportunity. Occasionally artists were invited individually to pursue special projects. Artists were given access to the building and studios twenty-four hours a day, seven days a week. LMCC provided artists with curatorial and technical support, and eventually garnered funding from the Jerome Foundation, which provided a stipend to each jury-selected artist to help with materials and supplies. Beyond the much needed studio space, artists had the opportunity to interact with peers, build a community and create new work in a truly extraordinary setting. Visits by critics, curators, art professionals and students were organized to create a dynamic space of exchange, learning and exposure. At the end of each cycle the studios were opened to the public, and thousands of visitors were able to experience the eccentric, alternative and daring qualities that characterized both the program and the city in which it was based.

This residency offered artists the rare opportunity to experience the intense rhythm and environment of the Financial District and to produce work in situ in one of the world's most renowned landmarks; it also offered corporate employees the chance for informal, spontaneous exchange with cultural producers and

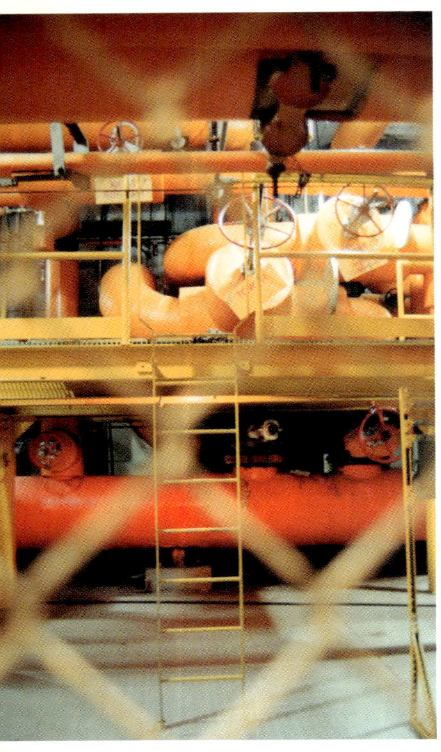

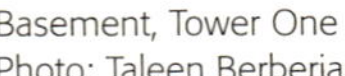

Basement, Tower One
Photo: Taleen Berberian

insight into their creative process. The artists slowly became part of the fabric of the complex, as the Port Authority took pride in the program and the Trade Center's staff, fascinated with the artists' presence and their projects, facilitated their needs and satisfied their curiosity. The late Bob Lynch, a property manager who perished in the attacks, took special interest in the program and was the first person to purchase a work from a resident artist. He volunteered to lead the popular basement tours that became a staple of the residency. Every cycle, artists, equipped with their cameras, were led through the depths of the complex to visit equipment rooms, abandoned spaces and secret passageways. The Port Authority used some artists' work for postcards and posters, and helped produce a mini retrospective exhibition in November of 1999 in the Tower One mezzanine. There was a kind of mutually beneficial exchange between LMCC and the Port Authority.

At the end of each cycle, an average of two thousand people made their way to the World Trade Center and up into the towers to meet the artists and see their work. These Open Studio events brought cultural producers, critics, collectors, writers and a variety of influential and esteemed individuals to a site they would most likely not have explored otherwise. LMCC partnered with the New Museum of Contemporary Art, the Whitney Museum of American Art, the Museum of Modern Art, the Guggenheim Museum, Americans for the Arts and others to expand audiences and help weave this work space program into the city's cultural fabric. In promoting the Twin Towers as a contemporary space that was worth experiencing for its cultural relevance as well as for its real estate and business significance, the program invariably helped thousands revisit, recontextualize and reconsider the World Trade Center. For instance, the number of applicants to the program grew exponentially from approximately sixty in the first cycle to almost nine hundred for the cycle that would have begun in the fall of 2001. Each one of these applicants, who in many instances hailed from across the country or abroad, had in some way researched the towers for their project proposal, which provided tremendous insight into the impact of the Twin Towers and a global perception of the complex. As a site that was loaded with symbolism and metaphorical meaning, the World Trade Center offered an unparalleled vantage point from which artists and others examined and reflected on our ever-expanding and rapidly changing global landscape.

Lab

We have traditionally come to think of site-specific art as an artist's intervention in a particular locale in the landscape (Robert Smithson), the public realm (Richard Serra) and, to a lesser extent, the gallery (Mel Bochner). Recent discussions about site-specific art acknowledge the ongoing permutations of the term and the practice. Context has become a central concern in investigating a site and its specificities. Not all of the artists who participated in the program created work that dealt with the World Trade Center site; many took the diverse opportunities that the program provided to delve deeper into their work, which was often identity-based and personal. A few produced works that were site-specific in the original sense of the term, where the

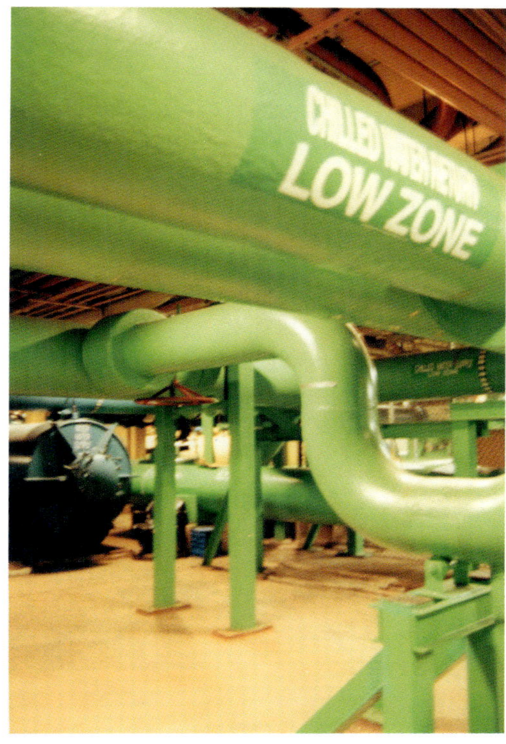

Basement, Tower One
Photo: Taleen Berberian

works were place-bound and so to move them was to destroy them; but most artists experimented with the context that the World Trade Center provided, where the site and the setting became both subject and stimulus.

Using a variety of means and media, the majority of artists engaged with the location, exploring and extracting its formal characteristics, its sociopolitical relations, its layered historic narratives, as well as the activities pursued within it. Drawn from a common site their individual interpretations help to reposition our notion of place and demonstrate the emergence of a variety of artistic and theoretical concepts, including site-determined, site-oriented, site-conscious, site-responsive and site-related.[2] It is interesting to think of the works produced by the artists during their residency period (and in some instances, years later) with material and documentation accumulated during their time at the World Trade Center as a collection of experiments that help inform and add to the ongoing debate of context and location-based artistic practice, which can allow us to reflect on the fundamentals and problematics of site-specific art.

In order to deepen one's understanding of a place, one needs to study not only the immediate site, but also the space in which the site is located and how this rapport informs the internal relationships within it. To know the World Trade Center from the inside was one thing, but it was another to look at the world from its windows and see how it related to the rest of New York City. Most people experienced the Twin Towers as structures that dominated the skyline, and in most instances, they were critiqued as architectural objects and cultural icons. Three distinct conceptual areas or frameworks have emerged from my thinking about this place and the works produced within it: supermodernity, vision and the iconographic. Together these three notions provide a broad matrix to understand the research that the artists undertook while in residence and to read the works reproduced in this publication. Meanings begin to emerge from the confluence of the physical specificity of the site, the world that it inhabits and the collective perceptions of it.

Supermodernity: The Internal

In contrast to its iconic presence in the landscape, the internal public spaces of the World Trade Center were not special or unique. Apart from their own peculiarities and specificities, they ultimately resembled spaces in which we spend an excessive amount of time: generic, soulless, transient spaces for commuting, communication, consumption and commerce that have increasingly come

Basement tour
Photo: Yigal Nizri

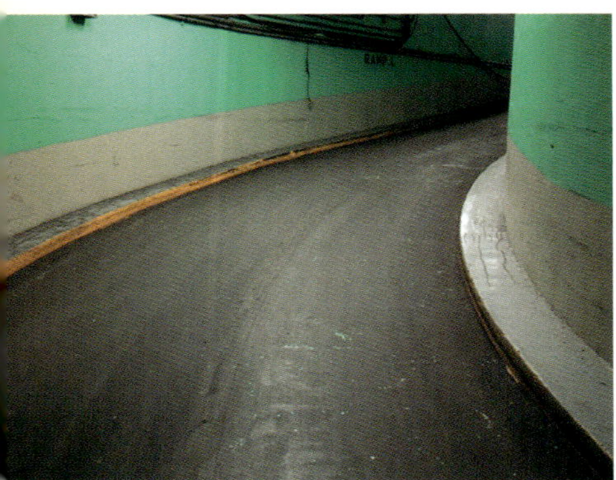

to represent late capitalism. In *Non-Places: Introduction to an Anthropology of Supermodernity*, Marc Augé defines such spaces as emblematic of supermodernity—a contemporary condition of general excess and acceleration with an overabundance of events, space and time.[3] If anthropologists have defined "place" as a space where there is a strong and cumulative relationship among culture, society and the individual, they have more recently begun to refer to a space that cannot be primarily defined in those terms as a "non-place." Walter Benjamin and Charles Baudelaire define "place" as a site that integrates old and new, and allows the modern *flâneur* to map an individual relationship to it. On the other hand, as contemporary authors such as J.G. Ballard and Don DeLillo note, in the new reality of human existence as described through the "non-place" of supermodernity, identity and history are only marginally significant; experience is likely to be commodified and mediated, with individuals connecting in a uniform and bureaucratic manner. What are the conditions created and contained within airports, rest areas, supermarkets, malls, hotels and office buildings? Do these sites warrant critical attention? How do individuals relate to them, and how do their reactions differ?

Any quick survey of global contemporary cultural production reveals that supermodernity and its non-places have been at the center of many artists' practice and analyses. A considerable number of artists in the program seemed to plug in to certain types of anxiety and alienation generated by these spaces. In one of Patty Chang's videos, we see a female office worker walking in a hallway. Suddenly the ground gives way under her feet and becomes liquid. She falls to the floor and struggles to get up as she is enveloped by the gray carpet. Wendy Chisholm cartoonishly depicts the experience of another worker, presumably gone mad, who runs through several walls and right out the building, leaving behind traces of her empty silhouette. In another video Patrick Meagher portrays a businessman destroying equipment and an office space in what appears to be a post dot-com act of vengeance. In Susan Kelly's performance, filmed primarily in a WTC staircase, a group of office workers walk from the ground floor to the ninety-first floor, completing ritualistic tasks as they struggle to make it through "the system." In a video by Christian Nguyen a worker's morning commute to his office space is depicted as a spiritual journey that transforms many of the building and corporate culture elements into sacred symbols. Edin Veléz's candidly beautiful video portraits of exhausted commuters riding escalators down to the subway record myriad individuals drifting in and out of their own reality. In his videotaped performances Torsten Zenas Burns hauntingly depicts zombie-like characters, workers that appear to be tortured and stuck within the confines of the office tower. Similarly, in *Five-Minute Break*, Kristin Lucas's video-game character appears to be lost and stranded in the basement of the building, unable to get to the next stage of the game. Another of her projects invited guests on nighttime tours in search of ghosts that may have lingered in the towers.

Many artists worked at uncovering what lay beneath the surface; the hidden histories, political realities and human conditions of the space. Caroline Birks, for instance, created an installation in which the visitor, caught between a drop ceiling and carpeting—the quintessential surfaces of office space—listens to a children's story about the 1993 bombing of the World Trade Center. The cold and quasi-official narrative emphasized the ideological implications of the script, while the hidden speakers underscored the burial of history in these non-places. Mary Jane Dean's suspension of a tiny plastic jet bomber in the WTC lobby, camouflaged among Christmas decorations, pointed to the interrelationship between the corporate and military industries. In her *Power Point* presentations Kelly Hashimoto played with the

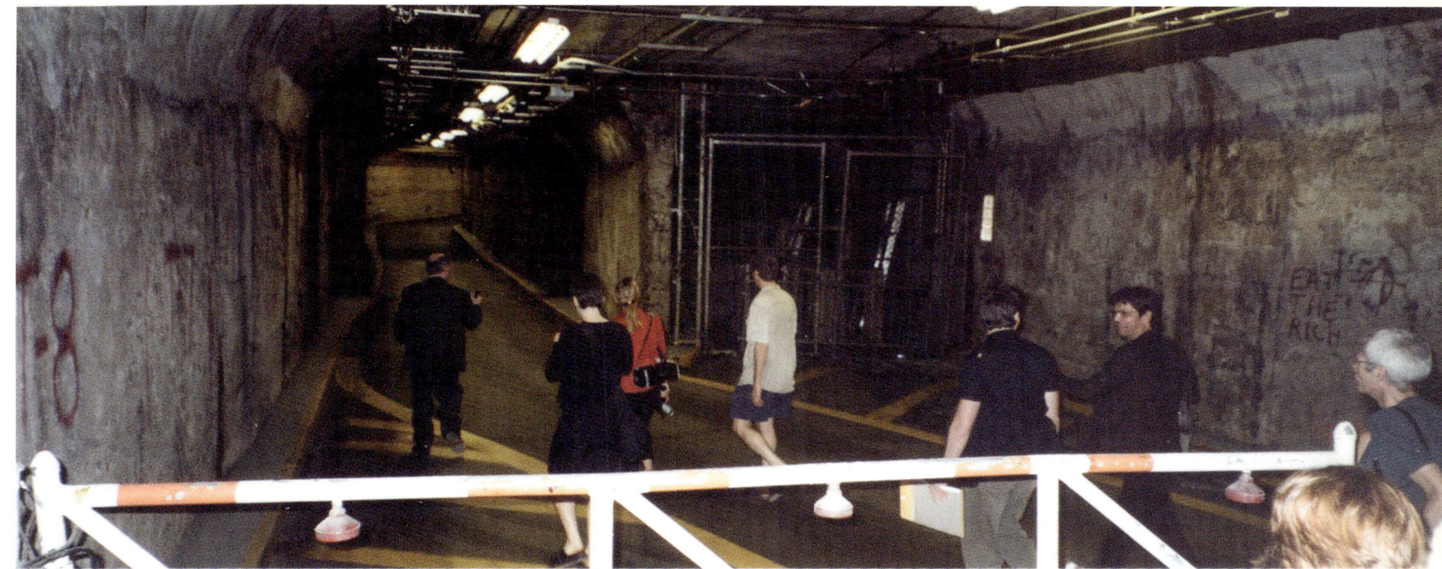

Basement tour
Photo: Yigal Nizri

hidden power dynamics and sexually laden dimensions of the workplace. Emily Jacir's installation, which documented and tracked the trajectory of an item she purchased in the Center's shopping mall, unraveled the effects of world trade and consumerism on human labor and the environment. In *Momento Mori* Paul Pfeiffer recorded his reaction to an event he witnessed on the WTC plaza: a performance by the Boys' Choir of Harlem, "displayed" at the Trade Center and sponsored, ironically, by a chocolate company. Nadine Robinson, intrigued by the changing program of Muzak played in elevators throughout the day, developed a project that explored the relationship of music to productivity and assigned each tenant in the building a traditional African-American work song.

Augé states that the contradiction and accelerated transformations of the contemporary world represented through supermodernity "offer a magnificent field for observation and, in the full sense of the term, an object of anthropological research."[4] Many of the artists in the program took on the roles of field researchers, social surveyors and investigators. However, the artists' experiences of the World Trade Center were not transient; they were not simply passing through. They inhabited the space for an extended period of time and gained access to its many layers, which in turn allowed the place's contradictions to challenge the artists' assumptions. It is obvious that the artists did not pursue authentic and exhaustive anthropological research but rather presented interpretative generalizations and subjective contributions about this place and its conditions.

Many of the artworks completed at the residency explored the social and psychological implications of the architecture. Rackstraw Downes' paintings of vacant, raw office floors attempt to record these spaces' own sense of existence, their own resonance and psychological weight. In her photographs of recently vacated office spaces, Martina Gecelli captures the wrecked state in which these spaces are left behind in this seemingly clean and ordered environment. One of Jennifer and Kevin McCoy's videos, *Airworld Probe*, simulates the entry of a human-guided robot into the vacant space of a trading floor, suggesting a scene of a crime or a scientific mission. In one of their mock advertising banners critiquing the virtual language of

Basement memorial
Photo: Douglas Ross

scientific, pharmaceutical and business ventures, the text simply states, "Welcome. We Are Air." Carola Dertnig attempted to pass through a revolving door with a loaded hand truck at lunchtime and recorded on video the way people reacted to her struggles. In one of her works Sally Gutiérrez interviewed a range of individuals and asked them to talk to her about the views they saw from both their work spaces and from the windows of their homes, charting an array of personal responses and information. And in one of his sound works Stephen Vitiello recorded the creaking and swaying of the building during a hurricane, which surprisingly captured the structure's shiplike feeling and fragility.

It is important to note that the spaces of supermodernity, these non-places, are not entirely or irrevocably alienating. There is much to be said about the human spirit and individuals' abilities to personalize their experiences and mark their differences in a seemingly oppressive and controlling system. Although forms of resistance were active throughout the seamless and finished areas of the buildings, they were mostly visible in its hidden and non-public spaces: the staircases where employees smoked, the freight elevators where smells and detritus were found, the loading docks where a docker's sharp tongue ruled, the walls of the basement levels where graffiti ranged from the base (sexual drawings) and the benign (a calculus assignment) to the personal (love declarations) and the political ("this is hell" and "eat the rich"). It is often in such spaces that organic culture is present and meaning is released. Employees in the basement built their own private memorial in honor of their friends who perished in the 1993 bombing. This construction was testimony to the natural possibilities that lie beneath the surface of non-places and the kind of rich human resistance that is possible to counter the flattening effects of supermodernity.

Stephan Apicella-Hitchcock's photo

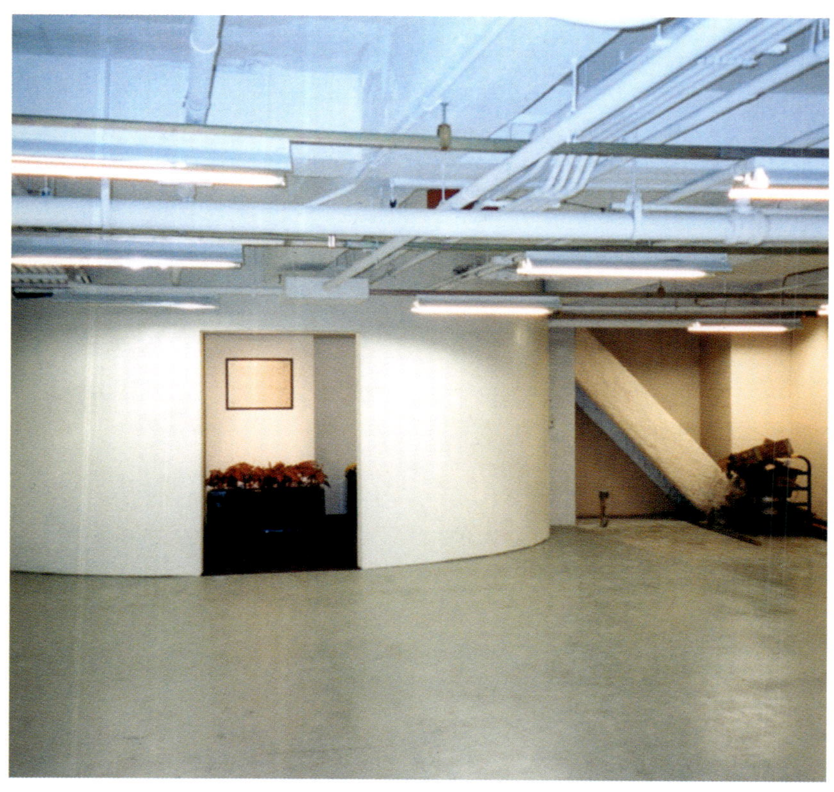

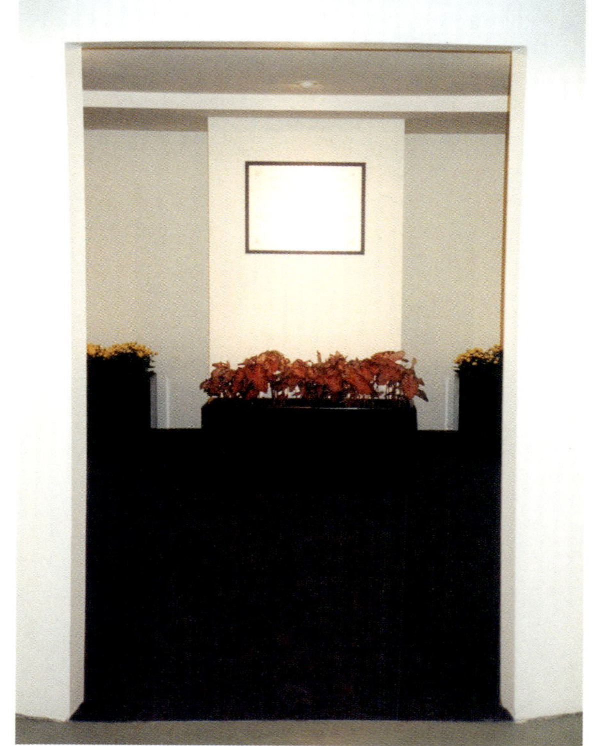

collages of audiotapes collected from his friends seem to suggest that despite their formal and orderly classification, these towering shapes contain a wealth of personal choices and layered identities. In his two-channel video installation, *Above The Grid*, John Pilson conveys the playful spirit of two middle-aged businessmen and their intimate relationship as we witness them walking through the building's hallways, elevators and bathrooms singing doo-wop tunes and playing ball. In his tiny sculpture Taketo Shimada illustrates a scenario in which two strangers meet and fall in love while riding the escalators in opposite directions.

Vision: The External

Representations of the aerial landscape in Western painting began to flourish with the Flemish masters of the fifteenth century. And it was in the late nineteenth century that Nadar took photographs of the Parisian landscape from a hot-air balloon: panoramic views observed from outside and above, the land surveyed from aloft as if by a powerful, omniscient viewer. A critical eye quickly reveals that landscape imagery does not simply denote nature's topography, but also represents how geography is shaped socially and culturally by human activity, as well as by the ideology inherent in the act of viewing. The process of observing a location from above allows us to more clearly study the dynamic between nature and culture and, in the process, foregrounds our individual methods of perception, cognition and evaluation. John Constable, the great landscape painter, said, "We see nothing until we truly understand it." In the act of looking, there is a convergence of the physical specificity of a place, the culture at large and individual perception. In other words we do not simply record landscapes; we interpret and envision them as a reflection of our own state of mind. The distance inherent in observing a landscape from above induces a kind of melancholy. It was

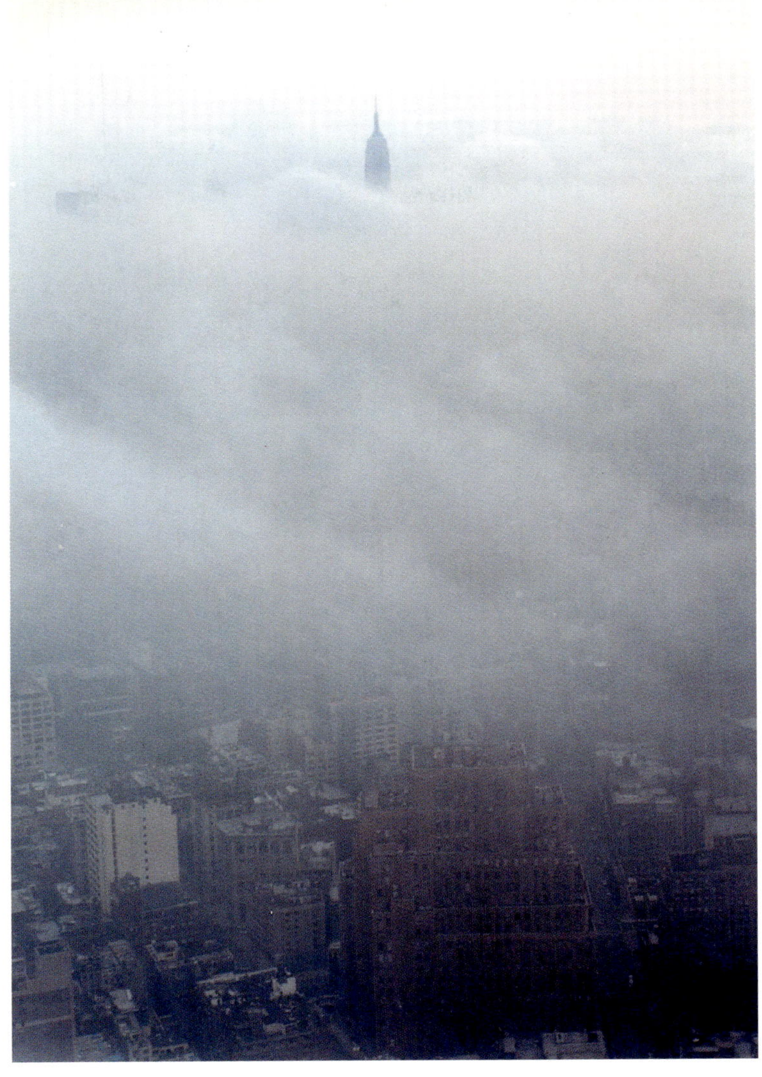

Empire State Building in fog
Photo: James Sheehan

common for the artists-in-residence to endlessly stare out the WTC windows, not unlike the solitary figures in Caspar David Friedrich's paintings, turned away and staring endlessly at the landscape beyond, as if on a spiritual mission to make sense of the world and their existence. From the towers the act of looking became a gesture in itself and produced a very modern form of solitude.

In the paintings and drawings of Olive Ayhens and Raoul Middleman, entirely fantastical worlds emerge from daydream interpretations of the city below. Their internal natures and energy are revealed in the compositions and brush strokes. For Jaime Davidovich, it is the scale of objects and icons like the Brooklyn Bridge that are lyrically reappropriated and push the medium of video further. In the work of painters Joellyn Duesberry, Jacqueline Gourevitch, Yvonne Jacquette, Daniel Kohn and Peter Ruta, the science of looking emerges in a variety of manners and techniques. Shapes and structures are isolated in the landscape, lines and horizons are explored, and color and reflections are redefined to liquid or blocky effect.

Some artists produced meditative projects, personal notions of how landscape has an ability to connect us with our core. Christian Nguyen, finding similarities in the building's window structures and the vertical panels of traditional Asian painting, produced an installation that recreated the fundamentals of a spiritual tradition. Tim Hailand's photographs of words spelled out on the windows allow the lonely onlooker to enter into a somewhat nostalgic dialogue with the city, where words suggest an exchange and a sense of personal reckoning in the metropolis. Italian artist Sandrine Nicoletta documented the changing landscape of New York and created unusual, almost alienlike, objects to represent each month of her stay in the city and its psychological effects on her.

The dominant form of perception in a city is visual. It is by looking that we attempt to contend with the built environment. While it is true one cannot intimately experience a city without being in it—navigating it horizontally and being immersed in its civic and cultural matter—the perspective from above provides us with the critical opportunity to unravel our collective and cumulative ideologies, traditions, plans and visions. Imagined logics and absurd systems of urban planning are delineated in the works of Marsha Cottrell, Hoon Kim, Mick O'Shea and Geraldine Lau. Adam Henry, Ron Milewicz and James Sheehan explored the political dimensions of architecture and cities, while relating their work to the history of painting and theories of sight.

It is hard to imagine that the views provided by the skyscrapers did not eventually become part of their function. Aside from the traditional association of height to spiritual achievement, there is a connection between the information and knowledge that such heights imply—an authority of the view seems to emerge. The gaze has often been associated with power; not just the power to control one's surroundings and the destiny of others, but also the power to have a sense of one's domain and its limitations. However, in New York, "to look down is not always to look down on."[5] Rather, it is a more intrinsic and collective experience of belonging to, and participating in, the metropolis. In *Delirious New York* Rem Koolhaas finds a direct correlation between New Yorkers' geographical self-consciousness and the intense culture of congestion, and the creative energy and megalomaniacal goals of its citizenry.[6] He attributes this dynamic to a constant desire for spectacle, not only from inside the skyscraper looking *out,* but also from outside looking *at*.

Indeed, no other city in the world has been "looked at" and reimaged more than New York. The mythic New York—Gotham, as it has been constructed in films and popular culture—adds an irrefutable ideological dimension to the city whenever one attempts to come to grips with New York's skyline and its identity as a metropolis.[7] Matthew

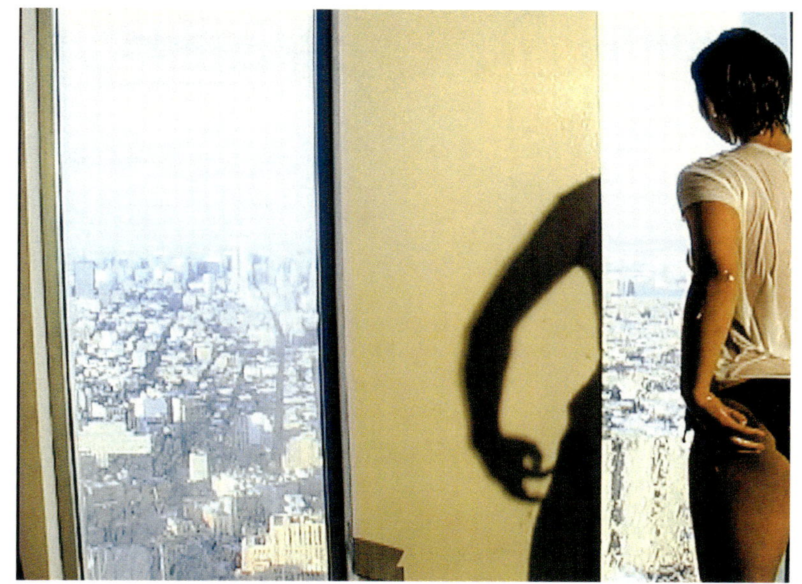

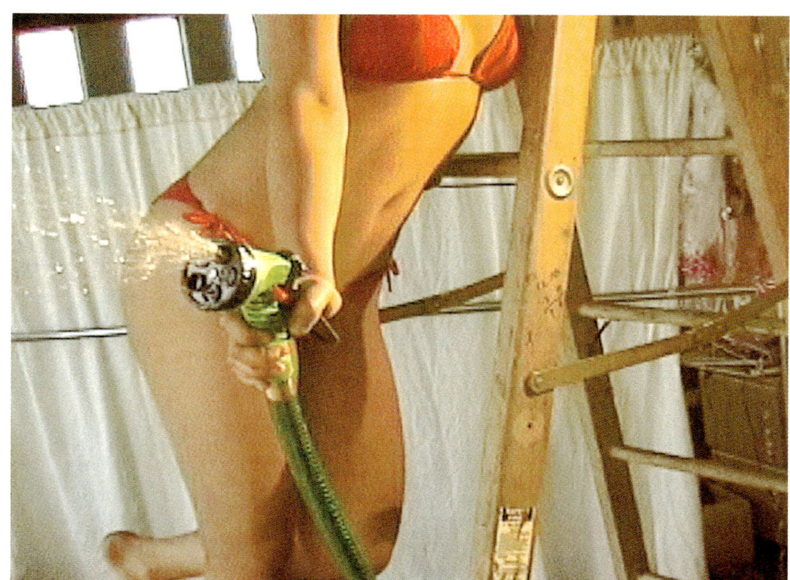

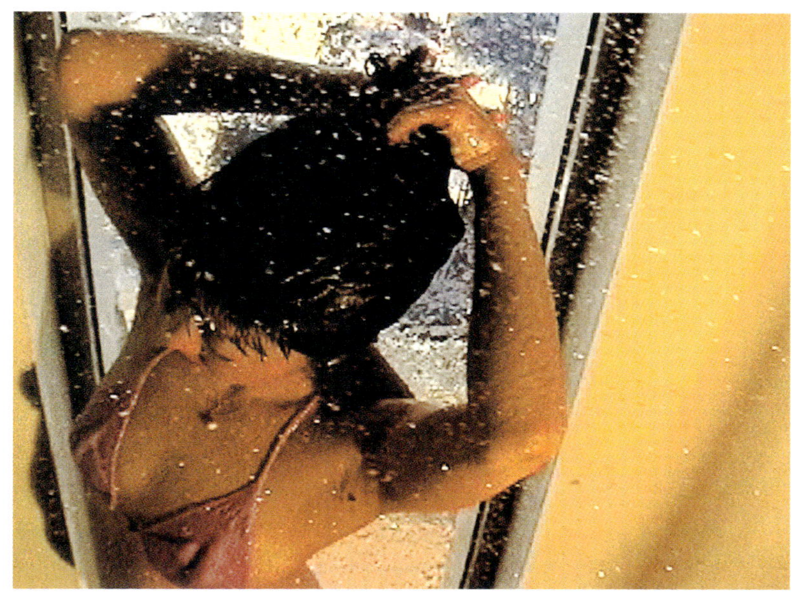

Patty Chang, Kelly Hashimoto and Kimberly SaRee Tomes
Angel Falls, 1999
Video (stills)

Bakkom's *1 WTC Cinema* explored the roles of ideology and history in the development of modernist architecture and New York City through a series of film screenings projected onto the studio windows. Here the backdrop of the city's skyline allowed viewers to drift back and forth between the two surfaces, between the projected and the real. Naomi Ben-Shahar invited friends to a party in the studios, where she provided everyone with headlamps and covered the room with Mylar so that city lights and the movement of the partygoers intermixed in a sort of liquid, reflective environment. Patty Chang, Kelly Hashimoto and Kimberly SaRee Tomes collaborated on *Angel Falls*, a humorous pseudo-erotic video referencing voyeuristic fetish films, featuring the "girls" playing in a shower against the backdrop of Manhattan. The artists successfully reversed almost every traditional power dynamic between subject and object, private and public, masculine and feminine and produced a hilarious yet critical piece that addresses issues of race and gender. In Mary Jane Dean's pinhole photographs of the city, produced by makeshift cameras she built to fit the entire window, a different kind of a New York emerges that almost disappoints in its lack of seduction. By allowing the building to literally record the city, or rather the city to project itself and produce images on its own, the role of humans in the construction of idealized representations of the city is revealed. For *Picture Motion* Douglas Ross installed motorized blinds on the windows which in a darkened room created a stroboscopic effect with the city inwardly projected in slow motion on the viewer's retina—reversing once again the order of things.

The Iconographic

Although it existed within New York City, in many ways the World Trade Center, which prided itself as being a city unto itself, was separate from it.[8] It was an internal universe for a select few. For most who lived in (or visited) New York, it was an icon to be observed from afar, a symbol. As such, its potency as a sign was not only projected onto the world by those who conceived and built it, but its potency was imbued with aesthetic, political and cultural significance from the outside. It is clear that the Twin Towers were built to convey a certain ideology. The developers were seeking to make a physical imprint on the New York skyline—a bold statement about American ingenuity and human possibility. The towers came to represent the United States' dominant position in the global economy and identified New York as the hub of that power. Their extreme height, their doubling and their minimalist form marked the city's psyche at the end of the 20th century as we slowly became accustomed to the shadows they cast onto us. The towers became the monument to "the system;" they were a modern version of the ziggurat, the obelisk, the pyramid, or the citadel. They became an emblem that was reproduced endlessly in images of the New York skyline, graphic logos and cinematic tropes. Advertisers and Hollywood filmmakers harnessed these qualities and used the towers to illustrate Machiavellian political strength, humankind's victory over nature, utopian idealism and dystopian visions.

Speaking about the towers, Jean Baudrillard observed the kind of reaction these symbols of authority elicited. "Allergy to any definitive order, to any definitive power, is happily universal, and the two towers of the World Trade Center were perfect embodiments, in their very twinness of that definitive order."[9] Critical representations of the Twin Towers began emerging as artists and cultural producers tapped into the material and metaphors they exuded.

As early as 1969, the artist Bill Bollinger, who was affiliated with the Fluxus movement, exhibited a piece consisting of two large boulders that were excavated from the World Trade Center's site. The work

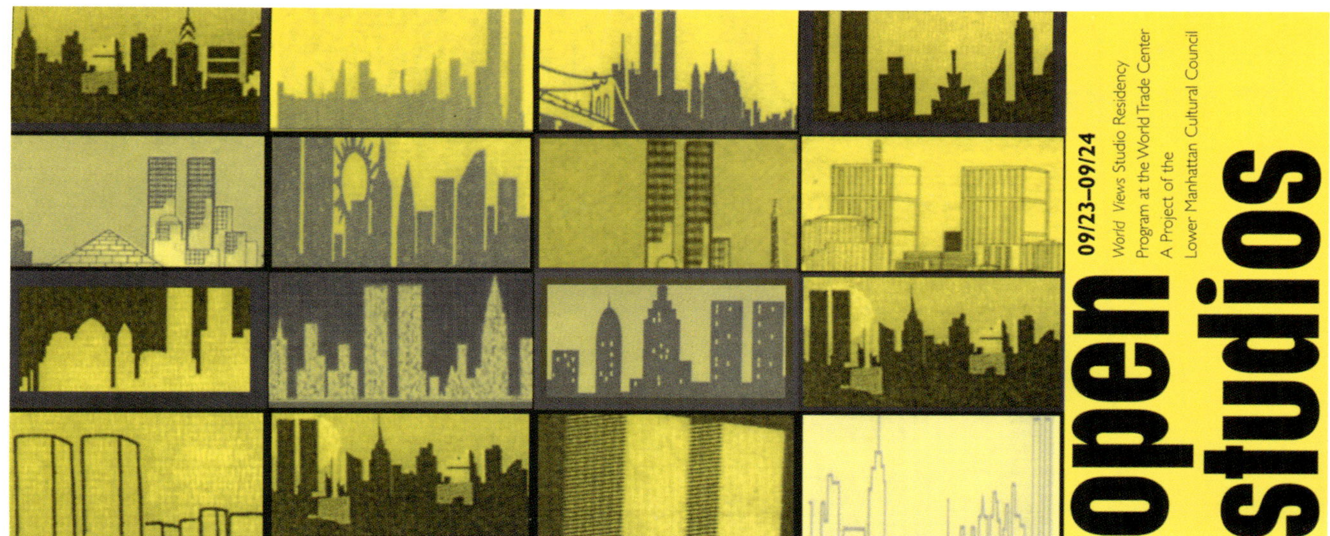

Images clipped from Manhattan Yellow Pages

was exhibited at the Whitney Museum of American Art in a show entitled *Anti-Illusions: Procedures/Materials*. In 1974, Joseph Beuys created *Cosmos und Damian*, a postcard that reproduced the Twin Towers with "Cosmos" scribbled on the North tower and "Damian" on the South. The piece made reference to the early Christian twin brothers who practiced the art of free healing in the eastern Mediterranean, propagating their faith widely. They were apprehended during the Diocletian persecution, and after miraculously surviving numerous attempts at torture and death, they were finally brought to their knees in a simultaneous public beheading. In 1979, Tseng Kwong Chi included an image of himself posing in front of the towers in his self-portrait series of photographs staged with famous world monuments. Taken from the ground up the image makes reference to the tourist snapshot but brings to mind official state photography and its power to convey ideology. The artist's light gray '50s-style suit adds to the Cold War political significance of the work. In 1980, Martin Kippenberger, one of the art world's darling hooligans, included a portrait of himself posing in front of the towers while leaning on a bomb in his photographic series, *Knechte des Tourismus*. With the casual pose and smirk on his face, the artist clearly intended this piece as a challenge to the world order that the towers represented.

In general, towers have often come to be seen as representing phallic symbols. In Lizzie Borden's 1983 film, *Born in Flames*, feminist terrorists perch on the quintessential symbol of male dominance and patriarchy and destroy the World Trade Center antennas. Gabriel Orozco's photograph, *Island into the Island*, taken on the West Side Highway in 1992, depicts a clumsy miniature reconstruction of the Financial District created out of found material and wood, set against the backdrop of the real city and the WTC. Although playful, the image is haunting in its rendition of scale and the omnipresence of the towers in Lower Manhattan. In addition to the numerous individual works dealing with the Twin Towers, *Art on the Beach*, which operated from 1978 to 1985, provided dozens of artists with the opportunity to produce site-specific work that, in most instances, directly interacted with the towers. Organized by the nonprofit Creative Time, and held on the Battery Park City landfill prior to the construction of the World Financial Center (on land displaced from the neighboring site of

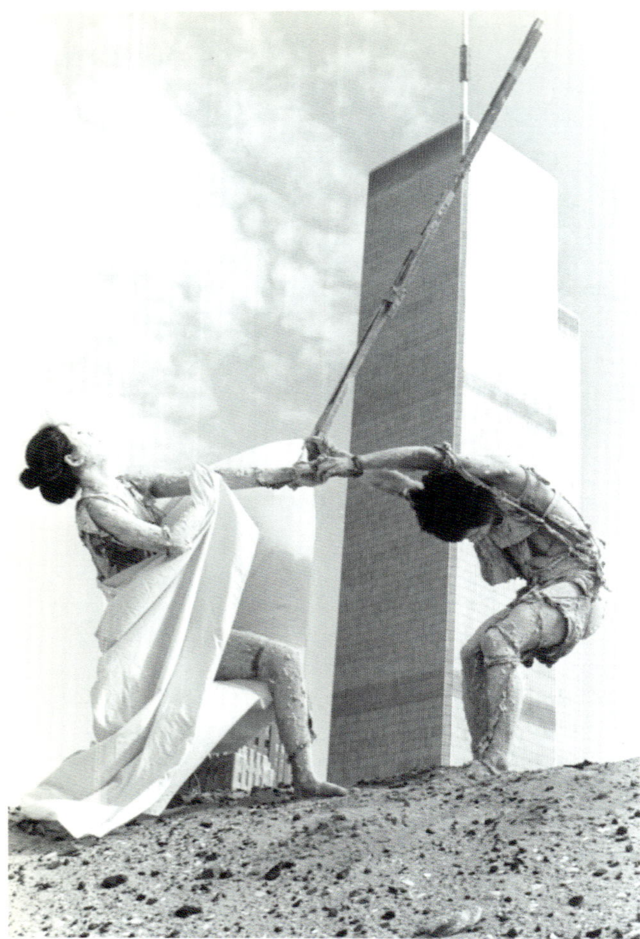

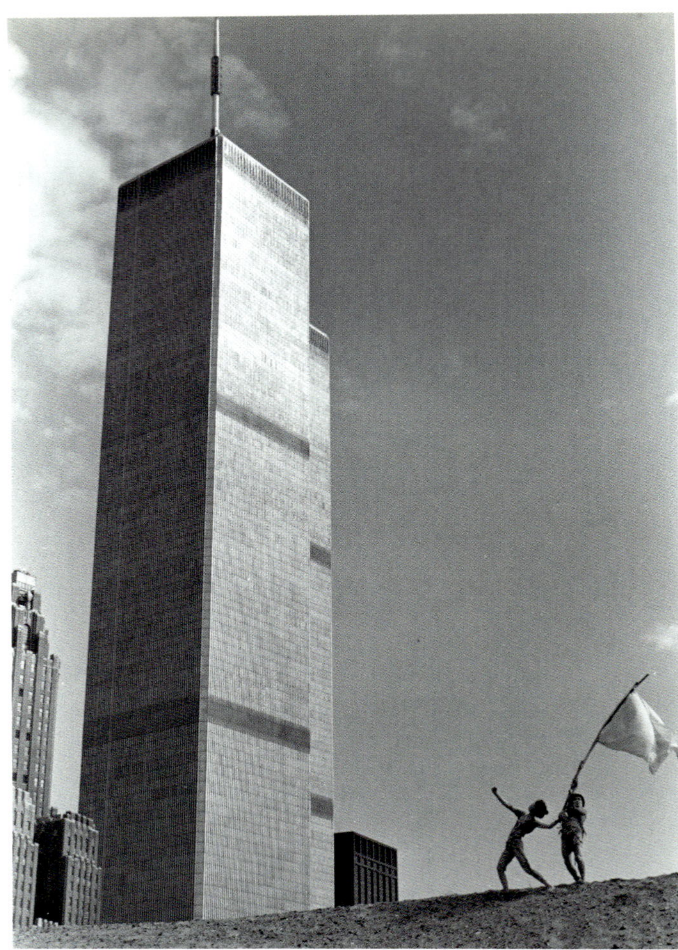

Eiko & Koma performance for **Art on the Beach**, 1980
Photo: Johan Elbers

the World Trade Center), the project allowed artists to rethink the existence of the towers through critical, temporary public art installations and performances.

Many artists in the residency program worked with the towers as signs, objects and sometimes as surfaces. Justine Cooper used the pattern created by the towers' facade at night to interpret their "genetic code" and produced a synthetic strand of the buildings' DNA, which blurred boundaries between the animate and the inanimate, as though the towers were some sort of living entity. In her drawings and childlike narrative, Carola Dertnig plays with the towers' visual presence and imagines myriad adventures and stories for the twin siblings. Susan Graham explored the relationship between the World Trade Center and the Empire State Building, once the two most prominent structures in the city. By re-creating them as sculptures and photographing them in different relational conditions, she questions their hegemonic power, the theoretical worlds they each represent and their philosophical rise and fall. Julian LaVerdiere and Paul Myoda worked relentlessly during their residency with Creative Time to find ways to realize their project, which included installing a beacon filled with bioluminescent algae on the antenna of Tower One, adding a sense of early science and World's Fair nostalgia to the structures.

Some New Yorkers often rejoiced in attempts to subdue the importance of

Gelatin
The B-Thing, 1999
Performance documentation

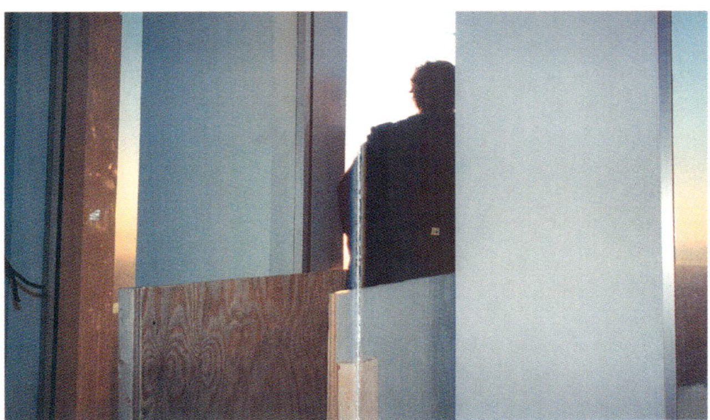

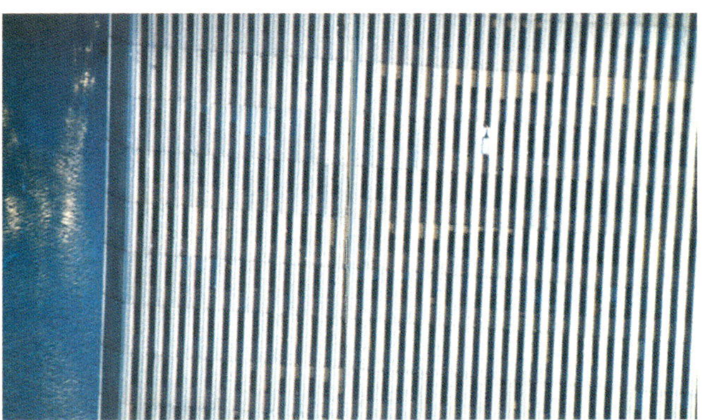

the towers and challenge their supremacy. In 1974, Philippe Petit performed his famous tightrope walk between the roofs of the two towers, and in 1977, George Willig climbed up the side of the south tower, earning himself the nicknames "human fly" and "Spider Man." Not unlike the above-mentioned daredevils, some artists attempted to mark the buildings in a personal way and exert some kind of whimsical authority over them, to penetrate their surface. In *127 Illuminated Windows*, The E-Team solicited the help of tenants in the building to cover their windows at the end of the work day in various formations in order to spell "E-Team" on Tower One, turning the exterior of the building into a gigantic LED screen. The group Gelatin produced an elaborate piece entitled *B-Thing* that involved the artists' covert removal of a window on the ninety-first floor early one morning and temporarily installing a balcony. One member at a time stepped outside the building to watch the sun rise over the city. The project, which was documented from a helicopter and from a nearby hotel room, was both a poetic and political action and clearly disarmed the building's Cartesian exterior and sense of order, allowing the organic human figure to emerge victorious from within.

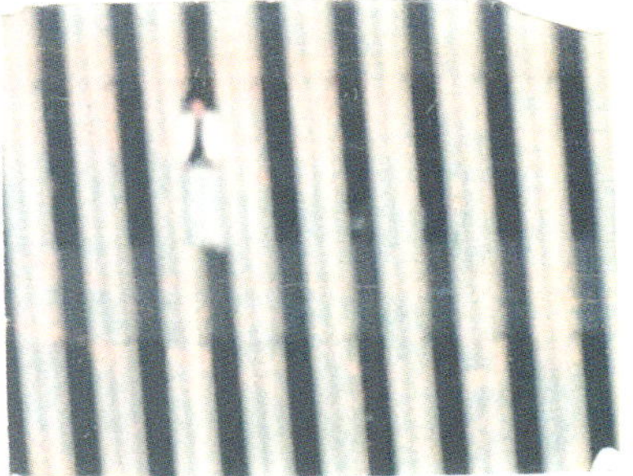

John Bennett and Gustavo Bonevardi,
Julian LaVerdiere and Paul Myoda,
Richard Nash Gould and Paul Marantz
A Tribute in Light, 2001

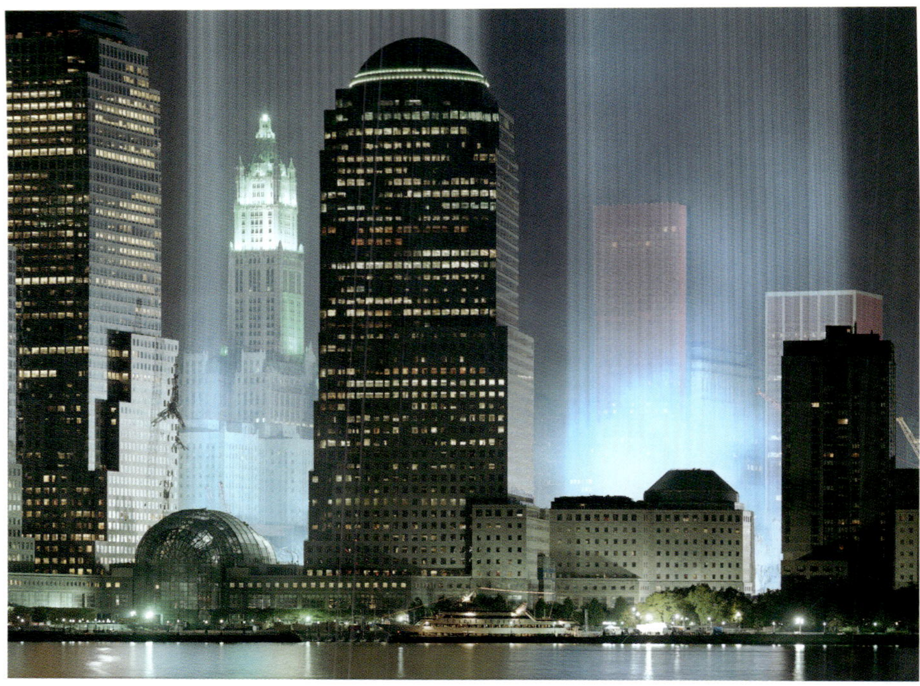

Erasure

The attacks on the World Trade Center in September 2001 were unprecedented in the histories of terrorism and architecture. The horror and scale of the event will forever remain unbelievable and unfathomable, despite the excessive mediation of the day. Artist Michael Richards was working in the studio on a new sculpture, part of his series on the Tuskegee airmen, African-American WWII pilots who never received their hero's welcome. He perished with thousands of others. The piece he was working on depicted a pilot cast in his likeness, riding burning debris and falling at great speed; man, metal and elements merging into one. Another artist who was in the building managed to escape just minutes before the towers collapsed.

The artists were in their final residency days and frantically preparing for the Open Studio weekend scheduled in early October. Many of the artists who were in residence during that last cycle in September were consequently challenged to balance emotional, intellectual and moral concerns in light of the disaster. They re-created work that had been destroyed, reconceptualized work in progress, or created new works from memory, archive material and documentation. In the aftermath of the attacks many of the artists were resolved to somehow pursue and complete their projects, and the LMCC staff worked to support their desires and needs. In December 2001, following an invitation by the New Museum of Contemporary Art, the fifteen jury-selected artists exhibited their work in a show entitled *World Views: Open Studio*. The exhibition, one of the best attended in the history of the museum, enabled New Yorkers to witness the resilience of our community and provided a place and opportunity to convene and reflect on the artistic process in the face of the tragedy and on the monumental erasure that had occurred in the city.

Julian LaVerdiere and Paul Myoda, past residents of the program, conceived one of the most celebrated commemorative public art works following the attacks.

The project, which consisted of two powerful beams of light shining upward from Ground Zero, used light to create matter. Its name changed three times in order to acknowledge the discrepancy that emerged between the loss of the towers and the individuals who perished within them. The project was first called *Phantom Towers*, then *Towers of Light*, and finally, *A Tribute in Light*.

It is intriguing that for the culture at large, the towers eventually took center stage, and in the months that followed 9/11, were fetishized endlessly. Their destruction in material form furthered their iconographic and symbolic states; experts, philosophers and media critics worldwide jumped at the task of analyzing, deciphering and critiquing them. In a strange way the residency program and its objectives gained considerable legitimacy and weight following the attacks. Perhaps this was due to the fact that the World Trade Center's destruction was perceived not as a mere attack on an architectural space, but rather an attack on a value system with its ideological, political and economic trappings. It was an attack on supermodernity and the Twin Towers represented the quintessential archetype of that concept. In his book, Augé notes that non-places—airports, aircrafts, big stores and railway stations—are particular targets for terrorism, not only because of the large number of people who frequent them but because "in a more or less confused way, those pursuing new socializations and localizations can see non-places only as a negation of their ideal. The non-place is the opposite of utopia: it exists, and it does not contain organic society."[10]

In an article about peculiar personas and activities at the World Trade Center that appeared in *The New York Times* a few months before 9/11, I was quoted as saying: "We no longer build things like this."[11] What I meant was that we no longer need to build structures like the Twin Towers, just like we no longer need to put a man on the moon; that the era and state of mind that culminates in such endeavors is over. Following the attacks I stumbled upon the Harper Collins *Atlas of World History*, printed in the early '90s, and hardly a politically correct edition. I noticed that each chapter cover was illustrated with an iconic photograph, a symbol of that civilization. The first chapter featured Stonehenge and the last chapter, titled "20th Century and Modernity," featured a picture of the World Trade Center with the Statue of Liberty in the background. If the Twin Towers came to represent modernity and the American empire that brought them to us, clearly their destruction must beg the question: What comes next and in what form?

Memories

It is important that this publication capture the unique experience that was the World Trade Center and the artists-in-residence program that it housed, lest our memories eventually fail us or become tainted by the tragedy and the times that followed. A residency of this sort was unprecedented; this book attempts to capture the spirit of this experiment where the Port Authority of New York and New Jersey, a public agency, in partnership with LMCC, a local arts organization, had the vision to take temporary vacant office spaces and convert them into creative laboratories that encouraged conceptual risk-taking and the production of art in a nonart environment. The works reproduced here hopefully will provoke us to think about the architectural, commercial and urban impact of the Twin Towers in aesthetic, psychological and political terms. It is clear that the context of the artworks has been affected by the attacks. It is possible that the works will forever carry the burden of explicating that tragedy or will be seen through a prism as sentimental mementos. However, it is my hope that we will be able to review them critically and independently from the events of September 2001. The World Trade Center's atmosphere gave artists many views to

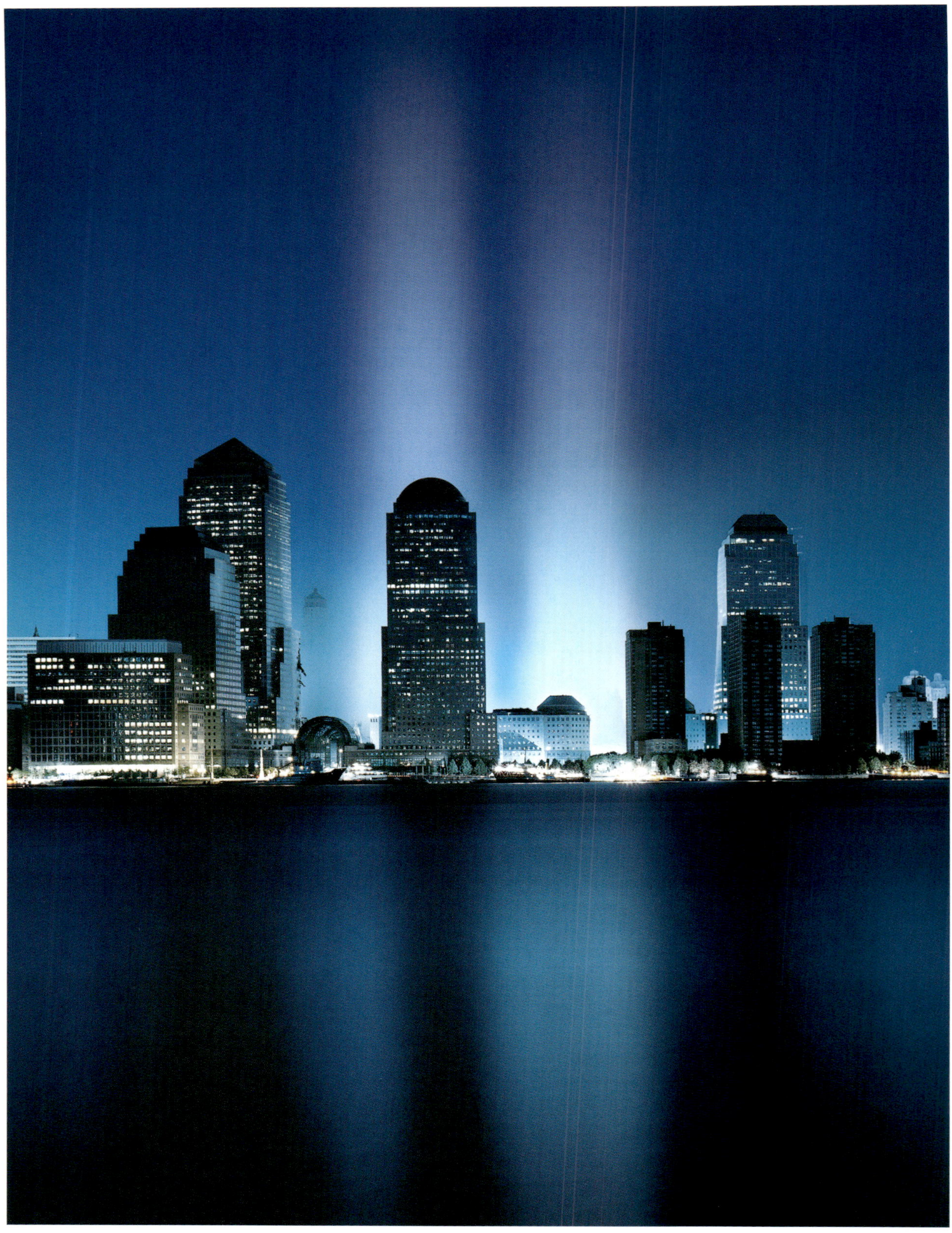

John Bennett and Gustavo Bonevardi, Julian LaVerdiere and Paul Myoda, Richard Nash Gould and Paul Marantz
A Tribute in Light, 2001

reflect on our contemporary landscape, our city and our notions of America while instigating a critical and playful look at urbanism, corporate and consumer cultures and global politics. I hope that this publication will provide an overview of the residency and capture the essence of what was a distinct project in New York City's cultural history. Most importantly though, this book gives us insight into the creative process and encapsulates the many methods and manners that artists use to record, examine, display and reinterpret the world we live in.

I carry with me the memories of this great adventure and the many anecdotes and experiences that emerged from this program. I love thinking about being lost in the basement and stumbling onto unexpected artifacts, like an archeologist on an excavation mission. I cherish my exchanges with Billy, who operated one of the freight elevators, whom I believe had lost pigmentation after being indoors for so many years and for whom banging on the elevator doors was the most assured way of getting picked up. I laugh at being chased from the plaza at midnight with Nadine Robinson after projecting text extracted from slave songs on Tower One, or at imagining the shock of the Japanese businessman from across the hall upon discovering Torsten Zenas Burns shaving half of his body in the men's room in preparation for his performance project. I cringe when I remember the phone call I received from a property manager informing me of the water damage in the offices directly below the studios as a result of the performance video, *Angel Falls*; or when I recall how I learned a year after the project was completed that Gelatin's *B-Thing* did in fact take place and was not an urban myth. The testimony, a large wad of orange chewing gum they used to mark the building with, was still stuck to the steel outside their studio's window. What a ruckus this project elicited! I take pride in the moments when property managers and security guards got passionate about some artist's work and visited the studios during their breaks. I often think of the outrageous parties we attended at Windows on the World on Wednesday nights, where DJ Mondo played carefully selected sets of shoddy retro beats and jet-set classics. I still think of the almost perfect melody that the creaking revolving doors near the Custom House created at rush hour. The sound was, in its own way, eerie and sublime. (I brought equipment in to record it but someone had decided to oil the hinges.) I witnessed so many spectacular sunsets in our studios, feeling like Saint-Exupéry, when as on clear days, I swear I could see the curvature of the earth. I smile when I recall the wonderful exchanges with tenants and workers in the building and the many private and ephemeral moments that they held; like the time when standing in Tower One, I waved at someone staring out the window from Tower Two, and they waved back at me.

Notes

1. For a fascinating and in-depth history and analysis of the World Trade Center, see Darton, Eric. *Divided We Stand.* New York, NY: Basic Books, 1999, as well as Glanz, James and Eric Lipton, *City in the Sky.* New York, NY: Times Books, 2003.
2. Kwon, Miwon. *One Place After Another: Site-Specific Art and Locational Identity.* Cambridge, MA: The MIT Press, 2002.
3. Augé, Marc. *Non-Places: An Introduction to an Anthropology of Supermodernity.* New York, NY: Verso, 1995.
4. Ibid. 30.
5. Gopnik, Adam. "A Walk on the High Line," *The New Yorker.* May 21, 2001. 44.
6. Koolhaas, Rem. *Delirious New York.* New York, NY: The Monacelli Press, 1994. 25.
7. For more on this, see Sanders, James. *Celluloid Skyline, New York and the Movies.* New York, NY: Alfred A. Knopf, 2003.
8. The World Trade Center was marketed as a place where one could work, shop, transact, and access transportation without ever leaving its premises. It is interesting to note that the WTC had its own zip code, 10048.
9. Baudrillard, Jean. *The Spirit of Terrorism.* New York, NY: Verso, 2002. 6.
10. Augé. 111.
11. Dewan, Shaila. "Twin Peaks Make A Vertical World of Their Own," *The New York Times.* February 27, 2001.

Uncanny Spaces: Notes on Art Created at the WTC

Anthony Vidler

Deserted escape stairs, abandoned offices, empty corridors, storage closets, machine rooms: the unseen and hidden spaces of the modern office building brought suddenly into focus, framed and revealed. We always knew they were there, the sordid underbelly of the real-estate image of clean, efficient, modern space. But their sudden reappearance in the many projects developed by artists in the Lower Manhattan Cultural Council's residency programs in the World Trade Center is disturbing.

It was natural for the artists, let loose in such an icon of corporate efficiency, to seek out the hidden and forgotten spaces, to point to the reality behind the facade, so to speak. It was equally natural for them to utilize the time-honored techniques of shock and disruption honed by generations of avant-garde artists to heighten the sense of discovery. Thus, the rough back rooms were exposed to view, with their decaying ducts, overstuffed closets and graffiti-scrawled walls, while the floors of public corridors were disrupted by unwonted shifts and splits in level. Offices in transition from one renter to another were viewed as sites of hasty departure, if not of vandalism and destruction. Windowpanes were removed from the closed facades of the building, the space between inside and outside invaded with vertigo-inducing effects. The video-narratives that recorded these projects work on our susceptibility to detective stories, holding us in suspense as we are led down corridors and stairs without end; a suspense that is never released as we recognize that the "crime," if one has been committed, is a crime committed by (and in) space itself, one perpetrated by architecture and its hidden dark side. Such images upset our normal view of life at the office and, like unwanted guests at a party, provoke anxiety.

Freud calls this feeling of vague anxiety—somewhere between outright fear and nervousness—the "uncanny." It is, he argues, a feeling that stems from a sudden withdrawal of what we might call the "homey" feeling of the familiar and everyday, which leads to a sense of estrangement and unreality. Taking the argument further, Freud defines the uncanny as a familiar feeling that is long-repressed on a conscious level but when it suddenly returns, is felt as shocking and disruptive.

In the context of the art projects conceived at the World Trade Center, we might then define their special kind of uncanniness as that stimulated by the shock of normality turned upside down, of the breaking down of the carefully preserved boundaries of everyday life at the office to reveal a far-from-reassuring reality behind or beyond. Or, more mildly, we could say that the projects created there act to heighten our consciousness of everyday actions—of walking along a corridor or down an escape stair, or looking through a window—by framing and gently disrupting them and that this heightened consciousness in itself destabilizes the everyday rhythms and routines of office life.

The artists were themselves self-conscious of the special nature of office space and, in particular, the space of the World Trade Center; space that was the very epitome of bureaucratic real estate and that from its inception had aspirations to be the most extreme example of its kind. For while the site as a locus for art was deliberately framed to heighten the strange contrasts embodied in every aspect of office life, in the context of these particular structures, the banality of everyday life in the office was seen juxtaposed against the scale of the Twin Towers themselves. On the one hand there was the infinite repetition of sameness, floor by repetitive floor; on the other, the unmatched height, within which the normal had to function. The apparent normalcy of each office floor was contrasted against the near impossibility of realizing its position in vertical space. Everything that the designers of the World Trade Center had done to obviate the natural vertigo of existence in the towers—lighting, deep offices, intimate cubicles, closely spaced exterior mullions—was shattered by these projects that revealed the real strangeness of the seemingly normal. We might say that from the outside, and viewed from a distance, the towers appealed to our sense of the grandeur of height and our wonder at human engineering ingenuity (something like the effect of great dams or alpine ranges) while from the inside they were supposed to seem ordinary and commonplace. All the artists' projects point to these dichotomies, each one in different ways focusing our attention on one or another aspect of this unlikely cohabitation of the sublime and the banal.

In this sense these projects are fundamentally modernist, their "shocking" qualities directed toward de-mythologizing and revealing aspects of contemporary modern life that those who manipulate the structures of economic and social existence would rather keep hidden. From the point of view of its builders and sponsors, this architectural complex was not a huge and unnecessary dinosaur of an office building, not an unsafe and ridiculously high venture in real-estate speculation, not a purely economic venture of a corporation shielded from public responsibility, nor even an example of the blatant use of state interests for political purposes. Rather, it was a sublime wonder, a great achievement of architecture and engineering, a new "cathedral" of commerce with elegant Gothic details. Beyond this, the towers were doubled to increase this effect.

There have been many precedents for tower-twinning in architecture: the double spires of cathedrals, the twin minarets of mosques and, in the modern period, the twinning of Mies van der Rohe's Lake Shore Drive apartment blocks in Chicago, and, even more recently, Cesar Pelli's towers in Kuala Lumpur. But the Twin Towers were special in that, as conceived in the early 1960s, they already seemed the last of a breed—the last gasp of modernism. They were the tallest, the most minimal, the biggest piling-up of real estate to be envisaged by modern architecture, and their twinning seemed at the time to double the already extreme effect of their bulk. Many of the LMCC artist-in-residence projects aimed to burst the inflationary bubble of such aesthetic pretensions, much in the same way that Freud implies that his investigation of the uncanny—a disturbing but not totally terrifying effect—can be read as his own deflation of the sublime in modern thought.

Continuing Freud's argument, one might propose that the Twin Towers were in themselves uncanny from the very fact that there were two of them. They were, in this sense, doubles of themselves. And the double, as Freud noted, was perhaps the most anxiety-producing phenomenon connected with the feeling of the uncanny. He gave the example of his own experience in a sleeping car of a train: When turning to the door he saw an elderly gentlemen entering the carriage and, jumping up to protest this invasion, realized that he was encountering his own reflection in the mirror of the car. If the uncanny was precipitated by the return of something familiar, then any sense of the repetition of the self was an extreme example.

But of course, in the context of our post-9/11 consciousness, these projects have gained an even more uncanny potency. Their very site-specificity—from the stairs, corridors, offices, store rooms and service spaces inside the World Trade Center to the surrounding panoramic views—invests them with a heightened and special significance following the destruction of the towers. It is as if a space that was once so real and tangible has been suspended in time. The normalcy of the spaces revealed in these projects, indeed their everyday banality, endows them with an unbearable effect of reality that is inevitably belied by the events of September 11, 2001. And while it is patently unfair to view these projects through such retrospective lenses—they deserve, after all, to be seen in the context of their conception and production—it is equally impossible not to see them as the spectral traces of a once potent reality. In the wake of 9/11, we experience the uncanny once again, but now redoubled, as a result of the destruction of the context that inspired these projects that provoked our uncanny feelings in the first place. We might describe this feeling as an uncanny that emerges as a ghost of a former uncanny.

It is often forgotten that Freud completed his seminal essay in 1919, the last in a series written during the First World War that reflected on its terrifying implications for human nature and the ideals of "civilization" that were being so brutally crushed by the wholesale destruction of European society and culture, essays with titles like "Mourning and Melancholia," "Thoughts for the Times on War and Death," and "On Transience." In treating these themes Freud was confronting his own incomprehension at the failure of culture in the face of the destructive instinct. It is obvious that for Freud the identification of the uncanny as a special case of anxiety was an important step in his analysis of the consequences of such a war. In reflecting on the projects published in this volume, and accepting all the resonance stemming from their original intentions and their inevitable place in the history of the recent terror, we might be led not so much to dispel an anxiety that has such real causes, but once more to use the sharp perceptions of art as a way of resisting the ever-expanding and opportunistic uses of the threat of terror as they seek to constrain, under the rubric of "security," our own public and private lives.

The Artist and the World Trade Center: A Fugue

Olu Oguibe

I

For several weeks during the summer of 2000, I worked as an artist-in-residence, along with a group of other artists, in a ninety-first floor studio in one of the Twin Towers at New York's World Trade Center. It was a most interesting experience, not only for the opportunity that it afforded one to work with a diverse group of artists in close proximity, but also for the uniqueness of the environment. That experience is made even more unique now, of course, by the unimaginably tragic manner in which the site was obliterated a year later on September 11, 2001. One of my more memorable works, a studio wall drawing of a ladder reaching infinitely upward yet casting a downward shadow, went down with the towers.

I arrived at the cavernous studio in mid-August, uncertain of what to expect. The other artists, who had come from different parts of the country, were already installed and busy at work. The open space had been carved up into little enclaves, which mediated its overwhelming emptiness. As my hundred canvases lay piled up in my corner, blank and intimidating, I was inescapably drawn to the huge, barren windows of the studio, which looked out on the rest of New York City. On a bright day the wall-to-wall, wrap-around windows offered a view of the city from borough to borough as far as the eyes could see. Standing at those windows, and taking in the city with its miniature streets and cars and people milling around far down under like the little hordes of Lilliput, one felt filled with the unmistakable authority of the site and one's location within it. The city lay literally at one's feet, and the sound of the name of the site rang clear in one's ear: the World Trade Center. It felt, indeed, like the center of the world. It was impossible not to recall poet Carl Sandburg's celebration of the human genius that created the earliest American skyscrapers and the marvel of the little two-legged creature that made these structures, steel rod upon steel rod, concrete floor upon concrete floor, glass pane upon glass pane.

Feeling both enamored and humbled by the presence and symbolism of the site, I decided on a theme that would parallel its global and monumental dimensions, something epochal and equally global that would constitute an epic when articulated, something in the vein of a modular history painting. I would make a hundred portraits of women from around the world—all cultures, all nationalities, all vocations, all tongues, women who in their numerous different ways helped shape the character and narrative of the twentieth century. I would call the series *Women of Substance.*

That summer I painted twenty-seven canvases in two weeks and made numerous sketches, working feverishly in the late afternoons, when it was easier to gain entry to the complex and more peaceful to work. During intermission I returned again and again to those windows and looked out on the city below with its collage of asphalt and steel and glass and vegetation, and twenty million people from every race and religion living together: working, laughing, loving, destroying, mourning and breeding. Doing that which is in their nature: being human.

II

Minoru Yamasaki's World Trade Center was a city unto itself, with enough space to accommodate a population the size of an average medieval city, even as it soared into the skies with its imposing solitariness and modernist insistence. It was also a formidable metropolis. In the daily traffic that coursed through its corridors and walkways, every nation on Earth was represented; every language, every polity and every shade of the human race. Tourists from every corner of the globe poured from wing to wing and milled indistinguishably with the workers and natives in an almost endless flood of human energy.

During the day its public spaces had the air of an ancient bazaar; its innumerable eateries and apparel stores collapsed a thousand markets into one and fed their voracious clientele one into another like the waters of a deluge. On their shelves every item of human manufacture could be found, and over the counters every imaginable item was exchanged. Goods from the farthest outposts of the world sat side by side with the commonest trifles of American industry: plants from New England conservatories and bananas from Latin America, electronic gadgets from Taiwan and American designer wear manufactured in Korea and Mexico, holistic incense from Jamaica and greasy snack packs from factories across the Hudson River. Up in the air, along its less obvious corridors, huge financial deals were cut and rare goods exchanged; diamonds and gold were traded over the telephone, petroleum and plutonium were bartered between states, mercenaries and spies were recruited and paid, and money in astronomical figures coursed through wires and bank ledgers.

The lobbies, with their queues of visitors, created scenes reminiscent of those of travelers at the gates of an ancient walled city, waiting their turn, presenting their passes, verifying their identities, sending word to expectant acquaintances inside the city, and waiting for word to return. After the complex was visited with a failed act of sabotage in the form of a bomb in 1993, this vague and incongruent air of siege thickened beyond measure and seemed to reinforce the thin, almost invisible but also seemingly impregnable, wall between the protected, inner quarters of the city and its more visible thoroughfares. The World Trade Center was not simply a city unto itself; it was indeed a city with two zones. There was the hidden and exclusive inner core, which was the real commercial heart of the complex, and there were the easygoing outskirts, a zone of vulnerability analogous to a reverse inner city that pulsated endlessly with the din of life yet was logistically degraded in the geography of capital that underlay the city.

Olu Oguibe
Women of Substance, 2000 (detail)

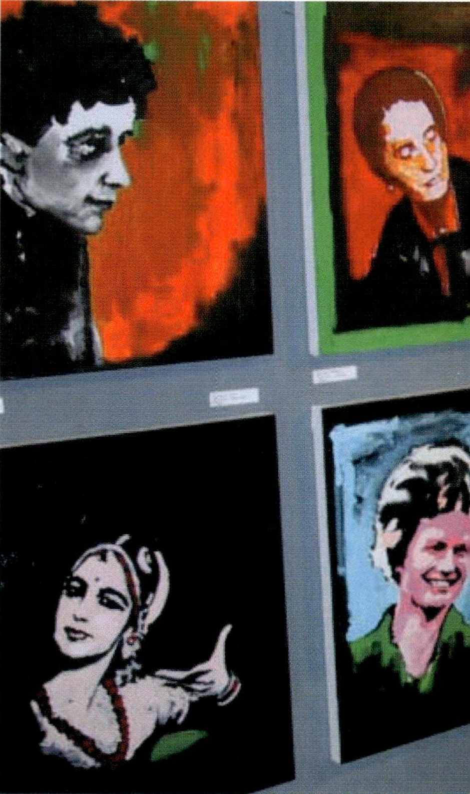

Except, of course, that there was one critical irony in the spatial dynamics of this geography. Each day at a certain hour that reverse inner city and zone of vulnerability became the inevitable meeting place for everyone who entered or left the complex as they poured out from or prepared to embark on their commutes. Bankers and equity brokers from the eightieth floor joined with florists and porters from the first; spies and agents from the Federal Bureau of Investigation stood with display assistants from the Banana Republic fashion outlet and five-dollar-per-hour "illegal" immigrants who serviced the food courts. Officials of global multinationals crossed paths with the menial laborers at the foot of the market ladder; together they emerged from or made for the A or the E trains. For that inescapable moment each day, the segregated city abandoned its hierarchies and securities, and reunited outside the invisible ramparts to reenact the ritual of intense energy that held it together.

Despite the stated, lofty vision of the complex as a "living representation of man's belief in humanity," as its architect described it, Yamasaki's World Trade Center was nevertheless designed like Plato's Republic, a metropolis in which there would be no place for the artist or the poet. Despite its huge expanse and staggering demographics, the World Trade Center was conceived with no spaces for culture in its original plans; no proper gardens, no theaters, no exhibition halls or museums, no libraries, no children's playgrounds and no leisure places that were not strictly subject to the exigencies of market returns. In the stiff dividend calculations and real-estate logic of dollar per square footage, such spaces and provisions seemed out of place. The architect and his patrons conceived of the millennial city as the supreme theater of exchange, but the perimeters of this exchange were narrowly envisioned to focus almost exclusively on the material, with scant regard for the spiritual.

As scholars have tried to establish, Yamasaki's architecture for the complex drew heavily on great Middle Eastern and Christian places of worship; the towering arches and sky-bound spires of its wall braces invoked the infinite oneness of the Divine, and the plan and location of its center court echoed that of the Islamic Holiest of Holies. Yet, of the thousands of words that were generated in the long, drawn-out discussions, debates and controversies that gave birth to the World Trade Center, art and culture were hardly among them. The shell of the great complex invoked and reflected the indomitable stature of man and the infinite beauty of Grace, yet at its heart it was conceived as a temple not for the elevation and enrichment of the human spirit, but for money changers.

Leaving gravity behind, the World Trade Center defied nature and eschewed art. In a sense, then, the complex represented a frightening epoch in the narrative of human civilization, one in which those preoccupations and rituals that offer us a handle on the metaphysical are methodically erased and pure consumerism becomes the order of the day. It also represented a divorce between art and public architecture never before seen since the advent of human shelter. Somehow the complex seemed to suggest that the sum of architecture's journey through the millennium was to arrive stripped of its ancient union with art and ritual; reduced, as it were, to a tiered shell.

However, if by default the World Trade Center embodied relative spiritual aridity, that lack did not reflect the life that surged within the complex or accurately represent the state of the world outside it. Inevitably, art, poetry, drama—those humane dimensions that sustain individuals and civilization beyond the mundane demands and material desires of the flesh—had to make their entry and find their corner in that global edifice.

III

With the introduction of LMCC's residency program, artists became a more integral part of the site and art appeared to reclaim something of its rightful place.

Through the program, artists from different parts of the world found opportunities to seek temporary retreat within the walls of the Trade Center. There they traded not in futures or the numerous other perishables for which the World Trade Center was known, but in the more lasting values and ideas that the place evoked or inspired. From far and wide they came to explore the magic of the site, as well as that mysterious energy that coursed through it and held it together. Some were fascinated by its elaborate geography, both physical and human. Others were inspired by the interior chemistry in all its elusive subtleties. Yet others came to listen to the sounds, the human din that ruled its day, but also the internal music of the structures, that mesmerizing, otherworldly sound that came through most remarkably in the quiet of night: the incantation of steel and concrete and silicon as the heat and wind and all the elements acted on them, releasing creaks and clangs and echoes that constituted the peculiar music of the site. Some artists sought to replicate, or perhaps represent, the majestic eminence of the structures; others the power and authority of their symbolism. Some levitated with the soaring towers; others were weighed down by the mass of steel and sweat that formed them.

As the autumn of 2000 drew near, and our studio efforts grew more spirited or drained, we were reminded that our period in residence at the World Trade Center would soon come to an end. It was time to conclude and then throw the studio doors open for all to see the results of our period of engagement with the site. Some of the manifestations were memorable, others were ephemeral, yet none was inconsequential. For each artist, in his or her own modest way, reaffirmed one historical truth, which is that no commune is complete without its artists and no city is whole without soul.

Critical Distance Erin Donnelly

If site was central to the Lower Manhattan Cultural Council's creative relationship to the World Trade Center, then it only became more so after its destruction. Marshall Berman, author of *All That is Solid Melts into Air* (a landmark text published on the experience of modernism nearly twenty years ago), recently stated: "... the World Trade Center is an important public space but I think it's become more of a public space [...] in its absence."[1] Commonly referred to as "the site" in the months following the disaster, the location of violent displacement, in a social sense, developed into a universalism around which many New Yorkers began to rebuild their relationship to place. This premise was central to LMCC in the programs it developed in response to September 11, 2001.

From across the East River in DUMBO to the edge of ground zero at the World Financial Center, LMCC's site-specific *New Views* residencies provided a framework for artists to consider the shattered cityscape as well as the process of healing and rebuilding. In addition to the temporary residency programs, LMCC assembled *Microviews*, an archive of artists' snapshots of the World Trade Center, which highlights the significance of everyday spaces and the importance of artists occupying nontraditional environments. During this two-year period, the resident artists' perspectives were shared with thousands of visitors in open studio events, exhibitions and artists' talks. These programs promoted dialogue and debate as ways of understanding public images, an ethos reflected in many other initiatives developed since September 11, 2001 by civic and cultural groups based in New York city.

In considering the artistic work created in relation to a site of absence, it is useful to think of the expanded definition of site-specificity that goes beyond the parameters of physical location to include the discursive field where cultural debate takes place.[2] The unprecedented public interest in the WTC site had been focused by the intense portrayal of September 11, 2001, in the media. In order to generate discussion about the ways in which this common experience was being defined, it became critical for LMCC to support the creation of artistic work that would offer alternative experiences and diverse points of view.

Conceived as iterations of LMCC's residency program in the World Trade Center, the *New Views* residencies were designed to explore the changed city at critical distances, including views of the Lower Manhattan skyline from Brooklyn and the immediate area surrounding the site in the Financial District. The concept of critical distance was crucial in a geographic sense but also established an ideological perspective. Critical distance implies an oppositional stance and challenges the modernist conception of the

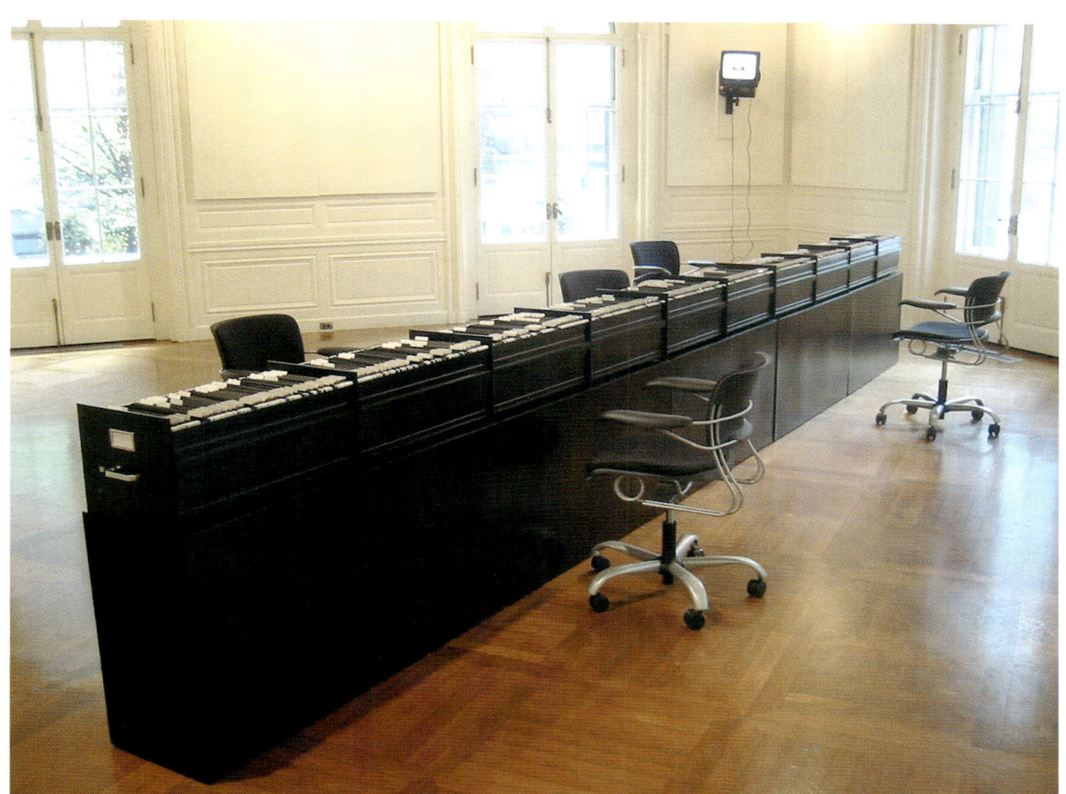

Installation view of **Microviews**
Municipal Art Society
September 4–October 10, 2002
Photo: Stephan Apicella-Hitchcock

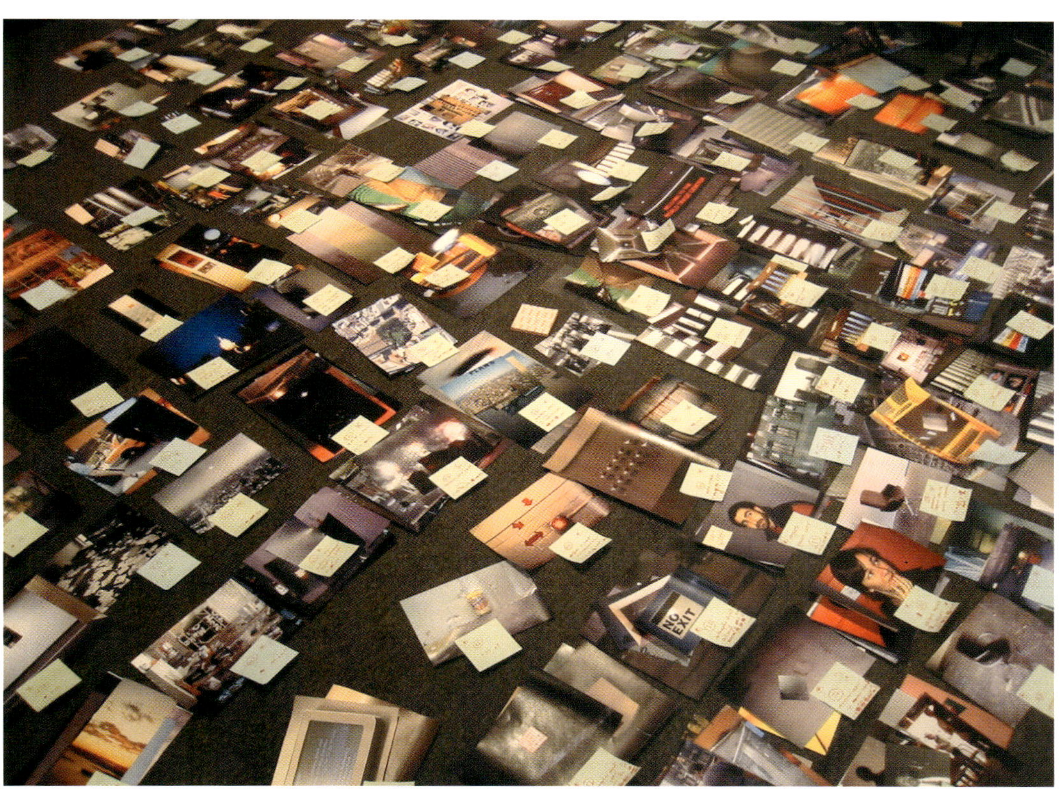

Organizing **Microviews** images,
Summer 2002
Photo: Stephan Apicella-Hitchcock

Amie Siegel
Establishing Shots, 2002 (stills)
Video
Produced during *New Views: DUMBO* residency

Sebastian Romo
Untitled, 2002
Strathmore board
Dimension variable
Produced during *New Views: DUMBO* residency

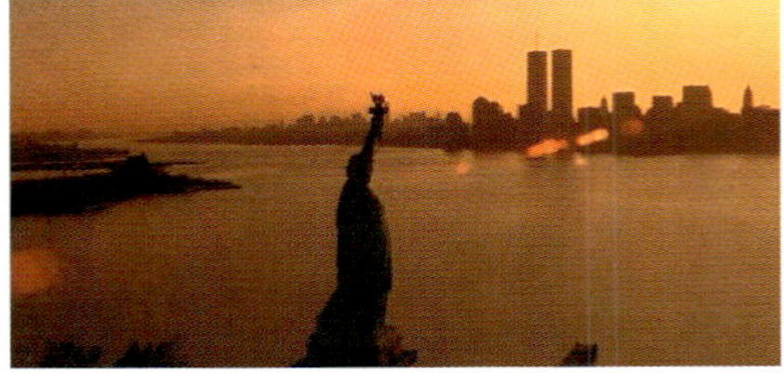

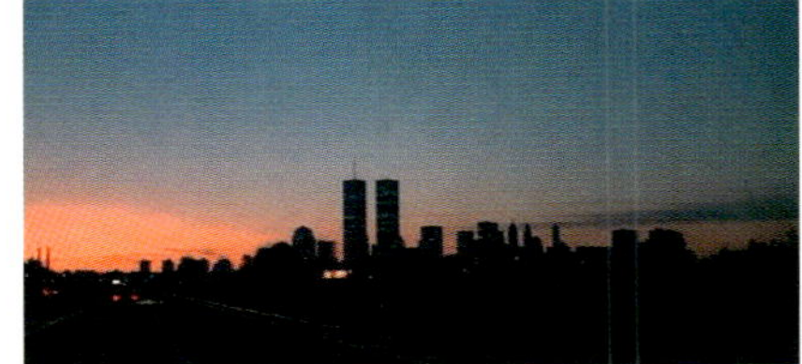

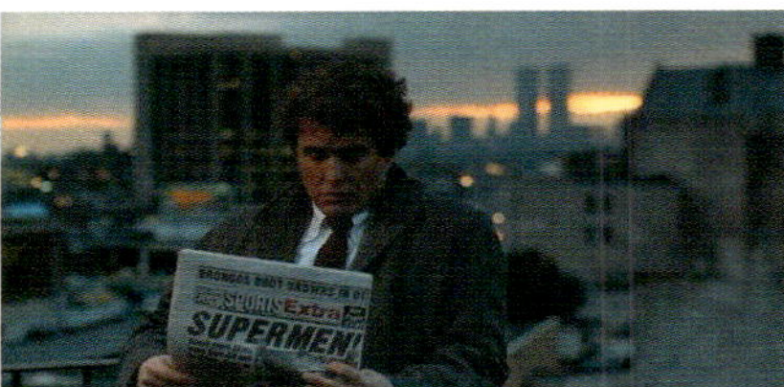

artist removed from everyday life—a condition many critics believe is no longer possible.[3] From a psychological viewpoint it is also important for the viewer to consider these works with perspective as critical distance also describes the conditioning of immediate emotional responses that become mitigated by unfolding circumstances and tempered by time.

The Lower Manhattan cityscape is seen from Brooklyn as a continuous horizon line from the neighborhood of DUMBO (an acronym for down under the Manhattan Bridge overpass) to the Brooklyn Heights promenade. For LMCC this view from across the East River established an important starting point from which to consider how the skyline had changed. Working in space donated for six months by Two Trees Management, LMCC established the *New Views: DUMBO* program to provide artists the chance to create new work and use the space as a laboratory to examine Lower Manhattan. In April 2002, six cityscape painters—Karin Batten, Megan Craig, Sjoerd Doting, Stan Friedman, Nancy Friese, Nedra Newby and Rhoda Ross—who had been in residence at the World Trade Center on September 11, 2001, were the first to participate in the program. This group, who had painted from the ninety-first floor of Tower One, created new work in the DUMBO studios that reflected a change in perspective, ranging from skyline views captured at different times of day and night to meditations on the soaring undersides of the Brooklyn and Manhattan Bridges seen from nearby Empire State Park.

The *New Views: DUMBO* program also provided eight new artists-in-residence (working in sculpture, sound, video and film) with an opportunity to contemplate the altered skyline. During the summer of 2002, Warren Neidich, Sebastian Romo, Sharon Paz, Jenny Perlin, Amie Siegel, Wolfgang Staehle, Valerie Tevere and Virgil Wong created works that engaged with the views, as the windows were central to the studio space. Their work, among other issues, looked at popular representations of the city and how viewing the skyline became an act of healing.

Given the nature of how the events of September 11, 2001, were televised and electronically distributed, these works underscore how the language of film and media produces familiar narratives about the city. Amie Siegel's video installation,

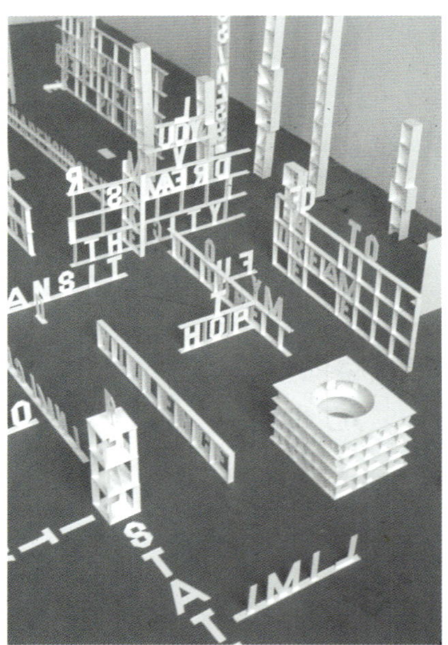

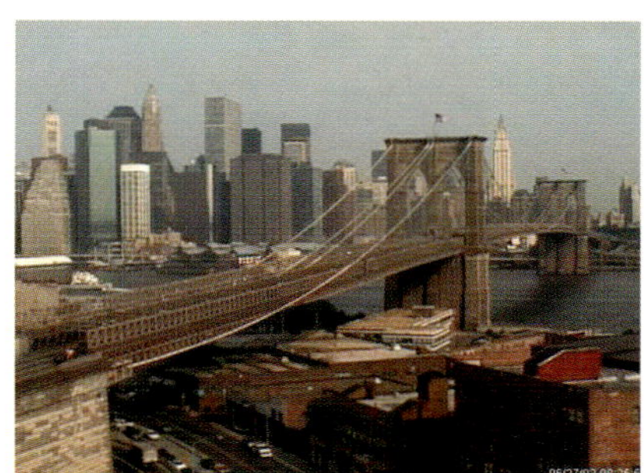

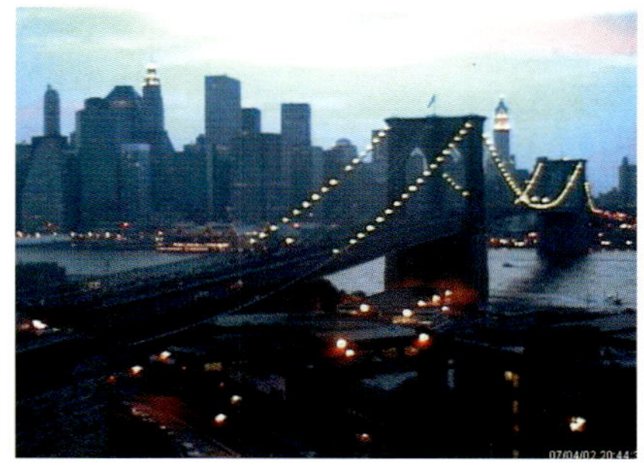

Wolfgang Staehle
Untitled, 2002
Live-feed video
Produced during *New Views: DUMBO* residency

Establishing Shots, investigated the Hollywood film device by creating a montage of collected film clips from the 1970s through the 1990s (including from such movies as *Working Girl*, *The Secret of My Success* and *Crocodile Dundee*) to illustrate how the towers served both as icon of power and banal backdrop in the popular imagination. To create *Out of Synch*, Sebastian Romo projected a super-8 print of Fritz Lang's 1927 visionary film, *Metropolis*, on the studio windows. The resulting photographs suggested a potential city or utopian ideal by transposing past ideas of its urban future onto the contemporary skyline.

Other artists explored themes of loss, healing and memory from the "objectivity" of science to visceral sensation to poetic elegy. Optics, neurology and technology are connected in Warren Neidich's installation, *After Image, After Image, After Image*. Viewers stood in front of a stroboscopic neon sign in the shape of the Twin Towers then stepped aside and blinked their eyes in front of a photo panorama of Lower Manhattan, revealing a phantom afterimage on the skyline where the Twin Towers once stood. Considering personal and collective acts of commemoration, Jenny Perlin presented two audio recordings of Mozart's *Requiem*, one rehearsed in the studio by the artist and the other recorded in concert at the Julliard Theater on the anniversary of the attacks. In another work, an untitled 16mm film depicts the skyline being "washed" by a hand cleaning the inside of the window. Sharon Paz's video installation, *In Between*, explored the sensation of ascent and falling by incorporating imagery such as a moving escalator that mimics the motions of a camera panning the vertiginous surface of a towering structure. And Virgil Wong's digital database, *PhineasMap: New York*, compiled injury, disease and medical-miracle stories that occurred in the urban environment and mapped them into a collective anatomical online body.

Other works made the spectator self-conscious of the very act of viewing. For most New Yorkers the everydayness of the city and the view was radically altered on September 11, 2001, when ephemeral images were made eternal and otherwise ordinary experiences were seared into memory. As part of the residency Wolfgang Staehle restaged a 2001 video installation that featured a continuous stream of panoramic images of Lower Manhattan uploaded to a Chelsea gallery via a live-feed camera from a rooftop in Brooklyn. While the original work was intended as a critique of the landscape genre, history reframed the images on view in the gallery on the morning of the attacks. In a new work, retraining his camera on the Brooklyn Bridge, Staehle created a seemingly unshifting image that was elongated into a timeless stillness that reintroduced monumentality into the urban landscape. For *Resounding Views*, Valerie Tevere interviewed subjects whose personal narratives formed audio portraits that the listener could hear while viewing the actual cityscape out the window, as if the thoughts were those of anonymous pedestrians crossing the Brooklyn Bridge immediately in the foreground or voices from farther afield

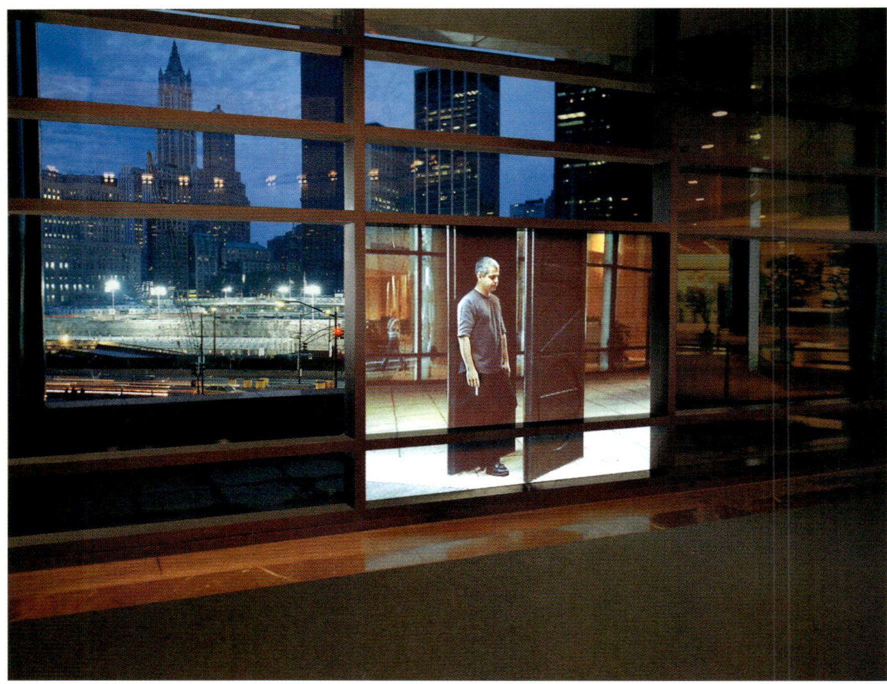

Alex Villar
Irrational Intervals, 2002 (installation view)
DVD projection, cabinet
Produced during *New Views: World Financial Center* residency

within the canyons of Lower Manhattan. By installing their work adjacent to the view, the *New Views: DUMBO* artists addressed how the continuous field of vision shaped their work and formed a dialectical relationship with the city.

This dialogue with urban space in transition continued in *New Views: World Financial Center*, a program created with the World Financial Center Arts and Events Program; however, here the context was even more dramatic. The nine artists-in-residence—Anne Beffel, Jane Benson, Curtis Cuffie, Charles Goldman, Elke Lehman, Pia Lindman, Brian McGrath, Andrea Ray and Alex Villar—were challenged to engage sensitively with an environment that had been violently destabilized by the disaster. Defined by its physical relationship to the World Trade Center and then cut off from the rest of the city, the World Financial Center community was severely traumatized during the attacks. While the center underwent construction and repair, only a small percentage of the population had returned to work there. And virtually no public visitors were in sight when the artists arrived in May 2002 to begin their five-month residency in the Courtyard Gallery, which had been converted into working studios. With these formidable struggles the goal of the program was to create site-specific public art projects to be displayed throughout the complex in a three-month exhibition from November 2002 through January 2003.[4]

The first point of entry into this complicated environment was to examine common assumptions about this kind of corporate space. Artists looked at how public areas are navigated and what contributes to the psychological climate of controlled spaces. For example, displayed in planters throughout one of the complex's gatehouses, Jane Benson's *Glory F Flora* was made of manipulated silk foliage cut into geometric shapes that disrupted and rendered visible the artificiality of the interior setting. In a performance-and-video installation, *Irrational Intervals*, Alex Villar addressed the unsanctioned use of leftover architectural spaces, laying bare behaviors that are accommodated by official structures and those that are not. Made from playful materials, Elke Lehman's quirky surveillance camera sculptures, entitled *Portraits*, subtly and explicitly questioned the uniformity and anonymity of the environment.

In several of the works, themes of trauma and recovery necessitated explorations of personal memory and interpersonal exchanges. Assembled from found objects collected from the local area, the ephemeral nature and altar-like appearance of Curtis Cuffie's *Untitled* sculptures were fitting in this environment, which was healing from trauma. To create *Lend Me A Memory*, Charles Goldman asked people to share a memory that the artist translated into an individual clay sculpture displayed along with more than one hundred other memories in a vast "storage bank" in the courtyard. Also incorporating personal stories, Anne Beffel's *Apologies* dealt with the cleansing act of apology with an installation including free glycerin soaps near the public bathrooms. These intimate gestures revealed a human element that transformed the otherwise isolating, even alienating, space.

Direct references to absence were not only evident in some of the works on view, but also expressed in the architecture itself. Around the first anniversary of September 11, 2001, a viewing wall looking east over ground zero was erected to coincide with the reopening of the Winter Garden, the World Financial Center's most well-known and public space. This manifestation, along with video paintings entitled *Waterline* and *Viewing Platform* by Pia Lindman, which were displayed on plasma screens throughout the complex, addressed how architecture shapes our emotional experiences, particularly mourning. In addition, Brian McGrath's animated topographical map and timeline, *New York Ascendant: Here and Now*, revealed what had been added and what had been removed from the urban landscape over decades of continual change. Exploring how loss is psychologically processed, Andrea Ray's installation, *Filter,* incorporated group seating and an audio narrative akin to a psychotherapy session. In addition, a large image depicting a mound of World Trade Center debris at the Fresh Kills landfill referenced the opaque film that once covered the windows to obscure views of the disaster site. Ray's landscape image showed that a year later, grass had grown amid the debris.

While the *New Views work* was created in a context of loss, the *Microviews* archive was conceived as a return to images of the World Trade Center. While LMCC had considered for some time creating a retrospective project that looked at resident artists' experiences, the *Microviews* project officially began in the summer of 2002, when LMCC circulated an open call to 140 past resident artists and artist collectives requesting snapshots and photographs from their residency experiences in the World Trade Center. These unusual images were quite different than the iconic images of the Twin Towers that were so dominant in the media and popular experience immediately following the disaster.

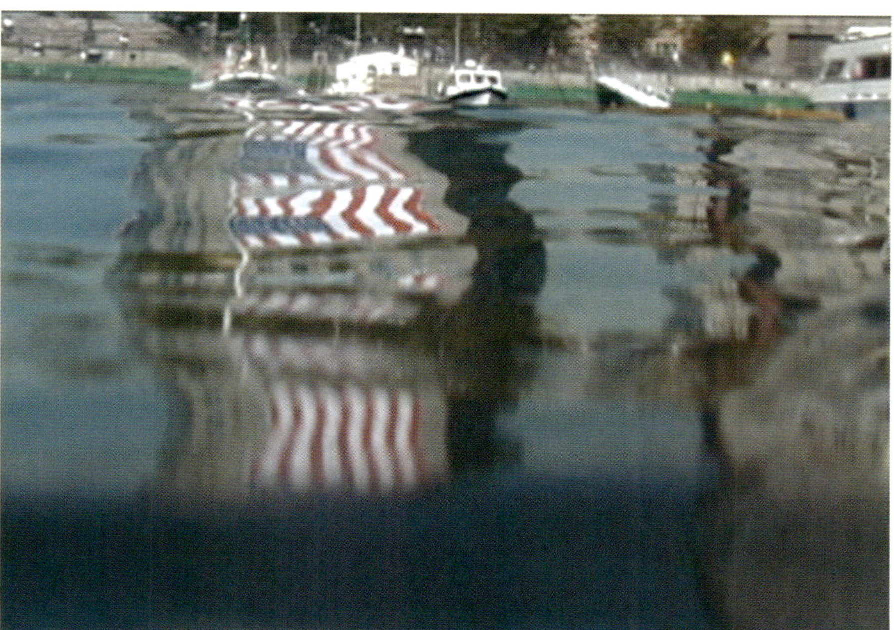

Pia Lindman
Waterline, 2002 (still)
DVD
Produced during *New Views: World Financial Center* residency

Past resident artists submitted hundreds of uncanny and familiar images of the hallways, bathrooms, basement levels, as well as views from the studios onto the city below. The challenge to curators Christopher K. Ho and Stephan Apicella-Hitchcock, working with Moukhtar Kocache and myself, was to organize and reconstitute this preexisting material in a way that honored the subject matter. More than 500 images in the archive were classified and cross-referenced on the basis of formal characteristics and arranged in open file cabinets positioned horizontally. In this way viewers were invited to sift through and handle the images and make their own meaning from any chosen direction or approach. First shown at the Municipal Art Society in September 2002, the presentation of *Microviews* was intended to emphasize the importance of everyday spaces as an alternative portrait of the World Trade Center. What had been a monumental structure from the exterior was humanized by a sense of its interior spaces.

Andrea Ray
Filter, 2002 (installation view)
Inkjet on vinyl, bleachers, two-channel audio track on headphones
Produced during *New Views: World Financial Center* residency

For the past two years LMCC has worked to reestablish its signature residency program with a juried process and rotating cycles of resident artists at the emerging and mid-career stages, working in all media. In April 2003, with the generous donation of space by The Witkoff Group, the establishment of *Workspace: The Woolworth Building* continued LMCC's tradition of enabling artists to occupy architectural icons, while providing much needed studio space, access to a community of fellow artists, and opportunities to present work to the public. Adjacent to the World Trade Center site, the Woolworth Building was a logical and interesting evolution of LMCC's site-based residency project. A monument to the first era of skyscrapers, the "Cathedral of Commerce" was the tallest building in the world when it was built in 1913, having been financed by Frank W. Woolworth's five-and-dime empire.

Like the other programs, the Woolworth residency challenged artists to connect their work to the urban, social and political landscape. Artists working from the thirty-third floor had views of City Hall, Battery Park and the harbor, the Hudson River and the WTC site, the East River and Brooklyn and Broadway, as it weaves uptown. This historic setting provided a framework for artists to consider today's downtown, from the new security environment to the rebuilding process. The first group of artists-in-residence—A.J. Bocchino, Megan Cump, Cecilia Galiena, Shin Il Kim, George Kimmerling, Catarina Leitão, Mary Magsamen & Stephan Hillerbrand, Conor McGrady, Diane Meyer, Matthew Northridge, Karina Aguilera Skvirsky, Dario Solman and Praxis (Delia Bajo & Brainard Carey)—produced a range of projects from solemn meditations on the shifting skyline to horror imagery inspired by the Gothic motifs of the building. The second group of resident artists—Jn.Ulrick Désert, Benj Gerdes, Andrea Geyer, Mariam Ghani, Jeff Grant, Patrick Jackson, Claudia Joskowicz, Angel Nevarez, Frank Parga, Trebor Scholz, Katrin Sigurdardóttir, Shelly Silver, Shinique Amie Smith and Bradley Wood—created works that engaged with the historic and architectural character of the building, as well as the social and political climate of the neighborhood.

By gaining critical distance and considering how the city has changed, these recent LMCC programs have encouraged

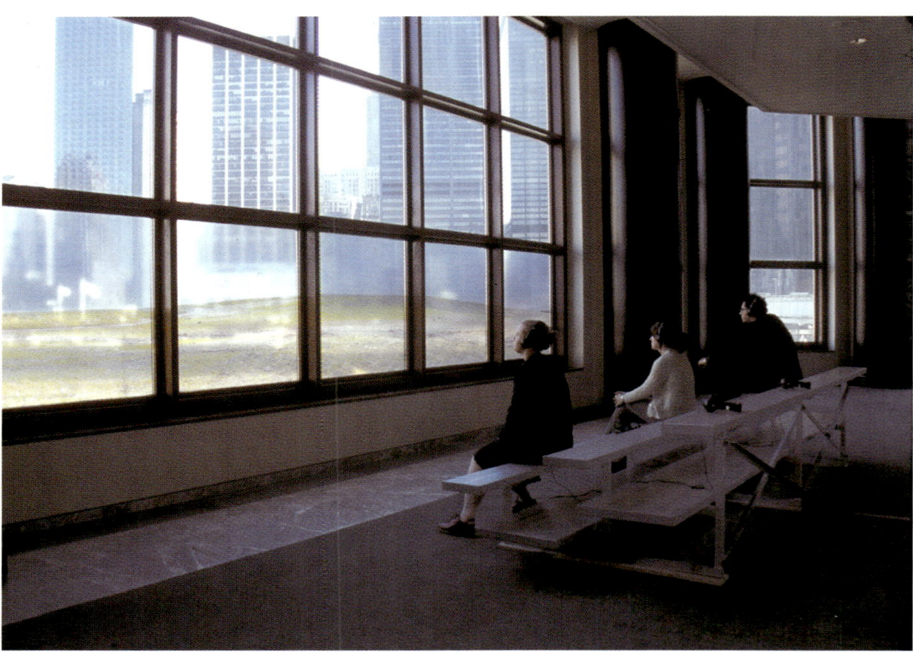

A.J. Bocchino
NY Times Headline
(February 1, 1993–July 28, 2003), 2003
(installation view with detail)
Produced during *LMCC/Workspace: The Woolworth Building*
Photos: Jason Mandella

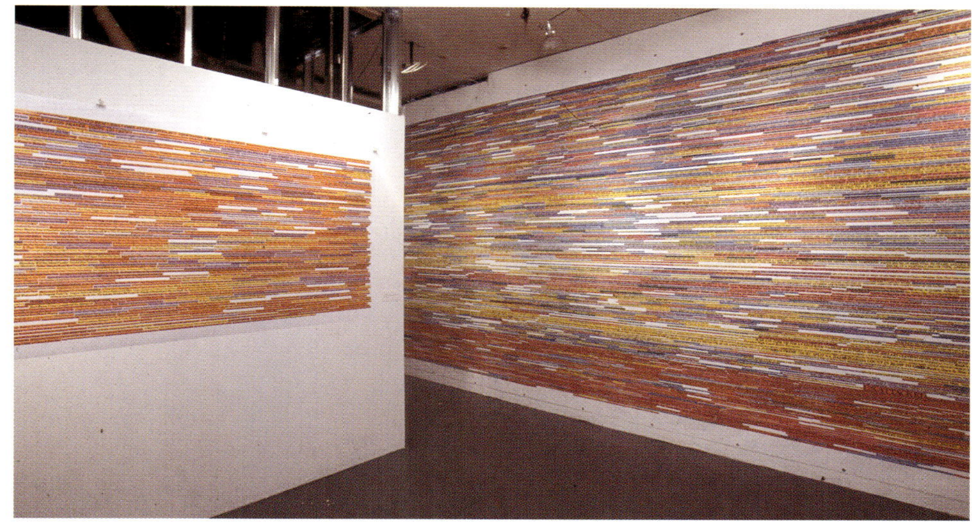

the discovery of diverse public images and experiences. Although much of the work was made in relationship to a site of absence, it does not approach sentimentality or nostalgia. And just as these works consider the urban landscape from various geographic vantage points, they also challenge the viewer to consider multiple critical perspectives. Since September 11, 2001, the residency programs have served more than fifty artists. LMCC's commitment to the role of artists in a rebuilt Downtown will ensure that many more follow in the years to come. Recognizing that context is constantly shifting, LMCC's programs will continue to engage artists, the Downtown community and viewers in a dynamic civic conversation by asking how a public relationship to an urban location is continually reinstated and reclaimed.

Notes

1. Berman, Marshall. "Image and Spectacle" panel, *WTC Forum,* Graduate School of Architecture, Planning and Preservation, Columbia University, February 2, 2002.
2. Kwon, Miwon. *One Place After Another: Site-Specific Art and Locational Identity.* Cambridge, MA: The MIT Press, 2002. 26.
3. Jameson, Frederic. *Postmodernism, or, The Cultural Logic of Late Capitalism.* Durham: Duke University, 1991.
4. Nuit Banai discusses the artists' interventions in fuller detail in her catalogue essay "Siting the Everyday." *New Views: World Financial Center.* Ed. Erin Shirreff. New York, NY: Lower Manhattan Cultural Council, 2003. 6–11.

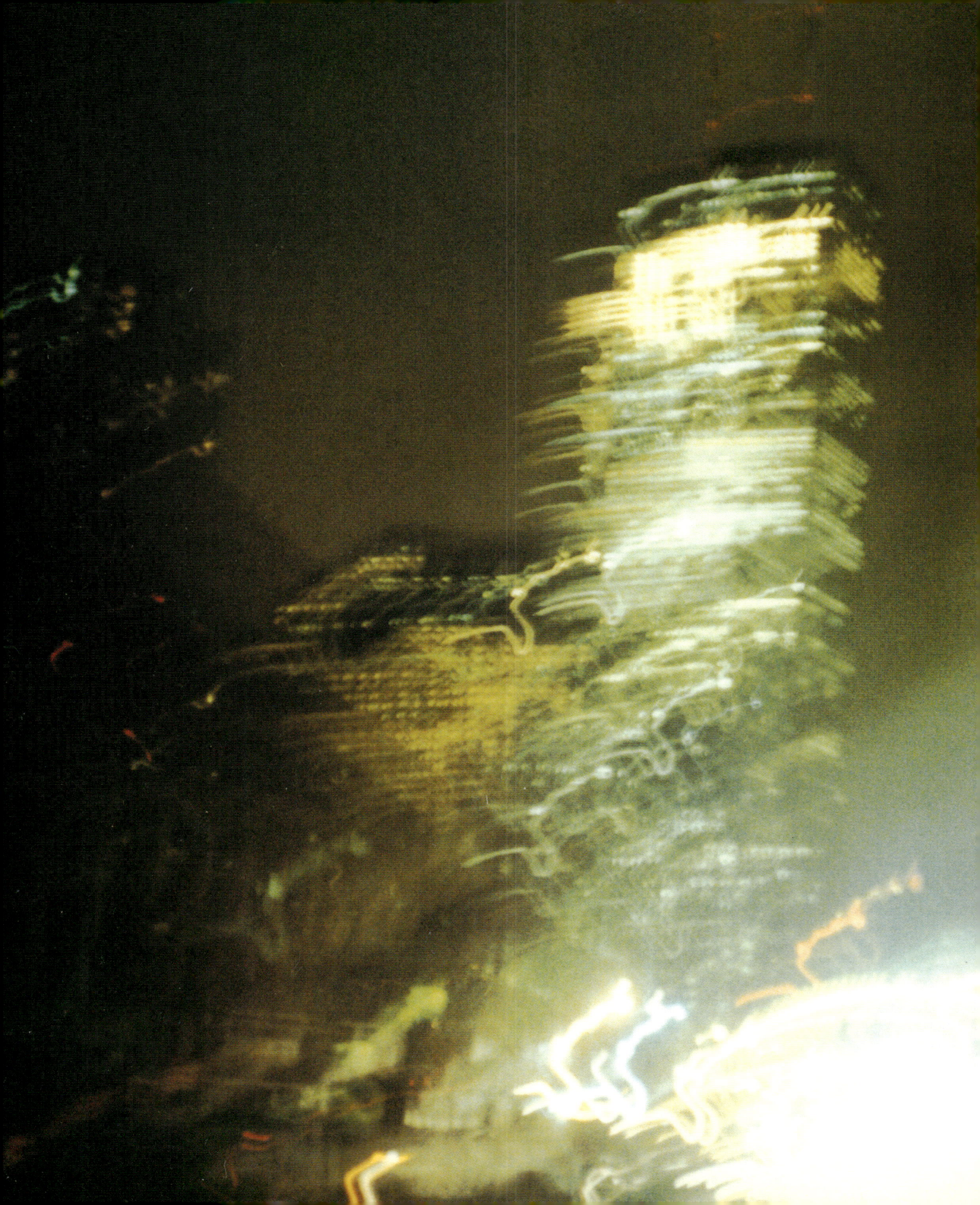

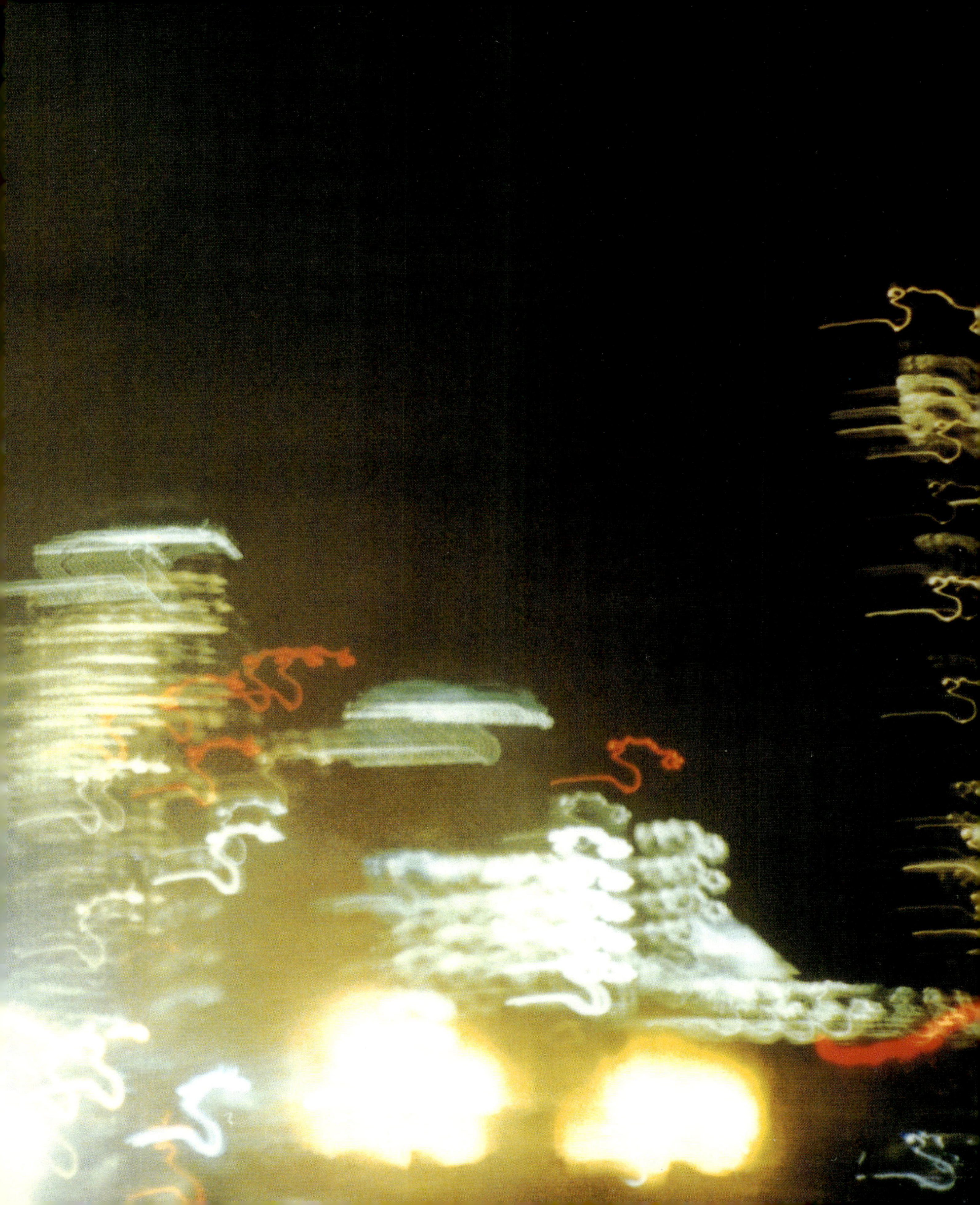

Pilot Project:
The Perceptual Painters (1997-98)

Gwinn Alderson
Donald Bracken
Lois Dodd
Rackstraw Downes
John Dubrow
Jessica Goodyear
Richard Haas
Susanna Heller
Diana Horowitz
Yvonne Jacquette
Elisa Jensen
Pamela Lawton
Eleanor Magid
Ron Milewicz
Marjorie Portnow
Carl Scorza
Torild Stray
Pola Wickham

Juror

Graham Nickson

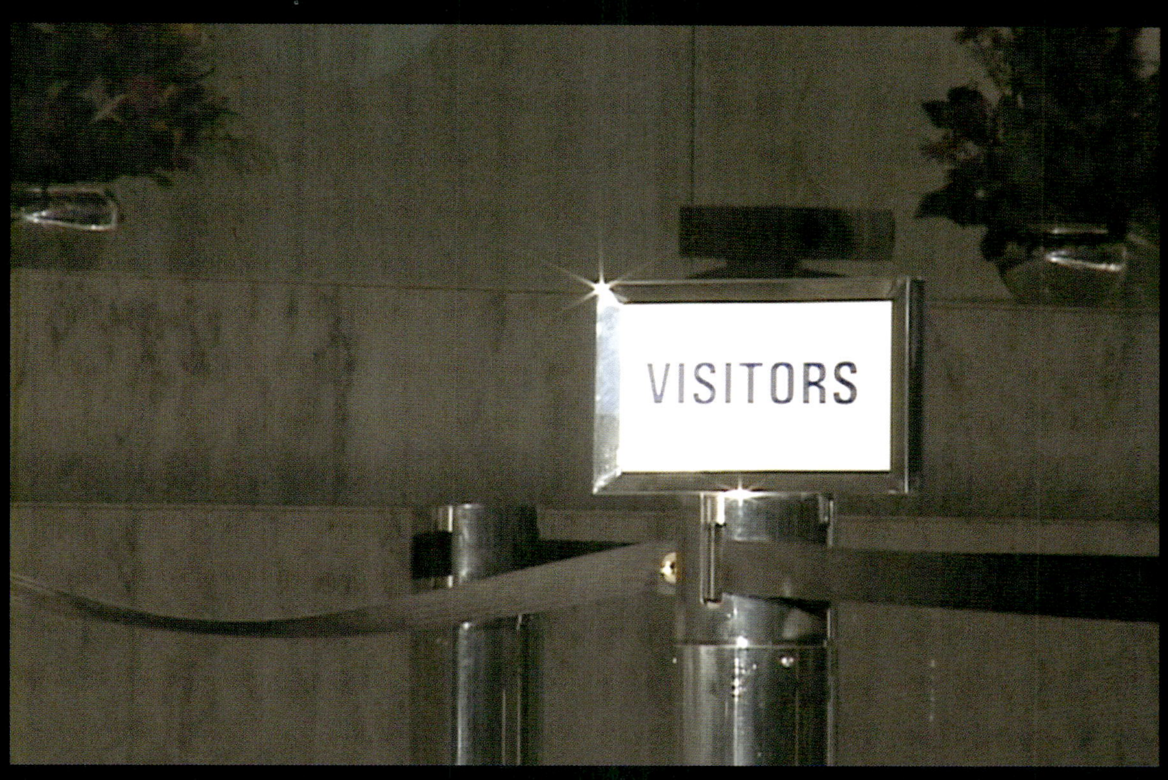
VISITORS

Gwinn Alderson

Summer Cityscape, 1997
Oil on canvas
20 x 16 inches
Collection of Peter and Mary Kelly
Photo: D. James Dee

Irregular Landscape, 1998
Oil on canvas
41 x 41 inches

Born 1963 in San Francisco, Calif.
Lives in Los Angeles, Calif.

Education

1994 The New York Studio School, N.Y.
1988 MFA, City University of New York, Queens
1987 BFA, Boston University, Mass.

Selected Group Exhibitions

2002 *25th Small Works Show*, 80 Washington Square East Galleries, New York, N.Y.
2000 *World Views*, Nabisco Gallery, East Hanover, N.J.
1999 *The 1999 National Competition*, First Street Gallery, New York, N.Y.
1998 *The Art Exchange*, New York, N.Y.
1994 *The Perceptual Pursuit*, Fordham University Plaza Gallery at Lincoln Center, New York, N.Y.

Awards

1994 The New York Studio School, Distinction in Painting
The New York Studio School, Seligman Von Simson Scholarship
1993 The New York Studio School, Ojeda Scholarship

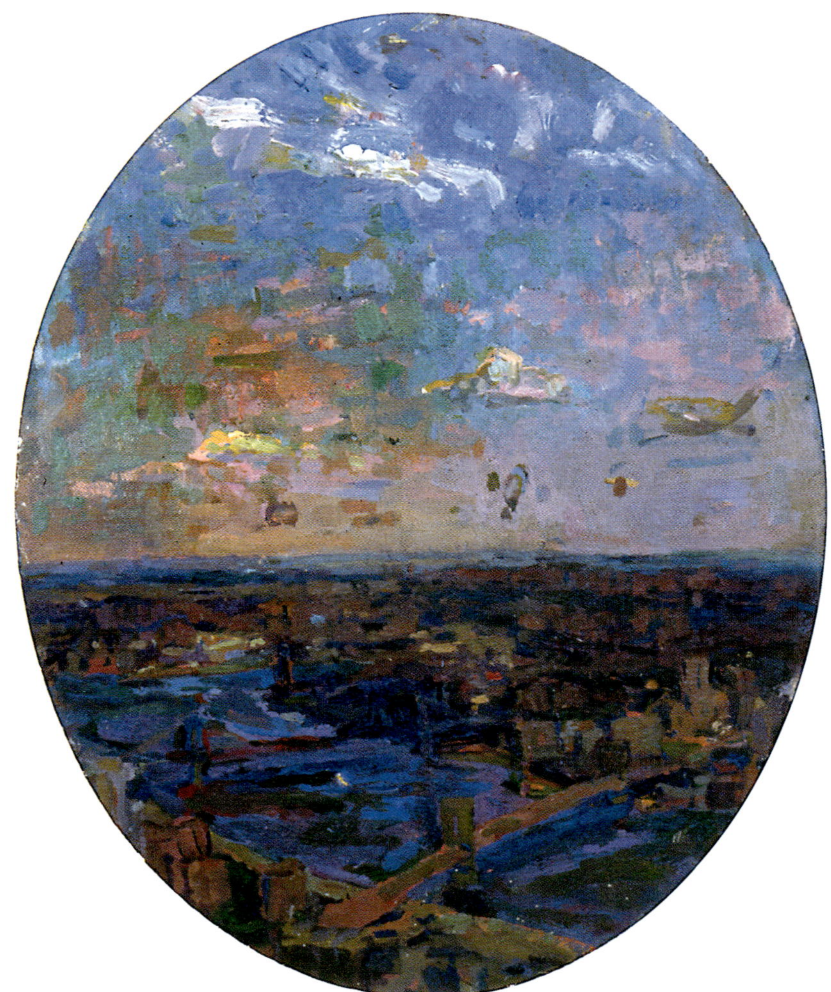

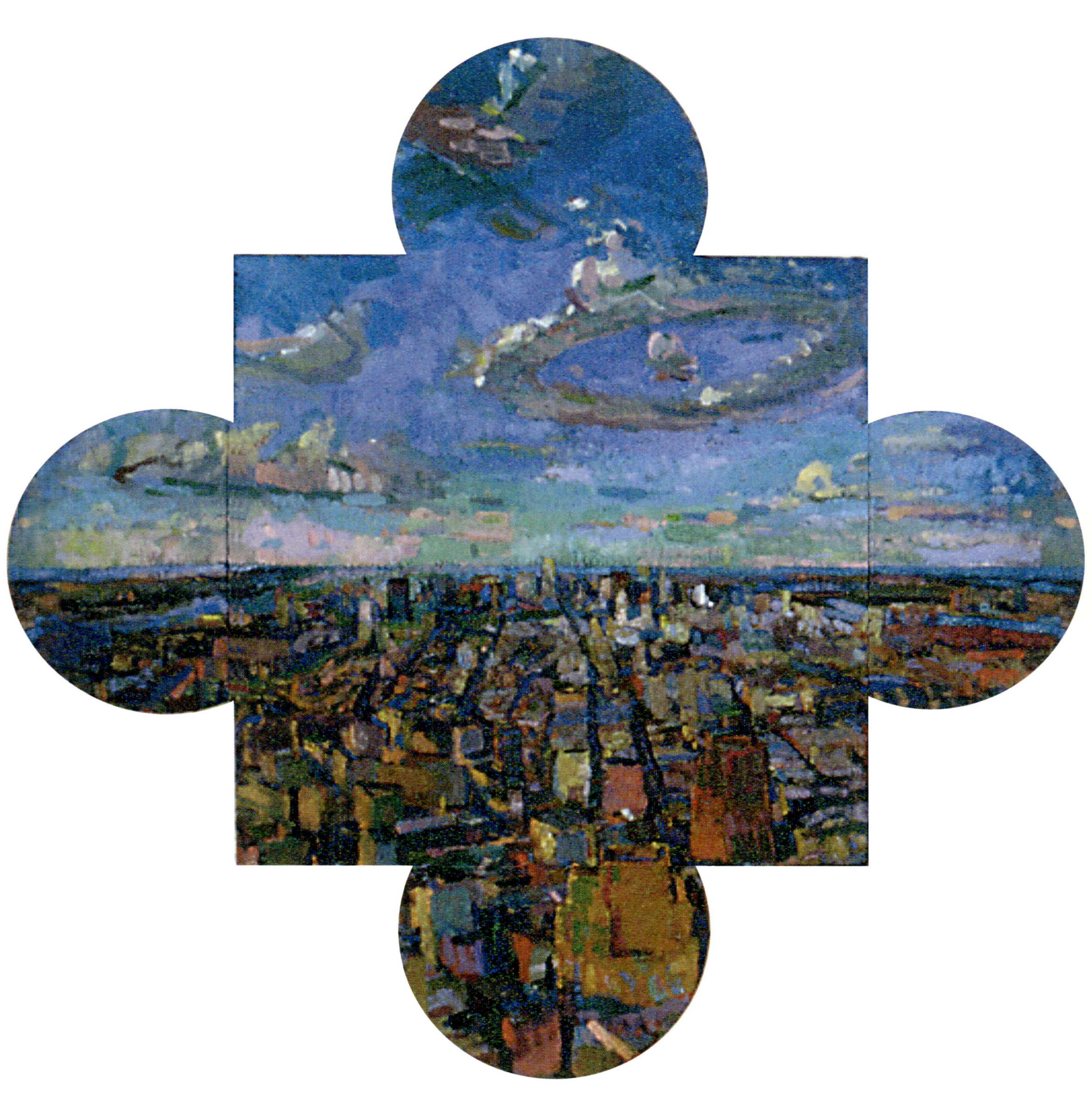

Donald Bracken

Fire Outside My Studio/World on Fire, 1997
Acrylic on plywood
23 x 96 inches

Untitled Premonition, 1997
Acrylic on plywood
58½ x 3½ inches

Born 1951 in Torrence, Calif.
Lives in West Cornwall, Conn.

Education

1973 BFA, University of California, Berkeley

Selected Solo Exhibitions

2002 *View from the 91st Floor,* New Arts Gallery, Litchfield, Conn.
1997 *91 Stories Above New York,* Good News Café, Woodbury, Conn.

Selected Group Exhibitions

2000 Bachlier Cardosky, Kent, Conn.
1999 Bachlier Cardosky, Kent, Conn.
1998 *Vertigo,* The New York Studio School, N.Y.
1997 Federal Reserve Bank, New York, N.Y.
1993 *New Worlds,* Mattatuck Museum, Waterbury, Conn.

Award

1997 Purchase Award, Federal Reserve Bank, New York, N.Y.

I painted in a cavernous 10,000-square-foot space on the ninety-first floor in the North Tower. The tiles of the floor had been ripped up, so the floor was the color of black mastic. The ceiling was gone, so you could see the pipes, wiring and insulation. There was no electricity and no reflected light in the space. I found the necessary items (a rolling scaffold and sheet rock) to make an easel that I could sit in and roll myself along from window to window so I could make large panoramic landscapes.

I came to work early one morning and the sun was rising on the eastern side of the building, burning through the backlit clouds with such brilliance that the sky appeared to be igniting through the rows of Gothic windows. Shafts of light came shooting across the black floor, setting the room aglow.

I felt magically separate from the world, yet very vulnerable, in this ivory tower. I created Fire Outside My Studio/World on Fire *in response to this experience, which became a portrait of my own fears for the future at that time.*

I created Untitled Premonition *using a metaphor of a plumb bob on a broken golden string. The plumb falls from the heavens, gravity causing it to take its Newtonian course.*

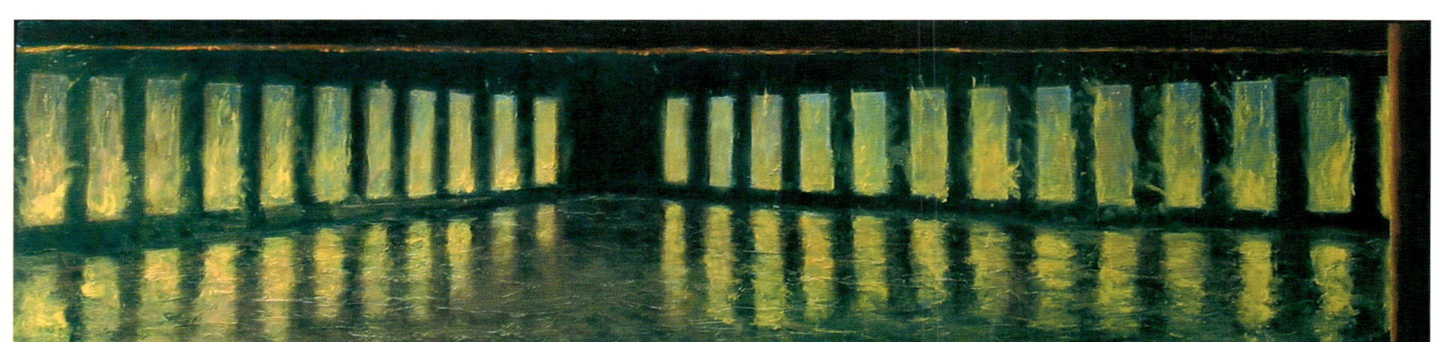

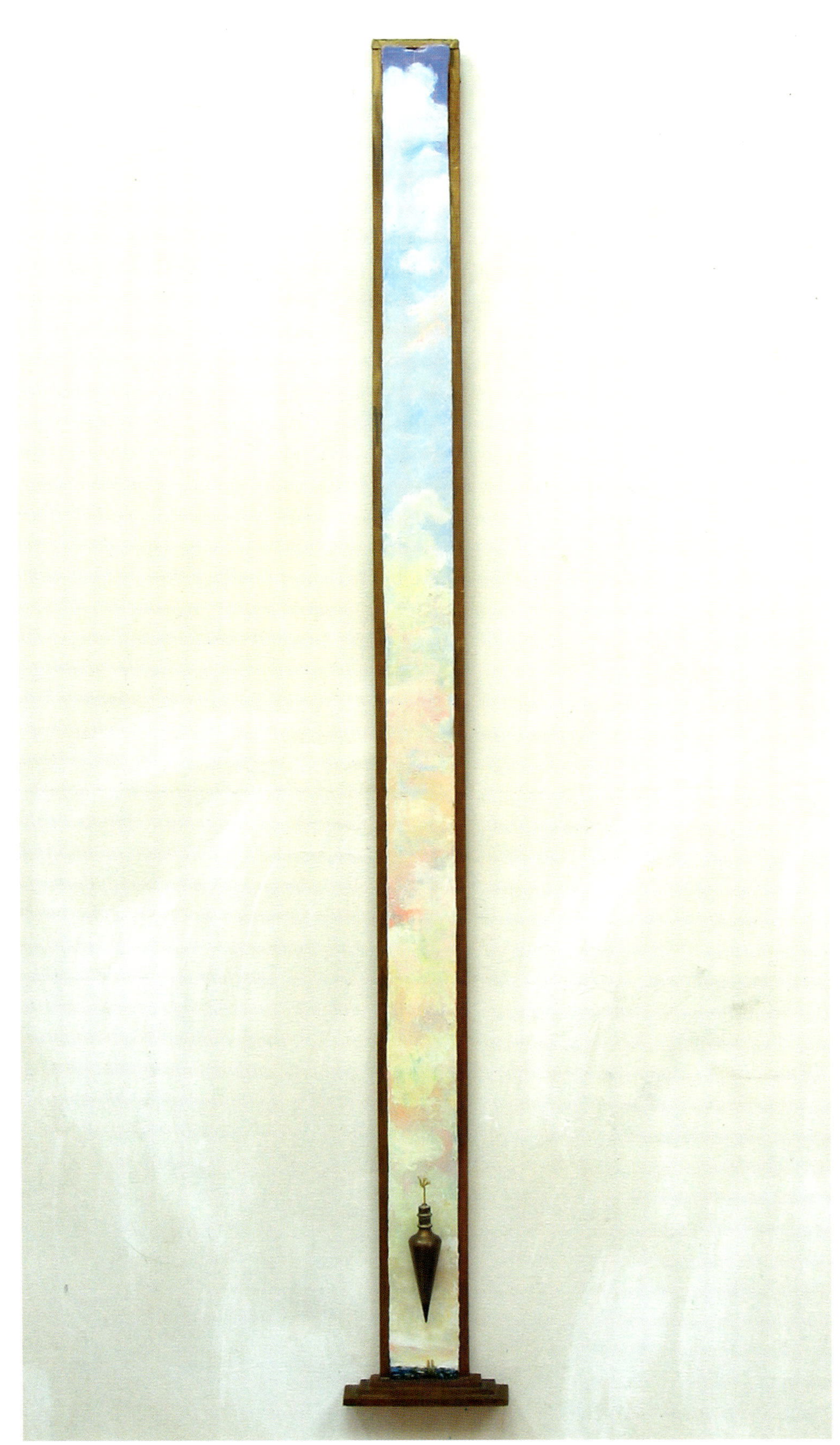

Lois Dodd

Governors Island and Verrazano Bridge, 1998
Oil on aluminum
5 x 7 inches
Gifted to the Lower Manhattan Cultural Council as honorees of the Skowhegan School Board of Governors (2002).

Statue of Liberty, 1998
Oil on aluminum
5 x 7 inches

Born 1927 in Montclair, N.J.
Lives in New York, N.Y.

Education
1948 The Cooper Union School of Art, New York, N.Y.

Selected Solo Exhibitions
2003 Alexandre Gallery, New York, N.Y.
Banana Factory, Bethlehem, Pa.
Caldbeck Gallery, Rockland, Maine

Selected Group Exhibitions
2003 *Women at Work*, The New York Studio School, N.Y.
Lyrical Landscapes, Trinity College, Hartford, Conn.
Maine Art Gallery, Wiscasset, Maine

Residency
2003 The Vermont Studio Center, Johnson

Lecture
2003 Round Top Center for the Arts, Damariscotta, Maine

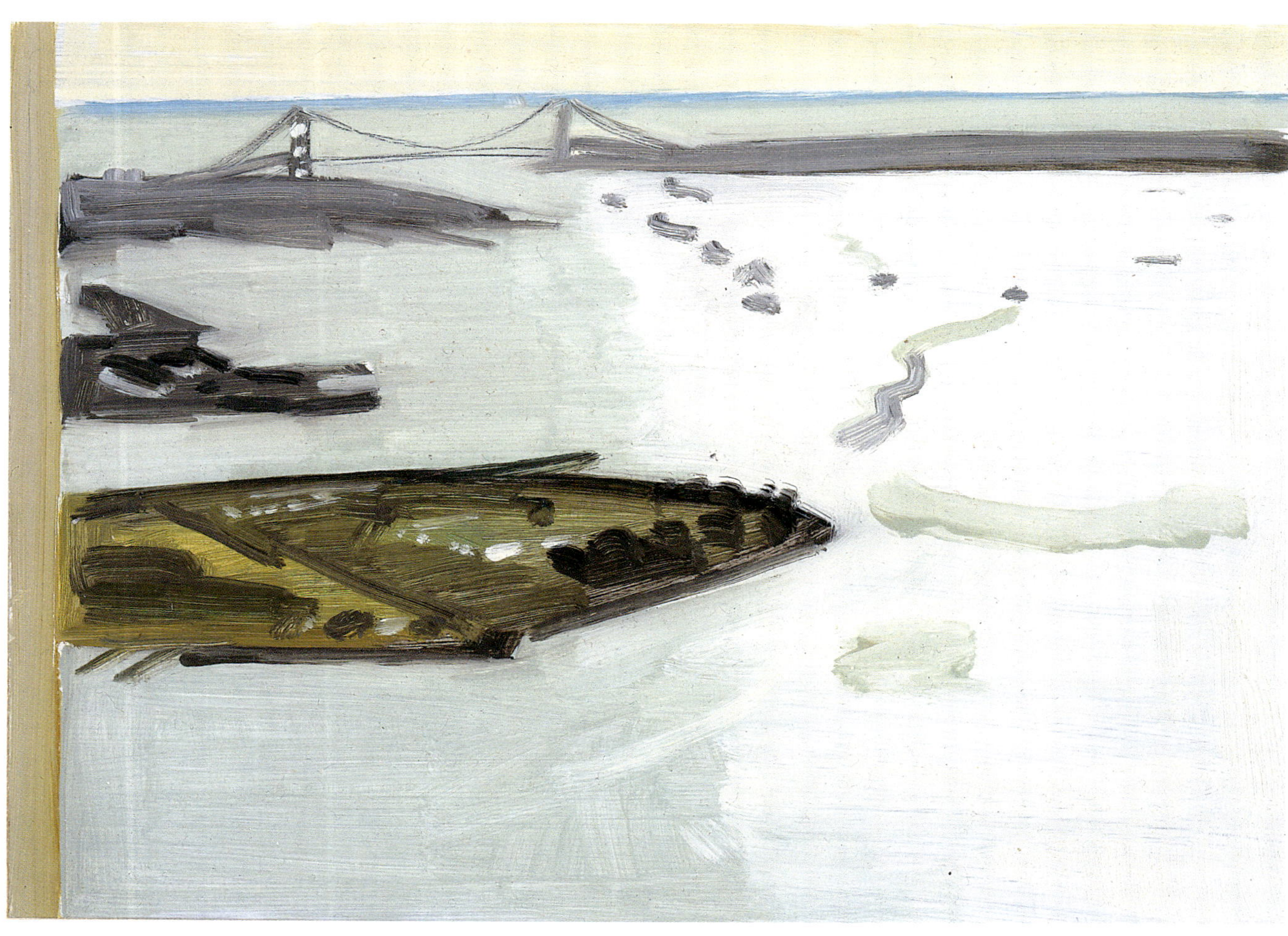

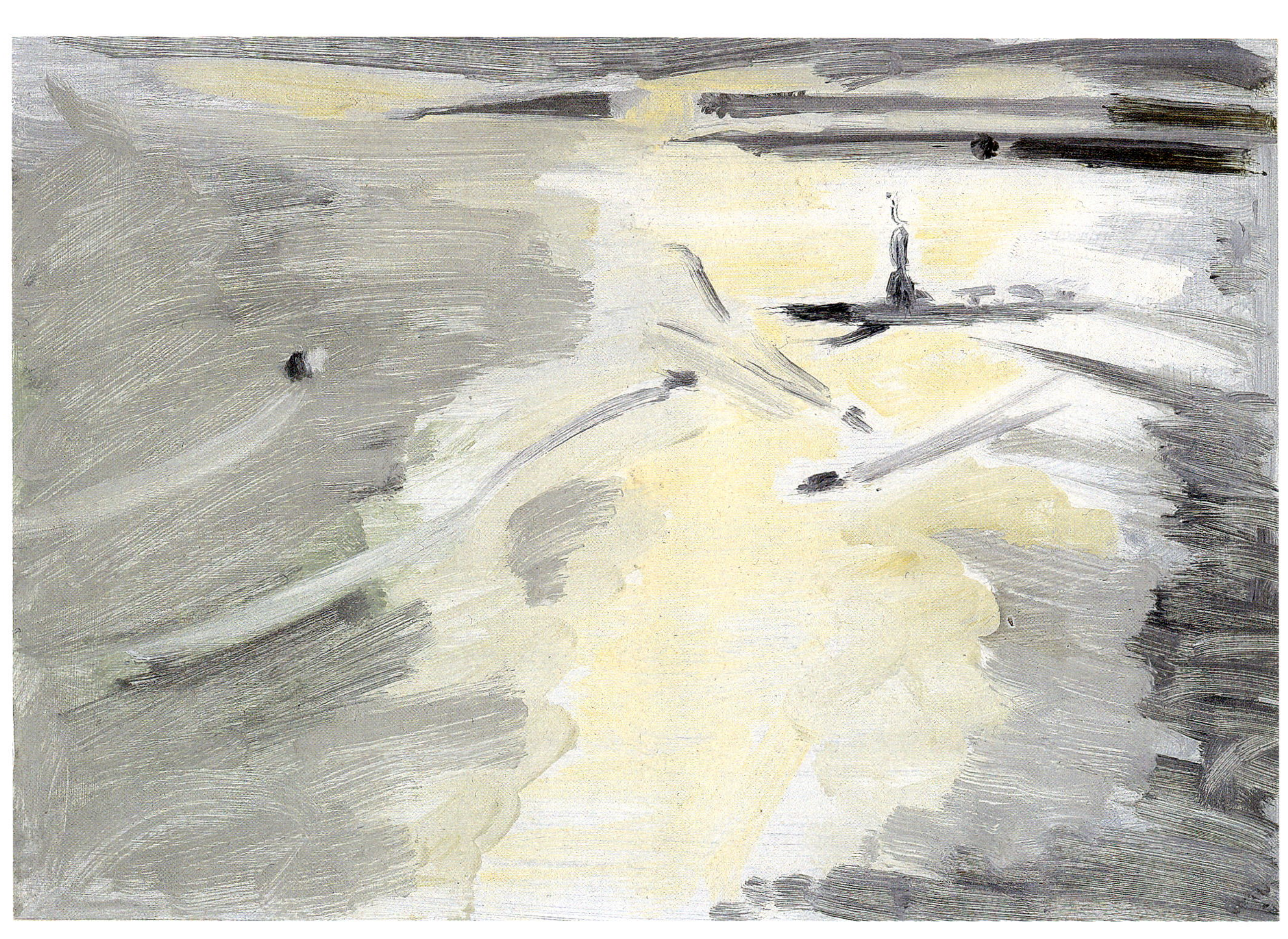

Rackstraw Downes

Untenanted Space with Four Exposures—World Trade Center—Study, 1998
Oil on canvas
10 x 44 inches
Courtesy Robert Miller Gallery, New York, N.Y.

Untenanted Space in the World Trade Center—Winter Sun, 1997
Oil on canvas
24 x 56¼ inches
Courtesy Robert Miller Gallery, New York, N.Y.

Born 1939 in Kent, U.K.
Lives in New York, N.Y.

Education

1964 MFA, Yale University School of Art, New Haven, Conn.
1961 BA, University of Cambridge, U.K.

Selected Solo Exhibitions

2000 Robert Miller Gallery, New York, N.Y.
1999 *The Chinati Paintings*, The Chinati Foundation, Marfa, Tex.
1998 *Drawings*, Texas Gallery, Houston

Selected Group Exhibitions

2002 *Curious Terrain*, Elizabeth Harris Gallery, New York, N.Y.
2001 *ReAppearance: Realism in Contemporary Art*, Brenau University Galleries, Gainesville, Ga.

Awards

1999 American Academy of Arts and Letters
1998 The John Simon Guggenheim Memorial Foundation
1980 The National Endowment for the Arts

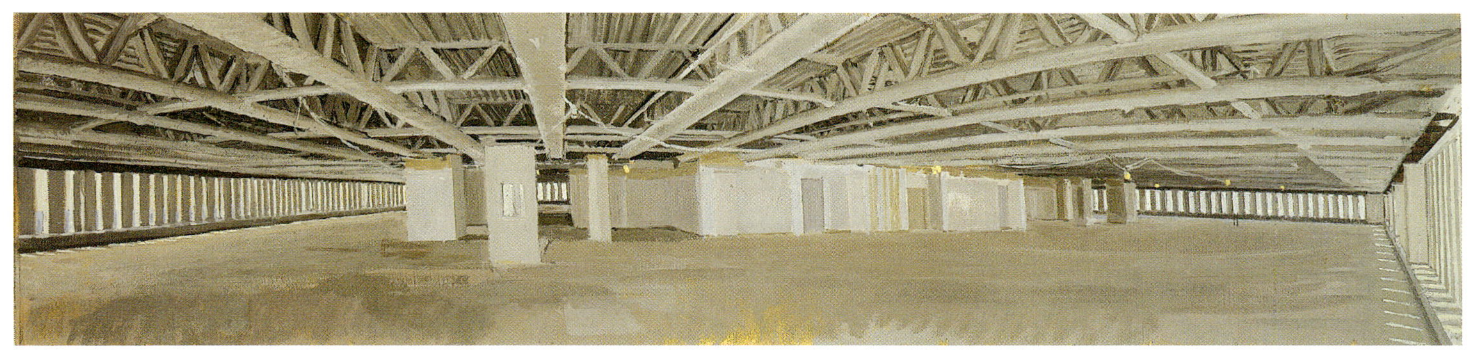

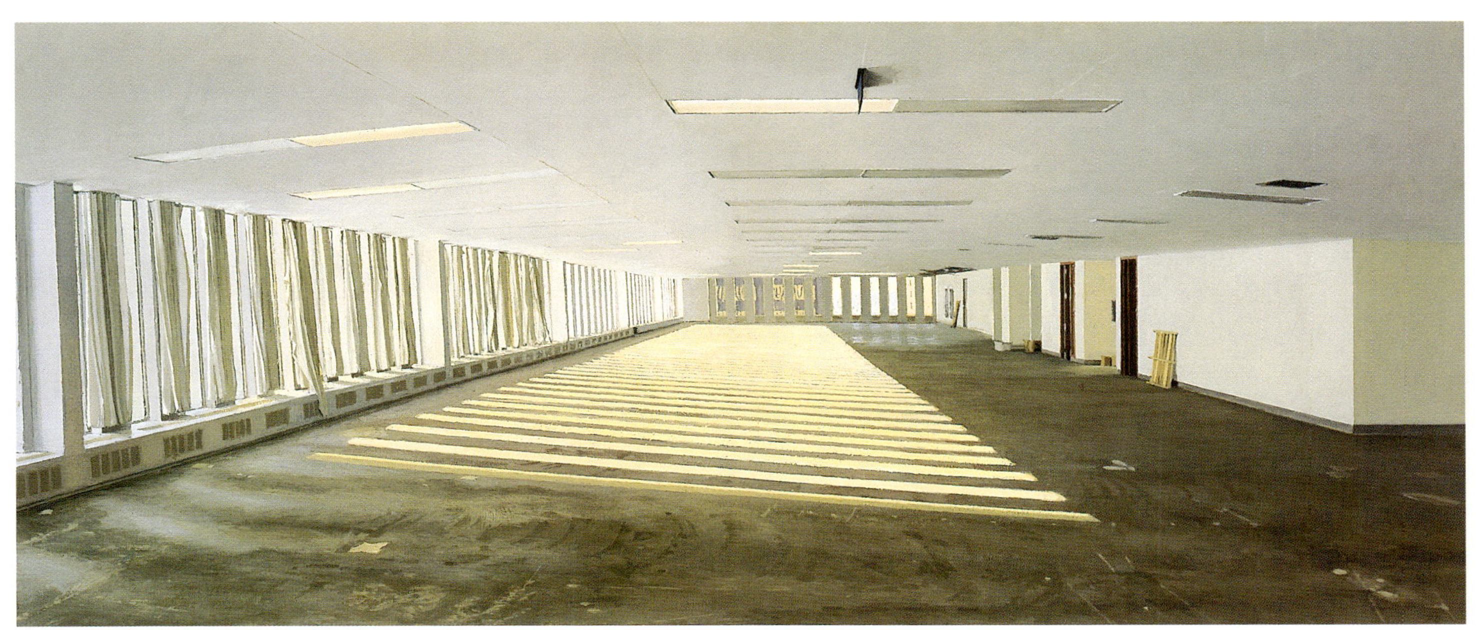

John Dubrow

World Trade Center, Harbor View, 1998
Oil on canvas
78 x 66 inches
Private collection
Photo: Paul Waldman

World Trade Center, View of Manhattan, 1997
Oil on canvas
90 x 96 inches
Private collection
Photo: Paul Waldman

Born 1958 in Salem, Mass.
Lives in Brooklyn, N.Y.

Education

1983 MFA, San Francisco Art Institute, Calif.
1980 BFA, San Francisco Art Institute, Calif.

Selected Solo Exhibitions

2003, 2000, 1998, 1996, 1993
Salander O'Reilly Galleries, New York, N.Y.

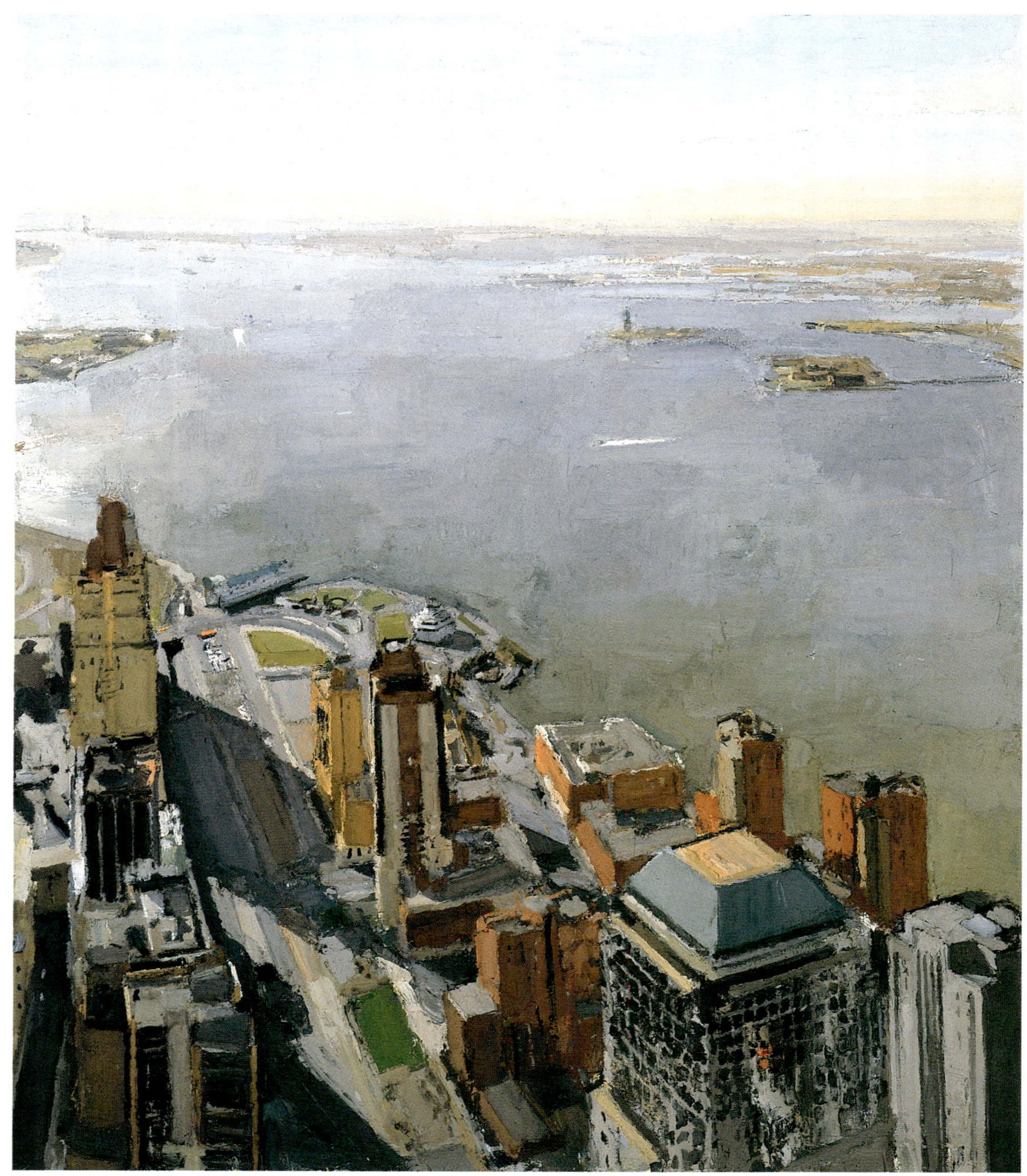

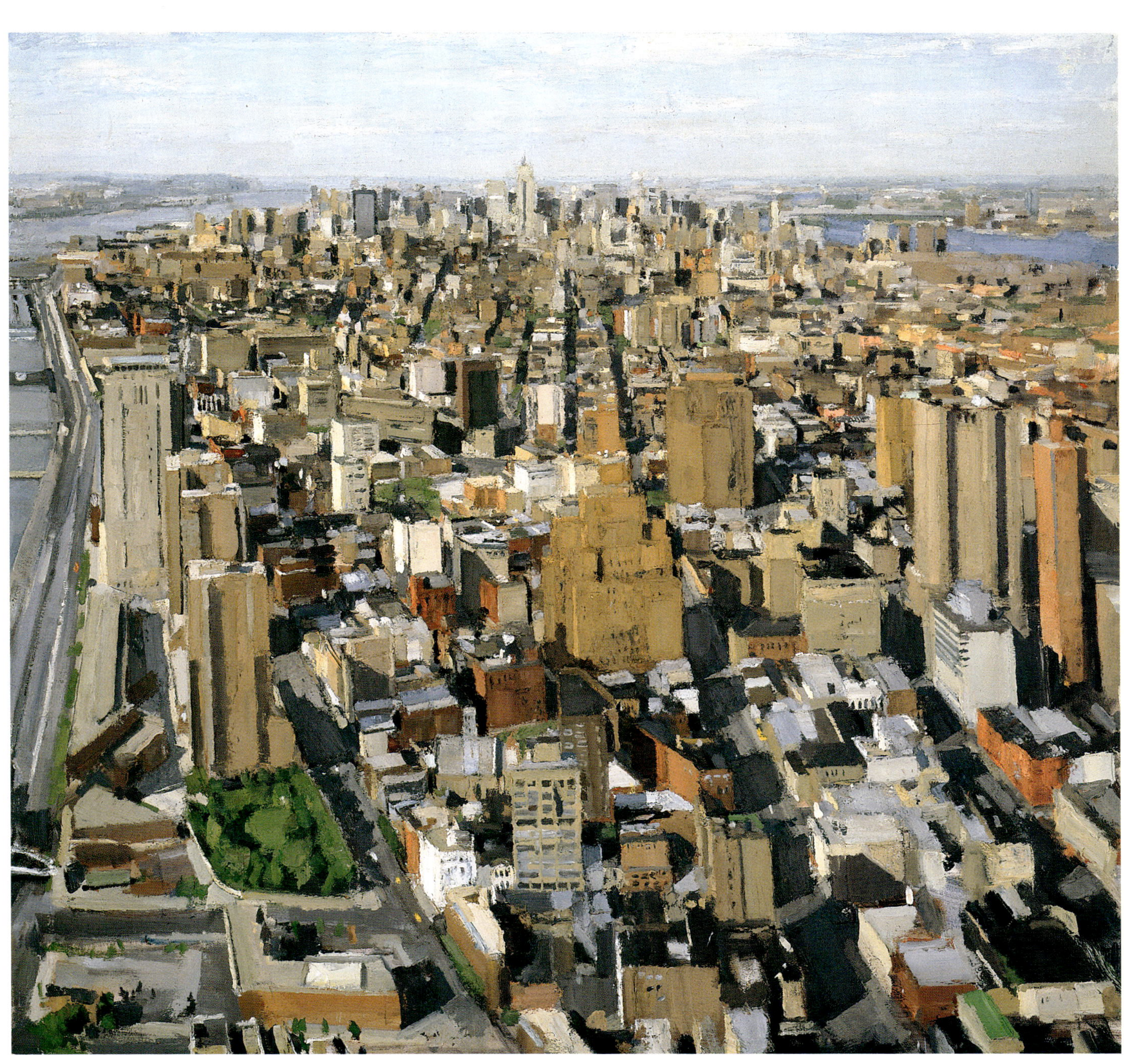

Jessica Goodyear

Overworked, 1998
Oil on canvas
24 x 34 inches
Collection of Michael Lacovara

Born 1946 in Carmel-by-the-Sea, Calif.
Lives in Branford, Conn.

Education

1980 BArch, Pratt Institute, Brooklyn, N.Y.

Selected Solo Exhibitions

1997 *Drawings of Lower Manhattan Landmarks*, India House, New York, N.Y.
1985 *The Serpent that Shakes the Earth*, Explorers Club, New York, N.Y.

Selected Group Exhibitions

2001 *Art of the Northeast*, Silvermine Guild Galleries, New Canaan, Conn.
1998 *Vertigo*, The New York Studio School, N.Y.
1996 *Design Your Cake and Eat it, Too*, Swiss Institute, New York, N.Y.
1995 Rene Fotouhi Gallery, New York, N.Y.

Performances

1979–83 New Wilderness Ocarina Orchestra
1980 Annual New York Avant-Garde Festival, Floyd Bennett Airfield, Cambridge, Mass., and World Trade Center, New York, N.Y.

I lived in the Wall Street area of Lower Manhattan for twenty-two years and would often observe men working late at night through distant windows, sitting at desks doing some kind of paperwork. Their late-night hours resonated with me.

Since 1980, I had been drawing Lower Manhattan landmarks and the LMCC residency was an opportunity to paint what I had only been drawing up until that time. This was my first painting in thirty-five years.

One day I was visiting the Broad Street offices of LMCC's Thundergulch program. Across the street was a nearby building facade. I spoke with the manager of that building and he allowed me to pose a model for a few hours in the empty office.

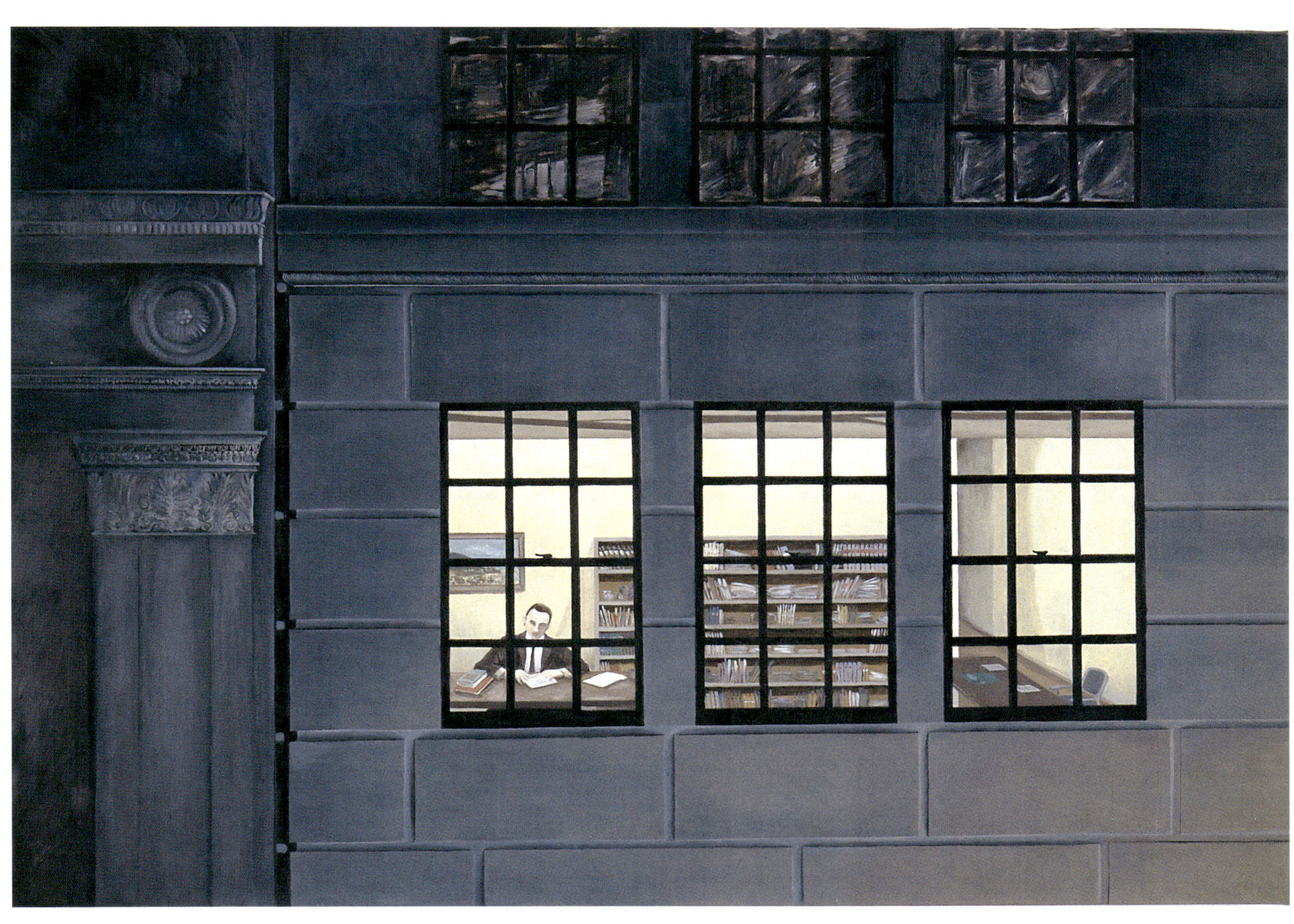

Richard Haas

Woolworth Building from WTC (Night), 1997
Pencil, pastel, gouache on paper
30 x 20 inches

Born 1936 in Spring Green, Wis.
Lives in Yonkers, N.Y.

Education

1964 MFA, University of Minnesota, Minneapolis
1959 BS, University of Wisconsin, Milwaukee

Selected Solo Exhibitions

2002 *Three Decades of Paintings, Prints and Works on Paper,* Michael Ingbar Gallery of Architectural Art, New York, N.Y.
Point of View, David Findlay Galleries, New York, N.Y.

Residency

2003 The MacDowell Colony, Peterborough, N.H.

Commissions and Awards

2003 Skowhegan School of Painting and Sculpture, Maine
Westchester Arts Council, N.Y.
2001 The Nashville Public Library, Tenn.
1989 Doris C. Freedman Award
1977 American Institute of Architects, Medal of Honor

When I was awarded a grant that allowed me to use four different spaces in both Tower One and Tower Two of the World Trade Center, I was excited because it gave me a permanent window on what before I had observed only by paying my fee and going to the observation deck in the South Tower. I could now study the transition of light from day to evening to night and see how weather affects the city from all vantage points. Each direction told a different story, but somehow I returned most often to the northeast corner of Tower One. I could stare down at the now toylike combination of the Woolworth Building, St. Paul's Church, City Hall and the Brooklyn Bridge, each a landmark of a different century of the city's history, and see how they were woven together as a foreground to the spreading metropolis. This was the quintessential New York that I had been trying to capture for over twenty-five years.

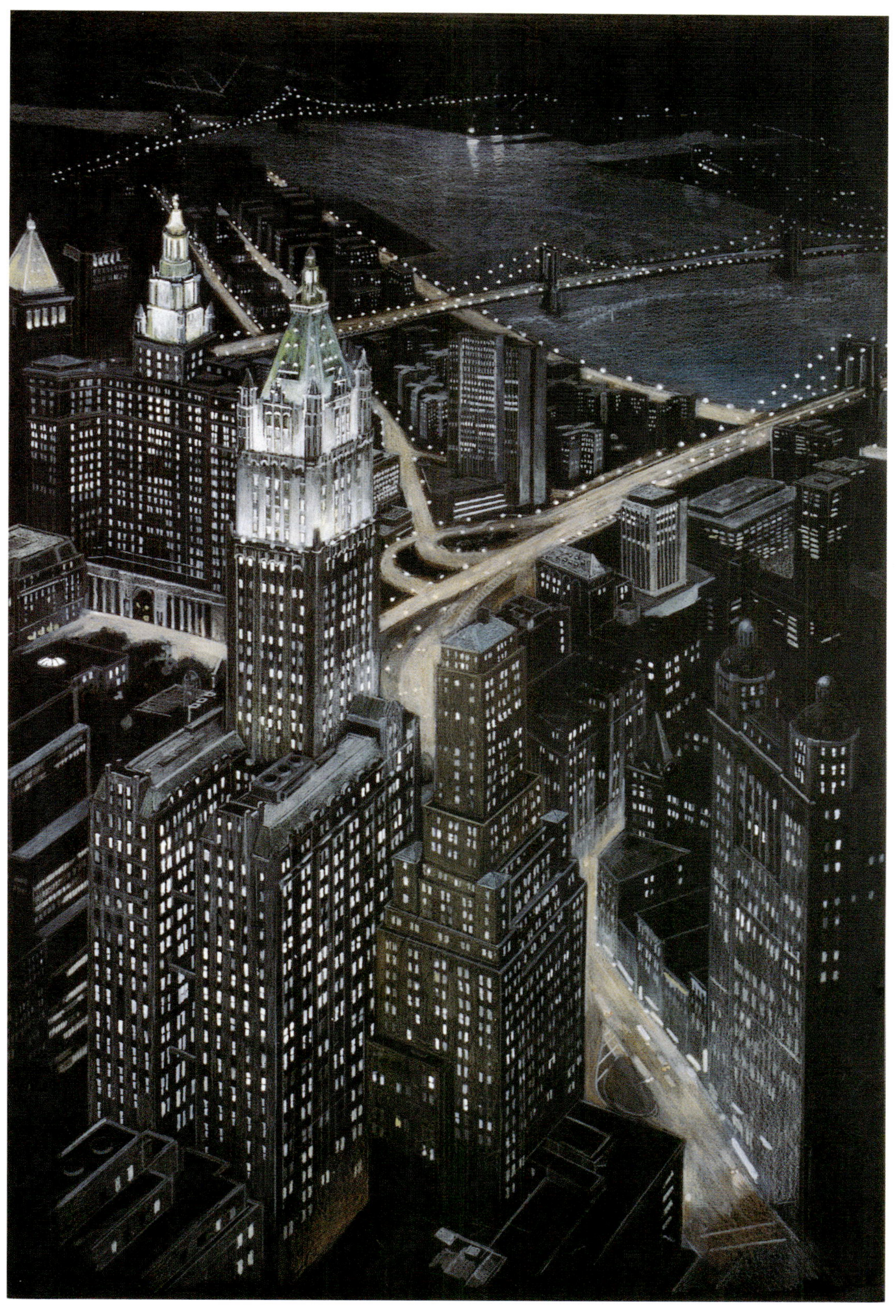

Susanna Heller

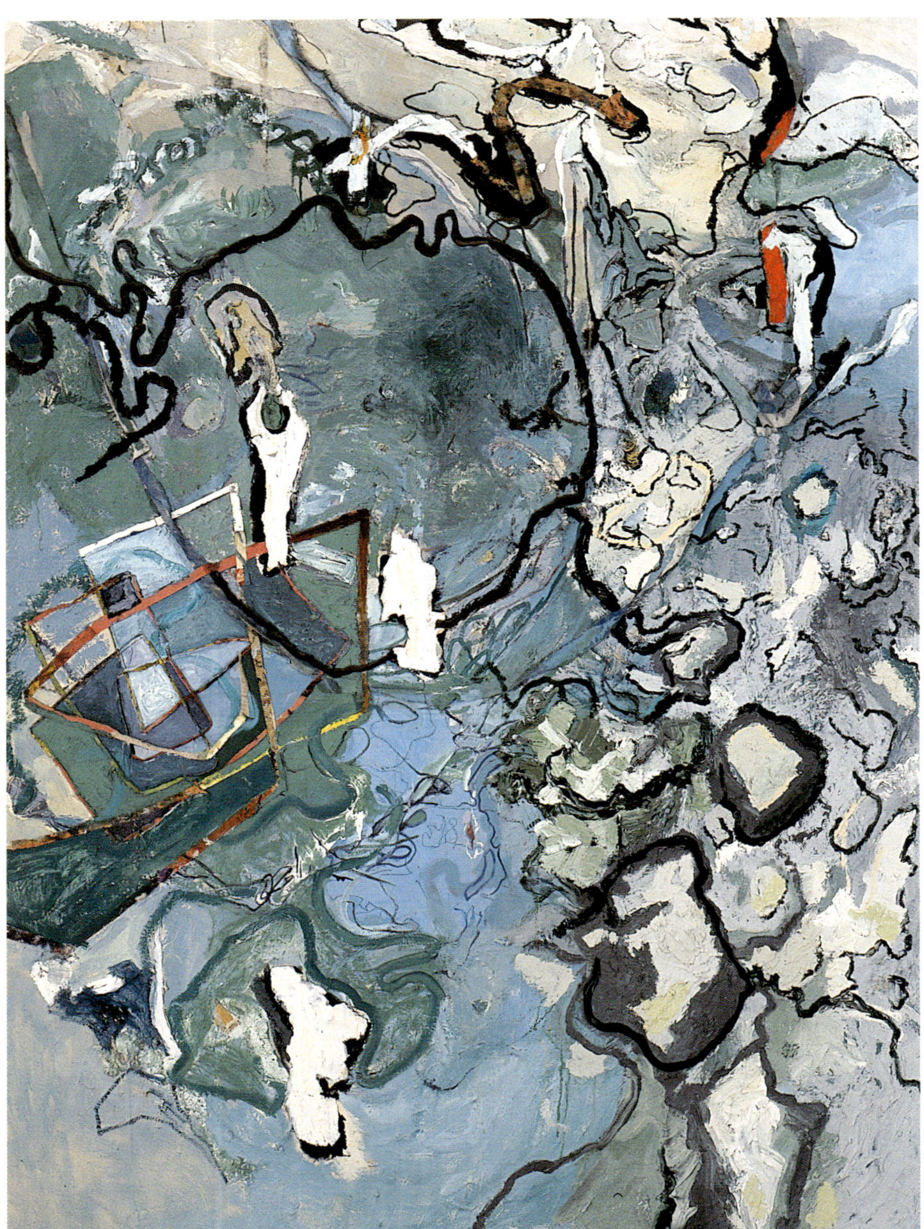

Harbor of Wakes, 2001
Oil and mixed media on linen
68 x 50 inches
Collection of Gilles and Julia Ouellette

The Big Drop, 2000
Oil on linen
78 x 60 inches
Collection of Donna Poile

Born 1956 in New York, N.Y.
Lives in Brooklyn, N.Y.

Education

1977 BFA, Nova Scotia College of Art and Design, Halifax

Selected Solo Exhibitions

2002 *From Here: New York City Paintings by Susanna Heller*, Museum London, London, Ontario
Olga Korper Gallery, Toronto, Ontario
Harbor of Wakes, Luis Ross Gallery, New York, N.Y.

1995 Galerie Paul Andriesse, Amsterdam, The Netherlands

Selected Group Exhibitions

2002 *Painters 15*, Shanghai Art Museum, China

2000 *Seven Hours: Art Berlin/New York*, New York, N.Y., and Berlin, Germany

Awards

1992 The National Endowment for the Arts
The John Simon Guggenheim Memorial Foundation

In my work I describe the experiences of living in New York City. In my painting and drawing the use of vertiginous, swooping movement shows the near with the distant, the clustered with the expansive and the continuous flux with the monumental. Almost daily I walk the city to understand and record these elusive and nonhierarchical ideas.

With this kind of exploration in mind, the view from the ninety-first floor of WTC1 was ideal: an eagle's nest location. It gave me the chance to watch and record these stories of the city in many new ways. From within the tower the space was a constantly changing map, and even the tower itself was in motion: rocking like a great ship suspended in the wind. I used my proximity to the ninety-first floor as a measurement, whether I was walking in the city or within the tower, so the building was like a magnet or an anchor for me. I used to stand and work for hours with my nose pressed against the glass. I looked straight down the side of the other tower to the tiny taxis below, or down and across the harbor from the swirling wakes of ships and the piers to the foggy horizon of the ocean beyond, or all the way north up the Hudson River to touch the tip of the Empire State Building. So instead of only walking the city to discover its illusively shifting stories, from the ninety-first floor I could actually fly through these spaces as well.

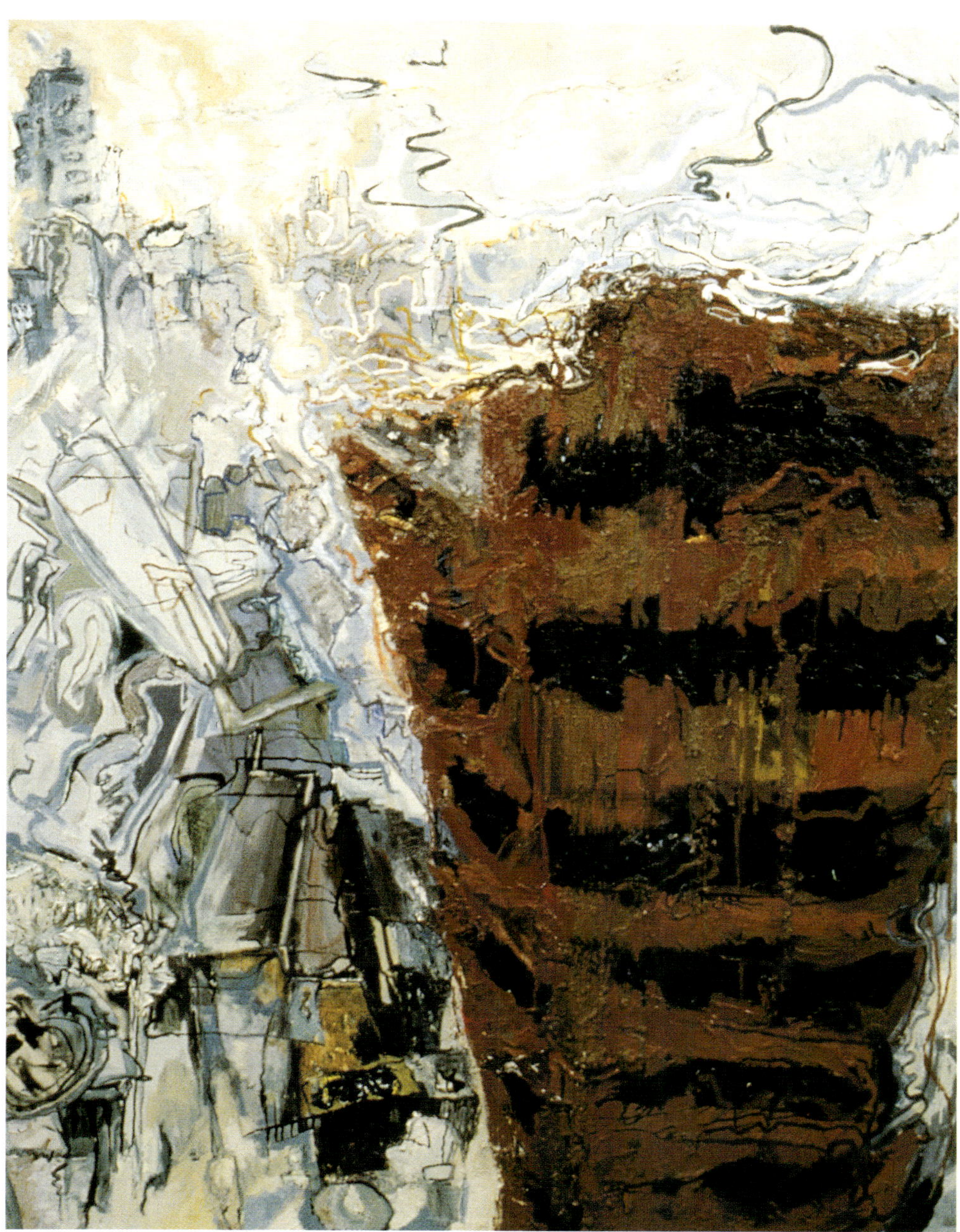

Diana Horowitz

New York Harbor and Ellis Island, 2001
Oil on linen
13 x 26 inches
Collection of the Museum of the City of New York
Photo: D. James Dee

Born 1958 in New York, N.Y.
Lives in New York, N.Y.

Education

1987 MFA, Brooklyn College, N.Y.
1980 BFA, State University of New York, Purchase

Selected Solo Exhibitions

2003 Hirschl & Adler Modern, New York, N.Y.
2000 MB Modern Gallery, New York, N.Y.
1999 Hirschl & Adler Modern, New York, N.Y.
1996 Hackett Freedman Gallery, San Francisco, Calif.

Awards

1999 Ballinglen Foundation Fellowship
1996 American Academy of Arts and Letters, Rosenthal Foundation Award
1993 The Pollock-Krasner Foundation
1988 The Ingram Merrill Foundation

Starting in 1985, I painted views of the city and New Jersey from the World Trade Center observation deck on the 107th floor. I would arrive each day with my easel and canvases and supplies, and I got to know the elevator and concession operators fairly well. When LMCC began its World Views residency program in 1997, I was lucky enough to be among the first group of artists to work on the ninety-first and eighty-fifth floors. The program provided an incredible freedom because it allowed me to leave all my things at the site and simply come to work each day, like so many other people in those buildings. I loved to paint the views of Brooklyn, New Jersey and the harbor. I also loved the atmosphere, the way that the buildings became small shapes at those distances, and the feeling of being in the sky with those sweeping views that dissolved into haze.

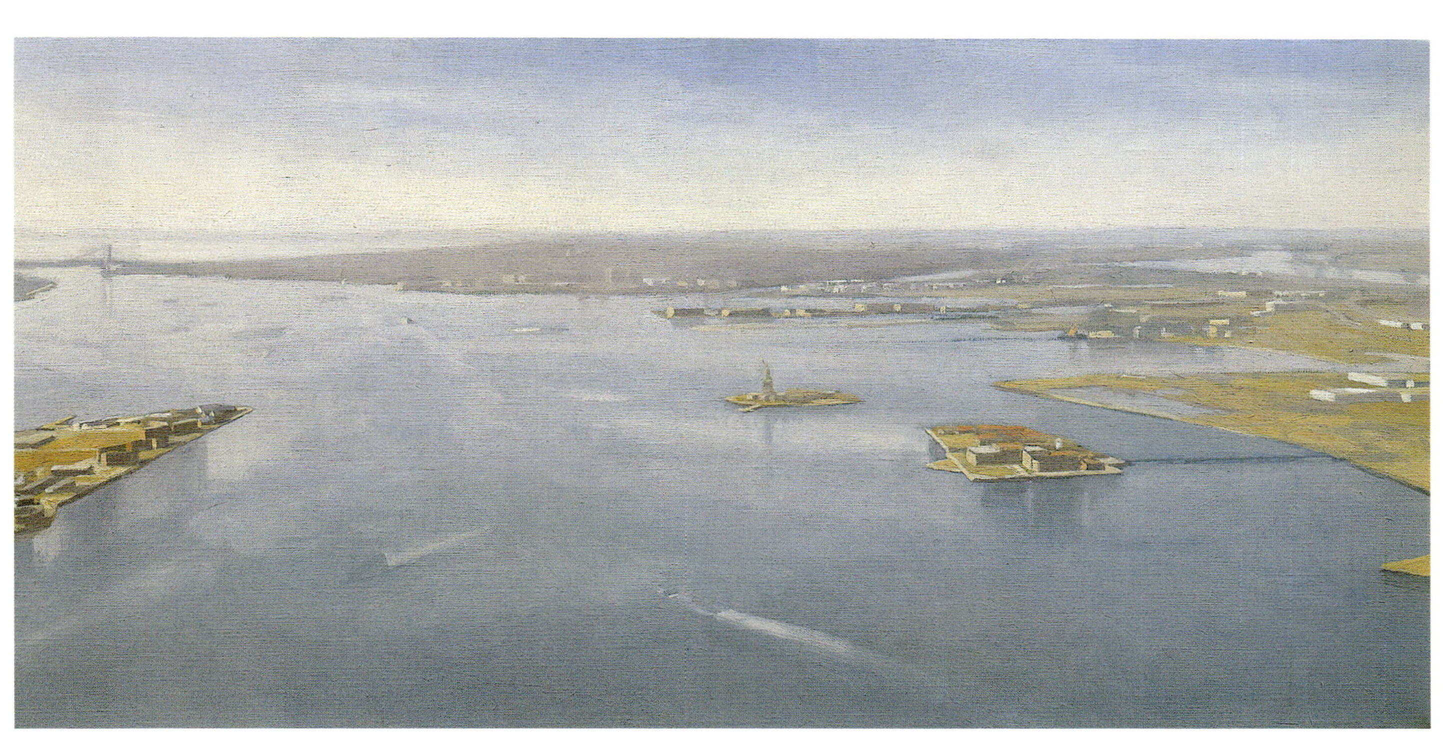

Yvonne Jacquette

South and West Views from World Trade Center II, 1996
Oil on canvas
53 x 144 inches overall
Private collection
Photo: Kevin Ryan

Southeast View from World Trade Center II, 2001
Oil on canvas
72 x 54 inches
Collection of Yale University Art Gallery, The Janet and Simeon Braguin Fund
Photo: Kevin Ryan

Born 1934 in Pittsburgh, Pa.
Lives in New York, N.Y.

Education

1952–56 Rhode Island School of Design, Providence

Selected Solo Exhibitions

2003 DC Moore Gallery, New York, N.Y.
2002 *Aerial Muse: The Art of Yvonne Jacquette*, Iris & B. Gerald Cantor Center for Visual Arts, Stanford University, Calif. (tour)
2000 *Evening: Chicago and New York*, DC Moore Gallery, New York, N.Y.

Selected Group Exhibitions

2003 *Mapping Maine: Four Contemporary Views*, Portland Museum of Art, Maine
2002 *Looking at America*, Yale University Art Gallery, New Haven, Conn.
2001 *Up on the Roof*, The New York Historical Society, New York, N.Y.

Awards

2003 American Academy of Arts & Letters
1998 The John Simon Guggenheim Memorial Foundation

I began drawing from the inside observation deck the year the WTC was opened, and continued frequently for the next twenty or more years. As a painter my fascination with the aerial view, then the night aerial view, was made possible by this vantage point. Where else would one have vertiginous understandings or distance excited by bridges, wharves, tankers, or clumpings of buildings? Key for me was the accessibility, especially at dusk or night, as my works were developed slowly and repeated visits were necessary. When the World Views *program began there were six or seven empty spaces available to the artists. That gave me the opportunity to composite sections from several different floors, or even from the two separate buildings, to continue my interest in radically changed scales or angles of vision. These works were very instinctual; if I had planned the units logically I wouldn't have made some "leaps." I'm indebted to that situation.*

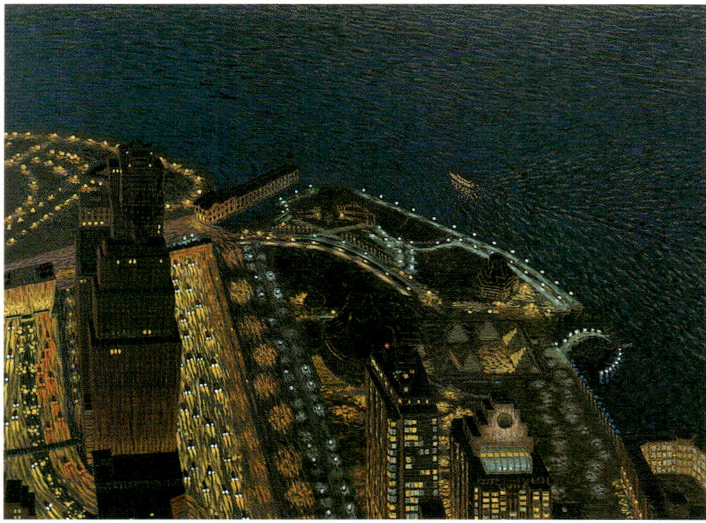

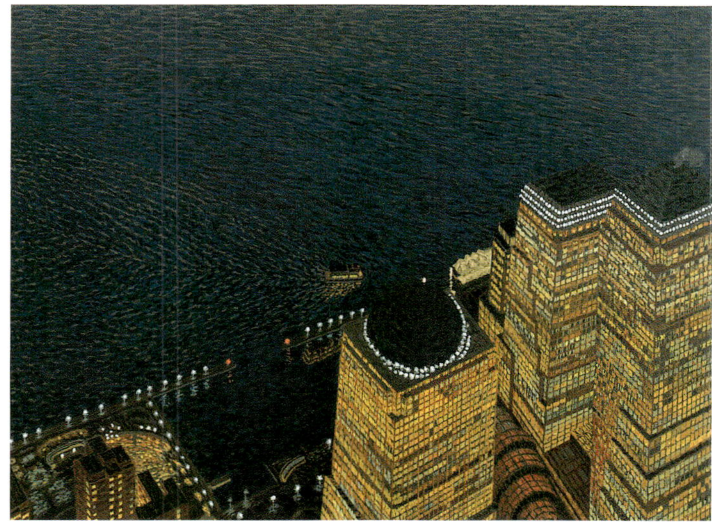

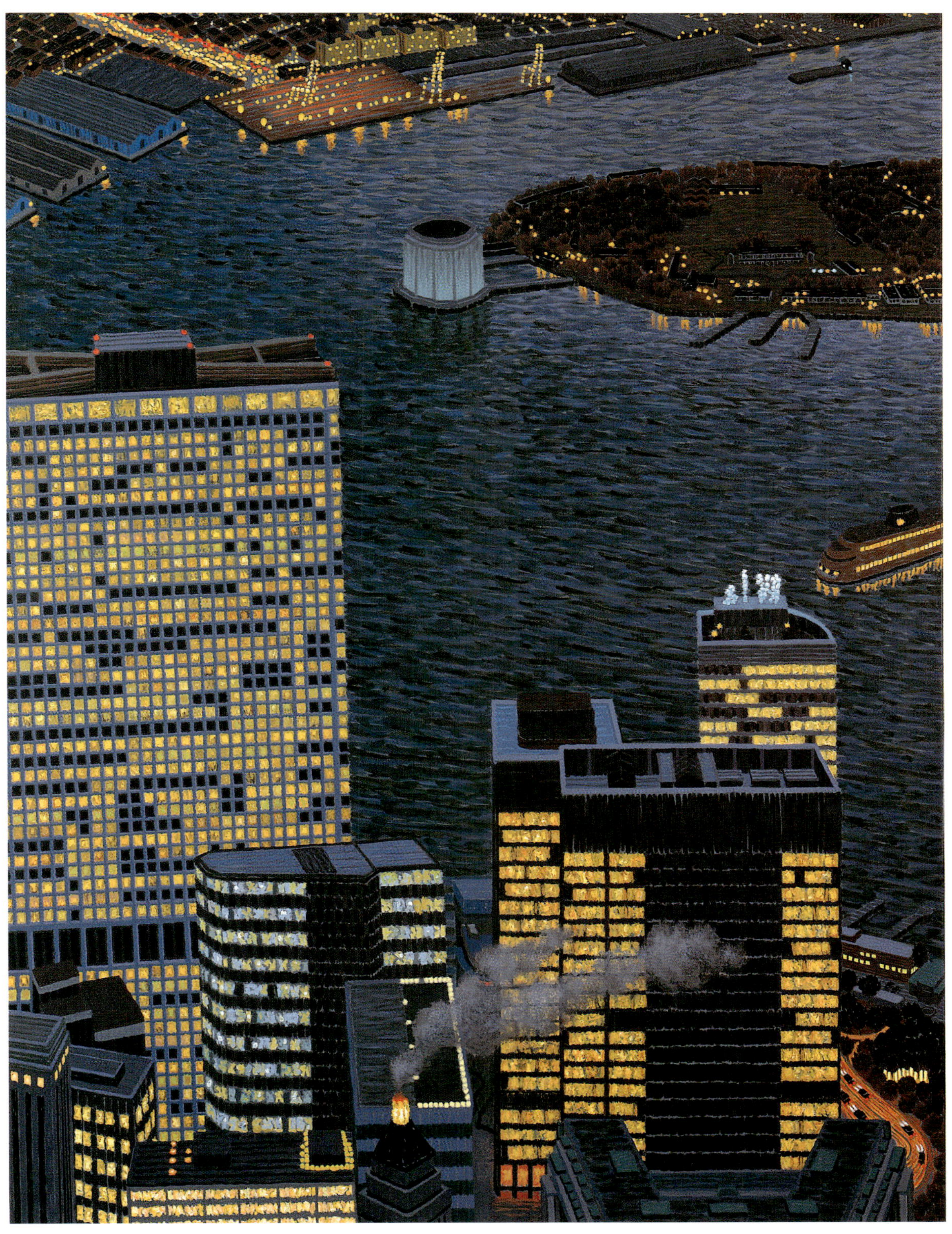

Elisa Jensen

New York Harbor from the 85th Floor, 1997
Oil on linen
18 x 36 inches

New York City, 1997
Oil on linen
30 x 34 inches

Born 1965 in Bridgeport, Conn.
Lives in Brooklyn, N.Y.

Selected Solo Exhibitions

2002 *Paintings*, Royal Danish Consulate General, New York, N.Y.
1999 *Umbria*Mors*Manhattan: Recent Work*, Ansonia Gallery, New York, N.Y.
1998 *Paintings and Drawings*, Suffolk County Community College, Newton, N.J.

Selected Group Exhibitions

2003 *Searching for the Image,* The Von Liebig Art Center, Naples, Fla., and Elliott Gallery, Eckerd College, St. Petersburg, Fla.
2002 *Take Five*, Yellow House Gallery, Greenport, N.Y.
2001 *Repainting Church's Territory*, Hudson Opera House, Hudson, N.Y., and Olana, Hudson, N.Y.
1998 *Languages of Reflection*, The Art Showcase XI, The Bond Market Association, New York, N.Y.
1997 *Paintings and Drawings*, Morsø Kunstforening, Nykøbing, Denmark

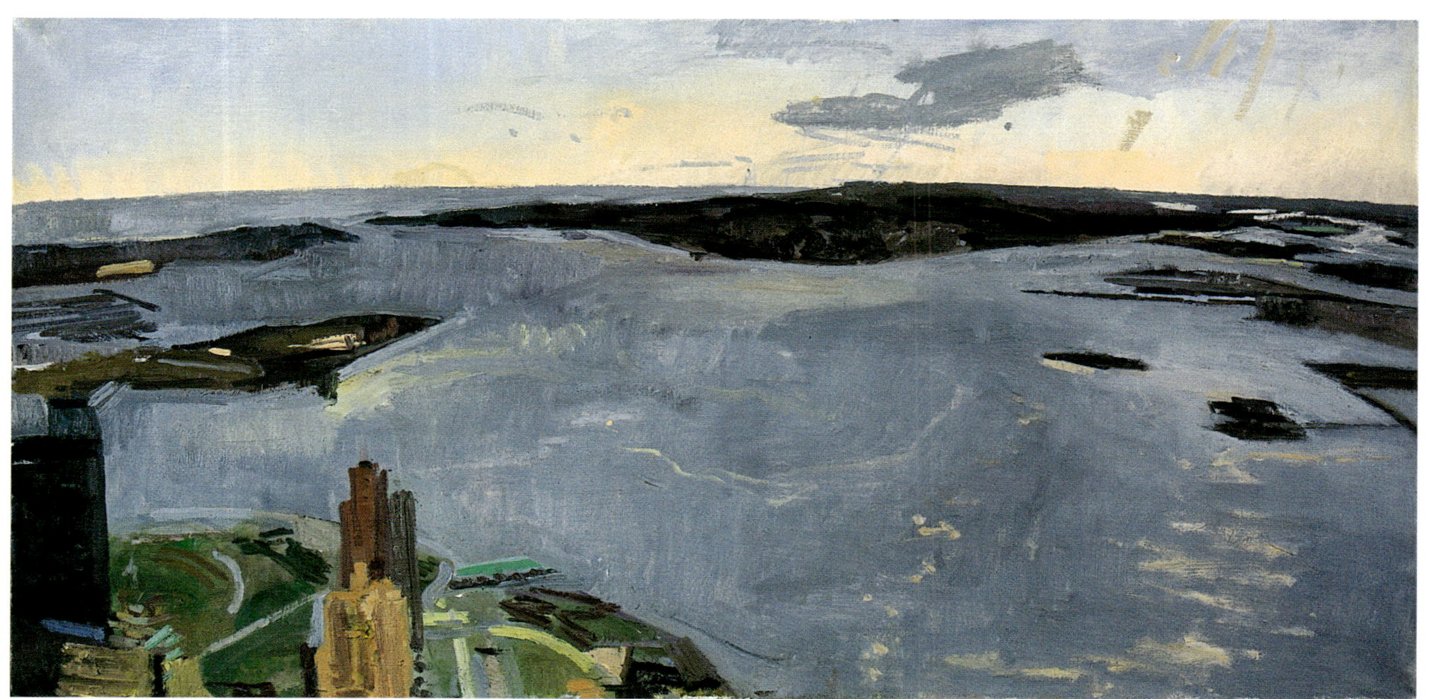

I was in the first group of artists selected to work up at the top of the World Trade Center in the World Views program. We felt like pioneers, doing something that had never been done before. What we saw and painted had never been painted or drawn before. The experience was exhilarating and changed the way I approached the city and the landscape. From that altitude I could see light and shadow and even weather move across the city, transforming it. It was a surprisingly intimate experience, in stark contrast with the feeling one has when one is walking down the avenue, with the light eclipsed by skyscrapers.

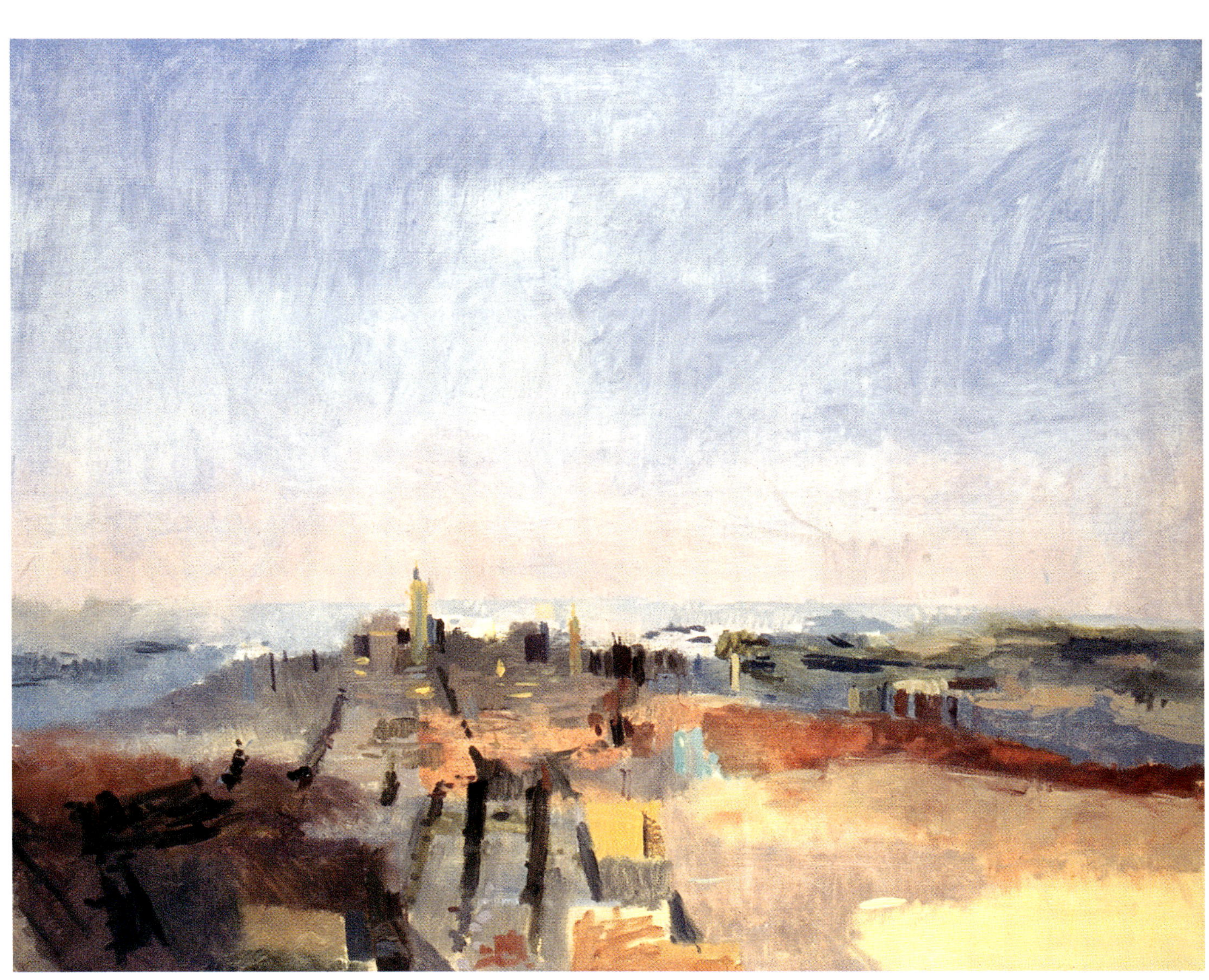

Pamela Lawton

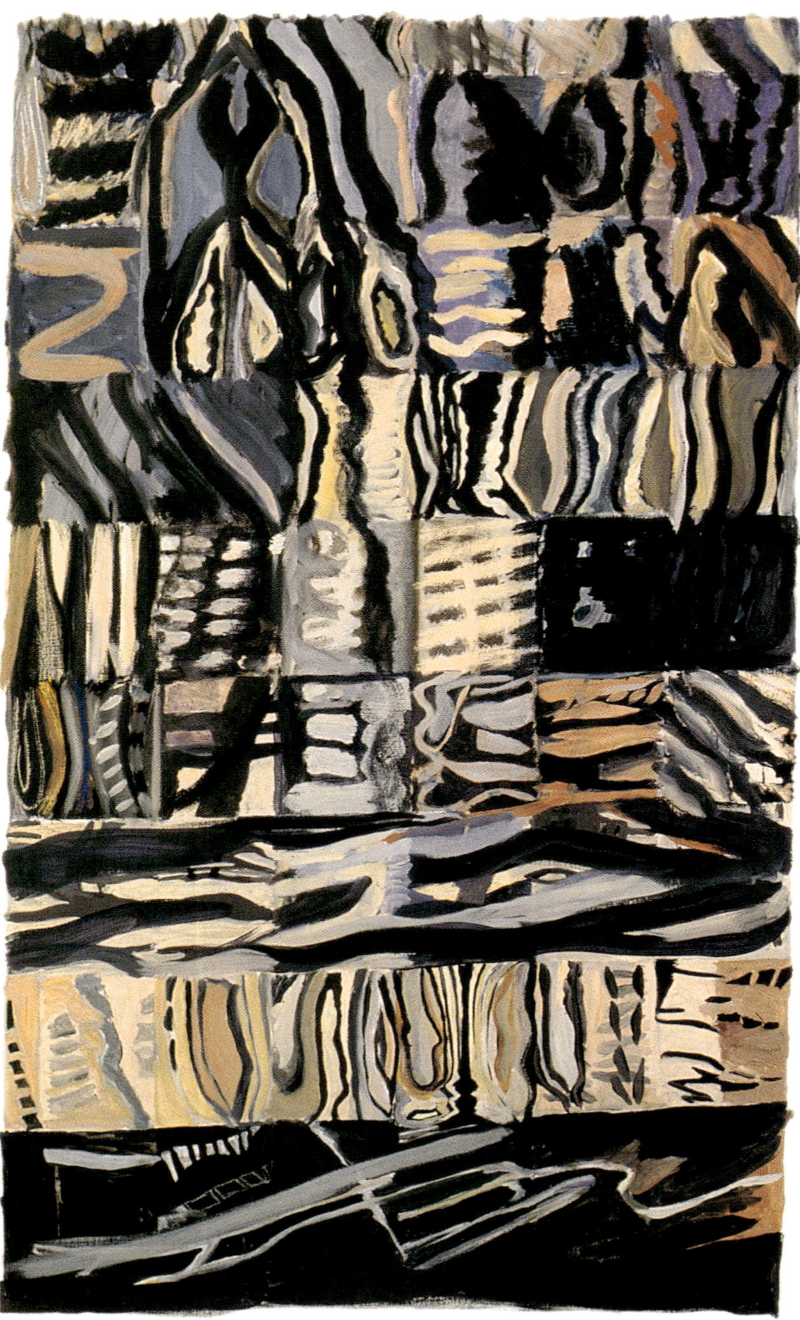

Tower 2, VI, 1998
Acrylic, pastel, charcoal on paper
72 x 45 inches
Private collection
Photo: Steven Bates

Tower 2, IV, 1998
Acrylic, pastel, charcoal on paper
72 x 48 inches
Private collection
Photo: Steven Bates

Born 1959 in Bryn Mawr, Pa.
Lives in New York, N.Y.

Education

2002 MFA, The City College of New York, N.Y.
1981 BA, Bennington College, Vt.

Selected Solo Exhibitions

2003 *The Annex*, White Box Gallery, New York, N.Y.
2002 The Isabel Ignacio Gallery, Seville, Spain

Selected Group Exhibitions

2003 *Grabado*, Galeria Nacionale, San Jose, Costa Rica
2000 *Remembering Rudy*, Tibor de Nagy Gallery, New York, N.Y.
Duchamp Traveling Exhibition, Emmanuel Heller Gallery, Tel Aviv, Israel

Curatorial Project

2004 The Painting Center, New York, N.Y.

Residency

2001 American University in Corciano, Italy

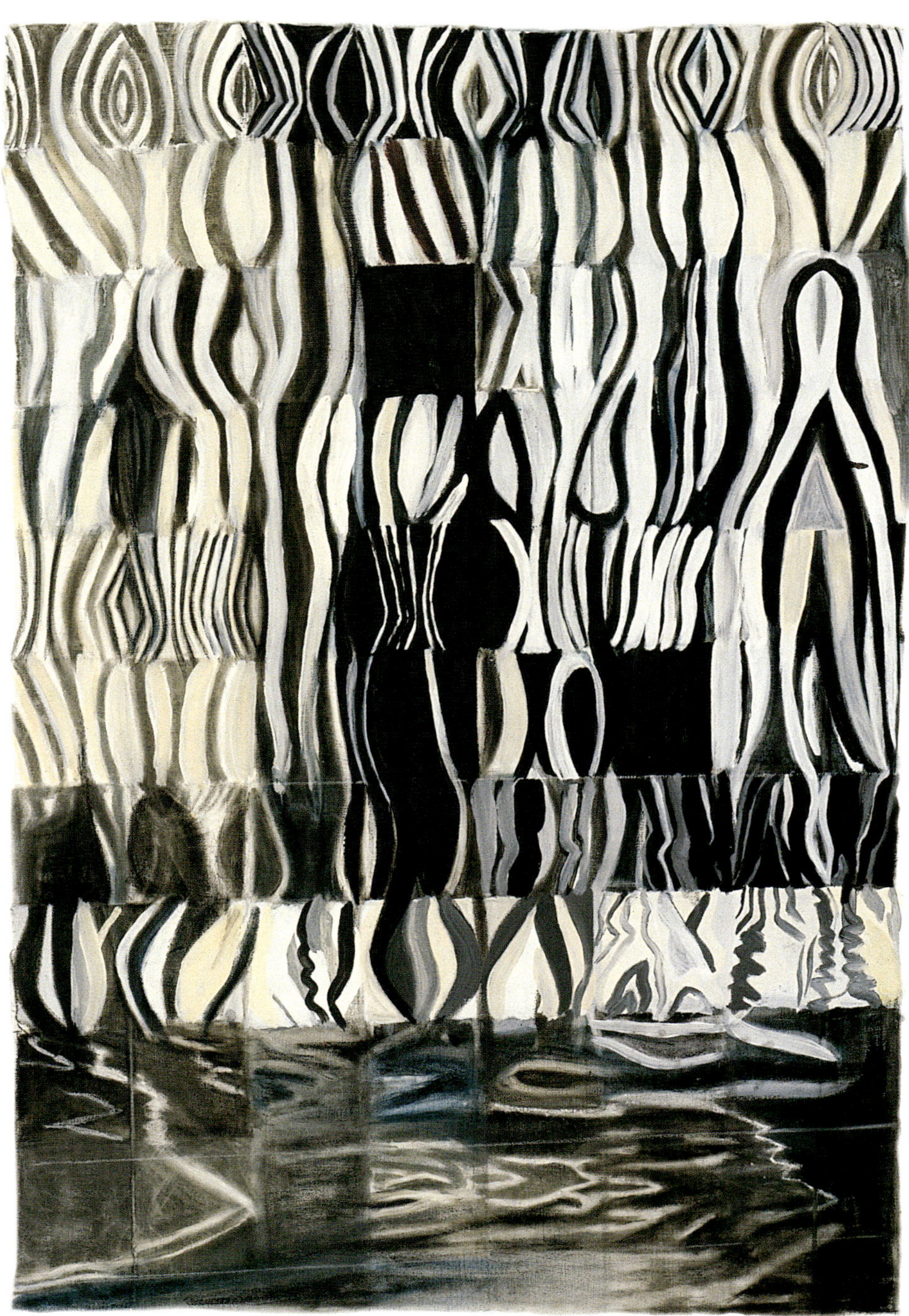

The vertigo I felt began with the vertical movement of the elevator ride. It continued with the sounds of the wind in the elevator and hallways; the sway of the building; the sensation of being in the long, low empty room where I painted; and led to the view out the window. In my works on paper I mapped my vertical and horizontal pathways through the gridded monolith, traveling through columns of rectangles.

I painted images of glass building facades that reflected my position—like a self-portrait in a mirror, but instead the self is the building reflected in mirrored windows. In reflections, solid form liquifies. These particular windows were flexible, moving in the wind. Their appearance changed with the weather and the time of day. The gridded glass curtain creates a further distortion, generating repetitious shapes. Buildings seen in glass dematerialize, multiply and fraction. These elements were the catalysts for the work, though not its final subject. The ambiguous and suggestive forms reflected my perceptions of a place that felt both shifting and groundless.

Eleanor Magid

Bridging 6, 2000
Ink and watercolor on paper
30 x 22½ inches

Born 1933 in Tiffin, Ohio
Lives in New York, N.Y.

Education

1985 MFA, Brooklyn College, N.Y.
1978 AB, Smith College, Northampton, Mass.

Selected Solo Exhibitions

2000 *Improvisational Bridges,* Trenton City Museum, N.J.
1997 Wilmer Jennings Gallery, New York, N.Y.

Selected Group Exhibitions

2003 *The Printmaking Tradition, in Memory of Robert Blackburn*, Kenkeleba Gallery, New York, N.Y.
2002 *From the Ashes: Sixth Annual Vision Festival*, Quando, New York, N.Y.
1985 *Art Works in City Spaces*, Tweed Courthouse, New York, N.Y.
The Gathering of the Avant-Garde: The Lower East Side, 1948–1970, Kenkeleba Gallery, Saint Mark's Church and Henry Street Settlement, New York, N.Y.

Other Projects

1992 *Art in the Scale of Being*, curator, Gaia Institute at the Cathedral of St. John the Divine, New York, N.Y.
1968 The Lower East Side Printshop, founder and first director, New York, N.Y.

For me East River bridges and Hudson River piers as seen from high up in the World Trade Center towers gathered complicated analogical meanings causing synapses to spark, connect, fade and spark again, making curious music.

In fact I began drawing from the observation deck years ago when the towers first opened to the public, but I owe some of the most intense working days of my life to an artist residency in 1998 under the auspices of the Lower Manhattan Cultural Council. When it was misty I'd sit up there on an otherwise empty floor in uncommon stillness, waiting for the Brooklyn Bridge to emerge below—a marvel every time.

The watercolor here is constructed directly over original drawings made on site. Ideas continue to build, and I believe I will be reshaping this imagery for the rest of my life.

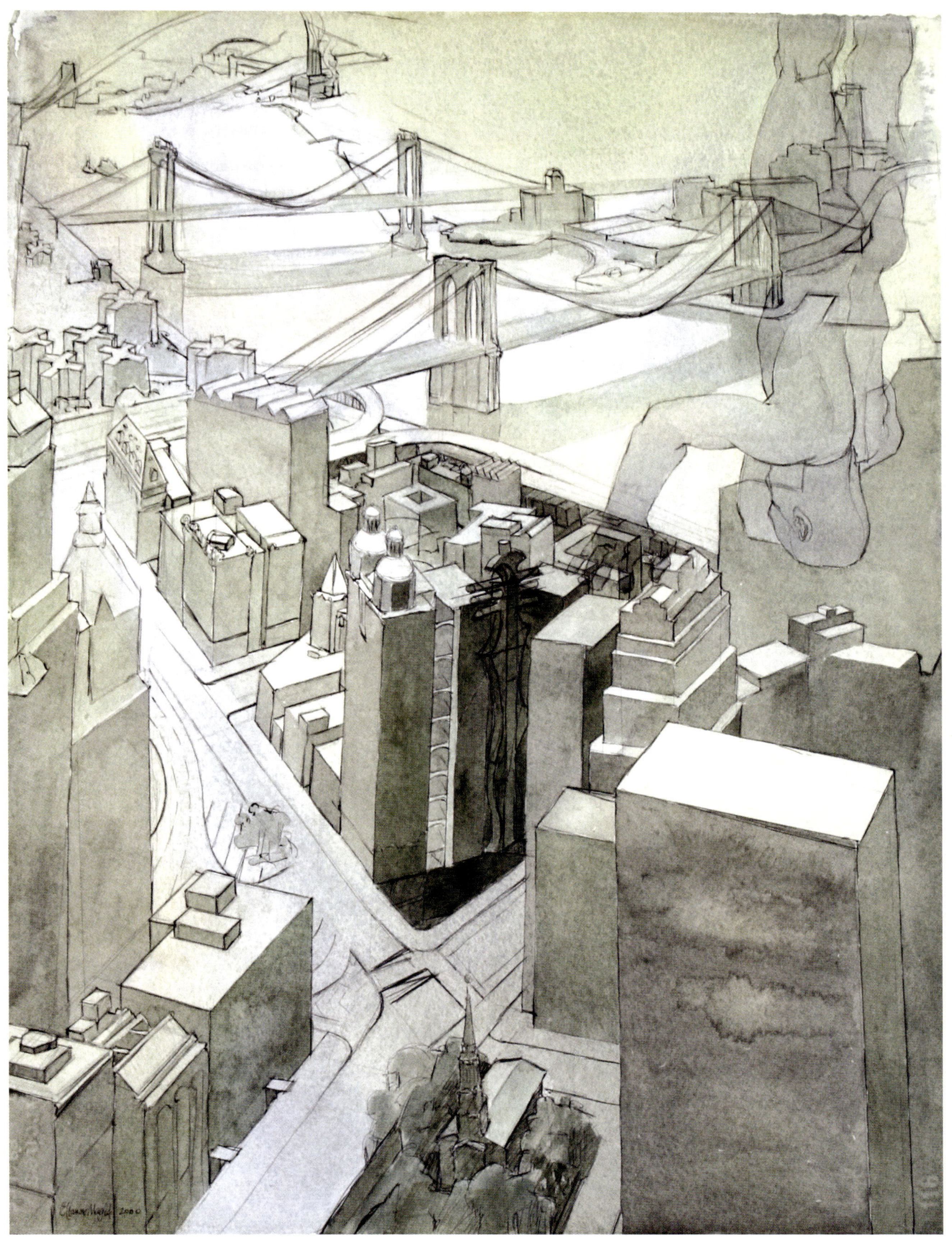

Ron Milewicz

Manhattan, 2, 1998
Oil on wood panel
8 x 11 inches
Collection of Nancy Whitney
Photo: D. James Dee

Queens/Manhattan, 2, 1997
Oil on wood
14¼ x 19 inches
Collection of Alice J. Raucher-Morra
Photo: D. James Dee

Born 1963 in New York, N.Y.
Lives in New York, N.Y.

Education

1994 The New York Studio School, N.Y.
1986 MArch, Columbia University, New York, N.Y.
1983 BA, Cornell University, Ithaca, N.Y.

Selected Solo Exhibitions

2003 George Billis Gallery, New York, N.Y.
2002 George Billis Gallery, New York, N.Y.
1999 Washington Art Association, Washington Depot, Conn.

Selected Group Exhibitions

2003 *Searching for the Image,* The Von Liebig Art Center, Naples, Fla., and Elliott Gallery, Eckerd College, St. Petersburg, Fla.
2002 *New York Studio School Alumni Exhibition*, Elizabeth Harris Gallery, New York, N.Y.
New York, A Tribute, Lizan Tops Gallery, East Hampton, N.Y.

Awards

1999 Cornell Council for the Arts
1994 The New York Studio School, Hohenberg Travel Grant

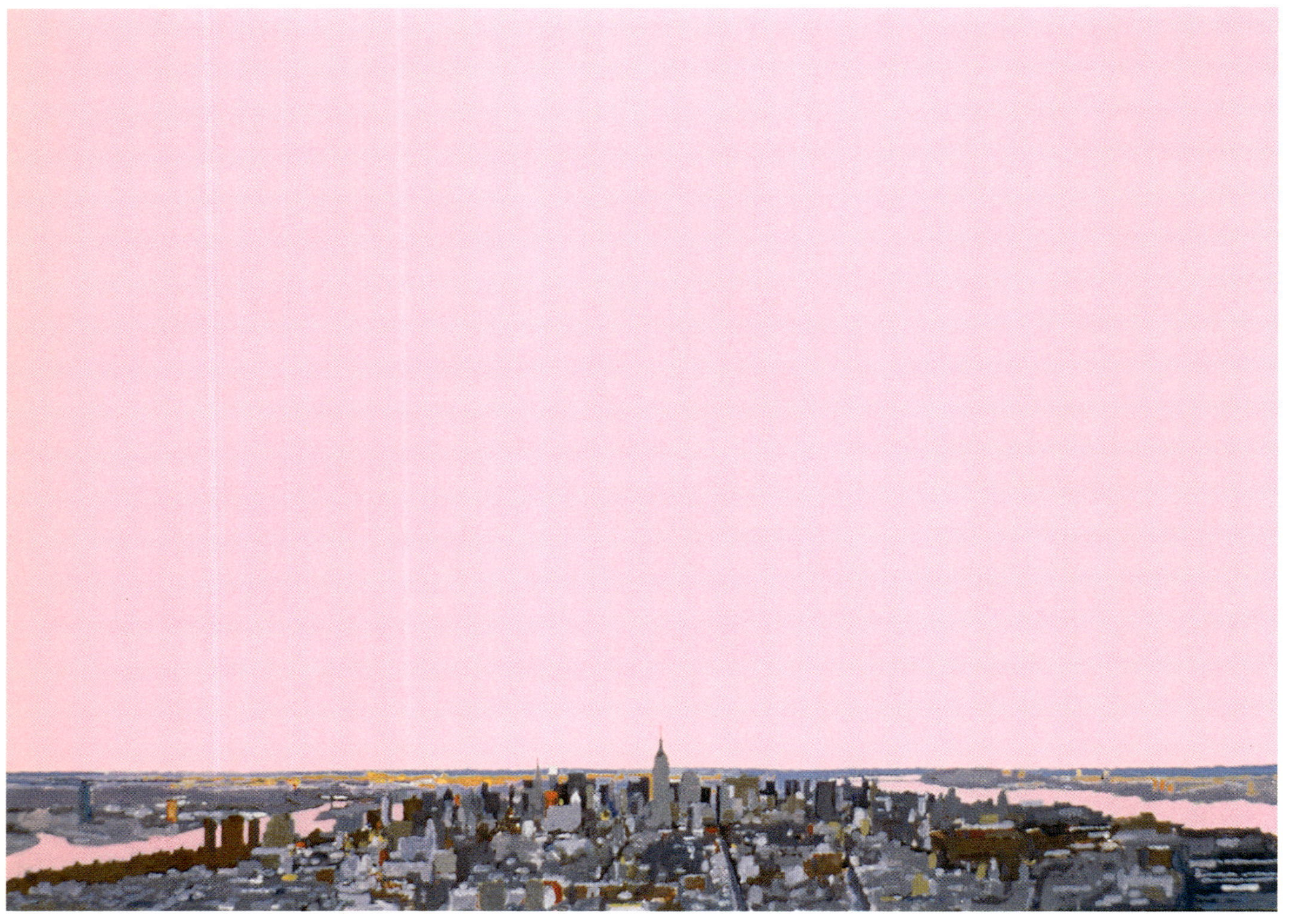

When I was offered a residency at the World Trade Center I was working on a series of cityscapes looking northward from my seventh-floor studio in downtown Manhattan. At the World Trade Center I continued to work from the same north view, but it was as if I had been pulled up and back. Because of the closeness of the vertical window mullions, I was painting, hundreds of feet up in the air, with my nose pressed to the glass. It seemed that the expanse outside was contained in a few inches. The distancing afforded by being high in the tower made the world remote and somehow more real—the other side of the glass being equivalent to the world on the other side of the painting. The immensity of the sky, expressed in my paintings through fields of color, revealed to me the smallness of giant buildings. This experience of a magical play between scale and size continues to be an important part of my work: the small format and intense color a consequence of compressing so much space into a panel just inches across.

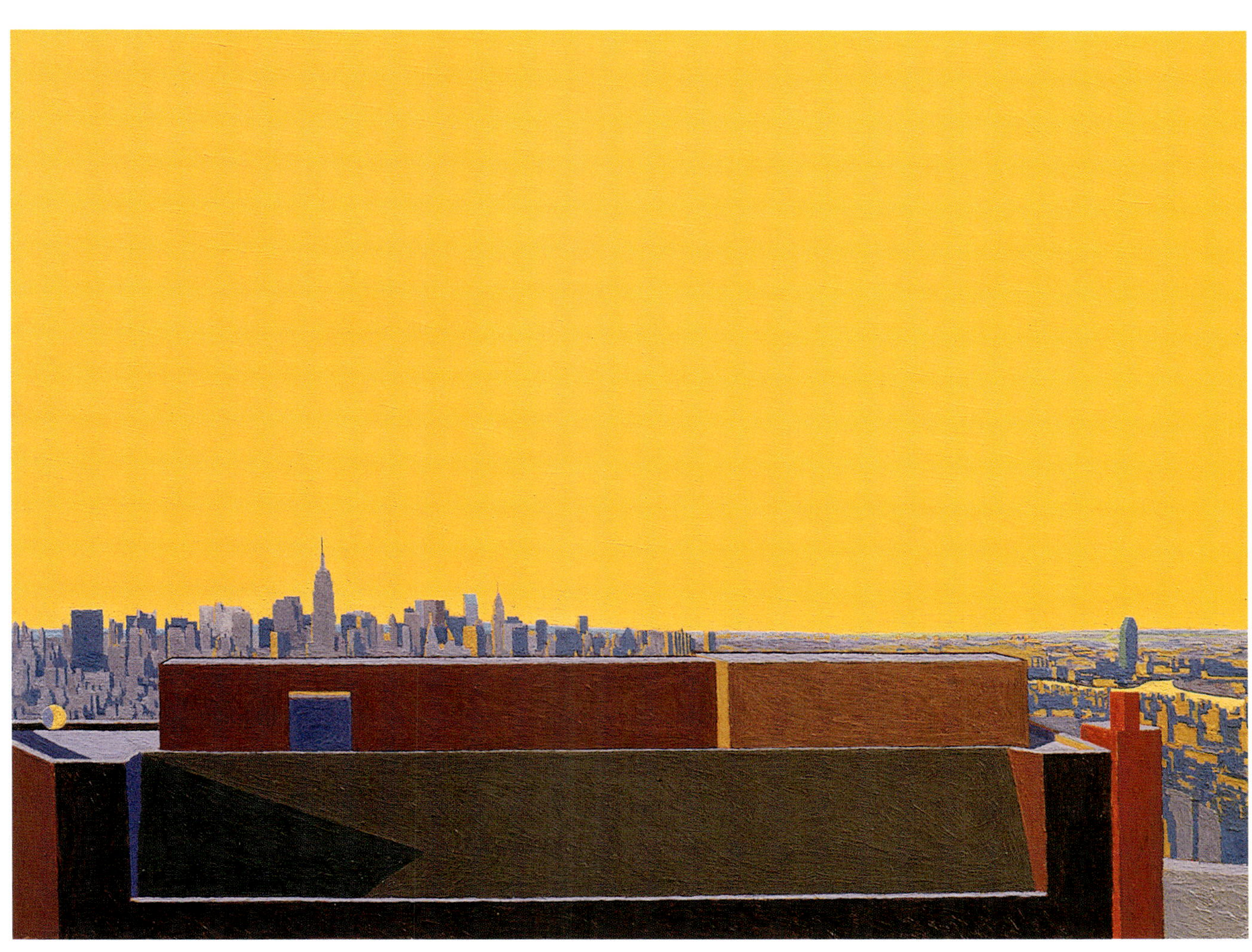

Marjorie Portnow

View From World Trade Looking North, Afternoon, 1998
Oil on panel
12 x 12 inches
Photo: Marty Heitner

Born 1942 in New York, N.Y.
Lives in New York, N.Y.

Education

1972 MFA, Brooklyn College, N.Y.
1964 BA, Western Reserve University, Cleveland, Ohio

Selected Solo Exhibitions

2000 Hollins University, Roanoke, Va.
1996 National Archives Building, Baton Rouge, La.

Selected Group Exhibitions

2001 *Cityscapes*, Lizan Tops Gallery, East Hampton, N.Y.
2000 *Repainting Church's Territory*, Olana, Hudson, N.Y.

Awards

2000 National Academy of Design
1995 American Academy of Arts and Letters, Hassam Purchase Prize
1994 The National Endowment for the Arts
1993 The Ingram Merrill Foundation

During my LMCC residency I painted the view from the ninety-first floor of the World Trade Center. I did plein-air, perceptual, panoramic views encompassing all of New York City, from river to river, below Canal Street and beyond the George Washington Bridge. I compressed this view (as New York City is so compressed) into 12 x 12-inch paintings. It changed my work. Some of the artists, with whom I painted and shared the space, also changed my life. It was a great idea and great experience to use empty office space with spectacular views for an artist residency.

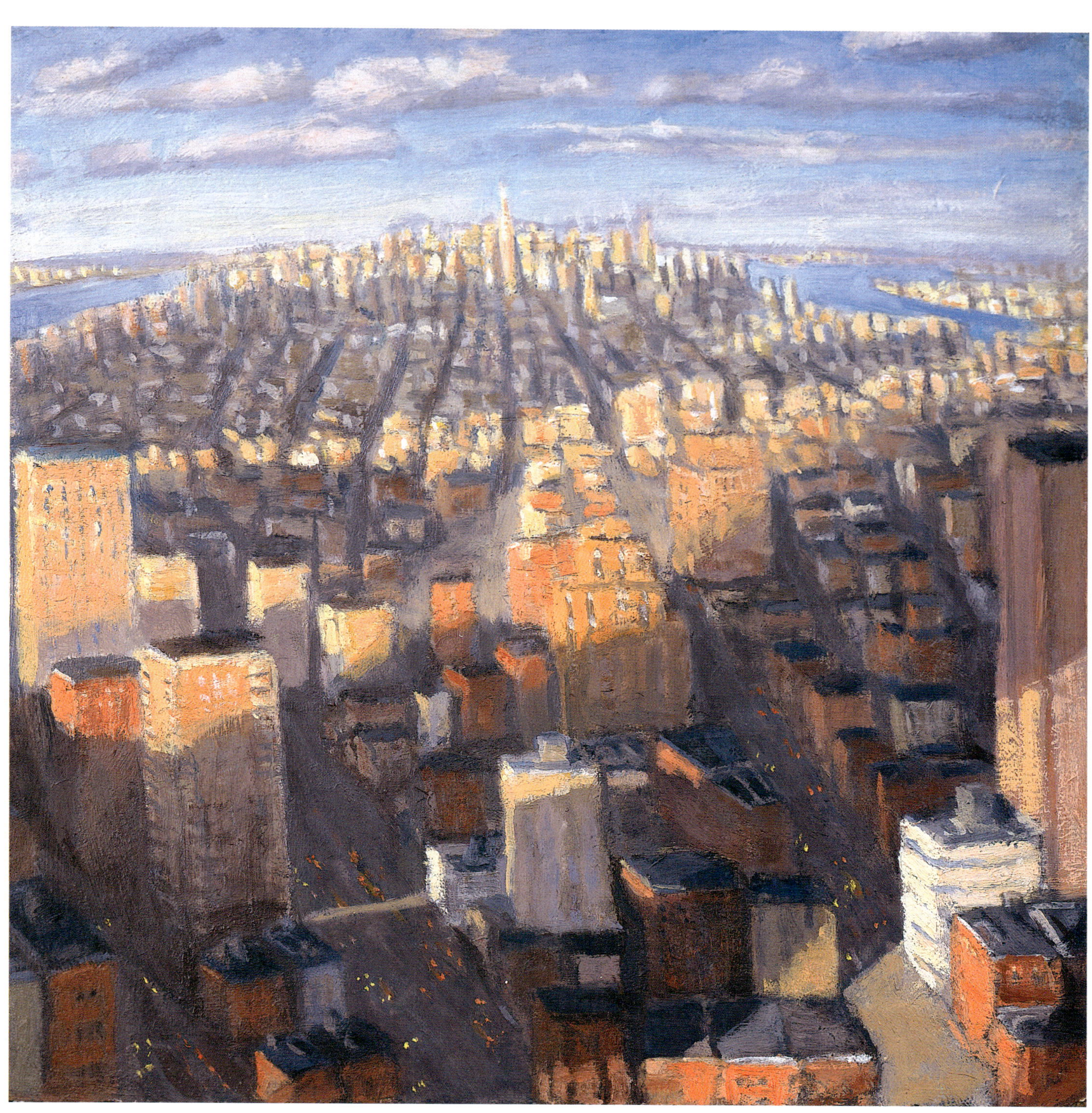

Torild Stray

N.Y. Metamorphosis, 1998 (with detail)
Charcoal on watercolor paper
72 x 168 inches
Photos: Ole Buenget

Born 1964 in Bodo, Norway
Lives in New York, N.Y.

Education

1994 The New York Studio School, N.Y.
1990 The Nordic School of Art, Kokkola, Finland

Selected Solo Exhibitions

2003 Gallery A, Oslo, Norway
2001 Anna K Gallery, New York, N.Y.
N.Y. Metamorphosis, Gallery 27, Oslo, Norway

Selected Group Exhibitions

2002 *NYSS Alumni Exhibition*, Elizabeth Harris Gallery, New York, N.Y.
Winter Invitational, Painting Center, New York, N.Y.
1998 Downtown Art Exchange, New York, N.Y.
Absolut Secret, David McKee Gallery, New York, N.Y.

Award

1992 Agnes Gund Scholarship Award

My inner vision directed me as I deconstructed the city and rebuilt it on canvas. The buildings, which I came to view as extensions of human beings, took the place of figures in my paintings. At a higher level of abstraction, the city itself was an organic being, alive and constantly changing.

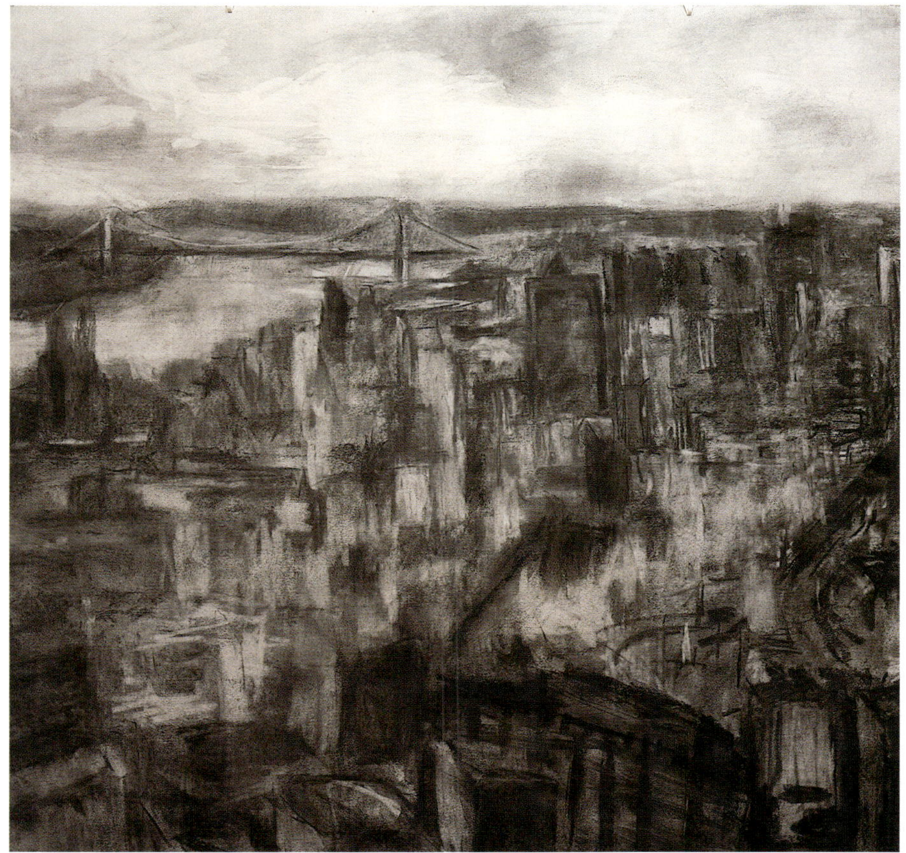

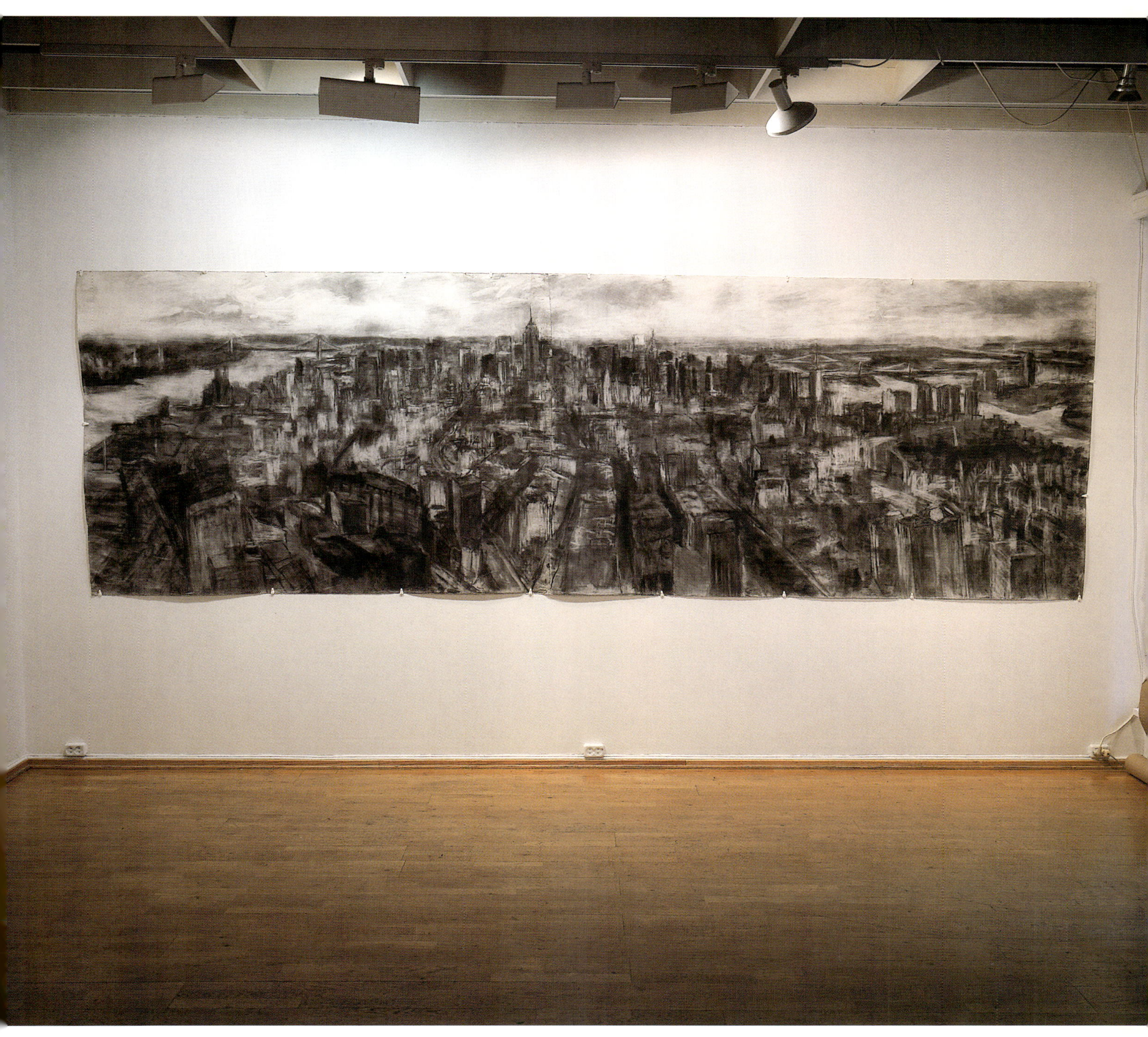

Pola Wickham

Wall Street, East River 1, 1997
Oil on plywood panel
12 x 10 inches
Private collection
Photo: Etienne Clermont

Born 1969 in London, U.K.
Lives in Barcelona, Spain

Education

1999 MFA, Yale University School of Art, New Haven, Conn.
1992–95 The New York Studio School, N.Y.
1989–90 The Leo Marchutz School, Aix-en-Provence, France

Selected Solo Exhibitions

2001 *Elgin*, Cassian de Vere Cole Fine Art, London, U.K.
2000 Galerie Atelier 408, Amsterdam, The Netherlands
1998 Washington Arts Association, Washington Depot, Conn.

Selected Group Exhibitions

2003 The Von Liebig Art Center, Naples, Fla.
2003 Elliott Gallery, Eckerd College, St. Petersburg, Fla.
2003 *The Urban Scene*, James Huntington-Whiteley Fine Art, London, U.K.

Awards

1998 Yale Norfolk Summer Fellowship
1996 The New York Studio School Hohenburg Travel Grant

Each painting I made was an unstudied response to the incredibly perpendicular experience—so vertical and yet so horizontal—of the ninety-first floor of the North Tower of the World Trade Center. All those long, skinny windows and the horizon spread out before one on the other side of the glass.

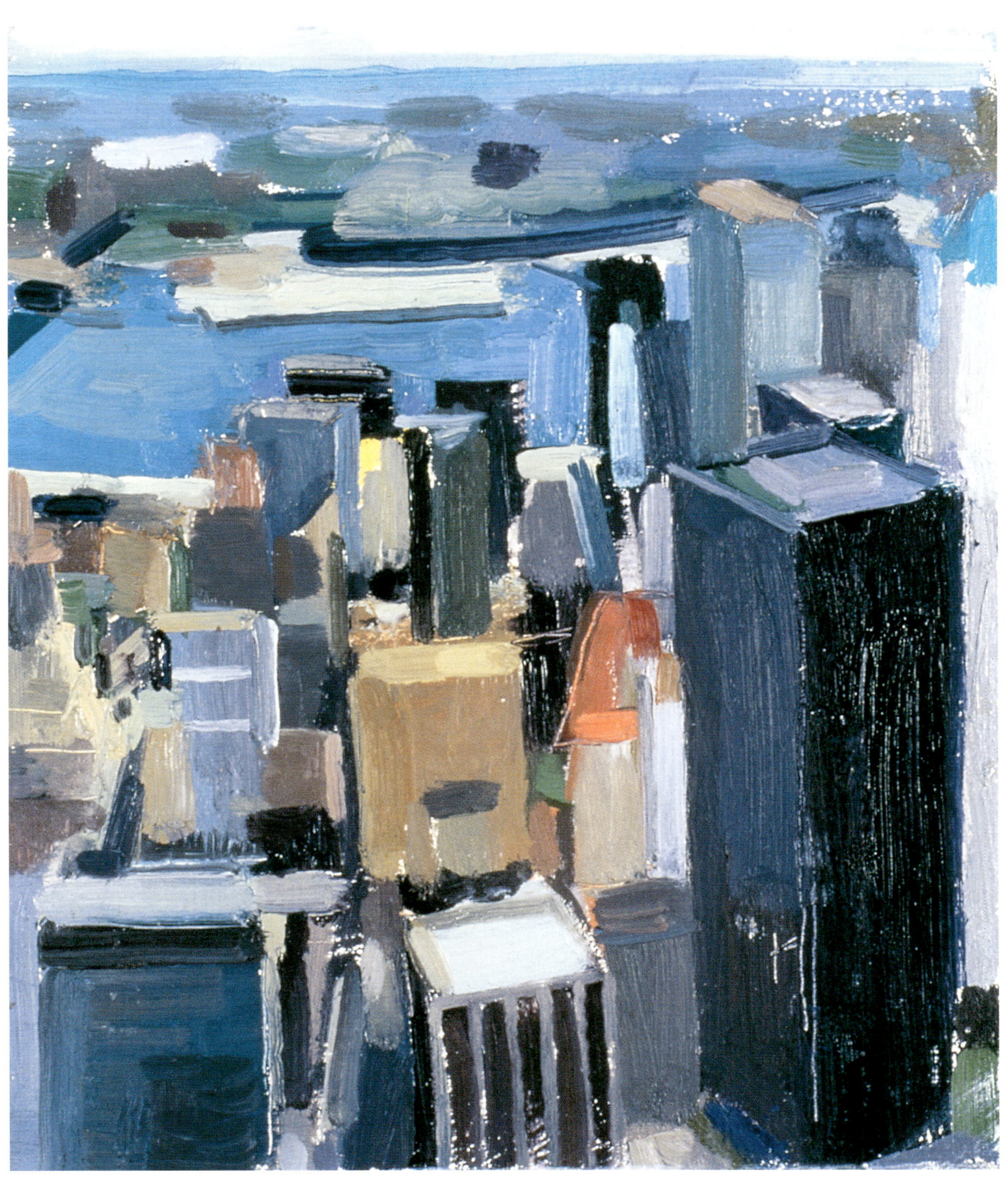

Winter 1998 through Spring 1999

Artists-in-Residence

Joellyn Duesberry
Matthew Geller
Terence Gower
Tim Hailand
Jennie C. Jones
Kim Sooja*
Diana Kingsley
Daniel Kohn
Sonya Sklaroff
Taylor Spence
Patrice Sullivan
Mette Tronvoll
Micki K. Watanabe

Jurors

Bruce W. Ferguson
Christian Haye
Rita McBride

Invited Artist

Nicole Carstens

*not represented

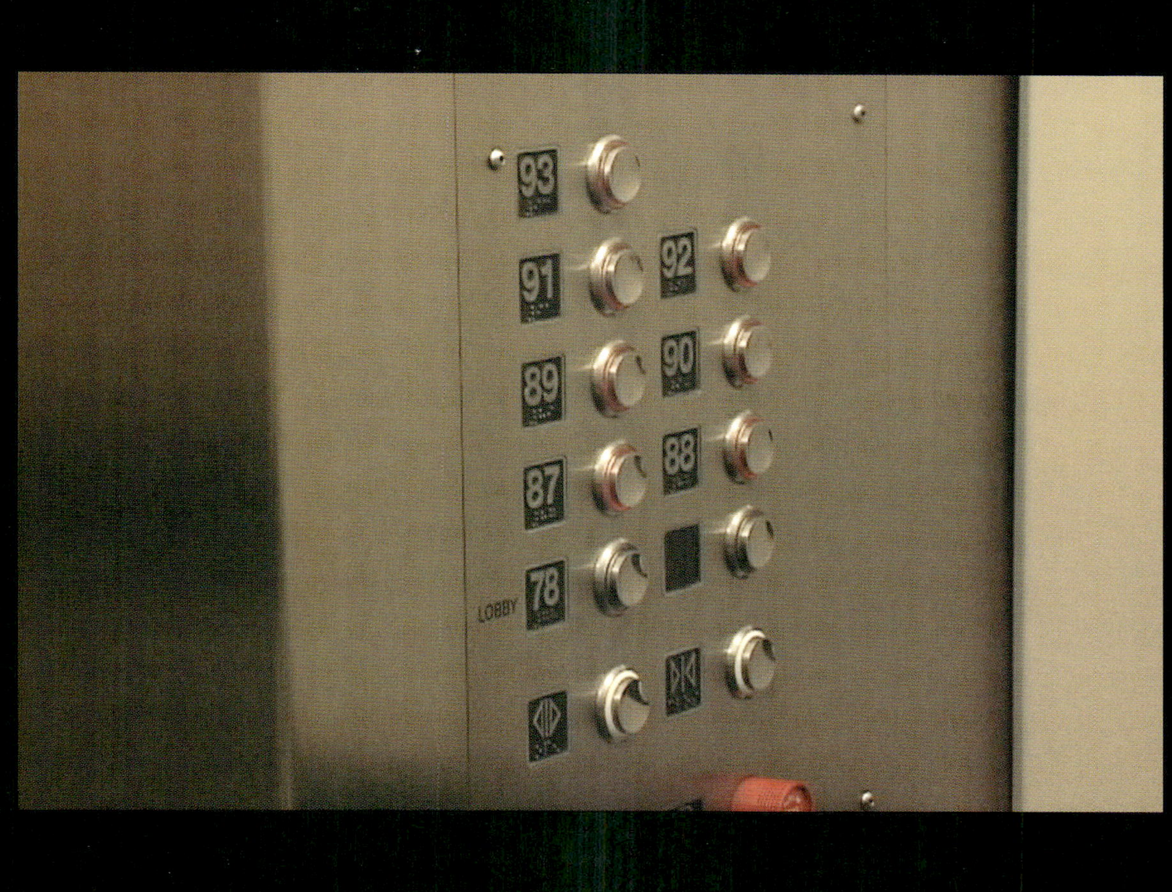
93
91
92
89
90
87
88
LOBBY
78

Nicole Carstens

Eight images from untitled series of b/w photographs, 1998–99
Dimensions variable

Born 1958 in The Hague, The Netherlands
Died 2001 in Amsterdam, The Netherlands

Education

1990 MFA, Pratt Institute, Brooklyn, N.Y.
1988 State Academy for Fine Arts, Amsterdam, The Netherlands
1985 University of Amsterdam, The Netherlands

Selected Solo Exhibitions

2002 *Artists' Studios in the World Trade Center*, International Press Centre Nieuwspoort, The Hague, The Netherlands
2001 *Blue Notes from Thin Air*, Netherlands Photo Institute, Rotterdam
1998 *Blue Notes from Thin Air*, Bronwyn Keenan Gallery, New York, N.Y.
1994 *Exchanged Heads* (two-person show), Contemporary Art Center, Moscow, Russia
1991 *Circumflex*, Ridge Gallery, New York, N.Y.

Selected Group Exhibitions

1996 *Wet Spirits*, St. Mark's Position, New York, N.Y.
1992 *Salon: More Than a Group Show*, Art in General, New York, N.Y.

Award

1994 Fonds voor Beeldende Kunsten, Amsterdam, The Netherlands

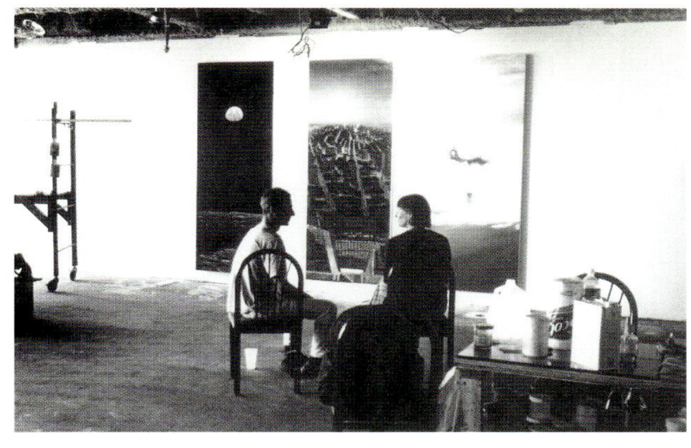
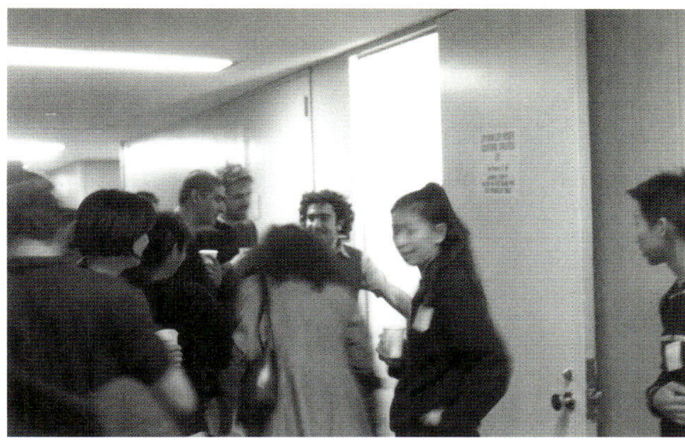
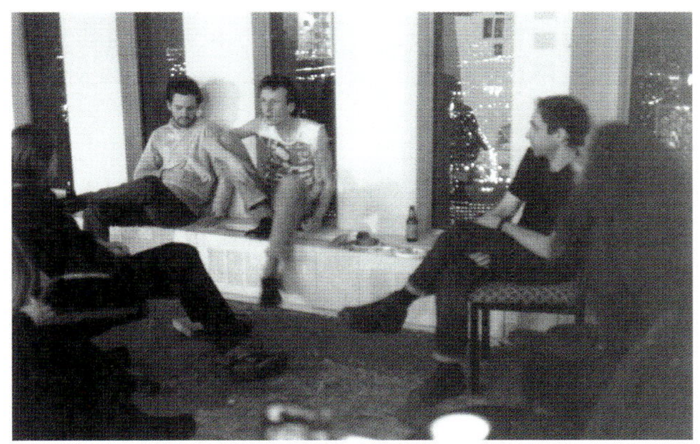
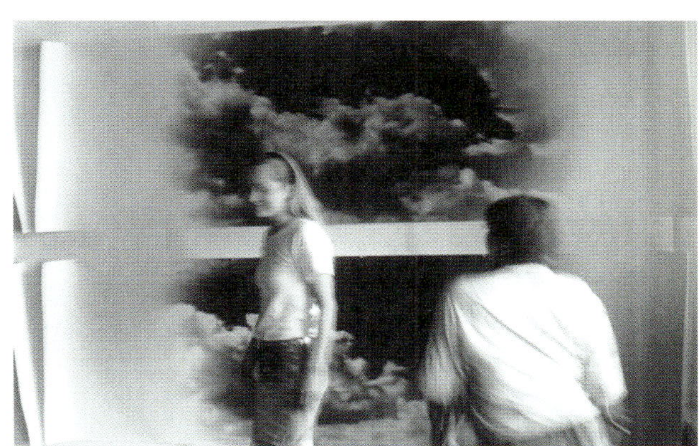
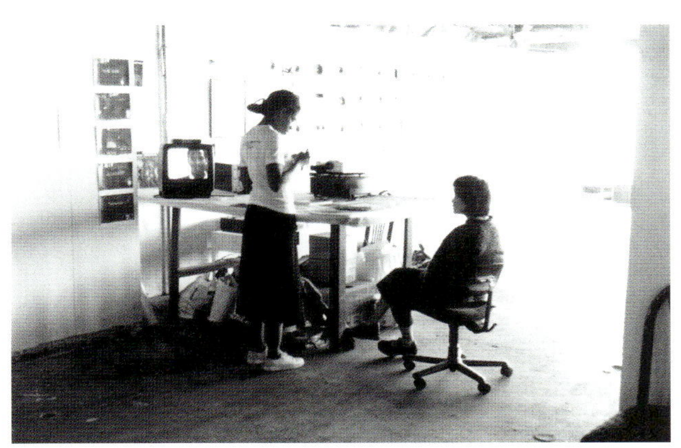
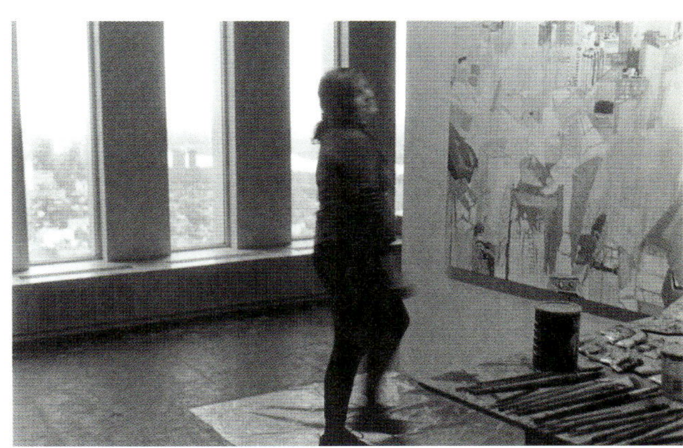
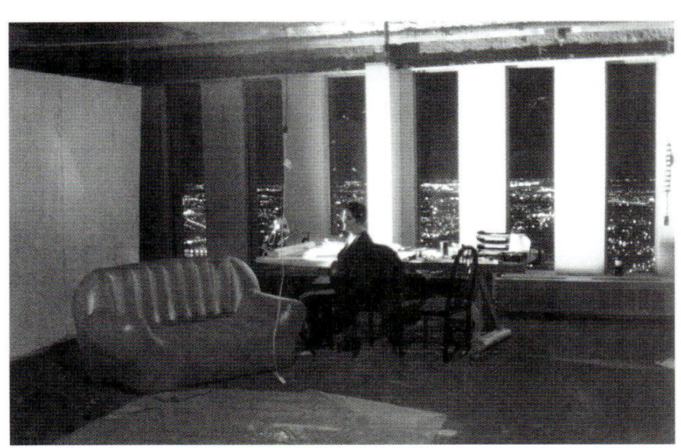
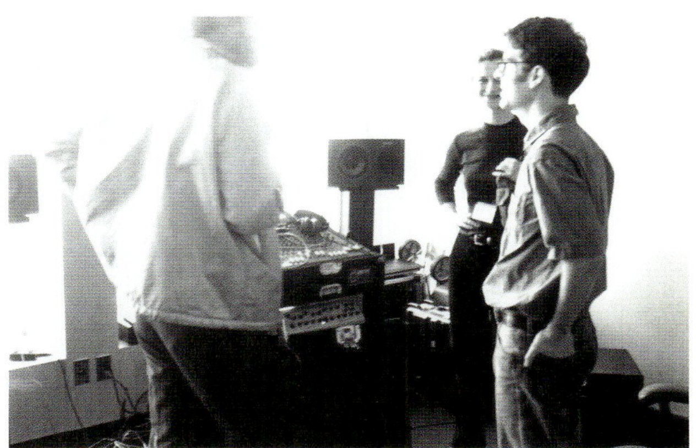

Joellyn Duesberry

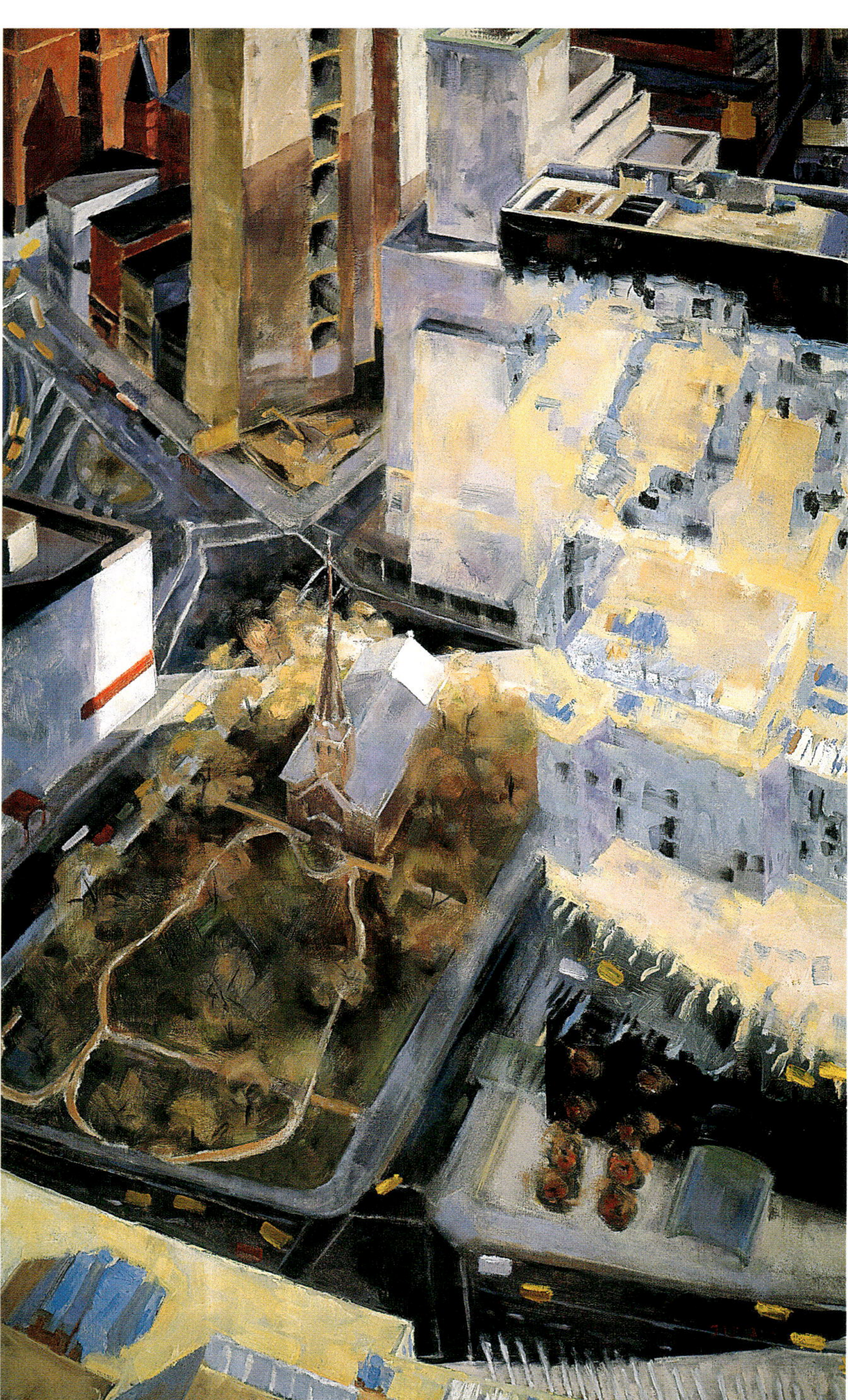

From the 91st Floor of the World Trade Center, Looking East, 1999
Oil on linen
50 x 30 inches
Courtesy James Graham and Sons, New York
Photo: 3 Peras

In spring, as midmorning light intensified, the reflected light bouncing off the North Tower dissolved the huge black and brooding Hilton Hotel across the street into blue veils, which were, in less dramatic light, the WTC entry facade and its shaded colonnades. From this towering height the graveyard across Fulton Street became a treed and turfed haven of paths, and the lovely old human-scaled Saint Paul's chapel, with its wooden steeple, clung earthward and welcomed the eye. By some fateful parallel, the giants surrounding Saint Paul's protected it during the attack of 9/11. This building was the emotional focus in almost all of my residency work: It was the unit of credible scale with which to measure the spectacle that overwhelmed from so high up.

Brooklyn and Manhattan Bridge, Night, 1998
Oil on linen
54 x 32 inches
Courtesy James Graham and Sons, New York
Photo: 3 Peras

Born 1944 in Richmond, Va.
Lives in New York, N.Y., and Denver, Colo.

Education

1994 The New York Studio School, N.Y.
1967 MA, New York University, N.Y.
1966 BA, Smith College, Northampton, Mass.

Selected Solo Exhibitions

2004 *New Paintings*, James Graham and Sons Gallery, New York, N.Y.
2003 Virginia Lynch Gallery (three-person show), Providence, R.I.
2002 *Points of View*, Gerald Peters Gallery, Santa Fe, N.Mex.
2001 *Duesberry Landscapes*, Gleason Fine Art, Camden, Maine
1998 *Covenant of Seasons*, Virginia Museum of Fine Arts, Richmond

Commission

2003 Red Rock Amphitheatre, Denver, Colo.

Residency

2001 Spring Island Institute, S.C.

My habit of hand and the content of my work has changed profoundly from those months up in the air. For a painter whose lifelong goal has been to paint geometry on the surface of a canvas and communicate the tension between this geometry and depth, the miles of space and infinite cubes bisected by the "smile" of the East River presented endless opportunities to develop my obsession. This view perished with 9/11, but the images have influenced three generations of my subsequent paintings, monotypes and drawings. I finished these works from a safe, sad, two-year distance from a time and place I loved.

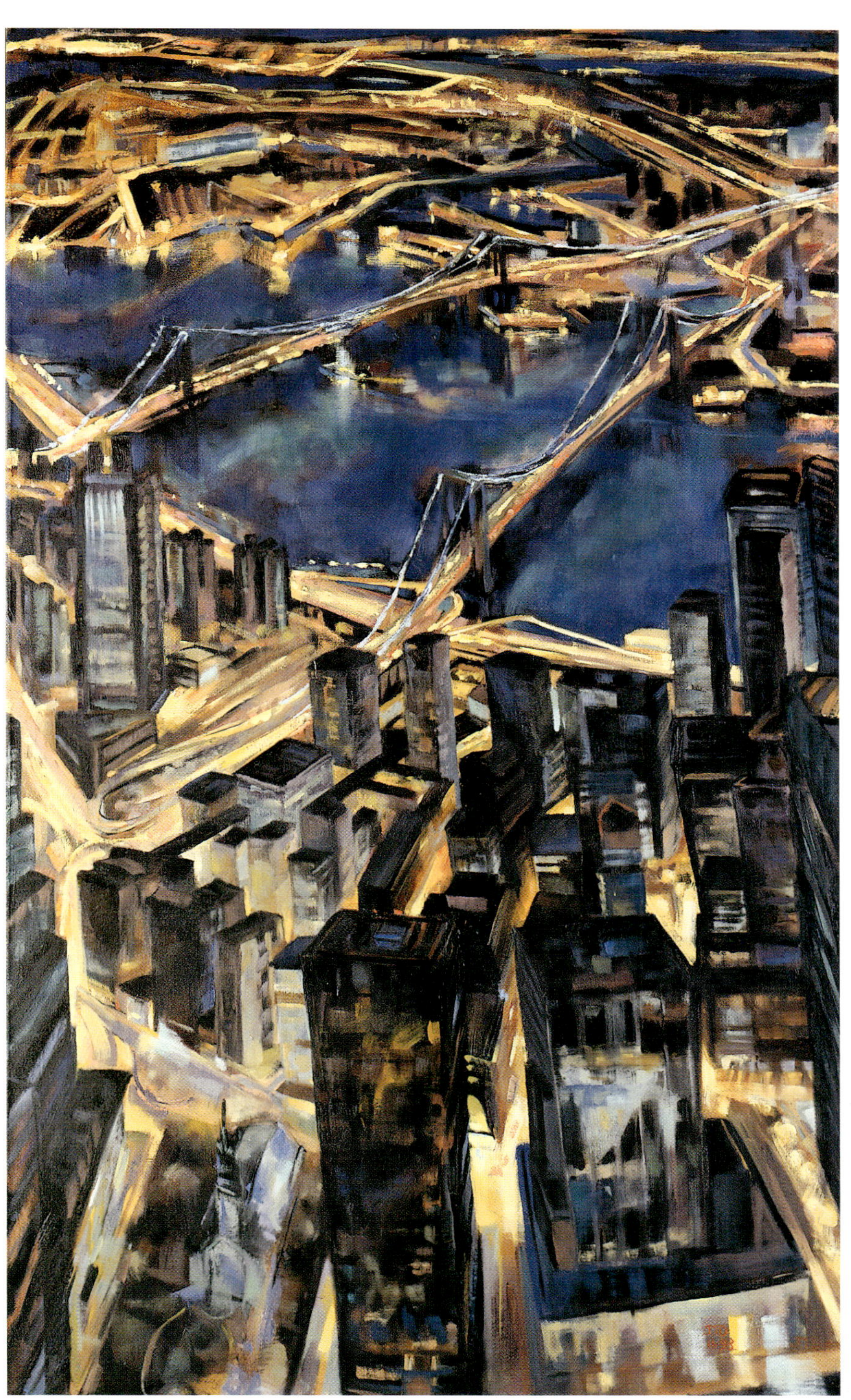

Matthew Geller

Quake, 1999 (detail)
Rockite, brass
37 x 6 x 7 inches
Photo: Jon Lamka

Partly sunny day, 1999
Rockite, brass, lights, fan, oil
A fan blows cool air and a sweet oil aroma through the shaftway
38 x 6 x 7 inches
Photo: Jon Lamka

Mostly cloudy day, 1999 (detail)
Rockite, brass, lights, styrofoam, motor
Cloud continuously revolves at 1.5 RPM
81 x 9 x 10 inches
Photo: Jon Lamka

Born 1954 in New York, N.Y.
Lives in New York, N.Y.

Education

1978 MFA, University of Delaware, Newark
1976 BA, Connecticut College, New London

Selected Exhibitions

2002 *Looking In*, Lower Manhattan Cultural Council, New York, N.Y.
1999 *Living with the Dutch*, London, U.K.
Space, Witte de With, Rotterdam, The Netherlands
1998 *Basements*, Hans Knoll Gallery, Budapest, Hungary

Broadcast

2002 *The Hagie C*, Kunst Kanaal, Amsterdam, The Netherlands

Commission and Awards

2002 Long Island Children's Museum, Garden City, N.Y.
2001 The Greenwall Foundation
2000 Creative Capital Foundation

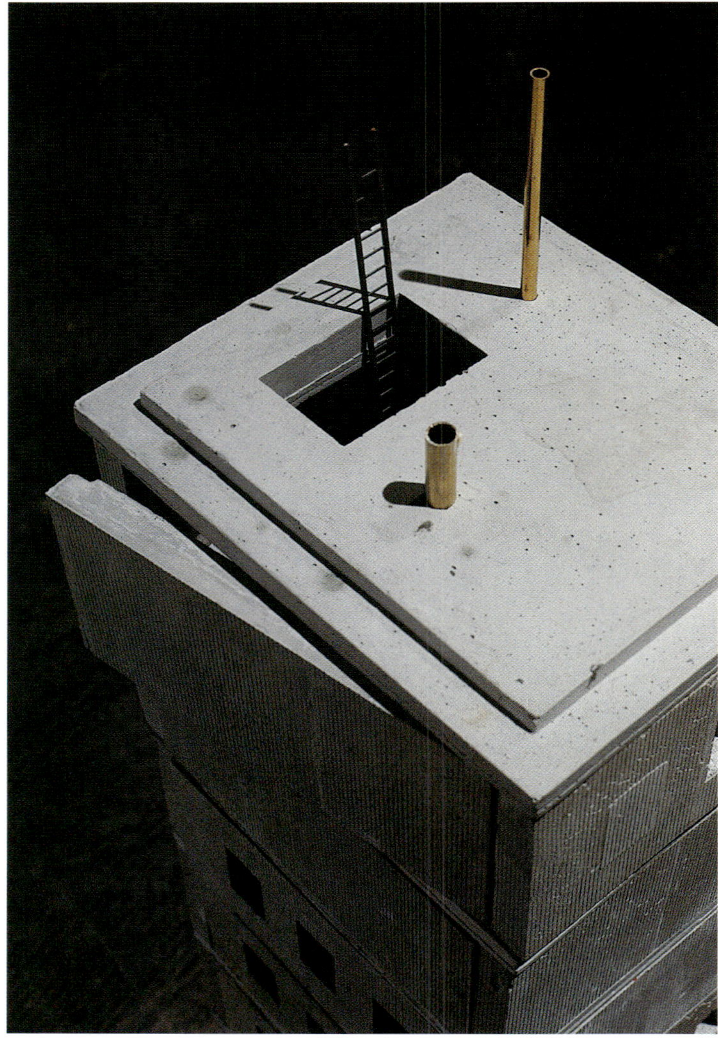

Tall buildings can be joyless and generic from the outside and at the same time elicit a sense of mystery and excitement about what is occurring inside. Endless spaces, rumbling machines and unknown inhabitants coexist anonymously; almost anything can happen, especially in the mind of the outsider looking in. My small-scale cement buildings engage these notions of concealment, suspense and revelation. Whether engulfed by another worldly weather pattern or permeated by an office light that never turns off, these structures become anything but neutral. Although they exhibit a certain charm that scaled-down things share, their size belies a sense of misdeed, a sense that things may have gotten slightly out of hand.

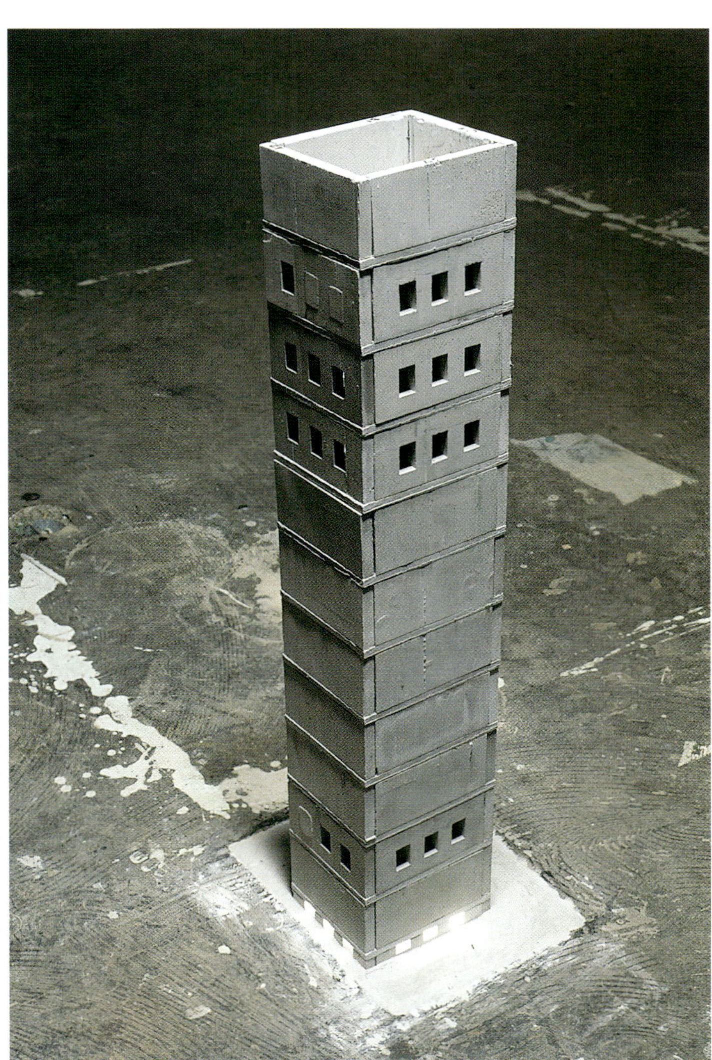

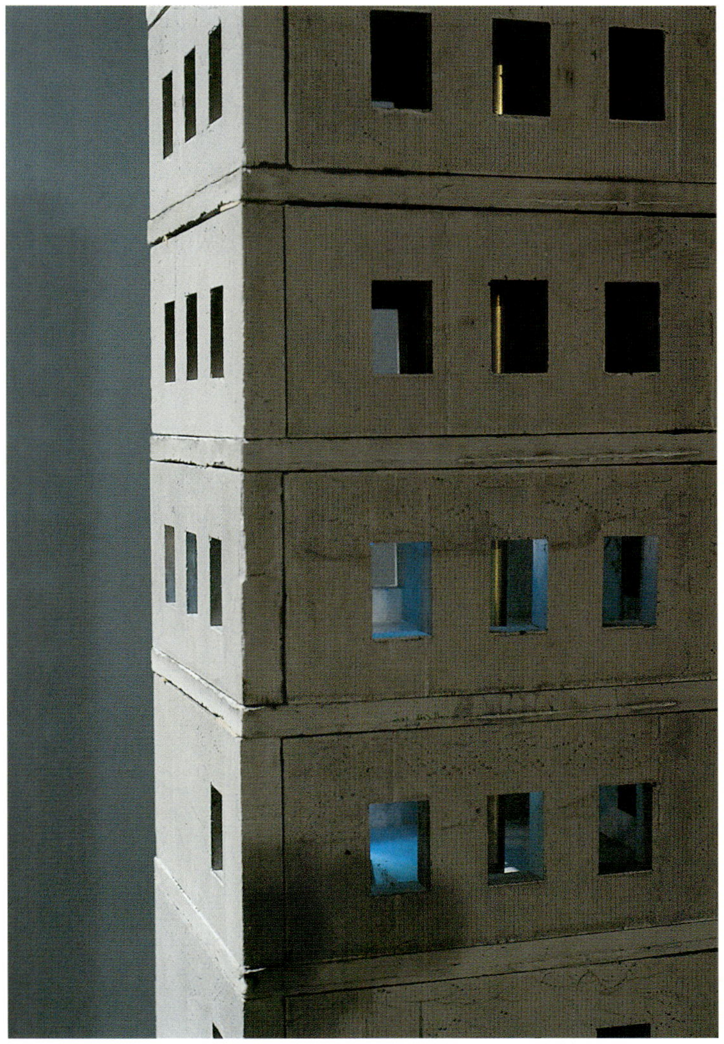

Terence Gower

The Corporation, 1999
Acrylic paint and adhesive vinyl
Performance History, 59 x 154 inches
Growth Comparison, 59 x 95 inches
Market Share, 95 x 53 inches

This piece consists of a series of graphs made with PowerPoint, the most popular software for business presentations. All line and text elements are vinyl transfer and all color elements are acrylic paint. The graphs show how three hypothetical companies—labeled a, b, and c—have competed against each other over a three-year period. There are three different chart types: a bar graph comparing each company's annual growth, an x/y graph comparing each company's quarterly performance (profit and loss), and pie charts comparing the three companies' market share for each year.

Born 1969 in Vernon, British Columbia
Lives in New York, N.Y.

Selected Group Exhibitions

2004 *Hecho en México*, Institute of Contemporary Art, Boston, Mass.
2003 *Stretch*, The Power Plant, Toronto, Ontario
2002 *Thisplay*, Colección Jumex, Mexico City, Mexico
2001 *La Estrategia*, Sala de arte público Siqueiros, Mexico City, Mexico
2000 *Critic as Grist*, White Box, New York, N.Y.
Greater New York, P.S.1 Contemporary Art Center, Long Island City, N.Y.
1999 *La formula*, Centro Cultural Recoleta, Buenos Aires, Argentina

Publication

1999 *Appendices, Illustrations & Notes*, Smart Art Press, Los Angeles, Calif.

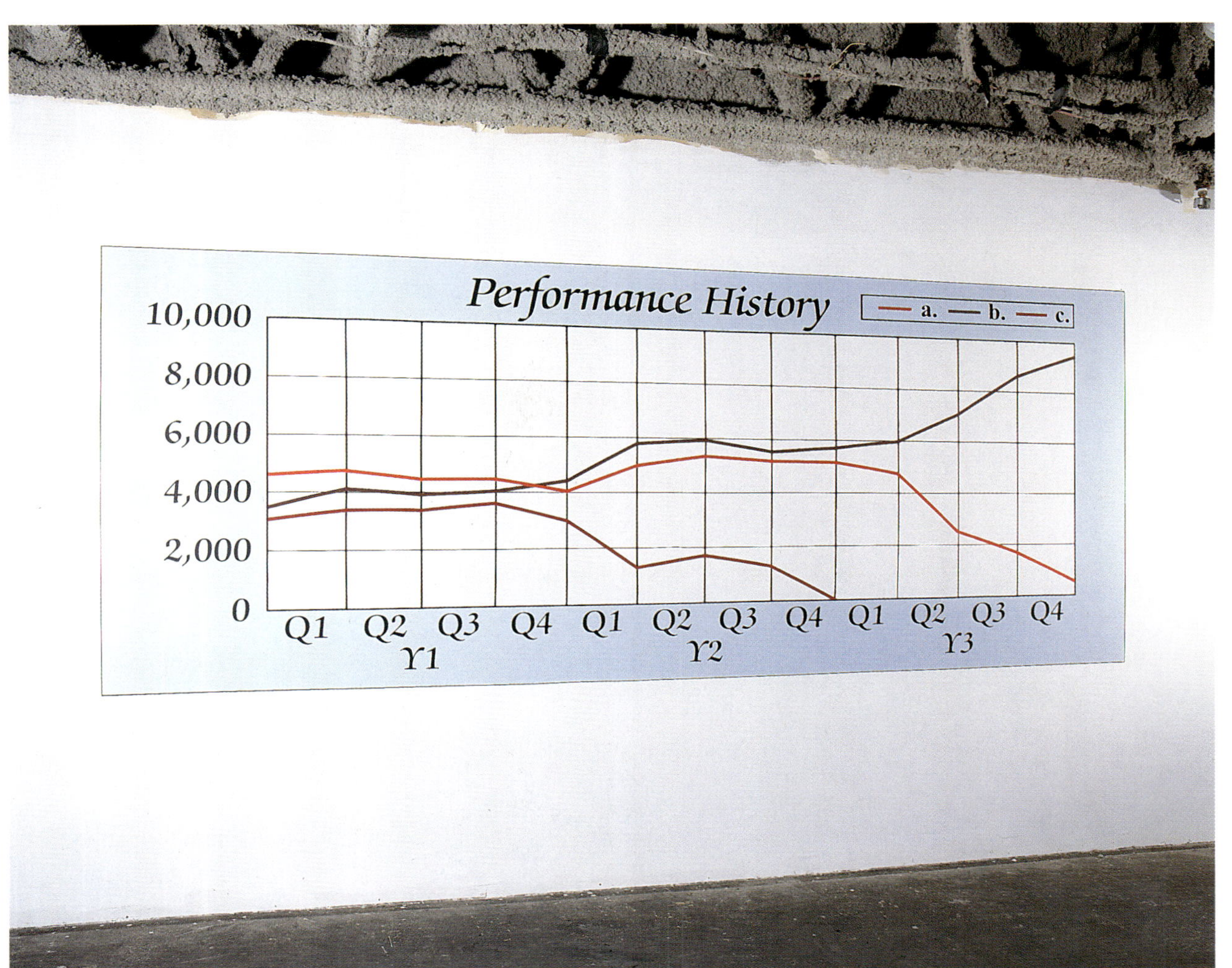

I began my residency at the World Trade Center at a time when the Asian economic crisis of the late 1990s was in full swing. Several of the occupants of the World Trade Center at this time were Asian banks and trading companies. It made an enormous impression on me when the Japanese bank across the hall from the studio program went out of business and abandoned its premises virtually overnight.

Before I began my residency at the World Trade Center I had worked briefly as an office assistant with a small investment firm on Wall Street. There, I was able to observe the competitive behavior of the business world. This research, brought into the intense financial climate of the Twin Towers at the time—in one office millions would be made, while next door millions would be lost—was the source for the work I did in the studio.

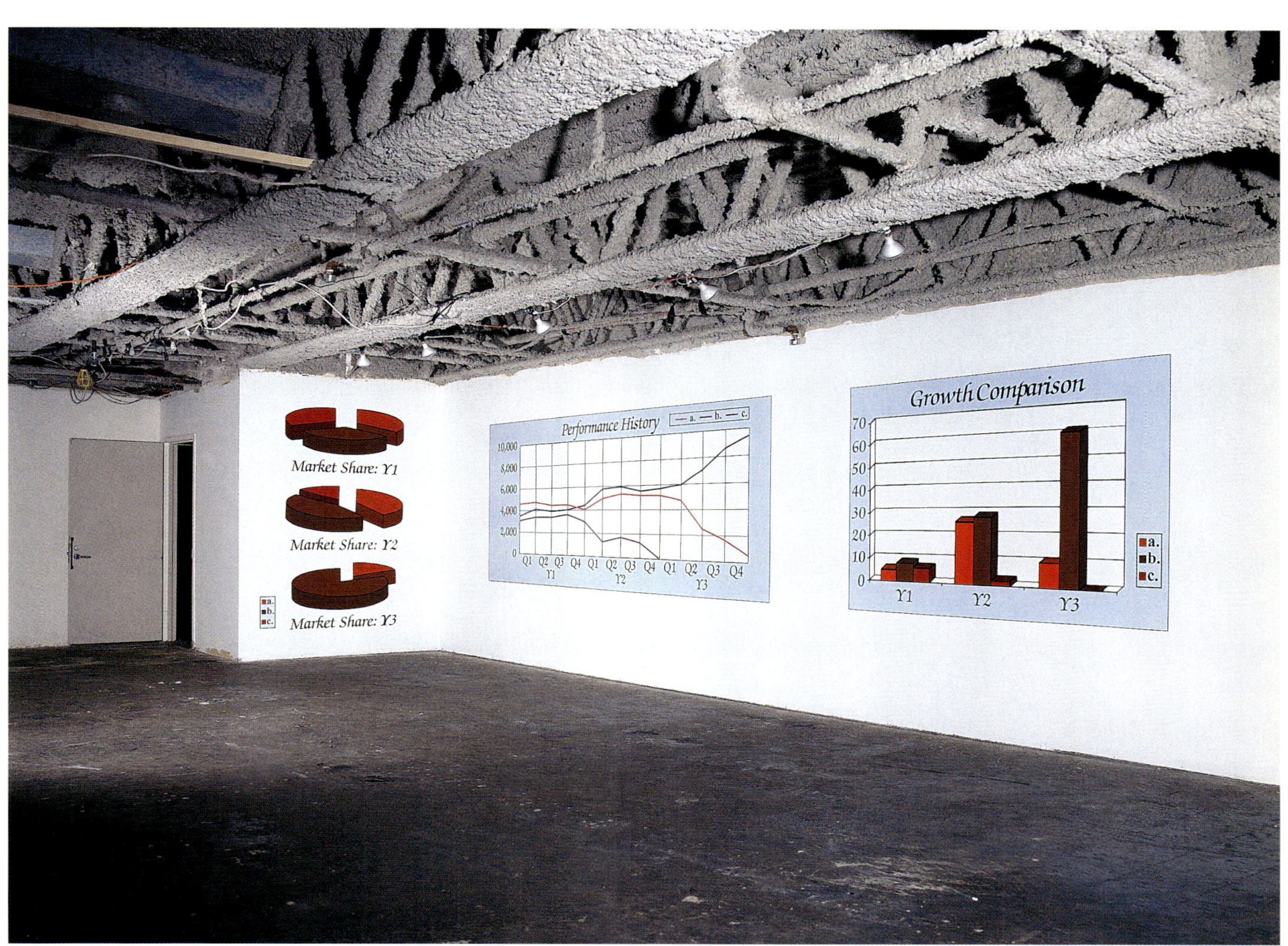

Tim Hailand

Untitled (DISTANCE), 1999
Eight iris prints
30 x 20 inches each

Untitled (BELIEVE), 1998
C-print
72 x 48 inches

Born 1965 in Buffalo, N.Y.
Lives in New York, N.Y.

Education
Parsons School of Design, New York, N.Y.

Selected Solo Exhibitions
2004 David Adamson Editions, Washington, D.C.
2001 Baldwin Gallery, Aspen, Colo.
2000 Lemon Sky Gallery, Los Angeles, Calif.
1999 Galleria Claudia Gian Ferreri, Milan, Italy
1997 CRG Gallery, New York, N.Y.
Rhona Hoffman Gallery, Chicago, Ill.

Publications
Work published in *Visionaire, W, V, Paper, Telerama, The New Yorker, Dutch, Elle* and *Aspen Magazine*

While in residence I continued my "word pieces" series, where I would place small plastic letters directly on the slender windows of the ninety-first floor and take a photo. The two pieces illustrated in this catalog, Untitled (BELIEVE) *and* Untitled (DISTANCE) *were created around the same time. It was actually Thanksgiving 1998. I had a disagreement with a friend that I was meant to spend the holiday with and was left stranded in the city by myself. Feeling a bit lost I decided to go to the studio and work. The various possibilities (the weather, the light, myself) all seemed to click that day.*

I loved how the city looked like a beautiful silent movie when way up high. How it has a sort of "make believe" quality about it, and how one had to have some sort of higher belief in this very reason for living in this, at times, very trying town.

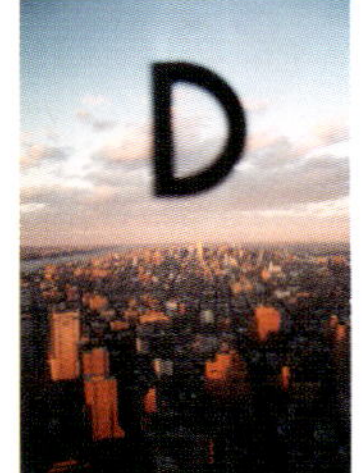

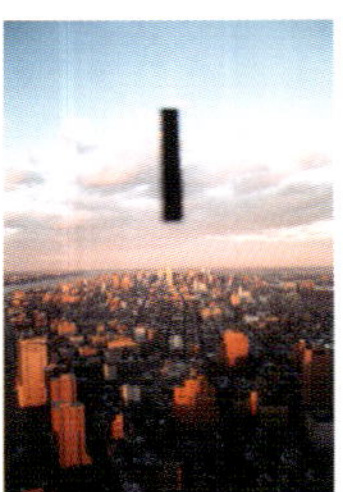

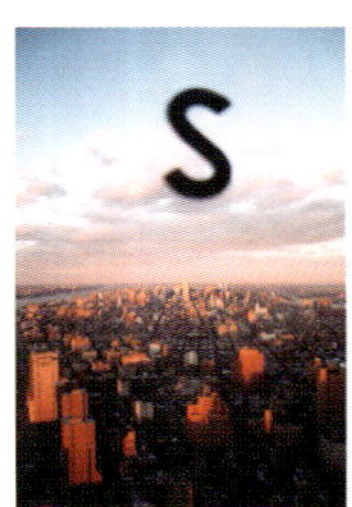

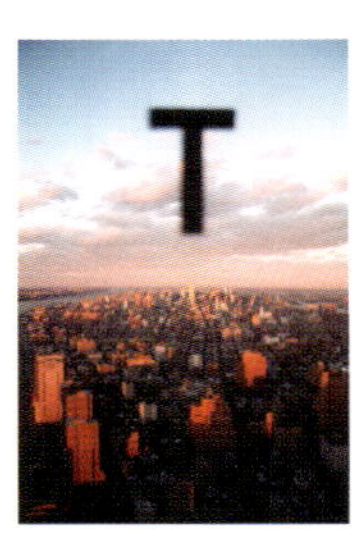

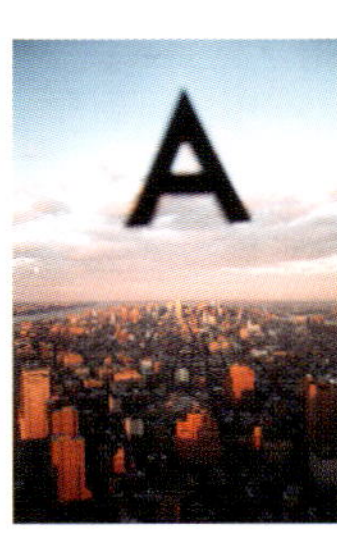

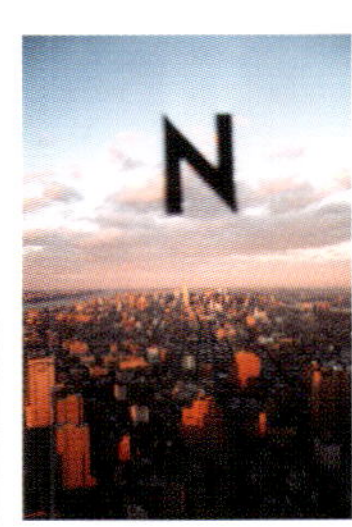

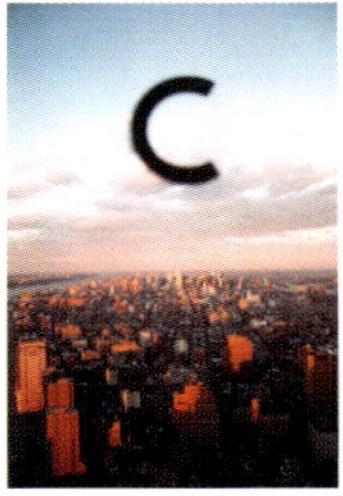

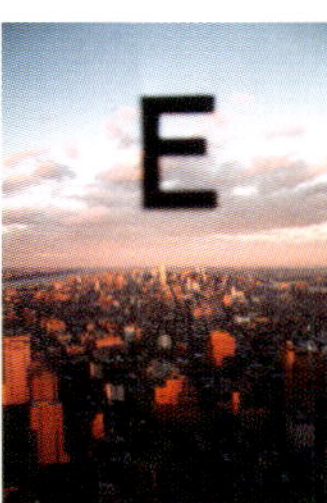

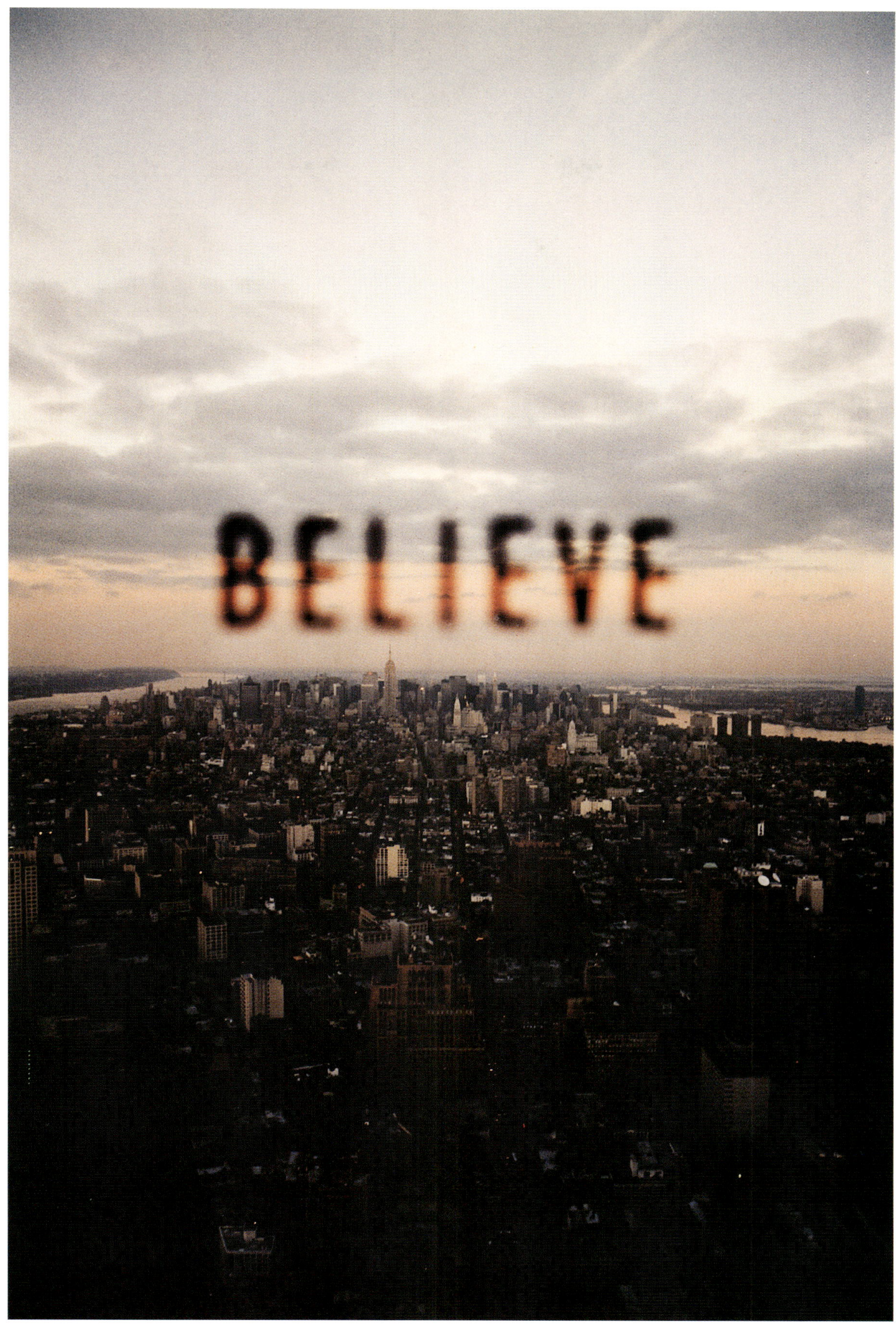
BELIEVE

Jennie C. Jones

Personal Options, 1999 (installation view)
Dimensions variable
(each box 12 x 12 / 14 x 14 inches)
Photo: Selina Rutovitz

Power, 1999
Acrylic, photo, plastic dome on wood
14 x 14 x 3 inches
Photo: Selina Rutovitz

Born 1968 in Cincinnati, Ohio
Lives in New York, N.Y.

Education

1996 MFA, Rutgers University, New Brunswick, N.J.
1991 BFA, The School of the Art Institute of Chicago, Ill.

Selected Group Exhibitions

2003 *Drawing*, G Fine Art, Washington, D.C.
AV audiovisual, Triple Candie, New York, N.Y.
2002 *Americas Re-Mixed*, Fabbrica del Vapore, Milan, Italy
2001 *Freestyle*, The Studio Museum in Harlem, New York, N.Y.
1999 *New York Big City of Dreams*, OpenSpace, Milan, Italy

Residencies

2004 Liguria Study Center for the Arts and Humanities, Genoa, Italy
2002 Cité Internationale des Arts, Paris, France
1996 Skowhegan School of Painting and Sculpture, Maine

Award

2000 The Pollock-Krasner Foundation

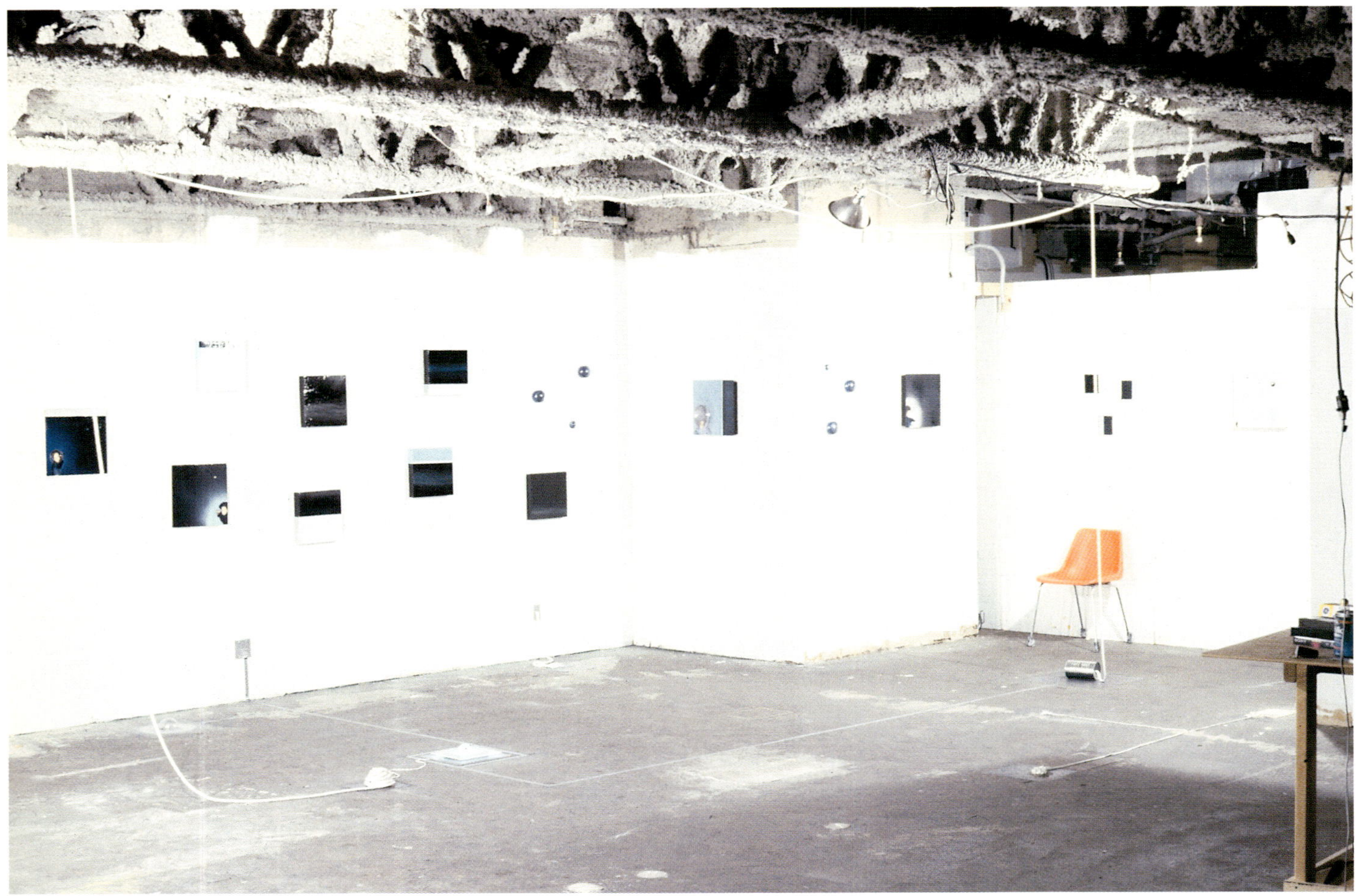

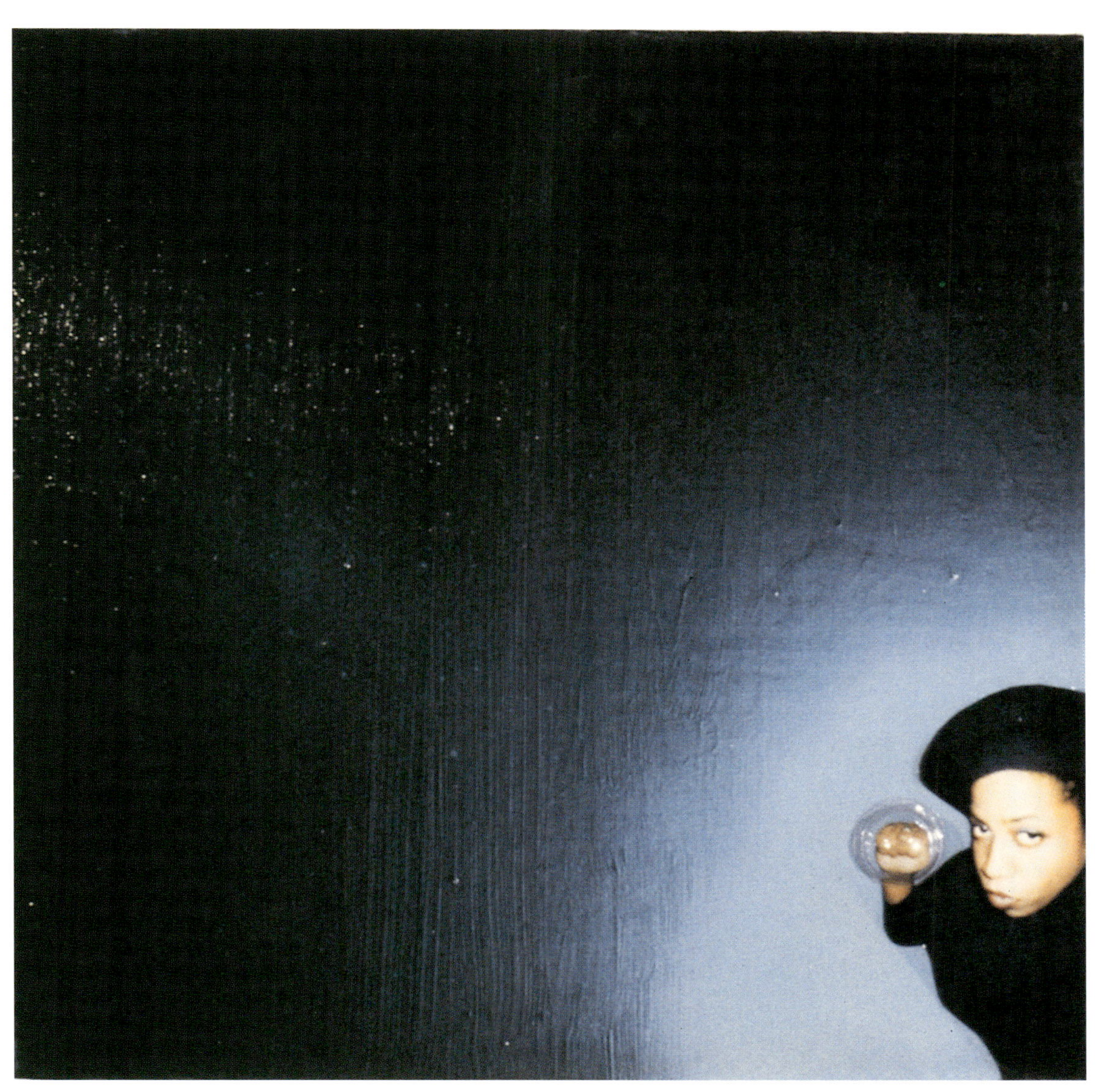

Diana Kingsley

Something Like That (Emerald), 1999
C-print
40 x 96 inches

In love a hundred times, 1999
Black-and-white photo
40 x 40 inches

Born 1964 in Philadelphia, Pa.
Lives in New York, N.Y.

Education

1997 MFA, School of Visual Arts, New York, N.Y.
1986 BA, Colgate University, Hamilton, N.Y.

Selected Solo Exhibitions

2002 *Lovely Swallowed Whole*, Bellwether Gallery, Brooklyn, N.Y.
1999 Derek Eller Gallery, New York, N.Y.
1998 Fotohof Gallery, Salzburg, Austria

Selected Group Exhibitions

2003 *Corner of Mine*, Leo Castelli Gallery, New York, N.Y.
Wormwood Hollow, Here Art Gallery, New York, N.Y.
2002 *End of the Rainbow*, Bellwether Gallery, Brooklyn, N.Y.
2001 *Out of Sorts*, Ormeau Baths Gallery, Belfast, Northern Ireland
Mnemosyne, Encontros de Fotografia 2000, Coimbra, Portugal

Elevator stuffed with canoe

We tried to stuff it into every elevator in Tower One. I had already spent days lugging 3,000 pounds of sand up to the ninety-first floor studios to create a setting for the beautiful big fourteen-foot canoe, and then the beautiful big fourteen-foot canoe wouldn't fit. The Port Authority staff alerted to the situation were not only rooting for me, they were also determined to help me make it happen. Finally they offered to keep it behind the Fire Emergency Command Center in the lobby so I could return after 1:00 A.M. to get a chance to try the Windows on the World elevator, allegedly the biggest. I came back and about a half dozen security guards and maintenance workers were gathered to help me try, but no go. Reluctantly, I whipped out a jigsaw from my backpack. (I had prepared myself by then for this possibility.) They were appalled at the prospect of my indelicate solution. I told them that the amputation and subsequent repair job was now officially part of its character, and the big canoe that was so alien to the Trade Center now became a small part of its lore.

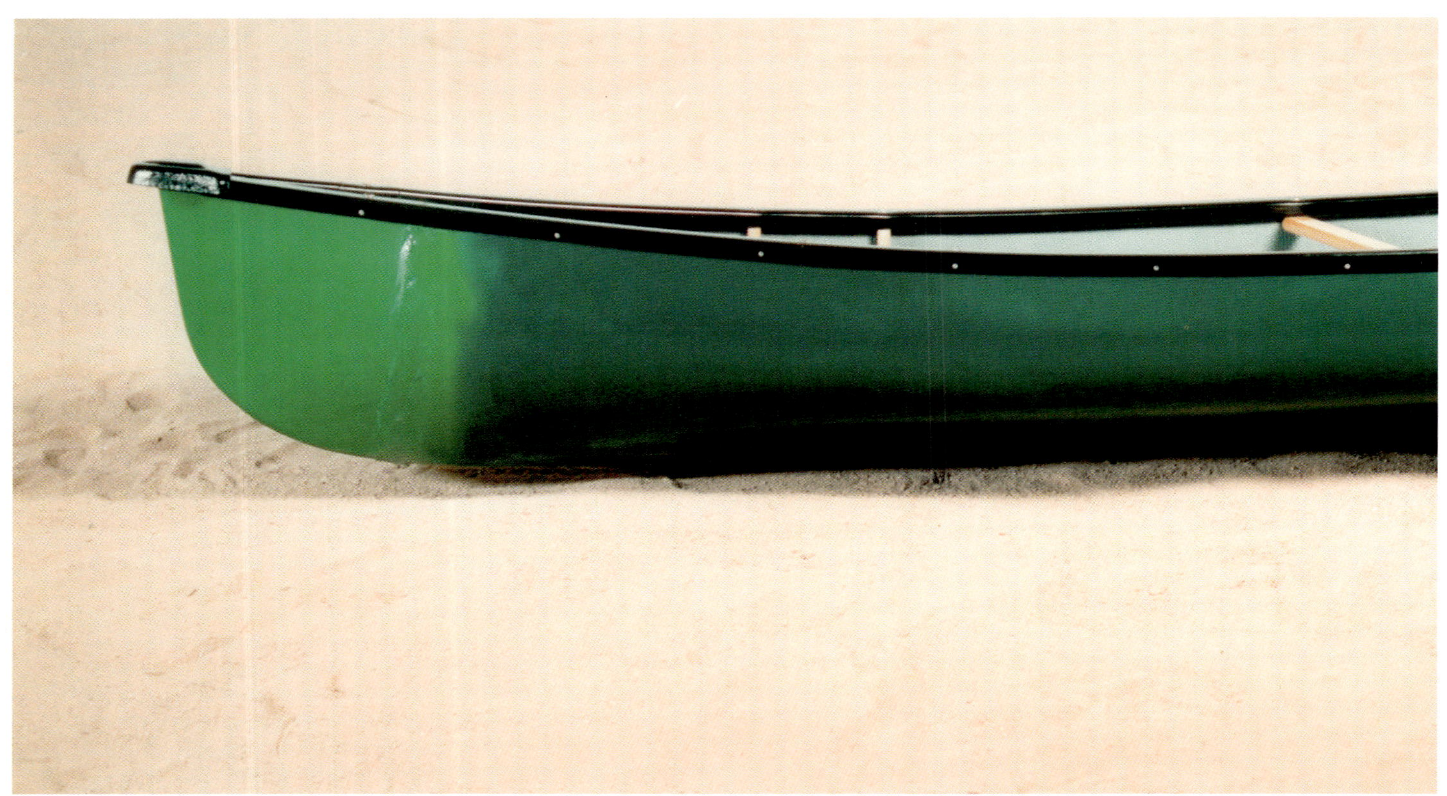

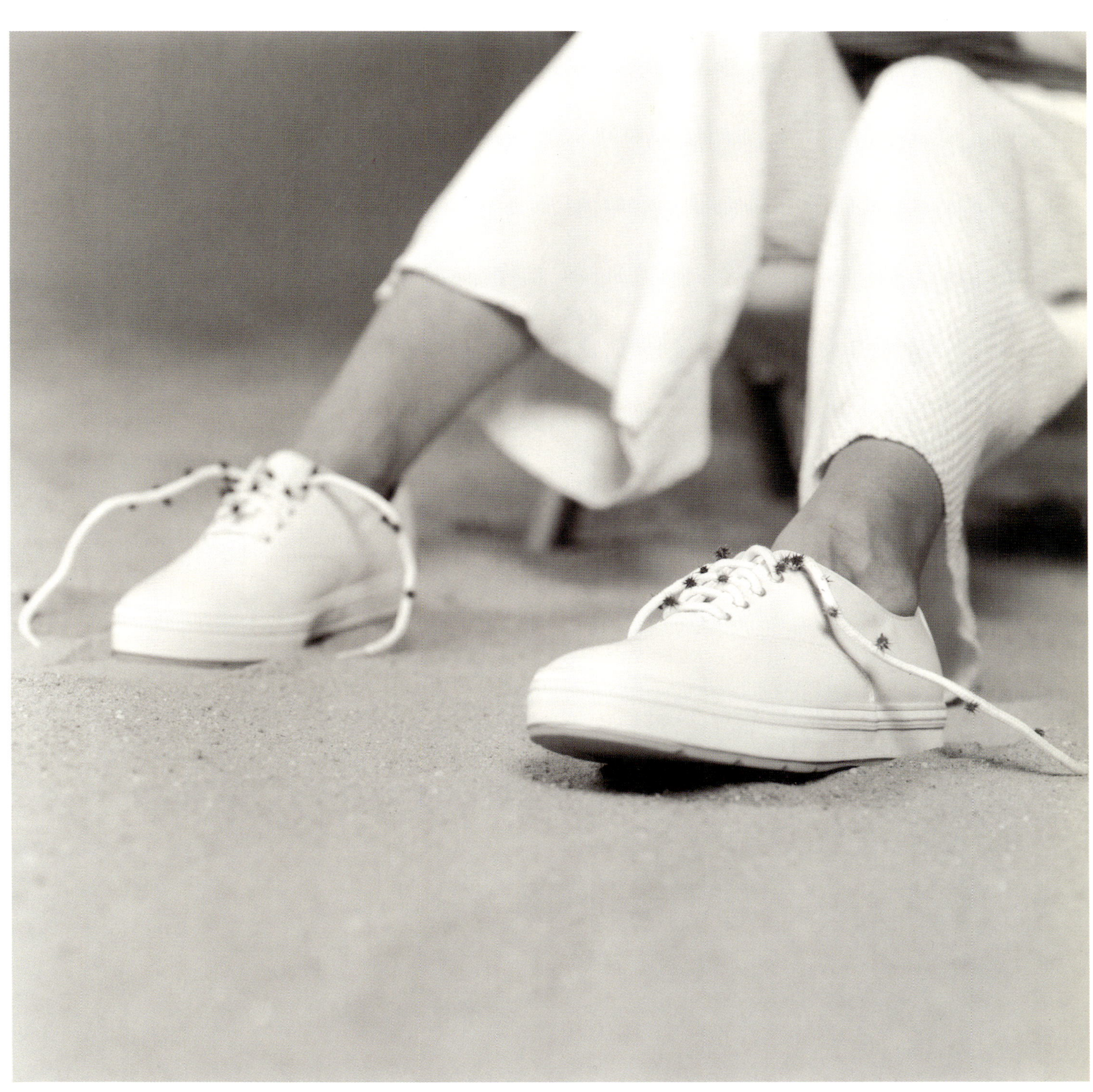

Daniel Kohn

Horizon 26, Brooklyn Trio 1, 2000
Oil on canvas
89 x 72 inches overall

Seen From Above, 2002 *(installation view)*
Oil on canvas
Twenty panels, 7 x 7 feet each,
35 x 28 feet overall

Born 1964 in Ahmedabad, India
Lives in Brooklyn, N.Y.

Education

1988 BA, Hampshire College, Amherst, Mass.

Selected Solo Exhibitions

2001 *Fragile Horizon*, Ute Stebich Gallery, Lenox, Mass.
1998 Montserrat College of Art Gallery, Beverly, Mass.
1997 Garcés y Veláquez Gallery, Bogota, Colombia

Selected Group Exhibitions

2003 *Horizon*, Reeves Contemporary Gallery, New York, N.Y.
2000 *Etats des Lieux*, Chapelle des Penitents, Clermont l'Hérault, France

Commissions

2003 Fiduciary Trust Headquarters at Rockefeller Center, New York, N.Y.
2002 Grand Central Station, New York, N.Y.
2001 Wheatleigh Hotel, Lenox, Mass.

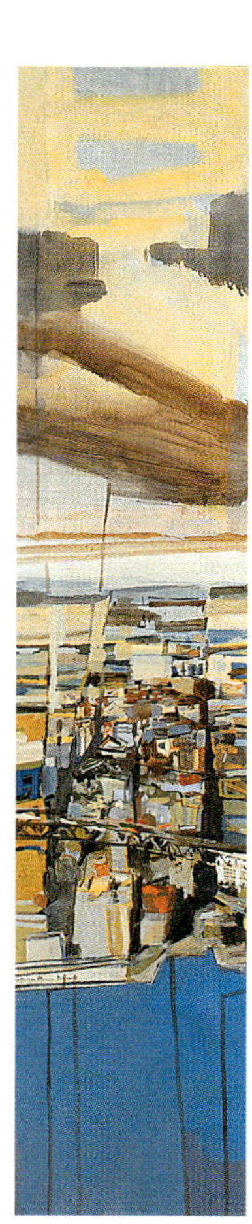

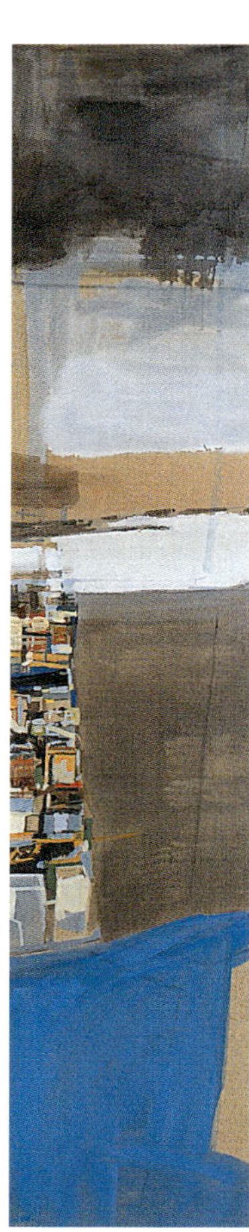

In 1996, I started two large still-life paintings that depicted objects on a round table. The scale (6 x 11 feet) and choice of colors made the rear of the table look like a horizon. When I visited the bar at the top of the WTC in 1996, I was completely taken by the view toward Brooklyn with its layered elements: the receding city, Far Rockaway, and the sea beyond. I became very excited when I found out there was a residency in which I might have the opportunity to develop such grand still lifes, while observing the actual horizon. I was curious to explore the effect of this superimpostition.

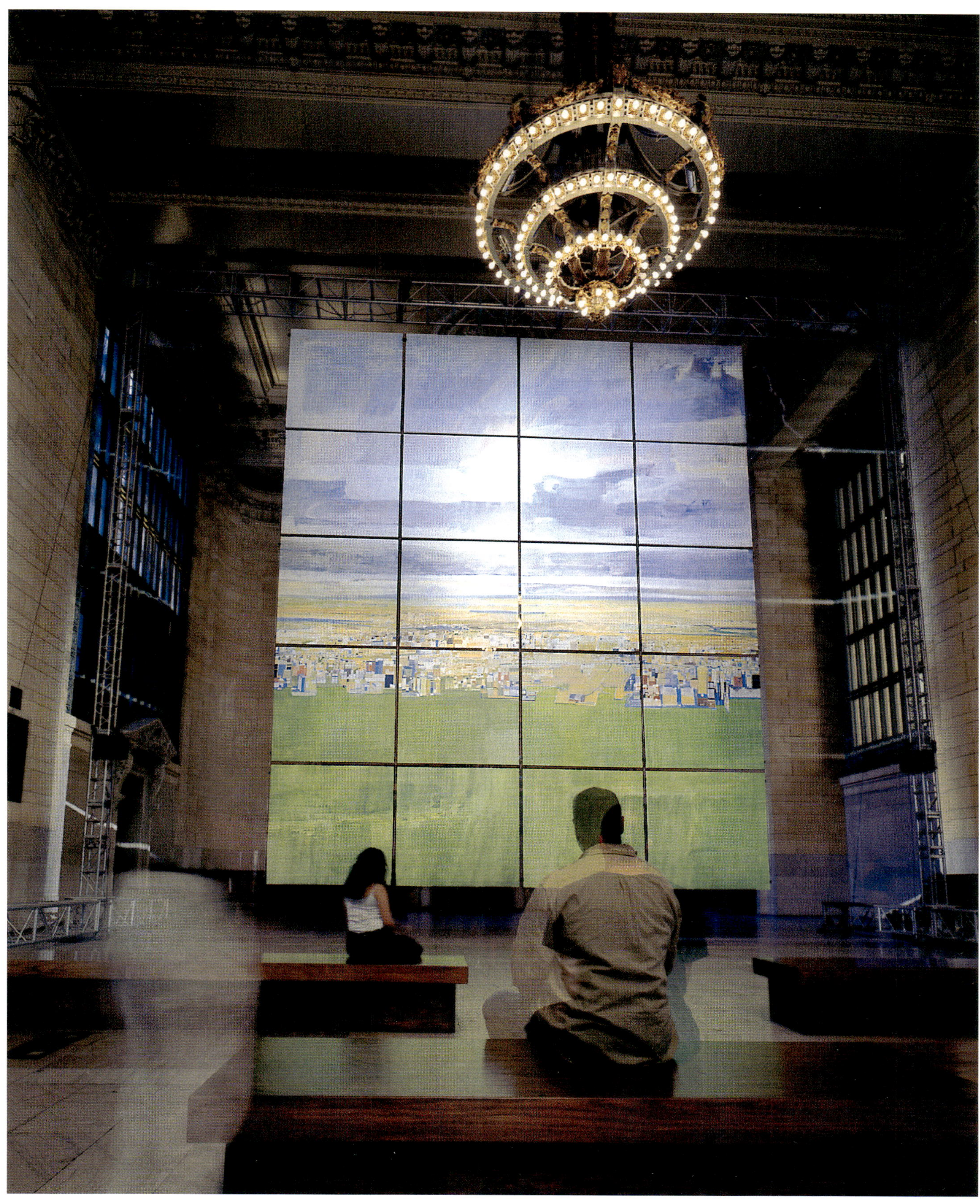

Taylor Spence

Radio Tower, 1999 (with detail)
Buon fresco, sand, lime putty, pigment, wire mesh, short-wave radio, wire
23 x 40 x 8 feet

Born 1967 in Eden, Wyo.
Lives in Brooklyn, N.Y.

Education

1998 MFA, School of Visual Arts, New York, N.Y.
1995 Akademija Likovni Umetnosti, Ljubljana, Slovenia

Selected Exhibitions and Projects

2002 *New Paintings*, Muse Gallery, Jackson, Wyo.
Invited Artists, Fine Arts Work Center, Provincetown, Mass.
1997 Collaboration with Marjetica Potrč, Skulptur Projeckte, Münster, Germany

Residencies

2001 Atlantic Center for the Arts, New Smyrna Beach, Fla.
1998 Skowhegan School of Painting and Sculpture, Maine

Awards

1999 Geraldine R. Dodge Foundation
1995 Fulbright Fellowship
1992 Mid-Atlantic Arts Foundation
Art Matters, Inc.

In my opinion a painter's primary concern is envisioning the fullest expression of him/herself. Regardless of what the artist depicts or creates, the self—the über-self—is the result. Creation is birth. Thus I seek to find a hole and a tunnel through the wall rather than a window or a door. Tunneling through the context of the World Trade Center was an impossible task. The yearning still remains.

Looking west I depicted all the mountains on the circumference of the globe from the point of Tower One. On the north I created a radio antenna that picked up the conversations of people below and other places.

I discovered myself standing in the middle.

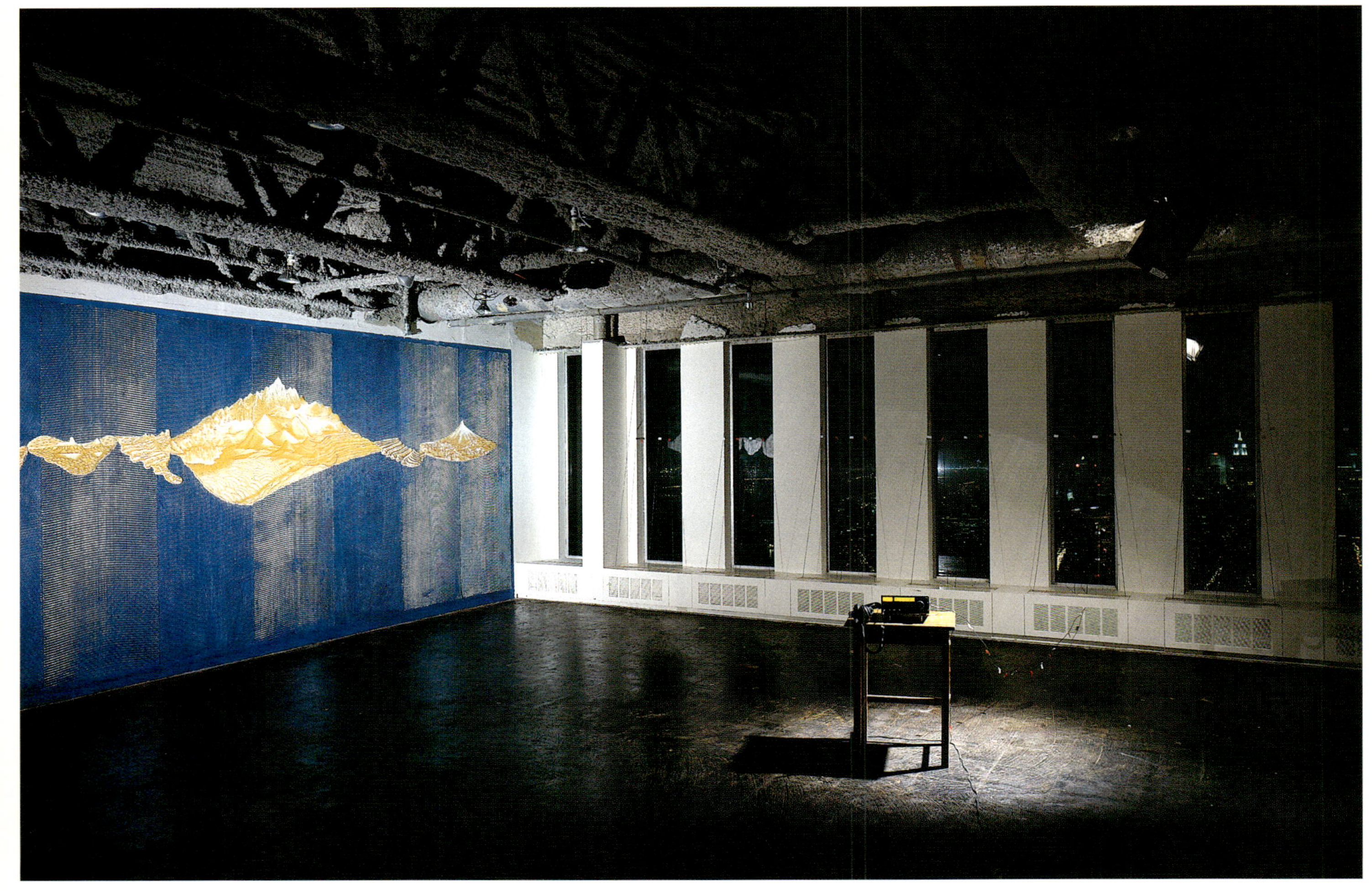

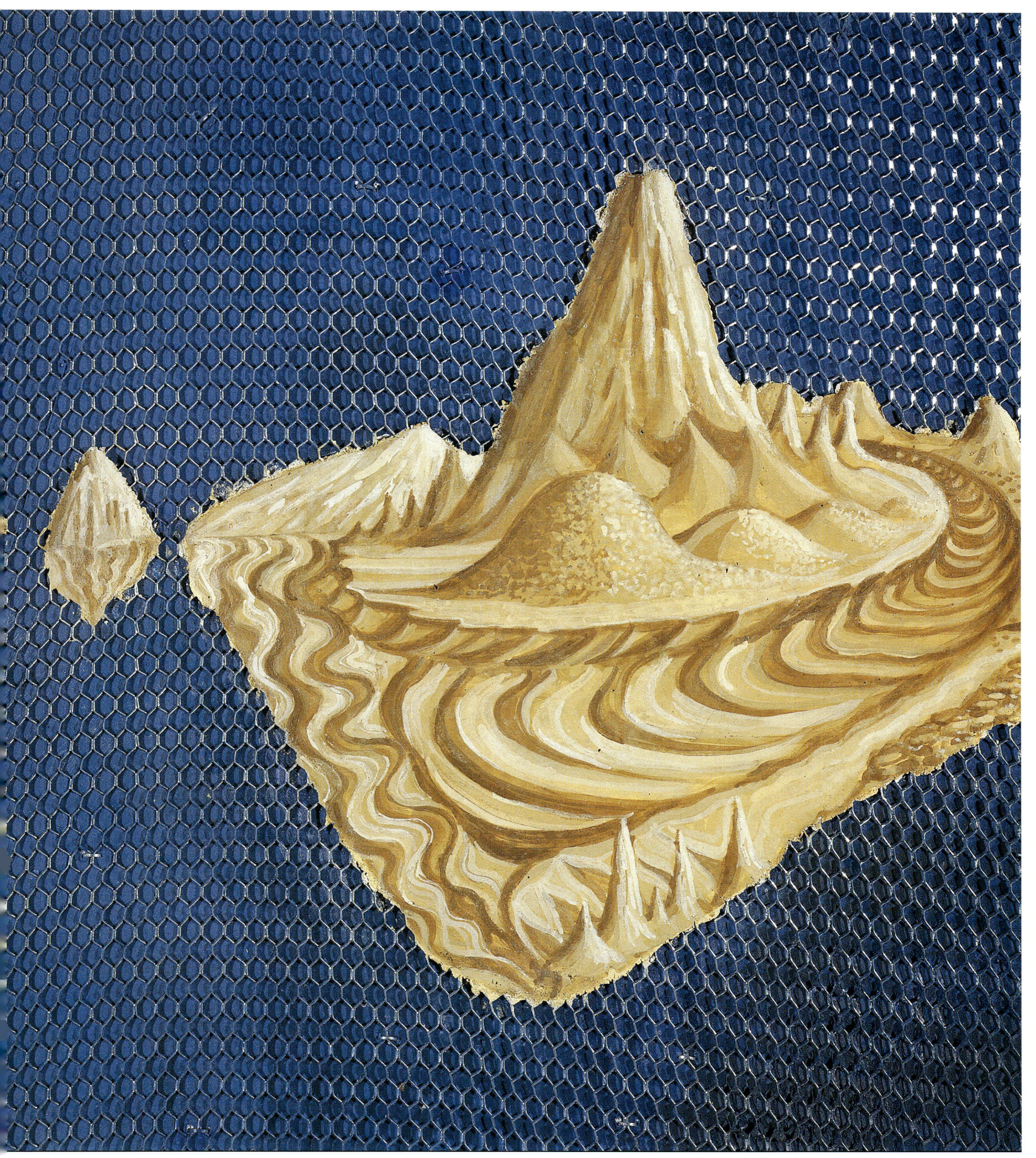

Patrice Sullivan

Fourth Grade, 2000
Oil on linen
8 x 12 inches

Birthday Poise, 2000
Oil on linen
18 x 18 inches

Born 1953 in Portland, Oreg.
Lives in Estes Park, Colo.

Education

1986 MFA, University of Pennsylvania, Philadelphia
1983 BFA, Massachusetts College of Art, Boston

Solo Exhibition

2003 Red Stallion Gallery, Glen Haven, Colo.

Selected Group Exhibitions

2003 *Alumni Exhibition*, University of Pennsylvania, Philadelphia
A.I.R. Gallery, New York, N.Y.
2002 *Icons*, Browdon Community College, Ft. Lauderdale, Fla.
1999 Gracie Mansion Gallery, New York, N.Y.
Jim Kempner Gallery, New York, N.Y.

Residency

1990 Millay Colony for the Arts, Austerlitz, N.Y.

Award

1998 Colorado Council of the Arts

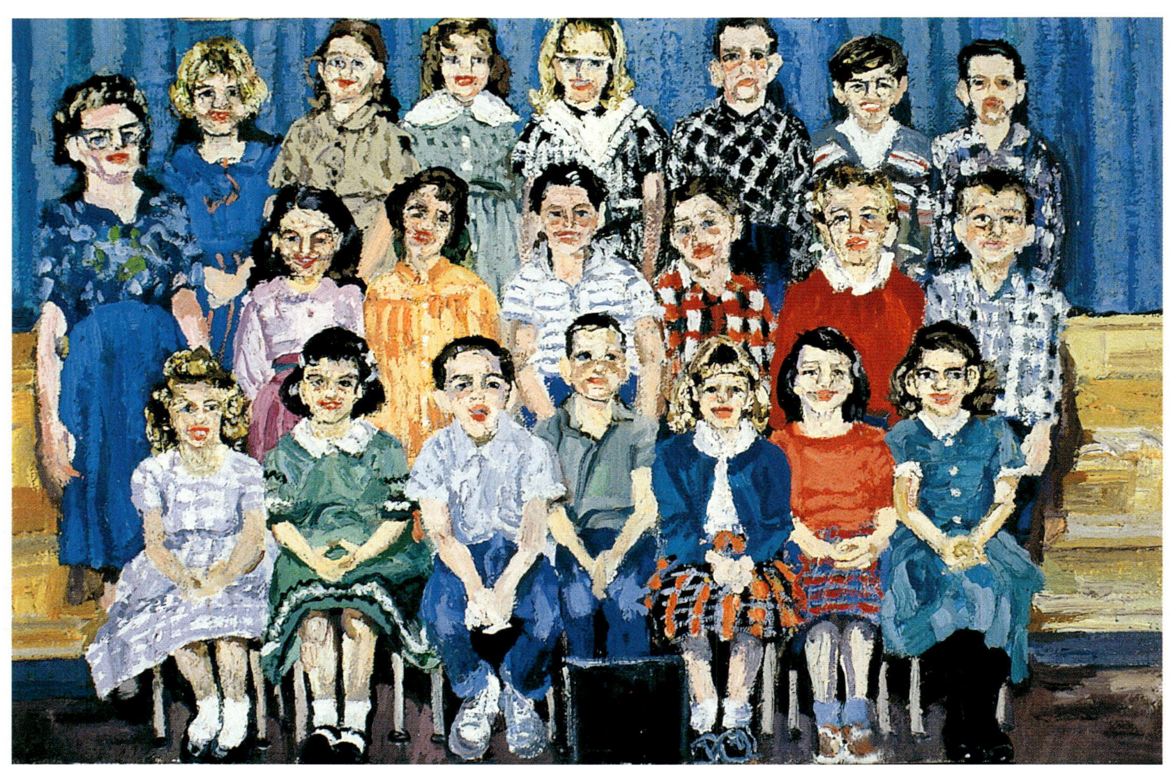

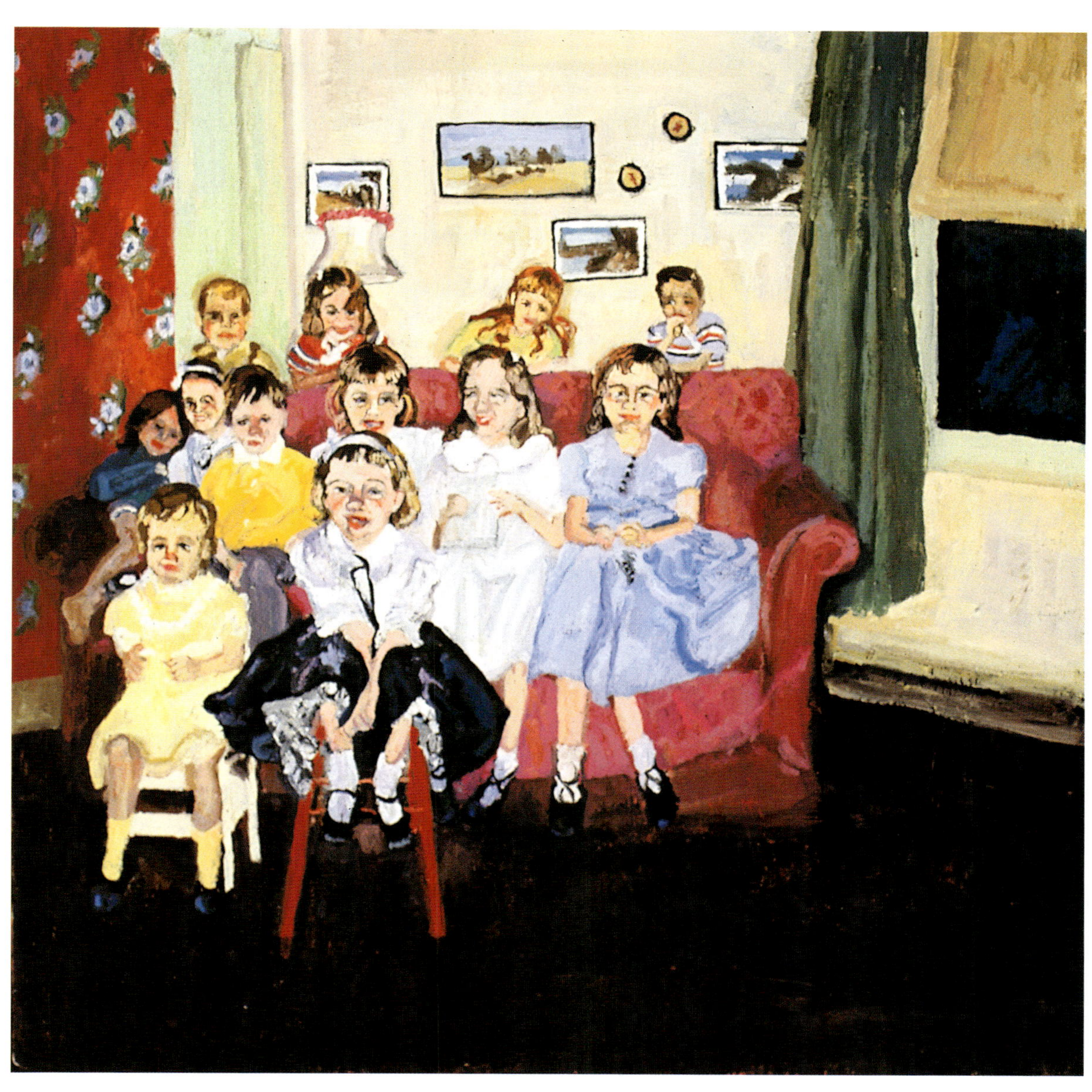

Mette Tronvoll

Valentina I & II, 1998
From the series *Double Portraits*
C-prints
62 x 100 inches overall

Isortoq Unartoq #11, 1999
C-print
29 x 35 inches
Collection of Jan Groth

Born 1965 in Trondheim, Norway
Lives in Berlin, Germany

Education

1992 BFA, Parsons School of Design, New York, N.Y.

Selected Solo Exhibitions

2002 Hippolyte Photographic Gallery, Helsinki, Finland
2001 The National Museum of Contemporary Art, Oslo, Norway
2000 Galerie Max Hetzler, Berlin, Germany

Selected Group Exhibitions

2004 Hamburger Bahnhof, Berlin, Germany
2003 *Happiness*, Mori Arts Museum, Tokyo, Japan
2002 *Beyond Paradise,* The National Gallery, Bangkok, Thailand (tour)

Residencies

2001 Cité Internationales des Arts, Paris, France
2000 Kunstlerhaus Bethanien, Berlin, Germany

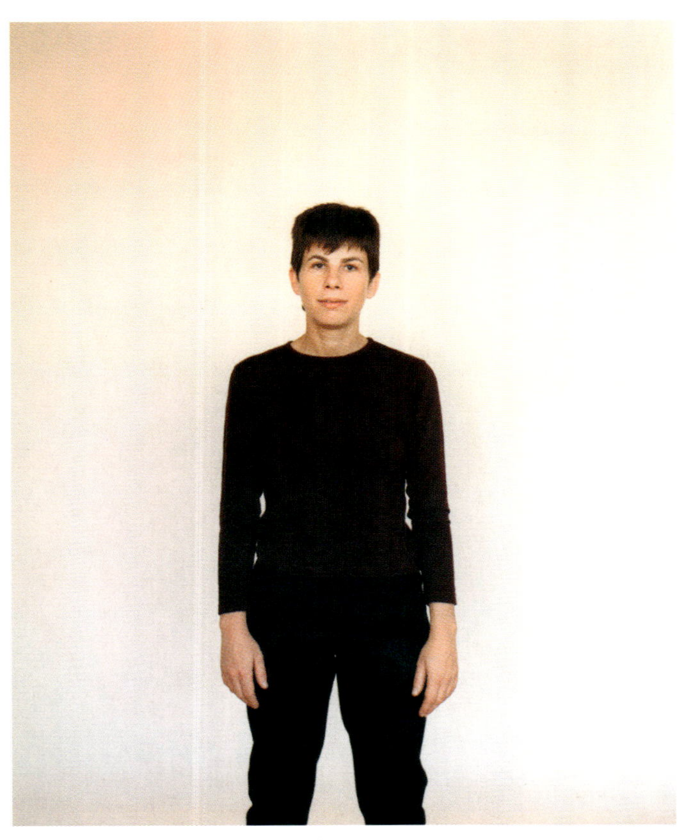

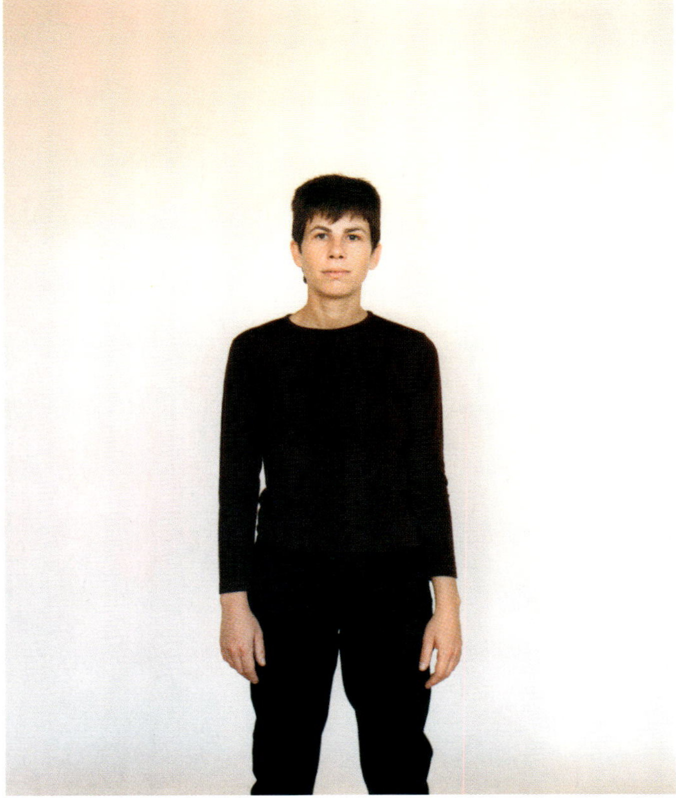

The Sky Lobby was the main point of departure and arrival for my expeditions up and down in the building. Offices moved in as others moved out. I capitalized on this process to collect used office furniture and furnish my studio on the ninety-first floor. Some pieces were too large to fit into the elevator, so I sought assistance in fitting the furniture into the freight elevator.

On one occasion the manager from the Port Authority helped me bring a huge flat file down to the basement in order to change to a different freight elevator and then return back to the ninety-first floor. The basement was enormous, and it took a while to orient myself to the space.

Numerous trucks were lined up with workers moving at a fast pace everywhere in a blur of activity. I had discovered an unknown world within the World Trade Center and felt completely lost there.

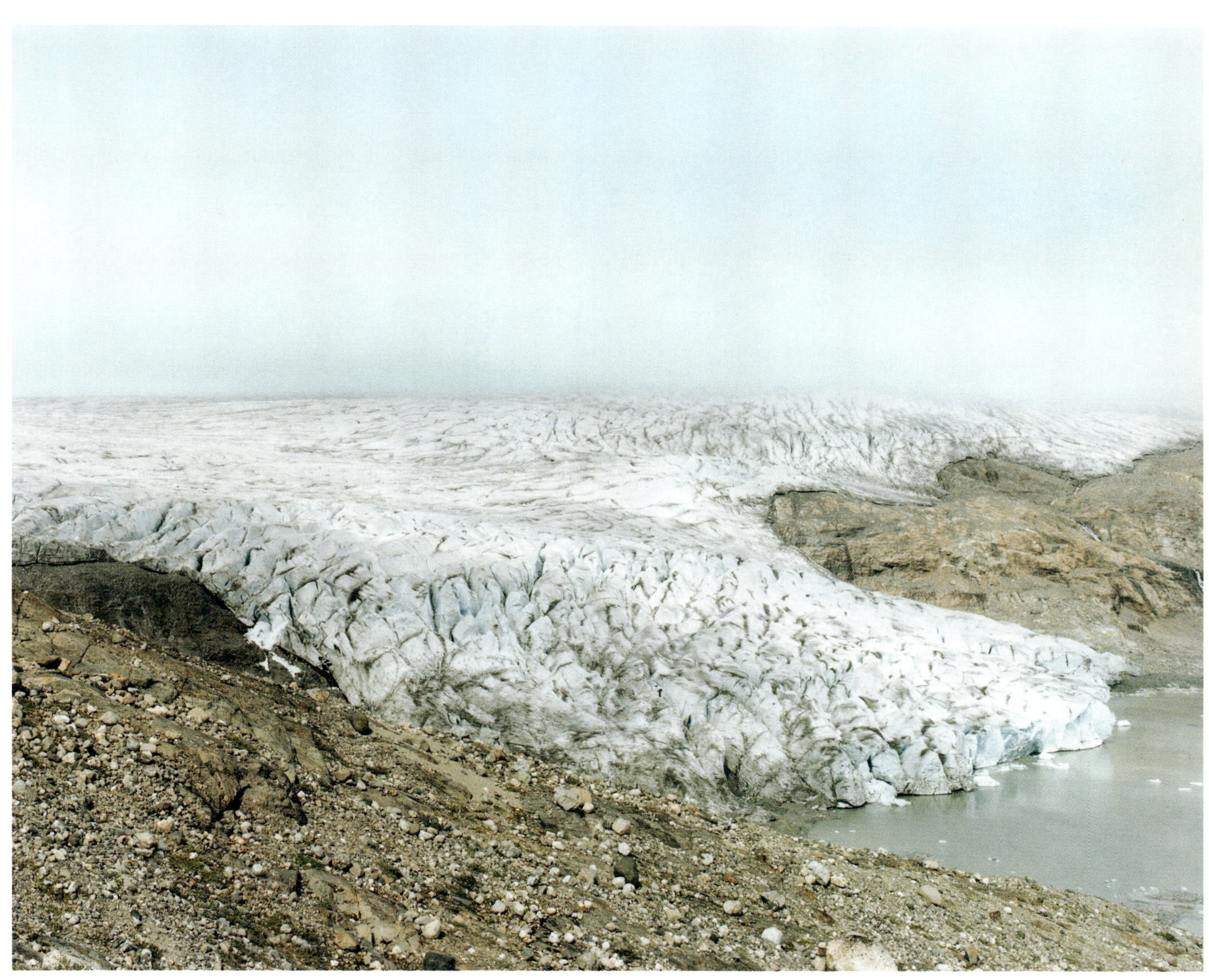

Micki K. Watanabe

Floorplan Collage: WTC 91st Fl. and 15 Park Avenue, 1999
Paint on concrete
1000 sq. ft.

Floorplan Collage: WTC 47th Fl. and Apt. on West End Avenue, 1999
Paint on concrete
Approx. 1000 sq. ft.

Born 1968 in Ehime, Japan
Lives in Brooklyn, N.Y.

Education

1993 MFA, Ohio State University, Columbus
1991 BFA, Kansas City Art Institute, Mo.

Selected Solo Exhibitions

2004 *Library as Reference/Library as Object*, Evergreen House Museum, Baltimore, Md.
2001 *Stories and Containers*, The College of Saint Rose Art Gallery, Albany, N.Y.

Selected Group Exhibitions

2003 *Macht Vergleichnar, New York Cross-Cut*, Kunstverein Firma Paradigma, Linz, Austria
Signs+Senses+Envelopes, Care/Of Gallery, Milan, Italy
Sculpture: A Matter of Soft and Hard, The Artists Alliance at Clemente Soto Velez Center, New York, N.Y.

Residencies

2003 Evergreen House, The John Hopkins University, Baltimore, Md.
2002 Bemis Center for Contemporary Arts, Omaha, Nebr.

Award

2001 The Pollock-Krasner Foundation

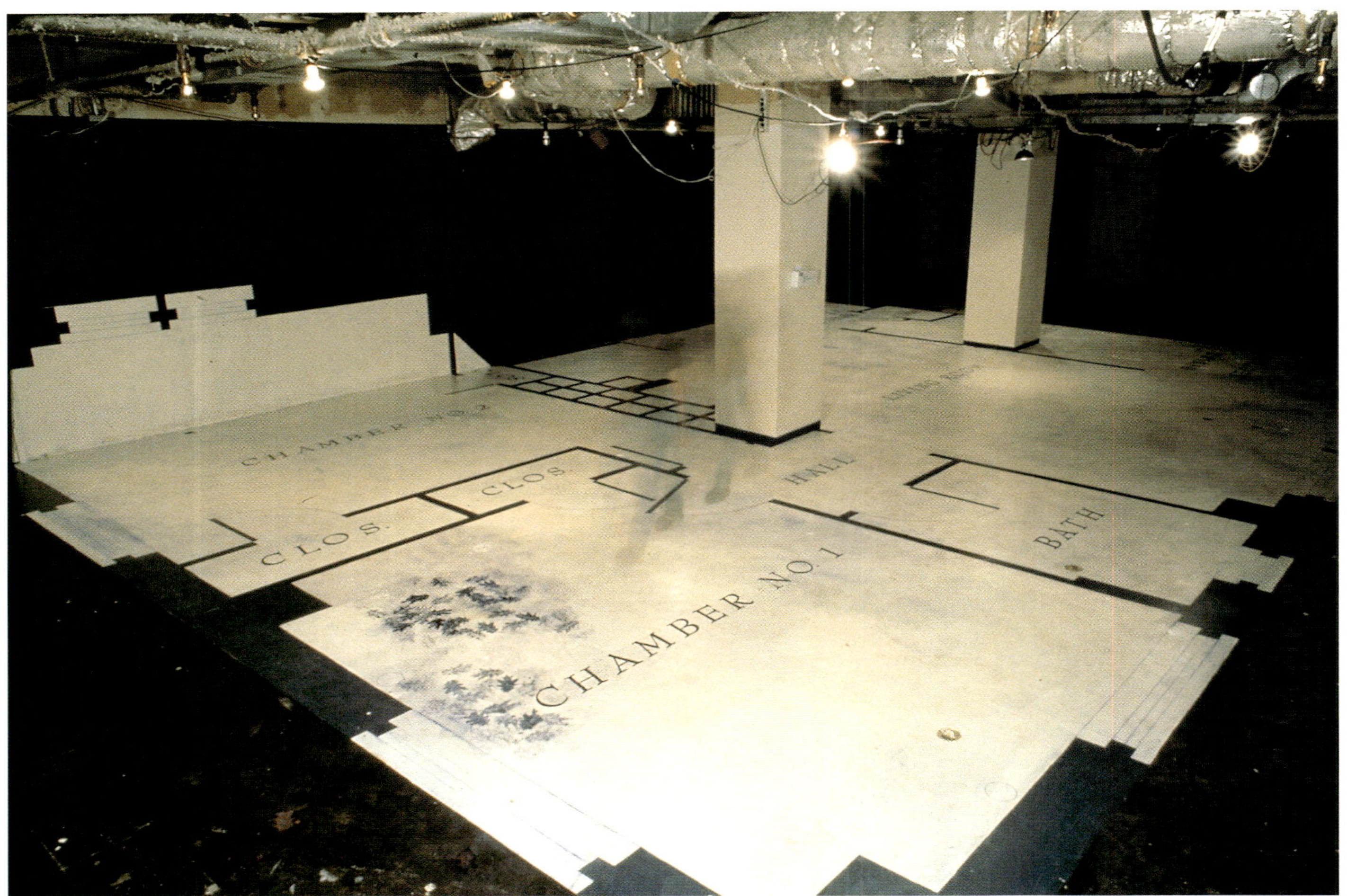

I remember early in November, a few weeks after I first stepped foot on the ninety-first floor, I saw from my new perch a soccer game being played in Battery Park. Sitting on one of the air ducts that delineated the space, I observed the white spots down below running in geometric diagrams which cast long shadows onto the playing field. This new perspective interested me a great deal. Then an hour later I sat on the train with one of the boys going home with his soccer mom. The white dot had no trailing shadow, and I thought it would be interesting if he still possessed the dramatic afternoon light there on the N train. I think that the residency had a great impact on how I perceive objects from great distances, and it changed the way I look at and use scale in my work. Though I didn't realize it until months after my tenure on the ninety-first floor ended, I had begun to work out the difficulties I was having with the differences between sculpture and installation, and how to resolve my interests in both.

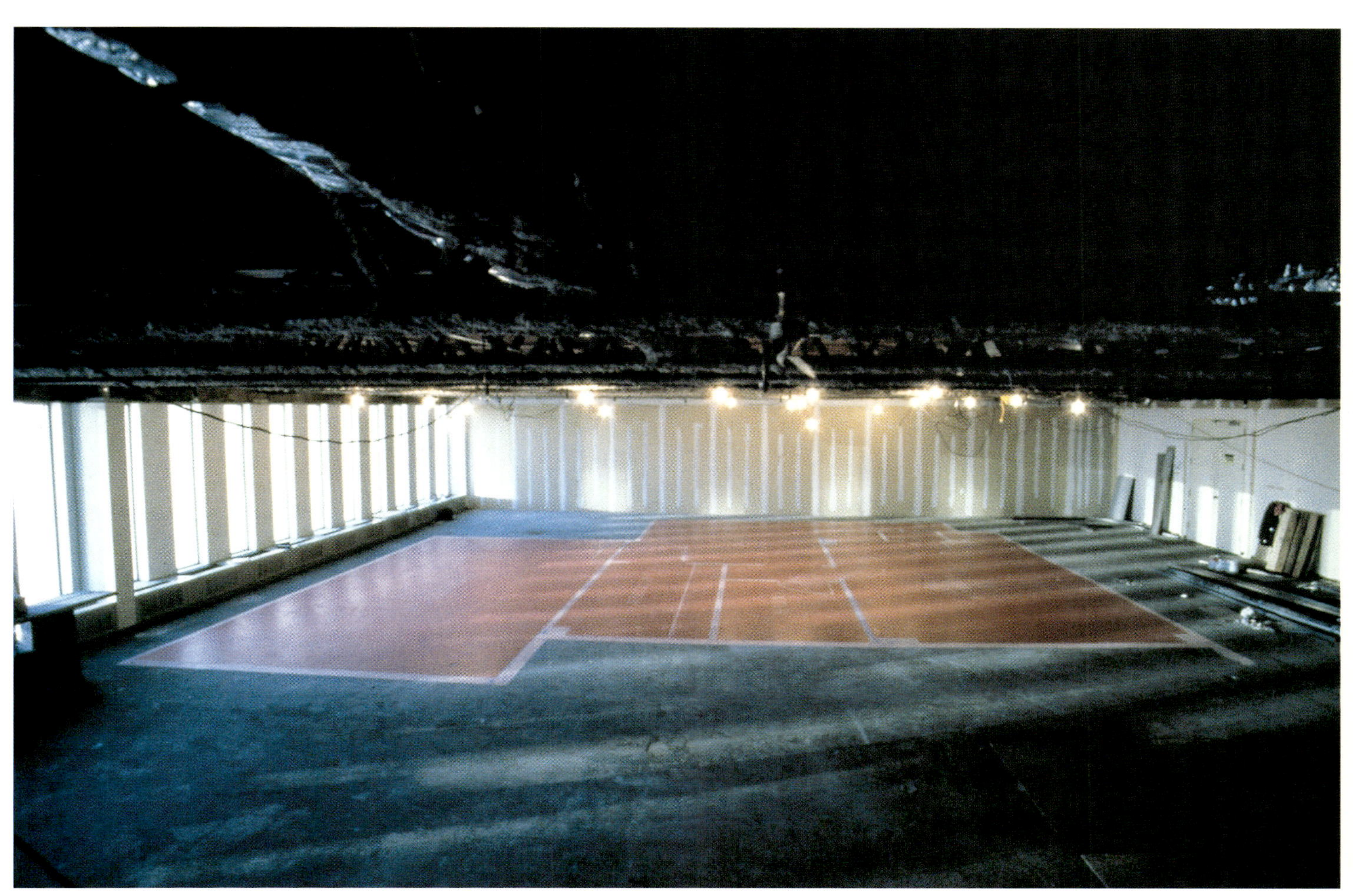

Summer 1999

Artists-in-Residence

Adriana Arenas Ilian
Olive Ayhens
Jennifer Bolande
Wendy Chisholm
Mary Jane Dean
Adrian Doura
Myong Hwa Jeong
Jennifer & Kevin McCoy
Mick O'Shea
Paul Pfeiffer
Nadine Robinson
Robert Selwyn
Taketo Shimada
MiYoung Sohn
Stephen Vitiello

Jurors

Lynn Cooke
Antonio Muntadas
Carol Parkinson
Lorna Simpson
Franklin Sirmans
Zhang Ga

Invited Artist

John Long

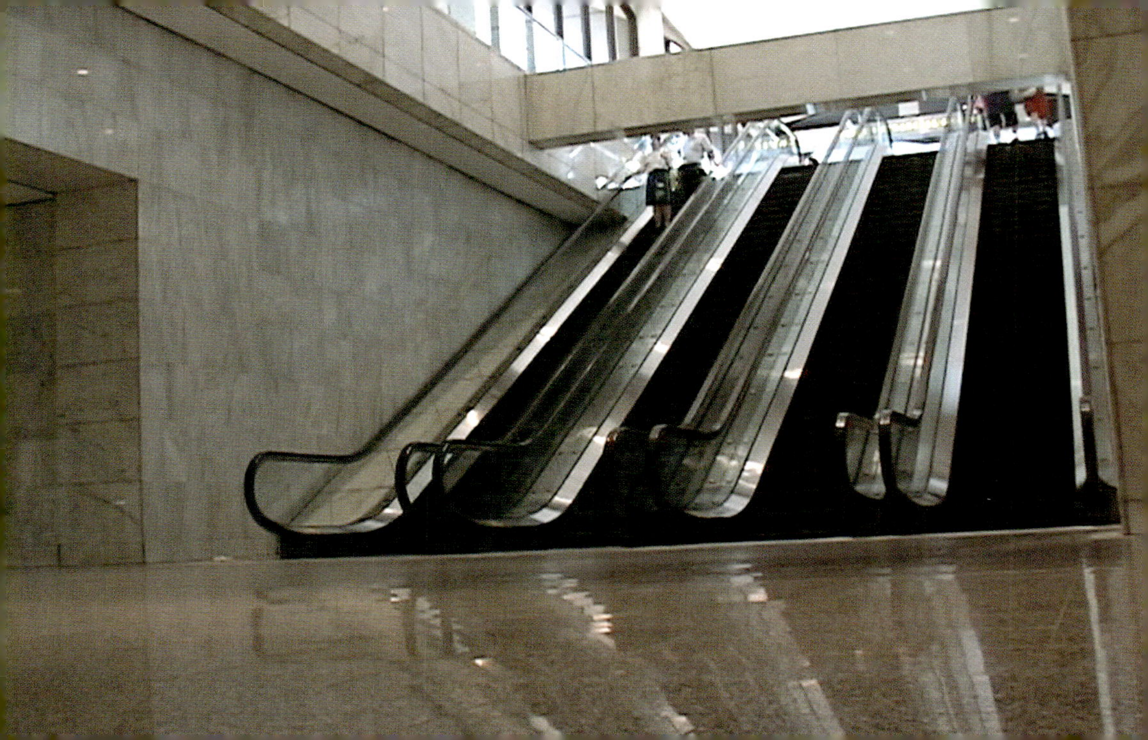

Adriana Arenas Ilian

Race Factory, 1999
Installation view and video stills

The viewer is lead into a space in which a large-scale projection and a monitor are situated opposite each other. Both display dancing figures, yet sound and rhythms have been omitted. In the video projection Adriana Arenas Ilian's gaze is not directed toward the camera; rather she seems to be dancing with the image of her own reflection. On the monitor, sixteen figures, originating from seventeenth-century colonial Mexican-Spanish *Casta* paintings, have been positioned in a circle. The circle of figures is an eschewed animation, reminiscent of an amorphoses in fifteenth- to eighteenth-century paintings taken from a text by Rike Frank.

Born 1969 in Pereira, Colombia
Lives in New York, N.Y.

Education

1999 MFA, Pratt Institute, Brooklyn, N.Y.
1994–95 Chelsea College of Art, London, U.K.
1988–92 Universidad de los Andes, Bogota, Colombia

Selected Solo Exhibitions

2002 The Bronx Museum of the Arts, The Bronx, N.Y.
Roebling Hall, Brooklyn, N.Y.
2000 *Sweet Illusion*, Contemporary Art Center, Cincinnati, Ohio
1999 The Museo de Arte de Pereira, Colombia

Selected Group Exhibitions

2001 *Video Jam*, Palm Beach Institute of Contemporary Art, Fla.
Digital, Brooklyn Museum of Art, N.Y.
2000 *Nomads*, Havana Biennial, Cuba
Greater New York, P.S.1 Contemporary Art Center, Long Island City, N.Y.

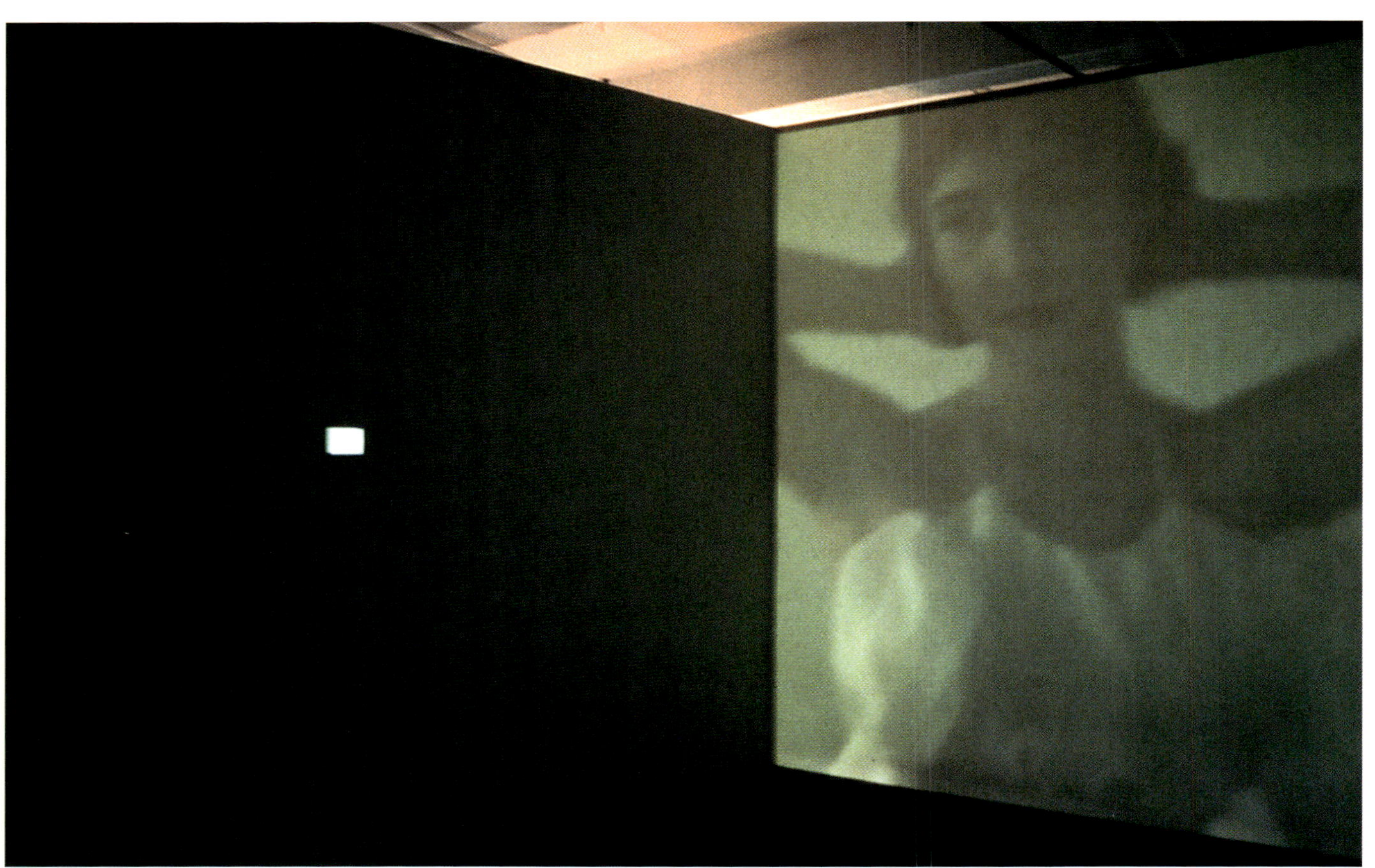

To have keys to a space on the ninety-first floor of the WTC and know that I could go to the space at any time and that I was part of the flow of activity there was quite empowering. I was familiar with the security guards and in a small way (because the building functioned like a town) with the dynamic of the social structure. Riding the elevator represents an icon of the WTC experience; changing elevators, sometimes without thinking, to ascend higher in the sky.

At the time of my residency, I was living in a street-level apartment where I had grown accustomed to street noise. One day while working in my studio I heard a cart pass and mistook the sound for a vehicle in the street. I realized it was actually a robotic window cleaner. This was a magical, however disorienting, experience that has stayed with me along with other quirky recollections, like the hammock I suspended from structural beams so I could watch the planes and take in the sunset above the city.

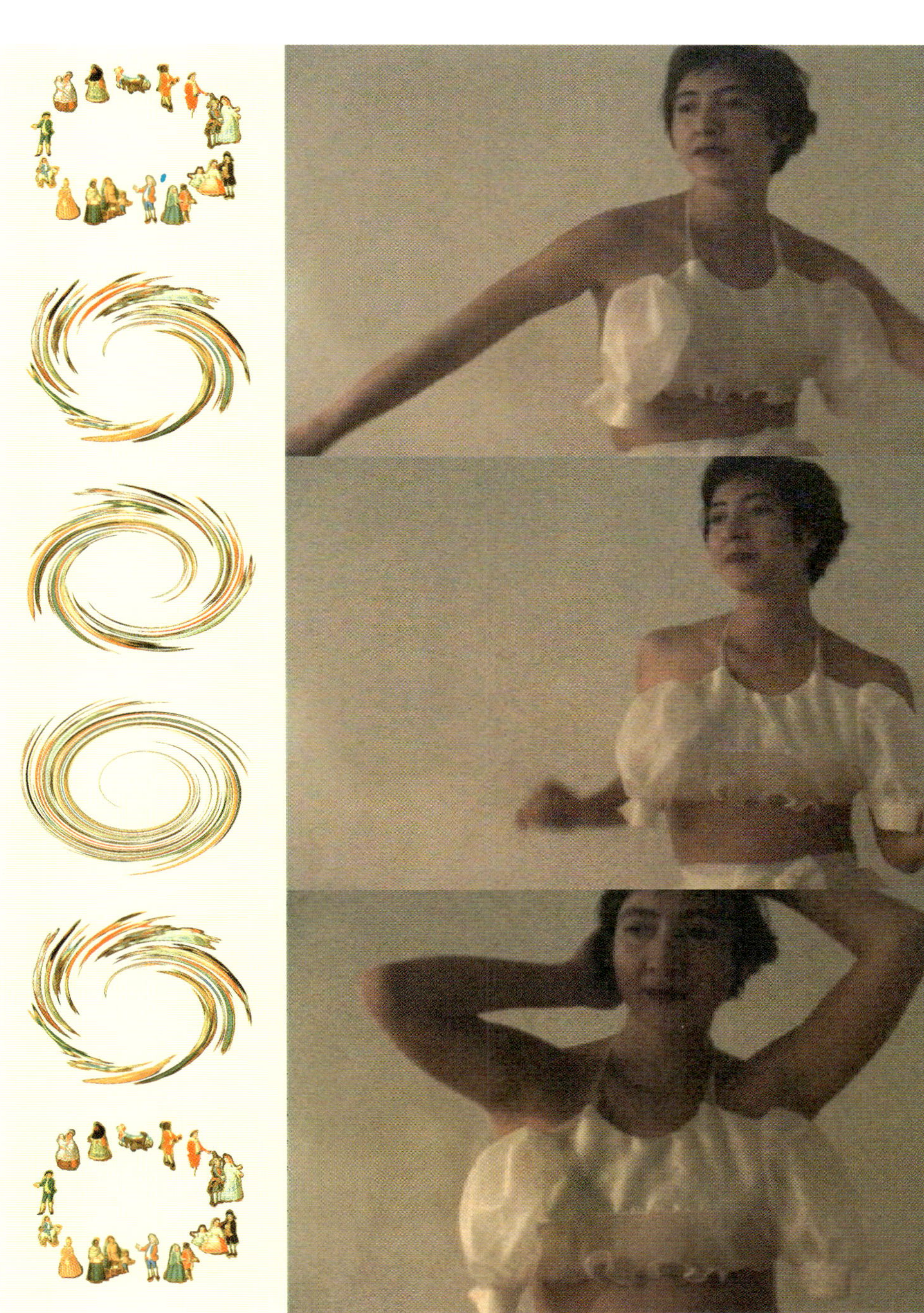

Olive Ayhens

Manhattan Rooftops, 1999–2000
Oil on canvas
48 x 68 inches
Photo: John Berens

Cat In the Night, 1999
Oil on canvas
68 x 58 inches
Photo: John Berens

Born 1943 in Oakland, Calif.
Lives in Brooklyn, N.Y.

Education
1969 MFA, San Francisco Art Institute, Calif.
1968 BFA, San Francisco Art Institute, Calif.

Selected Solo Exhibitions
2003 Gary Tatuntsian Gallery, New York, N.Y.
Pierogi 2000, Brooklyn, N.Y. (tour)

Selected Group Exhibitions
2003 *NY/SF/LA*, San Luis Obispo, Calif.
2002 *Artists to Artists: A Decade of the Space Program*, The Marie Walsh Sharpe Art Foundation, ACE Gallery, New York, N.Y.
Adam Baumgold Gallery, New York, N.Y.

Residencies
2003 Salzburg Kunstlerhaus, Austria
1999 The MacDowell Colony, Peterborough, N.H.

Award
2001 The Pollock-Krasner Foundation

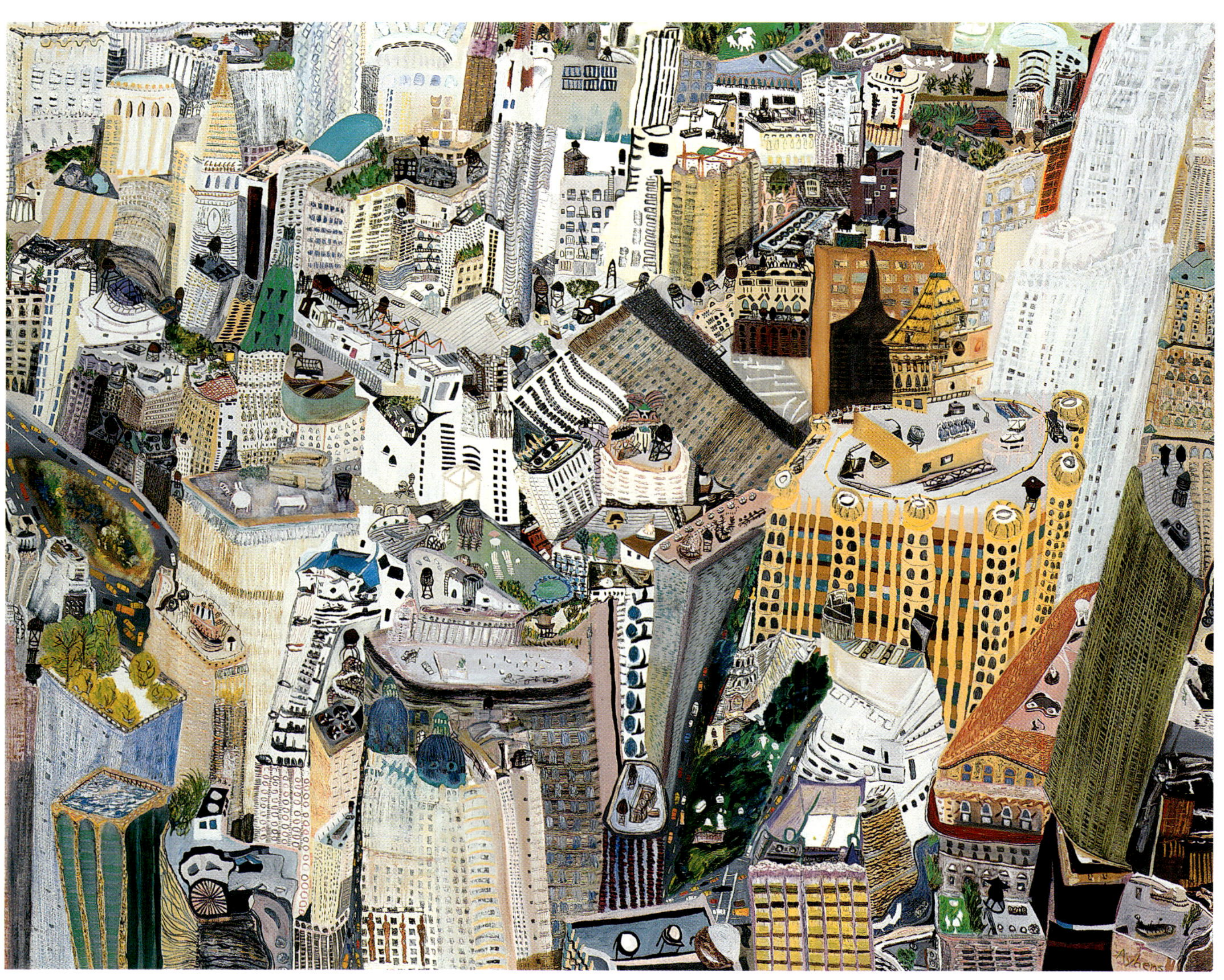

The experience of observing New York City from a highly elevated viewpoint is like watching a total "living being" that weaves its intricacies for organic purposes of its own. It's similar to studying an organism under a microscope. I was the voyeur, with binoculars, observing a variety of intimate rooftop scenes. My imagination got going while working in the now, elaborating, inventing, evolving. . . . The paintings reflected the fabric patterns of urban architecture, skyscrapers and gridlock.

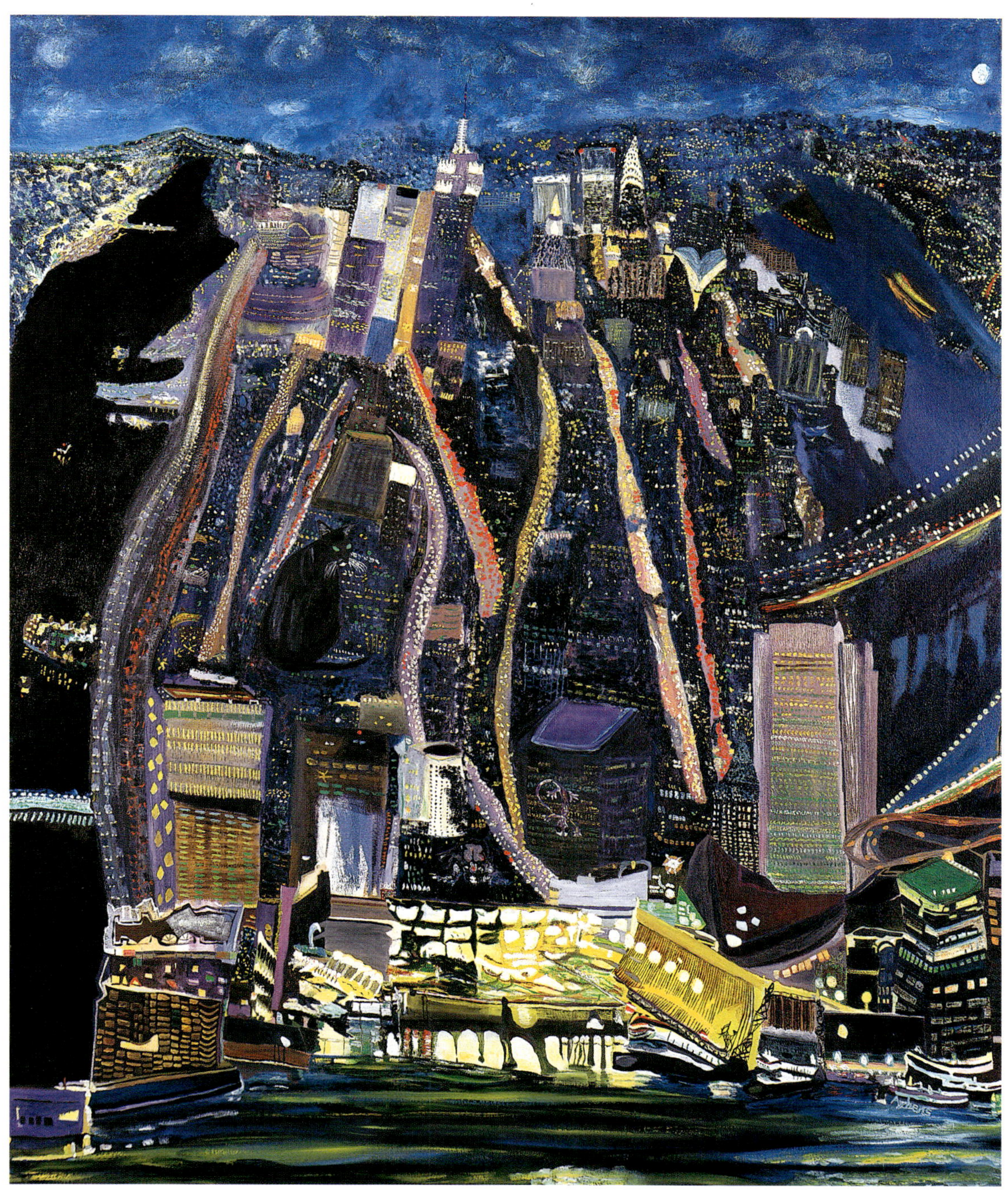

Jennifer Bolande

Appliance House, 1998–99
Two duratrans photographs in lightboxes with stainless steel frames and columns
91 x 51 x 5 inches
Courtesy Alexander and Bonin, New York, N.Y.
Photo: Orcutt & Van Der Putten

Born 1957 in Cleveland, Ohio
Lives in New York, N.Y.

Education

1979 BFA, Nova Scotia College of Art and Design, Halifax

Selected Solo Exhibitions

2001 Alexander and Bonin, New York, N.Y.
1999 P.S.1 Contemporary Art Center, Long Island City, N.Y.
1998 *Forest Spirits*, Patricia Sweetow Gallery, San Francisco, Calif.

Selected Group Exhibitions

2003 *Living Inside the Grid*, New Museum of Contemporary Art, New York, N.Y.
2002 *The Photogenic: Photography Through Its Metaphors in Contemporary Art*, Institute of Contemporary Art, Philadelphia, Pa.

Awards

1999 Tesuque Foundation
1985 The Canada Council

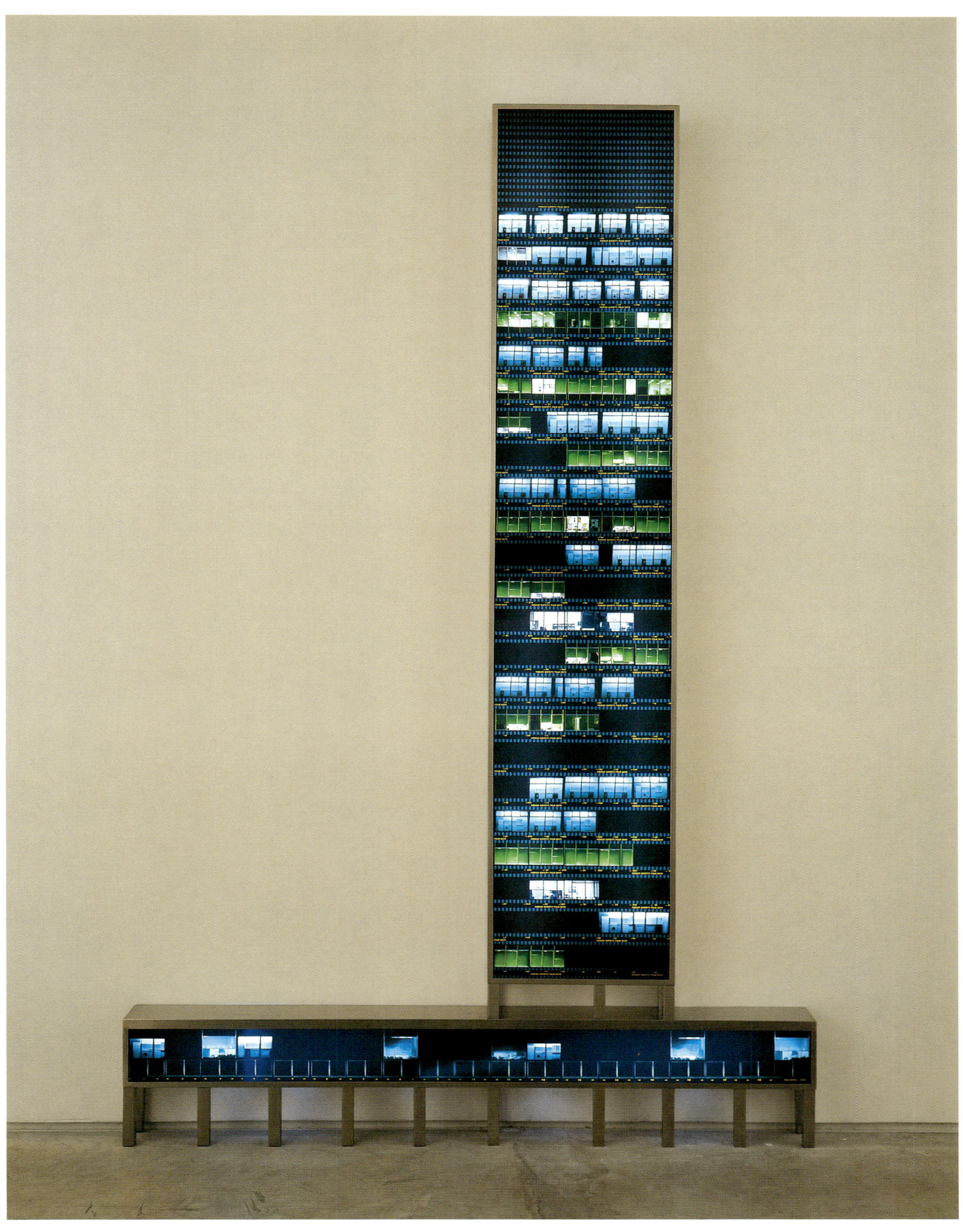

Wendy Chisholm

Badass, 1999 (installation views)
Drywall, wood, video projection
Approx. 20 x 4 feet

Badass was installed in Tower One of the World Trade Center in a ninety-first floor boardroom (Room 9165) with a westward view of New Jersey. Two freestanding walls (8 feet x 4 feet x 6 inches; drywall, wood, paint) with silhouette cut-outs (of myself, each in a different state of running) and corresponding (interior) silhouette cutouts were placed in a line toward the windows.

A new wall (mimicking the freestanding walls) was seamlessly built into the two middle windows, which provided a screen for a video projection. The video was a running silhouette—the inside of the silhouette being a moving image of the view from out the window. The overall effect was as if someone had run through two walls, and then continued through the wall of the building.

Born 1972 in San Jose, Calif.
Lives in New Orleans, La.

Education

1998 MFA, Rhode Island School of Design, Providence
1995 BA, University of California, Davis

Selected Solo Exhibitions

2003 *Wendar*, University of New Orleans Gallery, La.
1999 *PG*, Phoenix Gallery, New York, N.Y.

Selected Group Exhibitions

2003 *Superheroes,* Ruby Green Contemporary Art Center, Nashville, Tenn.
2002 *Bourbonization,* University of New Orleans Gallery, La.
2000 *ShowVIEW: Internationales Videoprogram*, Galerie 5020, Salzburg, Austria
1999 *The Millennium Exhibition*, The Alternative Museum, New York, N.Y.

Awards

2003 New Orleans Summer Scholar Program Grant
1999 *Artist in the Marketplace*, The Bronx Museum of the Arts, The Bronx, N.Y.

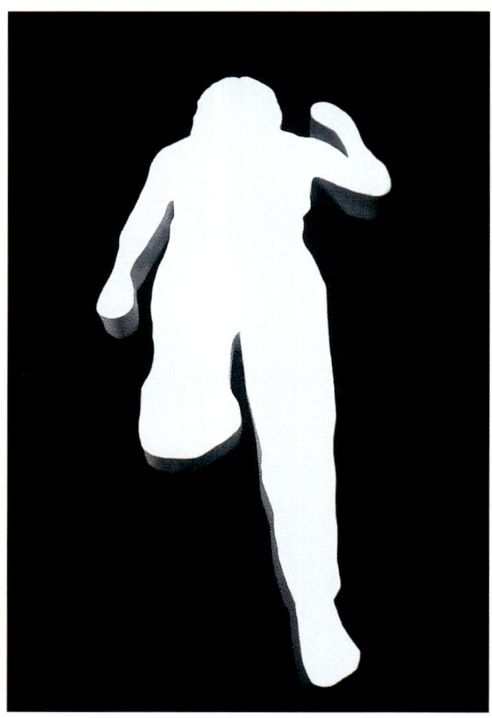

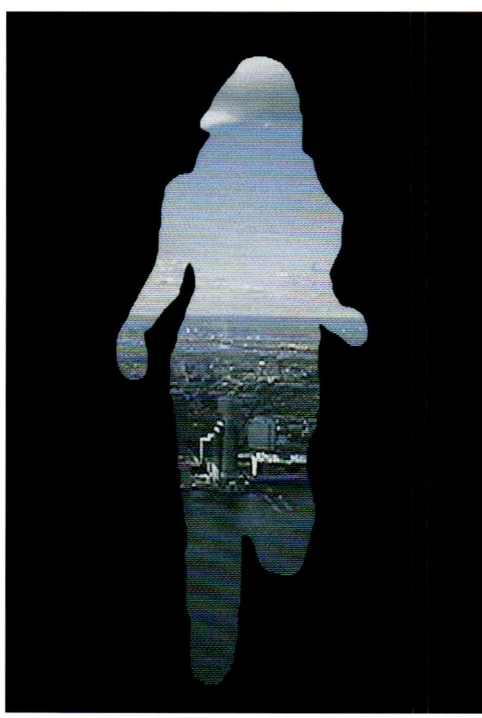

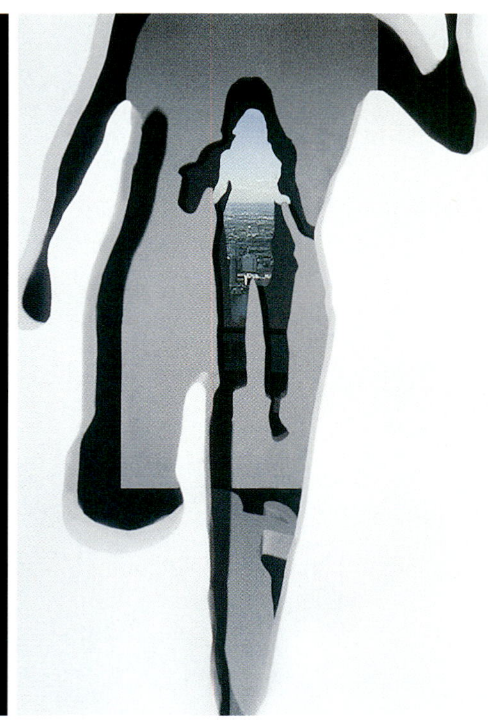

I never knew what to do once I finally got through security and rode the elevators up to the ninety-first floor. Usually I just wanted to go back down and get a sandwich. I spent more than a few late nights alone skateboarding across the studio space and smoking cigarettes. I was distracted by the view. Around 5:00 A.M. I would go down to the mall and eat bacon, egg and cheese on a roll with the building staff. I often got business men to jump up and down in the express elevator.

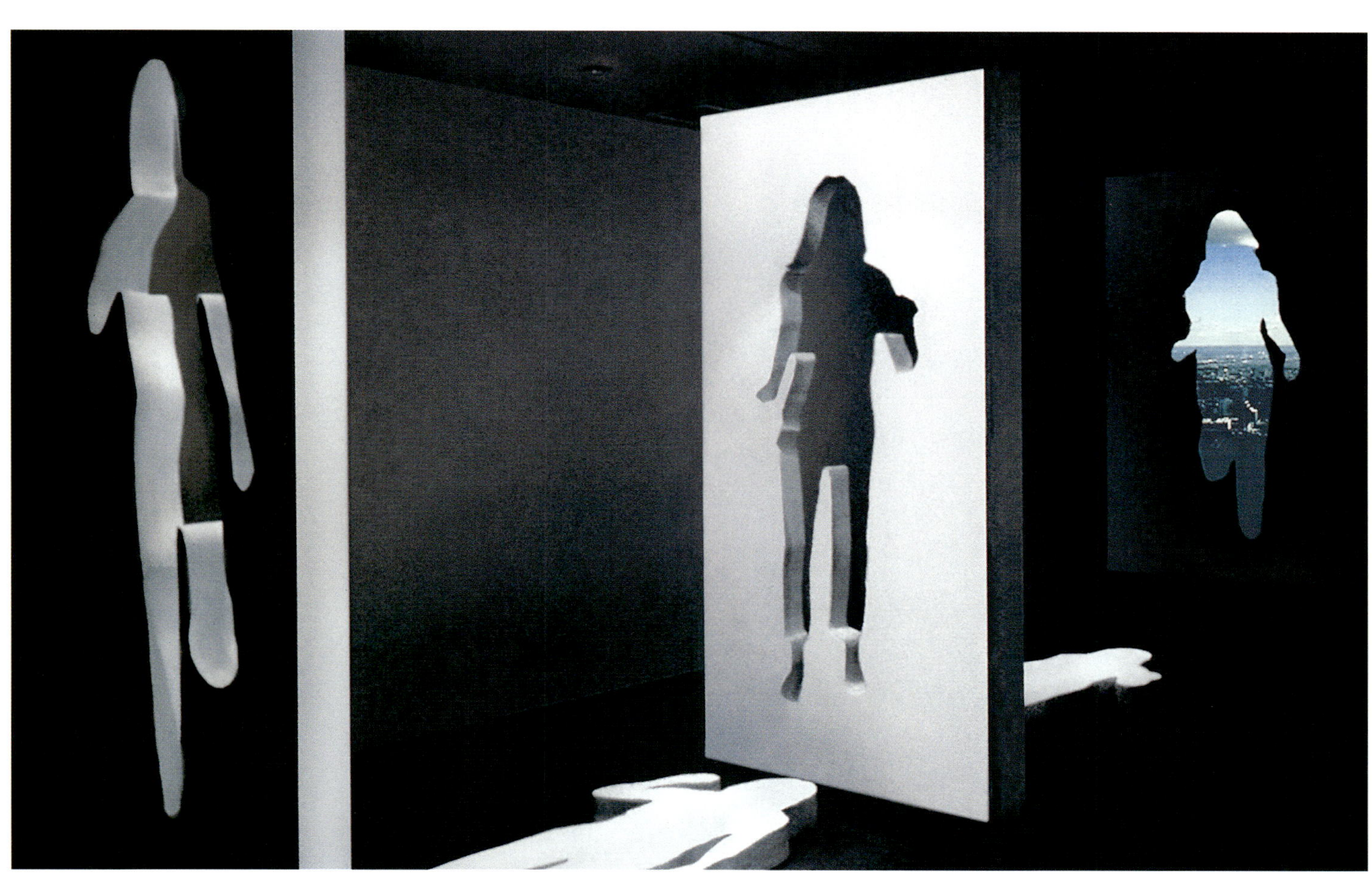

Mary Jane Dean

Optical Repository, 1999
Eight silver gelatin paper negatives
12 x 31 feet overall

A pinhole panoramic camera (4 x 4 x 1 feet) was made precisely for the architecture of the windows. Seven-foot negative photographs were taken of the different views and framed onto the window glass. These images were luminously backlit by sunlight.

Cumulus Blind, 1999
Pinhole panoramic camera, silver gelatin prints
42 x 144 inches each

A white iris frames and focuses vision on vast and dramatic skies. In each print, from out of shadows' depths, a minute and furtive craft emerges: Harrier jets hover, paratroopers dangle from ropes, machine-gun-laden helicopters advance and dive.

Born 1960 in San Francisco, Calif.
Lives in Provincetown, Mass.

Education

1998 MFA, University of California, Berkeley

Selected Solo Exhibitions

2000 *The Drift Bottle Project*, Hudson D. Walker Gallery, Provincetown, Mass

1999 *Moving Pictures*, Hudson D. Walker Gallery, Provincetown, Mass.

1998 Jack Hanley Gallery, San Francisco, Calif.

Residencies

2000 The MacDowell Colony, Peterborough, N.H.

1998 Skowhegan School of Painting and Sculpture, Maine

Awards

2002 Massachusetts Cultural Council

2001 Fine Arts Work Center Fellowship, Provincetown, Mass.

1995 The International Peace Center's Freedom Prize, Sarajevo, Bosnia-Herzegovina

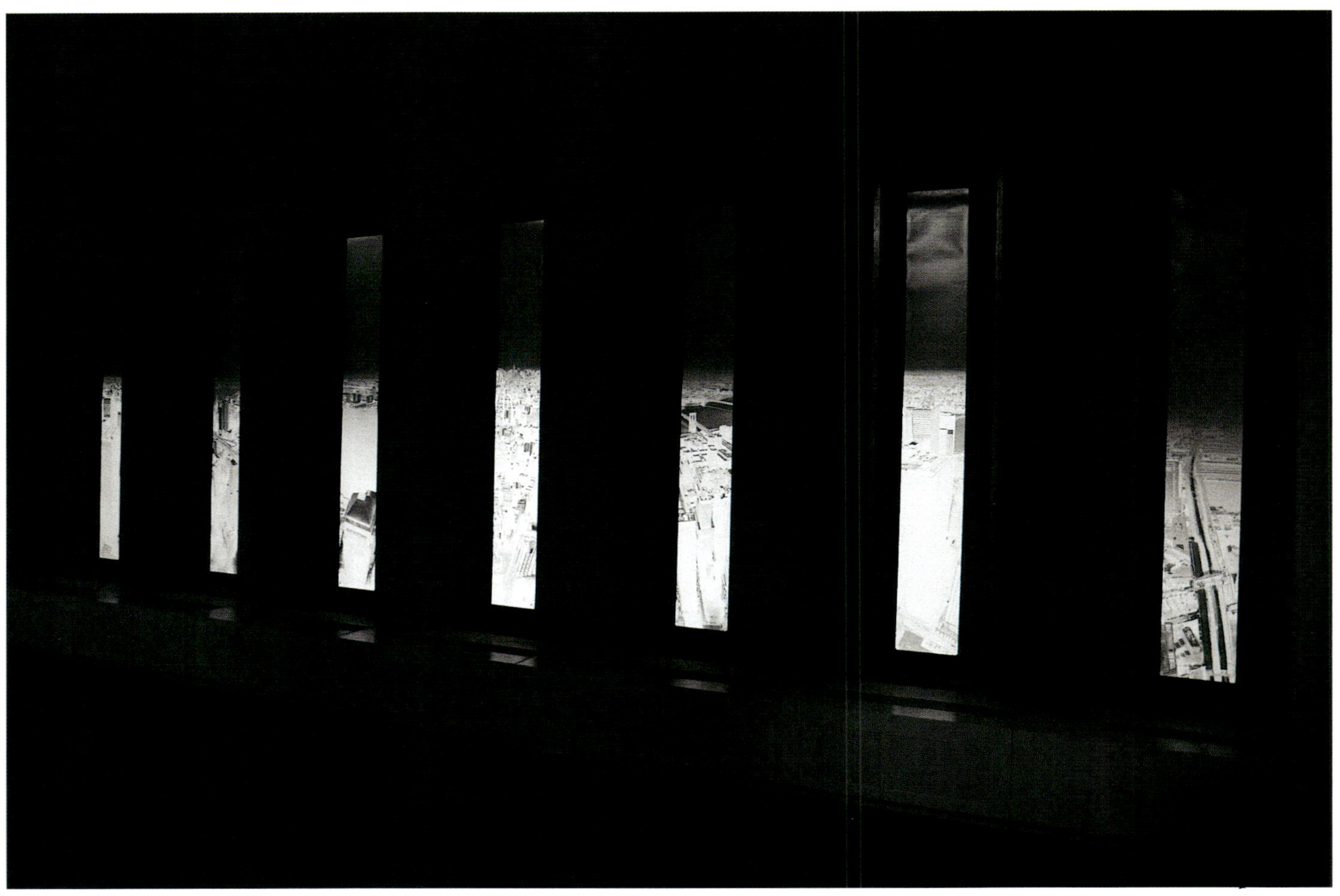

Through still imagery and time-based film projections, and using early photographic technologies, my work before the World Trade Center explored vast spaces swept and shrouded by atmospheric change and exploitation. These ruinous wastelands seemed to be either primordial or terminal: depleted mines, dry salt lakes, abandoned quarries.

Then, while in residence at the World Trade Center, in the confines of the city's depths and heights, I was compelled to examine notions of finality, menace and the expansive. I floated a minute F-16 fighter plane in the building's atrium. I built a large camera that took seven-foot negatives of the views surrounding us. Mounted onto the window glass, these backlit and reversed phantom images dissolved at sunset with the waning light. I filmed passing storm clouds, which both obscured and revealed the view beneath us. I shot photographs of the building from the ground looking up, attempting to dissolve its structure, evaporate the rigidity. Using old and intentionally impoverished media, this contemporary subject is removed from the present and placed into a past.

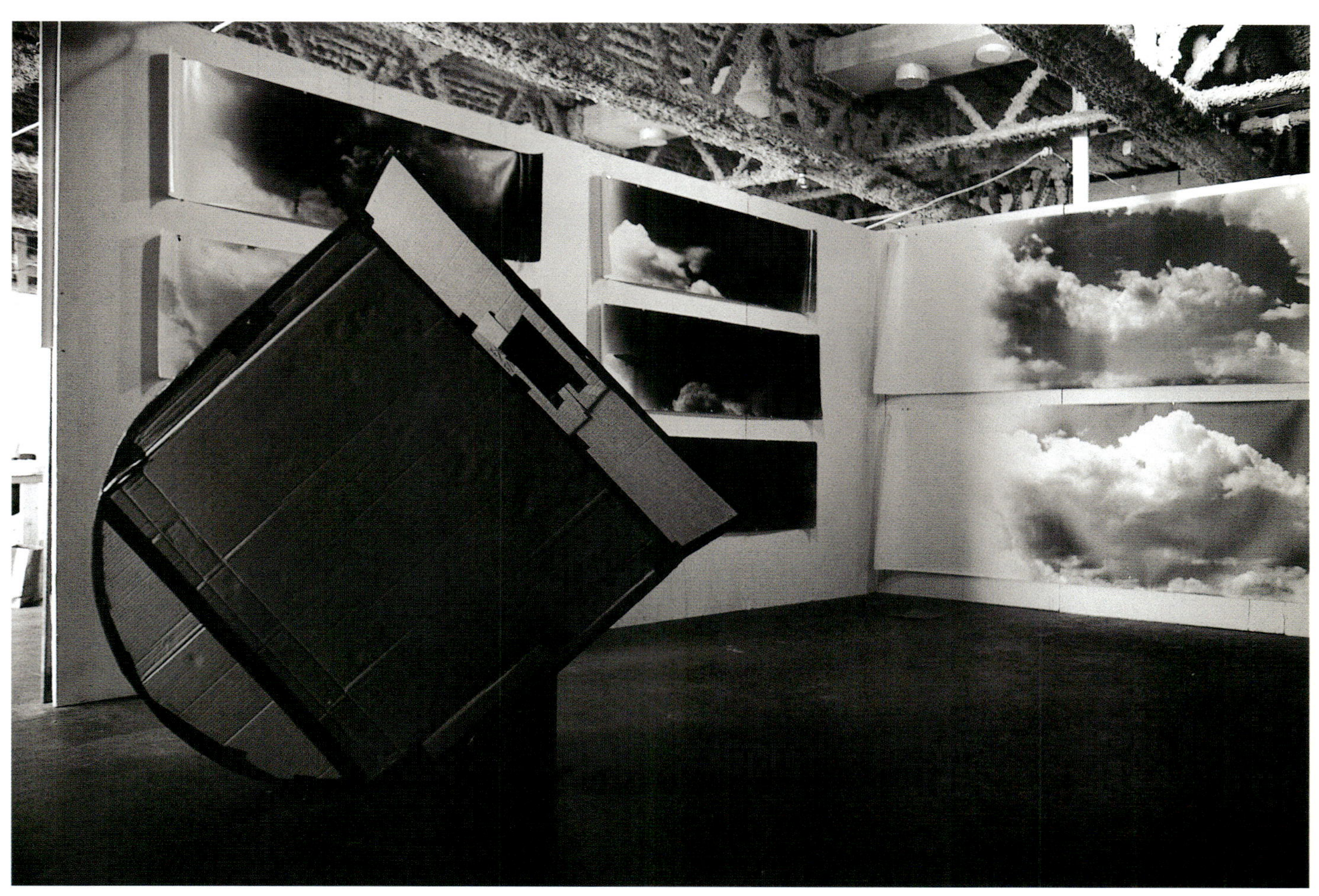

Adrian Doura

Landscape (Triptych U.S.A.), 1999
Oil on canvas
92 x 118 inches overall
Photo: Douglas Martin

Each panel represents an icon from the history and culture of the United States.

Born 1958 in Buenos Aires, Argentina
Lives in Marseille and Paris, France

Education

1989 Diplôme Supérieur d'art plastique, École Nationale Supérieure des Beaux Arts, Paris, France

Selected Solo Exhibitions

2003 Athanor Gallery (two-person exhibition), Marseille, France
2002 Miguel Frías Latin American Art, Buenos Aires, Argentina
2001 Miguel Frías Latin American Art, Buenos Aires, Argentina
1997 J.F. Meyer Gallery, Marseille, France
1993 Catherine Fletcher Gallery, Paris, France

Residency

1998 Triangle Artists Workshop, World Trade Center, New York, N.Y.

Awards

1999 Fondation Regards de Provence, Marseille, France
1990 Instituto de Cooperación Iberoamericana, Madrid, Spain

Bursting from the elevator onto the seventy-fifth floor, my ears still plugged from the rapid ascent, long corridors took me to smaller elevators servicing the ninety-first floor studios, where the raw space appeared as a flying platform far above the city. This huge capsule-like environment, with its continually recycled air, swayed in the wind. When a hurricane passed near N.Y.C. that summer, the entire building moved, making sounds like ancient gongs; the building was alive.

Through the windows, parades, traffic jams, planes, helicopters and even the Fourth of July fireworks seemed like part of a smaller world. Sunsets, the moon rising over the ocean and ever-changing meteorological events surrounded us, transforming the world below. The city glow lightened the studio at night, its energy keeping me company until sunrise.

The vastness of the view changed my perception of the cityscape, as if the buildings, highways, bridges and parks formed a thick sculpted crust on the surface of the earth. Immerged in this panorama and –confronted with this unsettling beauty, what else could I do but paint?

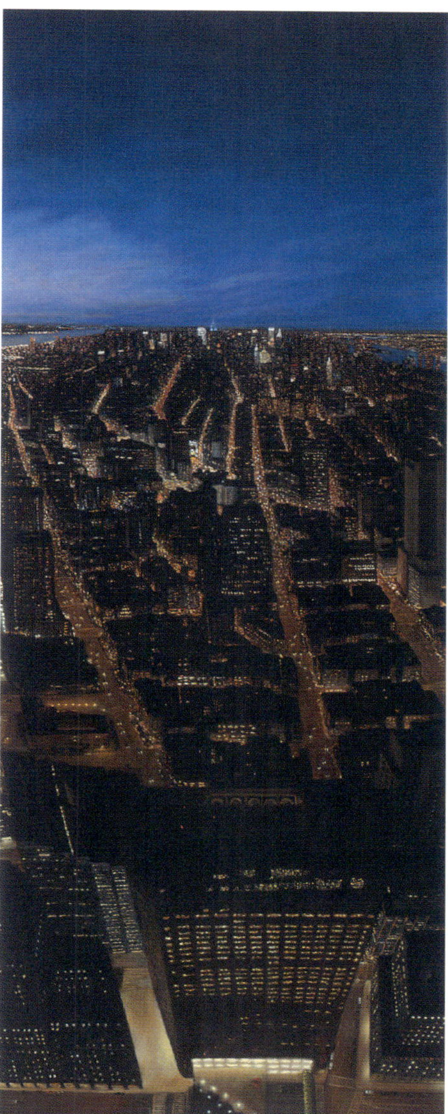

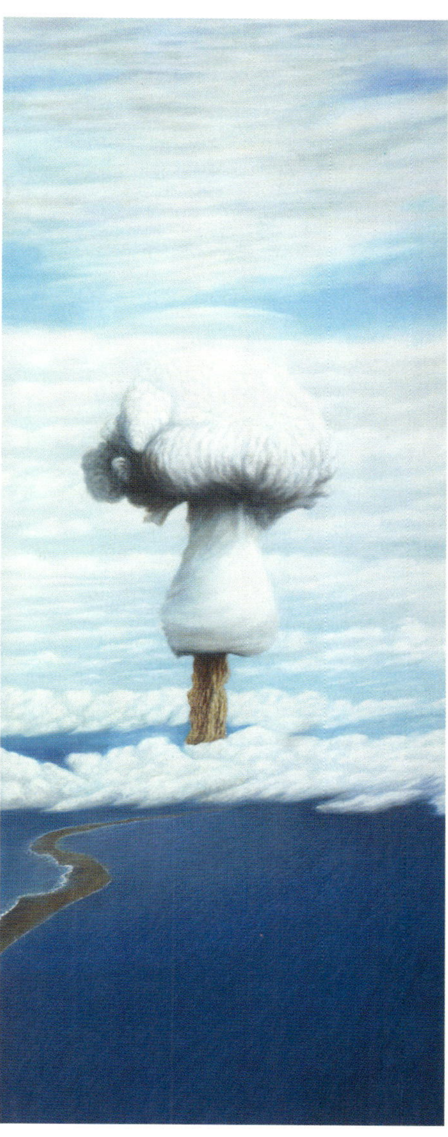

Myong Hwa Jeong

Subterranean State, 1999
Mixed media
4 1/8 x 3 inches

Subterranean State, 1999
C-print
24 x 30 inches

Born 1968 in Seoul, Korea
Lives and works in Seattle, Washington

Education

1998 Whitney Museum of American Art Independent Study Program, New York, N.Y.
1998 MFA, California Institute of the Arts, Valencia
1991 BA, Yonsei University, Seoul, Korea

Selected Group Exhibitions

2002 *Between Places*, Salena Gallery, Brooklyn, N.Y.
2000 *Pusan International Art Festival*, Pusan IAF, Korea
1999 *99 AIM Exhibition*, The Bronx Museum of the Arts, The Bronx, N.Y.
1997 *Kwangju Biennial*, Korea
Scene 97, Korean American Museum, Los Angeles, Calif.

Award

1999 *Artist in the Marketplace*, The Bronx Museum of the Arts, The Bronx, N.Y.

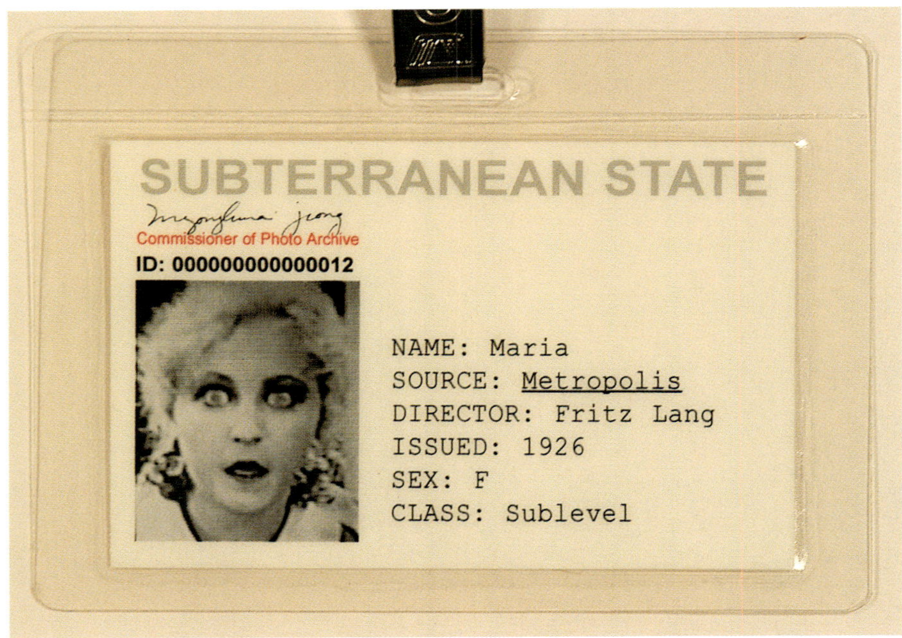

When I was contemplating a new project in the beginning of the residency, they took us on an underground tour of the WTC, which I found more intriguing than the rooftop tour. A spectacular view seemed less interesting than the anti-spectacle of the underground space where building-operations facilities spread across seven subterranean levels. My imagination avidly fed upon this dark, ungraspable terrain. Although the underground space of the WTC was well lit and completely tangible in its existence, my imagination traveled on its own to more remote subterranean worlds I had encountered in books, films and other media. The work I produced during the residency, Subterranean State, *includes photographs of New York subway tunnels and portraits presented in the form of identification cards appropriated from various sources such as* Planet of the Apes, The Invisible Man *and* The Mole People.

It was ironic working on this project that dealt with representing the underground while I was suspended ninety-one floors above what The Invisible Man *refers to as "the darkest spot of our civilization."*

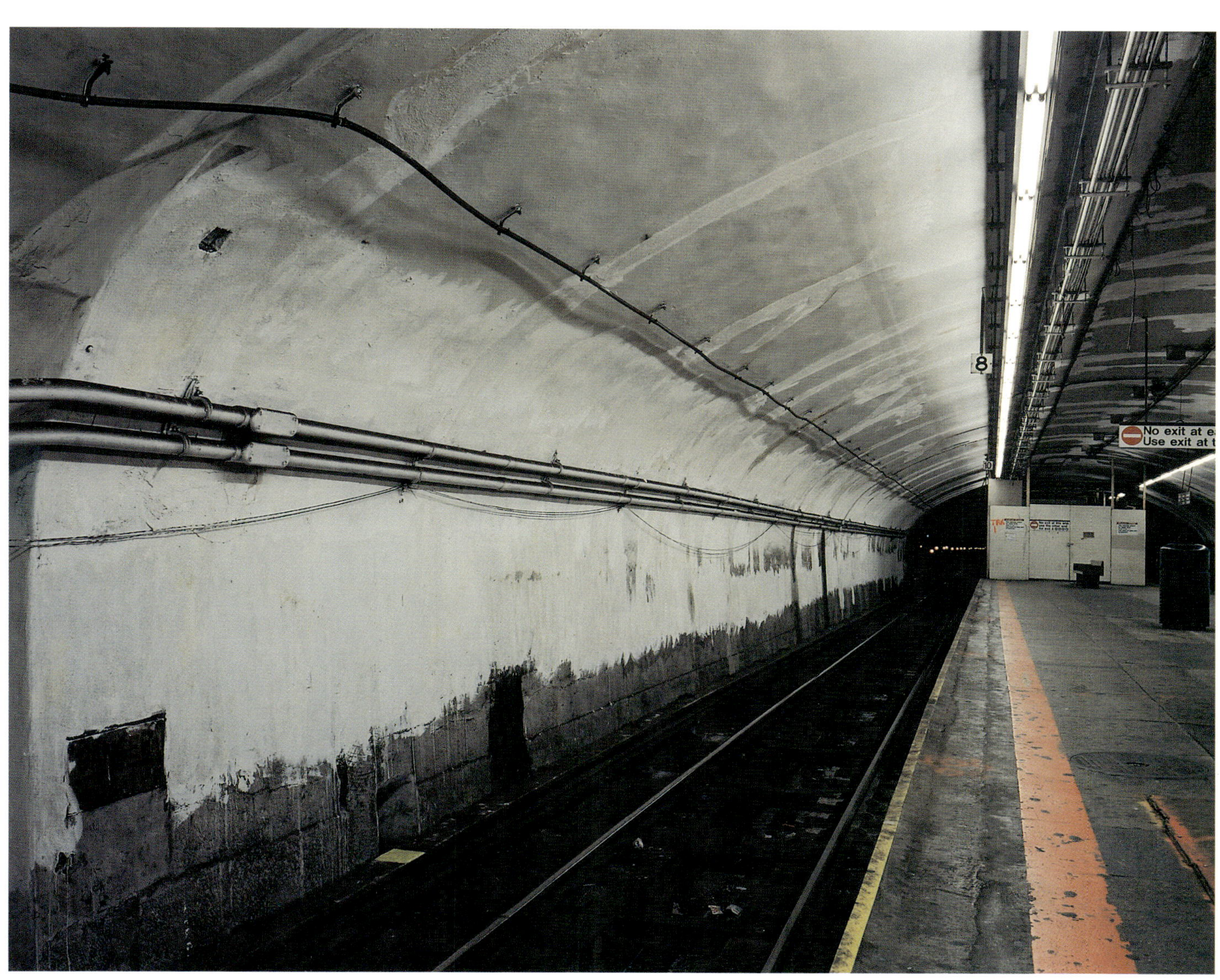

John Long

Revolving Door South Tower, 1999 (stills)
Video, 60 minutes

In August 1999, I hid a video camera in a suitcase and placed the suitcase in front of one of the revolving doors of the South Tower of the WTC. I had wanted to make a video of people coming in and out of the tower but whenever I pointed a camera at the building for more than a few minutes the guards would stop me. I stood next to the "suitcase with a camera" and taped an hour-long video of traffic through the door.

I incorporated this video into an installation in N.Y.C. for a performance of Heiner Muller's *Abandoned Shores* on September 11, 1999, in the Meatpacking District.

A revolving door was built in the back of a Ryder truck, and the video was rear-projected. I loved the way people entered the image and were sucked through the door while others were spit out only to disappear off-screen, existing for only a fleeting moment as a unique person.

Abandoned Shores, 1999
Performance poster
Ink on paper
18 x 24 inches each

I had photographed the cast members on the ninety-first floor for a publicity photo. Using shots of the members' arms, a photo looking down at the West Side Highway, and a shot of an Ethan Long sculpture of airplane seats, I created this poster. It was used to promote both the performance in N.Y.C. and in Paris. It represented both my hopes—that the project would travel—and my fears that we were a target for terrorists.

Born 1941 in Omaha, Nebr.
Lives in New York, N.Y.

Education
1970 MA, State University of New York, Buffalo
1967 BA, University of California, Davis

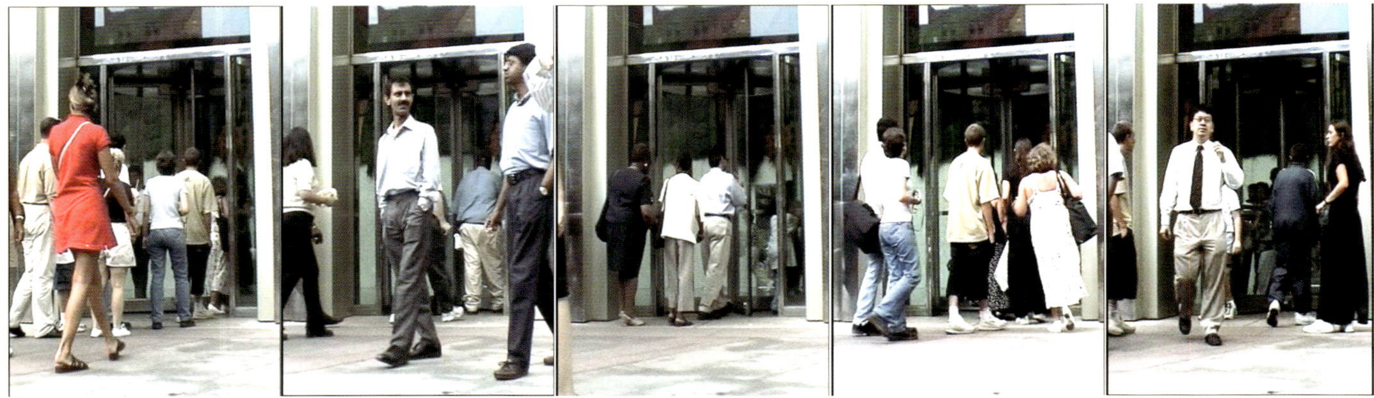

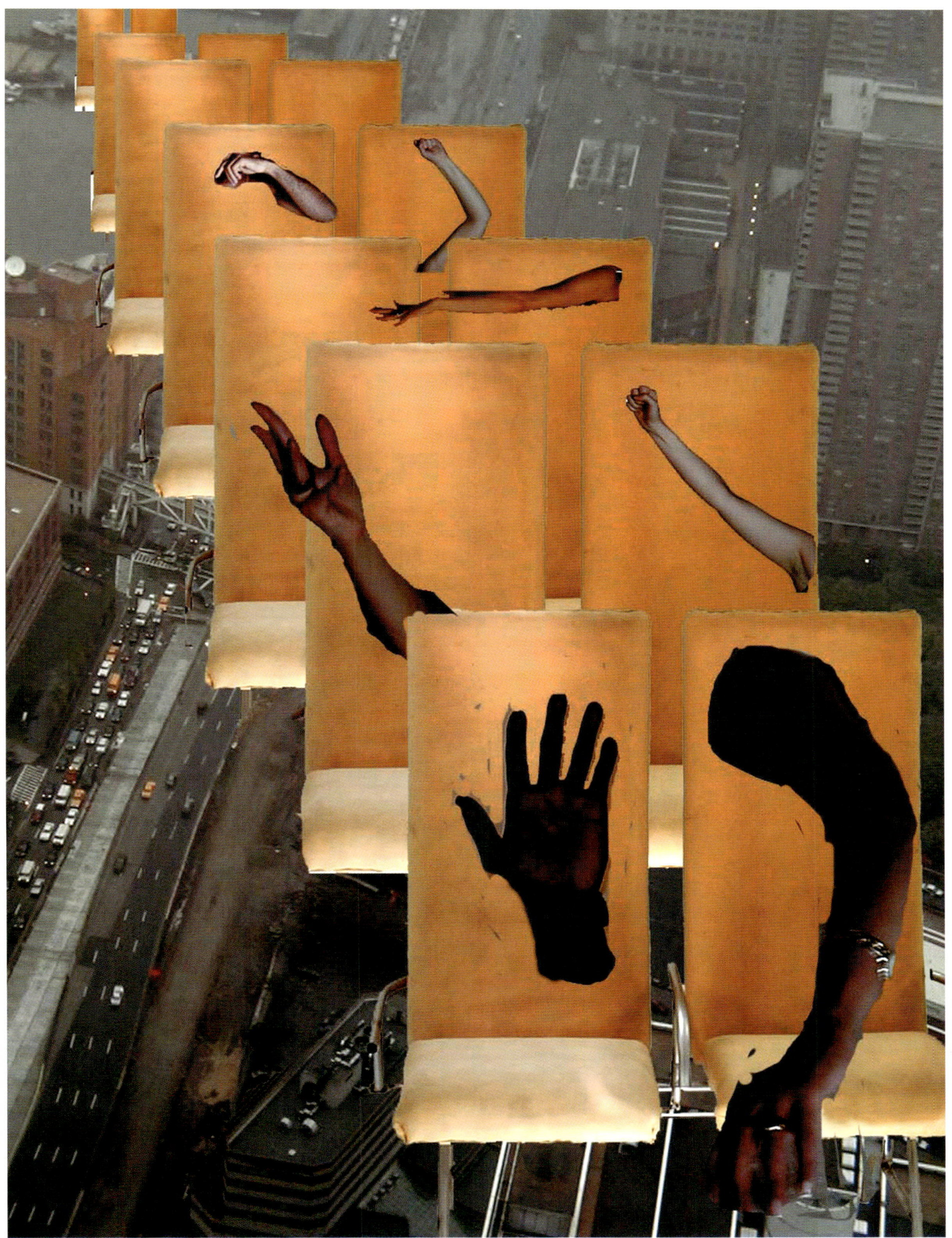

Mick O'Shea

Studioscape, 1999
Wood, enamel, glue
Dimensions variable
Photo: David Plakke

Prester World (World Trade), 1999 (details)
Various materials
12 x 65 feet
Photos: David Plakke

Born 1967 in Nahant, Mass.
Lives in New York, N.Y.

Education

1997 MFA, School of Visual Arts, New York, N.Y.
1995 BFA, Southern Methodist University, Dallas, Tex.

Selected Solo Exhibitions

2002 *(of) Field and the Fyce*, Roger Smith Gallery, New York, N.Y.
The Cattle Raid, mullerdechiara, Berlin, Germany
2001 *Wonder and the Palisades*, Roebling Hall, Brooklyn, N.Y.
2000 *Toy Box*, P.S.1 Contemporary Art Center, Long Island City, N.Y.
2000 *Your Industry, My World/My Industry, Your World*, Kunst-Werke, Berlin, Germany
La Ville, Le Jardin, Villa Medici, Rome, Italy

Selected Group Exhibitions

2002 *Sprawl*, Contemporary Arts Center, Cincinnati, Ohio
2001 *Troubleshooting*, Arnolfini, Bristol, U.K.

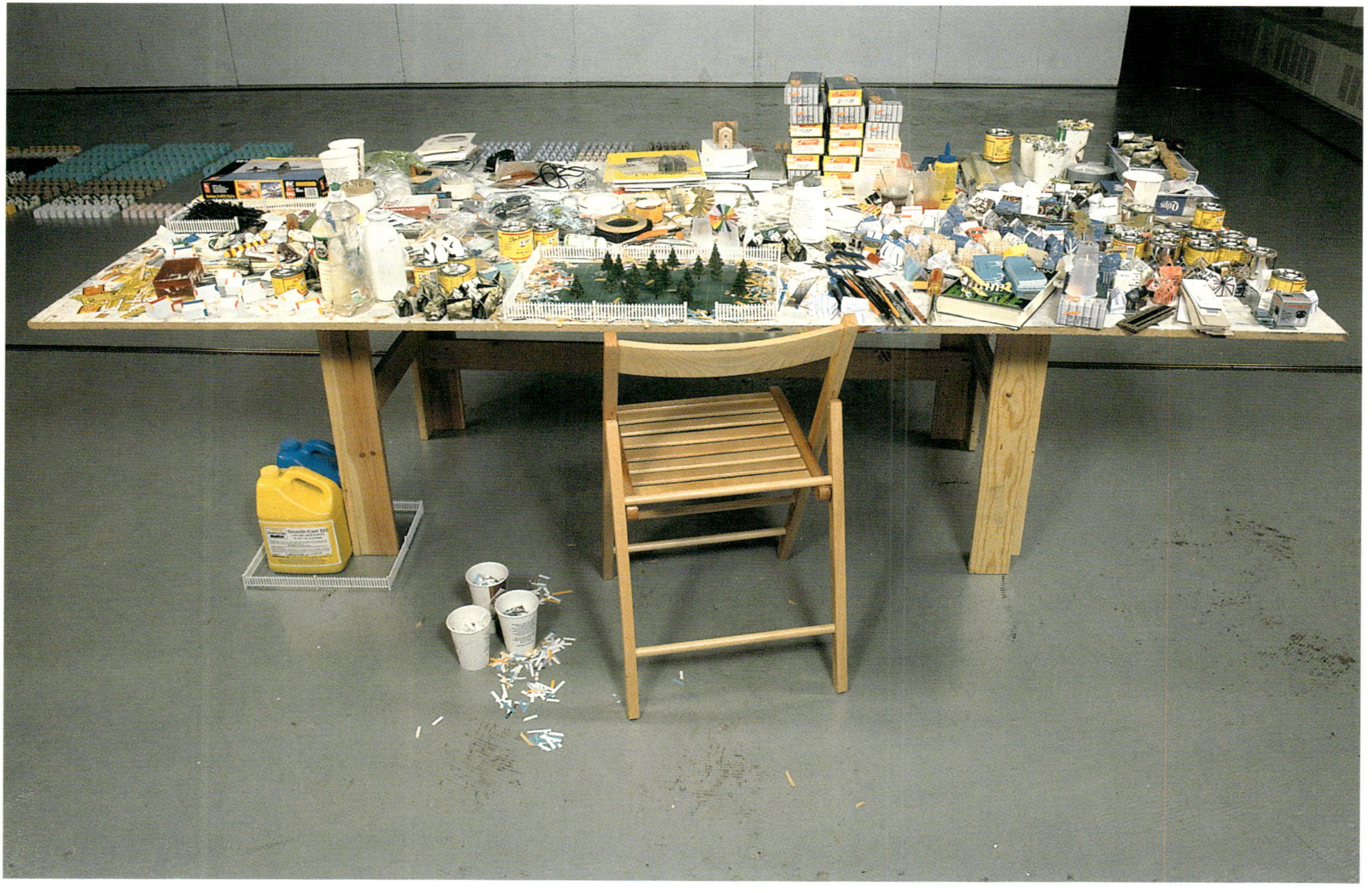

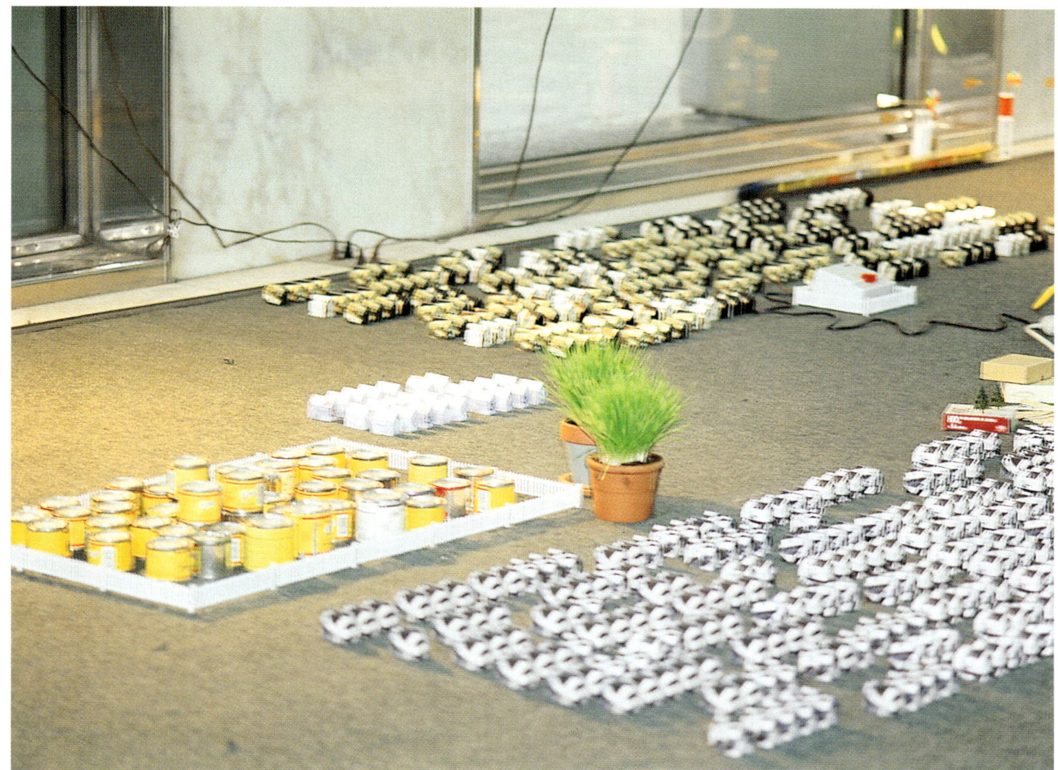

A residency can be a tricky thing. It is a time out of place. But perhaps because successful art so often is situated out of time, the residency's fleeting nature is apt to the creative process. What I remember is a place in the clouds that creaked against the wind the way a ship yawns against the tide. It was a place out of time for me, a place I can never go to again.

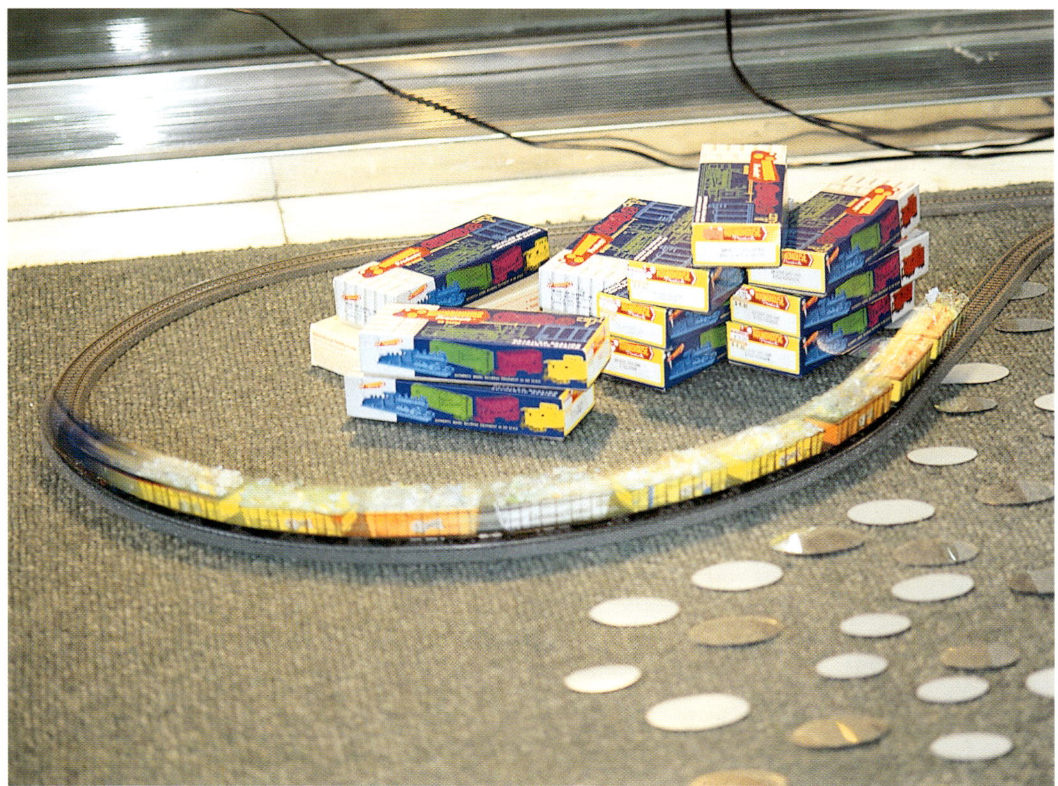

Paul Pfeiffer

Momento Mori, 1998
Plastic figures mounted in oak box and
CD recording of Handel's "Ode for St. Cecilia's Day"
20 x 24 x 7 inches
Courtesy The Project, New York, N.Y.

Born 1966 in Honolulu, Hawaii
Lives in New York, N.Y.

Education

1997–98	Whitney Museum of American Art Independent Study Program, New York, N.Y.
1994	MFA, Hunter College/CUNY, New York, N.Y.
1987	BFA, San Francisco Art Institute, Calif.

Selected Solo Exhibitions

2003	Museum of Contemporary Art, Chicago, Ill.
2001	*The Contemporary Series: Paul Pfeiffer*, Whitney Museum of American Art, New York, N.Y.
	Kunstaus Glarus, Switzerland
2000	Kunste-Werke, Berlin, Germany
1998	*The Pure Products Go Crazy*, The Project, New York, N.Y.

Residency

2001–02	MIT List Visual Arts Center, Cambridge, Mass.

Awards

2000	The Bucksbaum Award, The Whitney Museum of American Art
1999	The Public Art Fund, New York, N.Y.

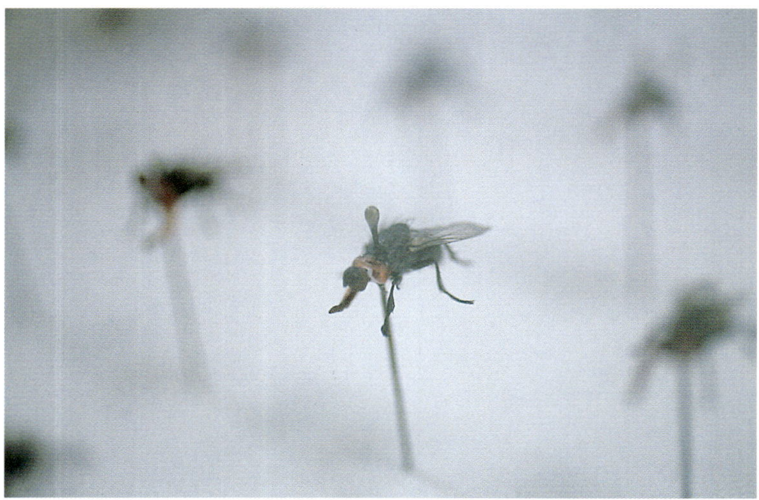

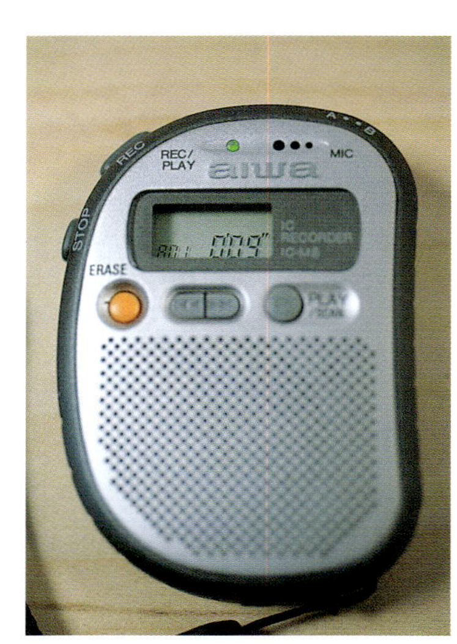

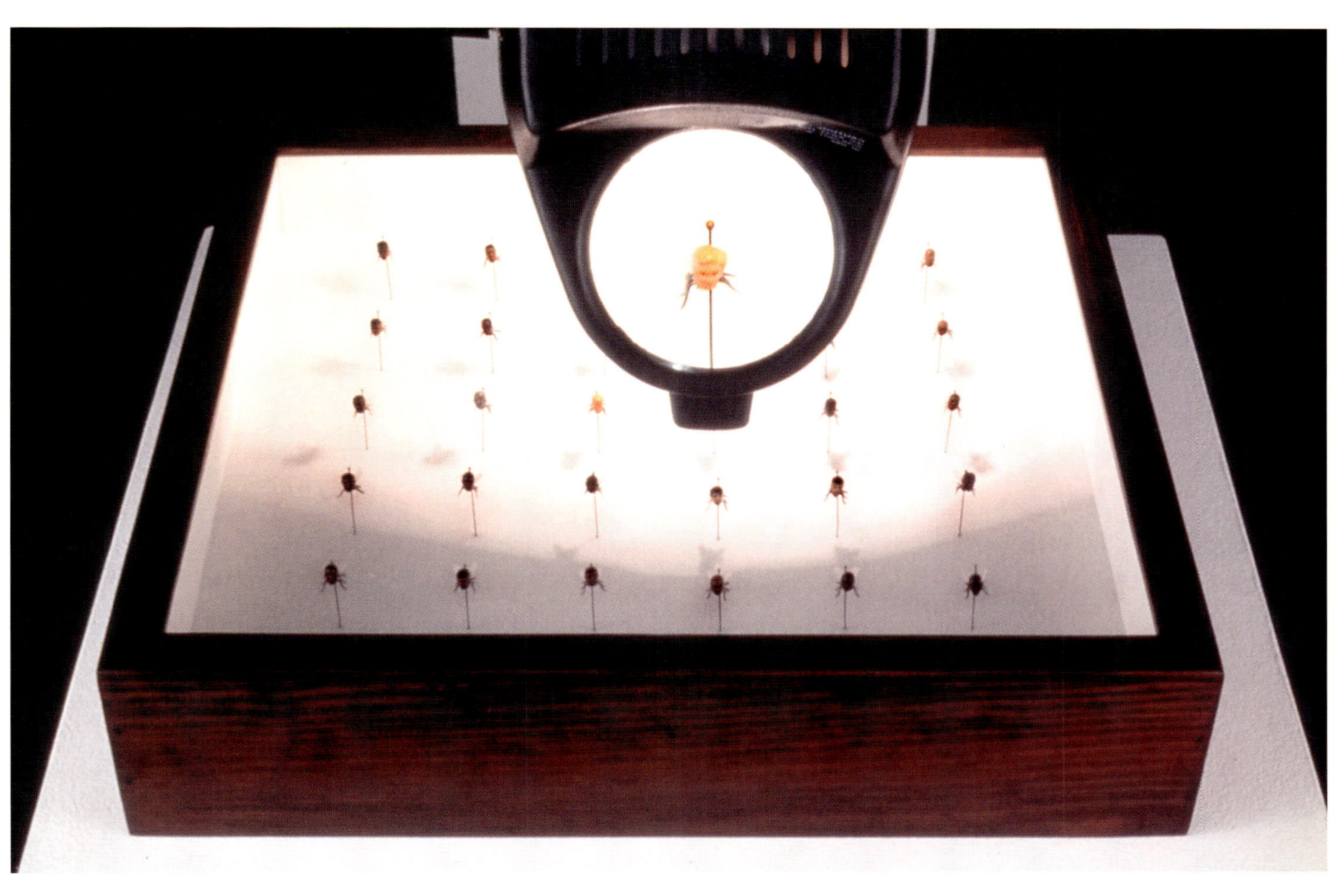

Nadine Robinson

Tower Hollers (Version One), 2001 (detail)
Four 14-minute records, four record players, 90 speakers, acrylic on canvas
10 x 26 x 5 feet
Collection of Peter Norton
Photo: Mark Luttrell

Born 1968 in London, U.K.
Lives in The Bronx, N.Y.

Education

1997 MA, New York University, N.Y.
1995 BFA, State University of New York, Stony Brook

Selected Solo Exhibitions

2003 *Ramp Projects–Das Hochzeitshaus*, Institute of Contemporary Art, Philadelphia, Pa.
White We, Caren Golden Fine Art, New York, N.Y.
1998 *Black Listing*, Longwood Arts Project, The Bronx, N.Y.

Selected Group Exhibitions

2003 *Hair Stories*, The Scottsdale Museum of Contemporary Art, Ariz. (tour)
Sound Systems, The Salzburg Kunstverein, Austria
2002 *Tempo*, The Museum of Modern Art, Queens, N.Y.

Residencies

2002 Smack Mellon, Brooklyn, N.Y.
1998 Millay Colony for the Arts, Austerlitz, N.Y.

Tower Hollers *has gone through many permutations since its conception during my 1999 residency in World Views. Most artists were invited to create art that was somewhat defined by the specificity of the unique location of our residency and there were many options to choose from. . . .*

Tower Hollers *was inspired by the ambient music, or Muzak, that I heard in an elevator ride I took to my studio on the ninety-first floor. Standing beside me was a cleaning lady with her work cart, and the song playing was a soupy rendition of "Here Comes the Sun." I began to think about the psychology of labor and modern attempts of harnessing the workforce of the world. Muzak in the workplace was a way to improve the mood and work environments and ultimately increase the productivity of each worker.*

For my final project I wanted to change the elevator music for a day, perhaps on a day during Open Studios, but the project became too complicated as it dealt with legal issues and the leaseholders of the Port Authority, even though the building management was encouraging through and through and felt enthusiastic about the project. In the end I presented the first version of the idea in the form of small speaker-paintings that I call "Boom Paintings." The installation of work songs playing from these speaker-paintings continues to be my strongest piece, conceptually and aesthetically. Working at the World Trade Center that year with many talented artists was an unforgettable experience. Each new venue where Tower Hollers *finds itself continues to reinforce this.*

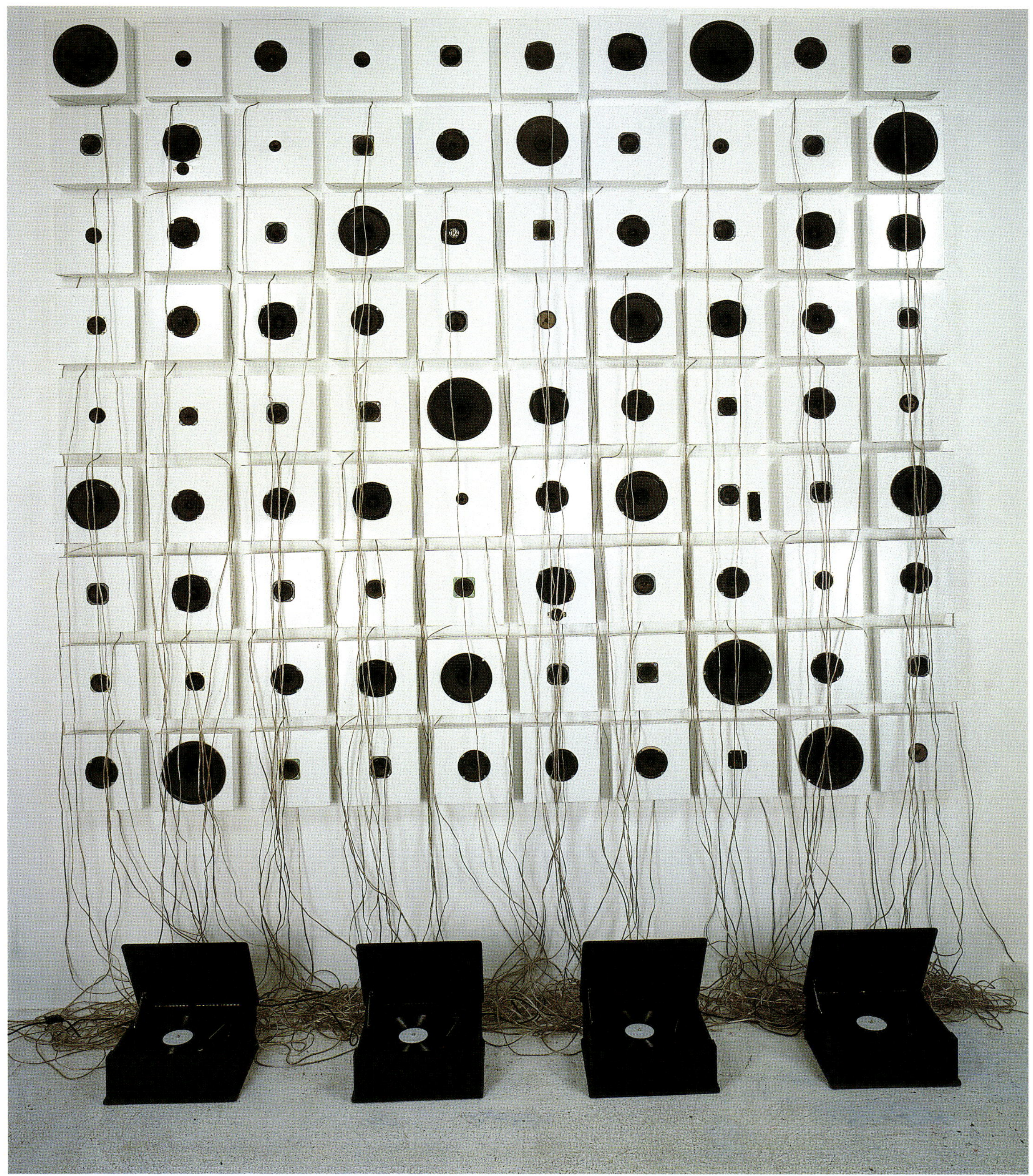

Robert Selwyn

Construction of World Trade Center, (1994–96)
Photographs from paintings
Dimensions variable

Photo and digital assistance: Ellen Page Wilson and Chris Whitlow

When I painted the construction of the World Trade Center in the mid-nineties, I lived and worked downtown in the shadow of the towers. They were my favorite buildings in New York. They changed with daylight, weather conditions, the vantage from where you viewed them. To me, they were an endgame of high modernism; massive, minimalist urban sculpture.

Born 1956 in Washington D.C.
Lives in Brooklyn, N.Y.

Education

1989 MFA, Yale University School of Art, New Haven, Conn.
1980 BFA, Pratt Institute, Brooklyn, N.Y.

Selected Solo Exhibitions

2000 Steffany Martz Gallery, New York, N.Y.
1999 Steffany Martz Gallery, New York, N.Y.
1996 Gary Edwards Photographs, Washington D.C.

Selected Group Exhibitions

2003 *New Photography*, Jim Kempner Fine Art, New York, N.Y.
2002 *25th Anniversary Exhibition*, The Drawing Center, New York, N.Y.
1997 *Disingenuous Images*, Galerie Renee Ziegler, Zurich, Switzerland
Emerging Artists, PaceWildenstein, New York, N.Y.
2002 New York Times Magazine (9/25), cover photograph

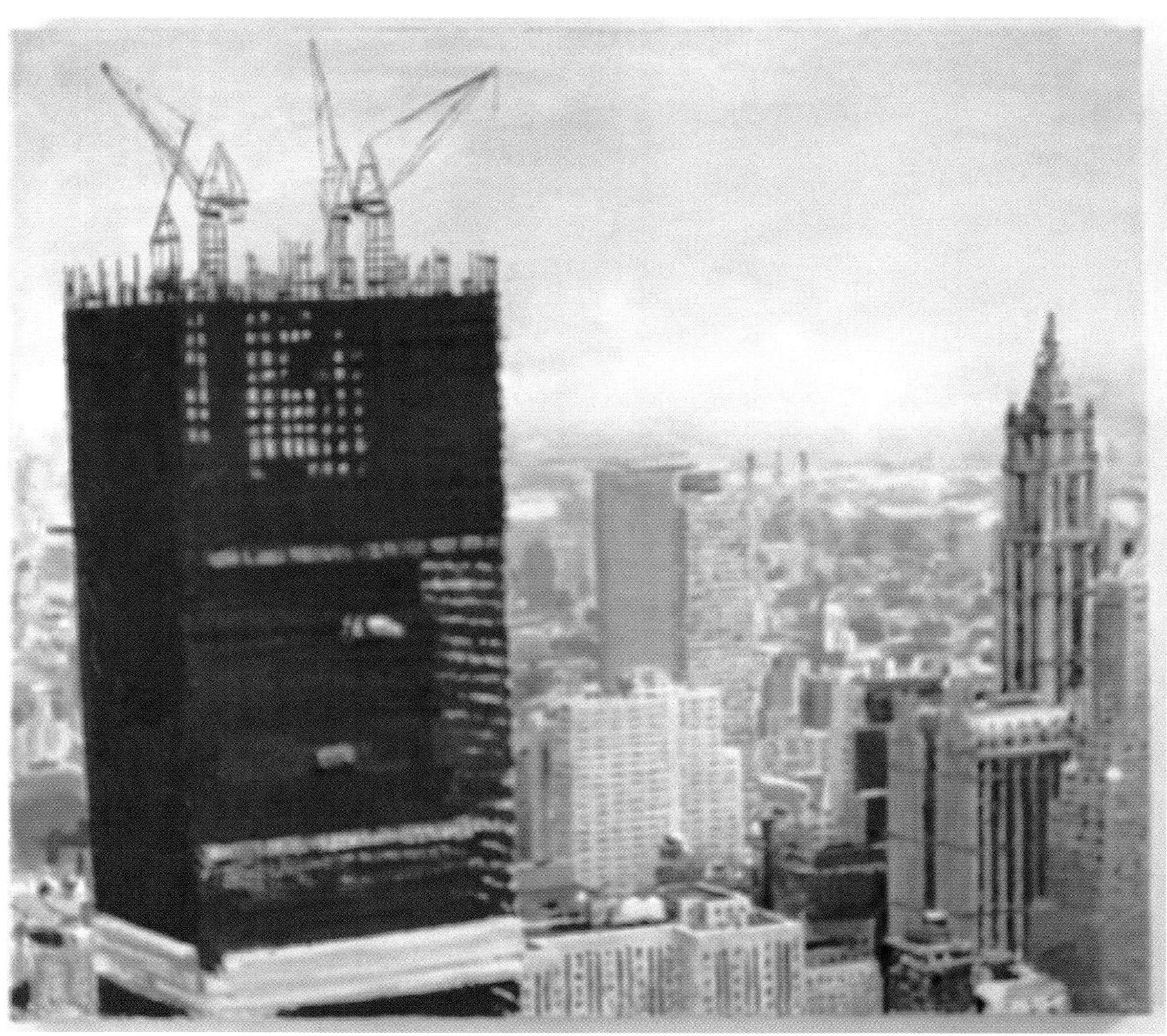

Two of my favorite times during the residency were looking down at the fireworks on the Fourth of July and being there during a strong tropical storm when you could feel the building sway and hear it creak. Mary Jane Dean, one of the artists, hung a plumb line with a pointed weight on the bottom going into sand, and it drew the movement of the building.

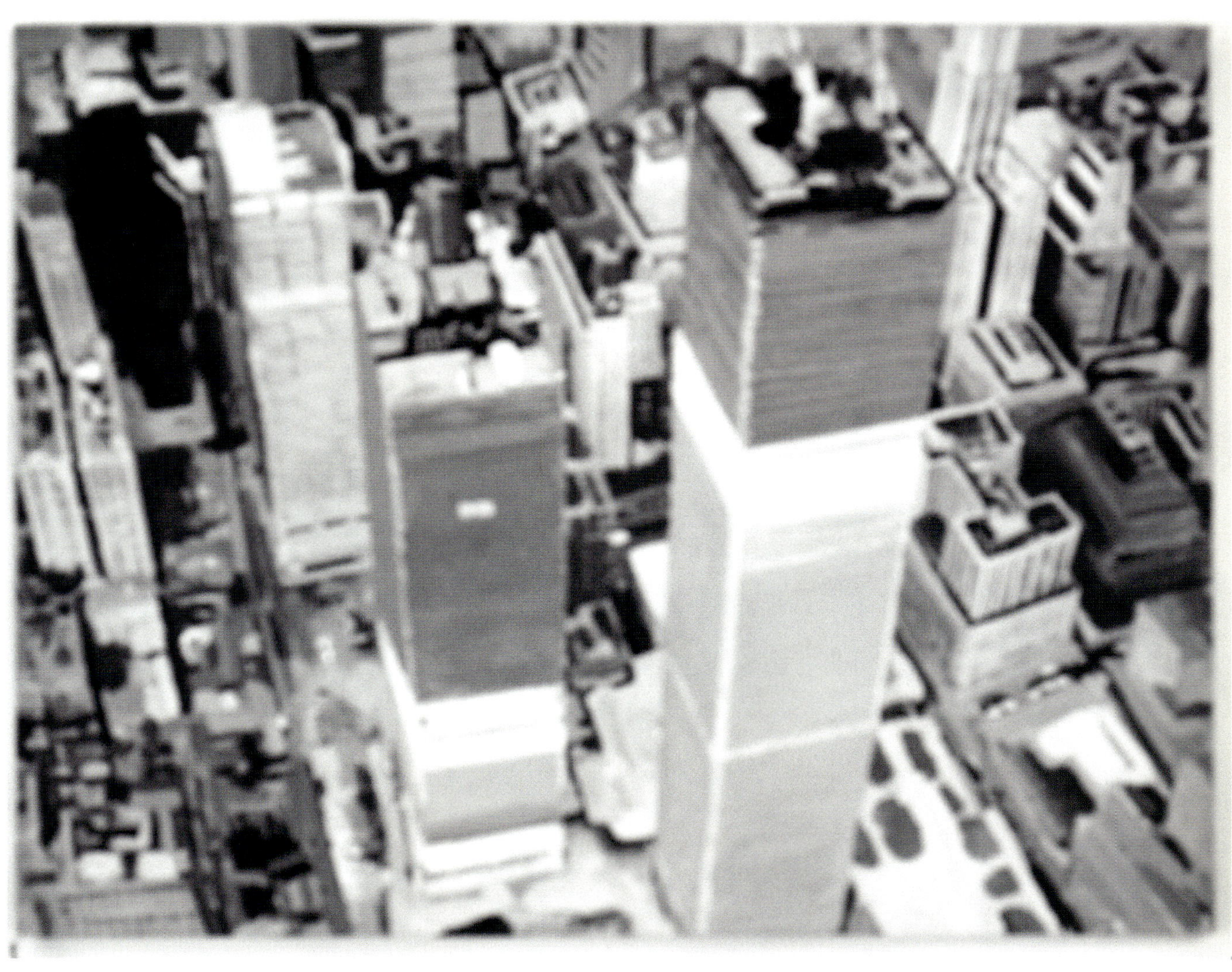

Taketo Shimada

Escalator Piece #1 (model), 1999
(installation view with detail)
Mixed media
12 x 2 x 6 inches

Born 1971 in Tokyo, Japan
Lives in New York, N.Y.

Education

1997 SMVisS, Massachusetts Institute of Technology, Cambridge

1994 BFA, School of Visual Arts, New York, N.Y.

Performances

2003 *SPINS* (with Charmaine Wheatley), The Knitting Factory, New York, N.Y.
Love Triangle (with Charmaine Wheatley), Cynthia Broan Gallery, New York, N.Y.

1999 *Center for Advanced Research in Music and Electronics* (with Toshio Kajiwara), Roullette, New York, N.Y.

Projects

2003 *Quack,* and *Resume,* Rammellzee LP from Gomma

2001 *TellusTools* (vinyl LP)

Awards

2002 Harvestworks Van Lier Grant
Experimental Television Center

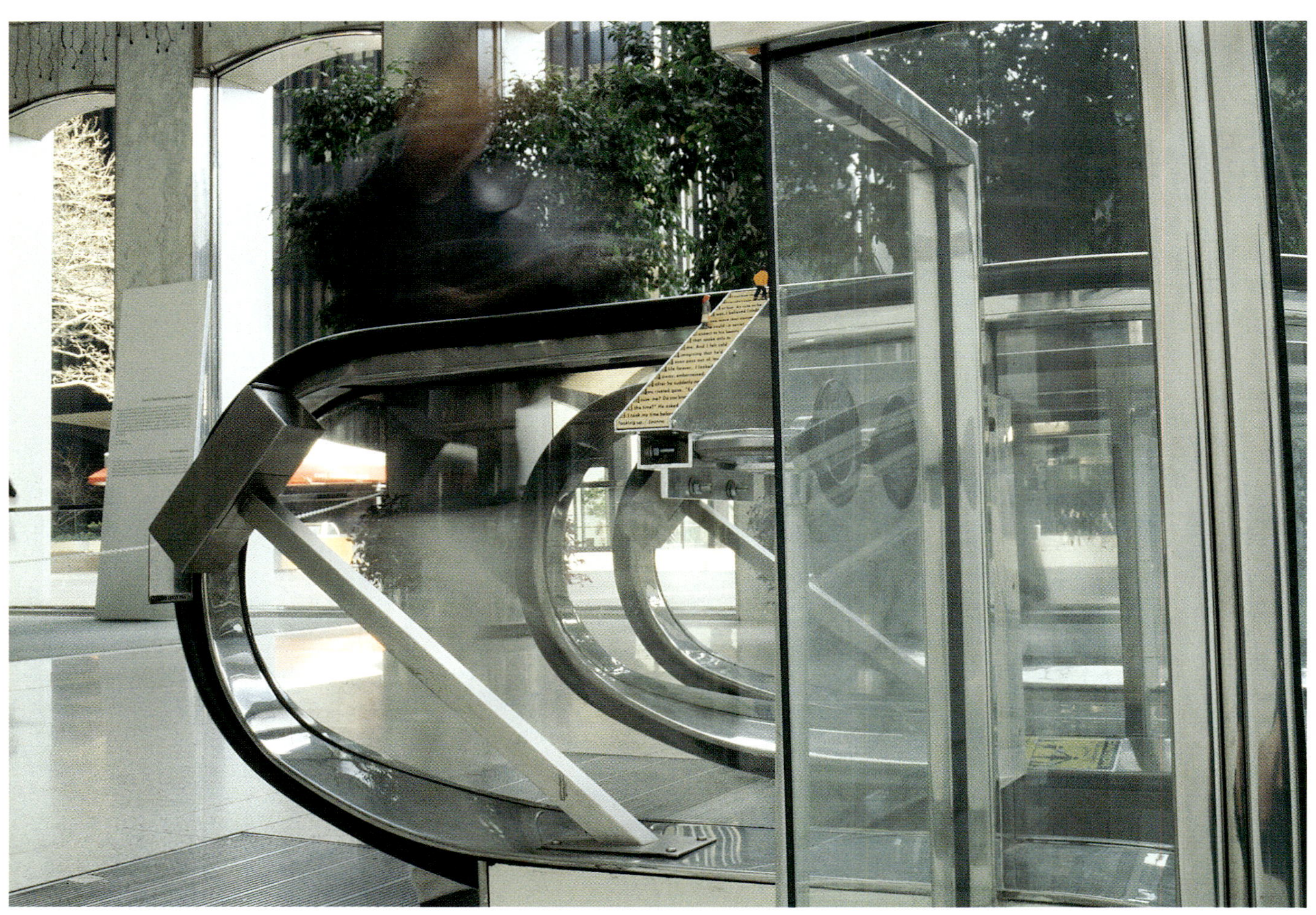

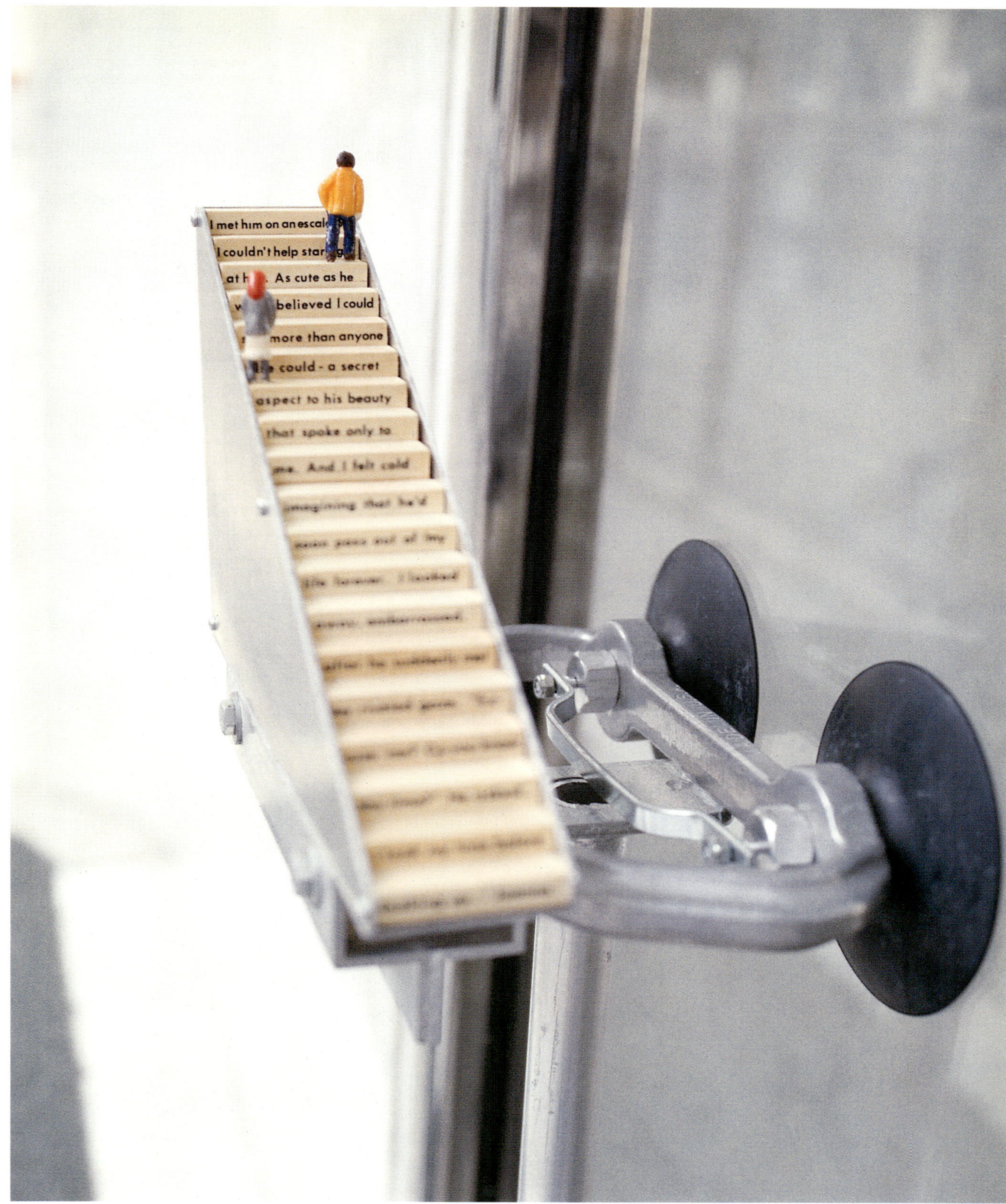
I met him on an escal
I couldn't help star
at h. As cute as he
believed I could
more than anyone
could - a secret
aspect to his beauty
that spoke only to
me. And I felt cold

Stephen Vitiello

World Trade Center Recordings:
Winds after Hurricane Floyd, 1999/2002
Audio recording from the 91st floor of the WTC
Approx. 8 minute loop
Courtesy The Project, New York, N.Y.

Winds after Hurricane Floyd is one of a number of sound recordings I captured during my residency in the summer and fall of 1999. Focusing on the sound outside the building and its absence inside, I affixed small contact microphones to the windows of my studio and captured recordings of passing planes, helicopters, thunder and rain, traffic below, church bells. Hurricane Floyd hit New York City in September of 1999 and was listed as one of the strongest storms to hit the city in ten years. The force of winds and the building's saturation from rain come through with an otherworldly (or out-of-time) feeling. One hears the building swaying and creaking like an old wooden ship. The force of nature and fragility of this mammoth structure are underlined through listening.

Born 1964 in New York, N.Y.
Lives in New York, N.Y.

Education

1986 BA, State University of New York, Purchase

Solo Exhibition

2000 *Tetrasomia*, Dia Center for the Arts, New York, N.Y.

Selected Group Exhibitions

2002 *Unknown Quantity*, Cartier Foundation, Paris, France
Musiques en Scene, Museum of Contemporary Art, Lyon, France
2002 Biennial Exhibition, Whitney Museum of American Art, New York, N.Y.
The Photogenic: Photography Through its Metaphors in Contemporary Art, Institute for Contemporary Art, Philadelphia, Pa.

Residency

1996 Harvestworks, New York, N.Y.

Awards

2001 Penny McCall Foundation
1999 Jerome Foundation/Media Alliance

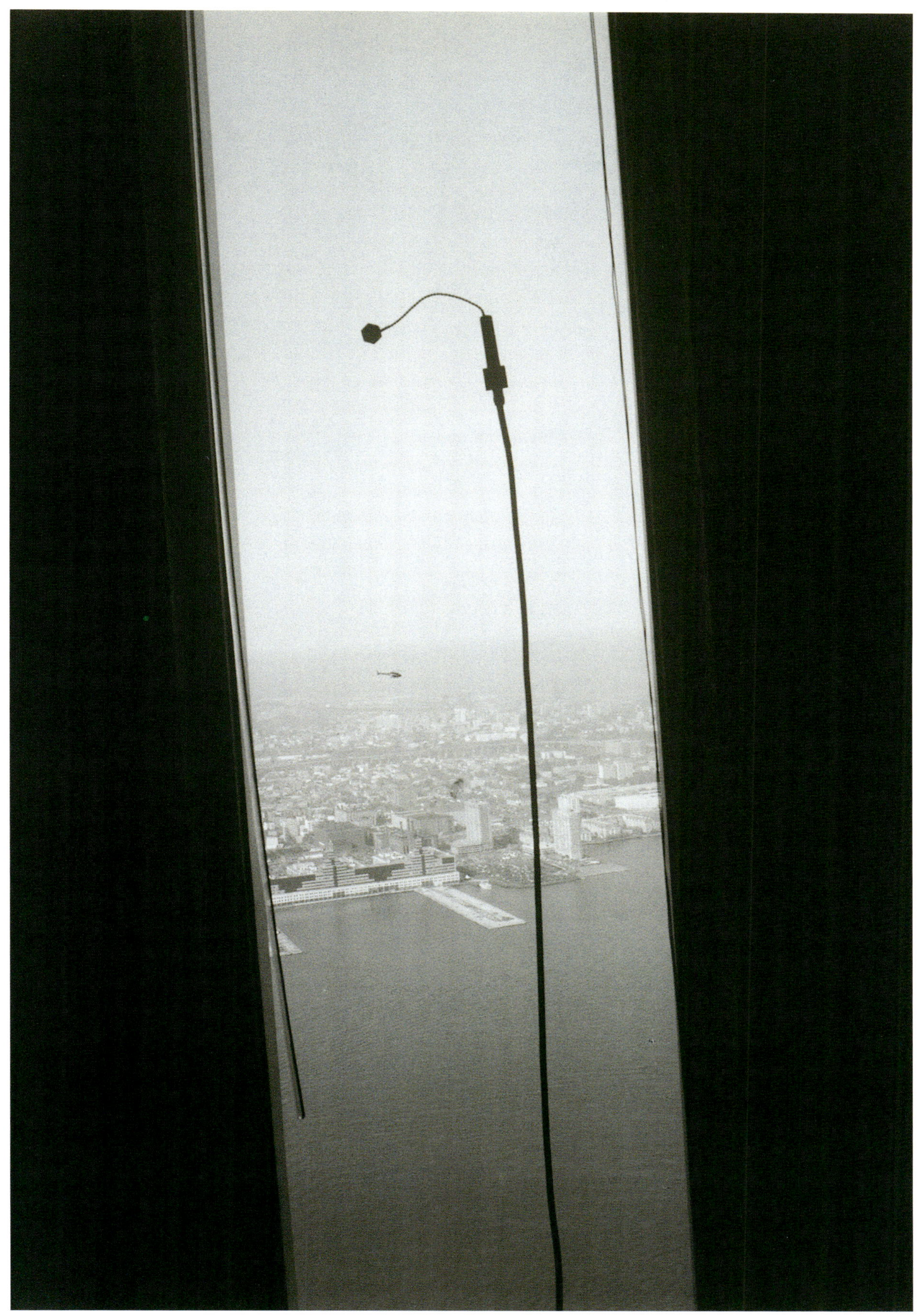

Winter 1999 through Spring 2000

Artists-in-Residence

Taleen Berberian
Bruce Brosnan
Patty Chang
Geoffrey Detrani
Martina Geccelli
Gelatin
Kelly Hashimoto
Emily Jacir
Susan Kelly
Diane Ludin
Tamara Mewis
Prema Murthy
Marcos Rosales
Slink Moss
Kimberly SaRee Tomes

Jurors

Kathy Brew
Lawrence Chua
Amada Cruz
Moukhtar Kocache
Kevin McCoy
Warren Neidich
Carol Parkinson

Invited Artists

Peter Ruta
Roman Scott*

*not represented

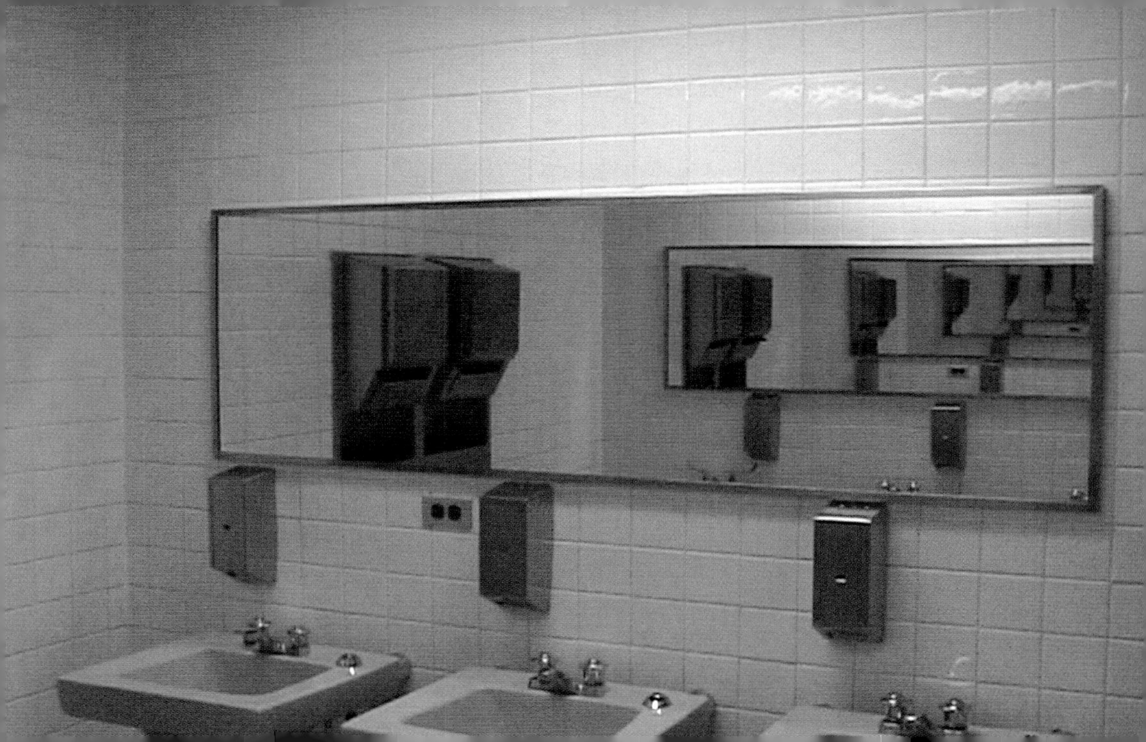

Taleen Berberian

Frenchy's Boudoir, 2000
(detail and installation view)
Mixed media
144 x 144 x 156 inches
Photos: Scott Davis

Initially inspired by French fashion and surrealism, the satirical sculpture and installation, *Frenchy's Boudoir,* playfully synthesizes sexual taboos and issues of body image as related to cultural icons like Barbie. Entering the circuslike boudoir, the viewer is invited to interact with Frenchy by changing the skirt and/or peeking under it. Standing firmly on three legs, this headless goddess is empowered by being frontal from all sides. In addition, copious breasts, ornamental vaginas and feathery high-heeled shoes make Frenchy an enticing and suggestively fertile force.

Born 1969 in Pasadena, Calif.
Lives in New York, N.Y.

Education

1998 MFA, Pratt Institute, Brooklyn, N.Y.
1995 BFA, California College of Arts and Crafts, Oakland

Selected Group Exhibitions

2003 *14th Annual Faculty Exhibition*, 92nd Street Y, New York, N.Y
2002 *Microviews*, Municipal Art Society, New York, N.Y
West Chelsea Arts Building Open Studios, New York, N.Y.
Armenian Women's Art, Armenian Center for Contemporary Experimental Art, Yerevan, Rep. of Armenia
2001 *St. John's University Fine Arts Faculty Exhibition,* Chung Cheng Gallery, Jamaica, N.Y.
2000 *Gyumri International Biennial Exhibition*, Style Gallery, Gyumri, Rep. of Armenia

Awards

2001 Artslink Grant, Republic of Armenia
2000 *Artist in the Marketplace*, The Bronx Museum of the Arts, The Bronx, N.Y.

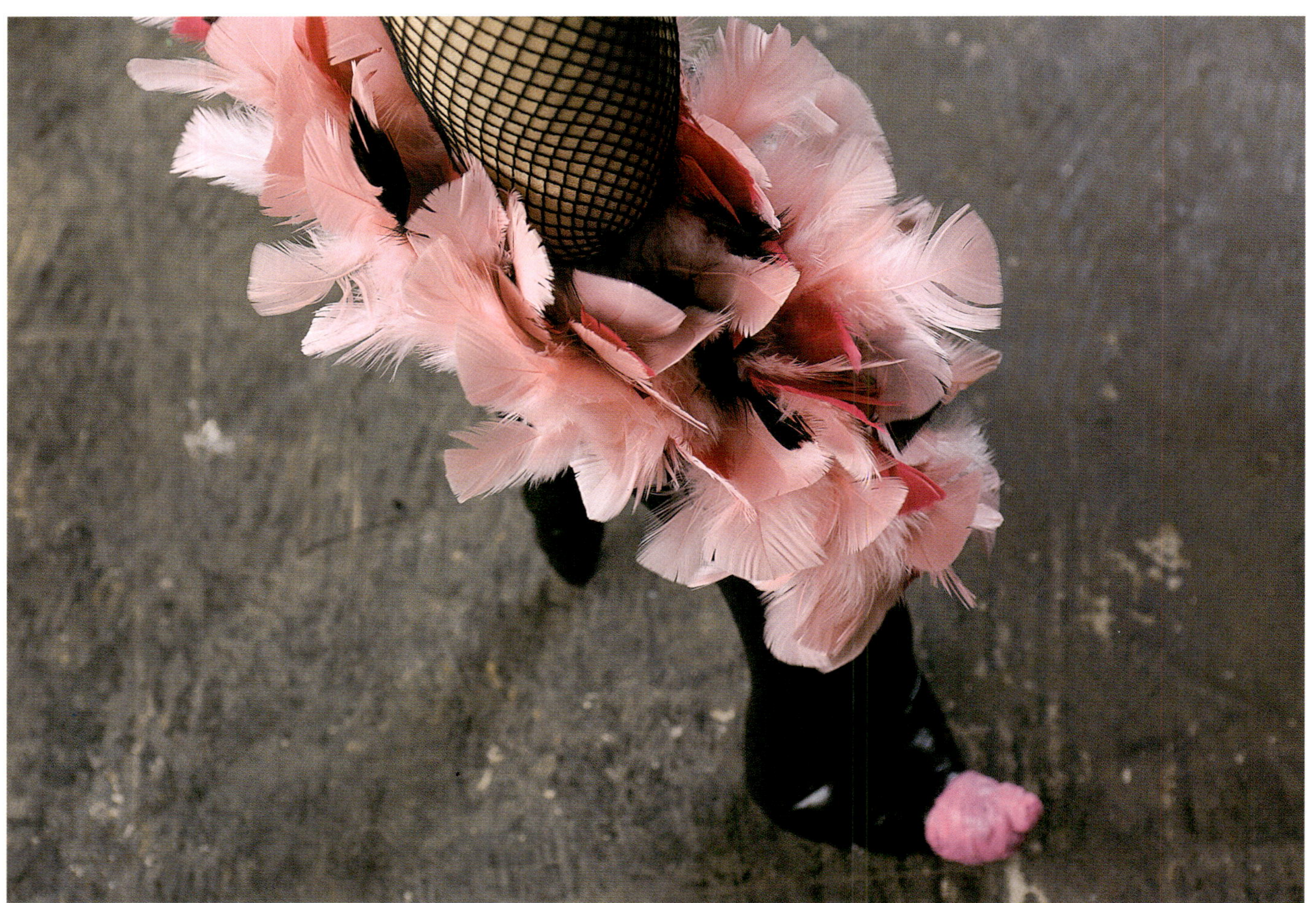

At 6:00 A.M. on weekday mornings, the subway station at 96th and Broadway was dense with commuters on their way to the Financial District. For the six months during my World Views residency, I would board a crammed Number 2 Express to reach my studio at sunrise. Entering the bustling concourse of the World Trade Center, I made my way to Tower One, flashed my WTC ID, and joined the group waiting to board the elevators. The elevator shot up like bullet—whistling its way to the seventy-eighth floor—the Sky Lobby. Fellow riders holding coffee and bagels in cardboard boxes would sometimes converse, exchange smiles and good mornings—expressions containing the affirmation of shared fortune: this unique relationship with our tower and city. A fraction of the people from the first elevator met in another that delivered us to the upper floors. On the ninety-first floor I was greeted by a raw studio space and a view. New York City resembled an intricate scale model bathed in the golden glow of sunrise. I worked for hours, enveloped in quiet grandeur.

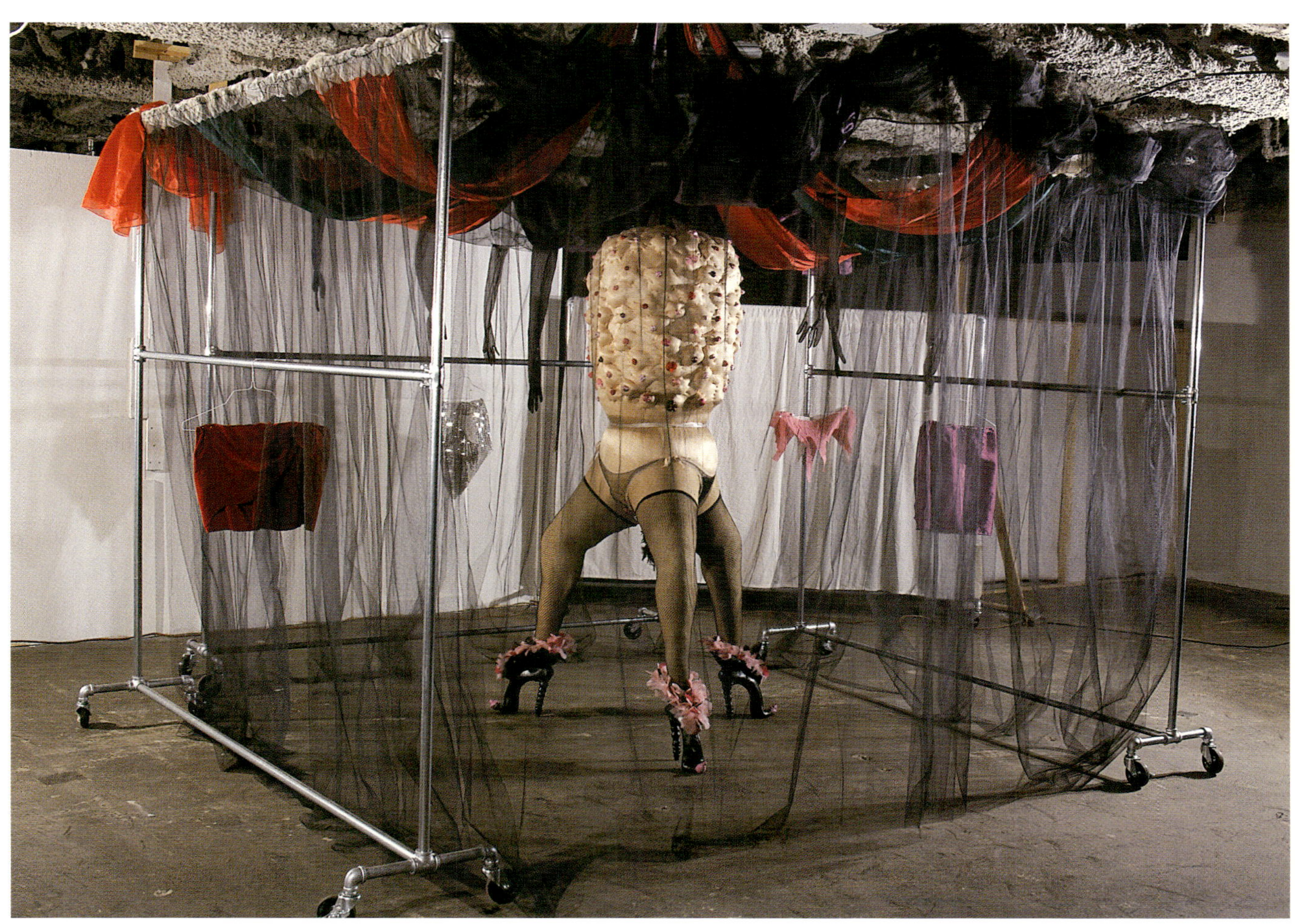

Bruce Brosnan

This page, studio view showing (L to R):

Untitled (Yellow Shade), 2000
Wood, masonite, Styrofoam, acrylic paint
40 x 50 x 14 inches

Daemons, 2000
Wood, masonite, monofilament, acrylic paint
22 x 62 x 56 inches

Untitled (Red Cast), 2000
Wood, Styrofoam, acrylic paint
38 x 42 x 30 inches
Photo: Karen Ostrum

Opposite page:

Lighthouse, 2000
Acrylic
9 x 15 feet
Photo: Karen Ostrum

Born 1968 in Hartford, Conn.
Lives in Brooklyn, N.Y.

Education

1998 MFA, Hunter College/CUNY, New York, N.Y.
1995 BFA, Maine College of Art, Portland

Selected Exhibitions

2003 *Series*, Grant Selwyn Fine Art, New York, N.Y.
Small-Scale Sculpture and Anonymous Tantra Paintings, Feature Inc., New York, N.Y.
Aniconica, Perugi, Padua, Italy
2002 *Inheriting Matisse*, Rocket, London, U.K.
Bruce Brosnan/Michael Rodriguez, M du B, F, H & g, Montreal, Quebec
2001 *Objective Color*, Yale University Art Gallery, New Haven, Conn.
2000 *Making Ends Meet*, Mills Gallery, Boston Center for the Arts, Mass.

Award

2000 Jerome Foundation

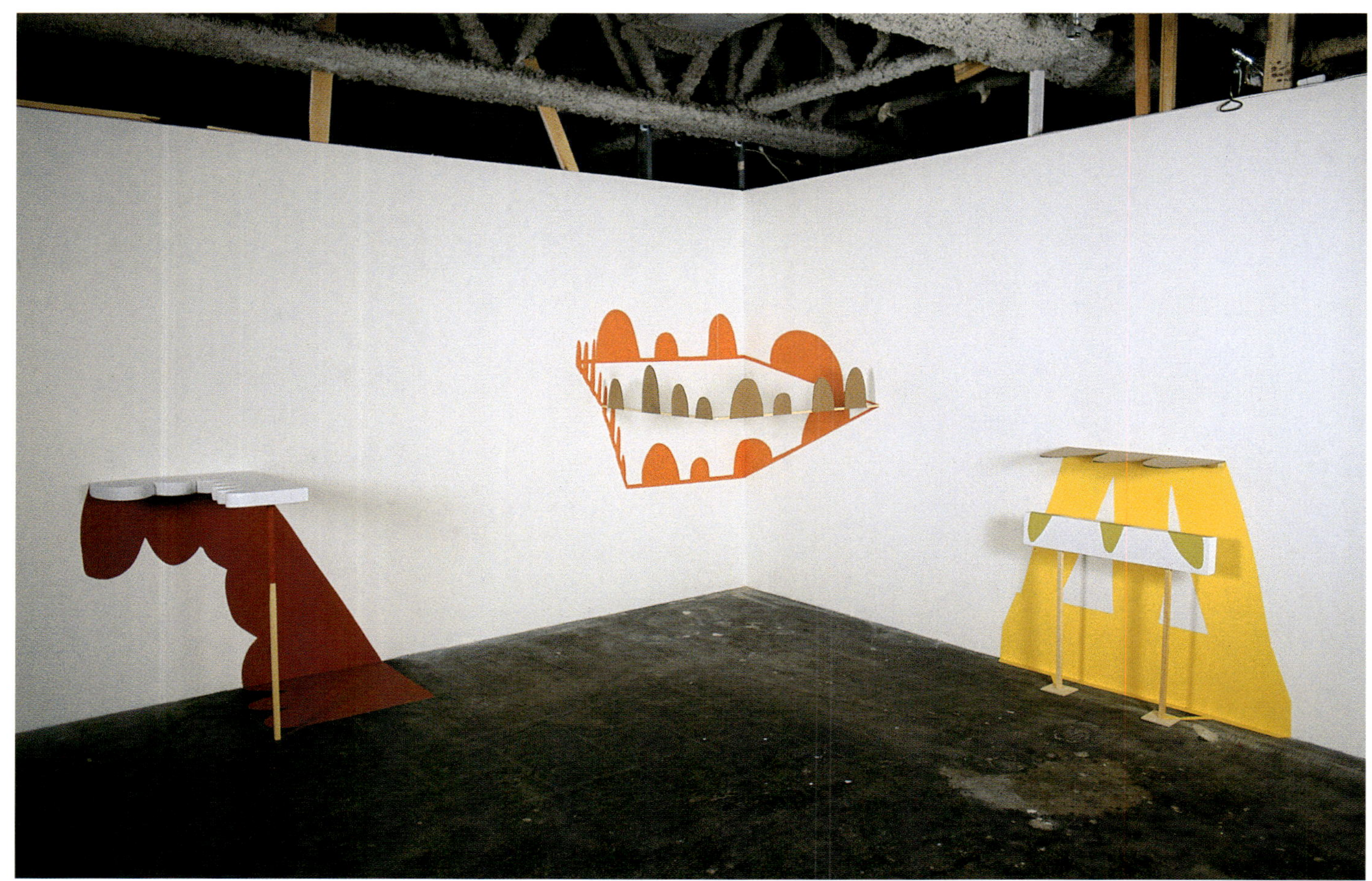

I stood in specific areas of the room and painted the image that lined up with the east and west outlines of Manhattan and the Empire State Building. If you moved your head slightly to the left or right, the alignment of this mural and the outside world would be centered, perfectly aligning the distant Empire State Building with its painted reflection.

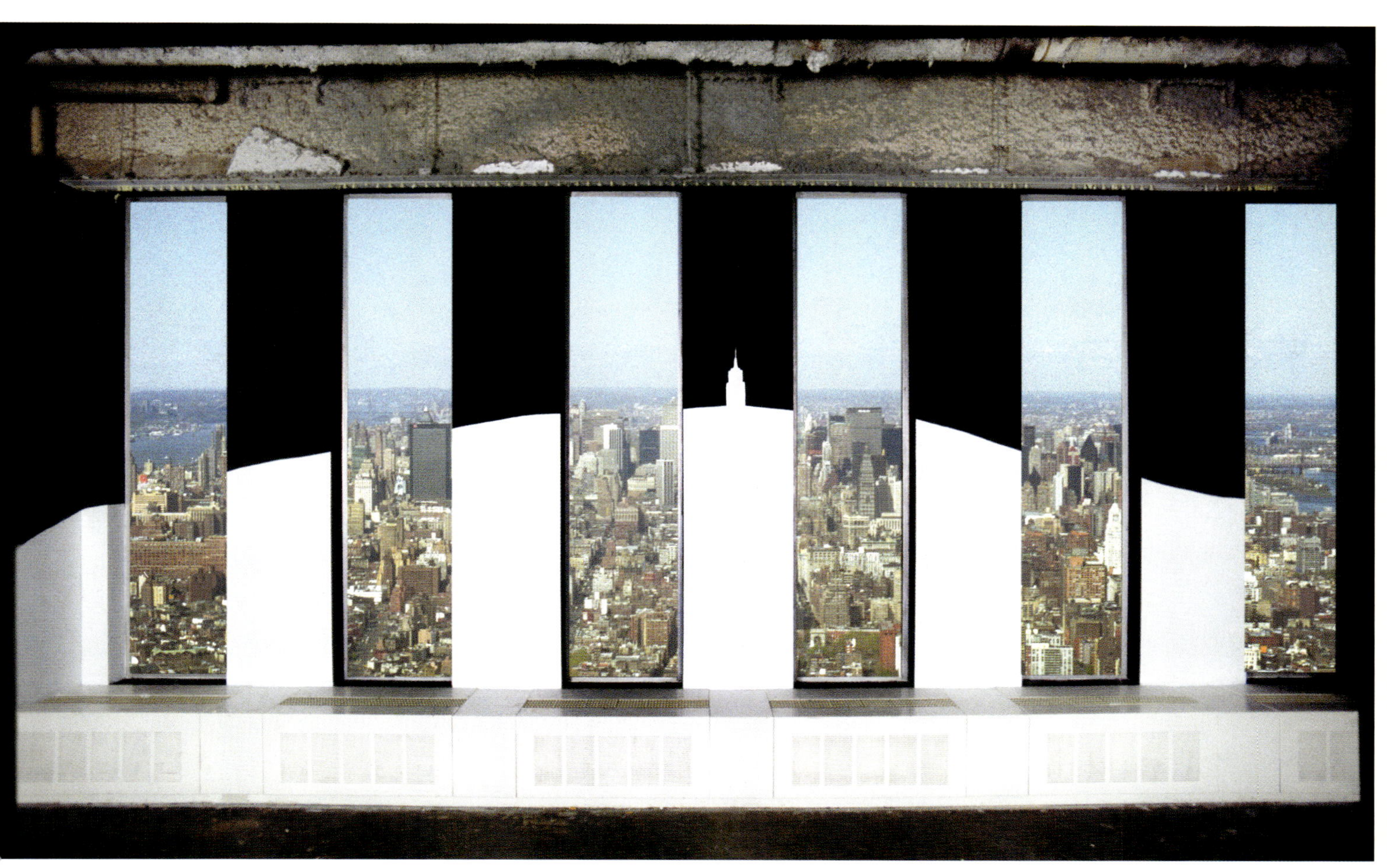

Patty Chang

Falling at 1120 ft. above Sea Level, 2000 (stills)
Video, 59 seconds

Born 1972 in San Diego, Calif.
Lives in New York, N.Y.

Education

1994 BA, University of California, San Diego

Selected Solo Exhibitions

2001 Entwistle Gallery, London, U.K.
2000 *Let Down and Release*, Yerba Buena Center for the Arts, San Francisco, Calif.

Selected Group Exhibitions

2003 *Uneasy Space*, SITE Santa Fe, N.Mex.
Somewhere Better Than This Place, Contemporary Arts Center, Cincinnati, Ohio
2002 *Moving Pictures*, The Solomon R. Guggenheim Museum, New York, N.Y.
Mirror, Mirror, MASS MoCA, North Adams, Mass.
2000 Museo Nacional Centro de Arte Reina Sofia, Madrid, Spain

Award

2003 The Rockefeller Foundation

Having to ride up the express elevators to the studio space made me extremely anxious every time I wanted to work. I'm sure that informed my choice for using the disconcerting, jerky movements of the video camera on the waterbed. Walking on the water indirectly controlled the movements of the camera: It was tossed by the waves and induced images suffering from whiplash. I imagine that falling at that altitude is something like flying: to be suspended for only a brief moment in the sky.

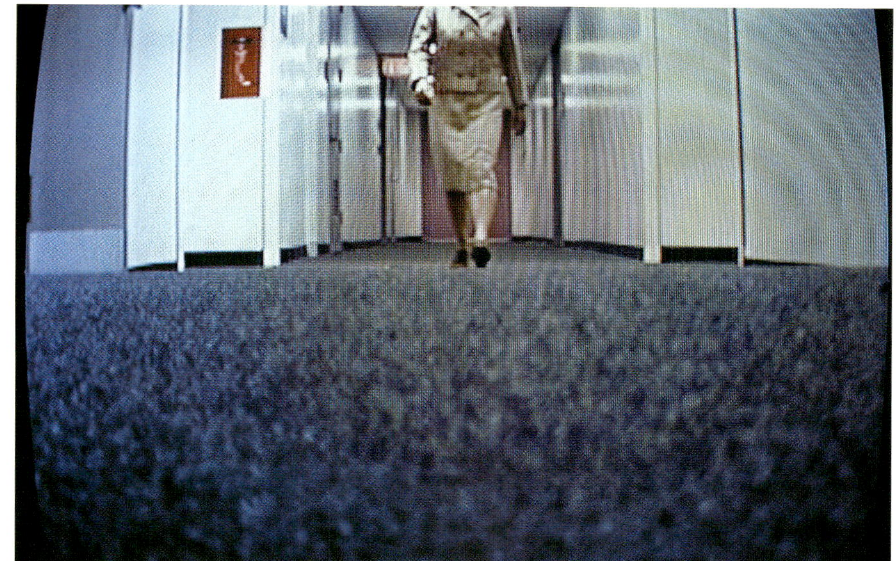
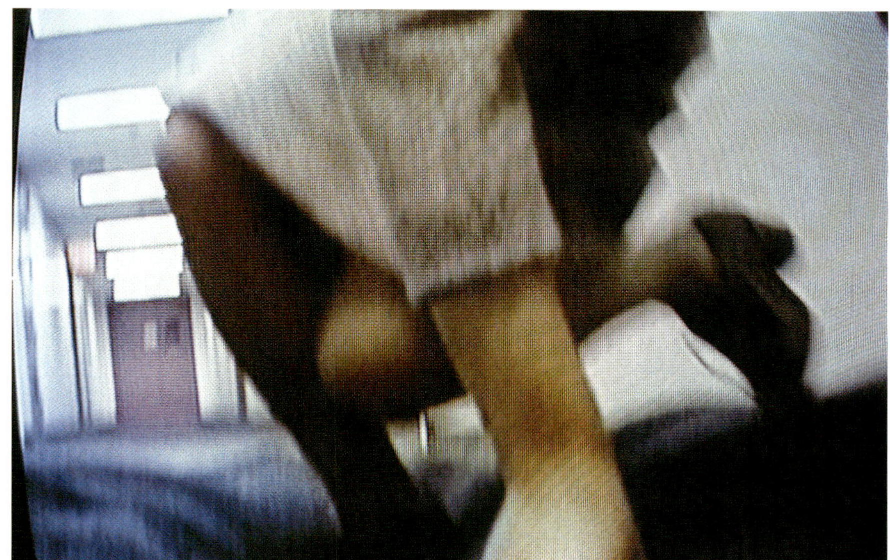
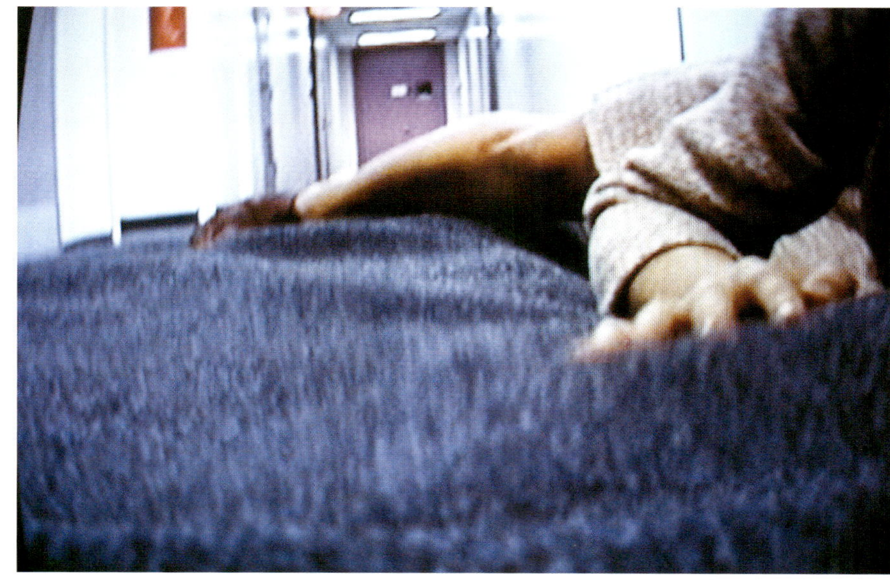

Geoffrey Detrani

A Jig at the Victory Party, 2000
Pencil, resin, mylar on panel
24 x 36 inches

This work was, in part, a reply to what I believed to be the sterility and resoluteness of the Twin Towers. In this piece, foliage, riotous in its abundance and disorder, overtakes and grows through an image of iconic architectural solidity.

Born 1970 in New York, N.Y.
Lives in New York, N.Y.

Education

1996 MFA, State University of New York, New Paltz
1993 BA, State University of New York, New Paltz and Hunter College/CUNY, New York, N.Y.

Selected Solo Exhibitions

2003 *New Work*, Philadelphia Arts Alliance, Pa.
Transverse, John Harms Center for the Arts, Engelwood, N.J.

Residencies

2004 Helen Wurlitzer Foundation, Taos, N.Mex.
2002 Rotunda Gallery/Brooklyn Community Access Television, N.Y.
2001 Vermont Studio Center, Johnson
Snug Harbor Cultural Center, Staten Island, N.Y.

Awards

1999 *Artist in the Marketplace*, The Bronx Museum of the Arts, N.Y.
New York Foundation for the Arts

As I write this text in May of 2003, it is impossible to remember my period in residency at the World Trade Center with any clarity. Any reflection on my original motivations and impulses for creating the work that I did while my site of production was integrated into the unique social/physical environment of the massive WTC complex is now strongly overshadowed by the atrocity of September 11, 2001. While in residence the towers seemed oddly stark, monolithic and inscrutable. In retrospect I understand that this perception was part of an arrogance of looking, merely a way of seeing that was fore-scripted with suppositions and presumptions. The buildings teemed with humanity and humanizing expressions of place with a unique and intriguing specificity. From the ninety-first floor the New York metropolitan area seemed to stream out in a pattern of incandescent marks from what felt like an axis mundi. *I am privileged to have been able to work there.*

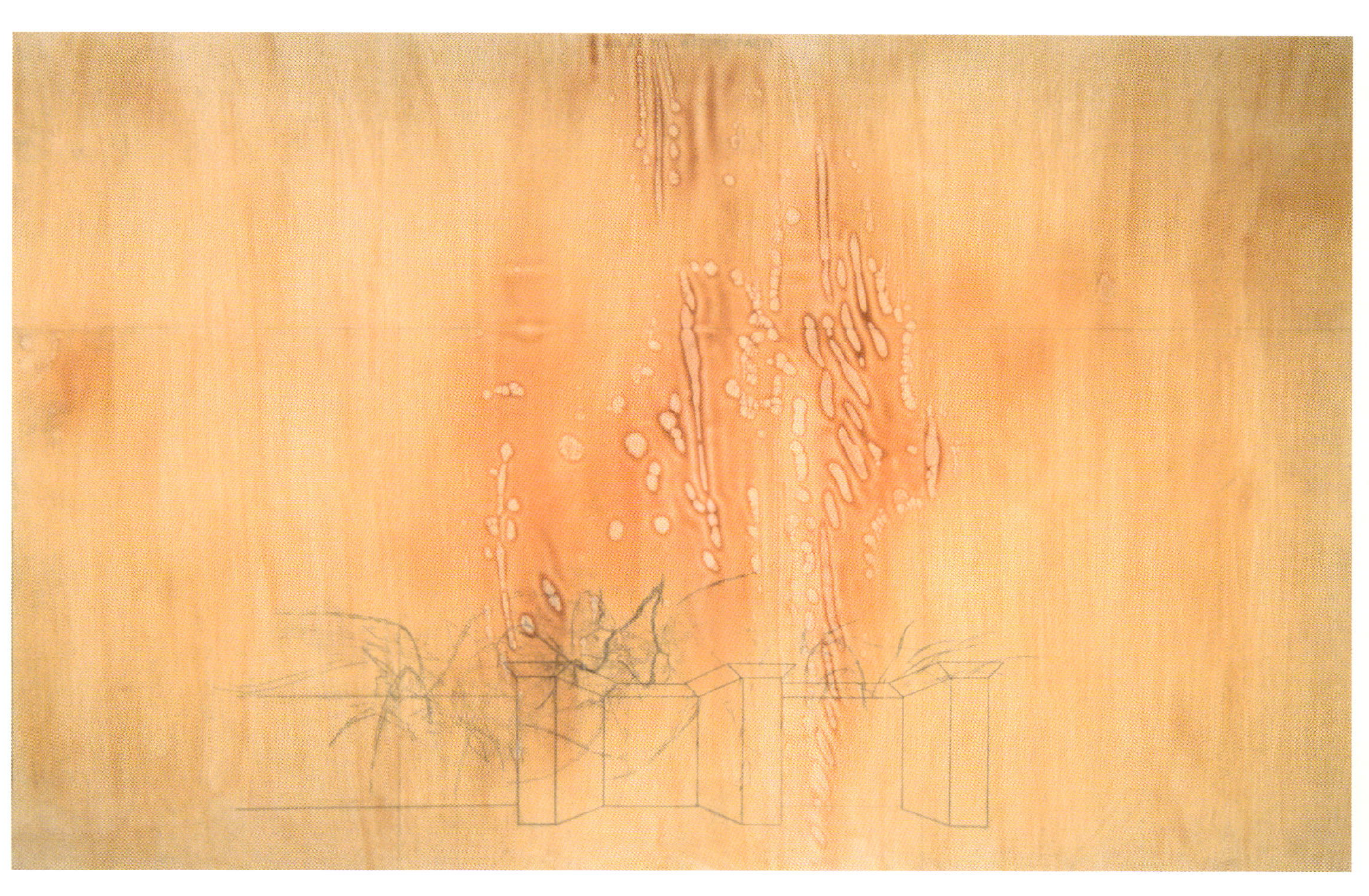

Martina Geccelli

Suite #8203, 2000
R-type print on aluminum
24 x 36 inches

Suite #4047, 2000
R-type print on aluminum
24 x 36 inches

Born 1957 in Mulheim/Ruhr, Germany
Lives in London, U.K.

Education

2003 Institute of Education, London, U.K.
1993 MFA, Kunstakademie, Dusseldorf, Germany
1988 Hochschule der Kunste, Berlin-West, Germany

Selected Solo Exhibitions

2003 *Still Lifes*, Gallery Stefan Rasche, Munster, Germany
2002 *Still Lifes*, Goethe Institute, London, U.K.
Suites (with Torsten Streichardt), Coop Space, Berlin, Germany
2000 *City Walks*, Transit Space, London, U.K.
1997 *Footsteps*, Kunstverein, Ludwigsburg, Germany

Group Exhibition

1998 *Homeless* (with David Goldenberg), Mot Gallery, London, U.K.

Publications

2001 *Why Drive Yourself Crazy?*, SITE Magazine, Dusseldorf, Germany
1998 *60 Minutes Walk London*, SITE Magazine, Dusseldorf, Germany

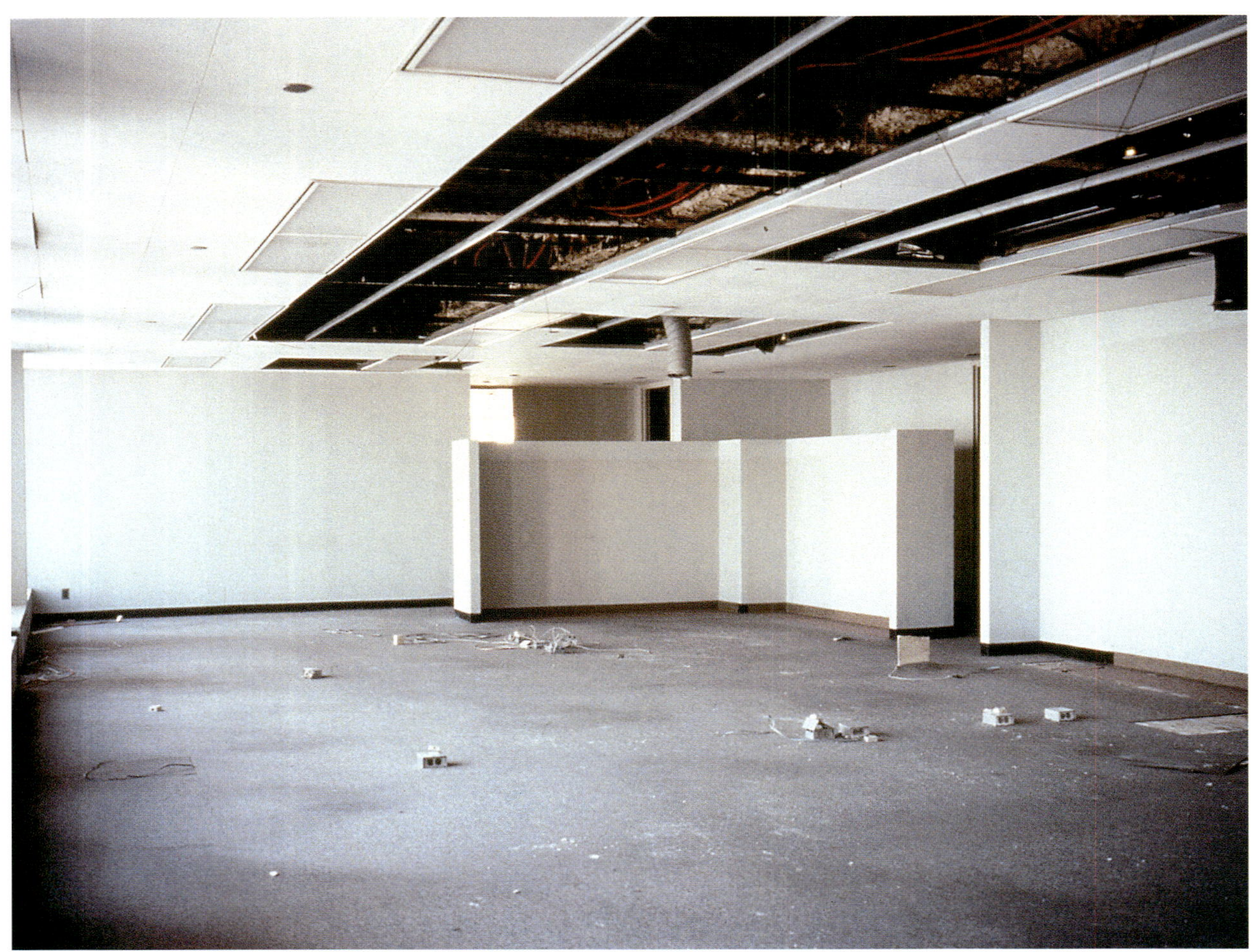

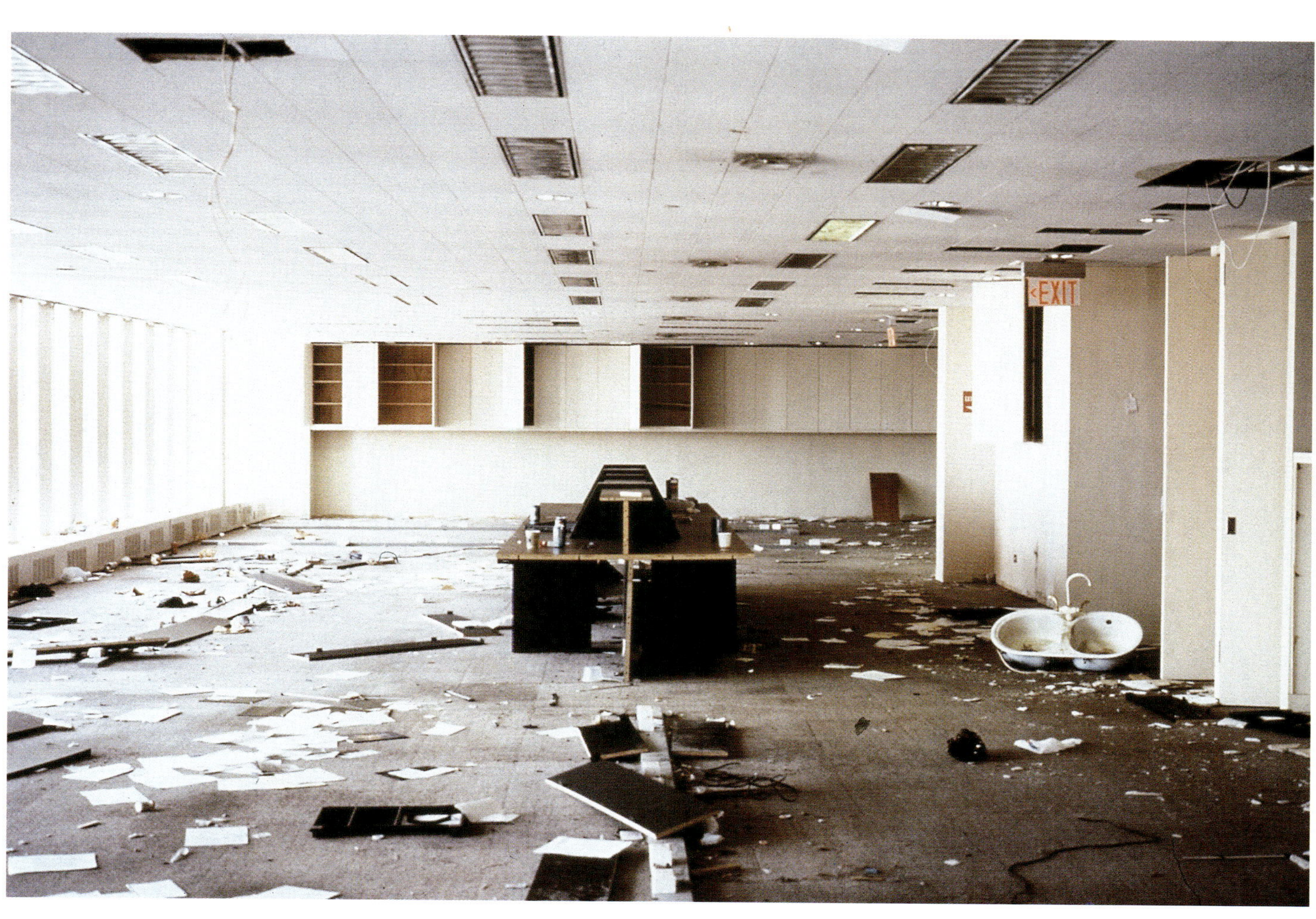
EXIT

Kelly Hashimoto

This page and opposite, top:

How I learned to suck the big corporate dick, 1999
Items from American Express with company logo (motivational flyer, bubble pen, stress horse), PowerPoint presentation
Dimensions variable

Opposite page, bottom:

KH & Her Boys: Eros, 1999
PowerPoint presentation

Born 1960 in Chicago, Ill.
Lives in Denver, Colo.

Education

1992 DAAD, Hochschule Für Bildende Kunst, Hamburg, Germany
1991 MFA, California Institute of the Arts, Valencia
1988 BA, University of California, Los Angeles

Selected Exhibitions

2003 *On my own time,* CH2M Hill/Colorado Business Committee for the Arts, Denver, Colo.
2001 *Peppermint*, Smack Mellon, Brooklyn, N.Y.
SMIRK: Women, Art and Humor, Firehouse Art Gallery, Nassau Community College, N.Y.
Office Hours, Meatmarket Art Fair, New York, N.Y.
2000 *Transparent Architecture*, GAle GAtes et al., Brooklyn, N.Y.
Electronic Easel, University Art Galleries, Bolder, Colo.
1999 *Alternative: Alternative*, Roebling Hall, Brooklyn, N.Y.

Conference

2000 *Multimedia and Interactivity: Where is the Body?,* Society for Literature and Science, Atlanta, Ga.

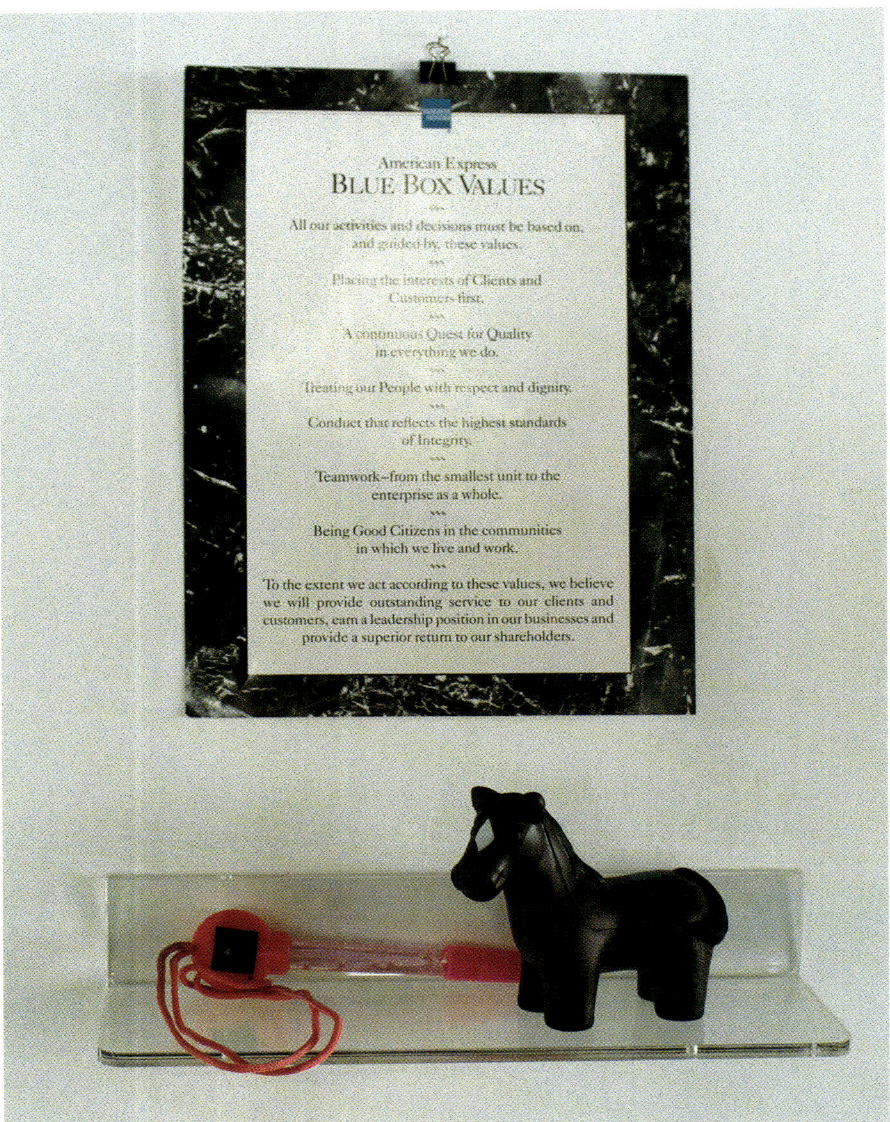

On the third day of the third month, she began a "duty." It was her job to be part of a productive economy, to sacrifice for something else — something larger than the self, a corporation, many interdependent people working together for the common good of an anonymous entity. Prior to this, she was a bad girl for not being more responsible, stable and family-oriented.

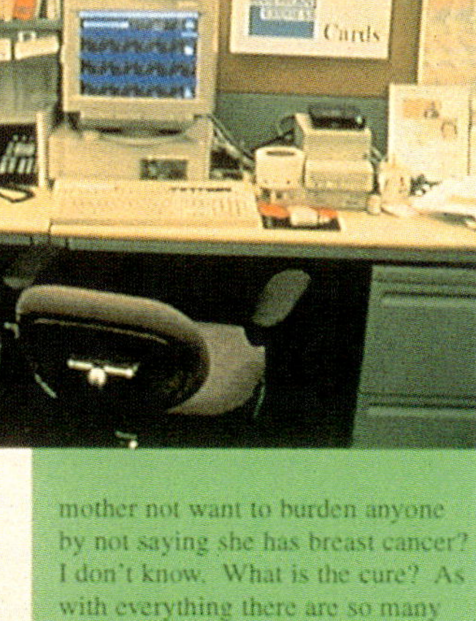

Why did she have this bad attitude towards marriage in the first place? Why didn't she want to get married in her 20's and go the family route, to get a good job, stay there and have children... why was she so selfish? She wanted to be an artist — to be irresponsible, and not have to commit to anyone or take of anyone else?

I feel so bad about this now, but it seems too late.

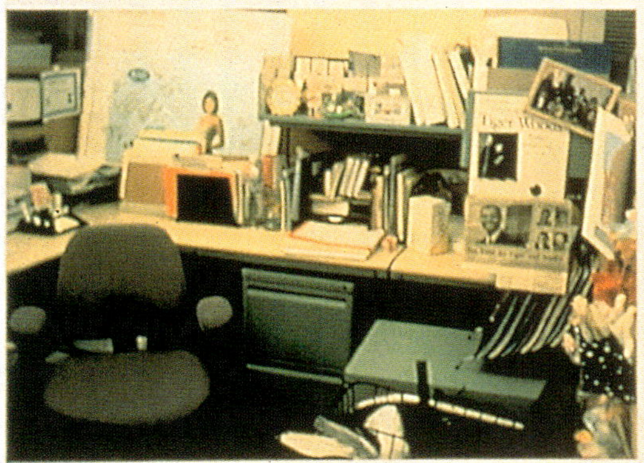

In the moment, I occupy the space or cubicle of someone out on maternity leave. I don't change much around, because my status is one of transience, technically, a freelancer. I am never permanent anywhere, such a fashionable nomad. No residue is left of my time spent, my labor goes unremarked except for the moment...time in and the more energy that is expended the more... In some ways, I want to clean this up, to organize it to make it my place... but for what? I am here such a short time anyway and I don't want to offend. I actually abhor the other's organization and style; it's visual shit, but it is her place and not mind—she is permanent and I am transient.

Why does it become like this?

The family thing, is not too too confining. But, now why did my mother not want to burden anyone by not saying she has breast cancer? I don't know. What is the cure? As with everything there are so many issues involved. Family, work... it is not entertainment. Oh, gee that was nice, the show at the Kunsthalle in Berlin, but I say that with a tinge of irony of course. Albert Oehlen, going digital, doing ads for his dealers, poster size. Well, nice touch. At least it is trying to look like he is trying to keep the wild boys style, the cutting and pasting can continue from painting to computer. But, wasn't he good at maintaining his style with whatever is trendy at the moment? Like a kid eager to play with the newest toy, but getting bored with it shortly?

Now that my original text was lost. It was so political too. Back to being an airhead. A symphonic addition, nice sweet touch, like a country breeze.

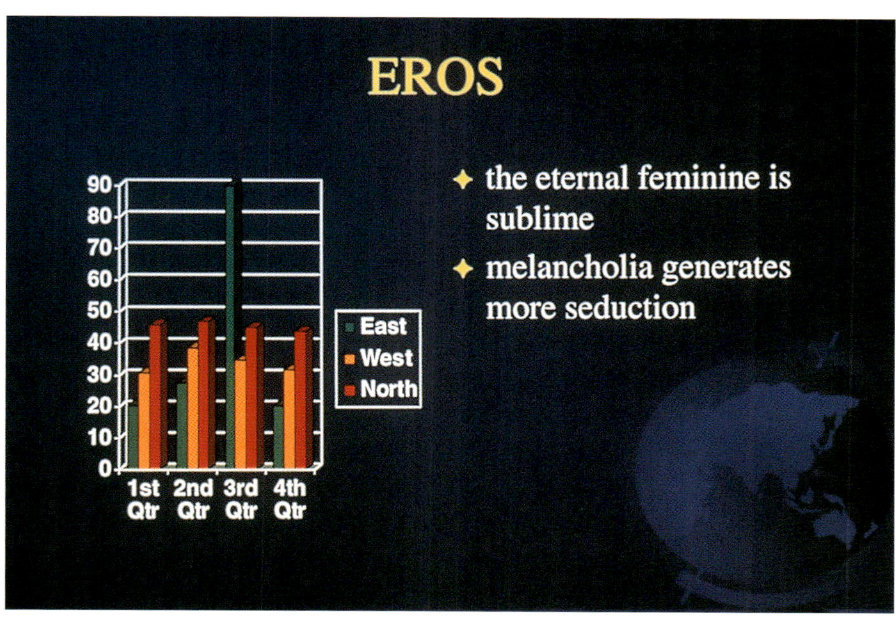

Emily Jacir

My America (I am still here), 2000
33 framed photographs and receipts, shopping bags
Dimensions variable

Photographs, receipts and shopping bags document the purchase and return of goods from every store at the World Trade Center Mall. This performance lasted one month, February 2000. The medium was my credit card, which marked the passage of time and my existence in a system.

Born in 1970
Lives in Ramallah, Palestine and New York, N.Y.

Education

1998–99 Whitney Museum of American Art Independent Study Program, New York, N.Y.
1994 MFA, Memphis College of Art, Tenn.
1992 BFA, University of Dallas, Tex.

Selected Solo Exhibitions

2003 *Where We Come From*, Debs & Co., New York, N.Y.
The Khalili Sakakini Cultural Centre, Ramallah, Palestine
The O.K. Center for Contemporary Art, Linz, Austria

Selected Group Exhibitions

2003 *Poetic Justice,* 8th International Istanbul Biennial, Turkey
Made in Palestine, The Station, Houston, Tex.
Homeland, Art Gallery of the Graduate Center/CUNY, New York, N.Y.

Residencies

2003 The Townhouse Gallery, Cairo, Egypt
2002 Al-Qattan Foundation, Ramallah, Palestine

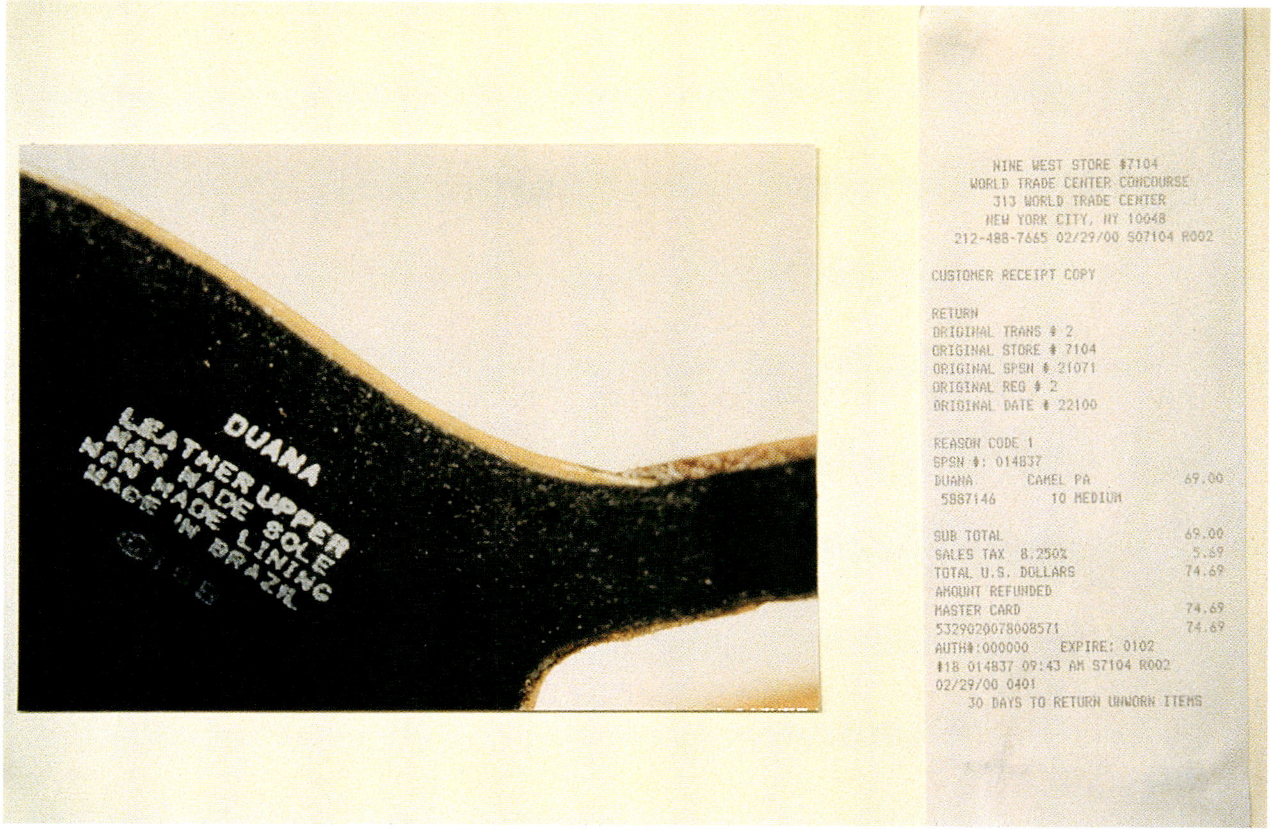

NINE WEST STORE #7104
WORLD TRADE CENTER CONCOURSE
313 WORLD TRADE CENTER
NEW YORK CITY, NY 10048
212-488-7665 02/29/00 S07104 R002

CUSTOMER RECEIPT COPY

RETURN
ORIGINAL TRANS # 2
ORIGINAL STORE # 7104
ORIGINAL SPSN # 21071
ORIGINAL REG # 2
ORIGINAL DATE # 22100

REASON CODE 1
SPSN #: 014837
DUANA CAMEL PA 69.00
5887146 10 MEDIUM

SUB TOTAL 69.00
SALES TAX 8.250% 5.69
TOTAL U.S. DOLLARS 74.69
AMOUNT REFUNDED
MASTER CARD 74.69
5329020078008571 74.69
AUTH#:000000 EXPIRE: 0102
#18 014837 09:43 AM S7104 R002
02/29/00 0401
30 DAYS TO RETURN UNWORN ITEMS

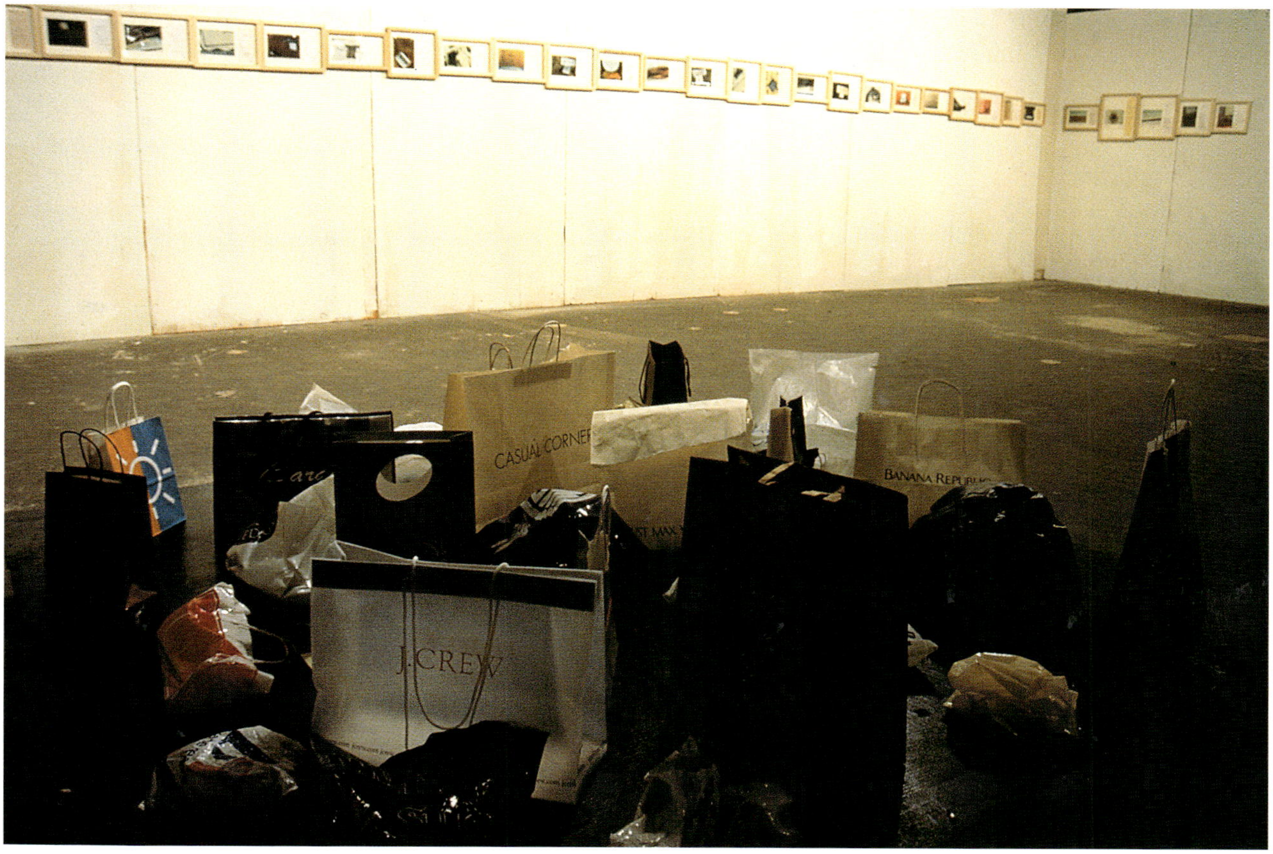

Susan Kelly

The Land of Far Beyond: Pilgrimage up the Center of World Trade, 2000 (stills)
Video documentation of performance
68 minutes

On March 11th, 2000, four pilgrims set off to climb the internal fire escape of the World Trade Center. Like the pilgrims in Enid Blyton's *Land of Far Beyond* (a children's story based on Bunyan's *Pilgrim's Progress*) we departed carrying our terrible burdens, meeting many obstacles on our way—the plains of weariness, the steps of tears, security cameras, disappearing staircases and an armed guard on the eighteenth floor. Five stations were set up where the weary pilgrims removed their shoes, gave up their money, imagined the view and drank cheap wine. We arrived at the windows of the ninety-first floor to a view of nothing more than the clouds of an incoming storm.

Born 1975 in Kilkenny, Ireland
Lives in London, U.K. and Tampere, Finland

Education

Current	PhD, University of London, Goldsmiths College, U.K.
1998–99	Whitney Museum of American Art Independent Study Program, New York, N.Y.
1997	BFA, National College of Art and Design, Dublin, Ireland

Selected Exhibitions

2003	*What is to be Done? Questions for the 21st Century* (with Stephen Morton), The Lenin Museum, Tampere, Finland
2003	*Amorph! 03* (performance), MUU Ry and various venues Helsinki, Finland
2002	*Are We Nearly There Yet?* (performance), Mercer Union, Toronto, Ontario
2001	*The Brewster Project*, Brewster, N.Y.
1999	*Open Studio Exhibition*, Whitney ISP Studios, New York, N.Y.

Screening

2002	*The Land of Far Beyond, Pilgrimage up the Center of World Trade*, City Museum of Skopje, Macedonia

Awards

2002	Arts Council of Ireland Travel Award
2001–04	Postgraduate Research Award, Goldsmiths College, U.K.

The Land of Far Beyond, *like many of my projects, labored to remember different histories of movement (migration, pilgrimage, journeys) and to articulate this space of displacement through a practice that can never reach a Promised Land. The vantage point or "world view" from the top of the World Trade Center was a largely disinterested, panoramic vision—a kind of detached observation that optically transformed the social space of the city into a naturalized urban landscape. This project took on the practice of Early Irish Christian ascetic pilgrimage to retain a sense of motion, to dislocate the false exit of a final world view. It sought to work on a kind of symbolic enactment, an ethical training of subject to physically remember those journeys, and the contingent and non-systematic politics of experience that are so important to forming a different knowledge of the places we inhabit.*

Having a studio at the World Trade Center was a contradictory experience. As the NASDAQ boomed, the many shipping companies housed on the ninety-first floor seemed out-of-date. We joked about its irrelevance and pondered the postmodern dilemma of where a terrorist could plant a bomb now? At one of the stations where we had to make toasts, Alia proposed a toast to us all "getting out of here in one piece, without being blown to bits." Now things seem more complicated. The gulf of misunderstanding, the gulf between beliefs about who or what is worth remembering has widened. Power has locations and targets. It seems to me the need to think about the materiality of the places we live, how they are intensely connected to other places in the world, and how we got to where we are has become even more crucial.

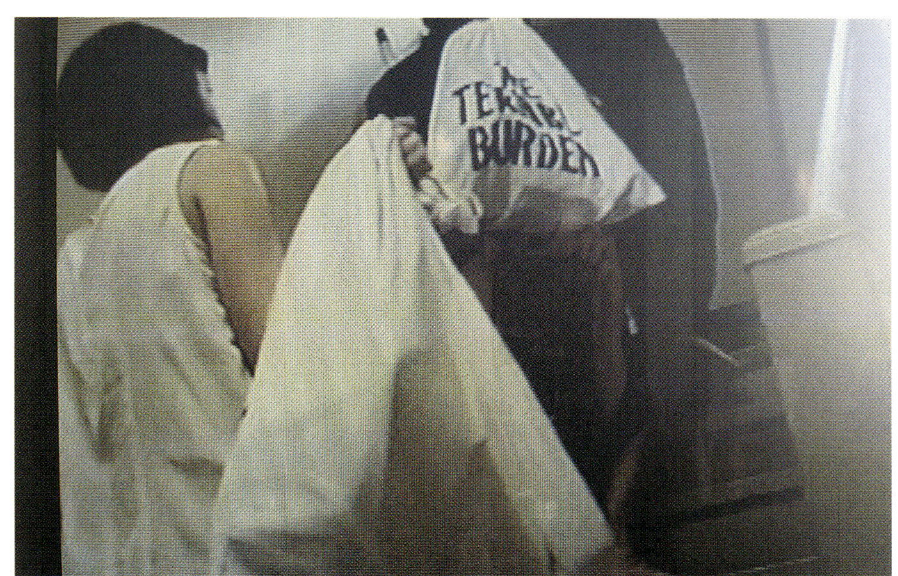
BURDEN

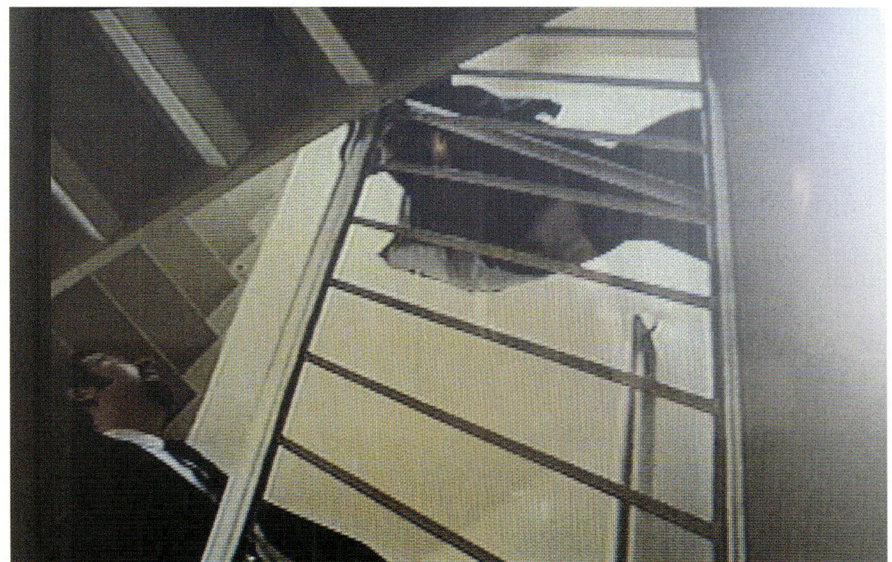

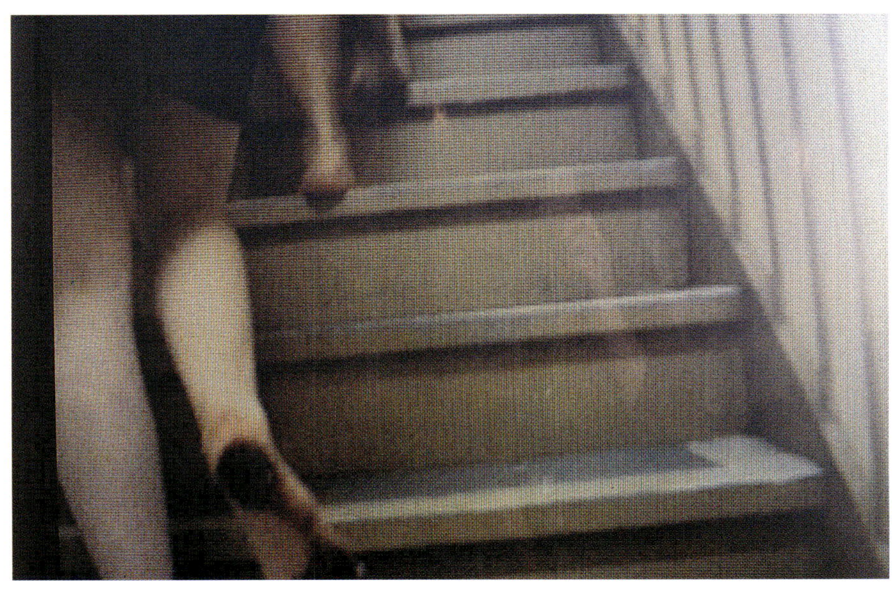

Diane Ludin

Pass the Bomb, 1999–2000 (installation views)
From the *Speed Economy Series*

Table, toy bomb, microsurveillance camera, playing cards, antistatic plastic curtains, inflatable chairs, text, drawings, event flyers, advertisement postcards and collages of Internet imagery of computer laboratories, women terrorists, women revolutionaries and economic forecasting

Born 1966 in Piermont, N.Y.
Lives in Brooklyn, N.Y.

Education

2000 MFA, School of Visual Arts, New York, N.Y.
1993 BFA, State University of New York, Purchase

Selected Group Exhibitions

2002 *Kingdom of Piracy* at *Unplugged: Art as the Scene of Global Conflicts*, Ars Electronica, Linz, Austria
2001 *Double Life*, The Generali Foundation, Vienna, Austria
2000 *Tenacity*, Swiss Institute, New York, N.Y.

Performance

2001 *Amnesia Interrupted*, Galapagos Art Space, Brooklyn, N.Y.

Commissions

2003 *Viral Portraits*, The Alternative Museum, New York, N.Y.
2001 *MemoryFlesh: Harvesting the Net*, Walker Arts Center, Minneapolis, Minn.
2000 *ID Runners: Re_flesh the body*, Franklin Furnace, New York, N.Y.
Genetic Response System: version 3.0, New Radio and Performing Arts, Inc., New York, N.Y.

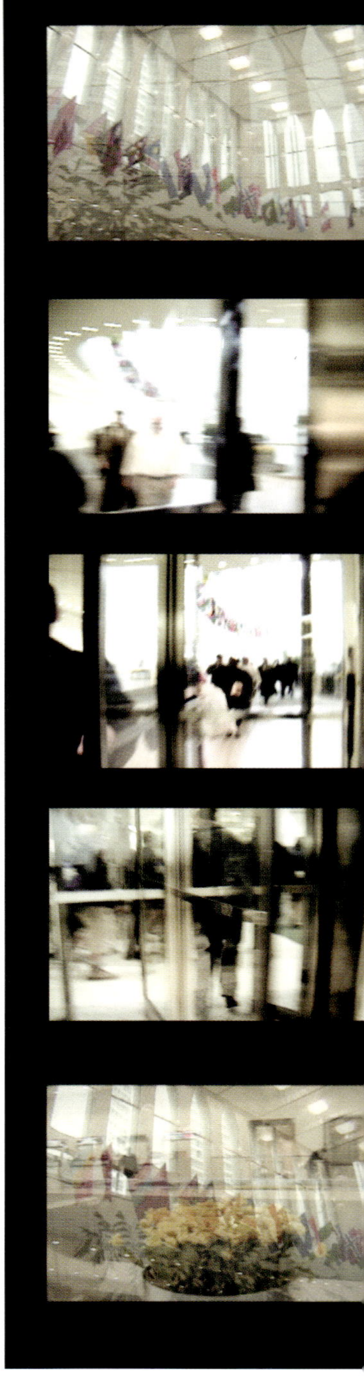

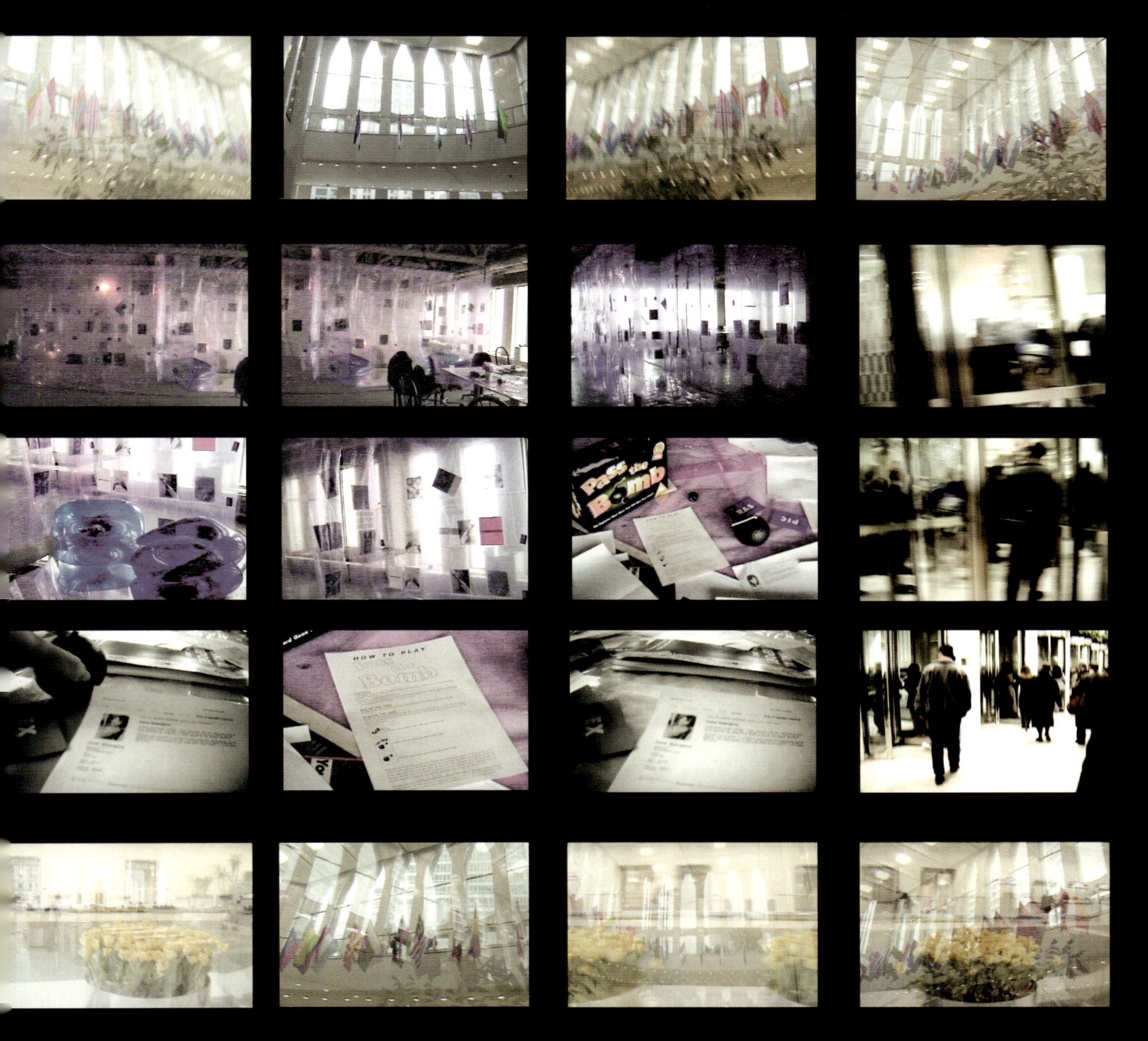
Pass the Bomb
HOW TO PLAY

Tamara Mewis

Prototype for WTC Fenestration— From Actual to Drawing, 2000
Wood, monofilament, photograph, graphite, ink
9 x 30 x 3½ inches
Photo: Adam deCroix

16 Beaver Street, 5th Floor, SE Corner, 2000
Monofilament, cotton string, construction chalk
20 x 32 feet
Photo: Adam deCroix

Architects use axonometric drawings to give a two-dimensional drawing a three-dimensional quality. Because it is closer to the way we perceive a space than a plan or an elevation, this technique employs a learned visual language to help convey complex spatial ideas. *16 Beaver Street, 5th Floor, SE Corner* is a three-dimensional representation of this two-dimensional drawing technique and depicts an actual space within a structure that exists in Lower Manhattan. This human-scale axonometric drawing can be seen in perspective as the viewer walks around and through it, thus conflating the languages of two-dimensional representation and three-dimensional space.

Born 1966 in Richmond, Tex.
Lives in New York, N.Y.

Education

1997–98 Whitney Museum of American Art Independent Study Program, New York, N.Y.
1997 MFA, California Institute of the Arts, Valencia
1990 BA, University of Texas, Austin

Selected Solo Exhibitions

2000 *Folded/Unfolded* (two-person show), P.S.122, New York, N.Y.
1999 *Interpolated Drawing Exercise*, Real Art Ways, Hartford, Conn.

Selected Group Exhibitions

2000 *Good Business Is the Best Art: Twenty Years of the Artist in the Marketplace Program*, The Bronx Museum of the Arts, The Bronx, N.Y.
1999 *AIM 19*, The Bronx Museum of the Arts, The Bronx, N.Y.
1998 *Open Studio Exhibition*, Whitney ISP Studios, New York, N.Y.
1997 *Attaché*, Gemini GEL Gallery, Los Angeles, Calif.
Uncommon Sense (part of GALA Committee with Mel Chin), MoCA at The Geffen Contemporary, Los Angeles, Calif.

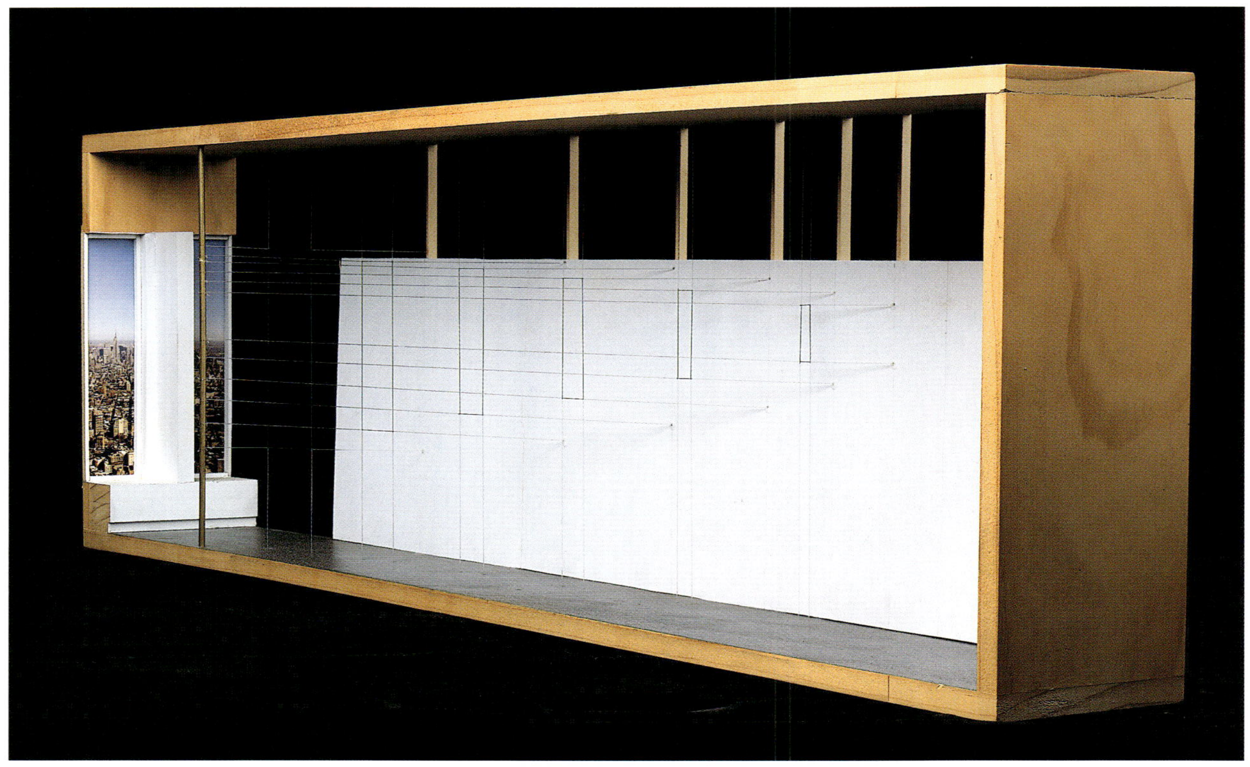

Each studio that I have ever occupied offered a particular context for me to think about my work and how it occupies space. The architectural space that surrounds us in never a "blank canvas," and my studio at the WTC was no exception. Although it offered ample room to experiment with large materials, I found the studio more conducive to thinking about the urban landscape that unfolded on the other side of the windows—how our vision renders the world around us and the ephemerality of each viewpoint.

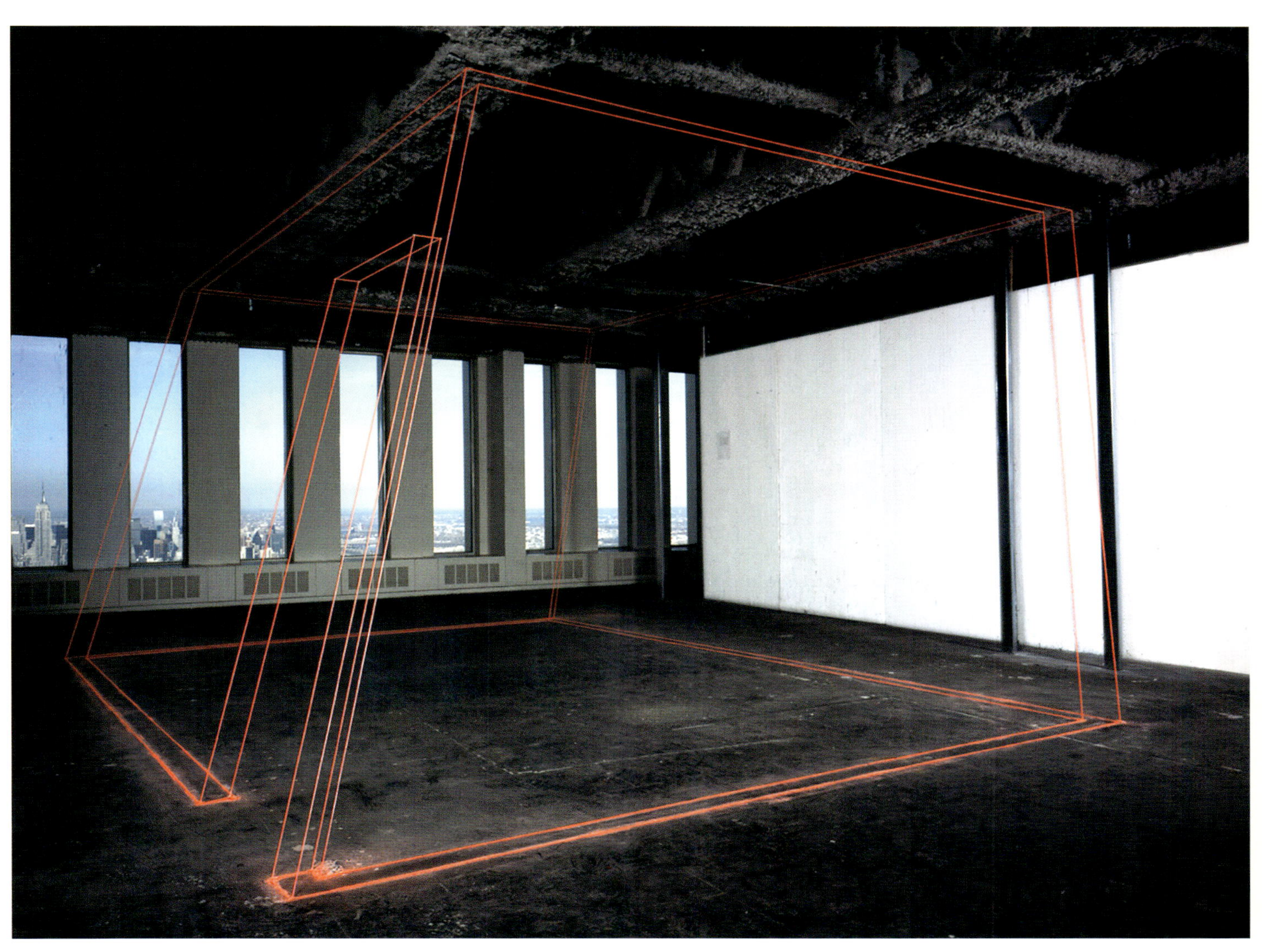

Prema Murthy

Bindigirl, 1999
Internet art

Bindi is a girl born out of the "exotic" and "erotic." She is the embodiment of desire for and of the "other"—the desire of wanting to be known or to know on an intimate level . . . and at the same time finding safety, even power, in distance, in being mysterious—liberation in not being easily categorized.

Bindi is my avatar. Not only is she my alias in the virtual world but a play on the word that in India means an incarnation of a Hindu deity, the embodiment of an archetype. In this case she is the embodiment of the "goddess/whore" archetype, which has historically been used to simplify the identity of women and their roles of power in society.

Born 1969 in Seattle, Wash.
Lives in New York, N.Y.

Education

2001 MFA, Goldsmiths College, London, U.K.
1994 BA, University of Texas, Austin

Selected Exhibitions

2003 *Atlanta Biennial*, The Contemporary Art Center, Atlanta, Ga.
2002 *New Contemporaries*, Shortlisted, Barbican Center, London, U.K.
Race and Digital Space, MIT List Center, Cambridge, Mass. (tour)
Un(suitable) Girls, Paisley Art Gallery, New York, N.Y.
2001 *Net.Ephemera*, Chapman Gallery, Manchester, U.K. (tour)
Crossing the Line, The Queens Museum, Queens, N.Y.
Double Life, The Generali Foundation, Vienna, Austria
2000 *2000 Biennial Exhibition*, Whitney Museum of American Art, New York, N.Y.

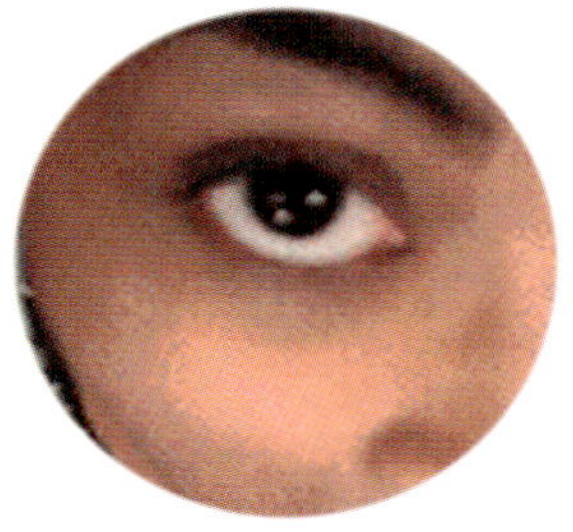

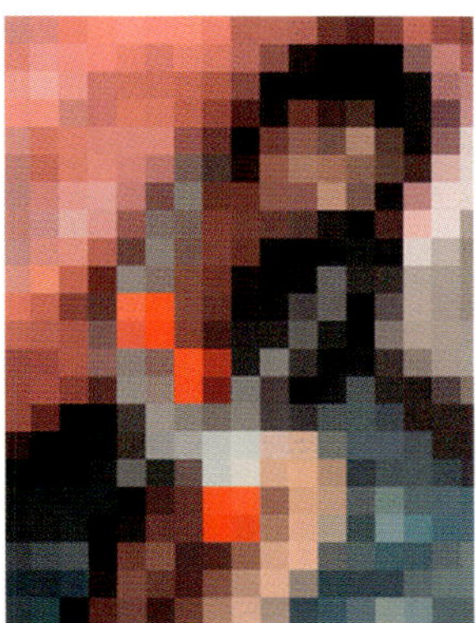

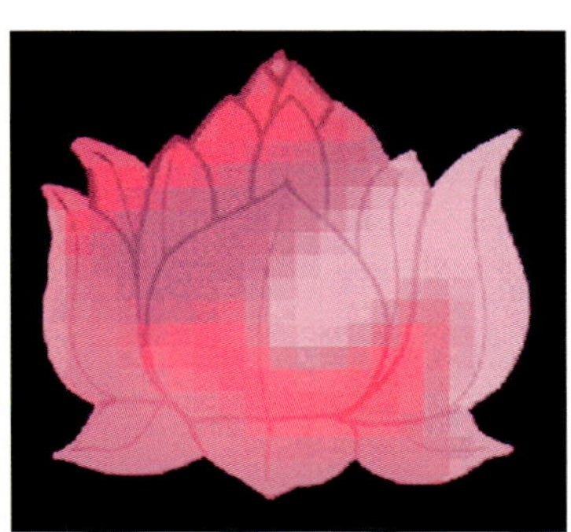

Peter Ruta

Manhattan View, 2000
Oil on canvas
54 x 64 inches

Born 1918 in Dresden, Germany
Lives in New York, N.Y.

Education

1947–49 Accademia di Belle Arte, Venice, Italy
1937–41 Art Students League, New York, N.Y.

Selected Solo Exhibitions

2004 *New York Paintings*, Museum of the City of New York, N.Y.
2003 *The Kennedy Years*, Banning Gallery, New York, N.Y.
2001 Academy Gallery, New Orleans, La.
1997 Munson Gallery, Santa Fe, N.Mex.

Selected Group Exhibitions

2002 *Re-imagining New York,* North Dakota Museum of Art, Grand Forks
1997 *Landscape Retrospective*, St. John's College, Santa Fe, N.Mex.

Residency

2000 Rochefort en Terre, Morbihan, France

Award

1995 The Pollock-Krasner Foundation

As I lay dying in a field hospital in the Philippines in 1945 (severely wounded in close combat in the retaking of Bataan), I vowed—if by some miracle I lived—to devote myself to painting. This determination carried me through the next fifty years as a painter. In winter/spring 2000 the Lower Manhattan Cultural Council staff, the kindest people in the world, gave me an official pass to the studio on the ninety-first floor of the North Tower of the World Trade Center, and while I had painted city views before, a new perspective opened up: Manhattan from above, in its shimmering vastness, shorelines, avenues, bridges and the sunset haze of late spring evenings. In August 2001, I returned to the ninety-first floor to paint Manhattan in the rosy glow of summer sunsets. The terrorist attack destroyed my best painting of this series, but as in 1945, the intrusion of violence only fortified my will and desire to go on painting, and my deep attachment to New York City.

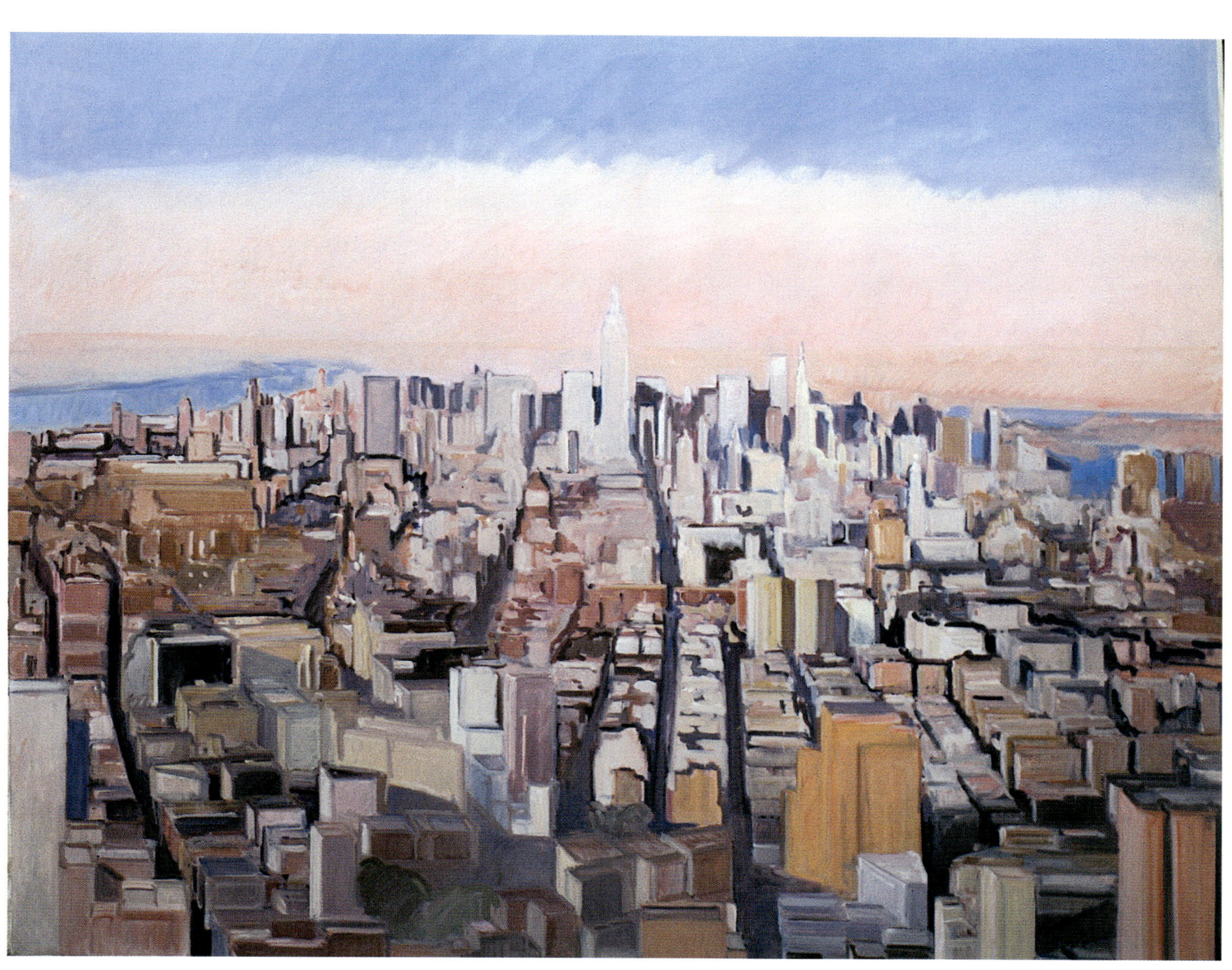

Marcos Rosales

Untitled, 2000
Polyester, cord, wire, wood
Dimensions variable

This piece was made slowly over a period of five years, with the largest parts created during two residencies. The first residency was at The Center for MetaMedia in Plasy, Czech Republic and the final section was completed during the World Views residency in New York.

I started making this piece while working in a mental health facility in Los Angeles. Macramé was a popular craft for the residents. Many of the pieces that were produced seemed to mark a passing of time yet had no particular goal. Plant hangers morphed into belts that morphed into wall hangings. This was the initial inspiration for the piece.

Born 1967 in Waco, Tex.
Lives in New York, N.Y.

Education

1995 MFA, California Institute of the Arts, Valencia
1990 BFA, University of North Texas, Denton

Selected Exhibitions and Performances

2003 *. . . and the black snakes* (with Luciana Achugar, Maria Hassabi and Jeremy Wade, with music by Pilgrim State, Movement Research), The Judson Memorial Church, New York, N.Y.
2002 *The Writing On The Wall,* Collective Unconscious, New York, N.Y.
sublimated, reduced and eventually annihilated, Angstrom Gallery, Dallas, Tex.
2001 *Mouthpiece* (with Jeremy Wade and Michael Floyd), Something Raw Festival, Frascati Theater, Amsterdam, The Netherlands
Presenting Miss World 1972, Daniel Reich, New York, N.Y.
Penny Dreadfuls, VTO Gallery, London, U.K.
2000 *The Back of Laughter (scenes from "The Glamour of Evil"),* 1234, Los Angeles, Calif.

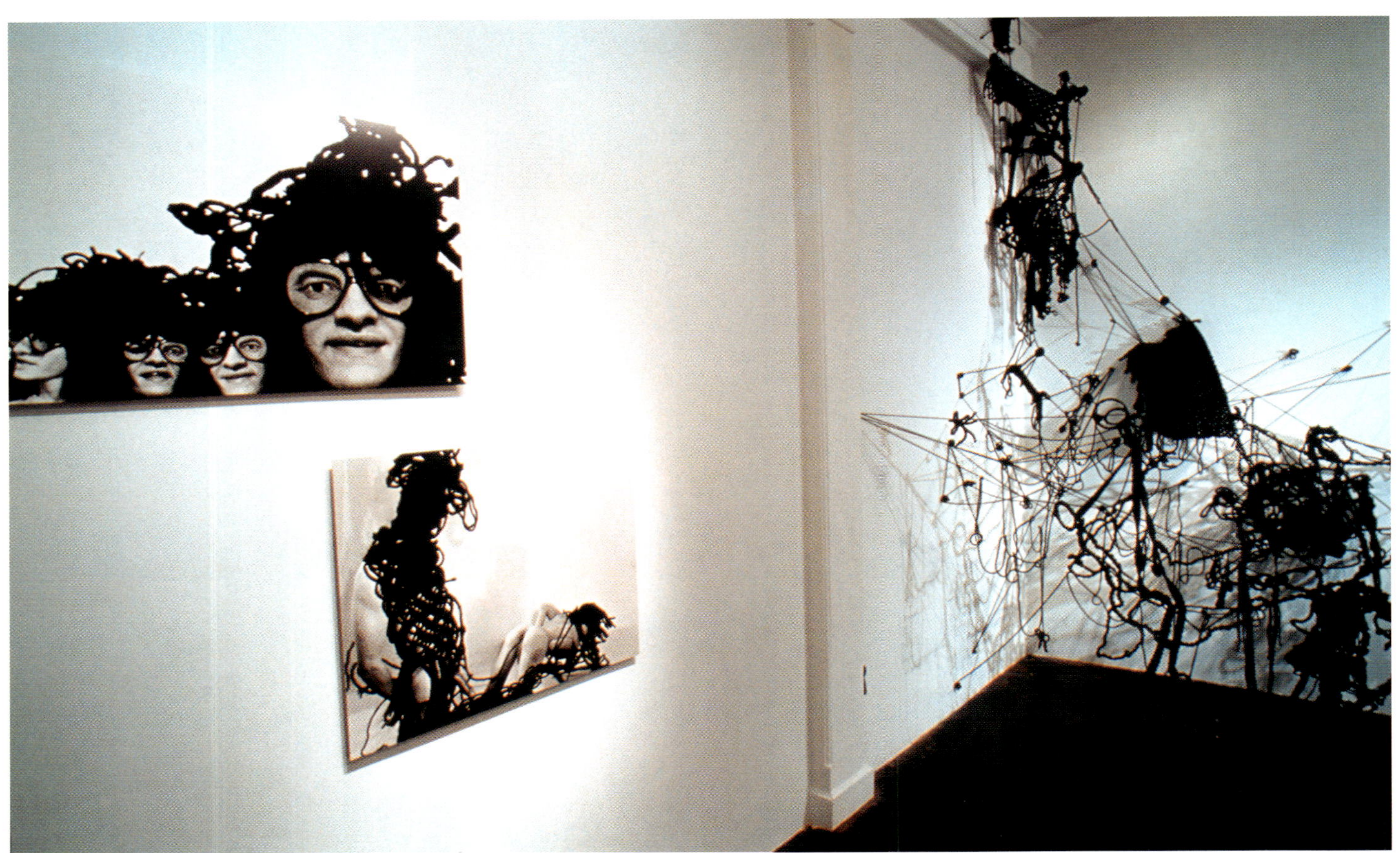

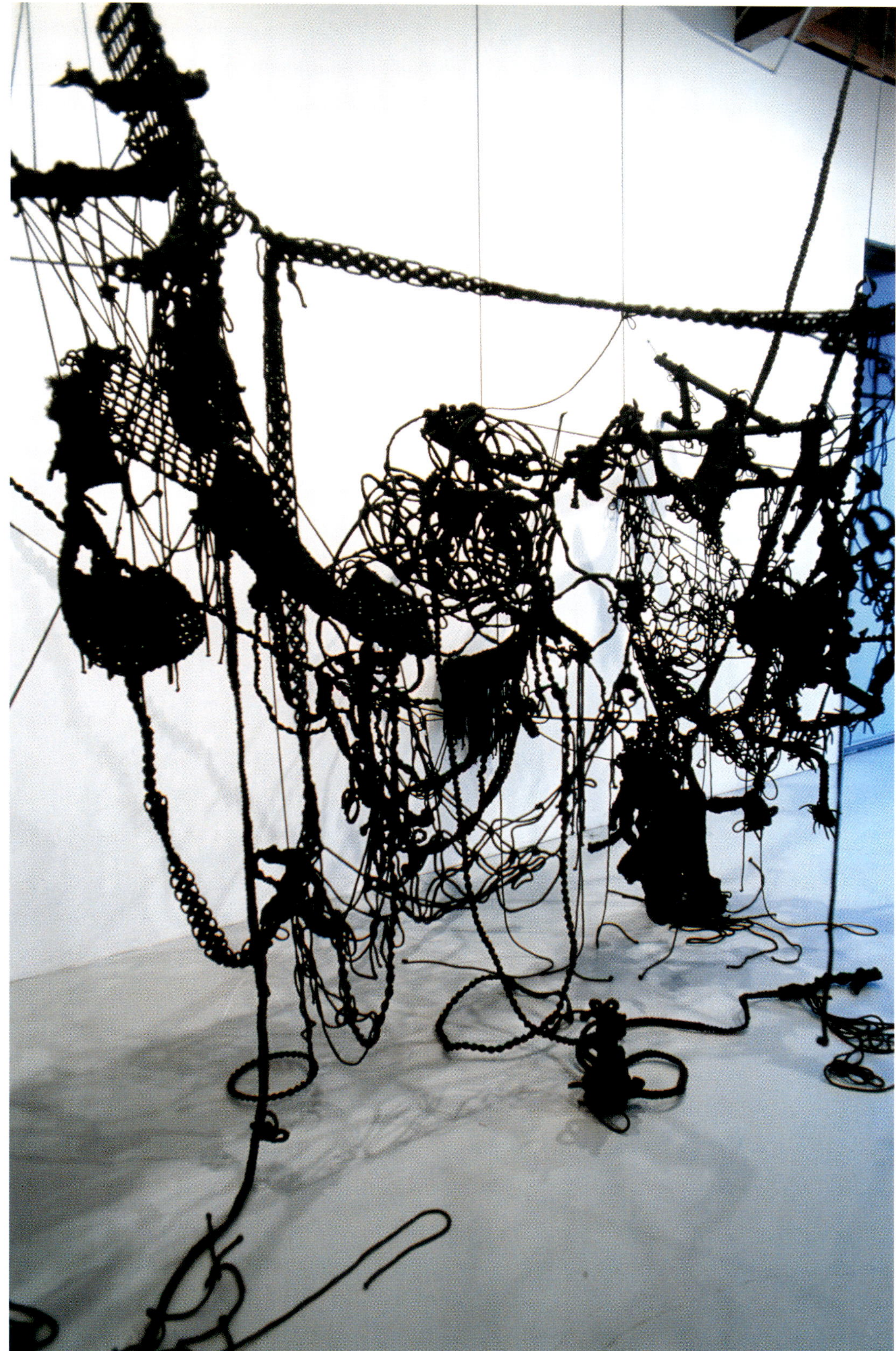

I remember many things from the residency. The crowds of business people rushing through the lobby of the World Trade Center and the sense of chaos upon entering the building. I always came to the studio in the thick of evening rush hour. Sometimes it seemed impossible to try and get my materials upstairs without getting trampled by hordes of business people. Once I got to the studios on ninety-one, I felt peaceful. I spent a lot of time watching details in the scene below or staring across at the Empire State Building while knotting my macramé piece. I never stopped being fascinated by the view and the idea of producing work so high above the city.

Slink Moss

Cathedral, 2000 (still)
Hand-processed super-8 film
Six minutes

Design for a Triangular House, 2000
Digital image of drawings

Born 1966 in Chicago, Ill.
Lives in New York and Hudson, N.Y.

Education

1996 BFA, The School of the Art Institute of Chicago, Ill.

Group Exhibition

2002 *Group Sex Show*, Art@Large, New York, N.Y.

Performances

2002 *Slink Moss Rockabilly Explosion*, "30 Bands in 30 Minutes," Metro, Chicago, Ill.
Slink Moss One Man Band, Uno A Go Go Festival, Abbey, Chicago, Ill.

2001 *Since I Lay My Burden Down*, DUMBO Arts Festival, Brooklyn, N.Y.

1999 *The Look of Love* (with Bengaloon), P.S.1 Contemporary Art Center, Long Island City, N.Y. and Mercury Lounge, New York, N.Y.

Screenings

2000 *Fresh Film*, Anthology Film Archives, New York, N.Y.
Super-8 World Tour, Robert Beck Memorial Cinema, New York, N.Y.

1999 *Hand-Processed Films*, ATA, San Francisco, Calif.

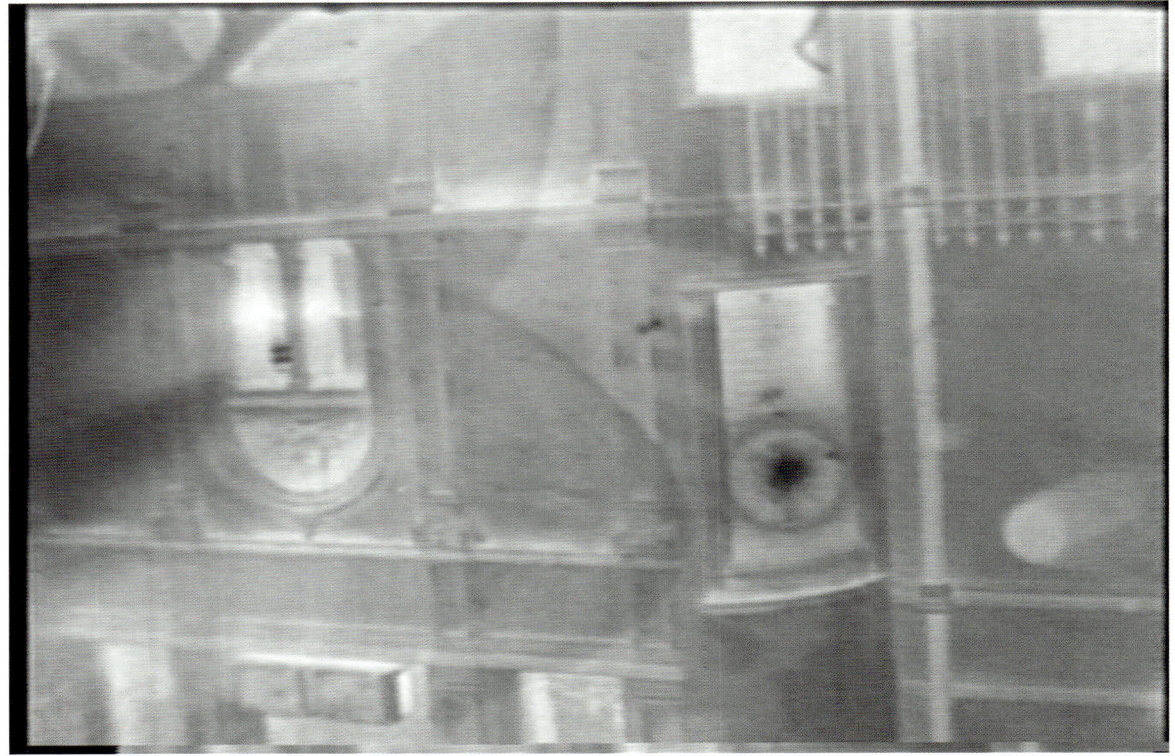

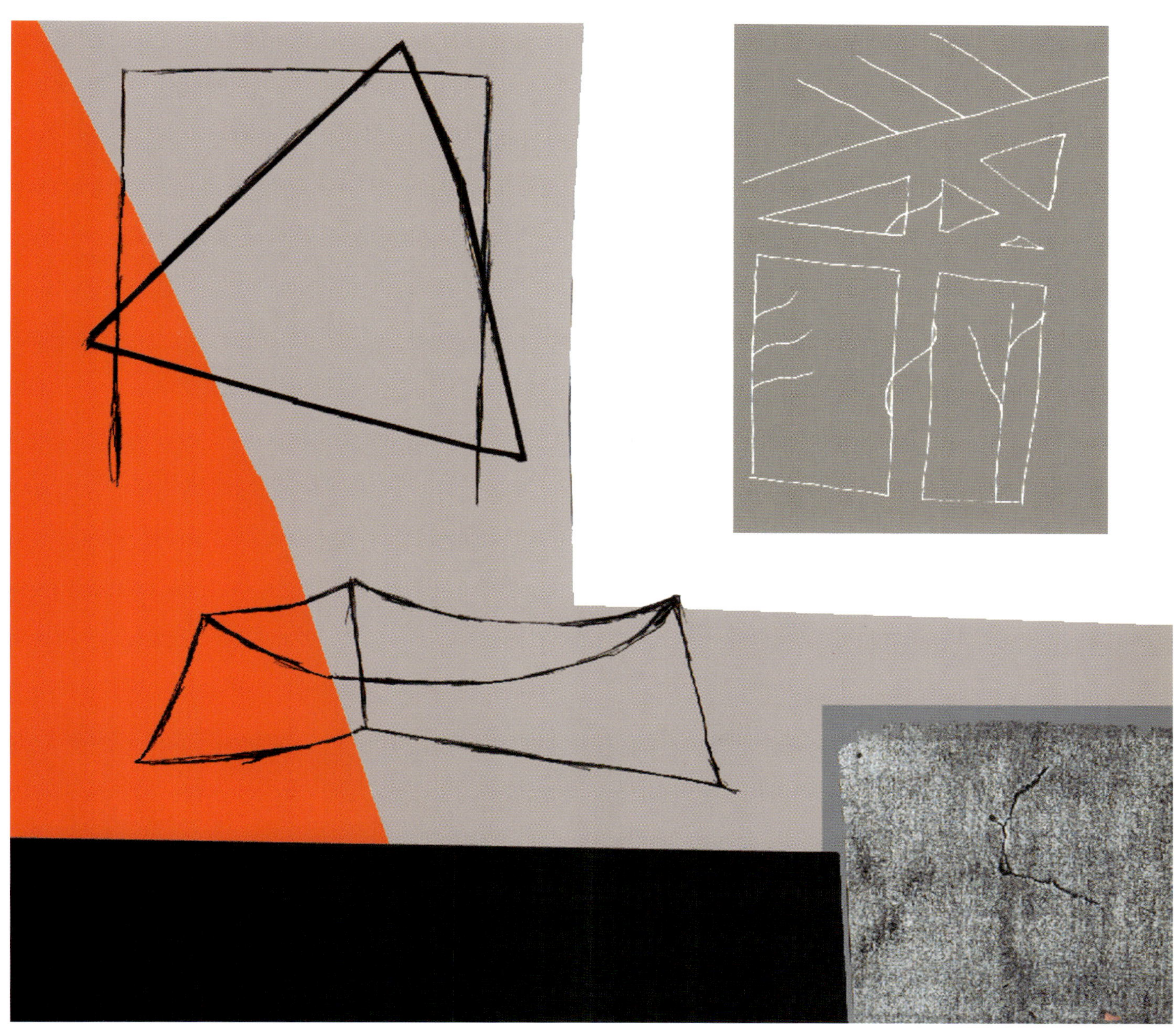

Kimberly SaRee Tomes

PLANT PROJECT 91, Model Organism, 2000
Arabidopsis seeds, soil, netting, photos
Dimensions variable

Born 1971 in Seoul, South Korea
Lives in New York, N.Y.

Education

1997–98 Whitney Museum of American Art Independent Study Program, New York, N.Y.
1997 MFA, Ohio University, Athens
1993 BFA, Truman State University, Kirksville, Mo.

Selected Group Exhibitions

2002 *Pause*, Kwangju Biennial, South Korea
2001 *SMIRK: Women, Art and Humor,* Firehouse Art Gallery, Nassau Community College, N.Y.
1998 *DNA Diaspora*, Plug-In Gallery, Winnipeg, Manitoba

Selected Screenings

2000 *EXIT*, Chisenhale Gallery, London, U.K.
Through the Lens, PBS, Philadelphia, Pa.
1999 *Asian Cine Vision*, Asian American Film Festival, New York, N.Y.

Residencies

2004 Civitella Ranieri Center, Umbertide, Italy
1997 The Banff Centre, Alberta

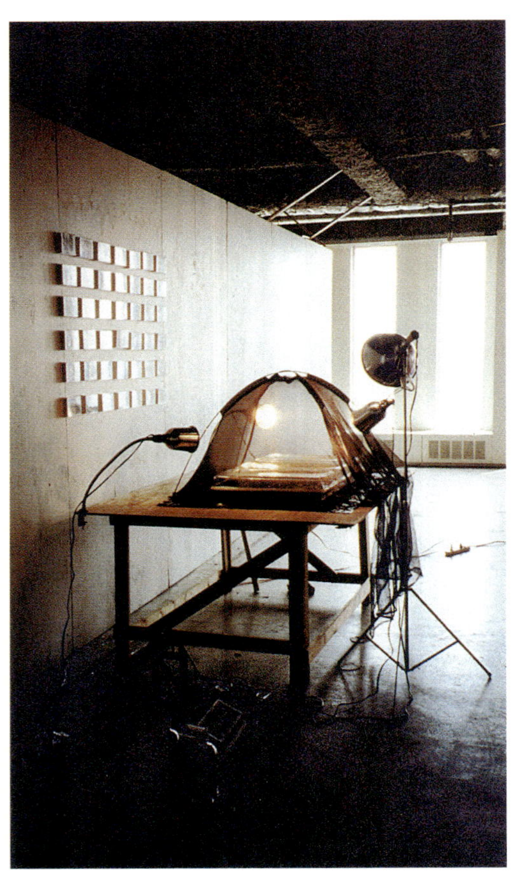

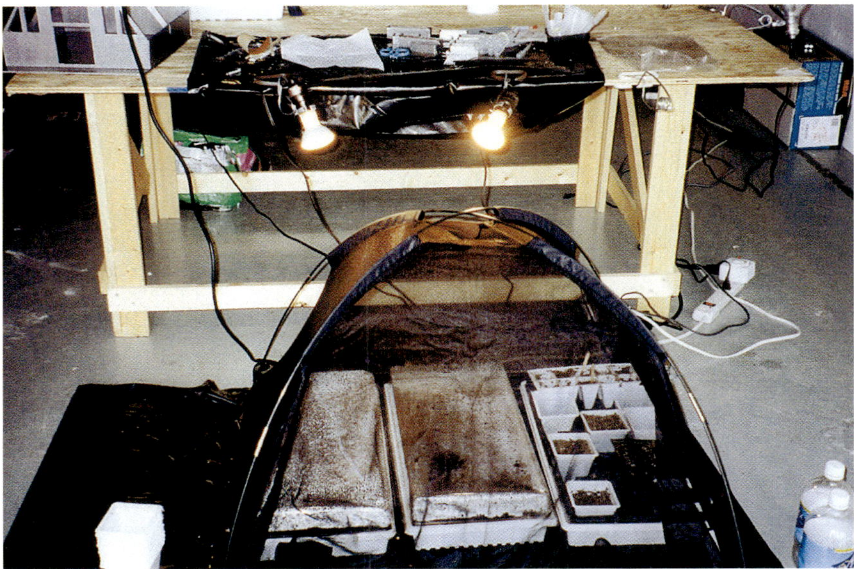

The 24/7 access to the World Trade Center studio was like being given health care insurance. Approval, privilege; something my father could tell his co-workers. I took some of his plant seeds used in the bio-engineering lab. Small seeds; thousands could fit in an eyedropper.

Plant Project 91
Relocate Arabidopis thaliana *seeds from father's biotech firm to ninety-first floor WTC1. Implement growth cycle. How do these plant "model organisms" fare? There are no other plants around. They are high in the sky, surrounded by the ebb and flow of financial transactions from the banking company next door. My plants did well at first but couldn't subsist in the dry environment.*

Playing with Patty and Kelly and making the video Angel Falls *was such a balm to pouring over botany texts* [for images see page 25]. *Pure bliss. It was lovely and definitely the most memorable part of the residency.*

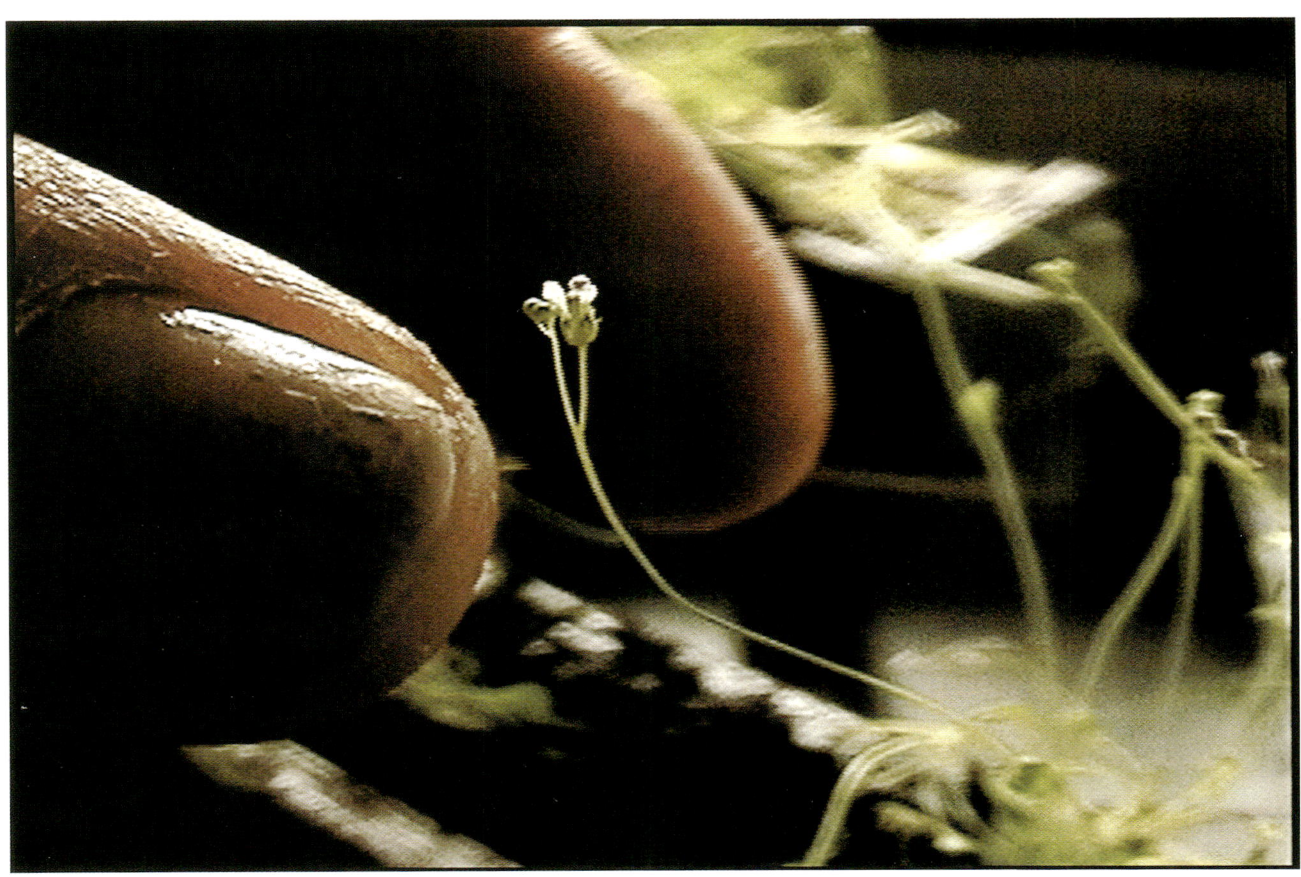

Summer 2000

Artists-in-Residence

Stephan Apicella-Hitchcock
Caroline Birks
Beth Campbell
Jaime Davidovich
Adam Frank
Susan Graham
Kira Lynn Harris
Kristin Lucas
Sergio Muñoz-Sarmiento
Christian Nguyen
Olu Oguibe
John Pilson
Douglas Ross
James Sheehan
Edin Veléz

Jurors

Kathy Brew
Kevin Duggan
Raina Lampkins-Fielder
Tom Finkelpearl
Moukhtar Kocache
Paul Pfeiffer
Bruce Wands

Invited Artists

Dennis D'Amelio
Joan Cobb Marsh

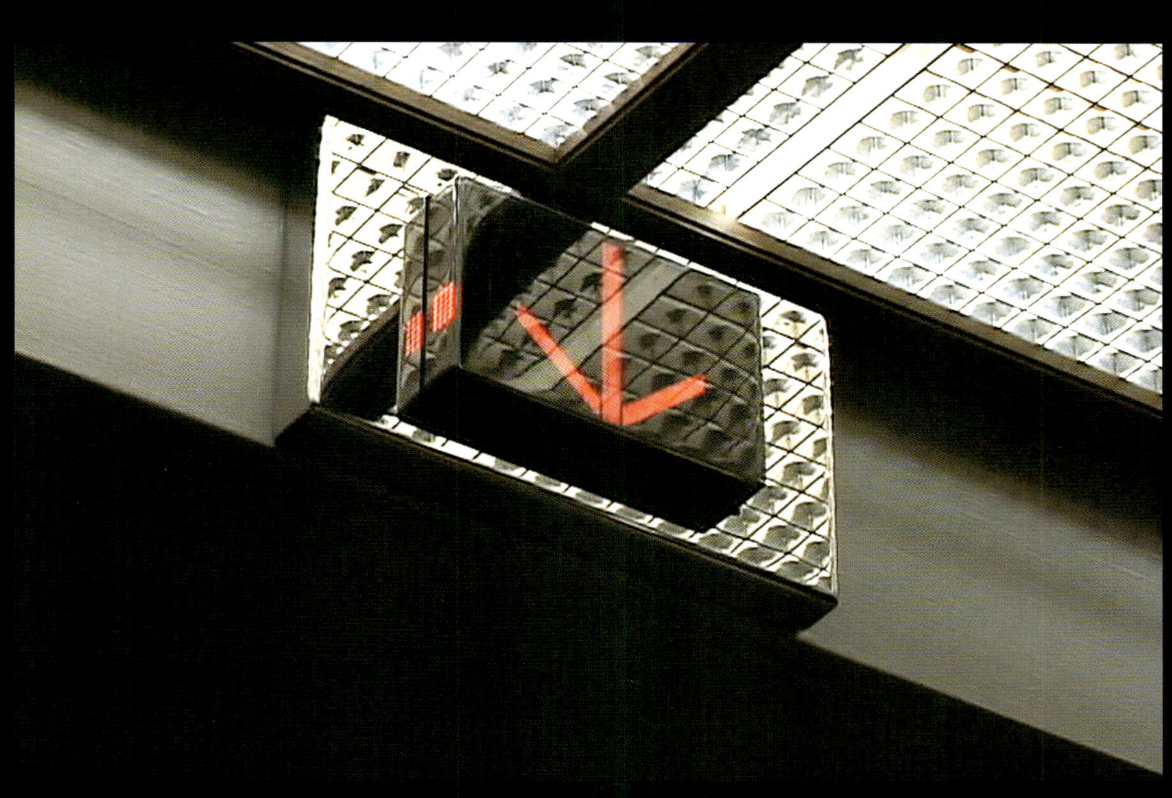

Stephan Apicella-Hitchcock

Core Samples, 2000 (with detail)
Digital C-print
9¾ x 15¾ inches

Core Samples catalogs the entirety of my high school cassette collection in miniature and presents it, in the spirit of the seventeenth century museum, with no regard to chronology or classification. Similar cassette collections of several key high school–era friends are included to indicate the collective taste of a time period. In *Core Samples* I am interested in paying homage to (and quantifying) elements and technology that no longer seem important. Any references to archeological measuring devices, geologic stratification and minimalist painting are entirely incidental, but nonetheless of interest.

Born 1968 in New York, N.Y.
Lives in Brooklyn, N.Y.

Education

1996 MFA, Rhode Island School of Design, Providence
1991 BA, Hampshire College, Amherst, Mass.

Selected Group Exhibitions

2003 *Inscribing the Temporal*, Kunsthalle Exnergasse, Vienna, Austria
Towards a Low-End Theory, Minnesota Center for Photography, Minneapolis
2002 *View*, Socrates Sculpture Park, Long Island City, N.Y.
Audio/Elevator, Art In General, New York, N.Y.
2001 *Points of Reference*, Visual Studies Workshop, Rochester, N.Y.
2000 *The Brewster Project*, Brewster, N.Y.
White Hot, Smack Mellon, Brooklyn, N.Y.

Lecture

2001 *Initial Public Offerings*, Whitney Museum of American Art, New York, N.Y.

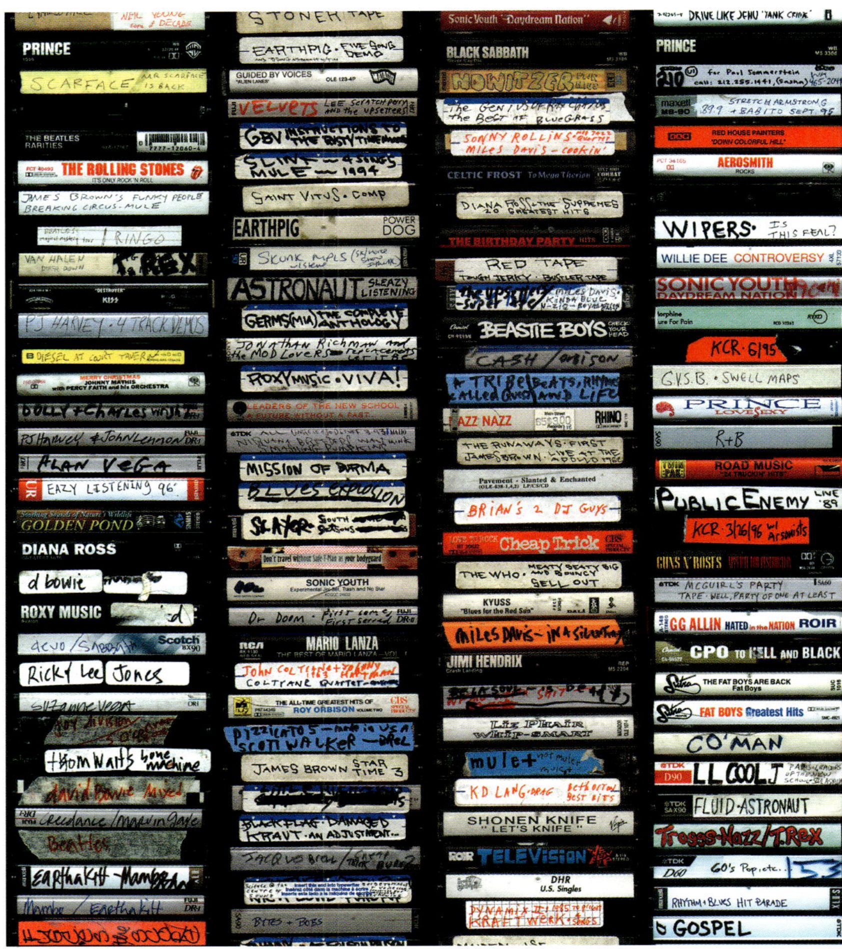

A finger is an exceptionally staggering device, and nowhere is this more evident than in the World Trade Center. Frank Lloyd Wright said in regard to technology (and fingers) that "if it keeps up, man will atrophy all his limbs but the push-button finger." I am not so sure that the great forward march of technology will turn us into bulbous headed stick people, but I do know for certain that the technology of the WTC, specifically the elevator button for floor ninety-one, did start to have a deleterious effect on my right index finger. In fact its functionality seems to be precisely the one and only thing that did not benefit from my World Views residency. Everything else was golden–ears finely attuned to the subtleties of borrowed Pierre Henri tapes; distance vision (and voyeurism) had never had such a solid workout; and I was totally in touch with the feel of that strange stuff that periodically dropped from the ceilings. I felt like a thoroughbred, except for one digit. Up and down almost every day for five months–you can imagine the wear–but pointing is rude anyway, so I believe it was a pretty sweet trade.

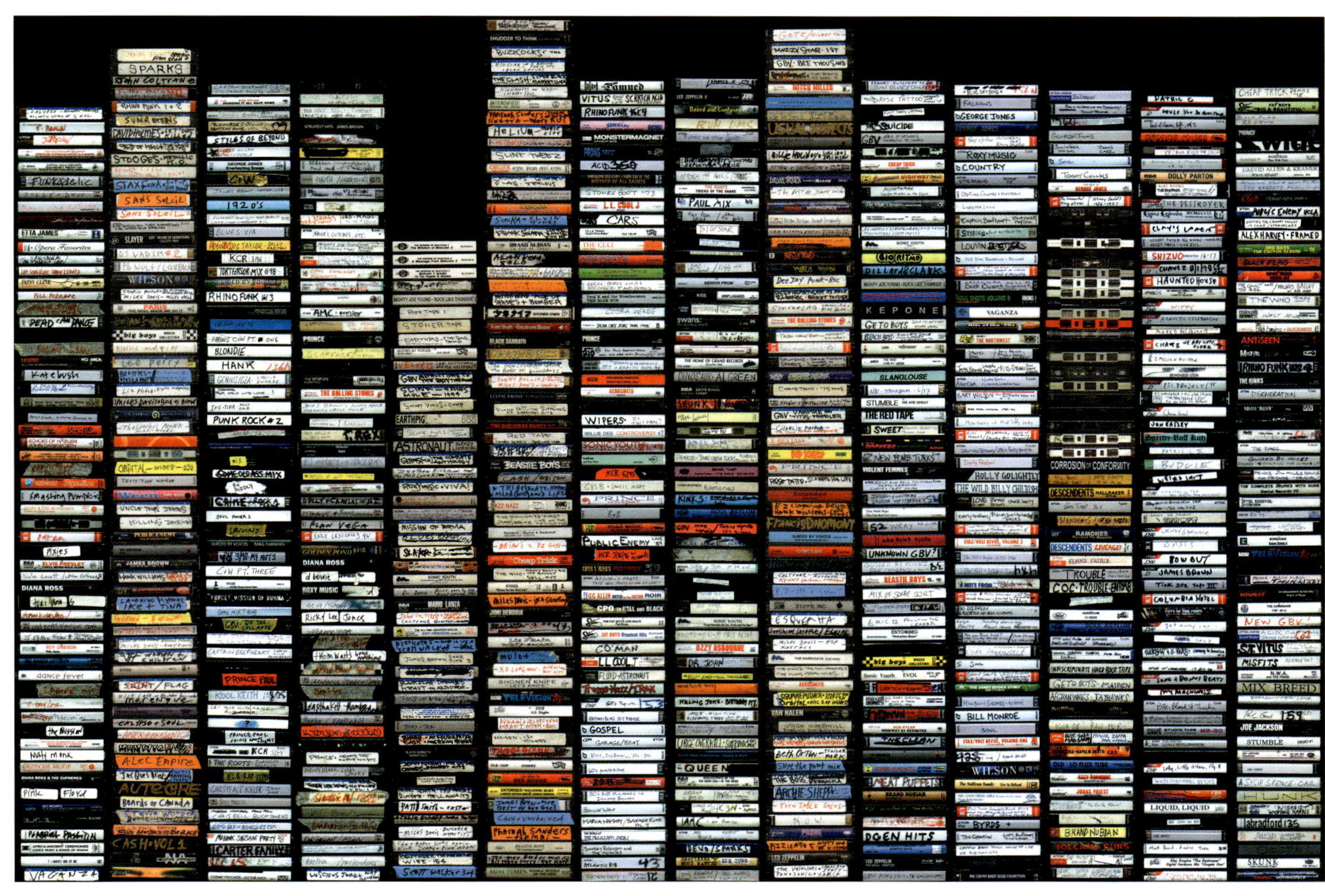

Caroline Birks

Terror in the Towers, 2000 (with detail)
CD, carpet, drop ceiling, speakers
8½ x 8 x 10 feet
Story adapted from Victoria Sherrow's book *The World Trade Center Bombing: Terror in the Towers*, 15:33 minutes

Terror in the Towers was inspired by the media frenzy that surrounded the World Trade Center bombing in 1993. A drop ceiling and carpet finish the raw space the World Views Studios occupied, and create a horizontal space for the viewer to stand in. Susan Genis reads an adapted version of Victoria Sherrow's *The World Trade Center Bombing: Terror in the Towers*, a children's story from the American Disasters series (Enslow Publishers, Inc.). It is played through speakers mounted in the drop ceiling.

Born 1966 in Montreal, Quebec
Lives in Toronto, Ontario

Education

1998 MFA, The School of the Art Institute of Chicago, Ill.
1987 BFA, Queen's University, Kingston, Ontario

Selected Solo Exhibitions

1995 *Exogyny*, The Red Head Gallery, Toronto, Ontario
1994 *Self Divisions*, The Red Head Gallery, Toronto, Ontario
1992 *The Tryst*, Hamilton Artists' Inc., Hamilton, Ontario

Selected Group Exhibitions

2000 *Retrospective*, The Red Head Gallery, Toronto, Ontario
1998 *Emerging Artists*, Vedanta Gallery, Chicago, Ill.
1998 *New Artists in Chicago*, Terra Museum of American Art, Chicago, Ill.

Set Installation

2001 *All I Want For Christmas*, The Canadian Film Centre, Toronto, Ontario

Award

1999 *Artist in the Marketplace*, The Bronx Museum of the Arts, The Bronx, N.Y.

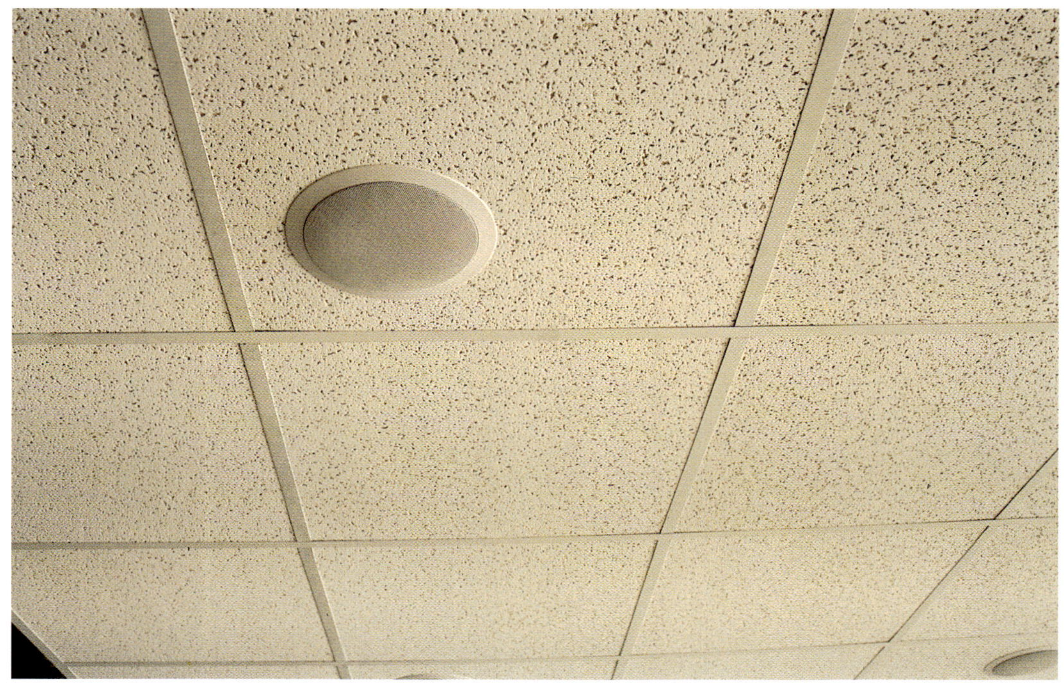

Mediated experience versus physical and personal knowledge of tragic events inspired Terror in the Towers. *My connection to the World Trade Center prior to my residency was formed by the media coverage of the 1993 bombing. Journalistic and dramatic realism, not reality itself, created my personal memories of the event, allowing me to reconstruct it dispassionately. Early in the residency a building engineer whose secretary was killed when the bomb destroyed his office gave our group a tour of the basement and garage where the blast took place. His loss made me realized how distant our experiences were, how superficial mine was in relation to his.*

This phenomenon of disparate memories formed around the same event was particularly strong after the September 11 attacks. It is impossible to reconcile the media representations with the real terror my friends and colleagues experienced. The schism between media realism and reality itself, between representation and its subject in time and space, affect our perception and understanding of what tragic events are.

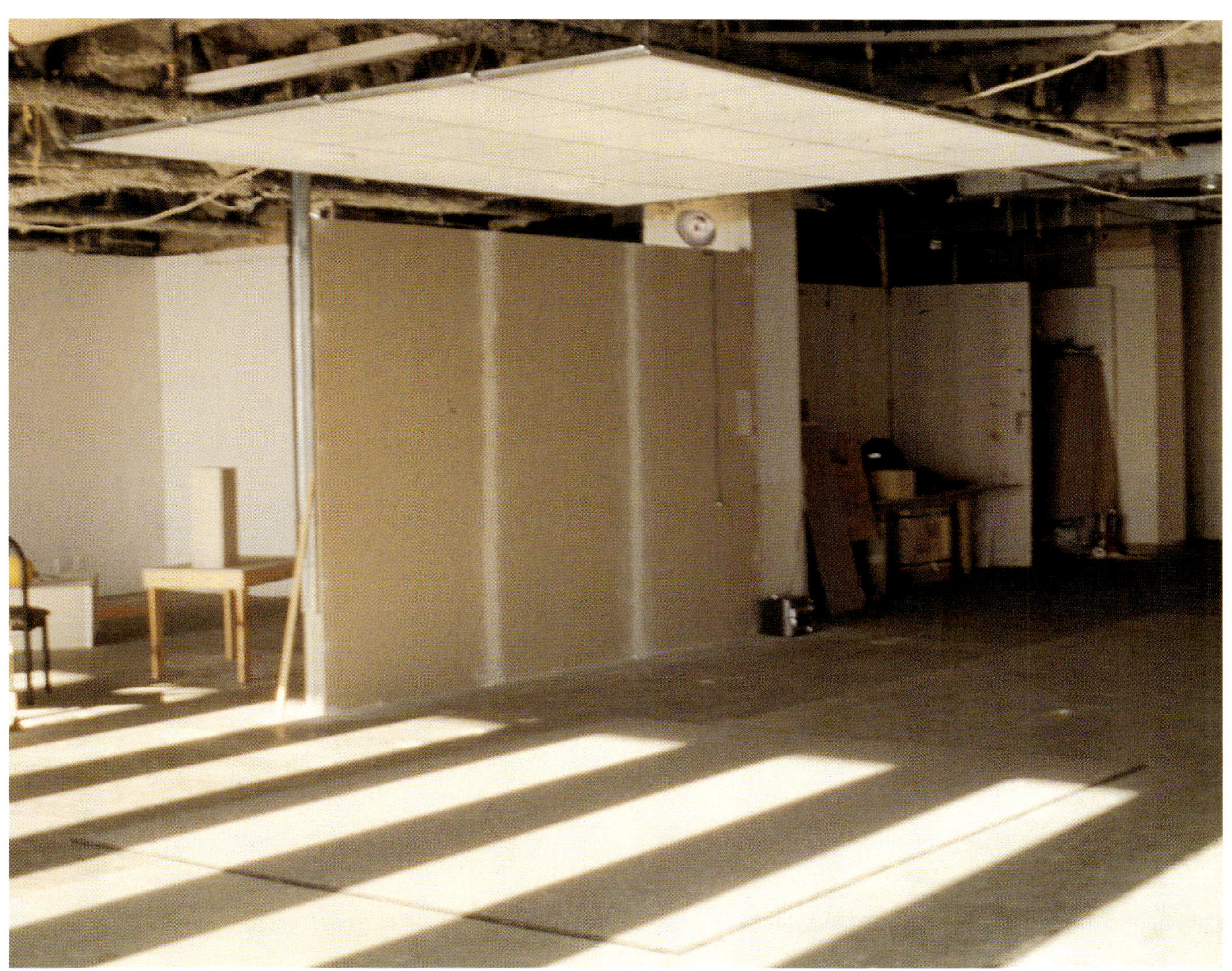

Beth Campbell

My Potential Future Based on Present Circumstances (6/7/00), 2000 (detail)
Pencil, paper
70 x 53 inches
Photo: Lori Nix

My Potential Future Based on Present Circumstances uses the simple gesture of pencil on paper to explore a far-reaching map of all the possible futures that might arise out of my simple everyday experiences. The charts also expose the various psychological locations the mind may occupy.

Born 1971 in Dwight, Ill.
Lives in New York, N.Y.

Education

1997 MFA, Ohio University, Athens
1993 BFA, Truman State University, Kirksville, Mo.

Selected Solo Exhibitions

2003 *Same As Me*, Sandroni Rey Gallery, Los Angeles, Calif.
2002 *Same As Me*, Roebling Hall, Brooklyn, N.Y.
2000 *House (A Standardized Affectation for Telepresence),* Roebling Hall, Brooklyn, N.Y.

Selected Group Exhibitions

2003 *Online*, Feigen Contemporary, New York, N.Y.
High & Inside, Marlborough Chelsea, New York, N.Y.
B-List, Hallwalls Contemporary Arts Center, Buffalo, N.Y.
2002 *Hello My Name Is . . .*, Carnegie Museum of Art, Pittsburgh, Pa.
2000 *White Room*, White Columns, New York, N.Y.

Residency

1997 Skowhegan School of Painting and Sculpture, Maine

I think about the residency and my experience in the World Trade Center all the time. I am sure part of this is due to what has happened since, but also because I could never quite get my head around those buildings. Most of my time up on the ninety-first floor was spent just looking out the window. The buildings always seemed impossible, the view made the streets of N.Y.C. look unreal, like a set or model. Standing at the base of the towers, the size and scale was inconceivable. I would often wonder about the future of the buildings. Would they become ancient remnants like the pyramids? Or would a future society implode them with the fall of capitalism? While riding the elevators up to the ninety-first floor I would eavesdrop on my fellow passengers. I would grab bits of information and wonder about their individual lives, their commutes, if their work was fulfilling or demanding. It felt like another world; the elevator transfer on the seventy-eighth floor felt like a space station.

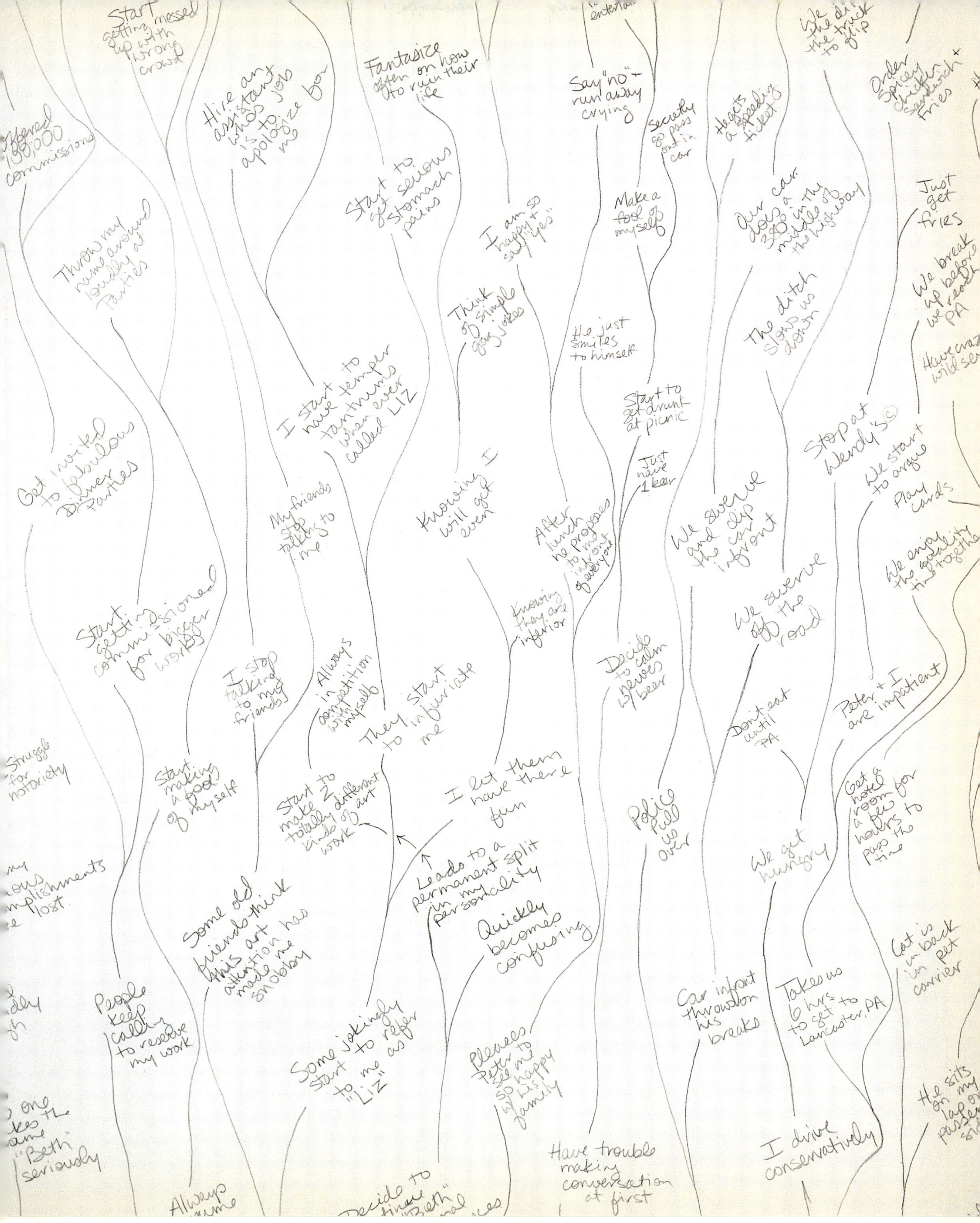
Start getting messed up with wrong crowd
Fantasize often on how to ruin their life
Say "no" + run away crying
We drive the truck to flip
Order spicy chicken sandwich + fries
Offered 100,000 commissions
Hire an assistant whose job is to apologize for me
Secretly go pass out in car
He gets a speeding ticket
Start to get serious stomach pains
I am so happy + say "yes"
Make a fool of myself
Our car does a 360 in the middle of the highway
Just get fries
Throw my name around loudly at parties
We break up before we reach PA
Think of simple gay jokes
He just smiles to himself
The ditch slows us down
I start to have temper tantrums when ever called LIZ
Start to get drunk at picnic
Stop at Wendy's
Get invited to fabulous dinner parties
Just have 1 beer
We start to argue
Play cards
My friends stop talking to me
Knowing I will get even
After lunch he proposes to me in front of everyone
We swerve and clip the car in front
We enjoy the quality time together
Start getting commissioned for bigger works
Knowing they are inferior
We swerve off the road
I stop talking to my friends
Always in competition with myself
They start to infuriate me
Decide to calm nerves w/ beer
Don't eat until PA
Peter + I are impatient
Struggle for notoriety
Start making a fool of myself
Start to make 2 totally different kinds of art work
I let them have there fun
Police pull us over
Get a hotel room for a few hours to pass the time
Leads to a permanent split in my personality
We get hungry
my accomplishments lost
Some old friends think this art attention has made me snobby
Quickly becomes confusing
Cat is in back in pet carrier
People keep calling to reserve my work
Car in front throws on his breaks
Takes us 6 hrs to get to Lancaster, PA
Some jokingly start to refer to me as "Liz"
Pleases Peter to see me so happy w/ his family
He sits on my lap on passenger side
No one takes the name "Beth" seriously
Have trouble making conversation at first
I drive conservatively
Always
Decide to

Jaime Davidovich

Mile-High Series, 2000
Rear video-projection on vellum of views from the ninety-first floor
Various durations, silent
8 x 10 inches each

Brooklyn Bridge Sunset, 2000
Video projection
7:30 mintues, silent
Real-time recording of the Brooklyn Bridge at sunset

Born 1936 in Buenos Aires, Argentina
Lives in New York, N.Y.

Education
Escuela Nacional, Buenos Aires, Argentina

Selected Solo Exhibitions

1999 *Paintings in Real Time*, Lehman College Art Gallery, N.Y.
1998 *Zocalo*, Museum of Modern Art, Buenos Aires, Argentina
1991 *Forces/Farces*, Exit Art, New York, N.Y.

Selected Group Exhibitions

2003 *View from Above*, Deep Listening Center, Kingston, N.Y.
1997 *Legacy/Legado*, The Old State House, Hartford, Conn.
1995 *Twenty-fifth Anniversary Exhibition, Part III: Reaffirming Spirituality*, El Museo del Barrio, New York, N.Y.
1994 *Recordando el Futuro*, ICI de Buenos Aires, Argentina
1992 *Americas*, Monasterio de Santa Clara, Moguer, Spain

During my residency I worked on the ninety-first floor regularly. I started very early in the morning, around 6:00 A.M., and videotaped the views from my assigned space. These views contained the night mist of the pre-awakened city. I came back later on in the afternoon and recorded the sunset. I was interested in capturing, in real time, the passing of time from this "mile-high" perspective.

My experience videotaping the New York landscape before and after rush hour made a significant impact on my work. When I look at the videos now, it is not a "past time" but a real time converted into mist and dust. The events of 9/11 have dramatically altered the context and meaning of my project. The landscapes I videotaped now exist in our collective memory and are full of anger, sadness and a range of other complex emotions.

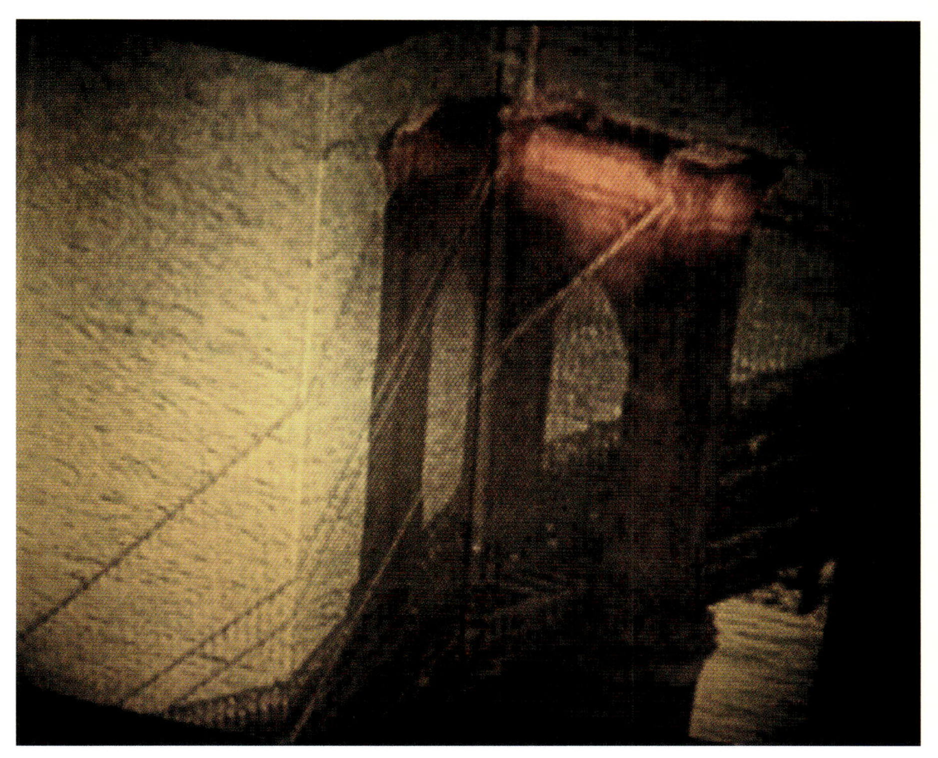

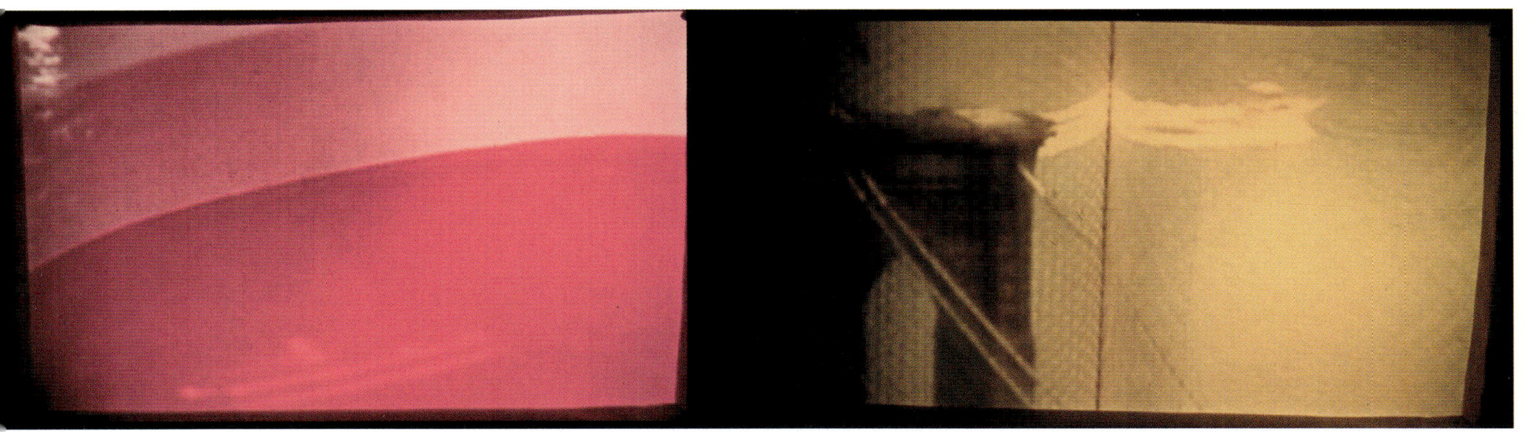

Adam Frank

Illuminator, 2000
Steel, mirror, lens, light bulb
24 x 9 x 8 inches

Illuminator uses a lens, a mirror and a common 200-watt light bulb to create something that is simultaneously a symbol, an image and a real thing.

Born 1970 in San Francisco, Calif.
Lives in New York, N.Y.

Education

1992 BFA, Rhode Island School of Design, Providence

Selected Group Exhibitions

2003 Eyebeam, New York, N.Y.
2002 *Meta-Forms*, Colgate University, Hamilton, N.Y.
1995 NTT InterCommunication Conference (ICC), Tokyo, Japan

Residencies

2003 Eyebeam Emerging Fields Residency, New York, N.Y.
2000 The Banff Centre, Alberta

Awards

2001 New York Foundation for the Arts
1998 *NewMedia* magazine's New Media Invision Award
1997 International Digital Media Award for Best Animation

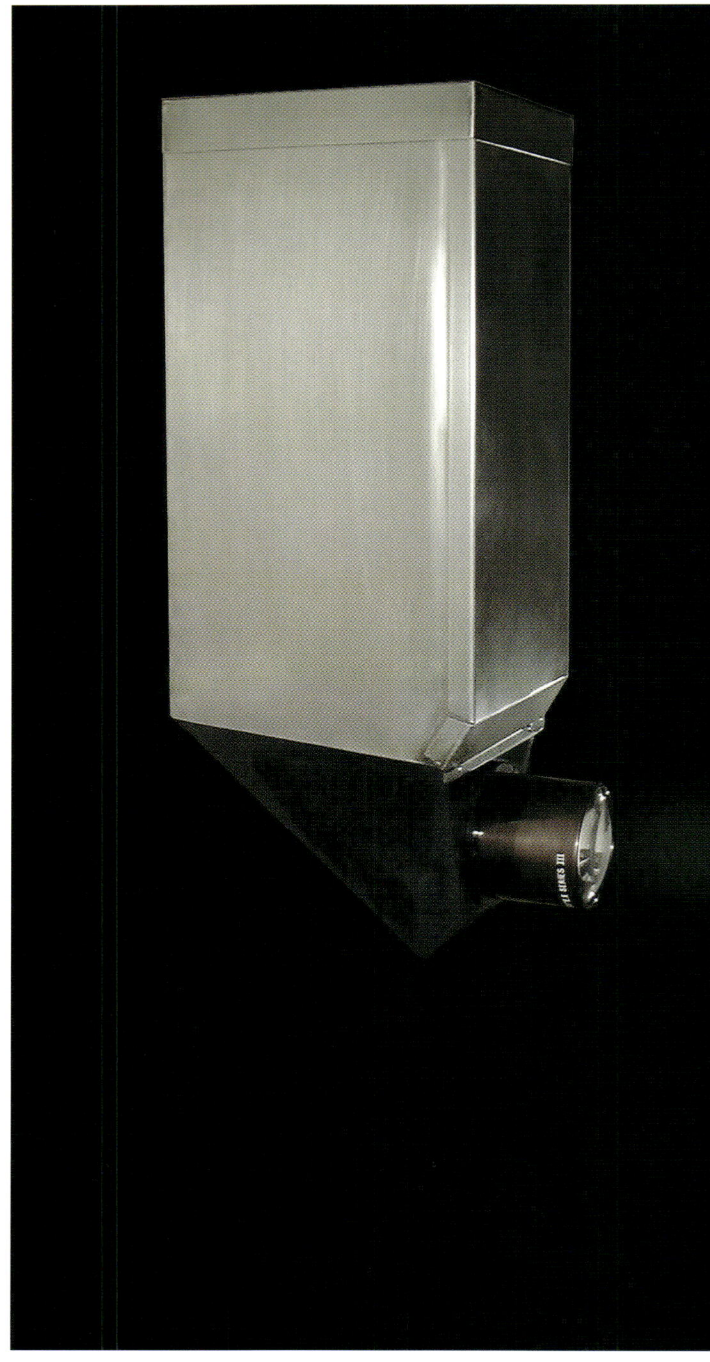

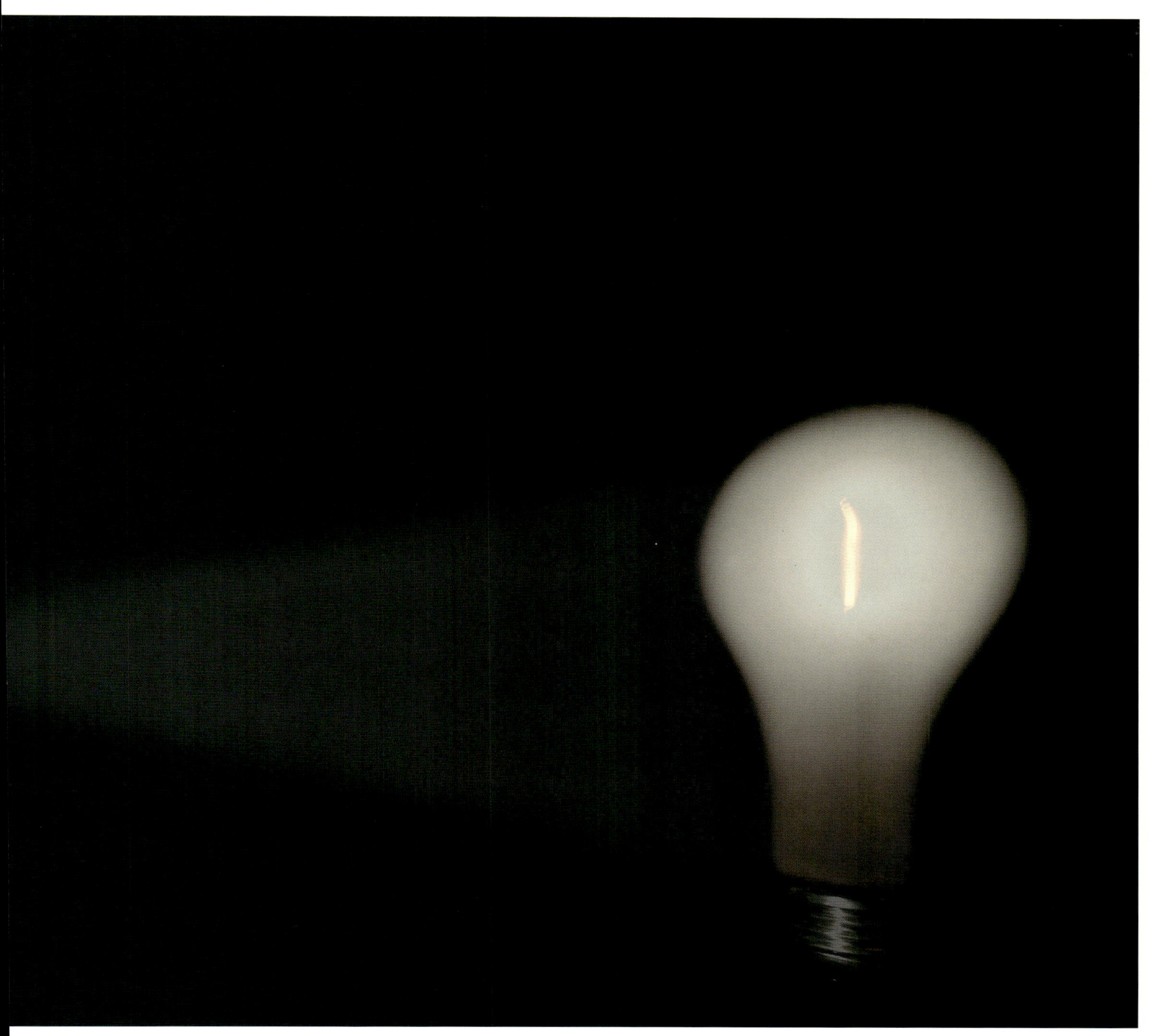

Susan Graham

Heaven or Hell, 2000
Series of six photographs
8 x 10 inches each

Born 1968 in Dayton, Ohio
Lives in New York, N.Y.

Education

1992 School of Visual Arts, New York, N.Y.
1990 BFA, Ohio State University, Columbus
1987 Ohio State University, Columbus

Selected Solo Exhibitions

2003 *Dreams and Arrays*, Avram Gallery, Long Island University, Southampton, N.Y.
2002 *Susan Graham and Julianne Swartz*, Schroeder Romero Gallery, Brooklyn, N.Y.
2001 *Insomnia: Project at the Chelsea Hotel*, Holly Solomon Gallery, New York, N.Y.
Insomnia, Photology Gallery, Milan, Italy

Selected Group Exhibitions

2002 *Five by Five*, Whitney Museum of American Art at Philip Morris, New York, N.Y.
Officina America/American Atelier, Galleria d'Arte Moderna, Bologna, Italy

Awards

2001 The Pollock-Krasner Foundation
1999 New York Foundation for the Arts

On the ground it was never so obvious to me how large the Empire State Building really is—there's always other tall buildings between myself and it—but my studio windows in the North Tower of the WTC looked straight into the windows of that building from a distance of more than fifty blocks. Looking down on the city, which was dwarfed from so high up, I had a view that was strangely dichotomous: A closeness to the openness of the sky or "heavens" was coupled with a view down onto the city that made the goings on below appear tiny and frantic. Thus the title I gave to the series of photos I ended up making, Heaven or Hell. *There was a dialogue between the Twin Towers and the Empire State Building that was really obvious only from the higher floors of these buildings. The three structures stood alone above the city. I found myself constructing the Twin Towers and the Empire State Building out of sugar and making landscape "portraits" in which the three buildings acted out some sort of triangular relationship.*

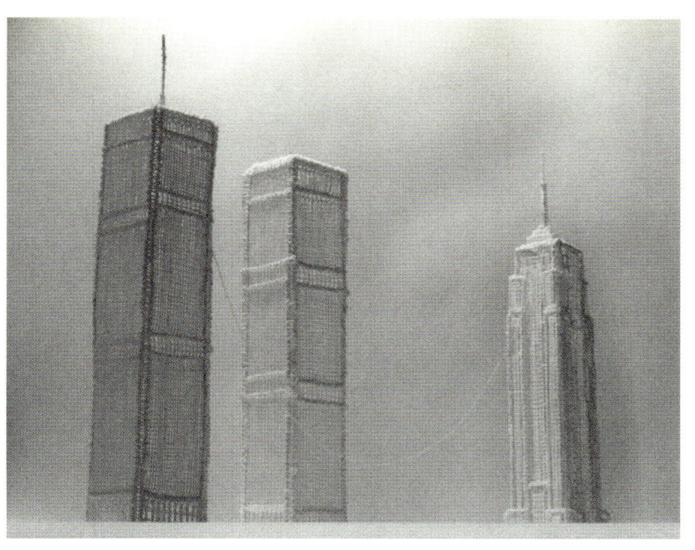
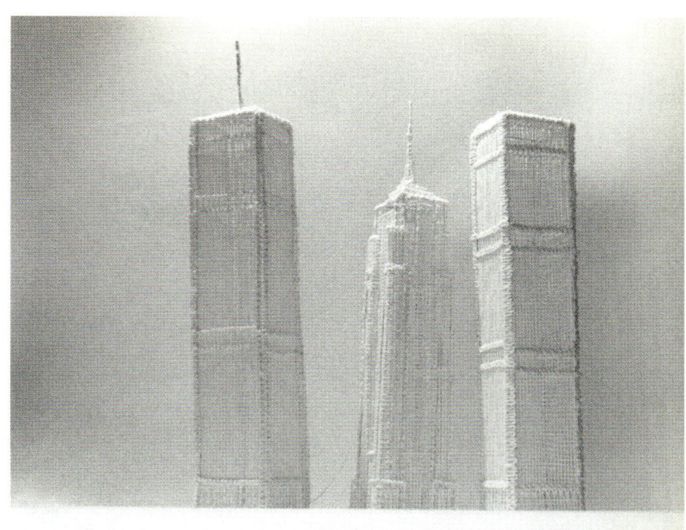
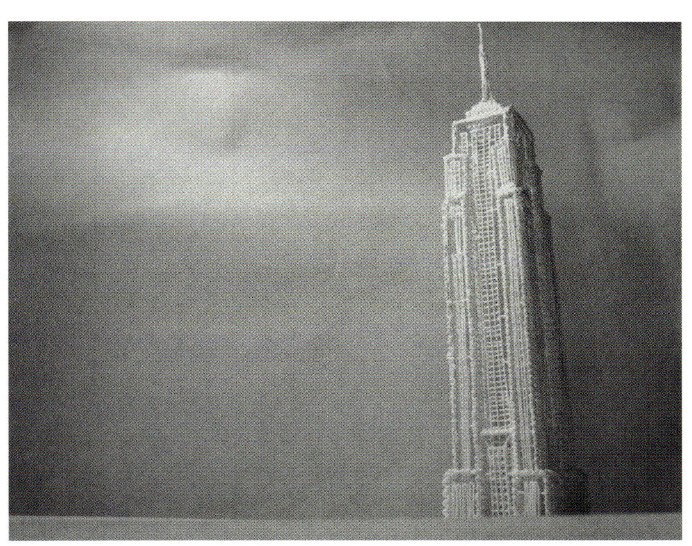
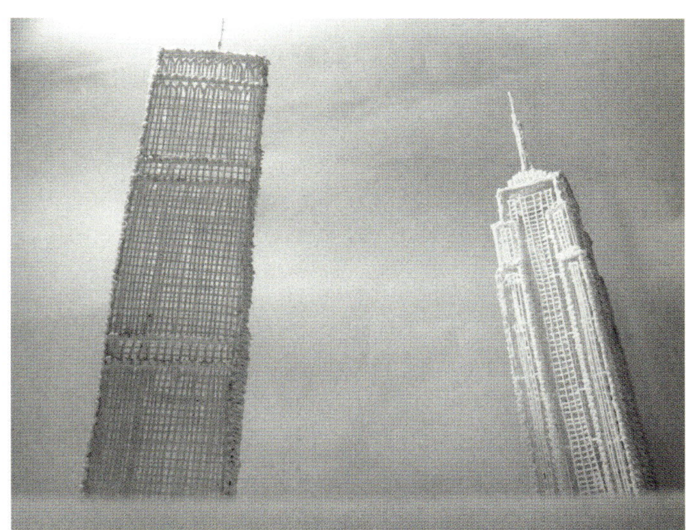
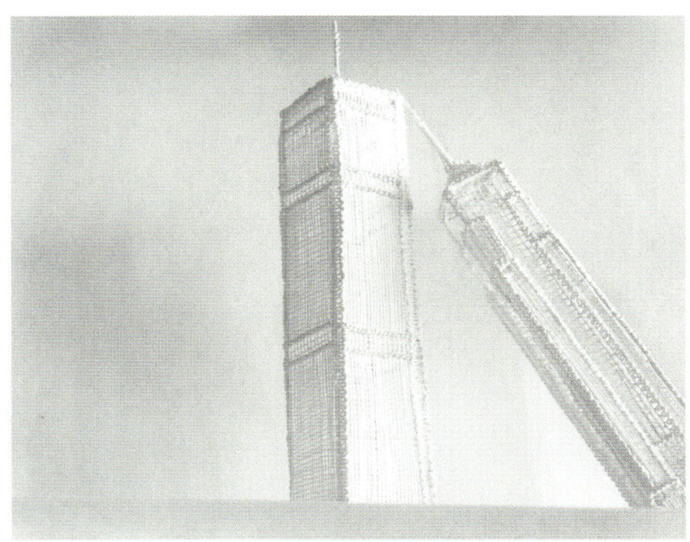
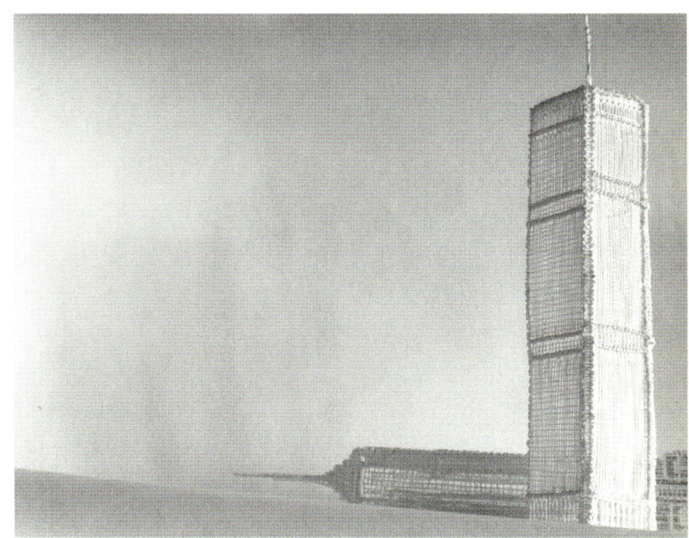

Kira Lynn Harris

River, 2001
Pigment print on paper
48 x 48 inches

Born 1963 in Los Angeles, Calif.
Lives in New York, N.Y.

Education

1998–99 Whitney Museum of American Art Independent Study Program, New York, N.Y.
1998 MFA, California Institute of the Arts, Valencia
1996 BA, University of California, Santa Cruz

Selected Group Exhibitions

2003 *Urban Aesthetics*, California African American Museum, Los Angeles
2002 *Ironic Iconic*, The Studio Museum in Harlem, New York, N.Y.
2001 *Freestyle*, The Studio Museum in Harlem, New York, N.Y.
2000 *The Light Show*, GAle GAtes et al., Brooklyn, N.Y.
White Hot, Smack Mellon, Brooklyn, N.Y.

Residencies

2003 Art Omi International Artists' Colony, Omi, N.Y.
Harvestworks, New York, N.Y.
2001 The Studio Museum in Harlem, New York, N.Y.

In the spring of 2000 I began a residency at the World Trade Center. Making art in a building that housed corporate and commercial enterprises was daunting and I reached an impasse. Since the mid nineties my work had consisted primarily of large-scale installations. These works composed my entry into the discourse of minimalism and the history of installations as investigations of space and perception. In many pieces I posited an intersection of the phenomenological with issues of culture, race and gender.

During my WTC residency I made a site-specific installation for an off-site show. I made polaroids of the changes I was creating in that space and those photos, scanned then enlarged, were exhibited at the WTC Open Studios. It was my first time exhibiting photos. Now, in addition to installations, my current media include photography, video and sound as well as installations that often provide a disorienting experience for the viewer.

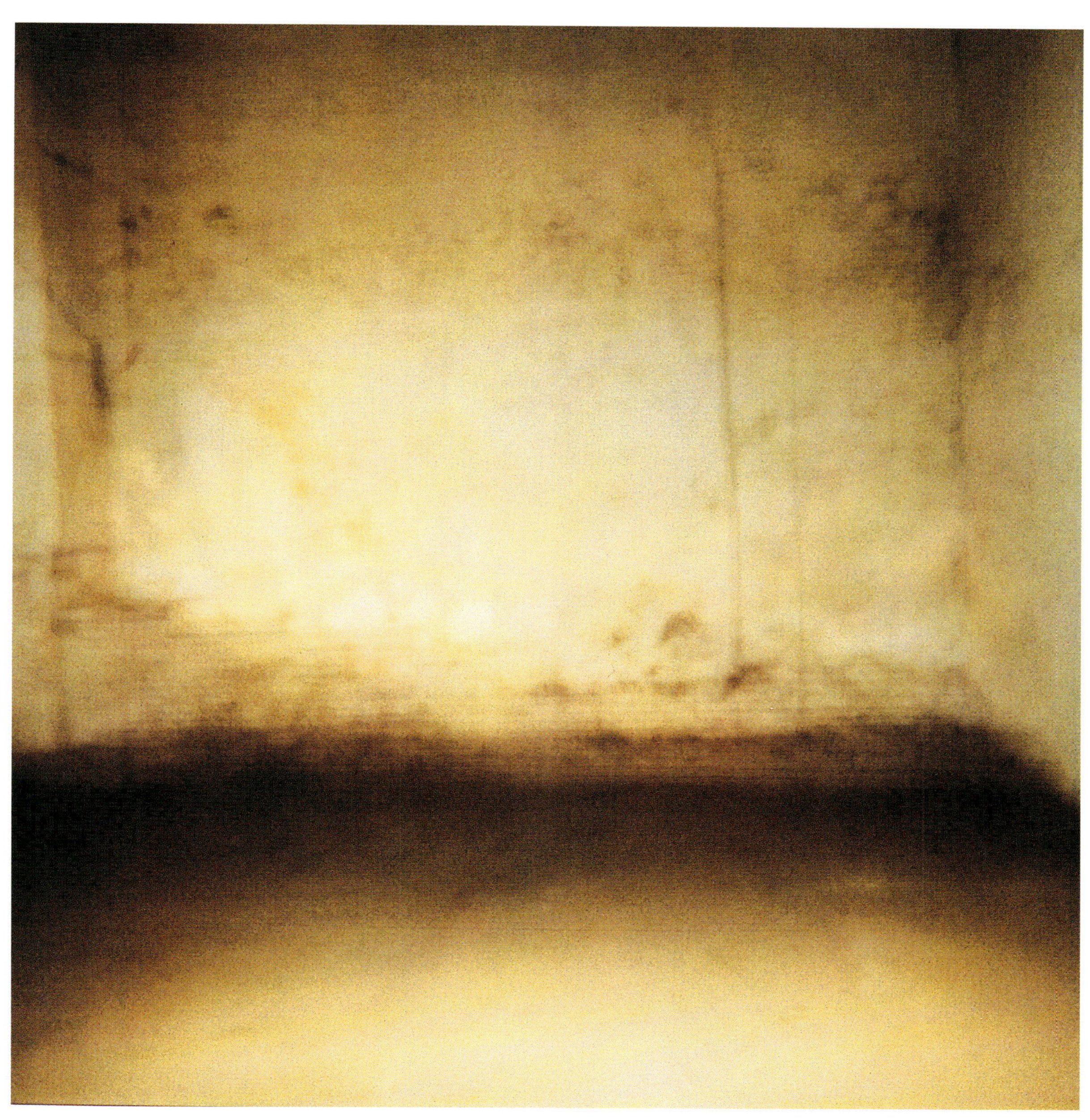

Kristin Lucas

5-Minute Break, 2001 (stills)
Video animation
4:35 minutes
Courtesy of Electronic Arts Intermix and Postmasters Gallery, New York, N.Y.

Born 1968 in Davenport, Iowa
Lives in Brooklyn, N.Y.

Education

1994 The Cooper Union School of Art, New York, N.Y.

Selected Solo Exhibitions

2003 *Celebrations for Breaking Routine*, Foundation for Art & Creative Technology, Liverpool, U.K.
2001 *Alias*, Postmasters, New York, N.Y.
2001 *The Electric Donut* (collaboration with Joe McKay), New Museum of Contemporary Art, New York, N.Y.
2000 *Temporary Housing for the Despondent Virtual Citizen*, The O.K. Center for Contemporary Art, Linz, Austria

Residencies

1999 ARCUS, Moriya Manabi-no-Sato, Ibaraki, Japan
1998 P.S.1 National Studio Program, Long Island City, N.Y.

Awards

2001 *Saint-Gervais Gevène Prix*, 9e Biennale de l'image en movement, Genève, Switzerland
2000 The Downtown Arts Project's Colbert Award for Excellence, New York, N.Y.

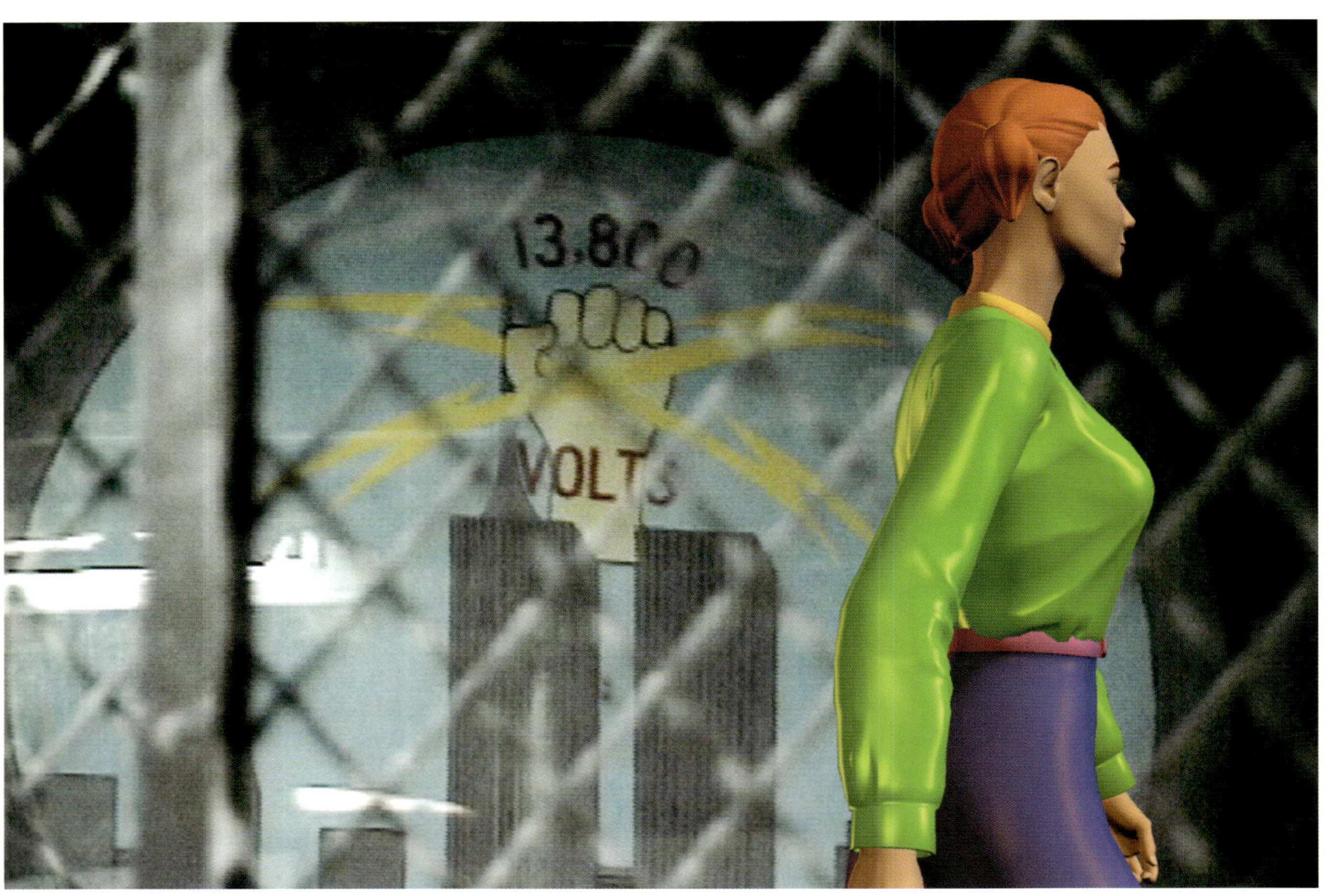

Getting there notes: A turnstile empties a body into a survivalist zone triggering muscle memory that has not been in use since that exact moment the day before. Blaring noise and bright fluorescent lights overwhelm and excite as you stand in line at a coffee shop that specializes in, yet peculiarly does not smell like, coffee. Security authorization acknowledgement by a red glowing panel on a three-foot-high metal box. Conversation in the elevator is again about the elevator—there are experts. Whoosh. Nervous smiles. Professional osmosis. Feeling confident that I am going to get through that stack of paperwork today. What paperwork? Sheepishly I wave and flash my pass to security guards en route to a second set of elevators. I spend this elevator ride alone wondering how to translate that paper-work vibe into something constructive.

My studio does not have a view. A howling draft from the freight elevator rolls through the gap in the doorway. I spend my after-noon lost in the core of the building, trying to figure out how to catch a ride from B2 to ninety-one—only to realize that I must first catch a freight elevator down to B6.

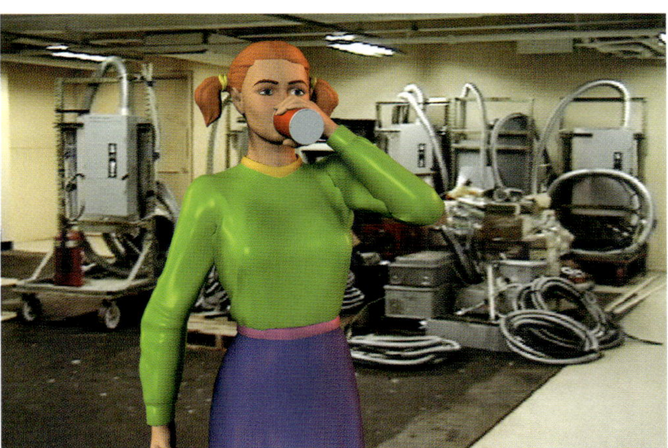

Joan Cobb Marsh

Plaza, WTC, NY, 2000
Oil on canvas
24 x 24 inches

Born 1938 in Long Island, N.Y.
Lives in Provincetown, Mass.

Education

1961 Castle Hill School for the Arts, Truro, Mass.
1960 BFA, Rochester Institute of Technology, N.Y.
1955–60 Cape Cod School of Art, Mass.

Selected Solo Exhibitions

1999 Eclipse Gallery, Boston, Mass.
1998 Addison Holmes Gallery, Orleans, Mass.
1997 Ellen Harris Gallery, Provincetown, Mass.

Selected Group Exhibitions

2002 Kiley Court Gallery, Provincetown, Mass.
1997 Berta Walker Gallery, Provincetown, Mass.
1996 *Secret Garden Tour*, Cape Cod Museum of Fine Arts, Brewster, Mass.
1995 *Trees*, Provincetown Art Association and Museum, Mass.

Residency

2003 C-Scape Dune Shack, Provincetown, Mass.

Although my residency was a short three months, it left enhanced memories. They stay with me even as I paint today. Manhattan's frenetic city life contrasted vividly with the silent cloud-lit WTC studio space.

Working early in the morning (6 A.M. till 11 A.M.) I found myself mostly alone. A big heavy metal door slammed noisily and securely behind me.

A clear, calm serenity saturated the studio. It inhabited my thoughts and influenced my paintings:

- *Windows engulfed in clouds, iridescent whites only a few sky blues could penetrate.*
- *Cloud-light tumbling in through wall windows—introducing new sensations, every day, every hour, every moment.*
- *The city, way below and far away, experienced with one sense only . . . the visual. Another sense . . . sound . . . unused.*
- *Long city vistas, glimpses of rare motifs—shadows and illuminations dancing quickly across buildings, bridges, roads . . . as clouds marched over Manhattan.*
- *And one day . . . a special gift . . . my most lingering memory. An intact 9 x 12 sheet of white paper—riding way up air currents . . . a free wind/cloud ride. Bubbling and bouncing over the silent city. For my eyes only.*

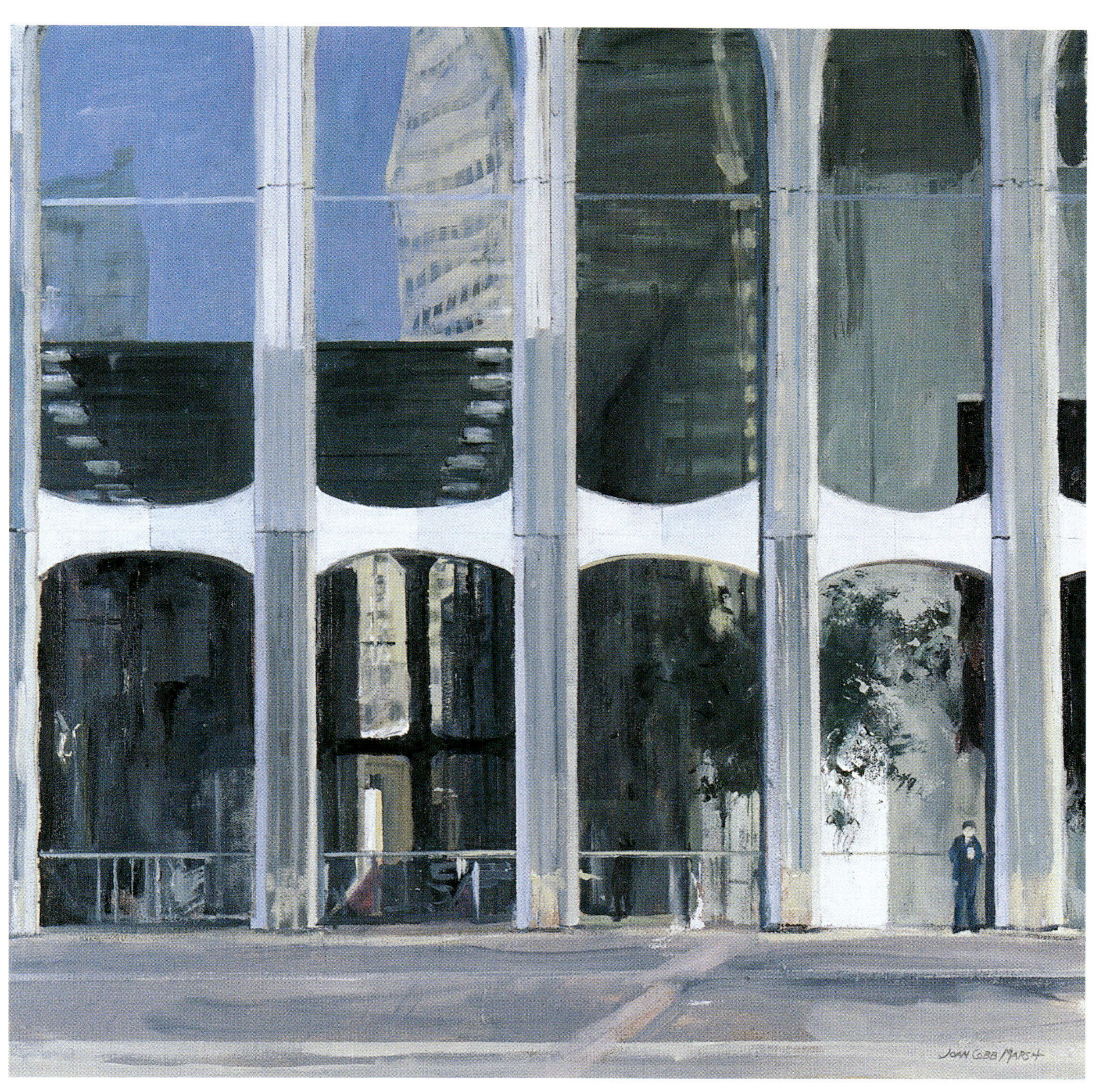
JOAN COBB MARSH

Sergio Muñoz-Sarmiento

Sculpture (with meaning missing) #2, 2000
Drywall, wood
37 x 73 x 60 inches

Sculpture (with meaning missing) #1, 2000
Drywall, wood, photograph
36 x 24 x 24 inches

Born 1968 in El Paso, Tex.
Lives in Ithaca, N.Y.

Education

Current J.D. candidate, Cornell Law School, Ithaca, N.Y.
1997–98 Whitney Museum of American Art Independent Study Program, New York, N.Y.
1997 MFA, California Institute of the Arts, Valencia

Selected Solo Exhibitions

2001 *In the Trace of the Law*, Deep River Gallery, Los Angeles, Calif.
1999 *Copula in Effigy*, Apex Art, New York, N.Y.
(Periods), Institute of Contemporary Art, Portland, Maine

Selected Group Exhibitions

2002 *Up Close*, Armory Center for the Arts, Pasadena, Calif.
What about Hegel (and you)?, Brigitte March, Stuttgart, Germany
2001 *Song Poems*, Cohan, Leslie & Brown, New York, N.Y.
Capital Art, Track 16 Gallery, Santa Monica, Calif.
2000 *ES2000 International Biennial of Standards*, CECUT, Centro Cultural Tijuana, Mexico
1999 *Five Continents and One City*, Museum of Mexico City, Mexico

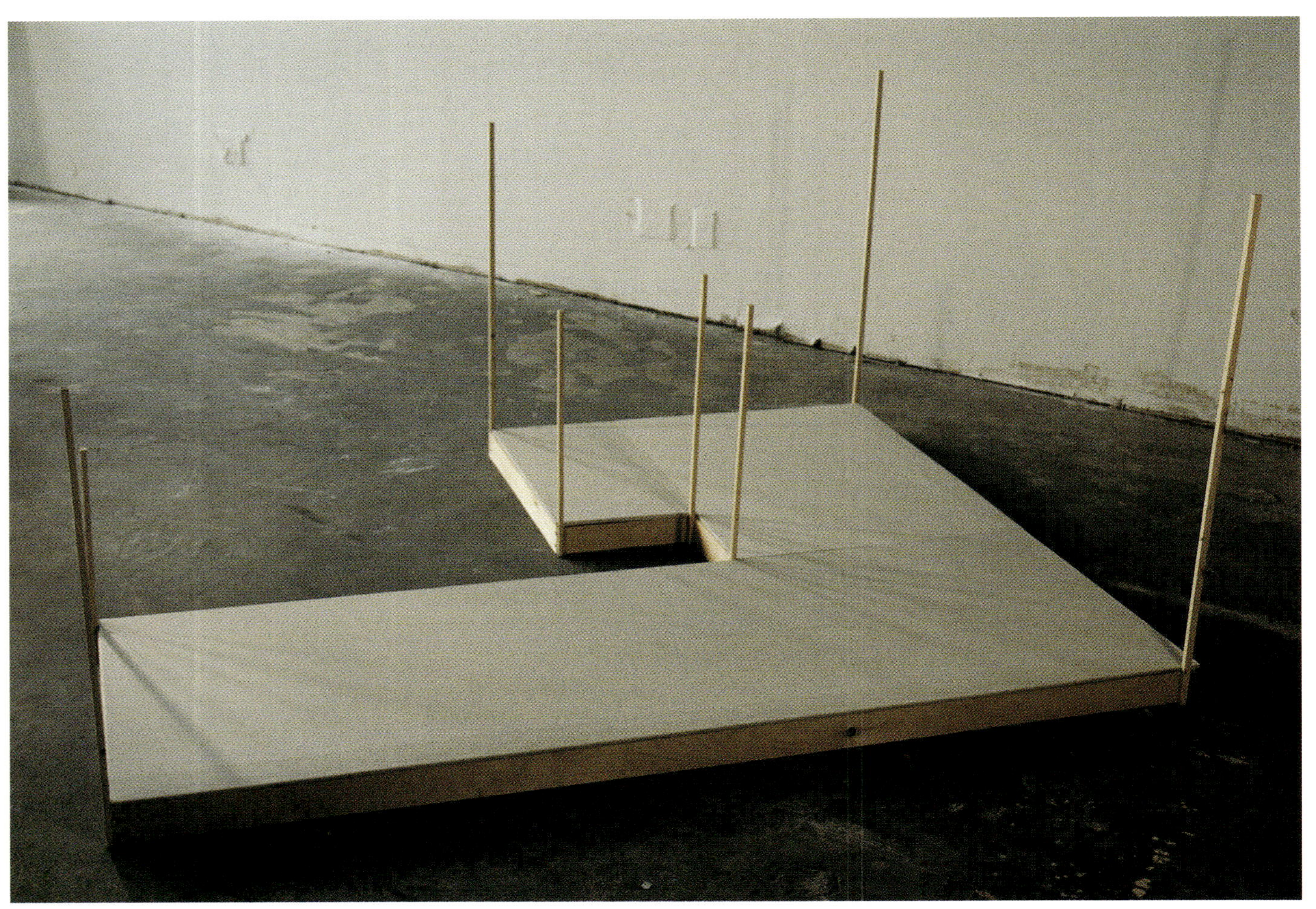

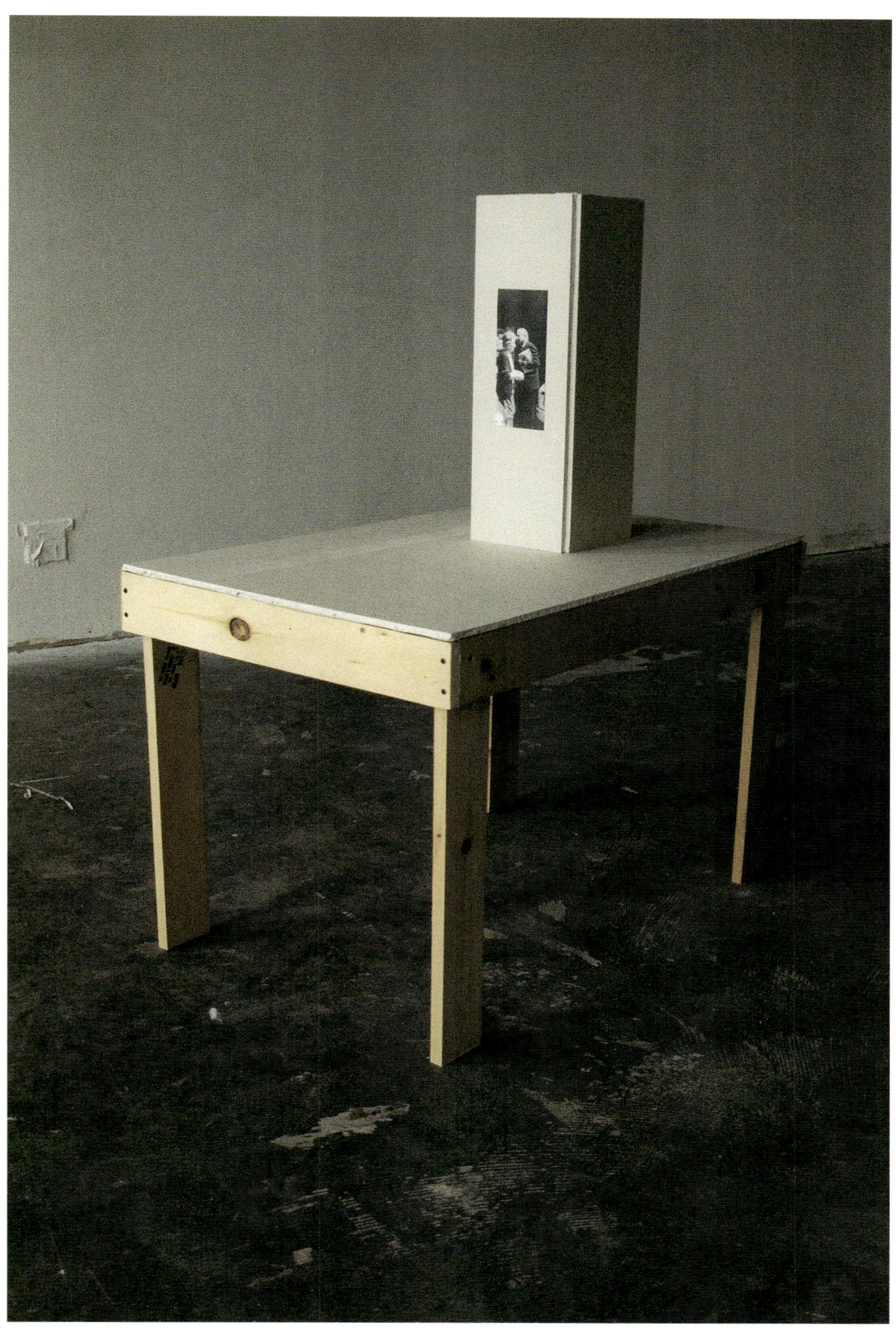

Christian Nguyen

The Lotus Eater, 2000 (still)
DVD, 7:20 minutes

A Thousand Peaks and Myriad Ravines, 2000
(Installation view during fog, sunset and evening)
Aluminum studs and drywall
85 x 180 inches

Born 1968 in Saigon, Vietnam
Lives in New York, N.Y.

Education

2000 MFA, Hunter College/CUNY, New York, N.Y.
1990 BFA, The Cooper Union School of Art, New York, N.Y.
1986 International Baccalaureate, United Nations International School, New York, N.Y.

Selected Solo Exhibitions

2003 *Novus Ordo Seclorum*, Diesel Denim Gallery, New York, N.Y.
Alteration & Habitation (two-person show), Cuchifritos, New York, N.Y.

Selected Group Exhibitions

2002 *Microviews*, Municipal Art Society, New York, N.Y.
Dining Haul: Unpacked No. 4—Food Inspired, Food Used and Food Digested Art, Meatpacking District, New York, N.Y.
Superlounge, GAle GAtes et al., Brooklyn. N.Y.
2001 *Something/Nothing: Passport to the State of Fluxus*, Art in General, New York, N.Y.
2000 *Havana Biennale*, Instituto Cubano del Arte e Industria Cinematograficos, Cuba
Foreign Bodies, White Columns, New York, N.Y.

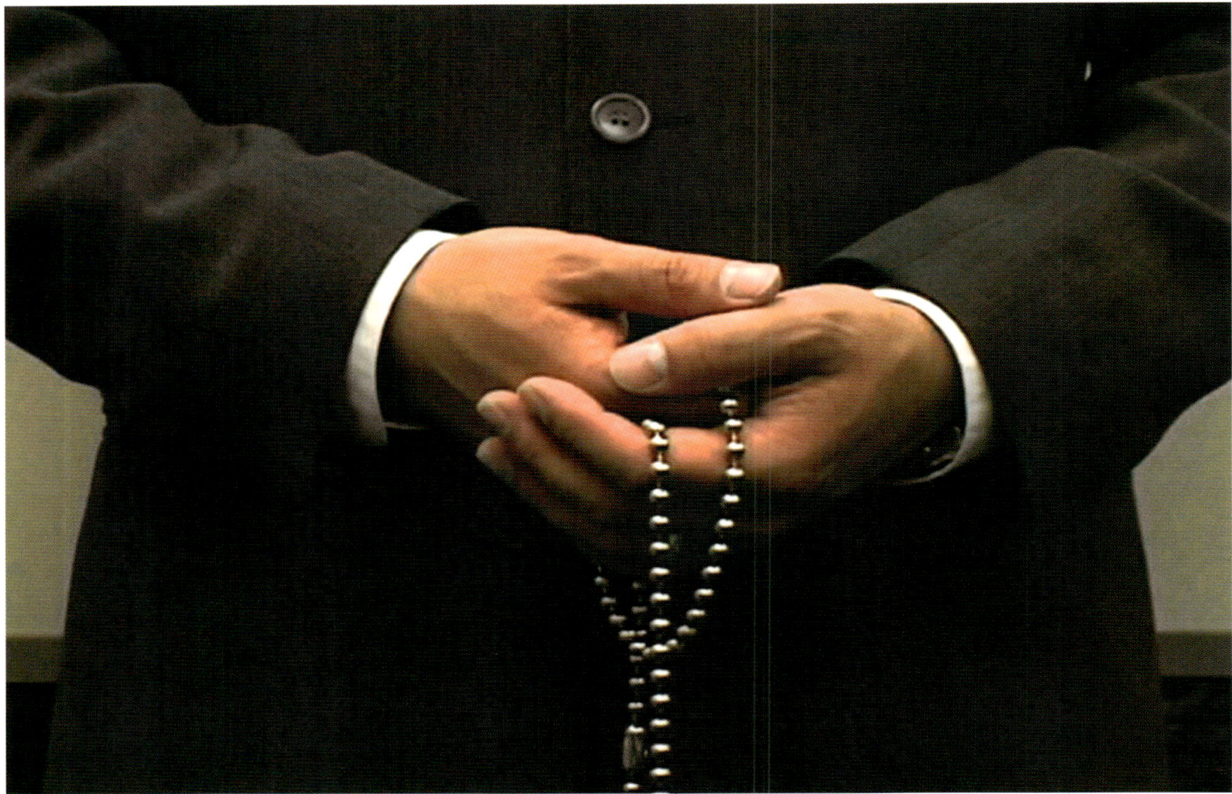

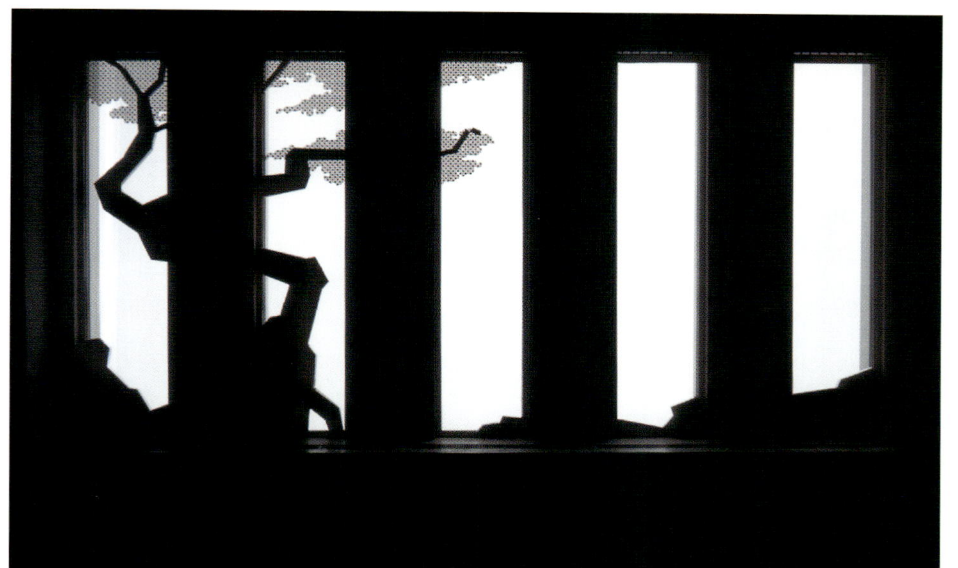

The site for the World Views residency was charged with an intensity that was impossible to ignore. The physicality of the building, the spectacular aerial views and the iconography of the buildings themselves inspired the work I made. The raw studio spaces provided a direct contact to the building. There were no carpets or layers of drywall or cubicles to mute the groans and rumbles of the building. I felt at times that I was inside a giant, seeing from his eyes the city as a big landscape, or the sun rising in a time zone far away.

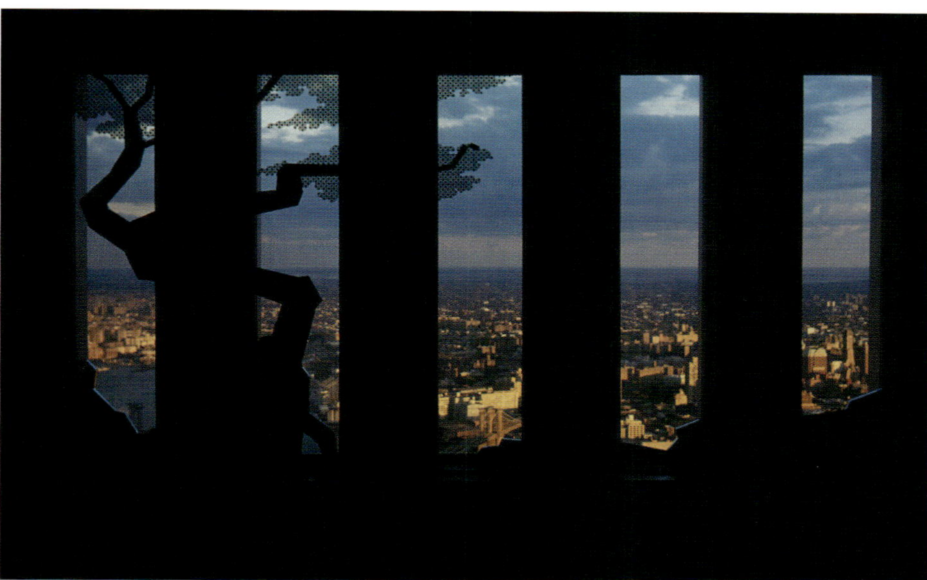

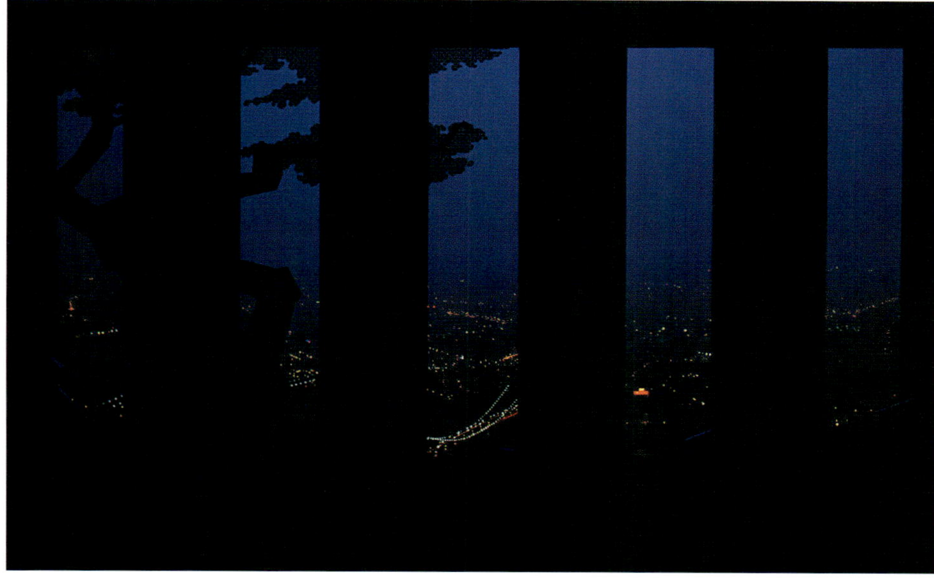

Olu Oguibe

Women of Substance: 100 Paintings, 2000
Installation view

Women of Substance: Ida B. Wells, 2000
Acrylic on canvas
24 x 30 inches

Women of Substance: Oum Kulthum, 2000
Acrylic on canvas
24 x 30 inches

Born 1964 in Aba, Nigeria
Lives in New York, N.Y. and Storrs, Conn.

Education

1992 University of London, U.K.
1986 BA, University of Nigeria

Selected Exhibitions

2003 *Olu Oguibe/William Kentridge: Next Flag 2,* Casino Luxembourg Forum d'Art Contemporain, Luxembourg
2nd Biennale of Ceramics in Contemporary Art, Studio Fontana, Albisola, Italy
The American Effect, Whitney Museum of American Art, New York, N.Y.
B.P.S Espace de Creation Contemporain, Chaleroi, Belgium
Black President: The Art and Legacy of Fela Anikulapo-Kuti, New Museum of Contemporary Art, New York, N.Y.
Migros Museum für Gegenwartskunst, Zürich, Switzerland

2002 *Family*, The Aldrich Museum, Ridgefield, Conn.
A Doll's House, Henie Onstad Kunstsenter, Oslo, Norway

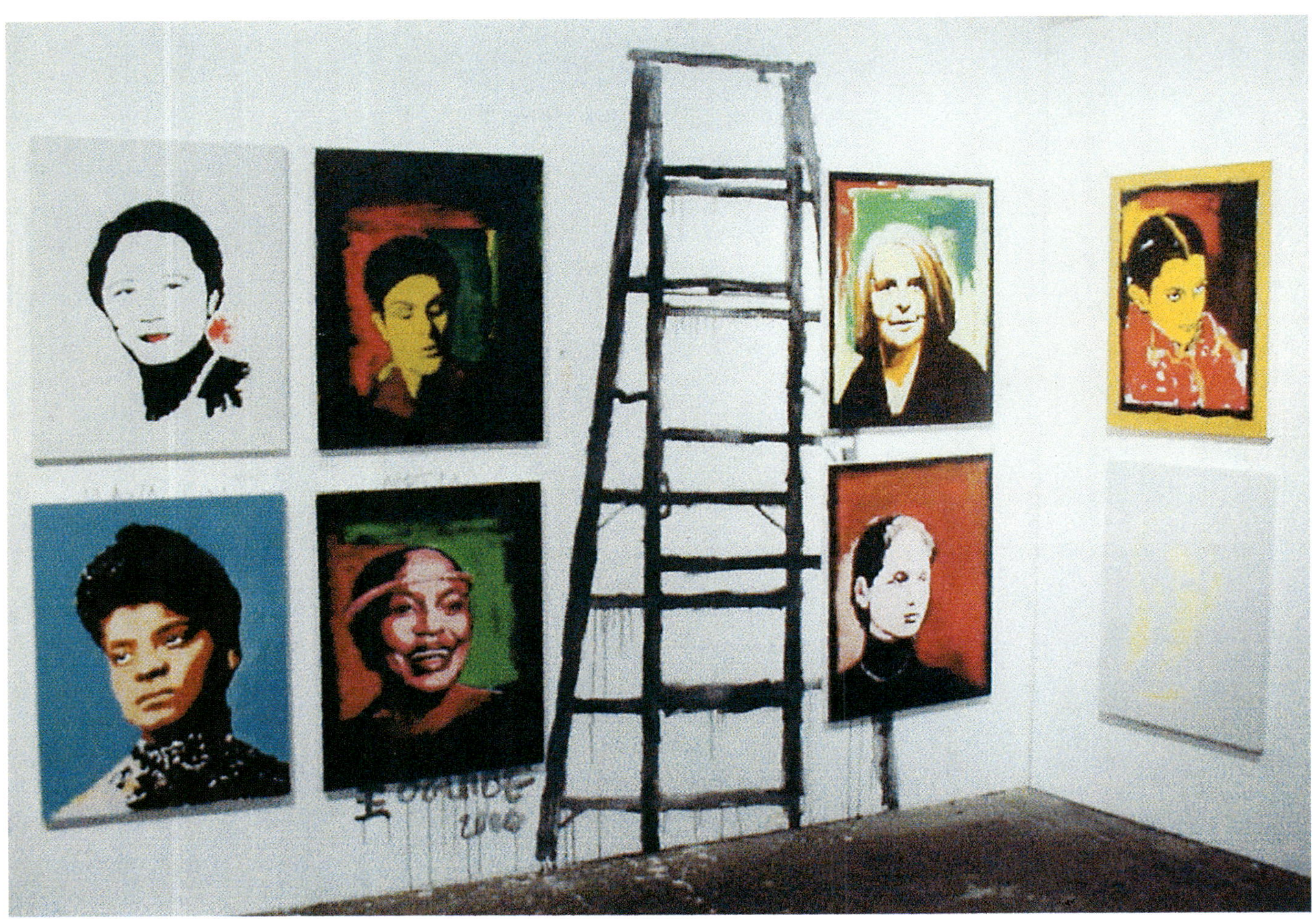

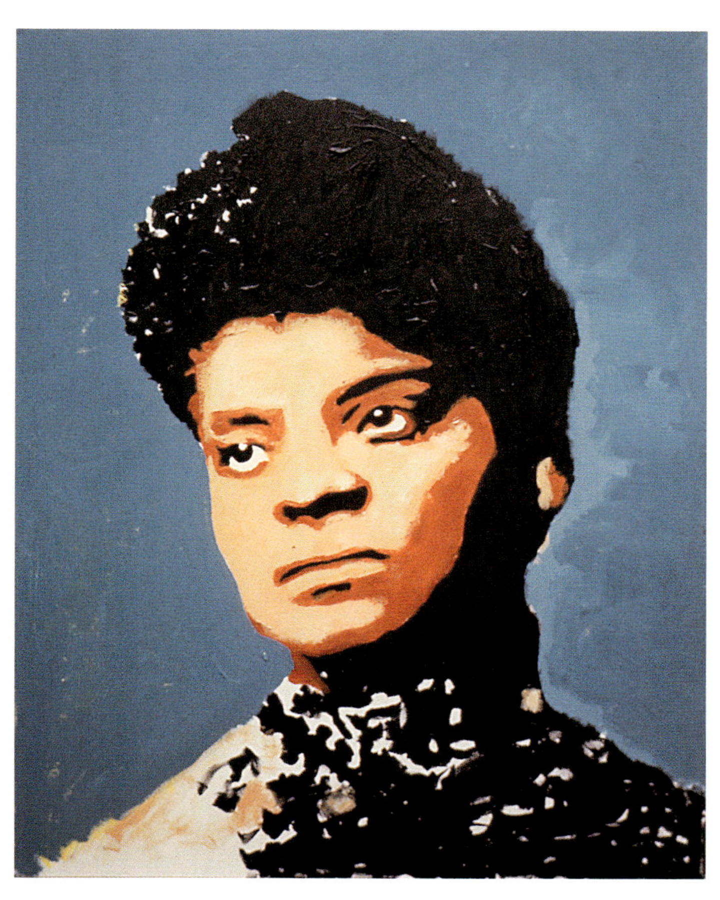

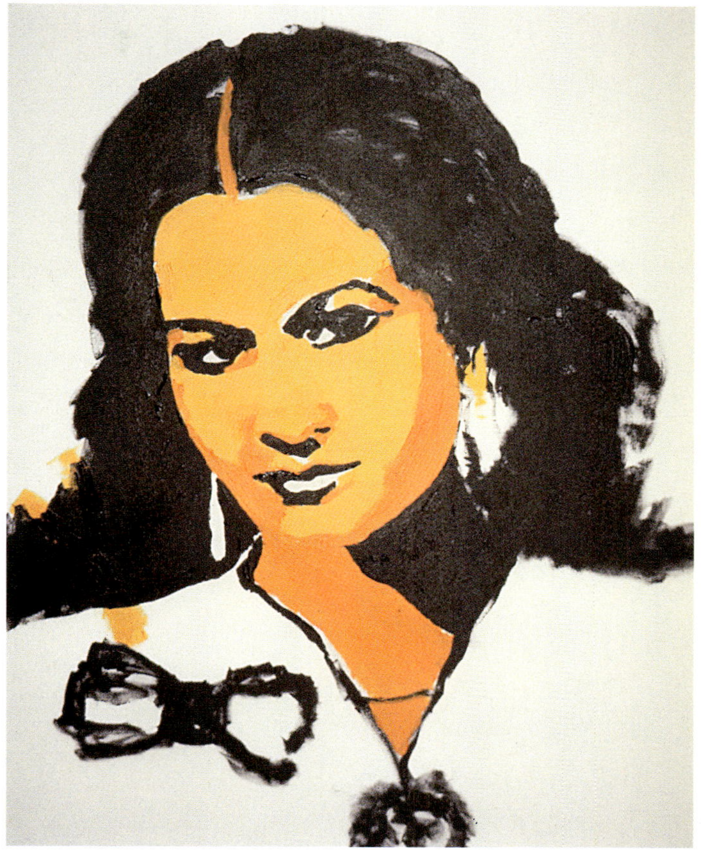

John Pilson

Above the Grid, 2000 (stills)
Two-channel video
9:30 minutes
Courtesy Nicole Klagsbrun Gallery, New York, N.Y.

Born 1968 in New York, N.Y.
Lives in New York, N.Y.

Education

1993 MFA, Yale University School of Art, New Haven, Conn.
1991 BFA, Sarah Lawrence College, Bronxville, N.Y.

Selected Solo Exhibitions

2003 *New Work*, Nicole Klagsbrun Gallery, New York, N.Y.
2002 *Clean Lines*, Nicole Klagsbrun Gallery, Art Basel 33, Switzerland
Annet Gelink Gallery, Amsterdam, The Netherlands

Selected Group Exhibitions

2003 *The Modern*, Castello di Rivoli, Museo d'Arte Contemporanea, Rivoli, Italy
2002 *Moving Pictures*, The Solomon R. Guggenheim Museum, New York, N.Y.
The Americans, Barbican Gallery, London, U.K.
2001 *49th International Exhibition of Art: Plateau of Mankind*, Venice Biennial, Italy

Award

2001 The Young Artist's Special Prize, Venice Biennial

Some people thought the ninety-first floor of the World Trade Center was a strange place to put an artists studio program. It was a strange place to put anything. The transition from subway to shopping mall to elevator to the hushed interior of the World Trade Center took only minutes, and there you were, suspended in air, looking down at your home. The long vertical window frames seemed the exact width of your shoulders. You spent the first week just staring at the city and pacing around the cavernous studio. It was quiet. All the screeches, crashes, horns and sirens were too far down to hear.

Walking the streamlined, vacuum-sealed corporate hallways, you left Manhattan and entered a parallel universe shared by office dwellers from Tokyo to Nebraska. Fluorescent light, chrome elevators and company logos on frosted glass doors. The empty corridors on a Sunday morning reminded you of the spaceship in 2001: A Space Odyssey. *The view on a cloudless night was pure* Blade Runner. *I never thought there was anything incongruous about the paint-splattered artists rubbing shoulders with the "suits." It was impossible not to dream on the ninety-first floor.*

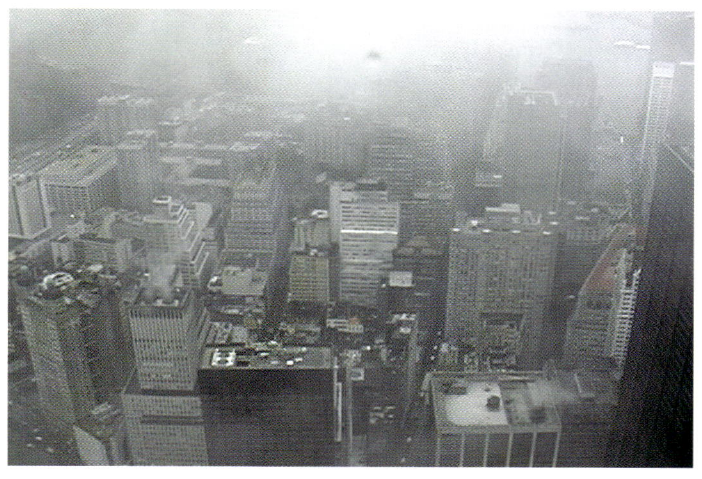

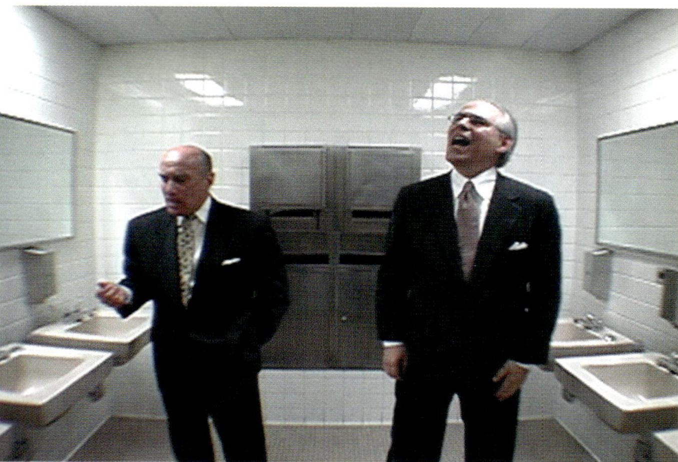

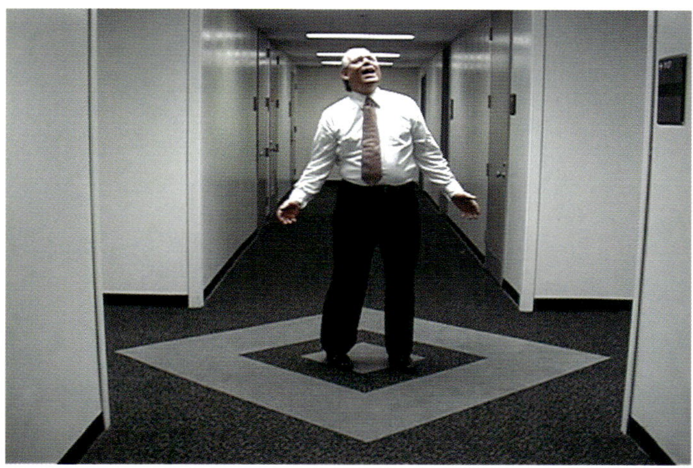

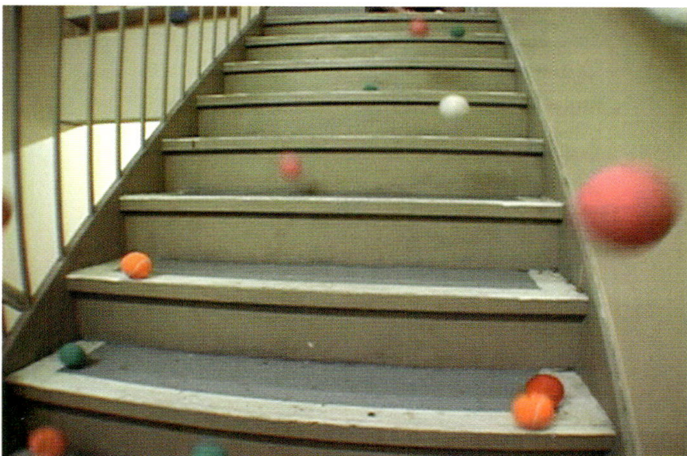

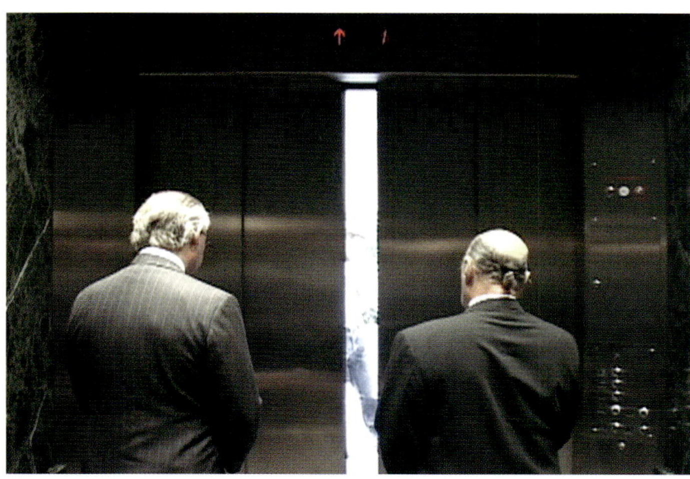

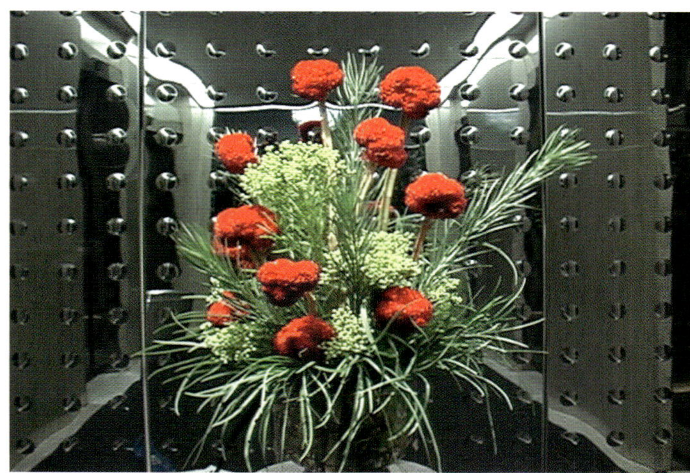

Douglas Ross

Picture Motion, 2000
Paper board, aluminum, acetal plastics, variable A/C motors, precision mechanical parts, natural/city light
Dimensions variable

Motorized horizontal blinds, made to fit two north-facing windows, rotate in unison, masking all outside light from the room eight times per second. The room flickers like the projection of early silent films. The world seen outside the room becomes filmic as it is animated through interruptions. Inside the room and out the windows the stillness and kinematics of bodies and objects appear greatly exaggerated as we are immersed in our subjective cinematographies.

Born 1969 in Brockton, Mass.
Lives in New York, N.Y.

Education

1998 MFA, School of Visual Arts, New York, N.Y.
1991 BFA, Parsons School of Design, New York, N.Y.

Selected Group Exhibitions

2002 *Walk Ways*, Independent Curators International, Portland Institute for Contemporary Art, Oreg. (tour)
2002 *ARCUS Projects*, Contemporary Art Factory, Tokyo, Japan
Listening to New Voices, P.S.1 Contemporary Art Center, Long Island City, N.Y.
2001 *One Planet Under A Groove: Hip-Hop and Contemporary Art*, The Bronx Museum of the Arts, The Bronx, N.Y. (tour)

Screening

2001 *Harmony*, New Museum of Contemporary Art, New York, N.Y.

Residencies and Awards

2002 ARCUS, Ibaraki Prefecture, Moriya, Japan
2001 P.S.1 National Studio Program, The Clocktower, New York, N.Y.
1999 Socrates Sculpture Park Emerging Artist Fellowship and Residency, Long Island City, N.Y.
1998 Skowhegan School of Painting and Sculpture, Maine

Earlier . . . while visiting New York City with an orchestra in 1985 I went to the observation deck of Tower Two. Up there I saw the whole city and then some falcons nesting between the roof security fences and machinery. From the outside so many ideas and feelings could be projected onto the building, even home.

Later . . . The persistent sensation in the studios of simultaneously flying and standing still is something I am consistently looking to reproduce somewhere, somehow. Curious that such a position of extraordinary visual privilege could induce the feeling that you are totally cut off from everything and everyone. Suspended in time and space, alone in our meditation bubble. People, NASDAQ, birds, elevators, airplanes, thunderclouds, PATH trains, alternating units of city light, are all the beautiful vicissitudes of weather. Despite our raw office it progressively seemed that we artists were not actually outlaws within the hive, as the material and social flows of our own field's economies were increasingly revealed. Mostly, no one was around. Occasionally the outdoor window-cleaning robot would visit.

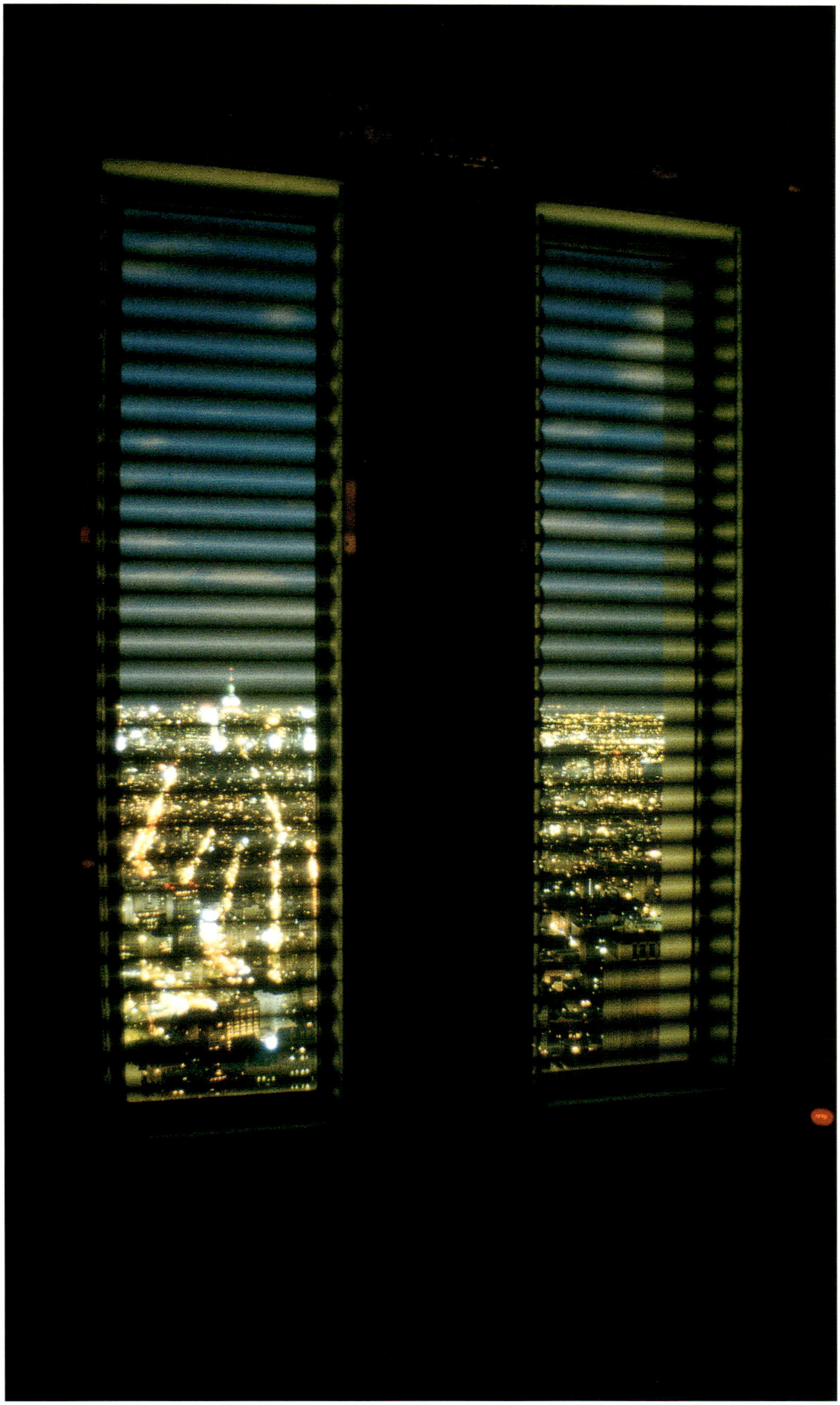

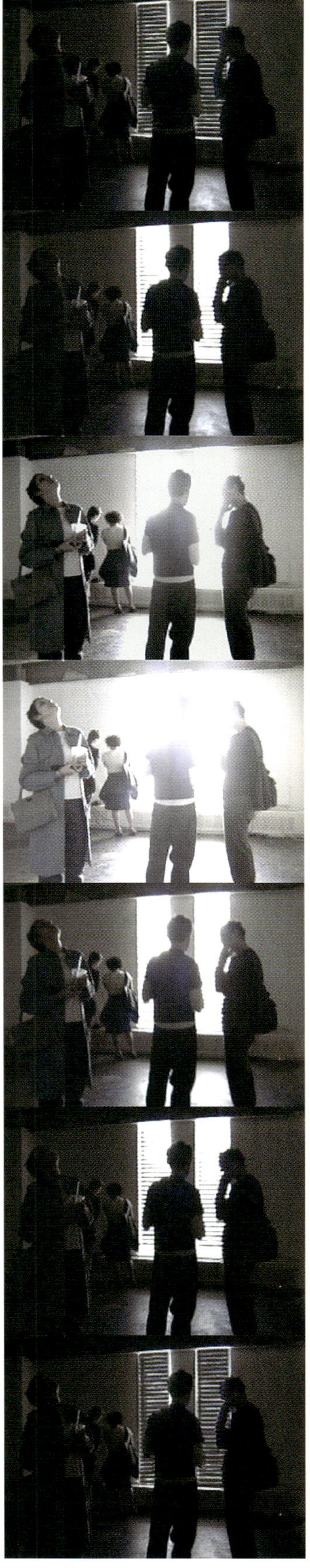

Winter 2000 through Spring 2001

Artists-in-Residence

Augusto Arbizo
Matthew Bakkom
Sanford Biggers
Torsten Zenas Burns
Marsha Cottrell
William Crow
Shelley Eshkar
Robert Grunder
Sally Gutiérrez
Adam Henry
Hoon Kim
Julian LaVerdiere & Paul Myoda
Patrick Meagher
Sandrine Nicoletta
Yigal Nizri

Jurors

Kathy Brew
Dan Cameron
Perry Hoberman
Barbara Hunt
Jennie C. Jones
Moukhtar Kocache
Jenelle Porter
Carol Stakenas
Bruce Wands

Invited Artists

Jerri Allyn
The E-Team
Eiko & Koma
Bart Elsbach
Jacqueline Gourevitch
Raoul Middleman
Kamilla Talbot

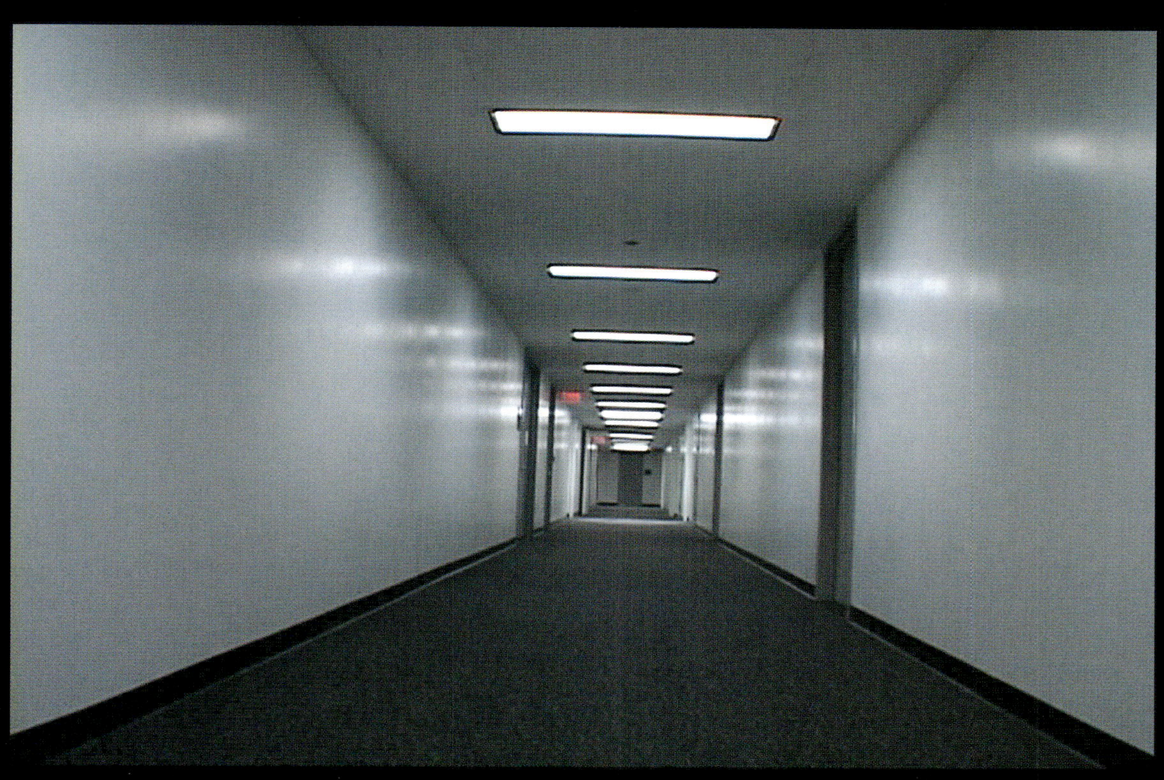

Jerri Allyn

A Chair is a Throne is a Freedom Fighter's Camp Stool is an interactive installation made up of twenty-one sculptural chairs and stools that act as portraits of people who have resolved conflicts creatively, and rendered thought-provoking alternatives to punishment. Stories about conflict resolution and soundscapes by Helene Rosenbluth and myself play on CD players incorporated into the design of each seat. The formation of chairs continuously changes which allows audience members to experience how seating arrangements effect communication.

The Cheyenne Portrait, 2002
Wood and paint
16 x 16 x 16 inches each chair
Designed and painted by artist;
built by Hanna Gafni

Portrait of a young man who, after witnessing his father's murder, came to terms with his anger and loss through art and poetry.

Born 1952 in Paterson, N.J.
Lives in New York, N.Y.

Education

1980 MA, Goddard College, Plainfield, Vt.

Selected Solo Exhibitions

2002 *A Chair is a Throne is a Freedom Fighter's Camp Stool*, public libraries, New York, N.Y.

1990 *Angels Have Been Sent to Me* (installation and performance), Creative Time, New York, N.Y. (tour)

Selected Group Exhibitions

2003 *High Performance: The First Five Years, 1978–1982*, Los Angeles Contemporary Exhibitions, Calif.

1994 *Six Moons over Oaxaca*, Artists Space, New York, N.Y and Galeria Arte de Oaxaca, Mexico

Residency

2002 The Rockefeller Foundation's Bellagio Study and Conference Center, Italy

Awards

2002 The Joan Mitchell Foundation Award

2001 New York State Council on the Arts, Film, Media & New Technologies Grant

1993 Arts International Lila Wallace-Reader's Digest Fund, Research and Residency Grant

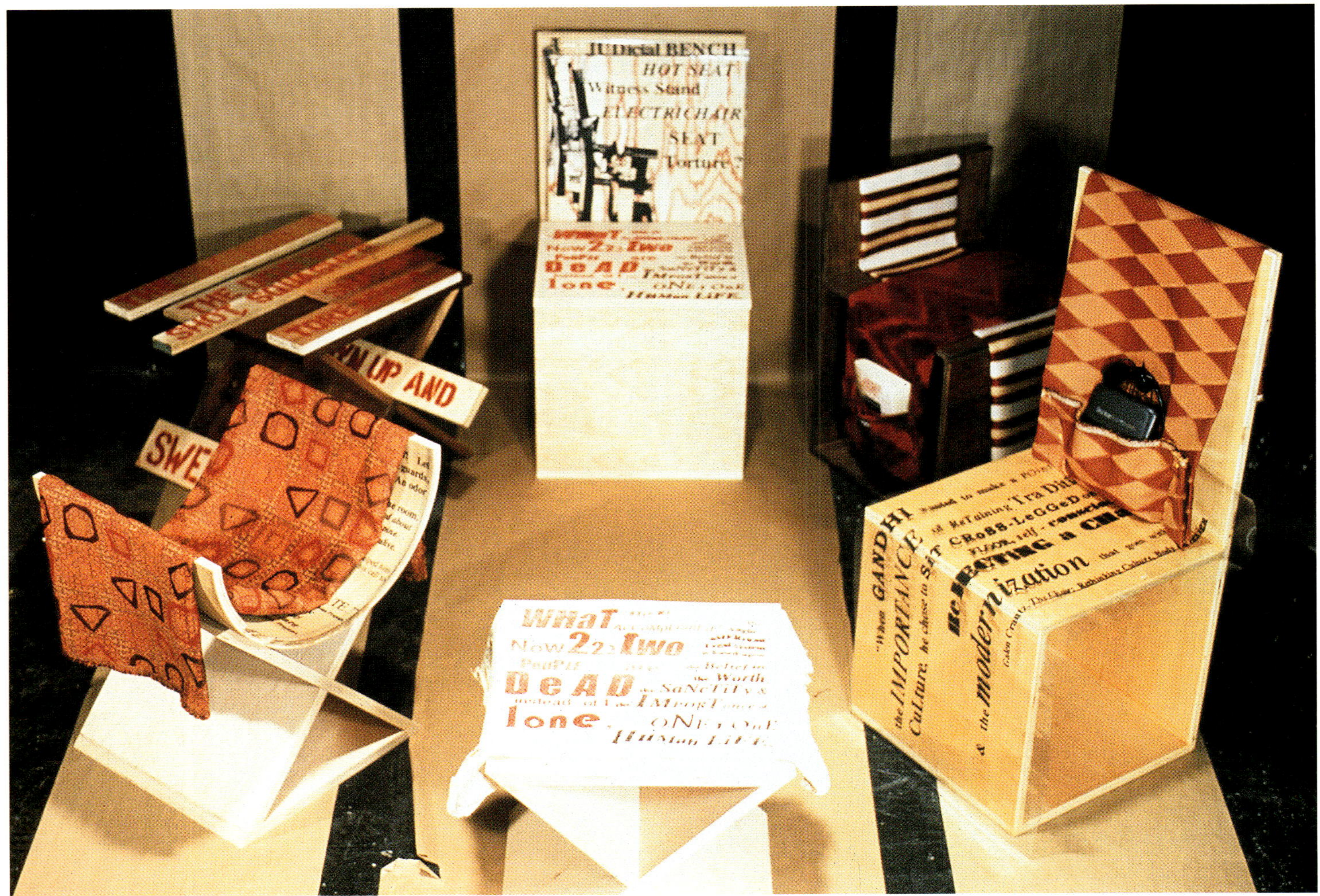

We were working in the clouds. Amazing to be at eye level with these natural wonders floating by. Awe-inspiring, this view, looking north at Manhattan and beyond. The resident artists shared windows the length of a football field, on two sides of Tower One. We could see both rivers flanking the island, Central Park, the Bronx in the distance and more. Sometimes surreal, looking down on traffic jams and people, relegated to the size of ants, scurrying below. I knew it would be chaos and intolerable noise on the streets, yet it was absolute quiet on the ninety-first floor. More often the view was serene, meditative, luxurious. We felt rich.

One day I thought the place had been draped with large white drop cloths. For what? Cleaning? Felt scary. Quickly pacing off the windows, I could see absolutely nothing beyond this white blanket. Went in search of the guards to ask how long the windows would be covered. Didn't want to work in this claustrophobic place. Total surprise when the guards told me it was fog! Thought I was imagining things early on, when the tower seemed to creak and groan and sway. Cautiously asked some fellow artists, did the building seem to be moving? Yes, they hesitantly answered. Again, went to question the guards. They reported that the tower was designed to move back and forth as much as three feet!

Nine months of coming and going, I got to know several guards, regulars on day, evening and overnight shifts. They had all kinds of tales about the tower. Everyone, to a tee, told stories about the tower by referencing the '93 bombing, without actually saying it. Everyone told stories with a before or after "it" happened. The building talked, the elevators included. Traveling fast in "normal" weather, slow during high winds, the lifts whistled shrilly through the five-minute ascent.

Several guards told me the morning "it" happened was the only time the tower was completely silent.

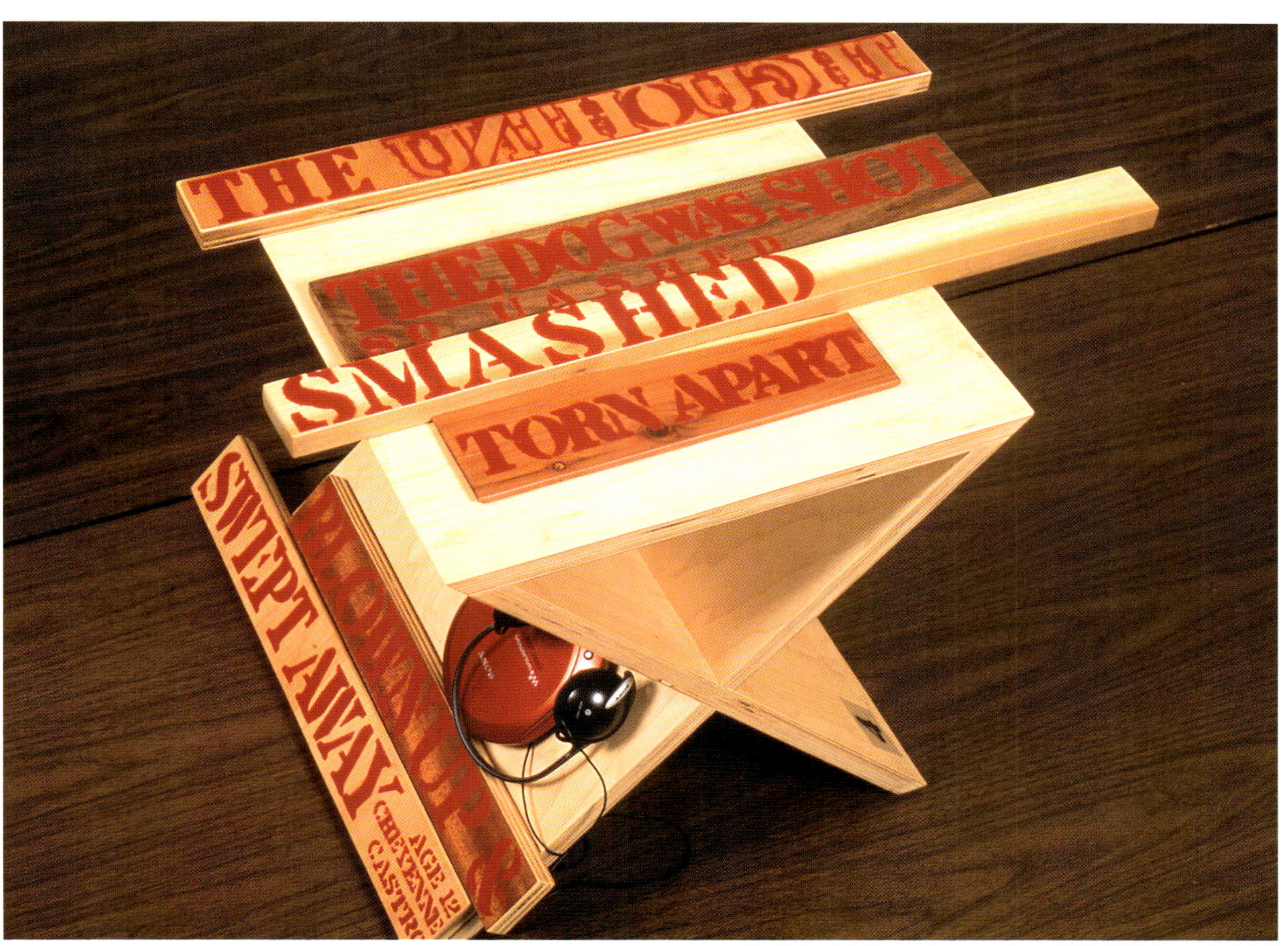

Augusto Arbizo

Untitled (Sky I), 2001
Acrylic on canvas
24 x 30 inches

Untitled (Sky II), 2001
Acrylic on canvas
24 x 30 inches

Born 1972 in Quezon City, Philippines
Lives in New York, N.Y.

Education

1997 MFA, University of Michigan, Ann Arbor
1995 BFA, The Cooper Union School of Art, New York, N.Y.

Solo Exhibition

2000 *White Room*, White Columns, New York, N.Y.

Selected Group Exhibitions

2003 *Giverny*, Salon 94, New York, N.Y.
After Matisse Picasso, P.S.1 Contemporary Art Center, Long Island City, N.Y.
2002 *The Queens International*, The Queens Museum, Queens, N.Y.
2001 *Arbizo, Iqbal, Raja*, Bellwether, Brooklyn, N.Y.

Residencies

2002 The Marie Walsh Sharpe Art Foundation, New York, N.Y.
Fondation Claude Monet, Giverny, France

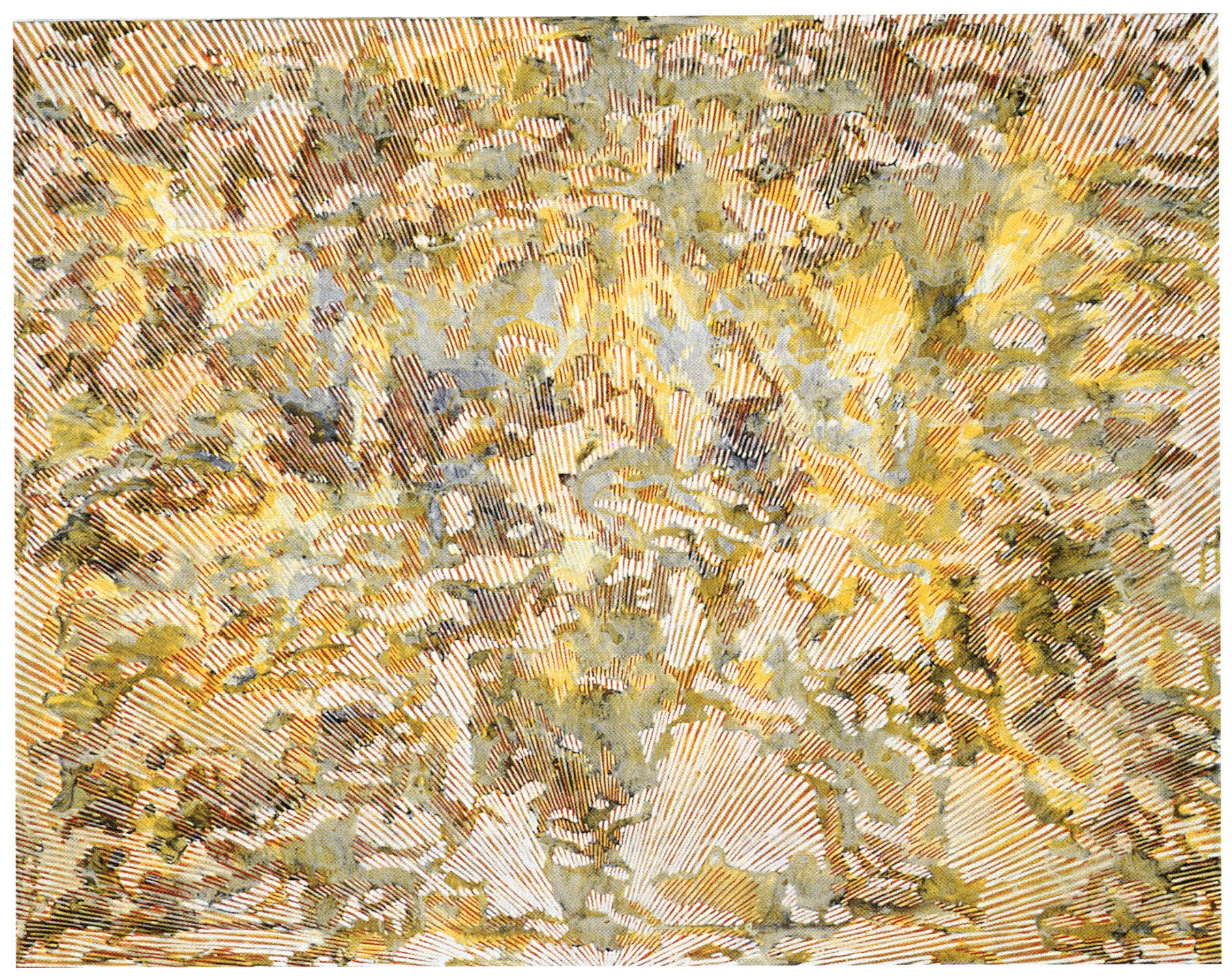

One of the things that became of interest to me while at the WTC was how the weather was different up there, ninety floors above ground. The light, cloud and wind changes (which you could feel even inside the closed spaces) were dramatic. And the views of sunsets were spectacular. I found that these observations had a strong impact on the direction of my work.

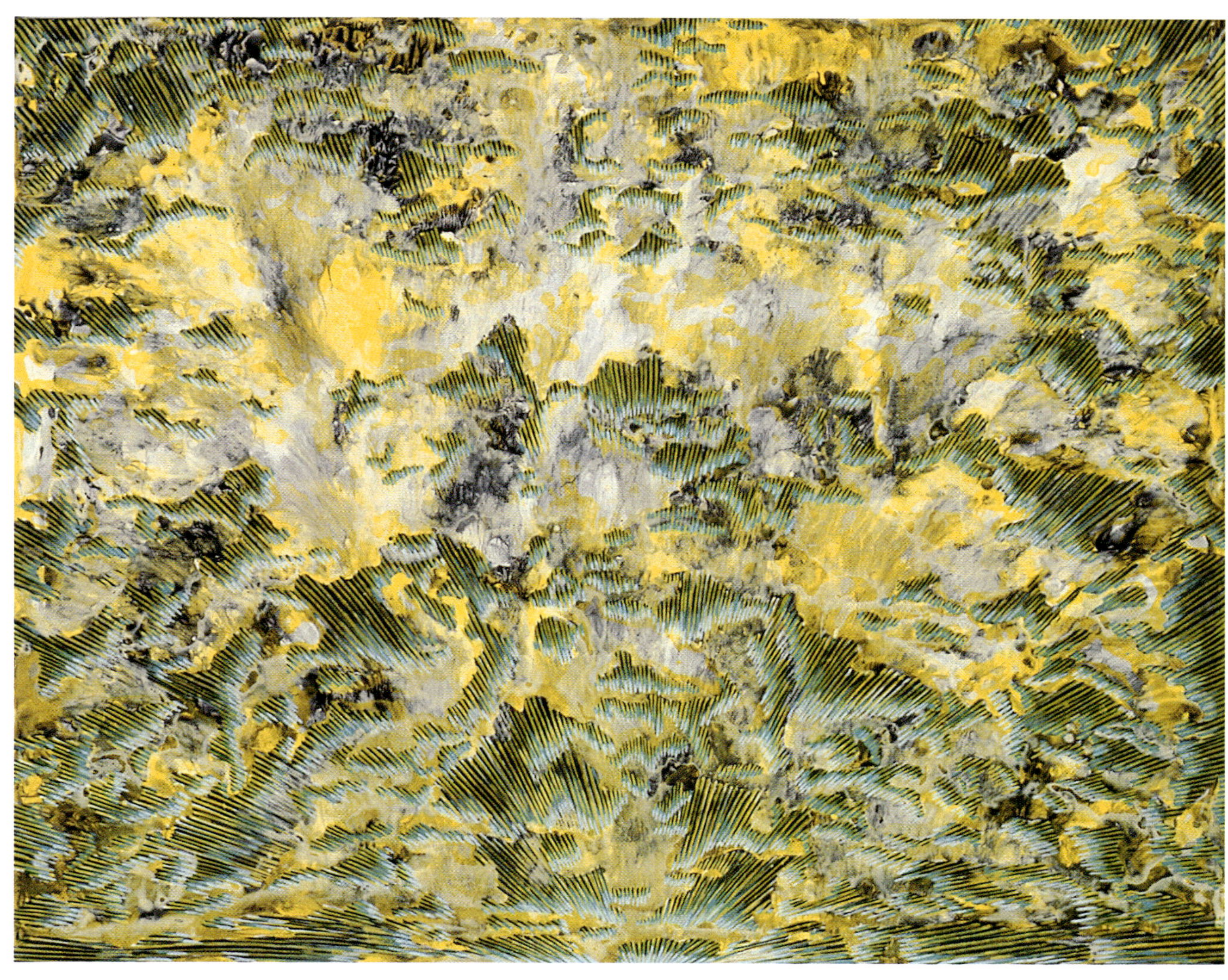

Torsten Zenas Burns

Selected Afterlife Characters–8:00–2001/03, ongoing (still)
Video, 8 minutes
Within expansive architectural and natural frameworks we see selected after-tomb personalities and explore improvisational humor, hygiene, memory and the arts.

Selected Lifespace–10:00–2000/03, ongoing (stills)
Video, 10 minutes
Saturated chunks of video bridged by earthsuits, payload specialists, bodynauts, texts and interface vehicles

While embedded within the speculative World Trade Center, I explored a fusion among improvisational video, micro/macro architectural set-ups and live performance body interactions.

Born 1968 in Laguna Niguel, Calif.
Lives in Brooklyn, N.Y.

Education

1993 MFA, San Francisco Art Institute, Calif.
1990 BFA, Alfred University, Alfred, N.Y.
1989 Studio Arts Center International, Florence, Italy

Selected Group Exhibitions

2003 *Lesson Stalls: Learning Nets* (collaboration with Darrin Martin), Electronic Arts Intermix, New York, N.Y.
2002 *The Omega Manual* (Halflifers collaboration and co-curator), Smack Mellon, Brooklyn, N.Y.
Beta Launch: Eyebeam Artists in Residence (collaboration with Darrin Martin), Eyebeam Atelier, New York, N.Y.

Screenings

2003 *New Social Modeling* (collaboration with Darrin Martin), Pacific Film Archive, Berkeley, Calif.
Currents (collaboration with Darrin Martin), Rencontres Internationales Paris/Berlin 5, Paris, France and Berlin, Germany
2002 *Inside/Out: The Spirits of Place and Medical Malaise*, The New York Video Festival, N.Y.
Video View Points, The Museum of Modern Art, New York, N.Y.

Award

2002 The San Francisco Foundation, James D. Phelan Video Art Award

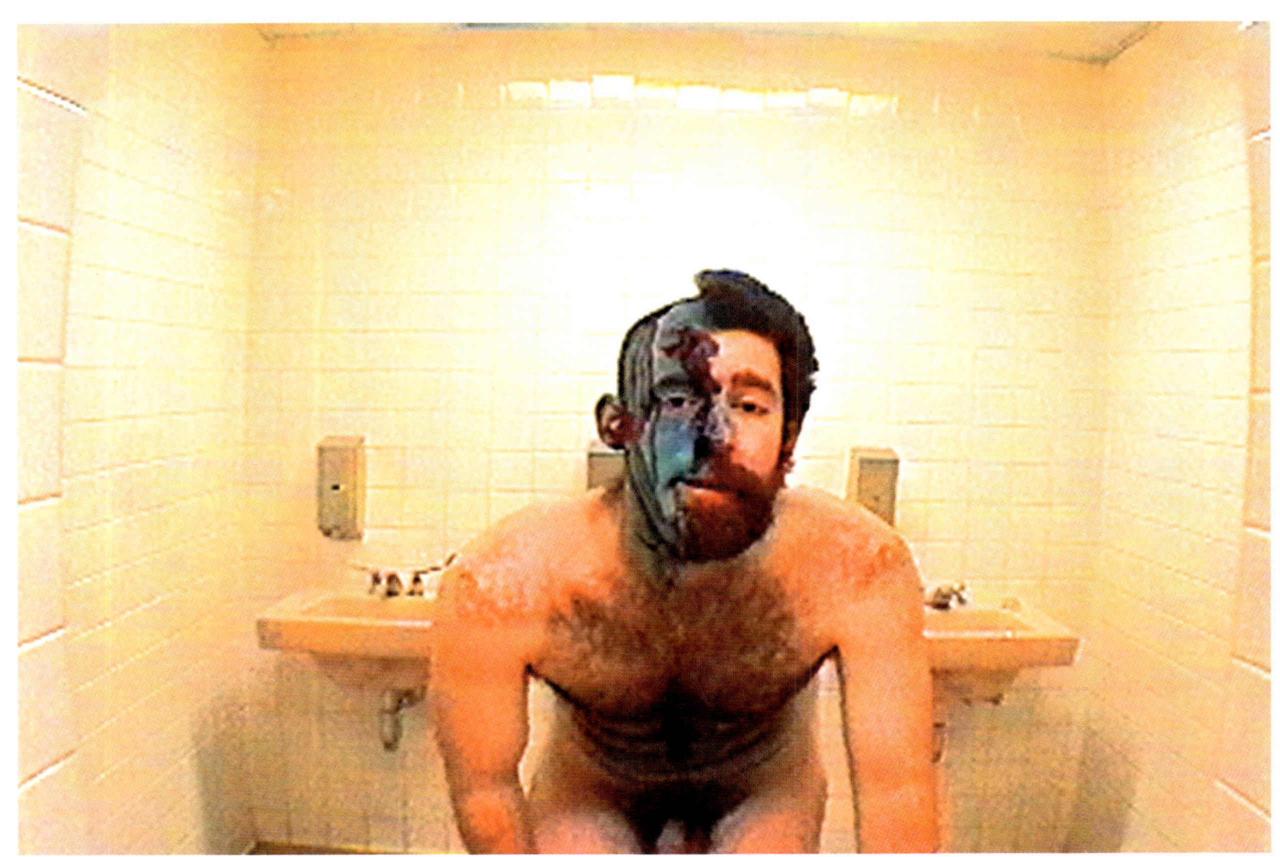

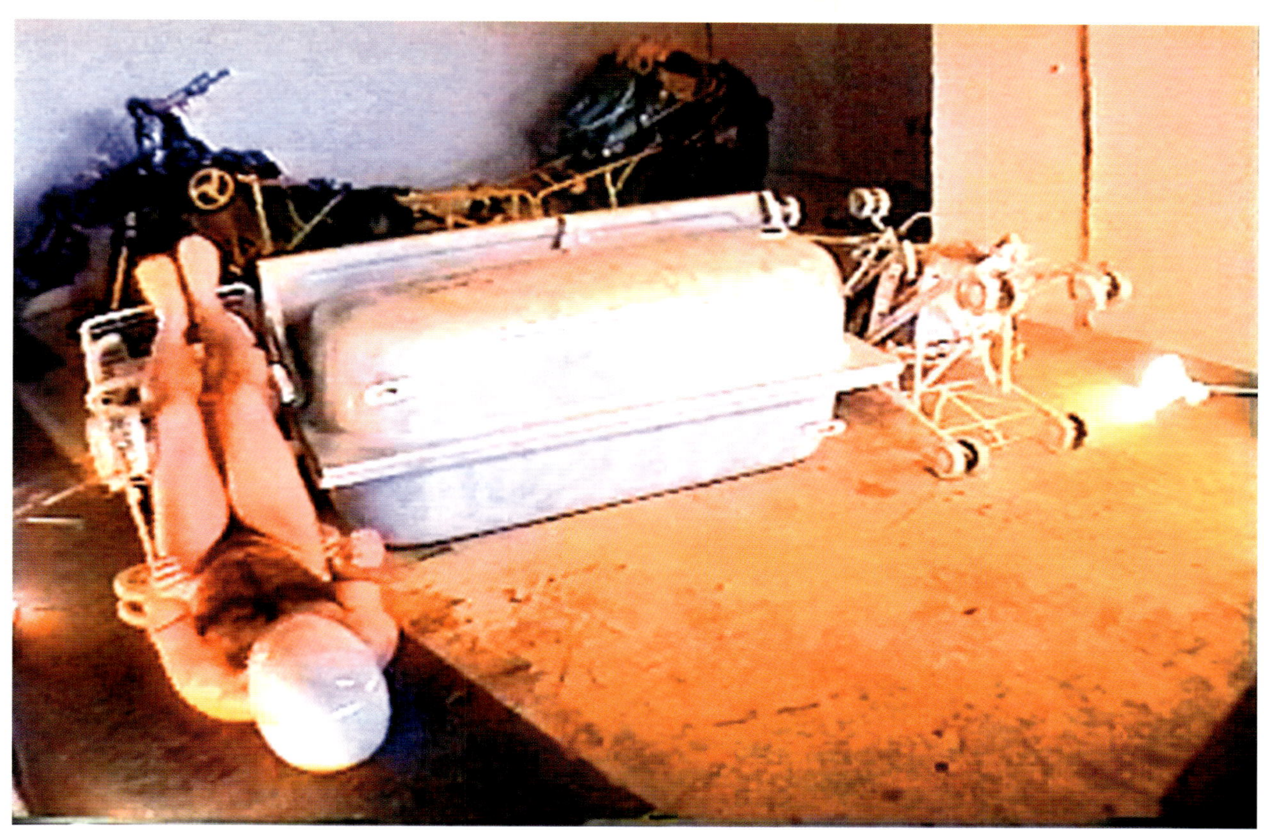

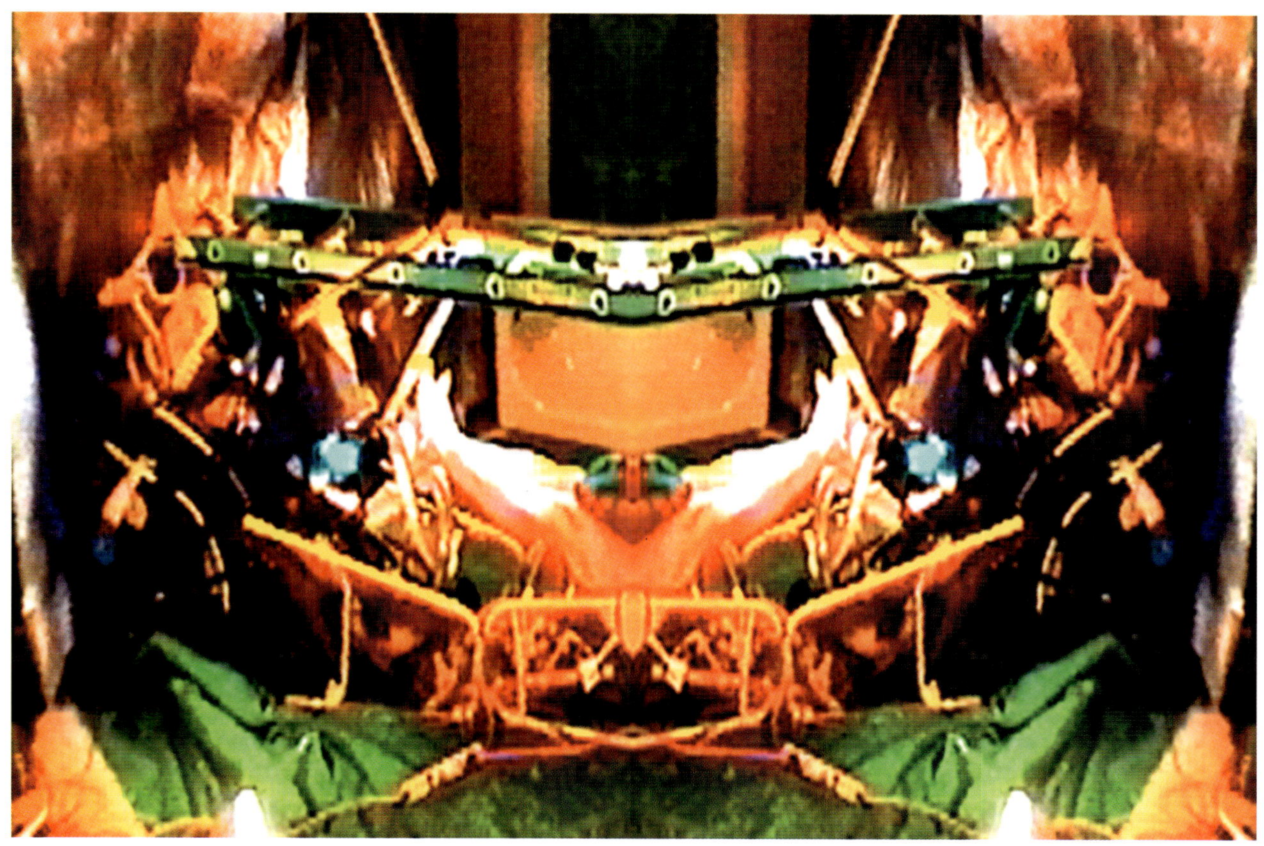

Marsha Cottrell

UNT.WT.5.3, 2001
Unique Océ print on mylar
24 x 36 inches
Collection of Susan Jacoby

UNT.WT.5.9, 2001 (with detail)
Unique Océ print on mylar
24 x 36 inches
Collection of Skadden, Arps, Meagher and Flom

Born 1964 in Philadelphia, Pa.
Lives in Brooklyn, N.Y.

Education

1990 MFA, University of North Carolina, Chapel Hill
1988 BFA, Temple University, Tyler School of Art, Philadelphia, Pa.

Selected Solo Exhibitions

2003 g-module, Paris, France
2002 *Out of Memory*, Henry Urbach Architecture, New York, N.Y.
2000 *Punctuation Drawings*, Revolution Gallery, Detroit, Mich.
1998 Derek Eller Gallery, New York, N.Y.

Residencies

2002 The MacDowell Colony, Peterborough, N.H.
1999 The Marie Walsh Sharpe Art Foundation, New York, N.Y.

Awards

2001 The John Simon Guggenheim Memorial Foundation
1999 New York Foundation for the Arts

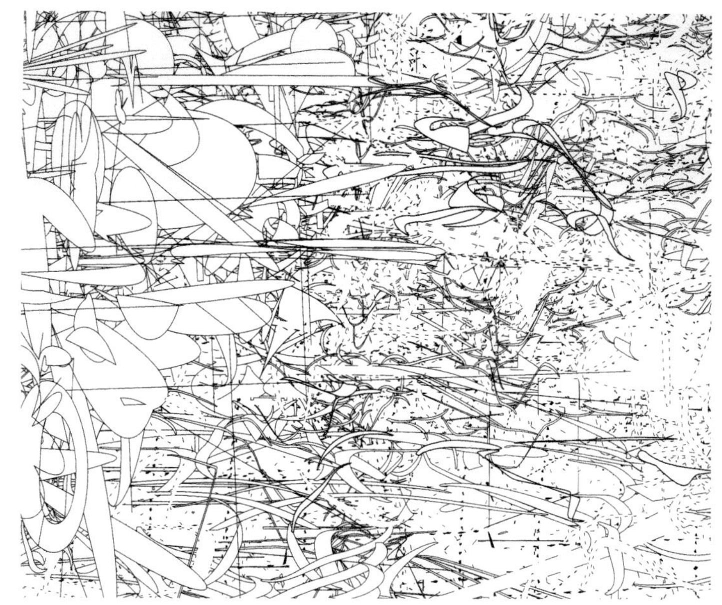

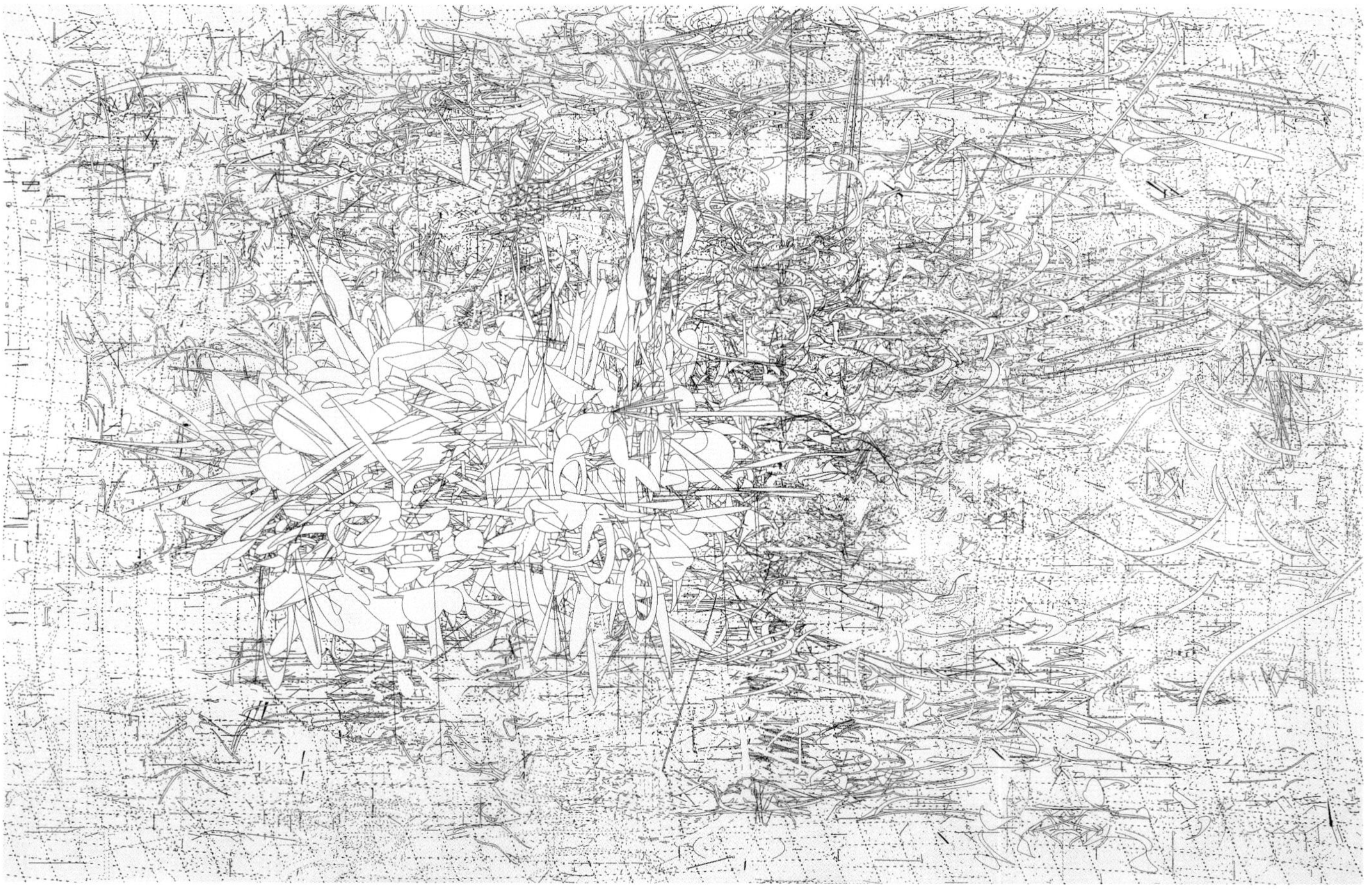

William Crow

Untitled (Spectator series), 2001
Oil and acrylic on wood panel
Dimensions variable

Born 1973 in Roanoke, Va.
Lives in New York, N.Y.

Education

1999 MFA, Hunter College/CUNY, New York, N.Y.
1995 BA, Wake Forest University, Winston-Salem, N.C.
1993–94 Universidad de Salamanca, Spain

Selected Solo Exhibitions

2002 *Recent Work*, Wake Forest University Art Gallery, Winston-Salem, N.C.
Discursive Spaces, Gallery 402, New York, N.Y.
Arrangements (two-person show), P.S.122, New York, N.Y.

Selected Group Exhibitions

2003 *Inner City*, Exit Art, New York, N.Y.
The Recession Show, Cynthia Broan Gallery, New York, N.Y.
2001 *Ripe and Hazy*, Goliath, Brooklyn, N.Y.

Residencies

2004 Longwood Center for the Arts, The Bronx, N.Y.
2003 Millay Colony for the Arts, Austerlitz, N.Y.

During the World Views residency I became immersed in the rituals and culture of the buildings and their inhabitants. Simple tasks such as moving through the underground mall with a current of commuters, or negotiating the elevators with office workers, heightened my awareness of the divisions between the group and the individual. I began to paint imagery of various spectator events in order to explore the dynamic that occurs when individuals convene on a site to witness an event or to become a member of that group. In this process, a portion of the individual identity is relinquished in order to become a part of the whole, and a new collective identity is created. These circular paintings contain imagery from an aerial or oblique perspective and distance the viewer so that the events depicted become ambiguous or even abstract. Crowds of onlookers become dabs of paint—marks that equalize or make ambiguous the presence of the individual.

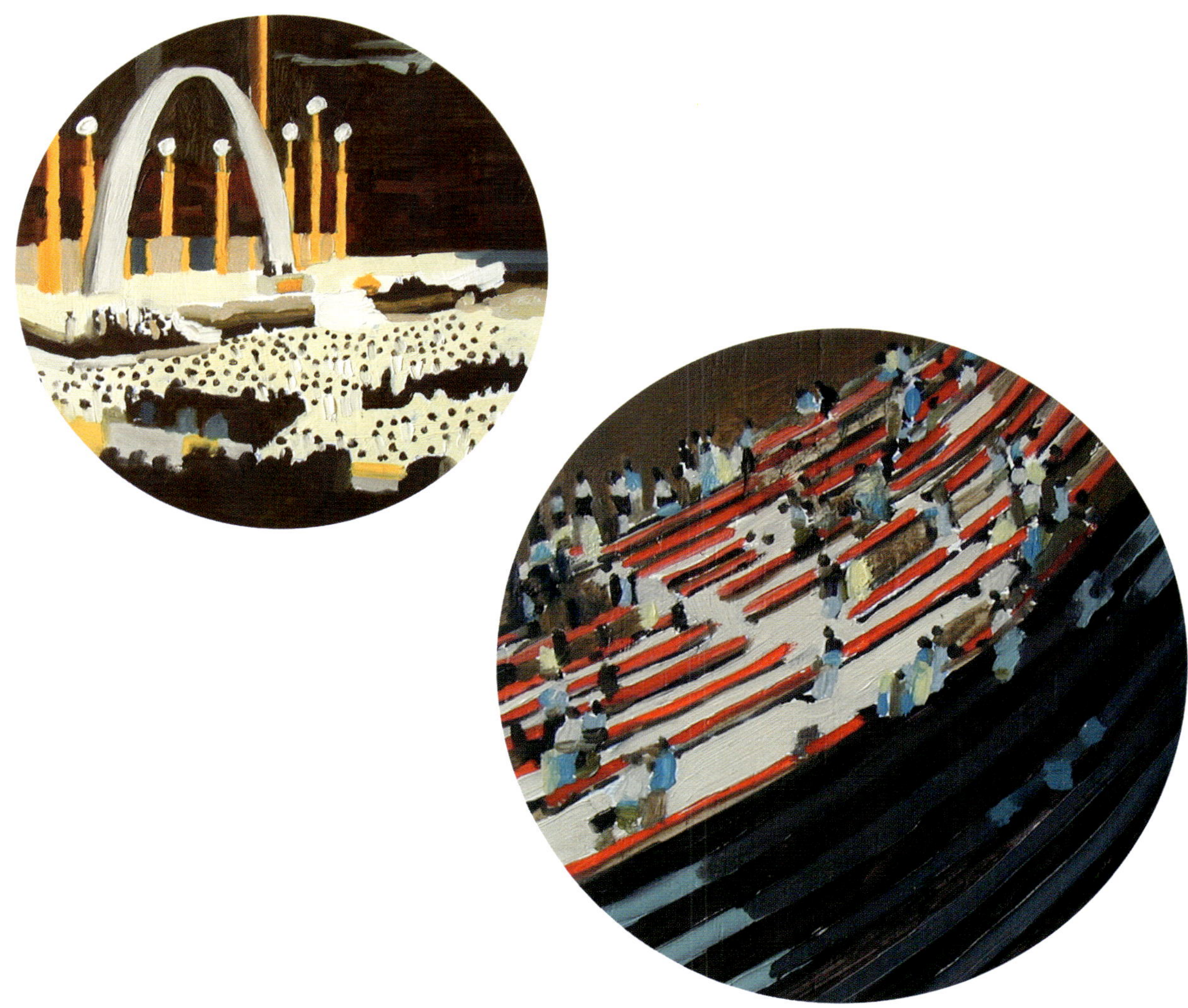

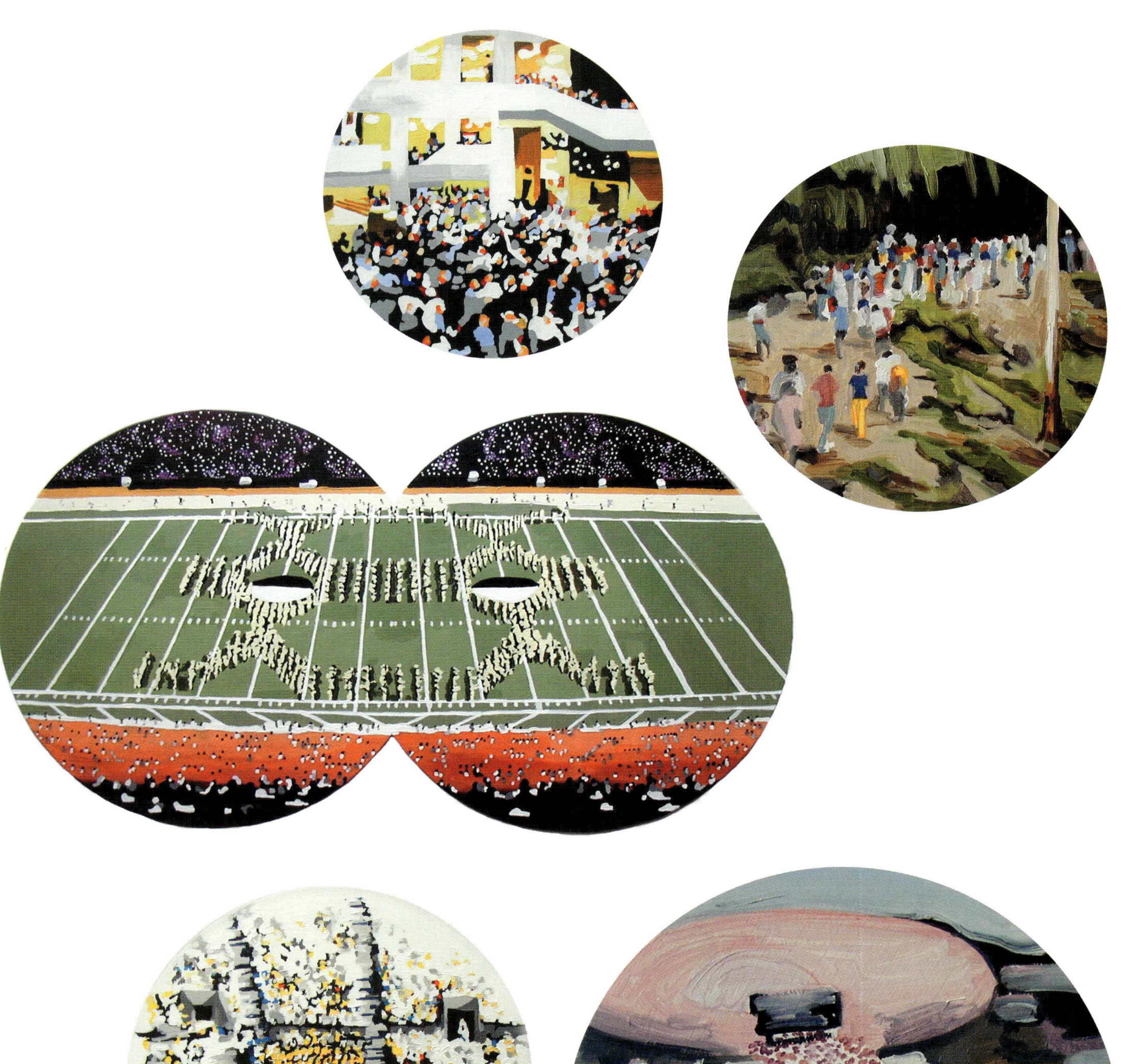

The E-Team

Quick Click, 4:30 P.M., March 31, 2001
Performance, photography

On March 31 at the World Views Open Studios, we staged *Quick Click*, an opportunity to have your picture taken inside the ninety-first floor from outside. Two E-Team members arrived in a helicopter outside WTC1 at 4:30 P.M., while the third member organized participants inside into a line. We communicated via walkie-talkie. With a limited time of twenty minutes we shot the photos, one by one, of sixty people as each stood in the designated window. The following day participants were able to pick up their free *Quick Click* portrait.

127 Illuminated Windows, April 29, 2001
Performance, photography

In order to billboard a phrase that did not have a particular meaning but could have a certain familiarity, we chose to present "E-Team," both a generic expression and the name of our collaboration, on the north face of WTC 1. To illuminate the word we needed 279 "dark" and 127 "light" windows on seven floors (floor 89 to floor 95). We contacted the fourteen respective offices and provided them with floor plans that showed which blinds should be closed or opened for the night of the lighting. Thanks to the cooperation of twelve participating offices, *127 Illuminated Windows* happened on the night of April 29, 2001.

Based in New York, N.Y.

Franziska Lamprecht
Born 1975 in Ilmenau, Germany

Education
1998 MFA, Bauhaus University, Weimar, Germany
1997 Art Center College of Design, Pasadena, Calif.
1997 School of Visual Arts, New York, N.Y.

Hajoe Moderegger
Born 1964 in Easton, Pa.

Education
1999 MFA, Bauhaus University, Weimar, Germany
1997 Art Center College of Design, Pasadena, Calif.
1997 School of Visual Arts, New York, N.Y.

Dan Seiple
Born 1973 in Harrisburg, Pa.

Education
1999 MFA, Cranbrook Academy of Art, Bloomfield Hills, Mich.
1996 BFA, University of Delaware, Newark

Selected Group Exhibitions
2002 *Brooklyn á Paris*, Chez Valentin, Paris, France and Momenta Art, Brooklyn, N.Y.
Supernatural Satisfaction, Soap Factory, Minneapolis, Minn.
2001 *Prankster*, White Columns, New York, N.Y.
To Market to Market (with Michael Smith), Rotunda Gallery, Brooklyn, N.Y.
Emerging Artists Fellowship Exhibition, Socrates Sculpture Park, Long Island City, N.Y.
Meineigenheim (web project), Palm Beach Institute of Contemporary Art, Fla.

Screening
2003 *How to Clean the Bottom of a Refrigerator* and *How to Catch a Millionaire*, Gallery 825, Los Angeles, Calif.

Award
2003 New York State Council on the Arts

The visual and spatial experience of being on the ninety-first floor was utterly impressive and overwhelming. The volume of the WTC and the city of offices that was contained within its hermetically sealed architecture were equally remarkable. Consequently, we chose to deal directly with the amazing view from the ninety-first floor, the building's uniform facade of roughly 51,000 windows, its unreachable height and the office workers inside. With each project we attempted to come closer to a "human" and individual detail of the austere towers in order to interrupt the corporate inaccessibility of the buildings.

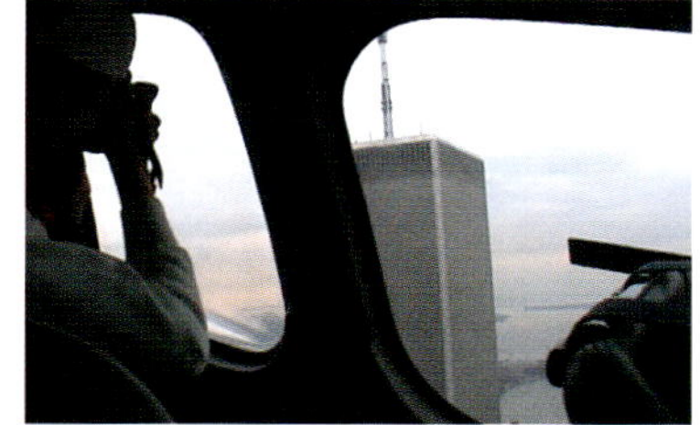

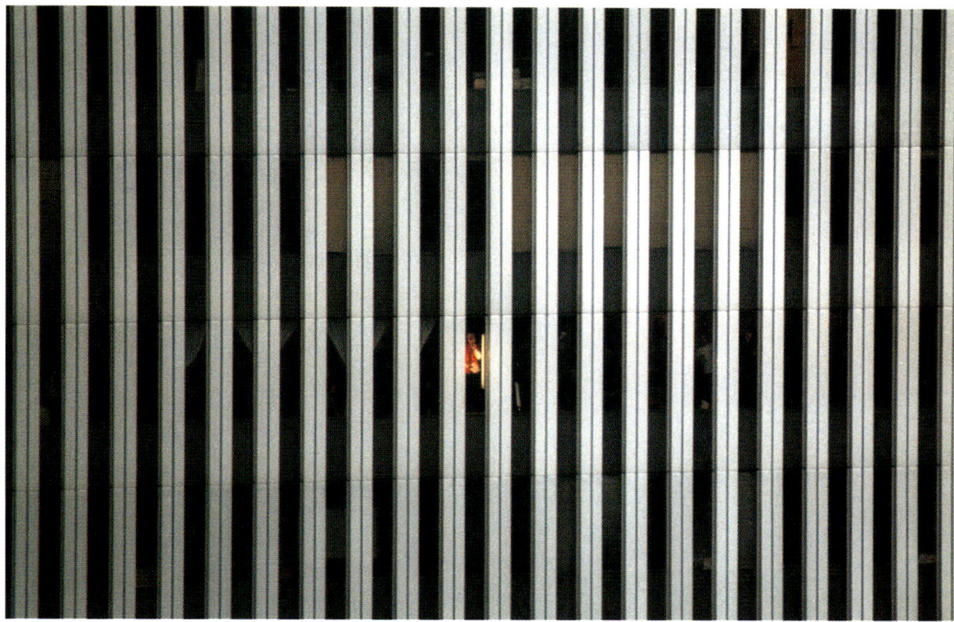

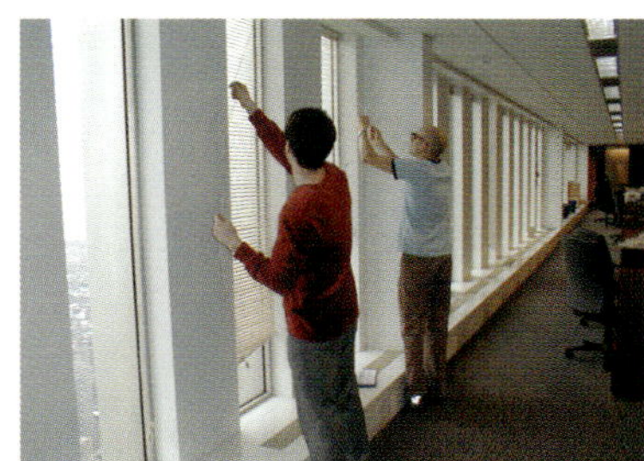

Eiko & Koma

When Nights Were Dark, premiered 2000
Photos: Eva Mueller and Tom Brazil

Eiko Otake
Born 1952 in Tokyo, Japan

Takashi Koma Otake
Born 1948 in Niigata, Japan

Collaborators since 1971
Based in New York, N.Y.

Selected Performances

2003 American Dance Festival, Durham, N.C.
2002 Joyce Theater, New York, N.Y.
2001 The Kennedy Center for the Performing Arts, Washington, D.C.
2000 Brooklyn Academy of Music, Next Wave Festival, N.Y.
1998 Whitney Museum of American Art, New York, N.Y.

Awards

1996 John D. and Catherine T. MacArthur Foundation Fellowship
1990 New York Dance and Performance Award (Bessie)
1984 The John Simon Guggenheim Memorial Foundation

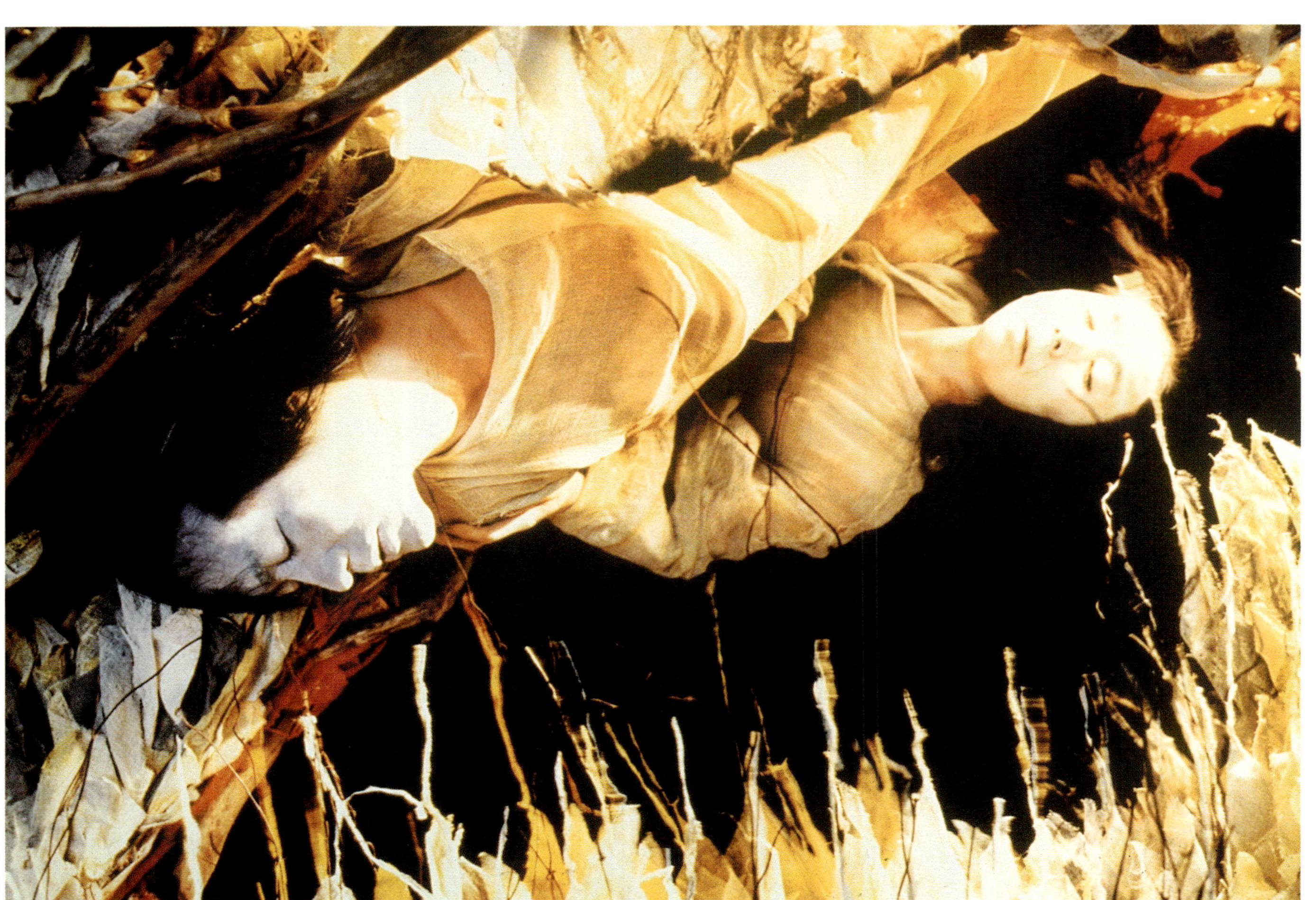

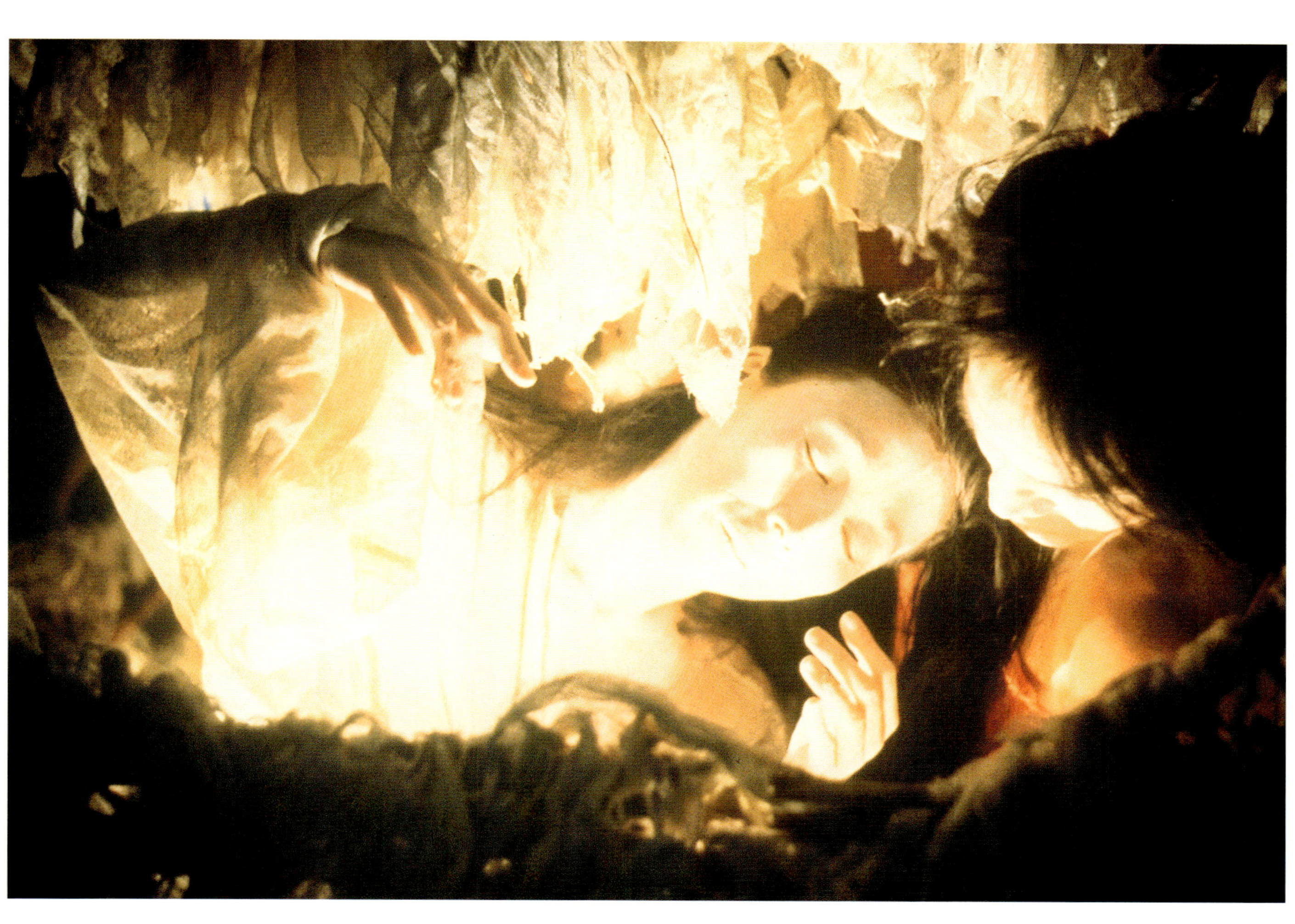

Bart Elsbach

Facade 237, 2001
Pen and ink
8 x 10 inches

Afternoon Light, 2001
Pen and ink
9 x 11 inches

Born 1961 in New York, N.Y.
Lives in Sheffield, Mass.

Education

1987 MFA, New York University, N.Y.
1984–85 Art Students League, New York, N.Y.
1983 BA, Hamilton College, Clinton, N.Y.

Selected Solo Exhibitions

2003 O.K. Harris, New York, N.Y.
2002 *Vanishing Point*, Fox and Fowle, New York, N.Y.
2001 Ute Stebich Gallery, Lenox, Mass.
1997 Wheatleigh, Lenox, Mass.

Selected Group Exhibitions

2001 Doran Gallery, Tulsa, Okla.
2000 David Klein Gallery, Birmingham, Mich.
Salisbury Association Invitational, Salisbury, Conn.

Award

2002 Malilangwe Artists Trust, Zimbabwe

The studio provided a dramatic viewpoint on a city that was my home for twenty-five years. I now experience the city as familiar, across the divide of fifteen years of partial separation.

Hanging 1,000 feet above Lower Manhattan, the studio faced north over the island past the Empire State Building, looked over the Hudson River to New Jersey and the George Washington Bridge, over the East River to Brooklyn and Prospect Park out to the bay, and over the marshes to the airports. Helicopters passed at or below eye level. Often accused of having my head in the clouds, at the studio, clouds often wisped by the windows, at times producing a complete white-out.

The perspective from so high a vantage was peculiar, particularly of nearby buildings and streets, with the role of rooftops accented. My vantage point on New York City has changed over time and distance. Returning to it to observe it with a changed eye was intriguing. My vantage point on this work and my time in the World Trade Center has now also changed dramatically. These subjects, and the space in which they were created, were a departure from my usual artistic experience, and now the whole experience which produced them has become a departure from my normal frame of reference. The already peculiar memory of working in that setting has been transformed into a wrenching dream I can step in and out of.

The enormity of the structures poised over the mesmerizing complexity of the city was often overwhelming. I tried to focus my view and energy into an area that welcomed a measure of intimacy. In the aftermath of the overwhelming events, I find myself again drawn to the solace of details and careful attention. I sense a familiar lesson, paying attention to that in my life that affords an opportunity for intimacy. I feel a strong reminder that the immense structures that overwhelm with their immutable permanence can vanish and leave us alone with only the permanence of our own vision and memory.

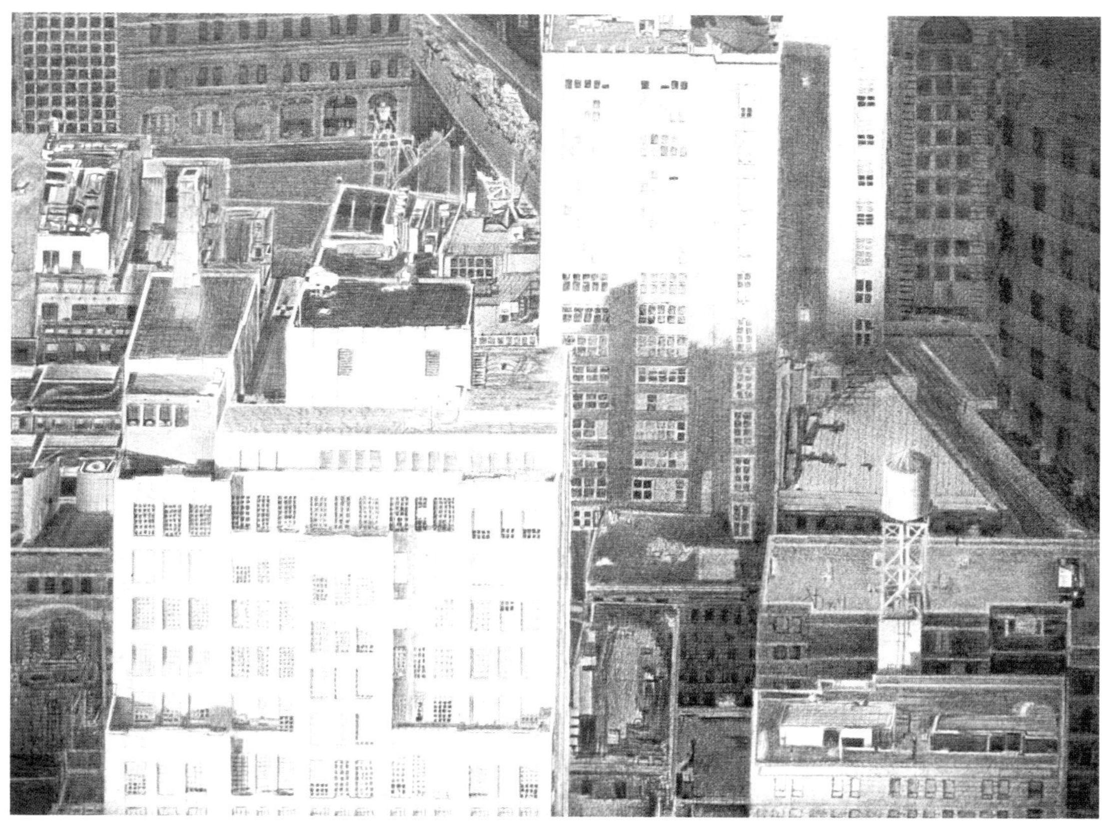

Shelley Eshkar

Public Seating, 2001
Concrete, wood, digital animation
26 x 36 x 36 inches

Pedestrian, 2002 (still)
Digital projection
13 minutes

From the windows on the ninety-first floor, pedestrians in the plaza below seemed far smaller than ants—in fact one needed a good pair of binoculars to identity them. This piece began with a concrete block, not out of place in the raw space of the studios, but whose scale referenced the public planters or benches found outside. When leaning over or sitting on the block, viewers could peer down into a "skylight" cut into it. There they would discover a virtual crowd circulating in a simulated plaza. The digital pedestrians go about their day, taking their time, walking and looking and gesturing with purposes we'll never know.

The animated figures of *Public Seating* were a sketch toward a larger public work entitled *Pedestrian,* a collaboration with Paul Kaiser, which appeared as a projection on Manhattan sidewalks in the winter of 2002. *Pedestrian* was co-produced by Eyebeam and the Art Production Fund.

Born 1970 in New York, N.Y.
Lives in New York, N.Y.

Education

1993 BFA, The Cooper Union School of Art, New York, N.Y.

Selected Group Exhibitions

2003 *Neuberger Museum of Art Biennial of Public Art* (with Paul Kaiser), State University of New York, Purchase

2002 *COPY,* Roth Horowitz Gallery, New York, N.Y.

2001 *ID/entity: Portraits in the 21st Century*, MIT Media Laboratory, Cambridge, Mass. (tour)

Public Art and Commissions

2002 *Pedestrian* (with Paul Kaiser), Rockefeller Center, Eyebeam Atelier, and The Studio Museum in Harlem, New York, N.Y. (tour)

1999 *BIPED* (with Paul Kaiser), Lincoln Center, New York, N.Y. (tour)
GHOSTCATCHING (with Bill T. Jones and Paul Kaiser), The Cooper Union School of Art, New York, N.Y.

Residency

2002–05 Institute for Studies in the Arts, Arizona State University, Tempe

Award

2001 New York Foundation for the Arts

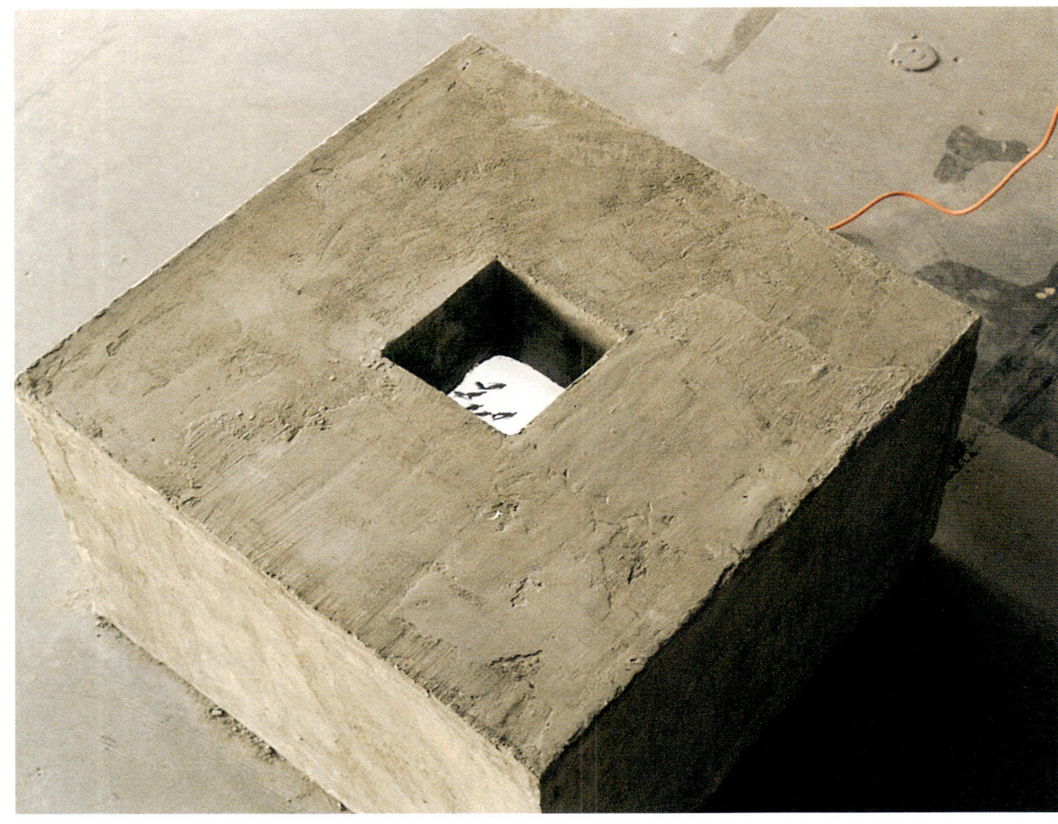

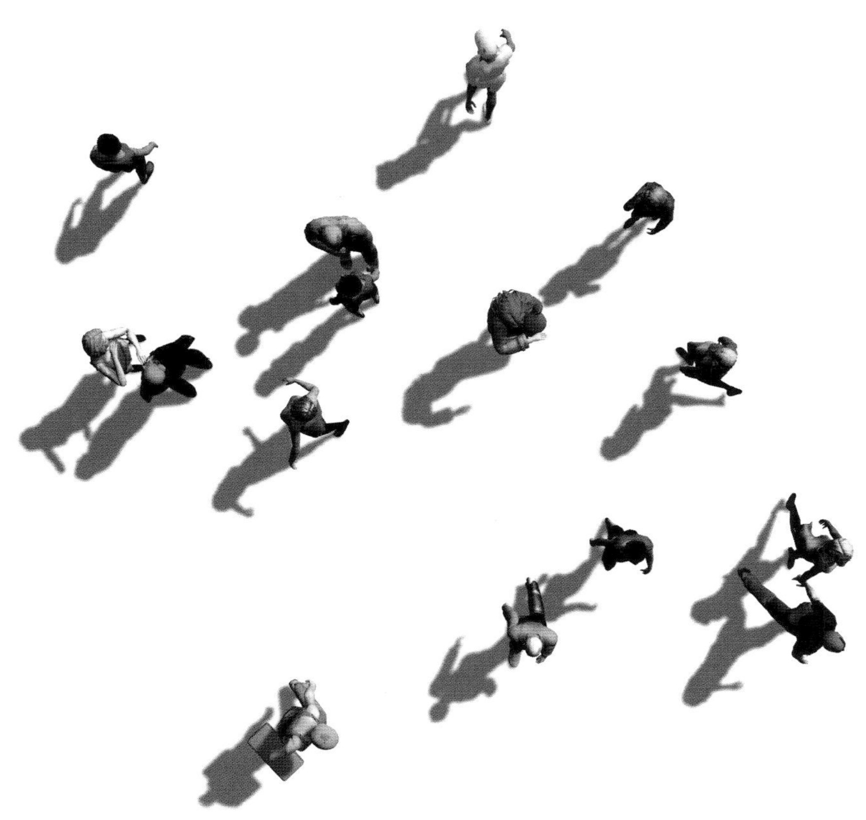

Jacqueline Gourevitch

WTC: Looking Down, North, 2000
Oil on canvas
14 x 11 inches
Photo: Adam Reich

Looking Northeast #2, 2000
Oil on canvas
28 x 24 inches
On extended loan to the Art in Embassies Program
Photo: Adam Reich

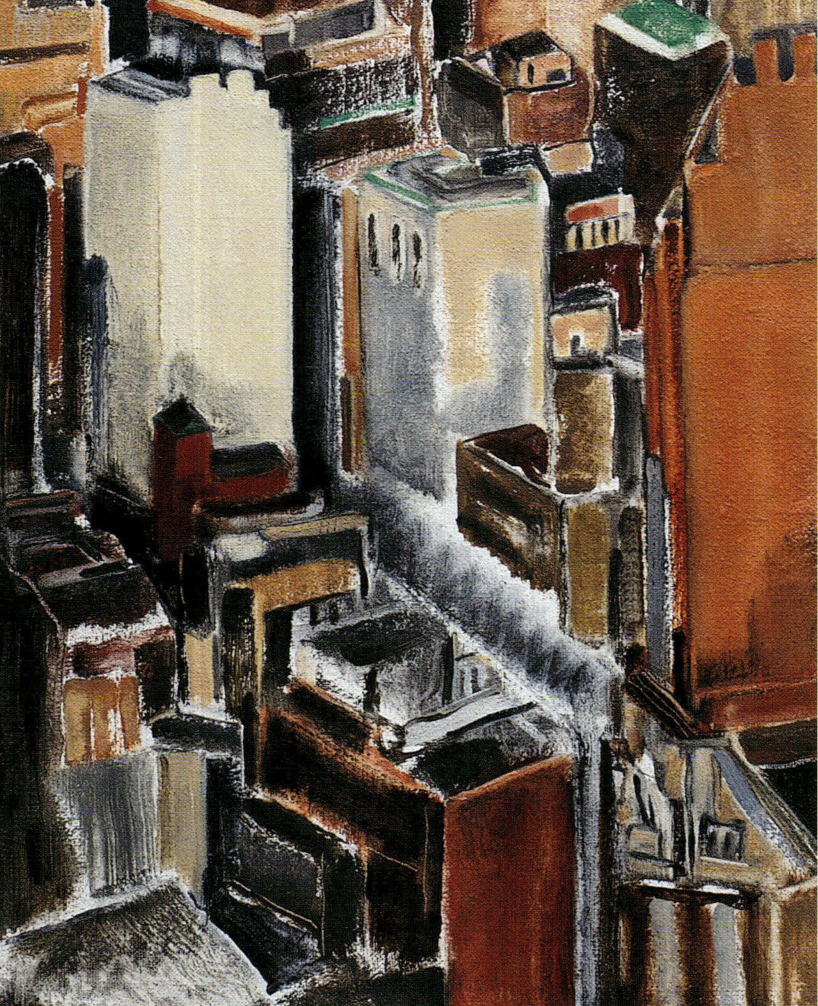

Born 1933 in Paris, France
Lives in New York, N.Y.

Education

1956 The School of the Art Institute of Chicago, Ill.
1954 BA, University of Chicago, Ill.
1950 Black Mountain College, N.C.

Selected Solo Exhibitions

2002 *Above and Below*, DFN Gallery, New York, N.Y.
1994 *Aerial Notations: Drawings and Paintings*, New Britain Museum of American Art, Conn.
1975 *Notations*, Matrix Gallery, Wadsworth Atheneum, Hartford, Conn.

Selected Group Exhibitions

2003 *Modern Shadows*, The Painting Center, New York, N.Y.
2002 *Invitational*, National Academy of Design, New York, N.Y.
Watercolor, The New York Studio School, N.Y.
1997 *Aerial Perspectives: Reality, Imagination, and Abstraction*, DC Moore Gallery, New York, N.Y.
1973 *1973 Biennial Exhibition*, Whitney Museum of American Art, New York, N.Y.

From my notes:

I was looking for a perch on high to serve as a periscope from which to see how it all hangs together, floorplan and elevation.

9.16.00 *Instead of the view running away from me as it does while in flight, here I can study it in stationary stillness and shifting light. My absorption in hard looking is intense. I feel myself seeing. Much of the time I'm alone. No phone.*

12.28.00, 5:10 P.M. *Facing east. The view is almost always oblique and receding. You can't escape the horizon. This is truly an island with waters beyond each river where distant bays and inlets empty into the Atlantic. Dark is settling in. At street level it has been dark for a long time. Up here the darkening is slower and palpable. For a short transition period the East River is clearly blue, then a glistening greenish blue-black.*

12.28.00, 5:25 P.M. *It is now probably as dark as it gets. There is much to see in the dark, so much color and so many darks. At dusk the tip of the towers' shadow extended toward Roosevelt Island and touched the East River. This is a permanent sundial.*

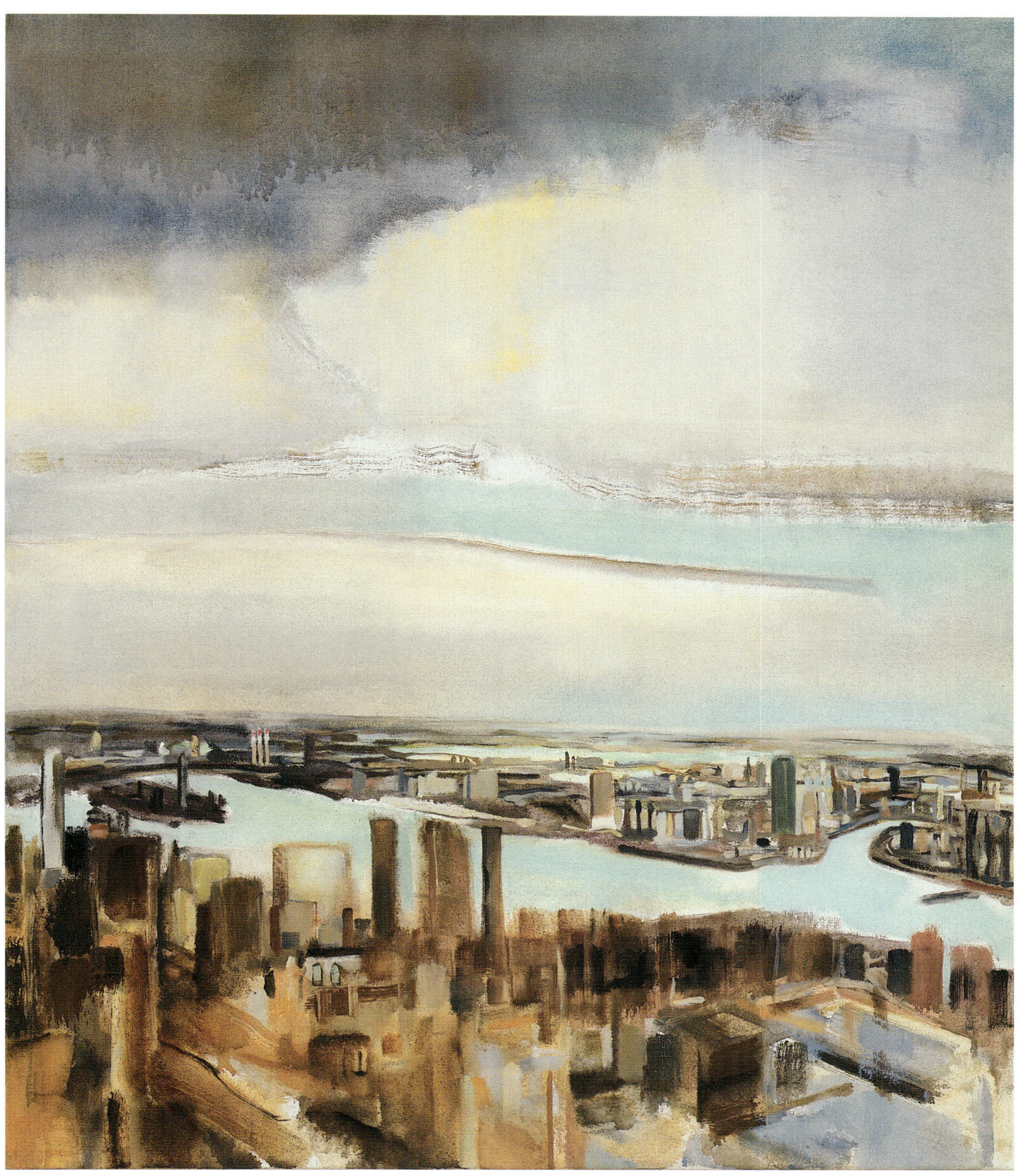

Robert Grunder

University Place Mall, 2001
Oil on canvas
80 x 40 inches

Born 1974 in Bethlehem, Pa.
Lives in New York, N.Y.

Education

1998 MFA, New York Academy of Art, N.Y.
1996 BFA, East Carolina University, Greenville, N.C.

Solo Exhibition

2003 *sixtyseven, Brooklyn, N.Y.

Selected Group Exhibitions

2002 *Night of a Thousand Drawings*, Artists Space, New York, N.Y.
Benefit Auction, Jersey City Museum, N.J.
2001 *Take Heart*, MPI Productions International, New York, N.Y.
Archipod, *sixtyseven, Brooklyn, N.Y.
2000 *Now*, New York Academy of Art Alumni Exhibition, N.Y.

Curatorial Projects

2000 *onomastix*, Exhibition Space 156, Brooklyn, N.Y.
1999 *ex-capillary*, Allen Sheppard Gallery, New York, N.Y.

Working in the World Trade Center, New York's most powerful symbol of American economic dominance, created for me a fascination with the architectural icons of commercial culture—suburban strip mall designs and aerial views of complex highway interchanges—that have in the past half-century become the archetypal American landscape.

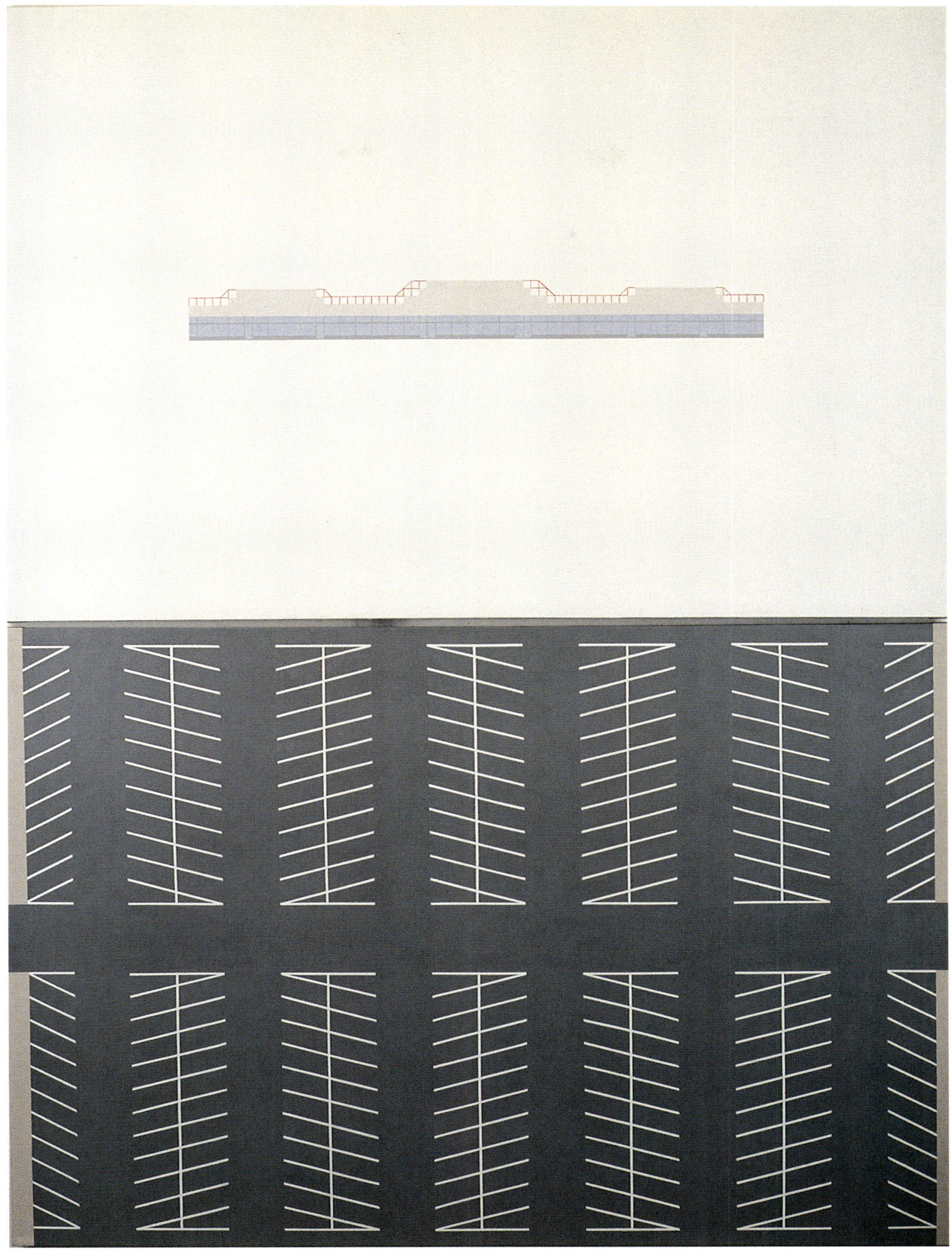

Sally Gutiérrez

City Game TV, 2002 (stills)
DVD, 14 minutes

City Game TV juxtaposes interviews with six WTC workers talking about the view from their windows at work, with footage shot from WTC windows at various times and seasons. The descriptions reflect personal feelings toward the building, its architecture and magnificent views, and at the same time they redefine the relationship of the individual to the city. I planned to show this piece in the elevators, halls and landings of the WTC; the scrolling subtitles, the constant movement of people and vehicles from the hierarchical height of the WTC, and the human aspect of the narratives were to be presented together as an ironic commentary on the various TV info/business channels shown continuously in the building.

In the wake of 9/11, *City Game TV* has been edited following the original idea, but also as a homage to Michael Richards, all the victims of 9/11 and to the hours, spaces and views lived in the WTC.

Open Windows, 2001
Eight cotton curtains, seven electric fans, seven wooden stools

Open Windows is a site-specific commentary on the institutional, commercial space of the WTC and its position of symbolic power. The white cotton curtains, reminiscent of southern interiors, moved with the breeze created by electric fans. As the public walked into the space they had the feeling that the windows were open and air was blowing. The curtains opened showing the spectacular views and gave the very masculine space a poetic and domestic feeling.

Born 1966 in Madrid, Spain
Lives in Madrid, Spain and New York, N.Y.

Education

2001 The New School for Social Research, New York, N.Y.
1999–2000 Whitney Museum of American Art Independent Study Program, New York, N.Y.
1990 MA, Facultad de Bellas Artes, Complutense University, Madrid, Spain

Selected Solo Exhibitions

2003 *Noise Trails,* Liquidación Total, Madrid, Spain
2001 *Scene of the Crime*, Whitebox Gallery, New York, N.Y.

Selected Group Exhibitions

2003 *Monocanal,* Museo Nacional Centro de Arte Reina Sofía, Madrid, Spain. (tour)
Raw, Smack Mellon, Brooklyn, N.Y.
2002 *Locations,* Rotunda Gallery, Brooklyn, N.Y.
Cine y Casi Cine, Museo Nacional Centro de Arte Reina Sofía, Madrid, Spain

Awards

2001 First Prize, Art and Technolgy, Fundación Retevisión, Barcelona, Spain
1998–99 Fulbright Fellowship

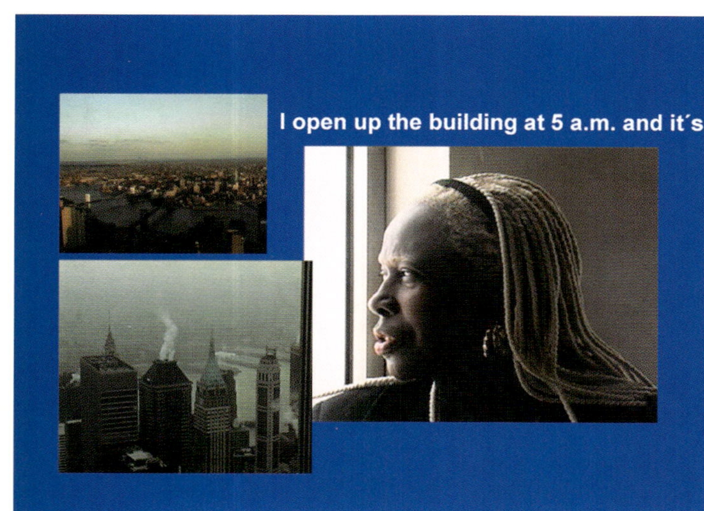

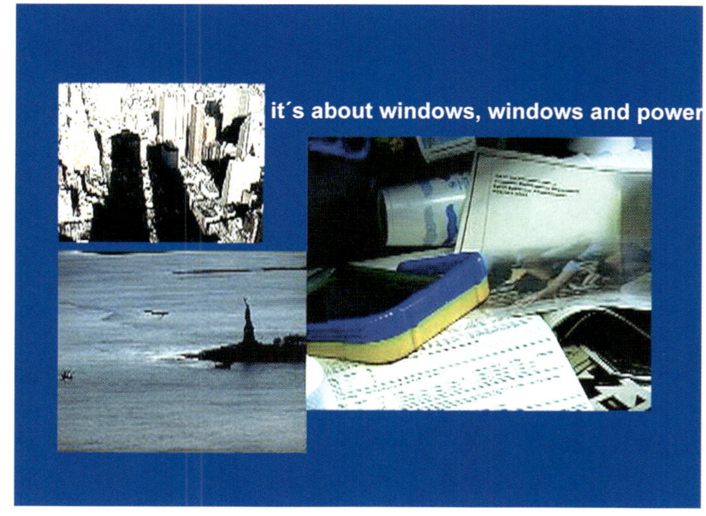

My artistic work is based on the perspective of how the individual perceives and inhabits urban space, so being in the WTC was both a unique and strange experience for me.

Early in the mornings, after the surrealistic ten-minute "commute" through the mall and elevators full of people and constant movement, I would open the door to those huge, empty studios and feel the physical impact of the view, the height, the silence and the openness. The fact that the building was the center and symbol of late capitalism made the contradiction between its fascination and decadence even greater. We were removed from the reality of the city below us but at the same time very much in the middle of it.

I was interested in finding out what the people working in that building felt about the WTC and how being there influenced their relationship to New York. I explored the top floors of the north building and got to know a lot of the security and cleaning staff, who helped me find the best places to film the views.

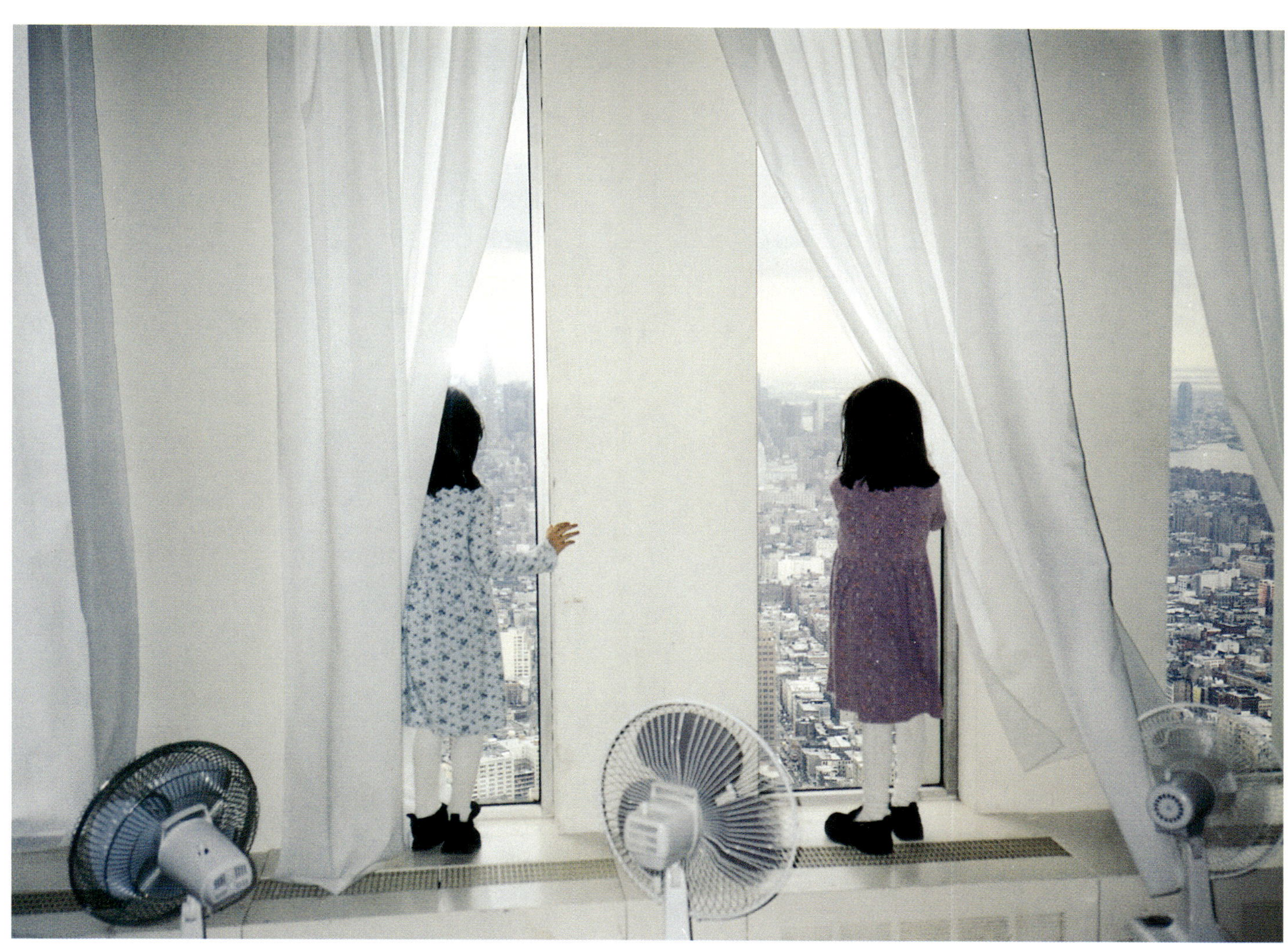

Adam Henry

A Few Things Have Happened #5, 2001
Photo collage
30 x 40 inches

A Few Things Have Happened #11, 2001
Photo collage
8 x 10 inches

Born 1974 in Pueblo, Colo.
Lives in New York, N.Y.

Education

2000 MFA, Yale University School of Art, New Haven, Conn.
1997 BFA, University of New Mexico, Albuquerque

Selected Group Exhibitions

2003 *Metastasize*, The Bronx River Art Center, The Bronx, N.Y.
Towards a Low-End Theory, Minnesota Center for Photography, Minneapolis
Labor Day, Rare Gallery, New York, N.Y.
2002 *Love and Ardor*, Geoffrey Young Gallery, Great Barrington, Mass.
2001 *On Location*, Midway Contemporary Art, Minneapolis, Minn.

Curatorial Project

2002 *Reconfigure*, Richard Levy Gallery, Albuquerque, N.Mex.

Award

2000 Richard Dixon Welling Award, Yale University

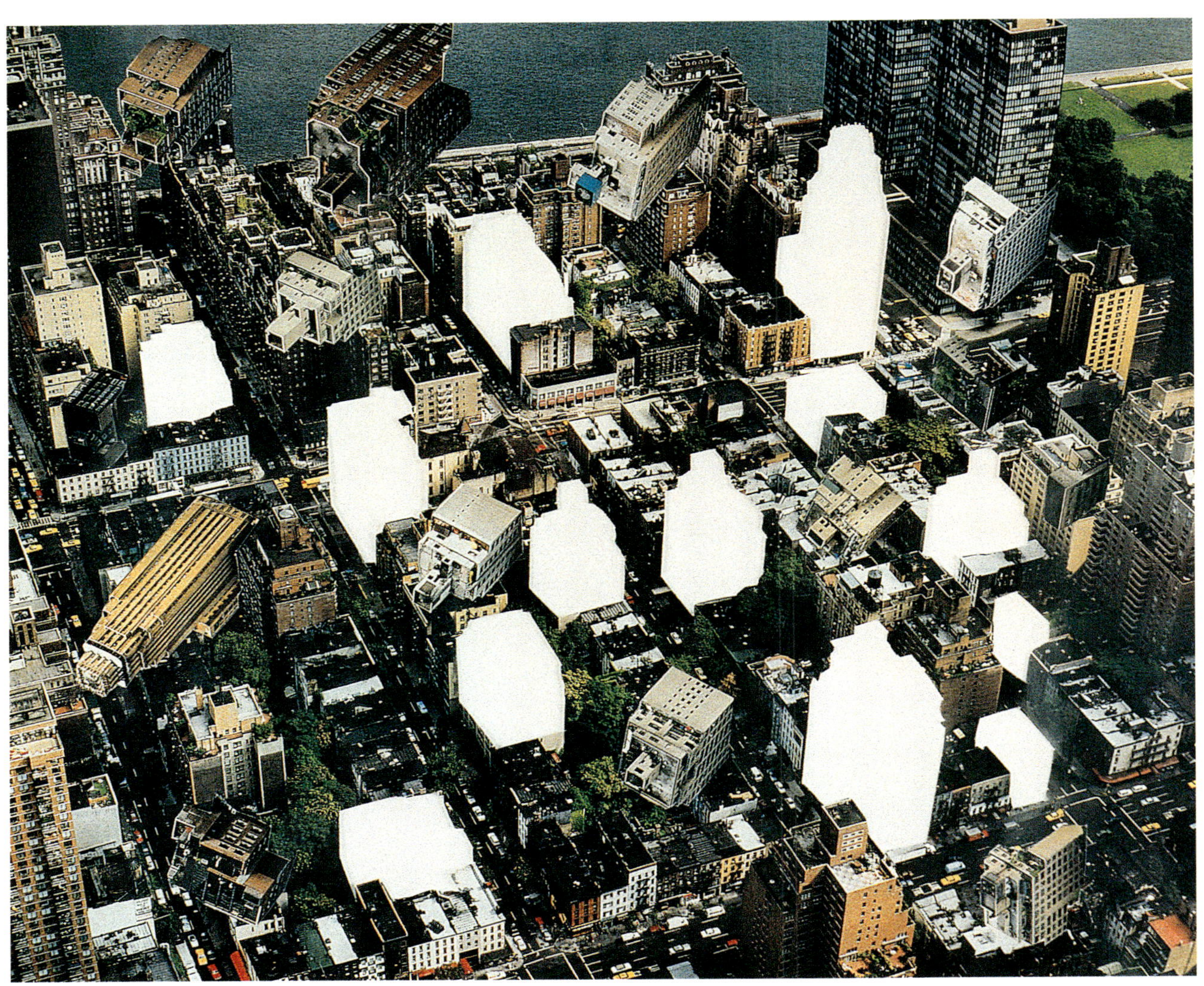

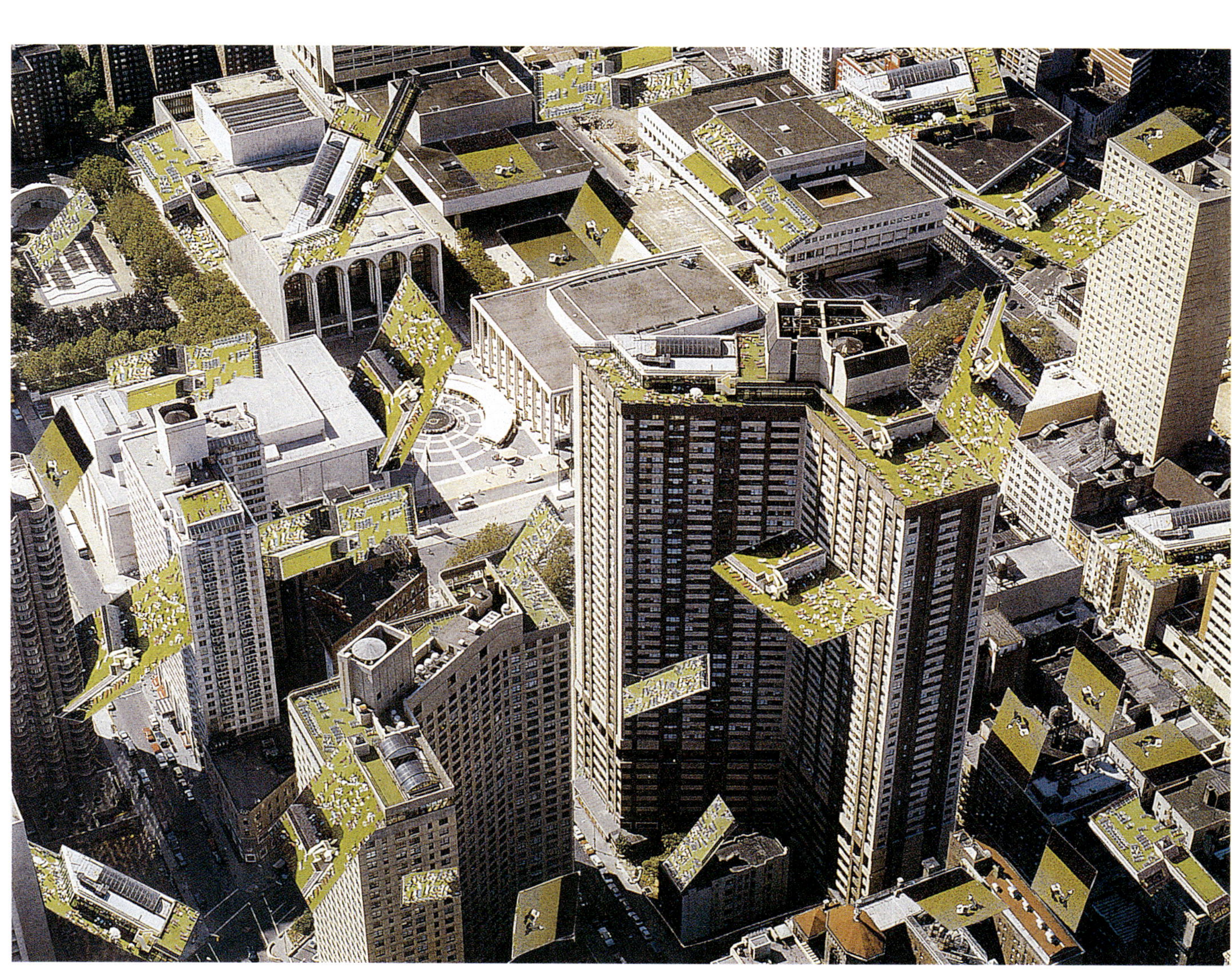

Hoon Kim

Electricity III, 2001
Mixed media installation
Dimensions variable
Photos: Young Sam, Kim

Electricity III was designed specifically for the ninety-first floor of the World Trade Center. Materials were gathered from every corner of the World Trade Center, and even the radio sound is a reproduction of the signals transmitted from the station on the roof. This site-specific installation comprises five different sculptures representing the electrical infrastructure of the city, including the Twin Towers, the Empire State Building, Times Square, Central Park and a computer control board.

The beautiful scenery of Manhattan at night can be seen as a chandelier. I view it as an electrical part whose function is limited and governed by bigger machinery operated by electricity. Humans think they are in control of electrical power, but we will soon be slaves to a company that is like a hybrid of Con Edison and Verizon.

The city is a living being that goes through a unique life cycle; a dormant city wakes up, evolves and dies. The electric current that courses through wires never stops, even when transmitted with wireless devices. This is equivalent to the endlessness of human desire.

This work revisits the New York blackout of 1977. A sudden blackout demonstrates the inherent imperfection of electrical power—a human product that could eventually destroy what humans have created.

Born 1971 in Daegu, South Korea
Lives in New York, N.Y.

Education

2000 MFA, School of Visual Arts, New York, N.Y.
1997 BFA, Kyung-Il University, Daegu, Korea

Selected Exhibitions

2000 *Moving Image: Ten Years of Video*, Anthology Film Archives, New York, N.Y.
Electricity I, Thread Waxing Space, New York, N.Y.
1997 *Turn around time*, Dong-Ah Gallery, Korea
1994 *Prelude-Newspaper*, Kyung-Il University, Korea

Publication and Performance

1994 *Mind*, Photography Journal No.1, Kyung-Il University Press, Korea
1993 *Prelude-Newspaper*, City of Daegu Police Department, Korea

Award

1999 School of Visual Arts Aaron Siskind Award

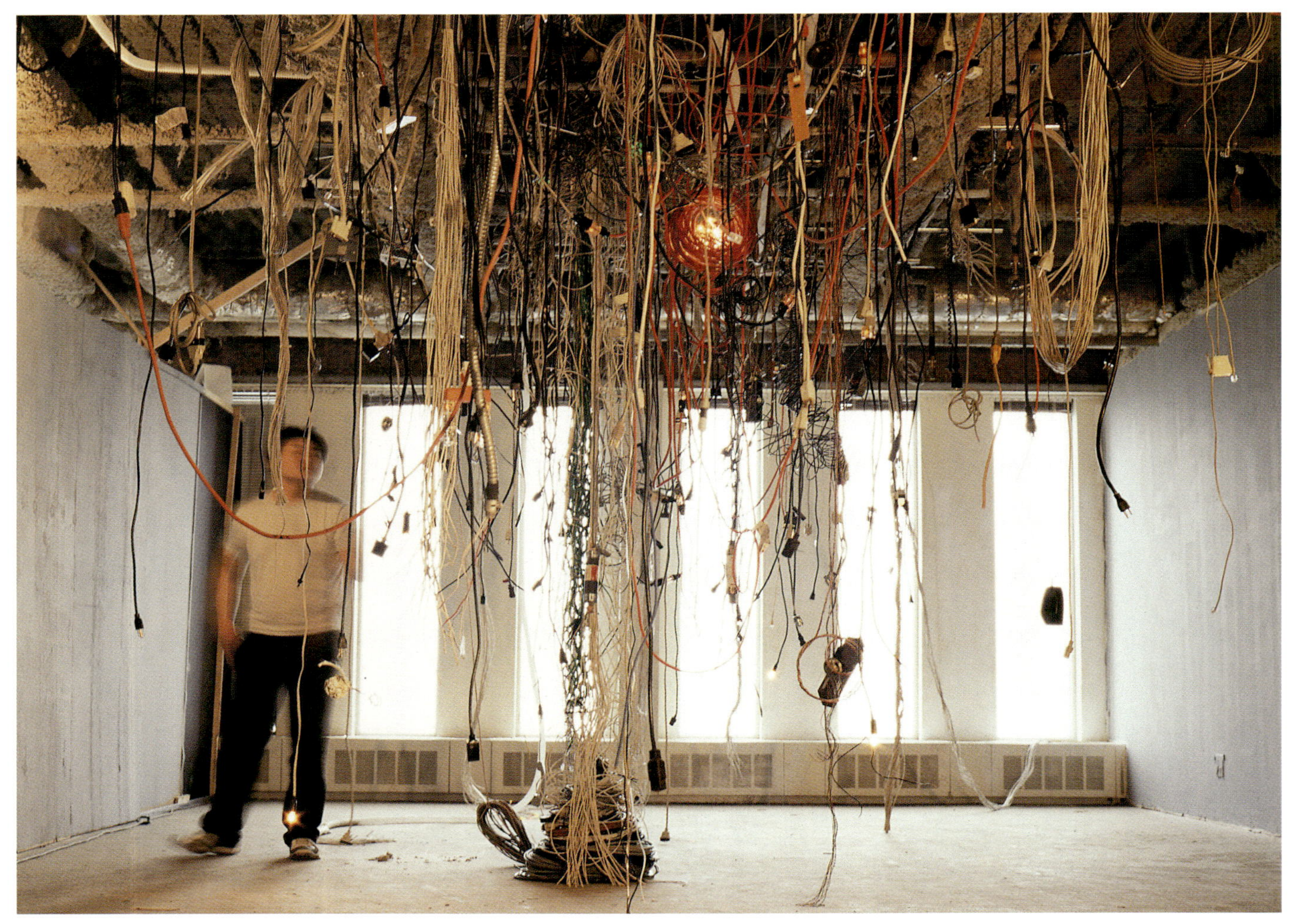

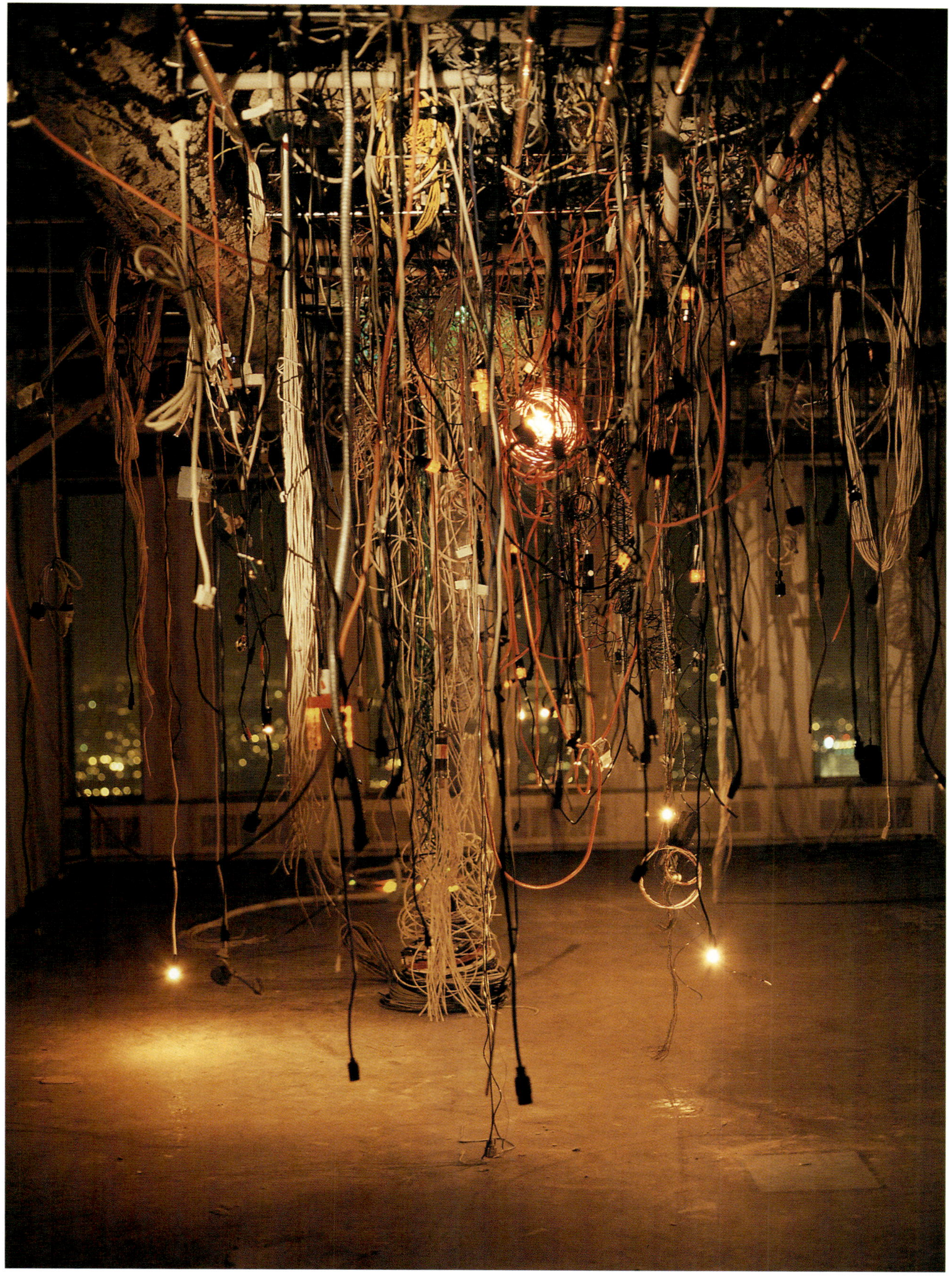

Raoul Middleman

View from Tower (2), 2001
Oil on canvas
48 x 48 inches

Born 1935 in Baltimore, Md.
Lives in Baltimore, Md.

Education

1961 Brooklyn Museum Art School, N.Y.
1959–61 Pennsylvania Academy of Fine Arts, Philadelphia
1955 BA, Johns Hopkins University, Baltimore, Md.

Selected Solo Exhibitions

2003 *Recent Landscapes*, C. Grimaldis Gallery, Baltimore, Md.
2000 *Recent Paintings*, MB Modern Gallery, New York, N.Y.

Selected Group Exhibitions

1995 American Academy of Arts and Letters, New York, N.Y.
1969 *Human Concern/Personal Torment*, Whitney Museum of American Art, New York, N.Y.

Residency

1997–2001 Hoffberger School of Painting, Maryland Institute College of Art, Baltimore, Md.

Awards

2003 Edwin Palmer Memorial Prize, The National Academy of Design
1997 Benjamin Altman Prize, The National Academy of Design

When I went up to the ninety-first floor of the WTC, I discovered that the horizon went up too, dragging the whole city along with it. Paradoxically, even though we were in the sky, perched among the hurtling clouds, there was very little left of the sky to paint. The studios looked straight down on St. Paul's Church and across the Financial District, Wall Street, the bridges of the East River and over Brooklyn, all the way, on a clear day, to Coney Island.

You couldn't paint everything. Sometimes you felt the building swaying under your feet from the strong wind. The windows were really narrow, only eighteen inches wide, just wide enough to catch you by the shoulders if you happened to fall through. So I ended up using a vertical format, looking straight down.

All around the younger artists were making videos and installations. They came from all over the world. There was a global density of artistic perspectives.

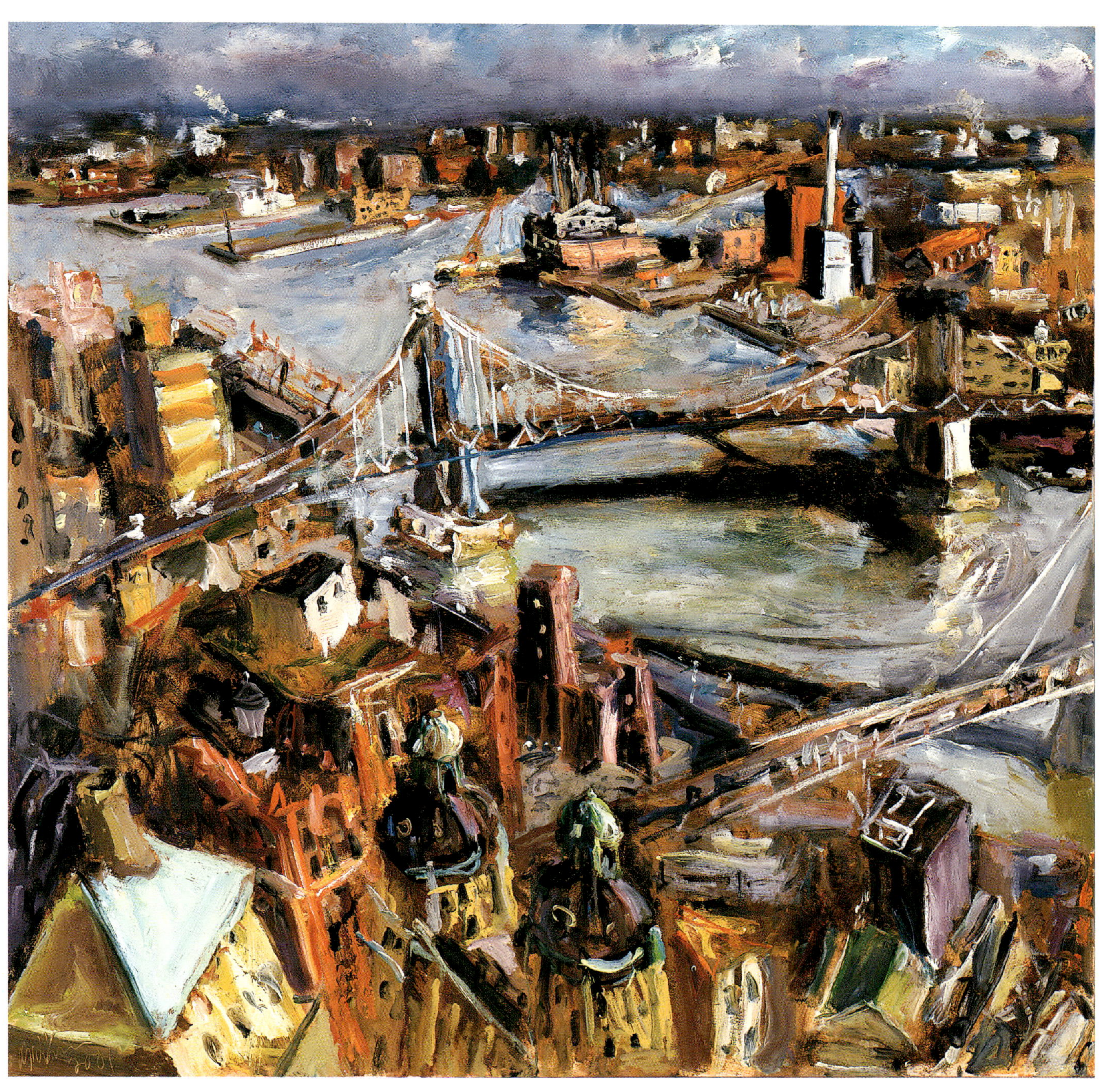

Sandrine Nicoletta

Thought (New York), 2001
Photos and sculptures
50 photos, 6½ x 8½ inches each;
5 sculptures, 16 x 79 x 79 inches overall
Courtesy Neon Gallery, Bologna, Italy

The pictures are meteorological and ambient notes. The sculptures are forms of the thoughts.

Born 1970 in Aosta, Italy
Lives in Bologna, Italy

Education

2000 Fondazione Antonio Ratti, Como, Italy
2000 University of Paris, France
1997 MFA, Academy of Fine Arts, Bologna, Italy

Selected Solo Exhibitions

2003 *mt 0,5 ——••• ∞*, Maze Gallery, Turin, Italy
2002 *Surplace*, Neon Gallery, Bologna, Italy
1999 *Demi bain*, ESBAM, Marseille, France

Selected Group Exhibitions

2001 *EurostAr*, Museum of Modern and Contemporary Art, Bologna, Italy
2000 *Emporio*, Viafarini, Milano, Italy

Public Art and Screening

2003 *Jump*, Tokyo Denki University, Japan
2001 *The secret of the archipelago*, San Sung Park Kongju, Korea
2000 *In video veritas*, The British School, Rome, Italy

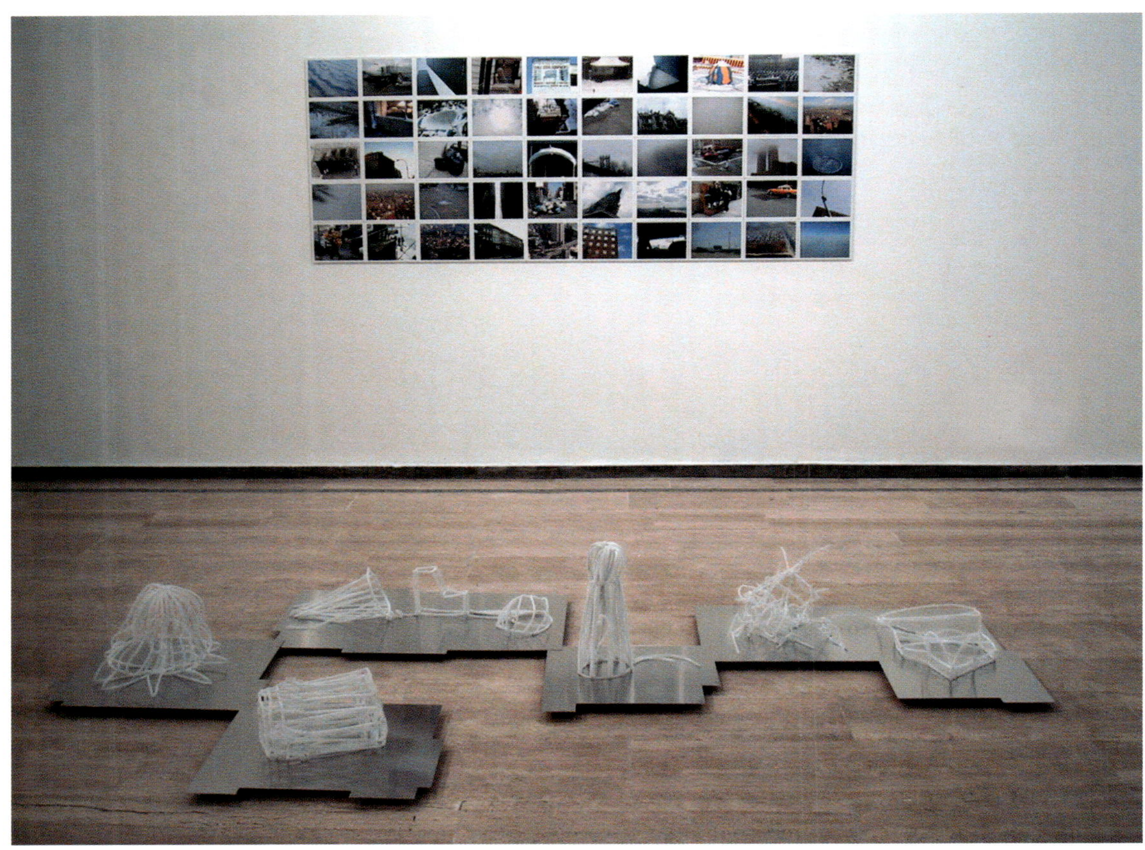

Each time I go to a new place I spend a lot of time observing the environment. 1) I listen to myself traveling the space. 2) I keep still and listen to everything that moves around me: the place, the people.

I take as many notes as possible (writings-drawings-photos-videos). Once I have observed all that needs to be observed, I transfer my work to the studio where I elaborate and reorganize the information —creating an emptiness. It is at this point that my project develops, as a result of my "encounters." Once I have completed my work I like to exchange opinions with people who go by.

The real point in my work is the tight connections: space, bodies and psychological aspects all linked in an indissoluble plot; the relations among verticality, horizontality and depth.

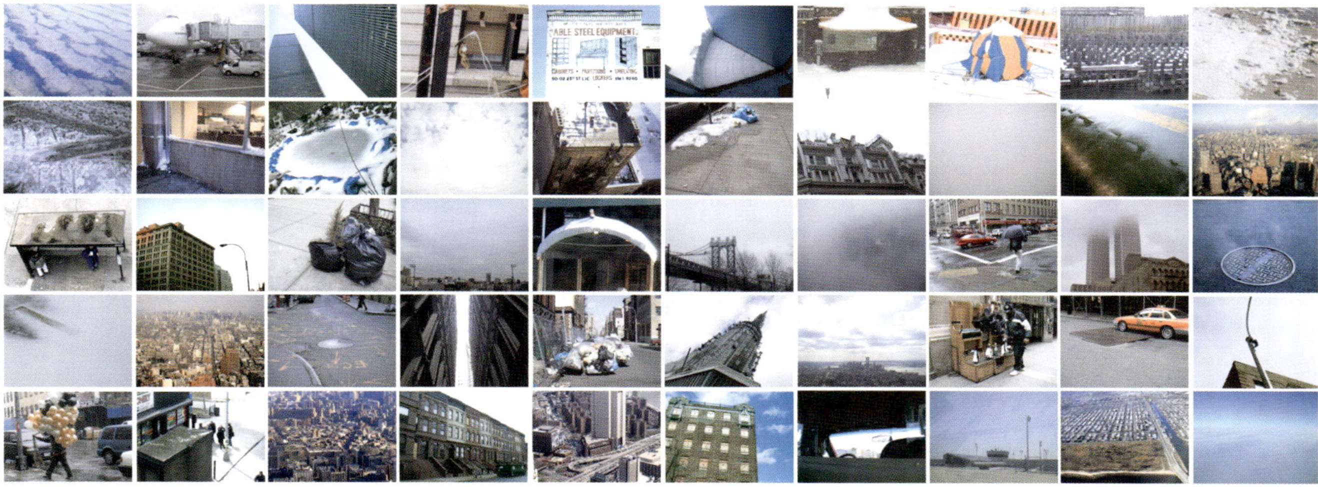

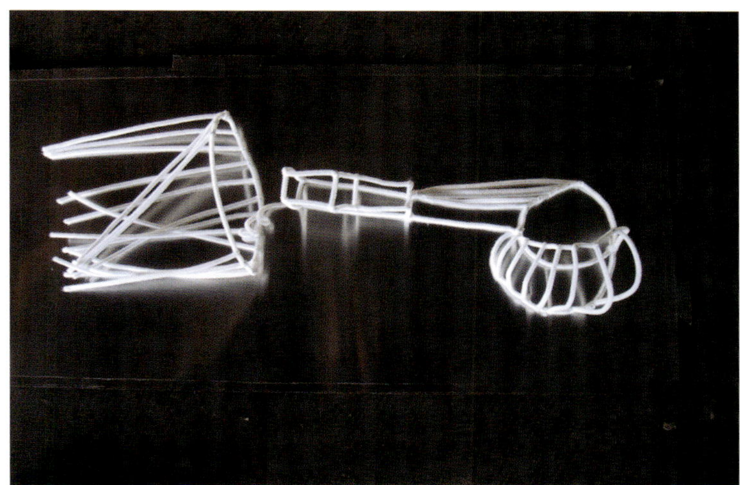

Yigal Nizri

Do you see Hebrew like you should? (gray cloud), 2001
Wood, slides, slide projectors
14 x 18 feet

Tiger, 2001
Wool, acrilan and Lycra
15 x 17½ feet
Photo: David Adika

Born 1973 in Haifa, Israel
Lives in New York, N.Y.

Education

1998 BFA, The Bezalel Academy of Art and Design, Jerusalem
1997–98 Student Exchange, The Cooper Union School of Art, New York, N.Y.

Selected Solo Exhibitions

2002 *Leaving Growing*, Dvir Gallery, Tel Aviv, Israel
1999 *, The Gallery of the Midrasha School of Art, Beit-Berl, Israel

Selected Group Exhibitions

2003 *The Promise, The Land: Artists in Relation to Politics and Society*, The O.K. Center for Contemporary Art, Linz, Austria
2002 *Mother Tongue*, Mishkan Le'Omanut at Ein-harod, Israel
2001 *Song Poems*, Cohan Leslie and Browne, New York, N.Y.
2000 *Not To Be Looked At*, The Israel Museum, Jerusalem
1999 *Ice Cream Van*, ArtFocus 3, International Biennial of Contemporary Art, Jerusalem

Award

2000 Anslem Keifer Award, Wolf Foundation, Israel

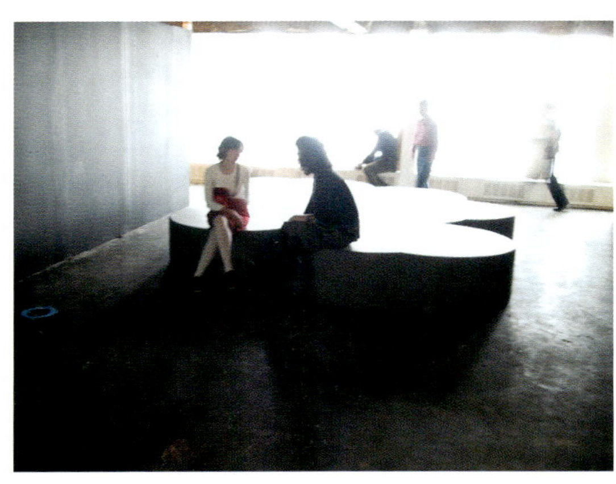

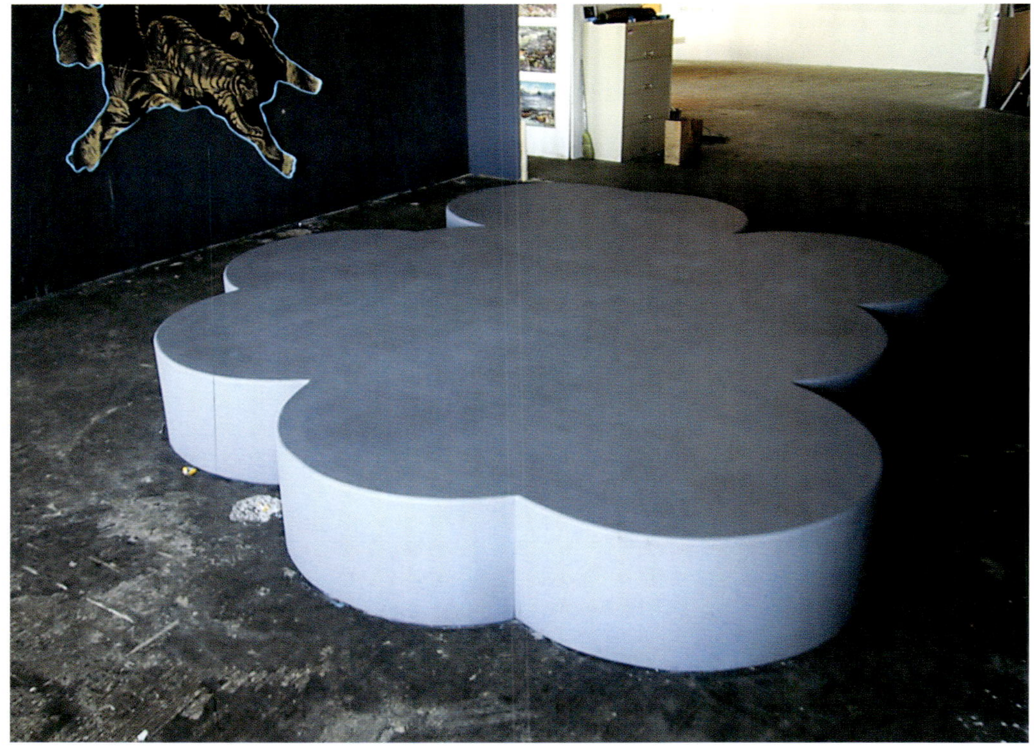

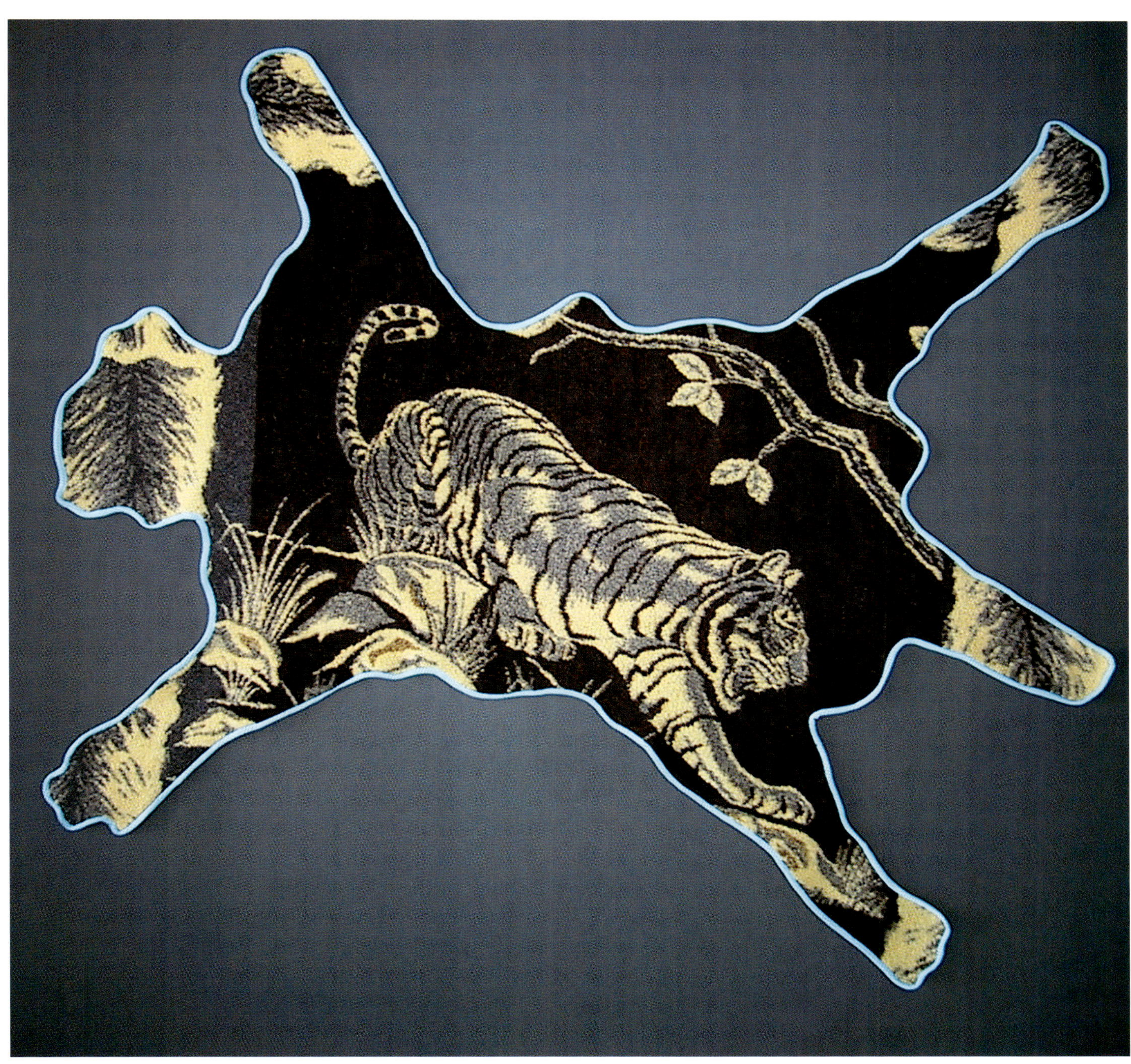

Kamilla Talbot

Huddle, 2001
Oil on linen
20 x 22 inches
Photo: D. James Dee

Born 1968 in Boston, Mass.
Lives in Brooklyn, N.Y.

Education

2000 The New York Studio School, N.Y.
1990 BFA, Rhode Island School of Design, Providence

Solo Exhibition

2002 Johannes Larsen Museum, Kerteminde, Denmark

Selected Group Exhibitions

2003 *Easter Exhibition,* Galleri Uggerby, Lønstrup, Denmark
New York Studio School Alumni Exhibition, The New York Studio School, N.Y.
2002 *Undoing the Landscape,* The Painting Center, New York, N.Y.
The Objective Landscape, Gallery North, Setauket, N.Y.
2001 *Juried Show*, Bowery Gallery, New York, N.Y.
Maryland Artists Equity Foundation Juried Exhibition, The Baltimore Museum of Art, Md.

Residency

2002 The Vermont Studio Center, Johnson

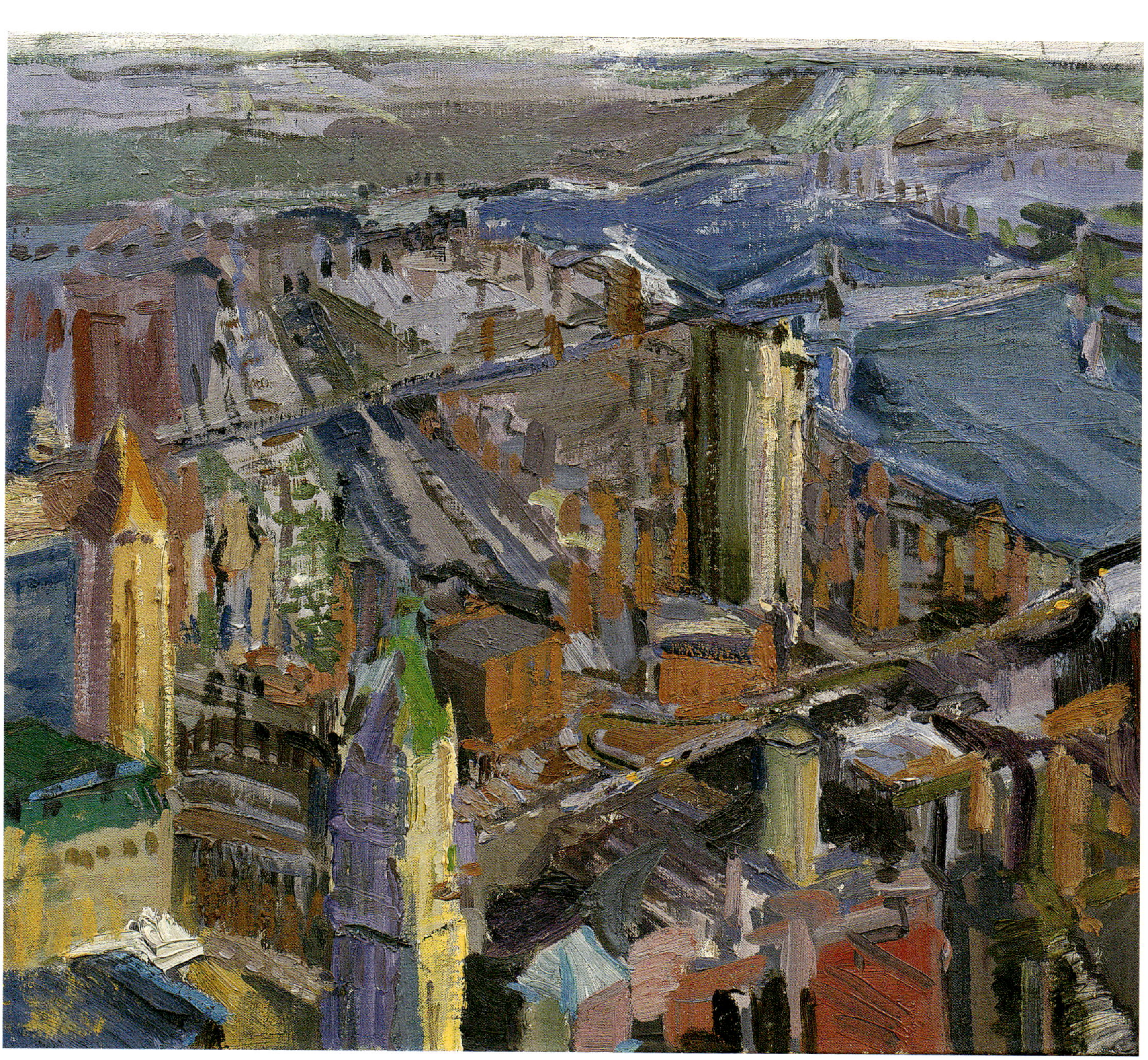

Summer 2001

Artists-in-Residence

Simon Aldridge
Naomi Ben-Shahar
Monika Bravo
Laurie Halsey Brown
Justine Cooper
Lucky DeBellevue
Carola Dertnig
Mahmoud Hamadani
Kara Hammond
Jeff Konigsberg
Motonobu Kurokawa
Geraldine Lau
Michael Richards
Nathan See
Hyungsub Shin

Jurors

Rachel Gugelberger
Hitomi Iwasaki
Karen Jones
Moukhtar Kocache
John Pilson
Sara Tucker

Invited Artists

Karin Batten
Jeff Byles
Megan Craig
Sjoerd Doting
Stan Friedman
Nancy Friese
Ellen Korbonski
Vanessa Lawrence
Nedra Newby
Ocean Earth

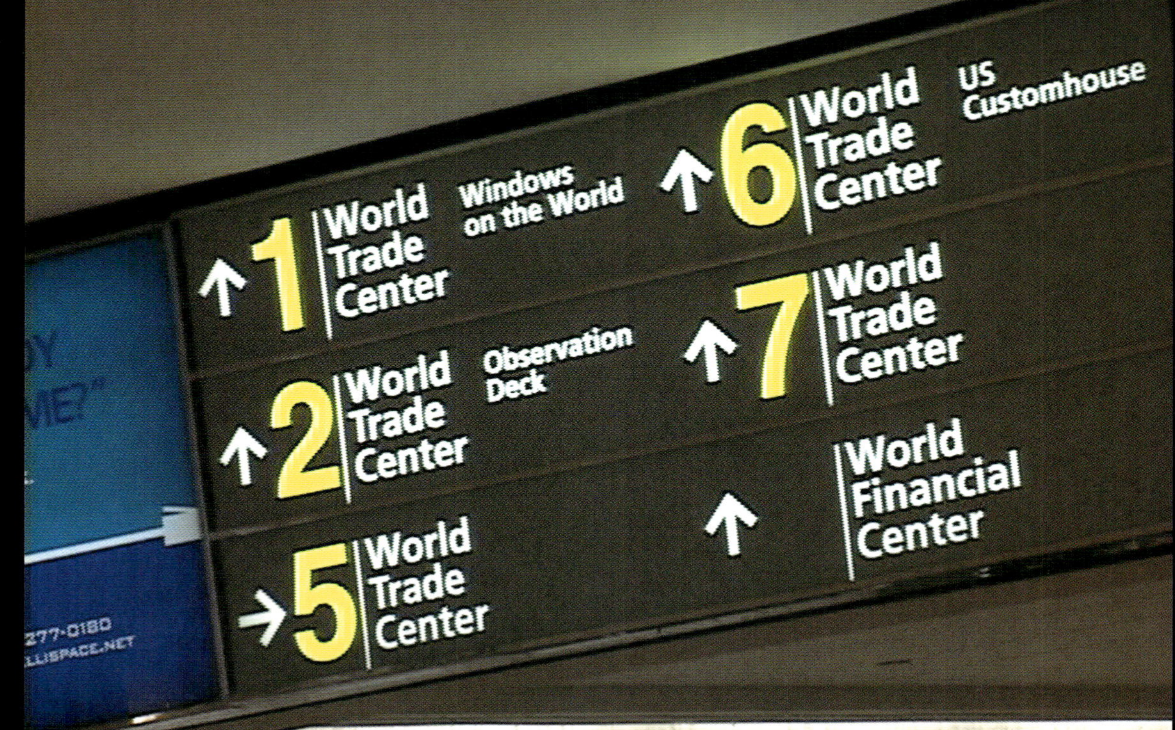
1 World Trade Center
Windows on the World
2 World Trade Center
Observation Deck
5 World Trade Center
6 World Trade Center
US Customhouse
7 World Trade Center
World Financial Center

Naomi Ben-Shahar

Floating Inside Out (WTC), 2001 (still)
DVD projection
15:08 minutes

Floating Inside Out (WTC) is one of several DVD projection works in which I utilized small lights to trace social events in the dark. In these works I filmed the interactions in three similar party situations that I created in different locations: the World Trade Center, a nightclub in Tel Aviv and a loft in Chelsea. They are poetic manifestations of structures created by interaction; structures that themselves can become composite, singular life forms.

The parties had DJs, bars and guests fitted with headlamps. The cameras were above or among the guests, recording the movements and energy of each party. *Floating Inside Out (WTC)* was recorded September 4, 2001, on the ninety-first floor of the WTC. It was probably the last party in this site. The night views, seen through the windows, became implicated in the piece as an echo and essential ingredient of the event.

Amber Latex A, 2001
C-print
40 x 30 inches

Amber Latex A is from a series of large-format photographs of reflections on latex rubber.

Born 1965 in Tel Aviv, Israel
Lives in New York, N.Y.

Education

1993 MFA, Hunter College/CUNY, New York, N.Y.
1990 BA, Empire State College, New York, N.Y.
1986 Tel Aviv University, Israel

Selected Solo Exhibitions

2002 *Can't Stop Wanting You (Tel Aviv),* Gorney Bravin + Lee Gallery, New York, N.Y.
1997 Feature, Inc., New York, N.Y.

Selected Group Exhibitions

2003 *Video Invitational*, f a projects, London, U.K.
2002 *Come to Life Benefit Show*, White Box Gallery, New York, N.Y.
2001 *Song Poems*, Cohan Leslie and Browne, N.Y. (tour)
Painting Not Painting, White Columns, New York, N.Y.
2000 *Not A. Lear*, Torch Gallery, Amsterdam, The Netherlands. (tour)

Award

2003 Edith Russ Grant for Media Art

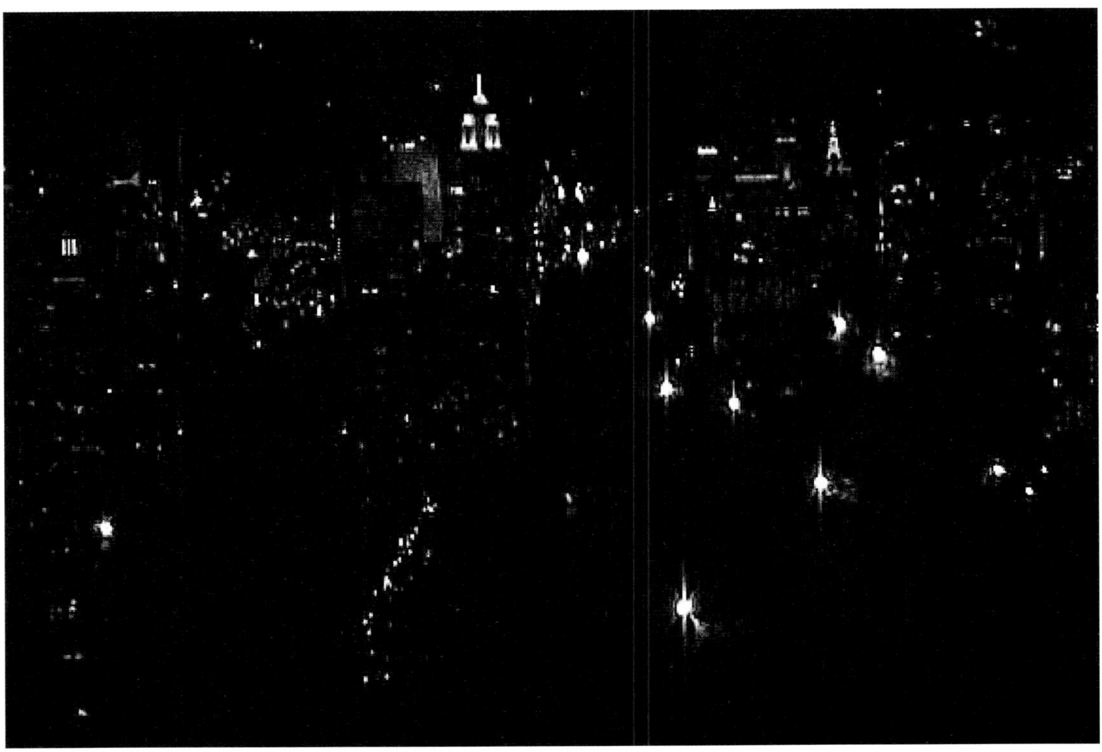

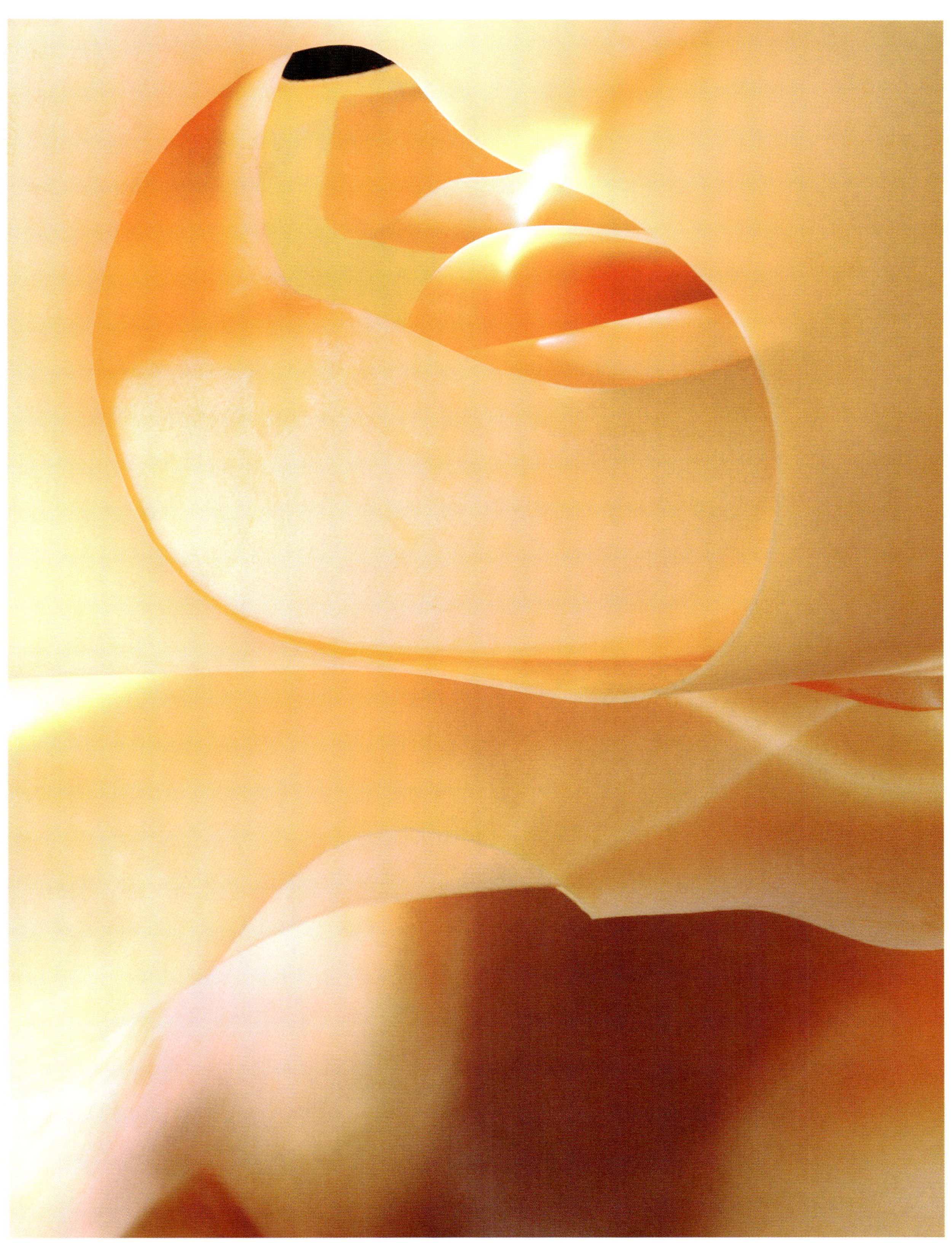

Monika Bravo

September 10, 2001, uno nunca muere la víspera, 2001 (stills)
Singe-channel video, color, 5:40 minutes
Soundtrack *Track 09, Schoehn* by Flora & Fauna, Codek Records (2000)
Courtesy of mullerdechiara, Berlin, Germany and Ciocca Arte Contemporanea, Milan, Italy

A time-lapse video recorded from the World Trade Center on September 10, 2001, that was originally intended to be part of an interactive video installation. The seven hours of condensed time capture an unusual thunderstorm, eerily foreshadowing the tragic events to come.

Born 1964 in Bogotá, Colombia
Lives in Brooklyn, N.Y.

Education

1995 International Center of Photography, New York, N.Y.
1989 London School of Photography, U.K.
1987 Ecole Esmod Guerre-Lavigne, Paris, France

Selected Solo Exhibitions

2002 *A_Maze*, mullerdechiara, Berlin, Germany. (tour)
Playing With Time, SITE Santa Fe, N.Mex.

Selected Group Exhibitions

2003 *Il Viaggio Dell'Uomo Immobile*, Museo D'Arte Contemporanea di Villa Croce, Genova, Italy
Der Rest der Welt, Neuffer im Park Pirmasens, Germany
2002 *9/11 Episodes*, The Kitchen, New York, N.Y.

Screenings

2002 *Visual Noise/Visual Memory: Recent Videos from Colombia*, Museum of Contemporary Art, Los Angeles, Calif. (tour)
2001 *Documentary Fortnight*, Roy & Niuta Titus Theater, The Museum of Modern Art, New York, N.Y.

Award

2002 New York State Council on the Arts, Electronic Media & Film Grant

It is clear to me that at times circumstances give us the opportunity to reflect on our condition and allow us to act purely on intuition, somehow guiding us to something nourishing, yet challenging. September 10 2001, uno nunca muere la víspera's *footage was rescued from total destruction on that same night. It also rescued me from feelings of helplessness the following days when I decided to edit it and share a copy with fellow residents and LMCC staff. The intention was far from creating a document that would travel the world as it has; in those moments my instincts told me that I still had the ability to create after all that had been destroyed.*

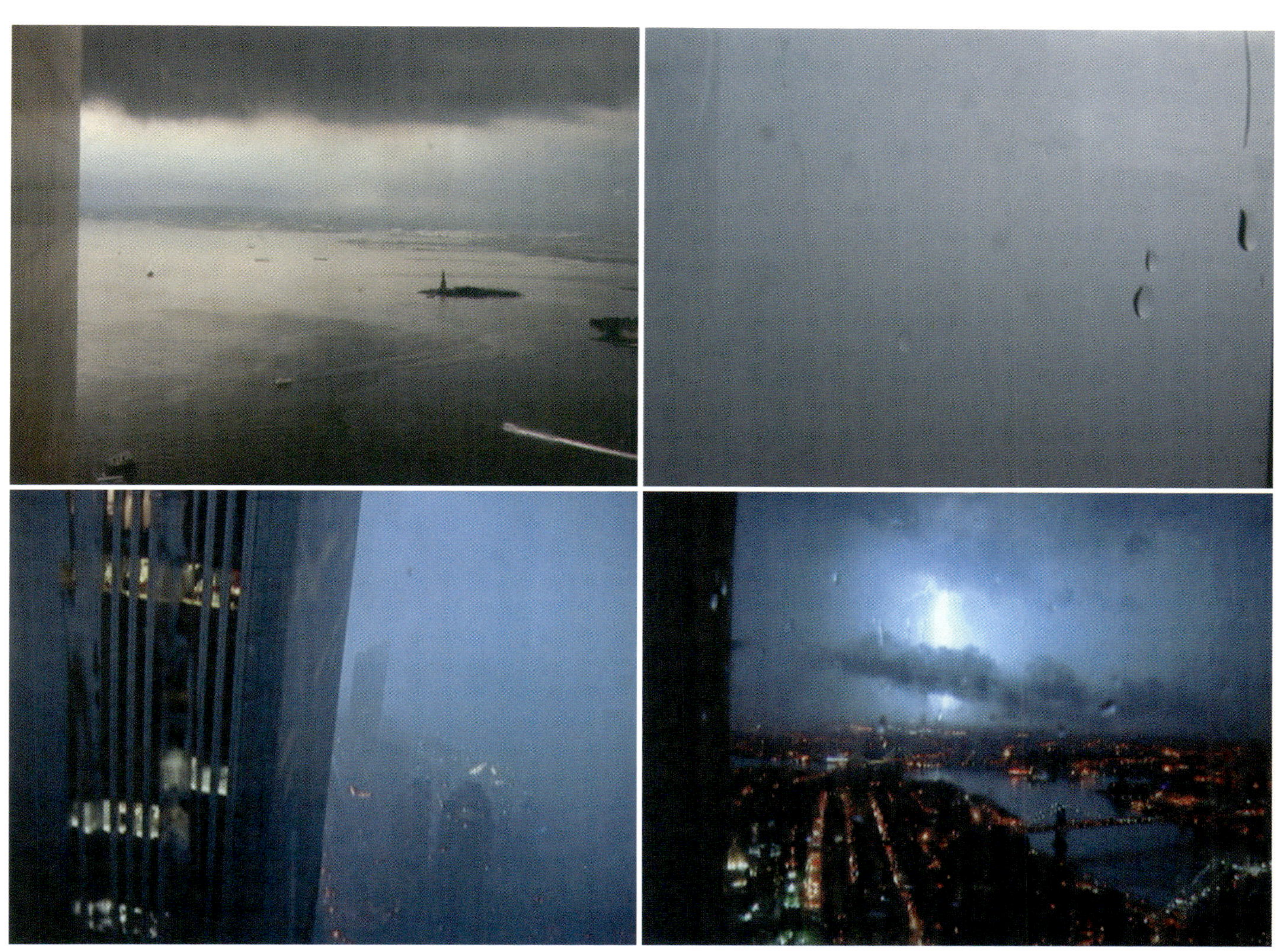

Laurie Halsey Brown

between looking right (when remembering) and looking left (when creating), 2001
Video, glass and photographic triptych

between looking right (when remembering) and looking left (when creating), 2001, is a site-responsive installation in which five panes of glass the same size of the windows in my WTC studio, are projected with video footage of different perspectives seen from the studio. The work refers to the memory of the experience of looking out the windows of the World Trade Center—a view that has now vanished. The low-tech aesthetic of the video projections refer to the process of memory—the images look faded from the originals the way that memory fades our perception over time. The glass reflects the viewer, including them in a mediation of the past that is juxtaposed with the present.

Born 1966 in Washington, D.C.
Lives in Rotterdam, The Netherlands

Education

1990 MFA, California Institute of the Arts, Valencia
1987 BFA, Corcoran School of Art, Washington, D.C.

Solo Exhibition

2003 *beingthere.v01.HOME*, CBK Gallery, Rotterdam, The Netherlands

Selected Group Exhibitions and Screenings

2003 *LIVE!NUDE!SPACE!*, TENT., Rotterdam, The Netherlands
2002 *Parallel Zone*, Cara Foundation, Miami, Fla.
Take Me From Nowhere to Nowhere, Artists Space, New York, N.Y.
2001 *Lecture Lounge*, P.S. 1/Clocktower Gallery, New York, N.Y.

Residencies

2002 Pilotprojekt Gropiusstadt, Berlin, Germany
2001 Santa Fe Art Institute, N.Mex.

Award

2002 Projectsubsidie, Centrum Beeldende Kunst, The Netherlands

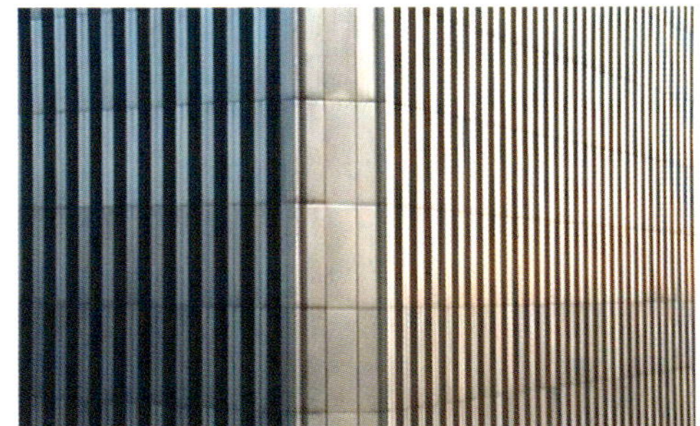

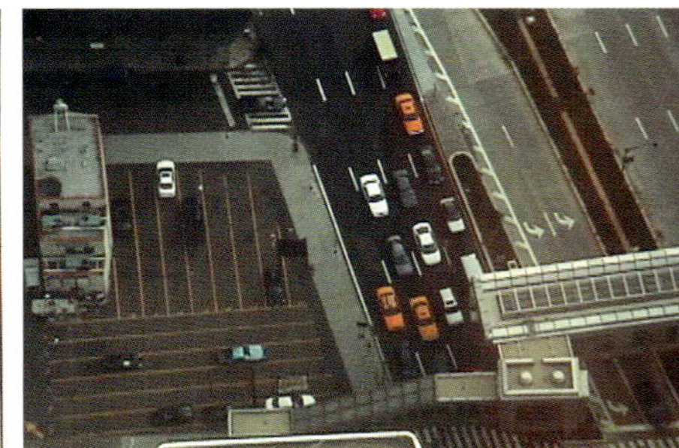

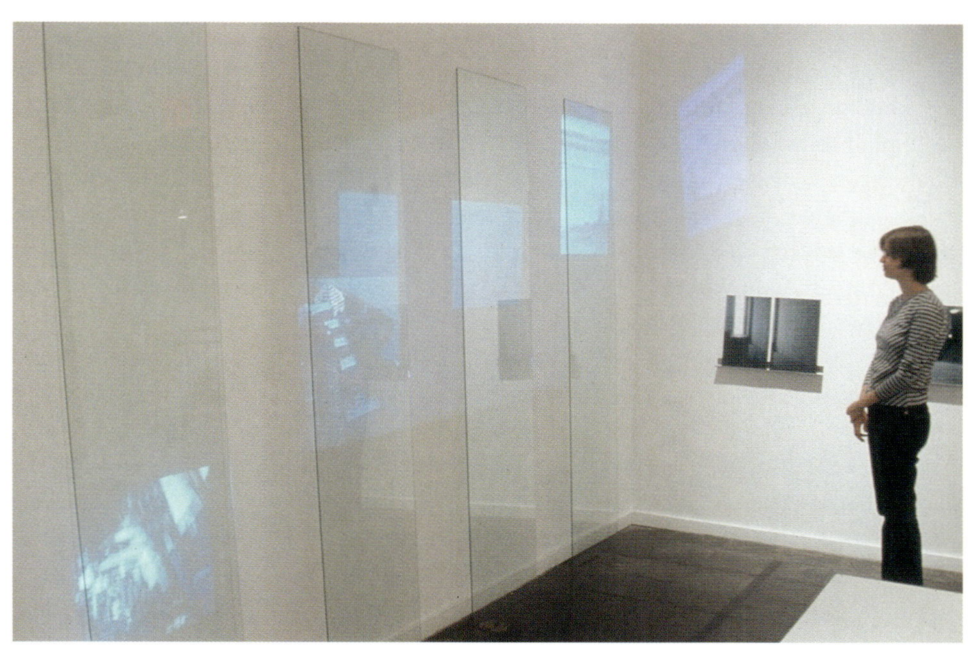

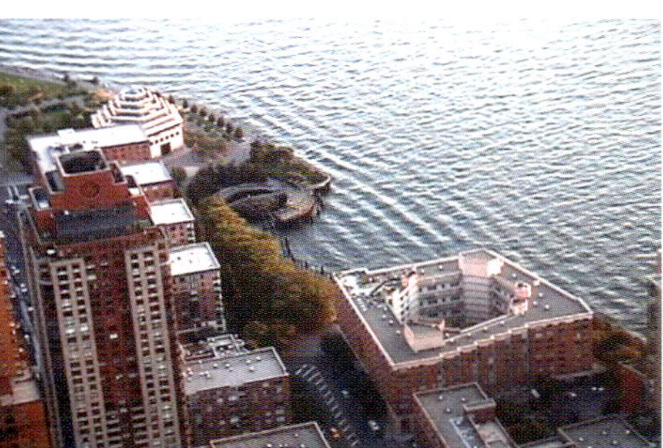

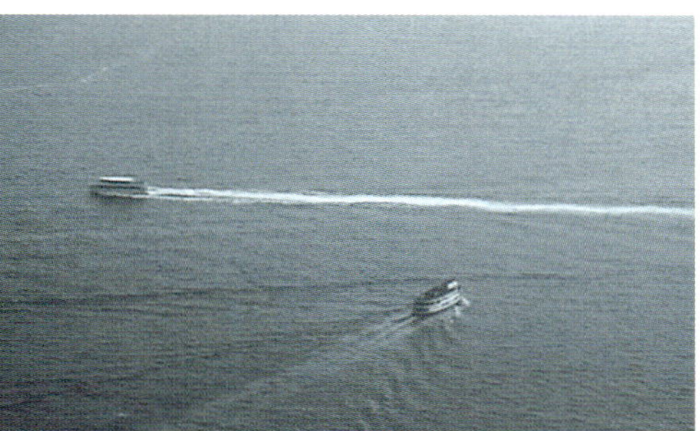

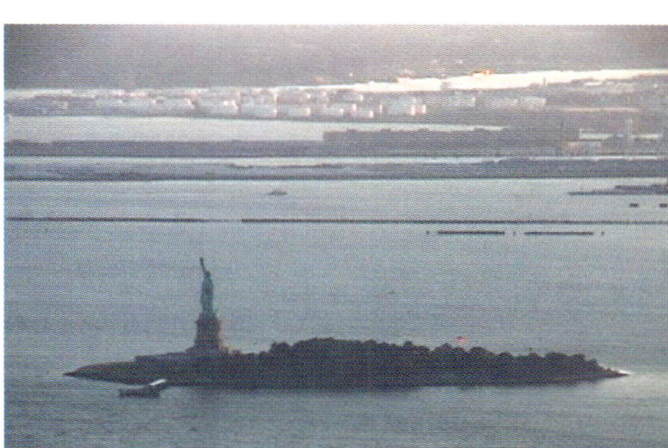

Justine Cooper

Evanition, 2001
Glass, stainless steel, DNA, LCD film, sensors
92 x 36 x 24 inches
Courtesy Julie Saul Gallery, New York, N.Y.
Photo: Bill Orcutt

The sequence for the DNA in the vial was created by translating the light patterns of Tower 1 of the World Trade Center into the four bases comprising DNA—guanine, adenine, thymine and cytosine—using a positional system.

The vial of DNA floats in an incision cut into the two-sided wall of the gallery. By approaching the work, proximity sensors alternate the state of the LCD glass panels between transparent and opaque.

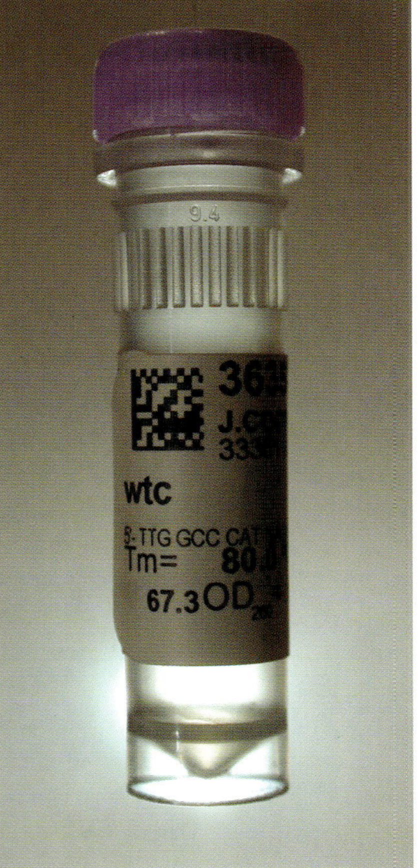

Born 1968 in Sydney, Australia
Lives in Brooklyn, N.Y.

Education

1998 MFA, Sydney University College of the Arts, Australia
1990 BSc, Syracuse University, N.Y.

Selected Group Exhibitions

2004 *TULP* (performance with Elision Ensemble and composer John Rodgers), Sydney and Brisbane Art Festivals, Australia
2003 *How Human: Life in the Post-Genome Era,* International Center of Photography, New York, N.Y.
2002 *PhotoGENEesis: Opus 2*, Santa Barbara Museum of Art, Calif.
ConVerge: Where Art and Science Meet, Adelaide Biennial, The Art Gallery of South Australia
2001 *hybrid <life>forms: Australian New Media Art*, Netherlands Media Art Institute, Amsterdam
2000 Kwangju Biennial, Korea

Residency

2002 *Moist*, Multimedia Arts Asia Pacific Festival, Beijing, China

Award

2001 Australian Network for Art and Technology grant for residency at The Museum of Natural History, New York, N.Y.

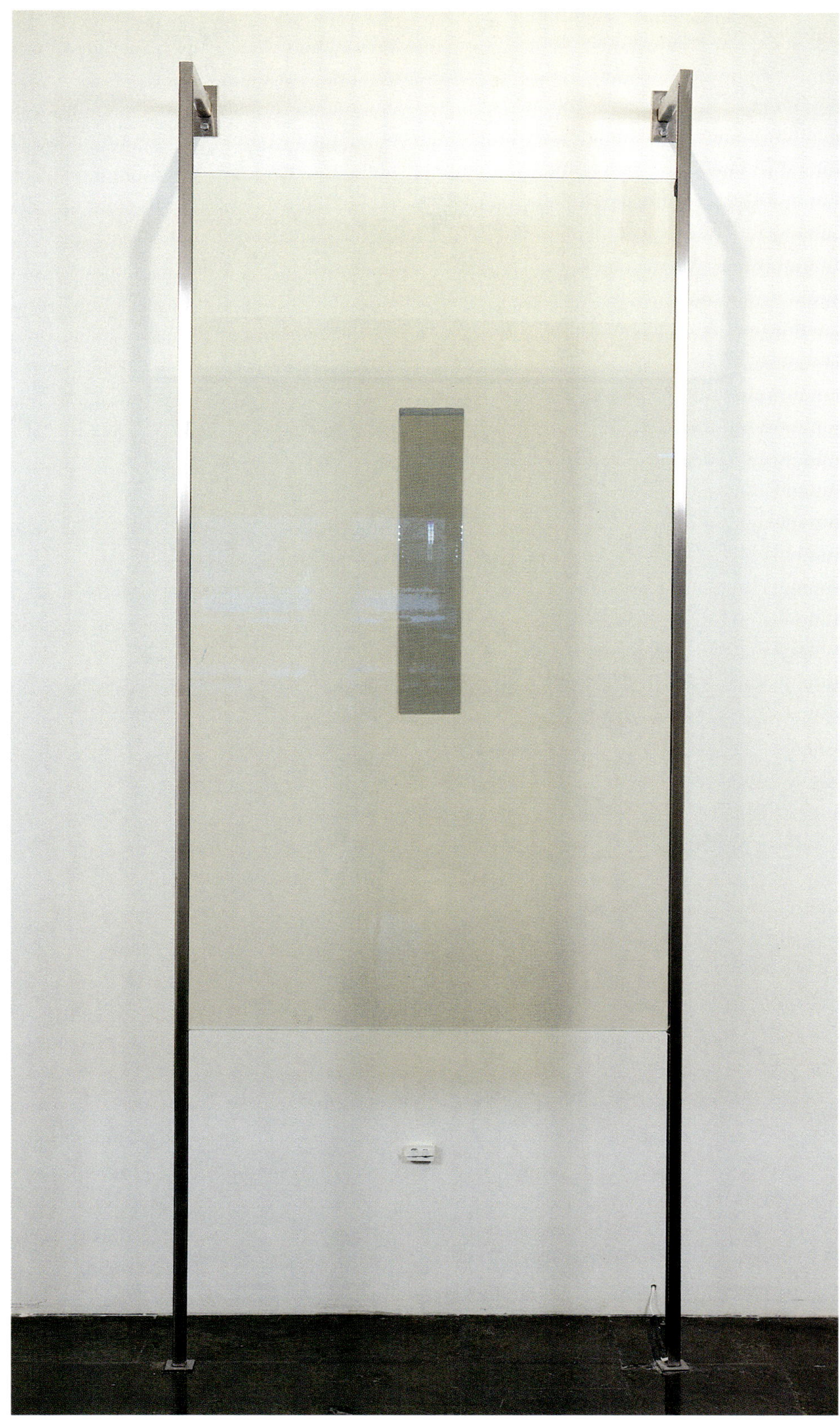

I had proposed my residency project based on the physical look of the buildings' offices lit up at night. I found them reminiscent of DNA autoradiographs. I wanted to take something physical, but not biological, and encode it using a system from biology. I started developing what physical form the project might take by looking at layering patterns and intertwining them with the inverse idea of randomness. Old computer punch cards and knitting patterns have a similar look to autoradiographs and function in the same way whereby the position of the "mark" essentially is the information. I was in the World Trade Center so I wanted to mesh patterns and randomness in economies as well. For instance, the way something random like a foot-and-mouth disease outbreak could affect the wool commodities market. So to tie all these fields and ideas together I thought I would use a knitting machine to relay the information and ideas into a physical form, with wool as the medium. Clearly that's not what I made. 9/11 destroyed my studio and the knitting machine, possibly saving me from my own process. Instead I built an installation where, in a strictly poetical sense, the DNA created becomes a biological transcription of an absent building, with the presence of the viewer affecting what is apparent or not.

Megan Craig

Calder's "Bent Propeller," 2001
Oil on masonite
5 x 7 inches

World Trade Center Plaza, 2001
Oil on gessoed paper
9 x 7 inches

Born 1975 in Potsdam, N.Y.
Lives in New Haven, Conn.

Education

Current	PhD, The New School For Social Research, New York, N.Y.
2001	MA, The New School For Social Research, New York, N.Y.
1997	BA, Yale University, New Haven, Conn.

Solo Exhibition

2004	*New Work*, The Mark Potter Gallery, Watertown, Conn.

Selected Group Exhibitions

2002	*Re-imagining New York*, North Dakota Museum of Art, Grand Forks
2001	*Illuminated Interiors*, Rubilad, Brooklyn

Residencies

2003	The Weir Farm Trust, Wilton, Conn. The Vermont Studio Center, Johnson
2002	C-Scape Dune Shack, Provincetown, Mass.

Awards

2002	New York Foundation for the Arts, Recovery Grant
2001	The Pollock-Krasner Foundation, WTC Emergency Grant

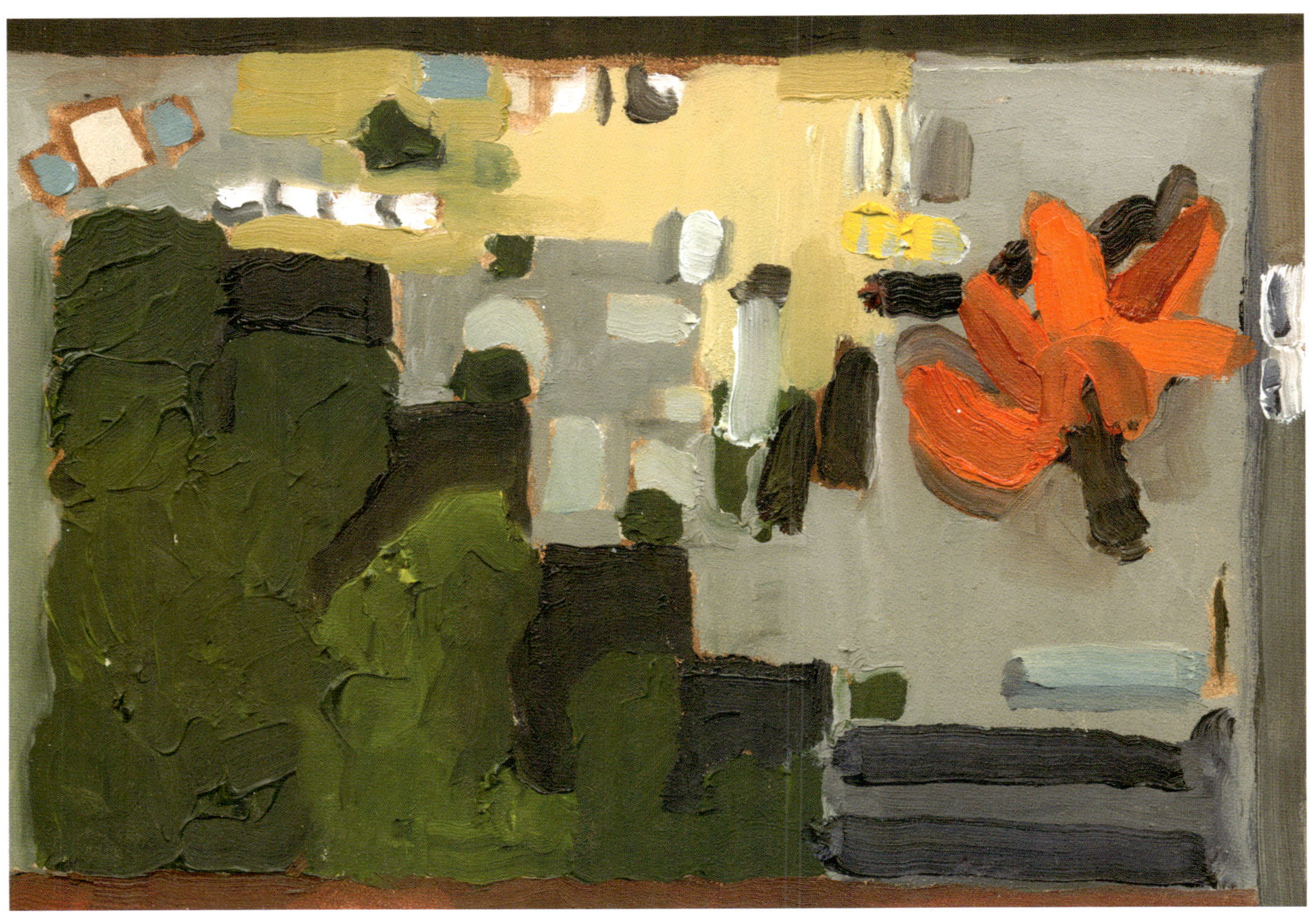

You could not hear the city from the ninety-first floor of the World Trade Center. From the north- and east-facing windows lining our studio, the city lay neatly stacked and sprawled far below in quiet order, settled between the expanses of the Hudson and East Rivers. Blimps and helicopters, like toys, passed below. Manhattan, Brooklyn and Queens were larger than one imagined, and yet smaller and more a part of the natural landscape surrounding and outstretching the concrete ribbons intersecting Manhattan's patchwork blocks. By 5 P.M., long, purple shadows lay over the West Side Highway and water towers spread their shadows across adjoining roofs. Between eight and nine the sky turned a uniform blue as the Empire State lit up, followed by dots of lights across the city, streaming up Fifth Avenue, the highway, the bridges, far over Queens and New Jersey, in yellow, white and red trails. My eyes are filled with that view, tracing the lines from the plaza directly beneath our windows to the George Washington Bridge, and the rooftops of everything in between.

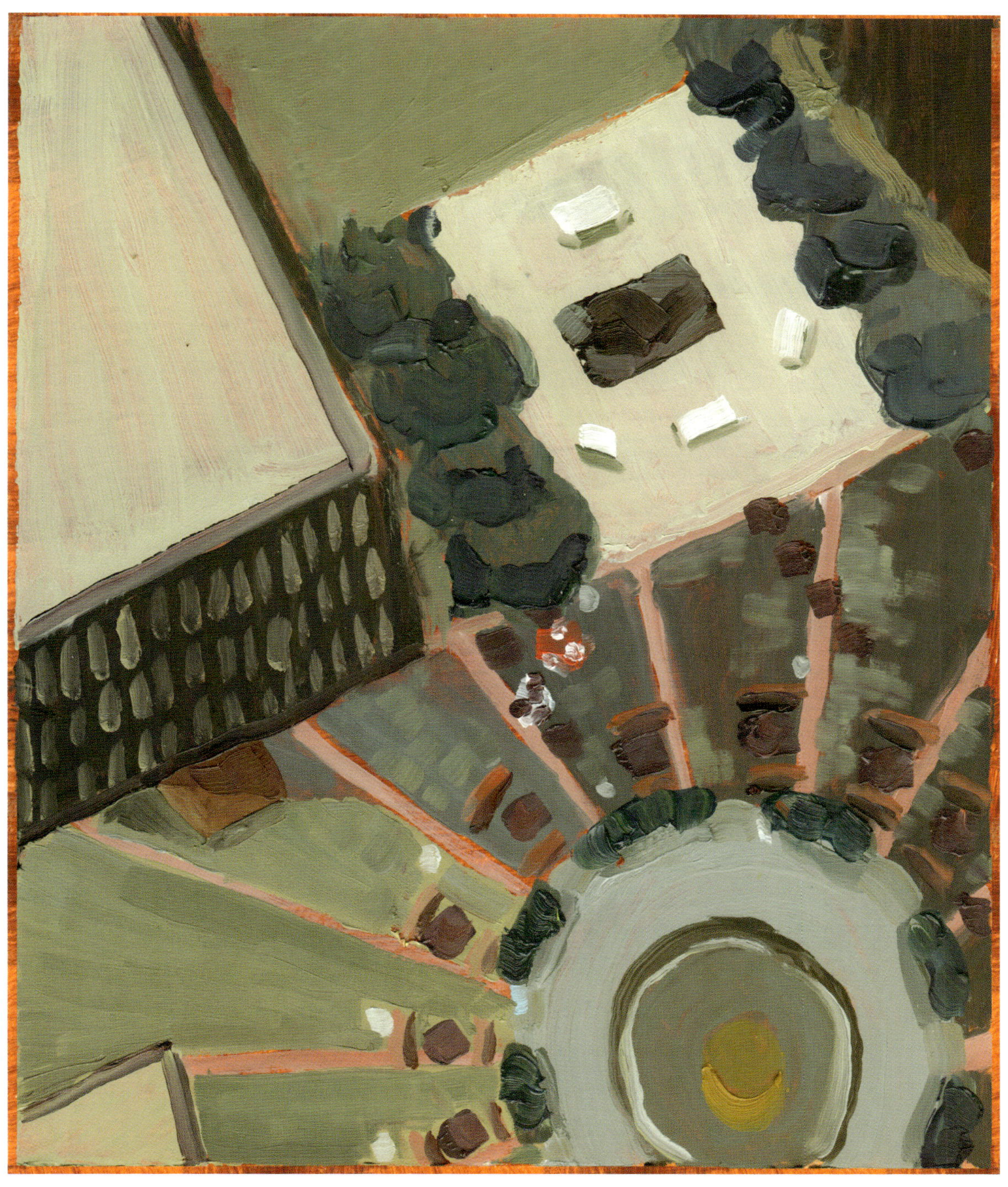

Lucky DeBellevue

Untitled, 1998
Plastic chain, cable ties
Variable height x 13 x 16 inches
Courtesy Feature Inc., New York, N.Y.
Photo: Peggy LeBoeuf

Untitled, 2001
Self-sticking dots
Dimensions variable
Courtesy Feature Inc., New York, N.Y.

Born 1957 in Lafayette, La.
Lives in New York, N.Y.

Education

1987 MFA, University of New Orleans, La.
1983 BFA, University of Southwestern Louisiana, Lafayette

Selected Solo Exhibitions

2002 *Karate, Tap Dancing, & Ping-Pong*, Roger Bjorkholmen Galleri, Stockholm, Sweden
Khlysty, The Owls, and the Others, Whitney Museum of American Art at Philip Morris, New York, N.Y.
2000 Feature Inc., New York, N.Y.
Johnson County Community College of Art, Overland Park, Kans.
1999 Lucky DeBellevue and Alexander Ross, Stephen Friedman Gallery, London, U.K.
1998 Galerie Emmanuel Perrotin, Paris, France
1997 Feature Inc., New York, N.Y.
Neuen Gessellschaft fur Bildende Kunst, Realismus Studio, Berlin, Germany

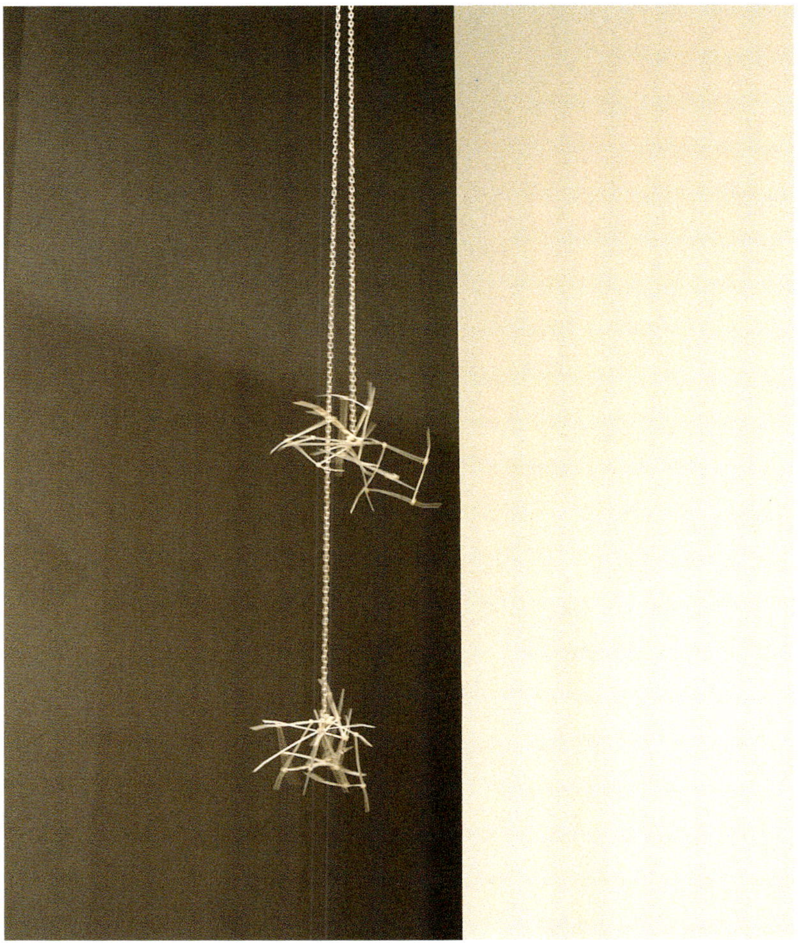

I was part of the last residency program in the World Trade Center. Aside from the enormous tragedy of the situation, a few random things stick in my mind. The Carr Futures logo was on the wall when I got off the elevator, and afterward I read in the paper about who worked and died there, people who I would nod to in the halls. Michael Richards, who died there, was in the studio the Sunday before the attack and at some point he was talking on the phone that was recently installed. He sounded very happy. One day someone found an abandoned office a couple of floors below us. It was a Japanese company, the door was unlocked, and inside was a computer room with printers and monitors still running, all scattered on the floor. In the conference room was food rotting as if the people fled in mid-sentence. At the time it seemed strange and funny, and there were vague plans of having a party there. Now it seems like an omen. I always felt a sense of dread going up in the elevators, saying to myself, "Relax, no one would try and blow up these buildings again." But once there, there was the incredible view, and intuition fades.

Carola Dertnig

. . . but buildings can`talk . . . , 2001 (details)
14 drawings, 14 photographs, story
Drawings: 16 x 12½ inches each

Born 1965 in Innsbruck, Austria
Lives in New York, N.Y. and Vienna, Austria

Education

1997–98 Whitney Museum of American Art Independent Study Program, New York, N.Y.
1992 MFA, École des Beaux Art, Paris, France
1987–91 Academy of Applied Art, Vienna, Austia

Selected Solo Exhibitions

2003 *Handlungsräume*, Kunstverein, Salzburg, Austria
1999 *Dancing with Remotes*, Artists Space, New York, N.Y. (tour)

Selected Group Exhibitions

2002 *Fabulation of Form*, Arthouse, Dublin, Ireland
2001 *A Room of One's Own*, Secession, Vienna, Austria
2000 *Flyby Productions*, P.S.1 Contemporary Art Center, Long Island City, N.Y.
1997 *The Digital Video Wall*, The Museum of Modern Art, New York, N.Y.

Curatorial Project

2003 *Mothers of Invention* (with Stefanie Seibold), MUMOK, Vienna, Austria

Screening

2003 International Short Film Festival, Oberhausen, Germany

When you entered the World Trade Center you passed thousands of people and thousands of people passed you at the same time, especially at rush hour. Sometimes I had a lot of things to carry. I had to pass through this revolving door with all my belongings and materials. I walked around with a dolly, and once got stuck in the revolving door. I was unable to move forward or backwards. I was stuck between the entrance of the first tower and the plaza. A well-dressed man came along and pushed me through the door. He pushed so hard that all my belongings fell on the floor. Loads of art supplies and myself on top of them. . . . Art supplies can appear strange and dangerous, so security came to inspect, and then took me to the security department to investigate further, asking to see my social security number and passport. My inactive cellular phone from Austria had somehow set off their alarm because of the magnetized security system. Finally the guards let me go, but not before taking my photograph and personal information in order to create an identification card for me to display when entering the tower.

There are Siamese twins living in a big city, they are called One and Two. They are busy with being busy and eating. They mostly eat take-out moneydinners, which they

take out of cash machines. Sometimes they are sick of it and they try to change their bad habit and instead of eating so much junk money they try to eat more organic food. In 1971, soon after they were born, they had diarrhea from sour moneymilk, which turned the Hudson River into raw sewage. It became a big

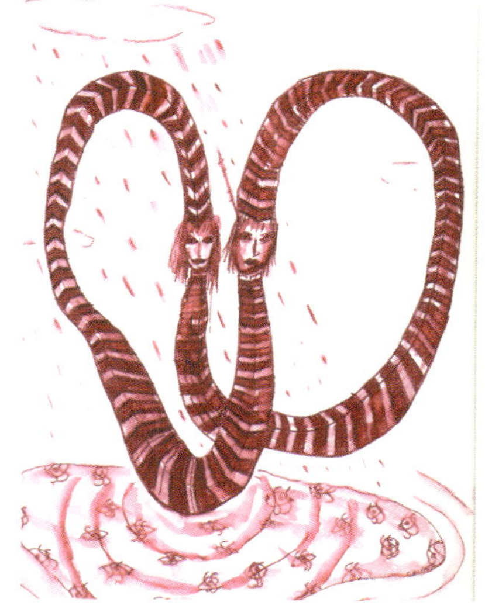

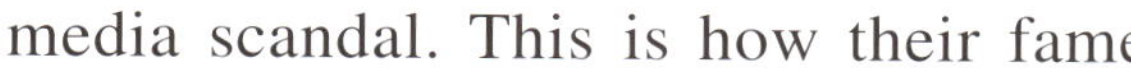

media scandal. This is how their fame started. Two is in love with someone named Elisa Islanda, who is at least twenty years older than the twins are. Elisa is a cool dancer and singer. She looks a little like Kim Gordon from Sonic Youth. She has a travel agency and through her business she gets to know millions of people. In her travel

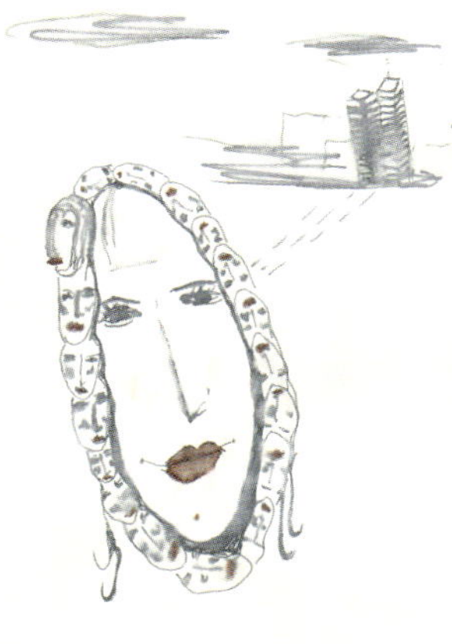

agency she runs a backroom business, which is to organize visas for aliens so that they can stay in the country. Sometimes a visa cannot be obtained when the alien is sick. The IRS will deport those people. It always upsets Elisa; she feels her mission failed.

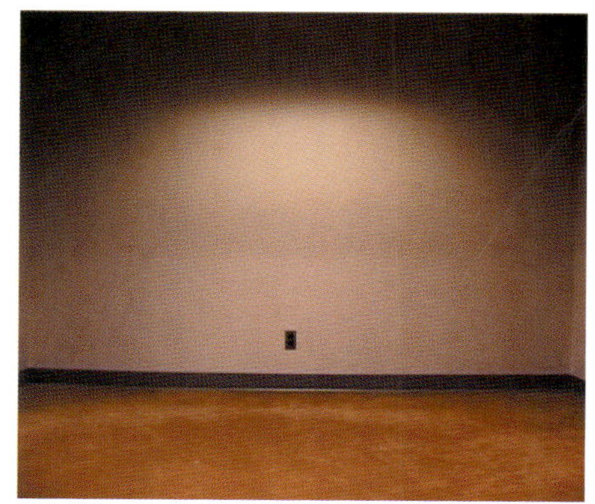

Sjoerd Doting

Rainy Day, 2001
Oil on board
10 x 12 inches
Photo: Sheldan Collins

From World Trade Center, Looking Northwest, 2001–02
Oil on canvas
62 x 46 inches
Photo: Sheldan Collins

Born 1955 in Wymbritseradeel, The Netherlands
Lives in New York, N.Y.

Education

1987–93 Art Students League, New York, N.Y.
1985–89 National Academy of Design, New York, N.Y.
1980–81 University of Amsterdam, The Netherlands

Solo Exhibition

1993 Forum Gallerie, Amsterdam, The Netherlands

Selected Group Exhibitions

2002 *Re-imagining New York*, North Dakota Museum of Art, Grand Forks
2000 *175th Annual Exhibition*, National Academy of Design, New York, N.Y.
1998 *62nd Mid-year Exhibition*, Butler Institute of American Art, Youngstown, Ohio
1998 *35th Juried Exhibition*, Parrish Art Museum, Southampton, N.Y.

Award

2002 The Pollack-Krasner Foundation, WTC Emergency Grant

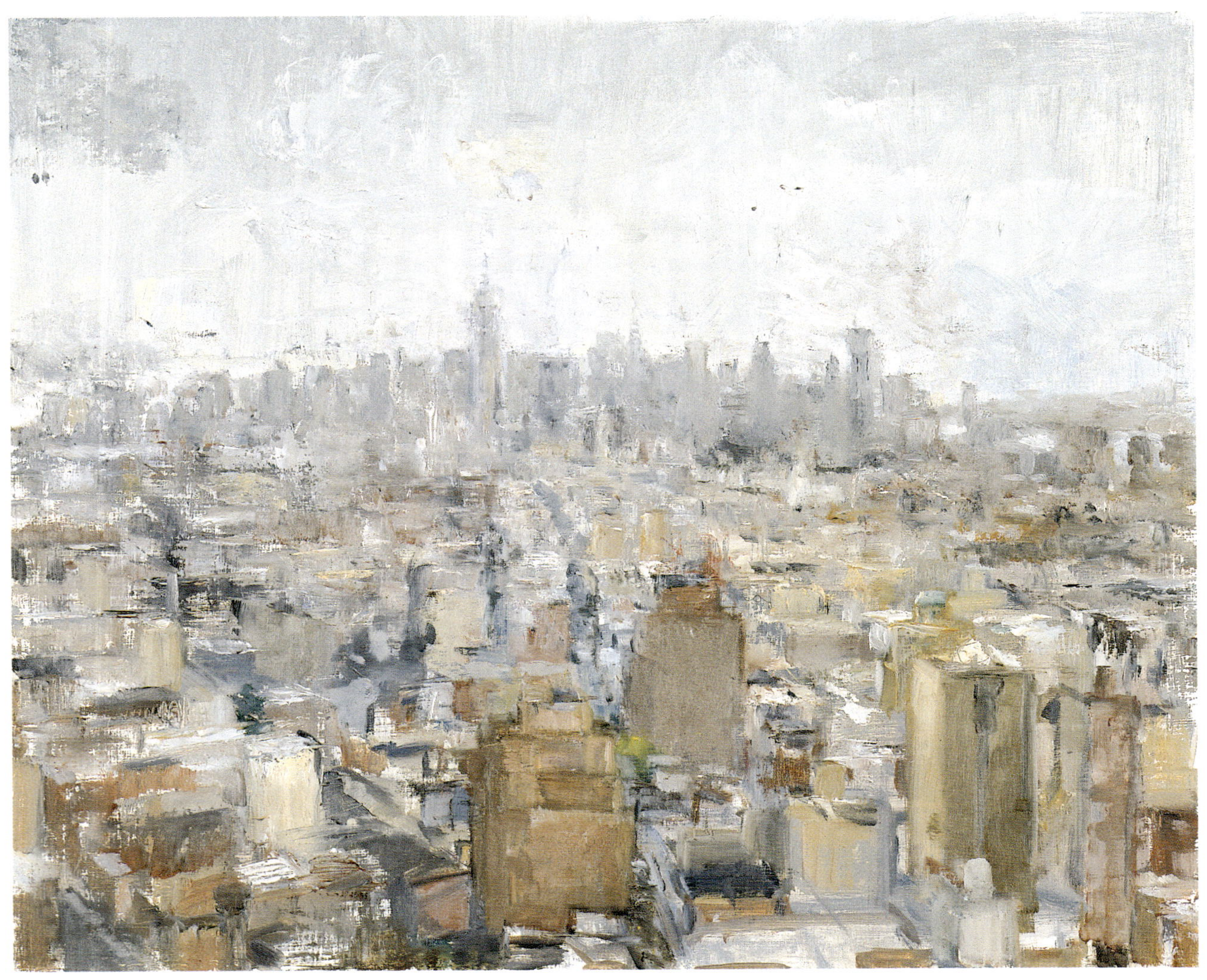

I have focused on cityscapes for the last ten years, so working at the WTC during the summer of 2001 was an amazing, often overwhelming experience. I became aware of the city's geography, its place in the greater landscape, surrounded by water. I could see so many places I had painted or had considered painting over the years, neighborhoods I had cycled through, where I lived, where I worked—the city finally came together for me.

*I had been productive during my WTC residency, working there usually every day. I lost many paintings on 9/11, including several large cityscapes. Fortunately, I did take home about fifteen small oil sketches a few weeks earlier. In the months that followed, I re-created, as best I could, one lost painting—*From World Trade Center, Looking Northwest*—using some sketches and photos I had made. The original was fresh in my mind and I think the re-creation is fairly accurate, though of course quite different. It was strange to be working on that view again, but it was cathartic. The views are still etched in my memory.*

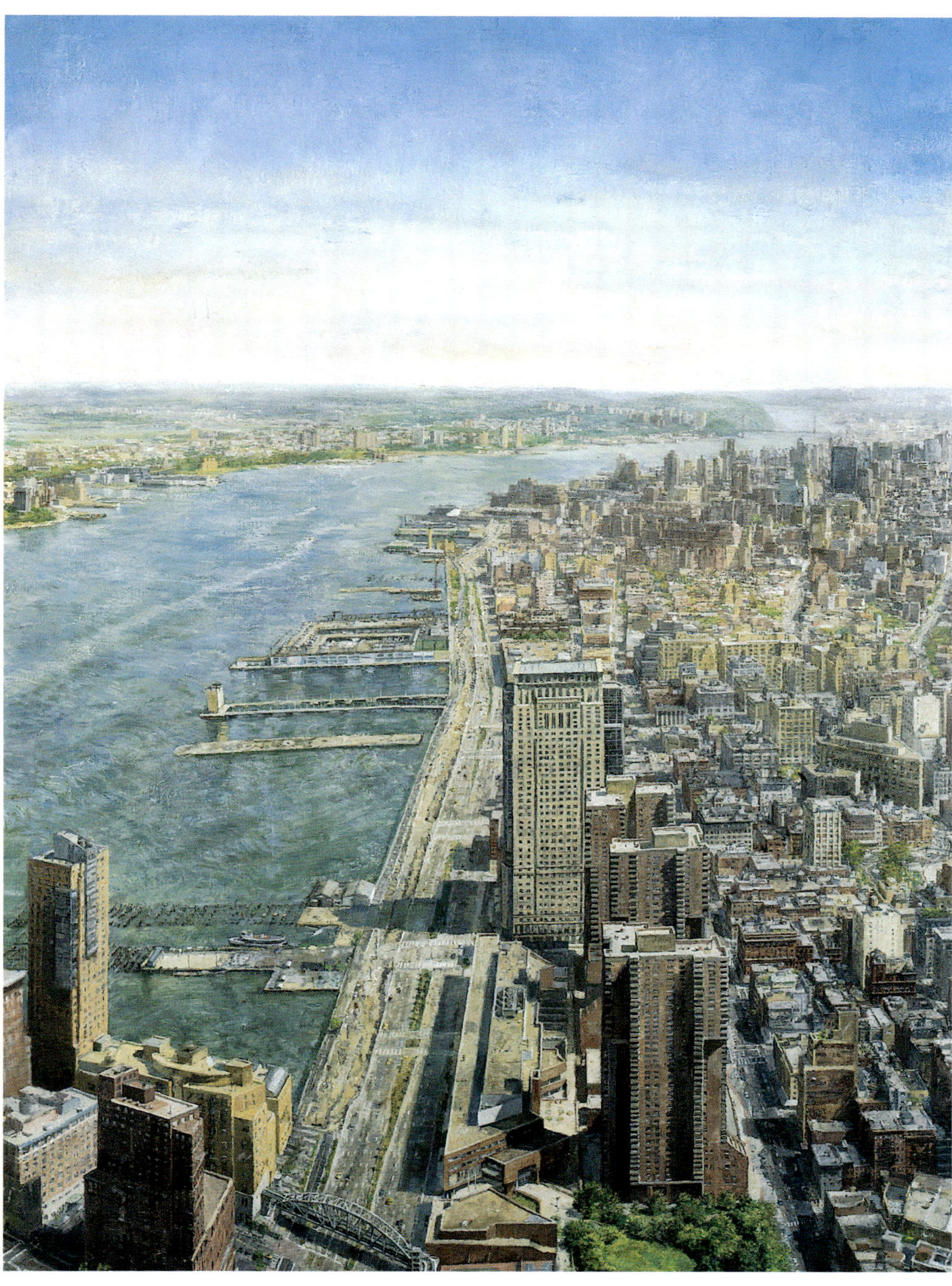

Stan Friedman

Night Painting from WTC, Downtown, 2001
Oil on hardboard
16 x 11¾ inches

Born 1941 in Newark, N.J.
Lives in New York, N.Y.

Education

1966 MFA, Brooklyn College, N.Y.
1964 BFA, Pratt Institute, Brooklyn, N.Y.

Selected Solo Exhibitions

2000 Walter Wiokiser Gallery, New York, N.Y.
1988 Contemporary Realist Gallery, San Francisco, Calif.
1983 Sid Deutsch Gallery, New York, N.Y.

Selected Group Exhibitions

2003 *Uncommon Perspectives,* Hermithae Foundation Museum, Norfolk, Va.
2002 *Re-imagining New York,* North Dakota Museum of Art, Grand Forks
1994 *Invitational Exhibition,* Academy of Arts and Letters, New York, N.Y.

Awards

1986 Mellon Foundation
1985 The National Endowment for the Arts

Painting a cityscape at night from the ninety-first floor was both a wonderful and sometimes strange experience. I remember working alone many nights past midnight. I had painted ground-level skylines before, but this was different—airplane-like. At night, Suite 9166 was both quiet and dark. Few lights were turned on, so that one could get the full effect of the night-lit city. And this city seemed vertical, not horizontal, like a vast curtain tilted up in front of the windows. The light and dark areas made exciting patterns of luminosity and void—no longer streets, bridges and buildings, but galaxies and voids filled with movement. My favorite thing about working in the dark was holding a pen flashlight in one hand while I painted with the other, trying not to lose my place due to afterimages.

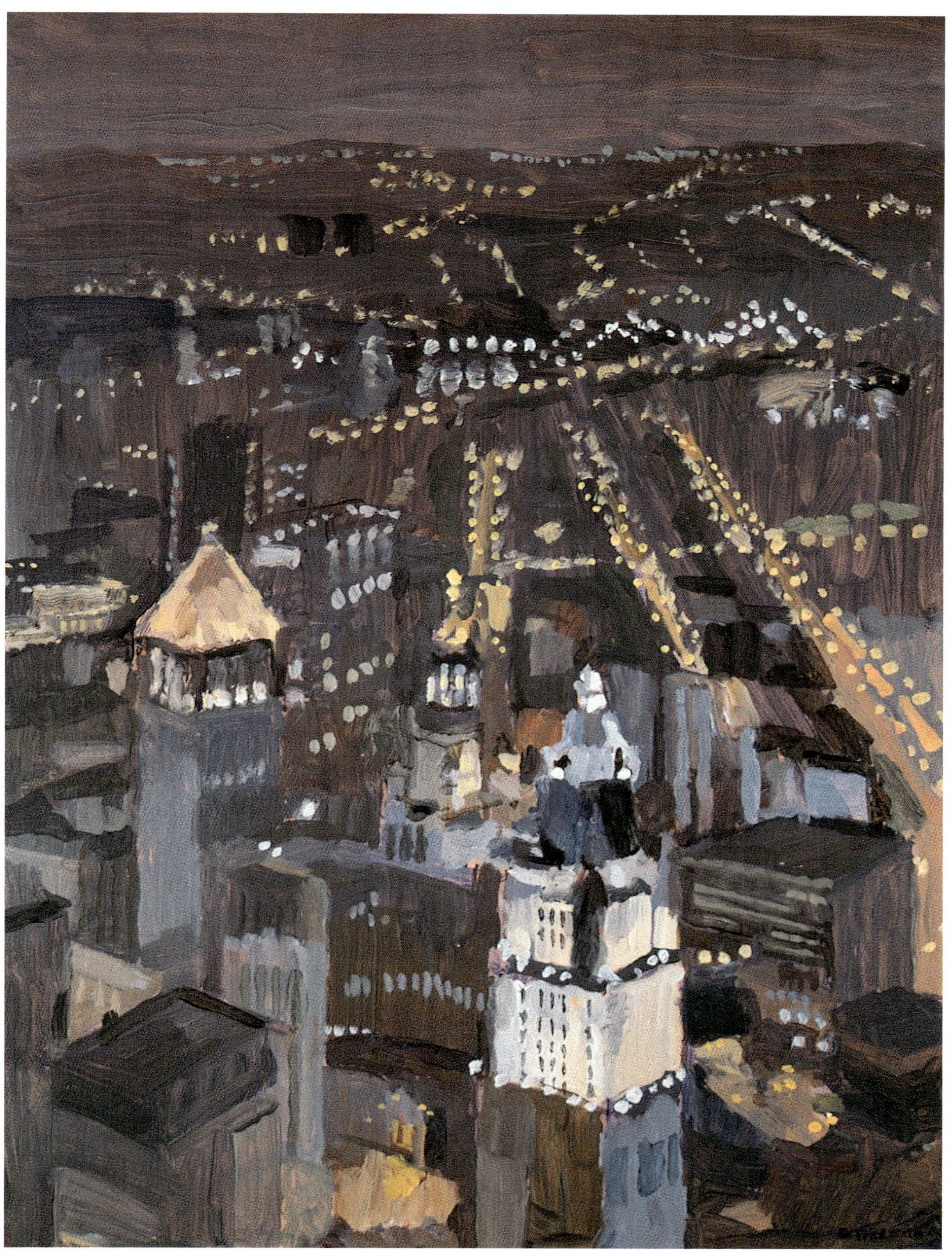

Nancy Friese

From Within, Remembered View, 2003
Oil on linen
30 x 30 inches
Courtesy Pepper Gallery, Boston, Mass.
Photo: Cathy Carver
With support from and credit to: I-Park Residency, East Haddam, Conn. and The Pollock-Krasner Foundation, WTC Emergency Grant

Born 1948 in Fargo, N.Dak.
Lives in Providence, R.I.

Education

1980 MFA, Yale University School of Art, New Haven, Conn.
1977 Art Academy of Cincinnati, Ohio
1970 BS, University of North Dakota, Grand Forks, N.Dak.

Solo Exhibition

2001 Pepper Gallery, Boston, Mass.

Selected Group Exhibitions

2002 *The Contemporary Landscape,* College of Wooster Art Museum, Ohio (tour)
A Legacy in Landscapes, The New York Public Library, Print and Stokes Gallery, New York, N.Y.
Re-imagining New York, North Dakota Museum of Art, Grand Forks

Residency

1999 Musée de Pont-Aven Residency, France

Awards

1992 The National Endowment for the Arts
1991 The National Endowment for the Arts
1987 The National Endowment for the Arts

Storms arose, lightning moved, twilight merged with reflections, clouds built up and diminished, fog settled and lifted, light and shadow lined the land, water and buildings. The view added to us. It formed the towers. At that height the action of the city and waterways seemed peopleless. The colors of the buildings turned into human tones in the different lights; the city took on a winding, human-touched character through the irregularities and the stance of the building forms. Human references pervaded everything. It was always a macro-view. I wanted to paint from a remarkable vantage and to see city scenes as a type of landscape with new intersections of clouds and earth. One could emphasize this juncture in panoramic drama from the towers. My city views were equaled by skies. I deciphered forms from an immense range and distance and painted new cloud views from morning to dusk. I began to pull the edge of the windows into the paintings to push the viewer into the inside space and to show a version of the real situation. All of the works were lost; I took no photographs of the work, studio or view.

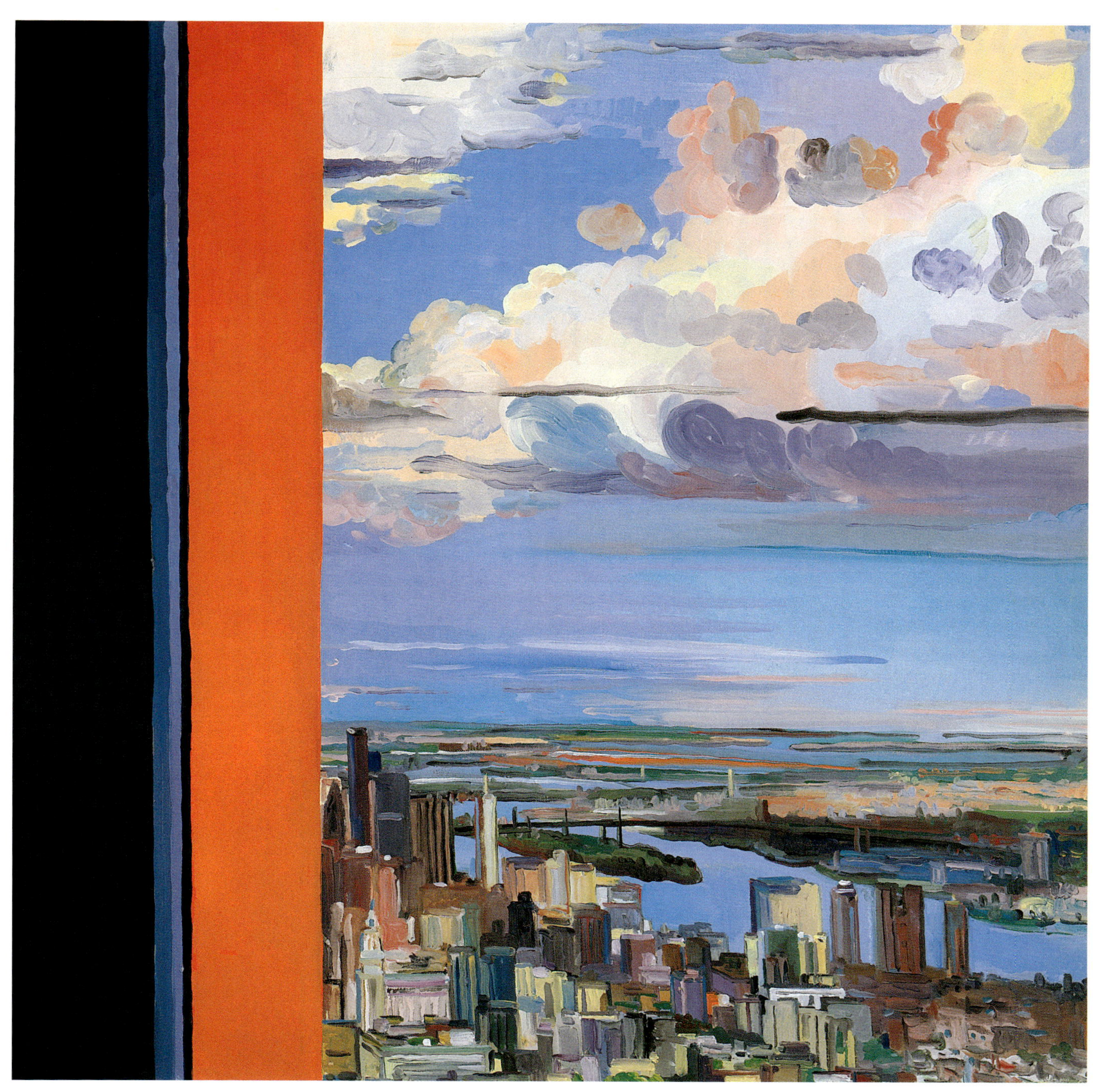

Mahmoud Hamadani

Ode to New York, 2001
Wood
4 x 8 x 4 feet

Ode to Kabul, 2001
Ink on paper
100 x 100 inches

Born 1958 in Rasht, Iran
Lives in New York, N.Y.

Education

1992 MPA, John F. Kennedy School of Government, Harvard University, Cambridge, Mass.
1981 BA, State University of New York, Oswego

Solo Exhibition

1999 Karen McCready Fine Arts, New York, N.Y.

Selected Group Exhibitions

2003 Korea Gallery, New York, N.Y.
2002 The Work Space, New York, N.Y.
New York University Small Works Exhibition, Washington Square East Gallery, New York, N.Y.
2000 Percy-Miller Gallery, London, U.K.
New York University Small Works Exhibition, Washington Square East Gallery, New York, N.Y.

Residencies

2002 The Ucross Foundation, Wyo.
Santa Fe Art Institute, N.Mex.

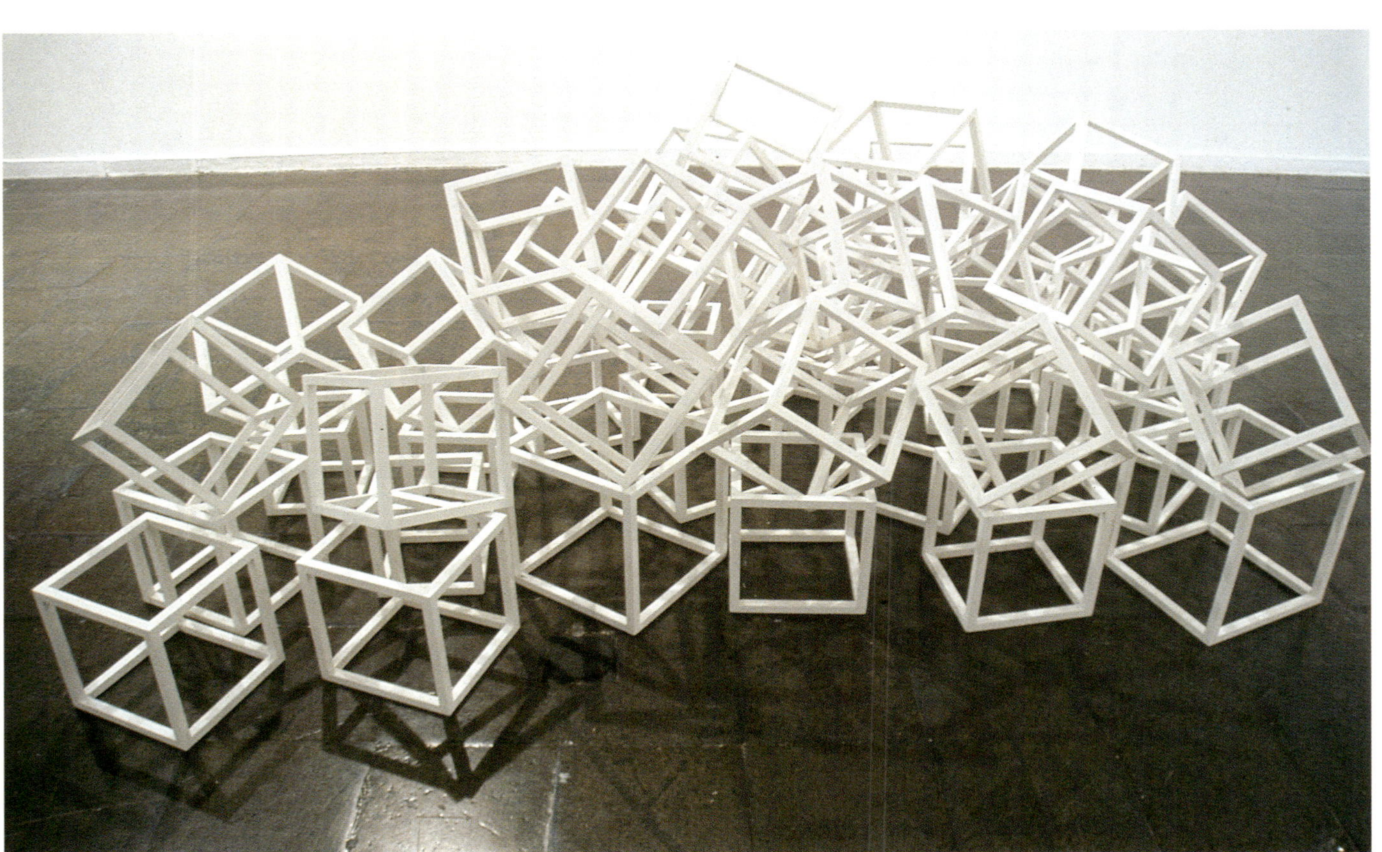

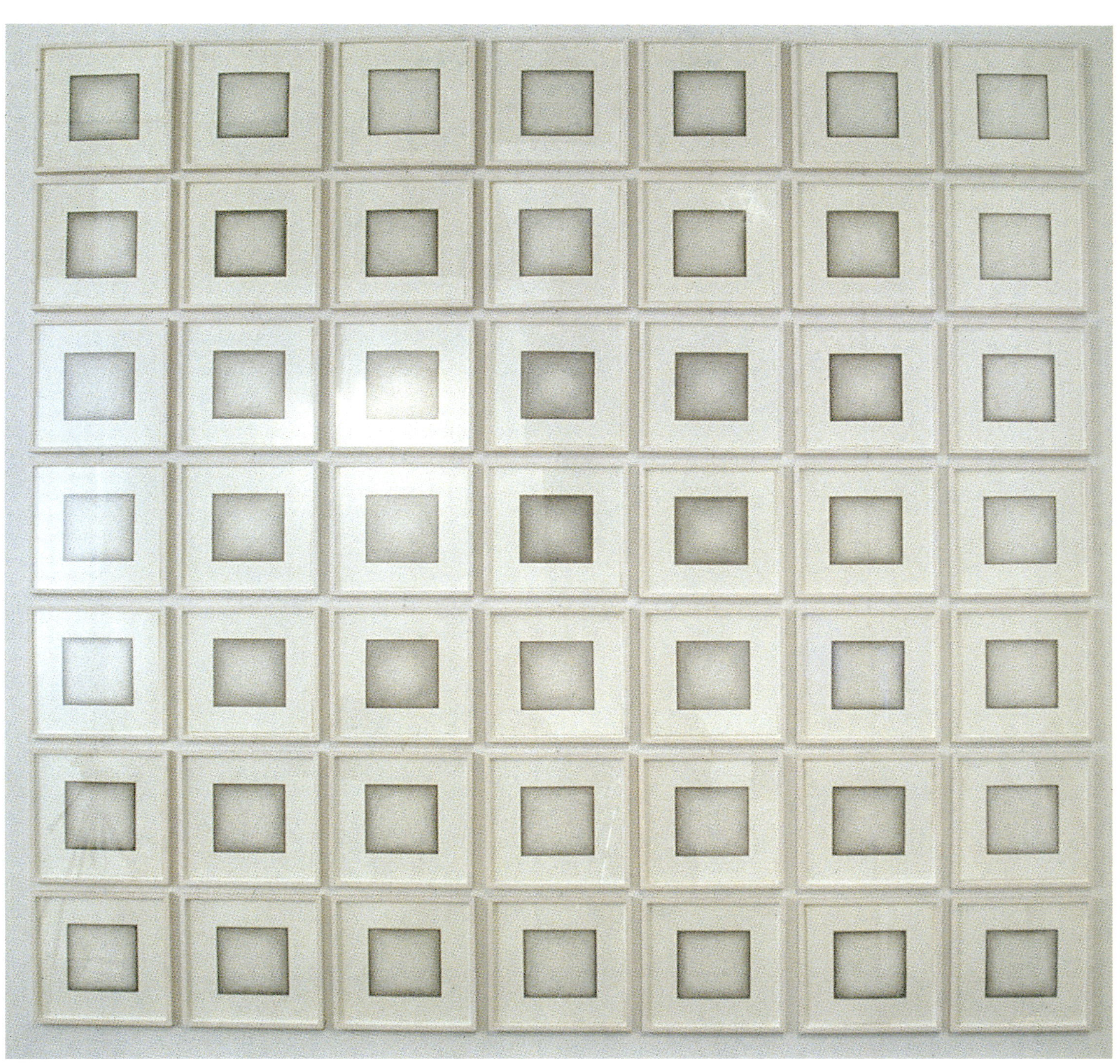

Kara Hammond

Cenotaph, 2001
Graphite
27 x 22 inches

St. Louis Arch, 1965, 2001 (detail)
Graphite
22 x 22 inches

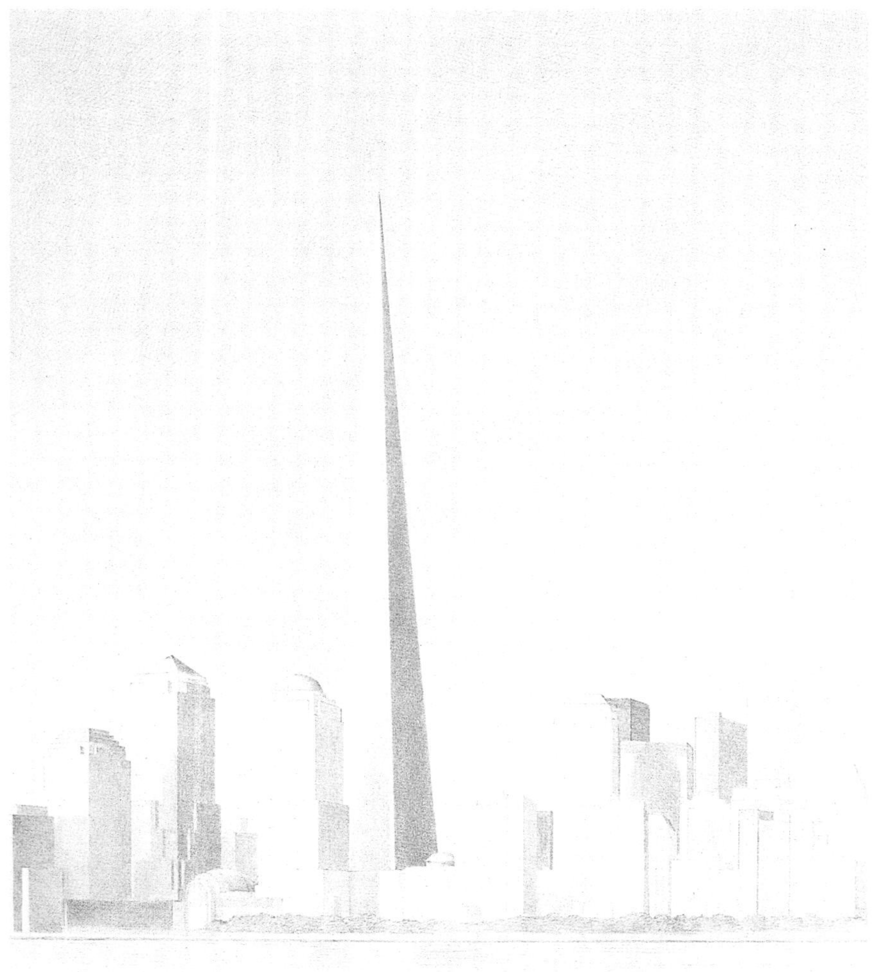

Born 1963 in Winston-Salem, N.C.
Lives in Brooklyn, N.Y.

Education

1989 MFA, Temple University, Tyler School of Art, Philadelphia, Pa.

Solo Exhibition

2001 Joseph Rickards Fine Art, New York, N.Y.

Selected Group Exhibitions

2003 *Defying Gravity: Contemporary Art and Flight*, North Carolina Museum of Art, Raleigh
2002 *Crafting Space*, The Smart Project Space, Amsterdam, The Netherlands
2001 *The (Ideal) Home Show*, Gimpel Fils, London, U.K.
1999 *Science Fictions*, White Columns, New York, N.Y.

Residencies

2002 Santa Fe Art Institute, N.Mex.
The Ucross Foundation, Wyo.

Award

2001 The Pollock-Krasner Foundation

For a long time I have maintained an interest in the extremes of human accomplishment, including all the positive and negative effects of such activities. The Trade Center happened to fit into that fascination rather nicely. Having a studio there inspired a whole new group of paintings and drawings for me.

St. Louis Arch, 1965, *was a drawing I had been working on when the Trade Center was attacked. I lost the resource material along with everything else there, so went looking for something suitable to replace what I had. I ran across an image where the two halves of the arch were almost together, still under construction, meeting with a girder in the center.*

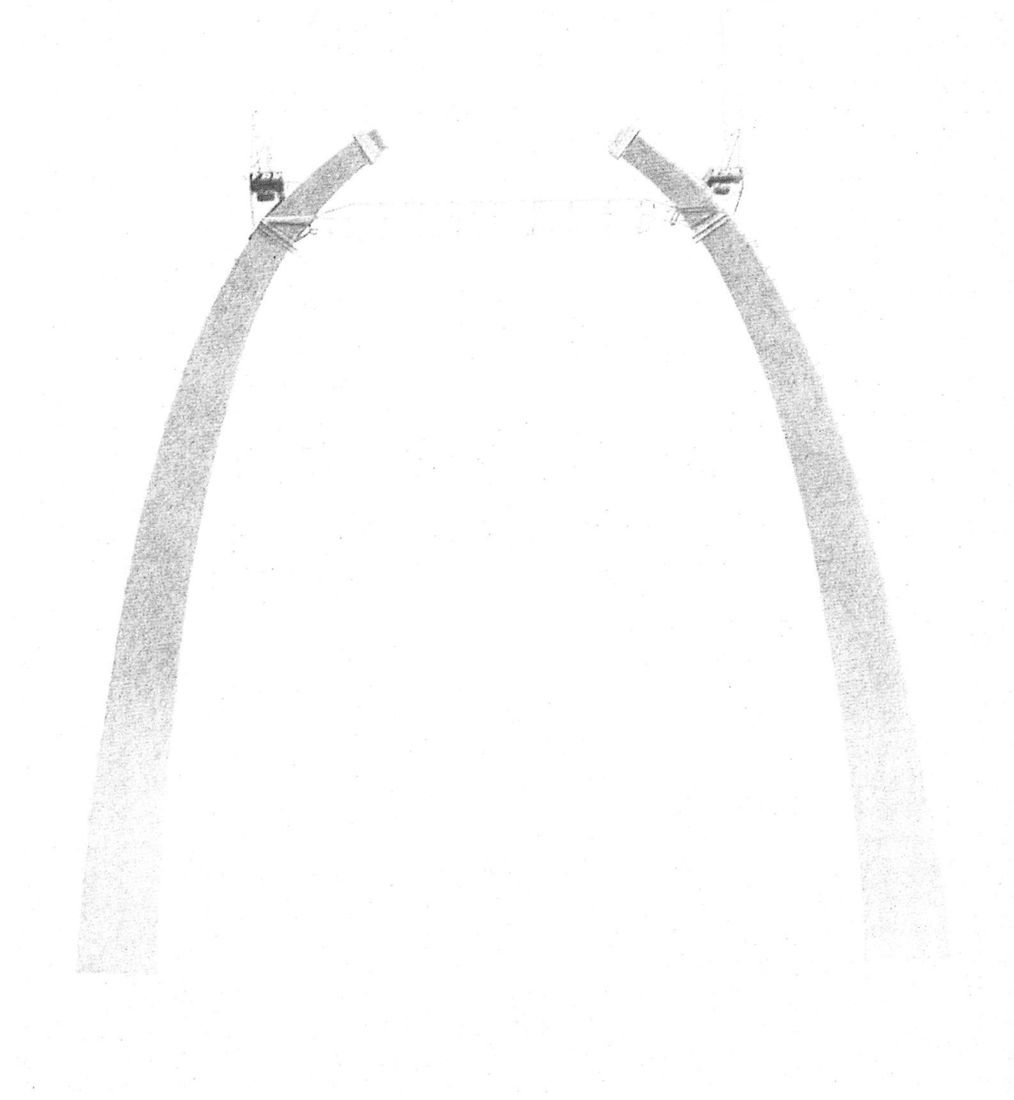

Jeff Konigsberg

Wallwork, 2001 (in progress)
Sheetrock, marker, acrylic
Wall dimensions: 9 x 18 feet

Reconstruction of Wallwork, 2001/2003
Digitally manipulated c-print
9 x 12 inches

Image of unfinished installation lost on 9/11, digitally reconfigured to convey an impression of the finished piece.

Born 1969 in New Rochelle, N.Y.
Lives in Brooklyn, N.Y.

Education

1997 MSAE, Massachusetts College of Art, Boston
1991 BFA, Carnegie Mellon University, Pittsburgh, Pa.

Selected Solo Exhibitions

2003 *Sample and Hold*, Clifford Smith Gallery, Boston, Mass.
2000 The Queens Museum of Art, Bulova Corporate Center, Queens, N.Y.

Selected Group Exhibitions

2003 *Selections: Fall*, The Drawing Center, New York, N.Y.
2002 *AIM 22*, The Bronx Museum of the Arts, The Bronx, N.Y.
The Accelerated Grimace, Silverstein Gallery, New York, N.Y.
Loaded, Midway Contemporary Art, St. Paul, Minn.
2000 *Greater New York*, P.S.1 Contemporary Art Center, Long Island City, N.Y.

Award

2001 New York Foundation for the Arts, Lily Auchincloss Fellow

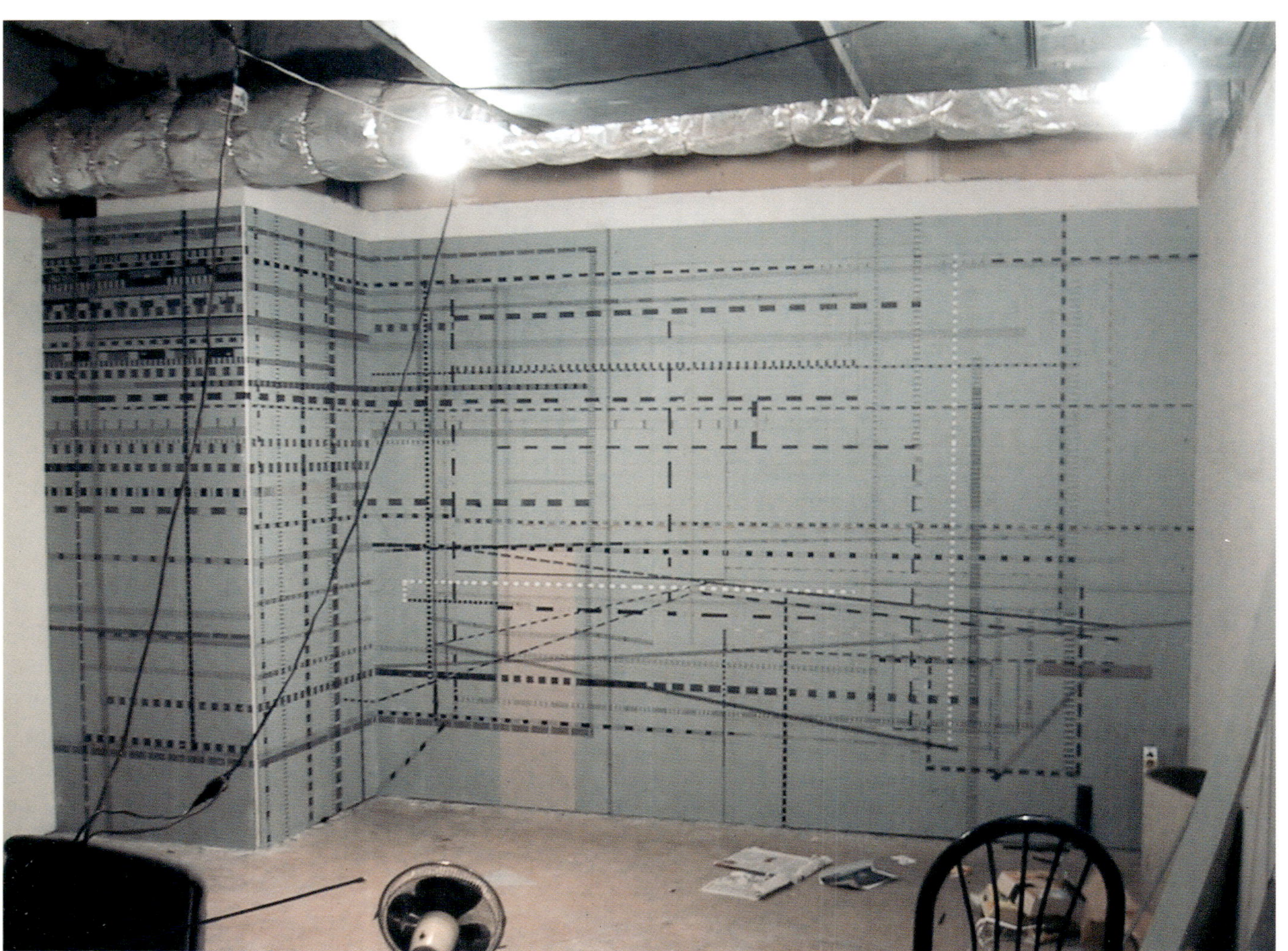

Aside from exploring the vacant office spaces, I loved looking out the windows. The lights of the Verranzano and George Washington bridges flickering wildly were a nighttime favorite. On my last night there Geraldine and I watched an incredible thunderstorm. We were surrounded by thick, dark, glowing clouds and bursts of lightning.

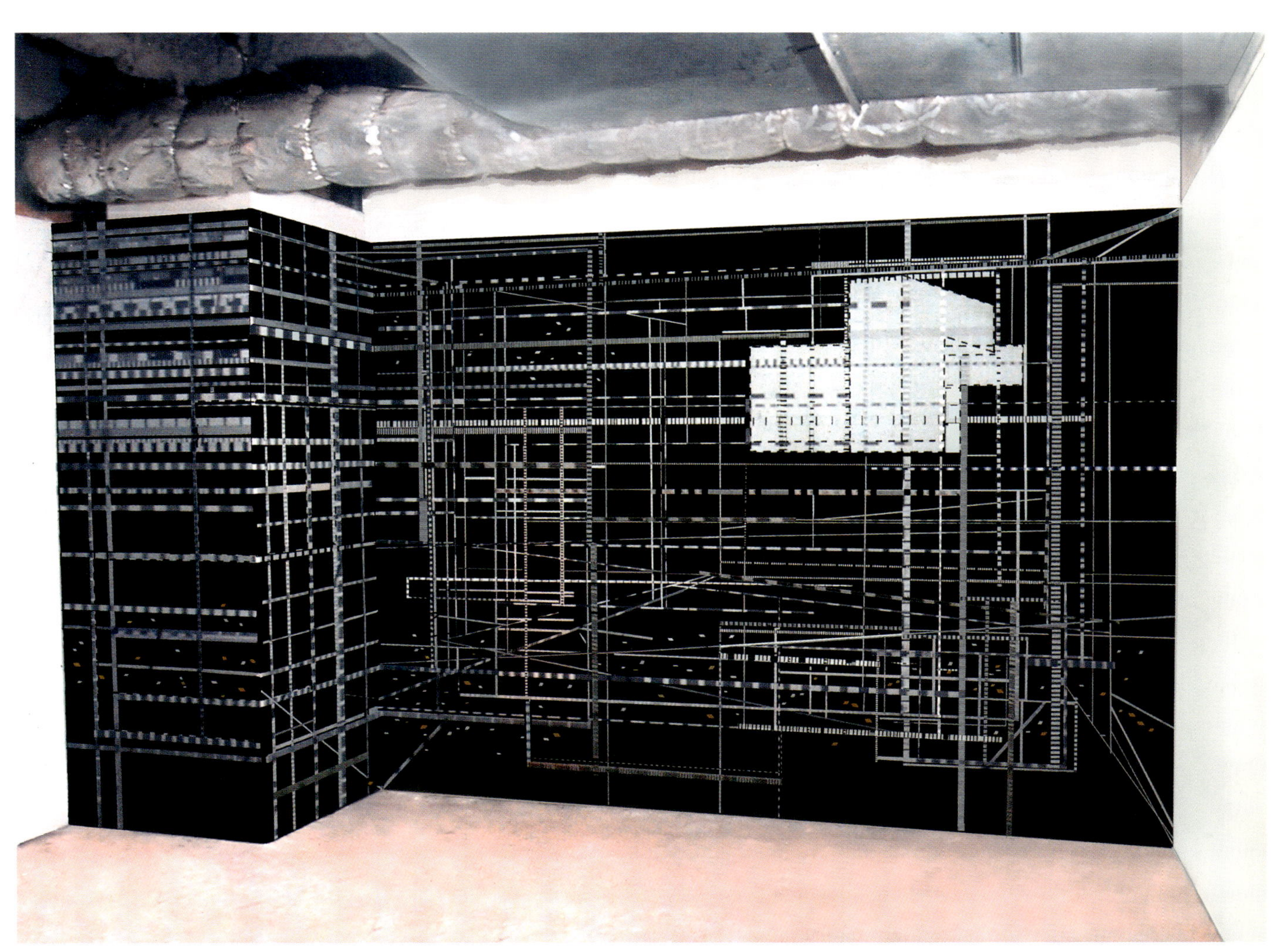

Ellen Korbonski

Nocturnal Twins, 2001
Watercolor
24 x 18 inches

Battery Park City, 2001
Watercolor
24 x 18 inches

Born 1963 in Los Angeles, Calif.
Lives in New York, N.Y.

Education

2000 MFA, New York University Film School, N.Y.
1985 BA, Wesleyan University, Middletown, Conn.

Group Exhibition

2002 *Living in the Shadows*, The Bronx River Art Center, The Bronx, N.Y.

Screenings

1999 Millennium Film Workshop
1998 Palm Springs International Film Festival
1998 Sinking Creek Film Festival

Filmography

1999 *Center of Gravity,* 16mm short
1998 *Say It with Flowers*, 16mm documentary short
1997 *Ladrao*, 16mm short
1996 *Salada Mista*, 16mm short
1995 *Rose*, 16mm short

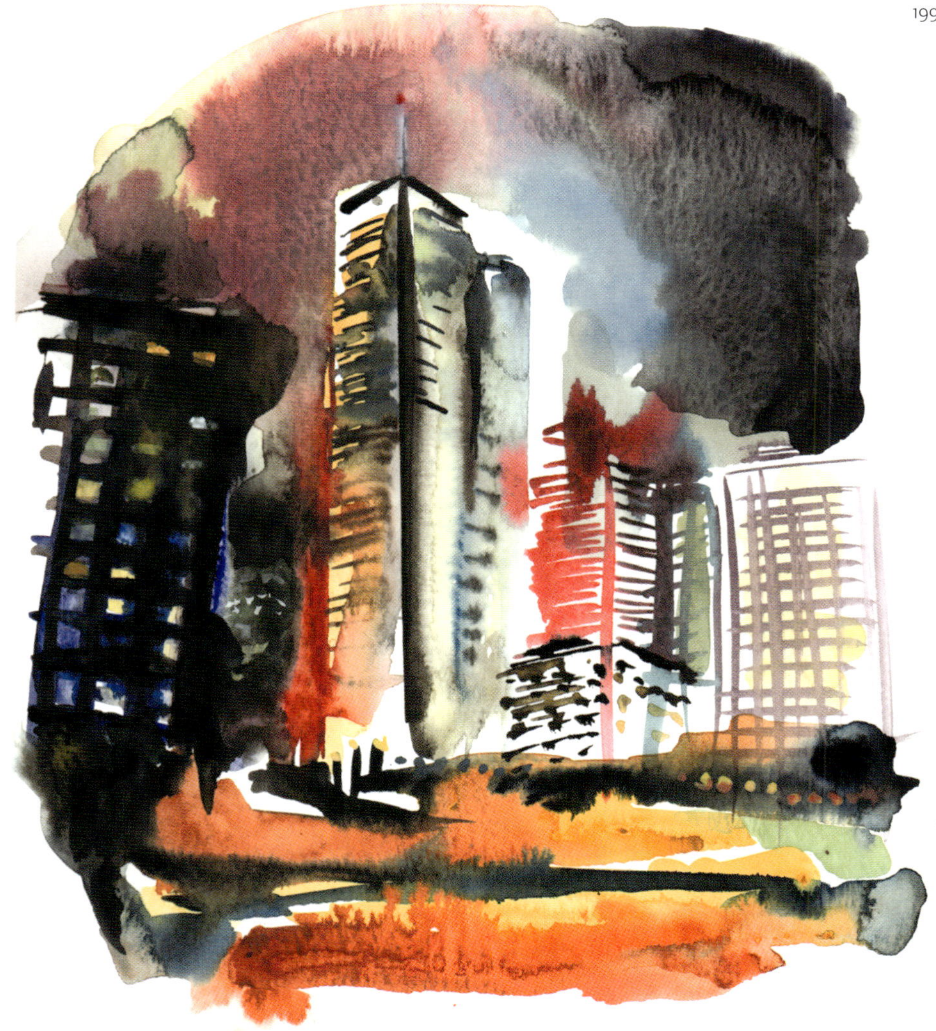

My paintings attempt to express the drama of the New York skyline and its myriad architectural wonders, which resemble a cast of characters with their own stories to tell. I feel the loss of the World Trade Center like the passing of a great movie star or public figure but am comforted that its presence will be immortalized through images.

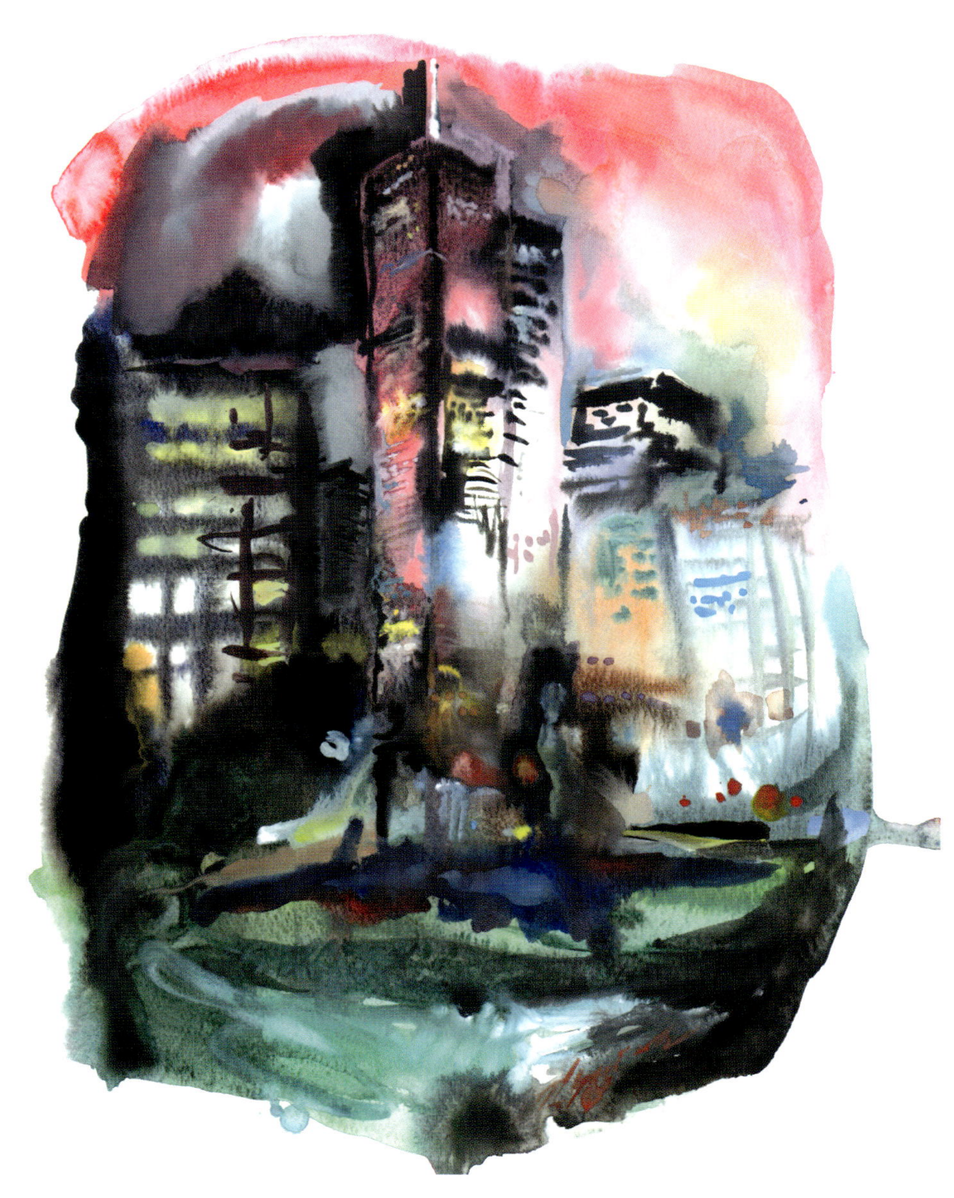

Motonobu Kurokawa

Untitled, 2001
Neon straws
11 x 11 x 11 inches
Photo: Bill Orcutt

Greenness of straw is as artificial as it gets, yet how the piece is put together is organic. This multidirectional chain formation allows dynamic, infinite and complex growth.

Born 1971 in Tokyo, Japan
Lives in New York, N.Y.

Education

1998 MArch, Columbia University, New York, N.Y.
1994 BSc, Cornell University, Ithaca, N.Y.

Selected Group Exhibitions

2003 *Athens-scape: The 2004 Olympics and the Metabolism of the City,* Royal Institute of British Architects Gallery, London, U.K.
Ephemeral Structures in the City of Athens, Byzantine & Christian Museum, Athens, Greece
Reconfiguring Space: Blueprints for Art in General, Art in General, New York, N.Y.
The HOME House Project Design Invitational, Southeastern Center For Contemporary Art, Winston-Salem, N.C.
2002 *Storage and Retrieval*, Midway Contemporary Art, St. Paul, Minn.

Awards

2003 First Prize, Architectural Competition, Hellenic Cultural Heritage SA, Athens, Greece
2002 The Pollock-Krasner Foundation, WTC Emergency Grant

This was my very first residency program. More importantly it was my first time sharing space and ideas with other artists. As much as I hated the idea of a 110-story building and its monolithic/scaleless striped facade, the studio space on the ninety-second floor became my second home. The work I produced during the residency did not necessarily respond to the uniqueness of the site; it was more of a "soul searching" for my creative process.

Currently I've been working on architectural/landscape projects, and my works are all about repetitive and compulsive linear stripes. . . .

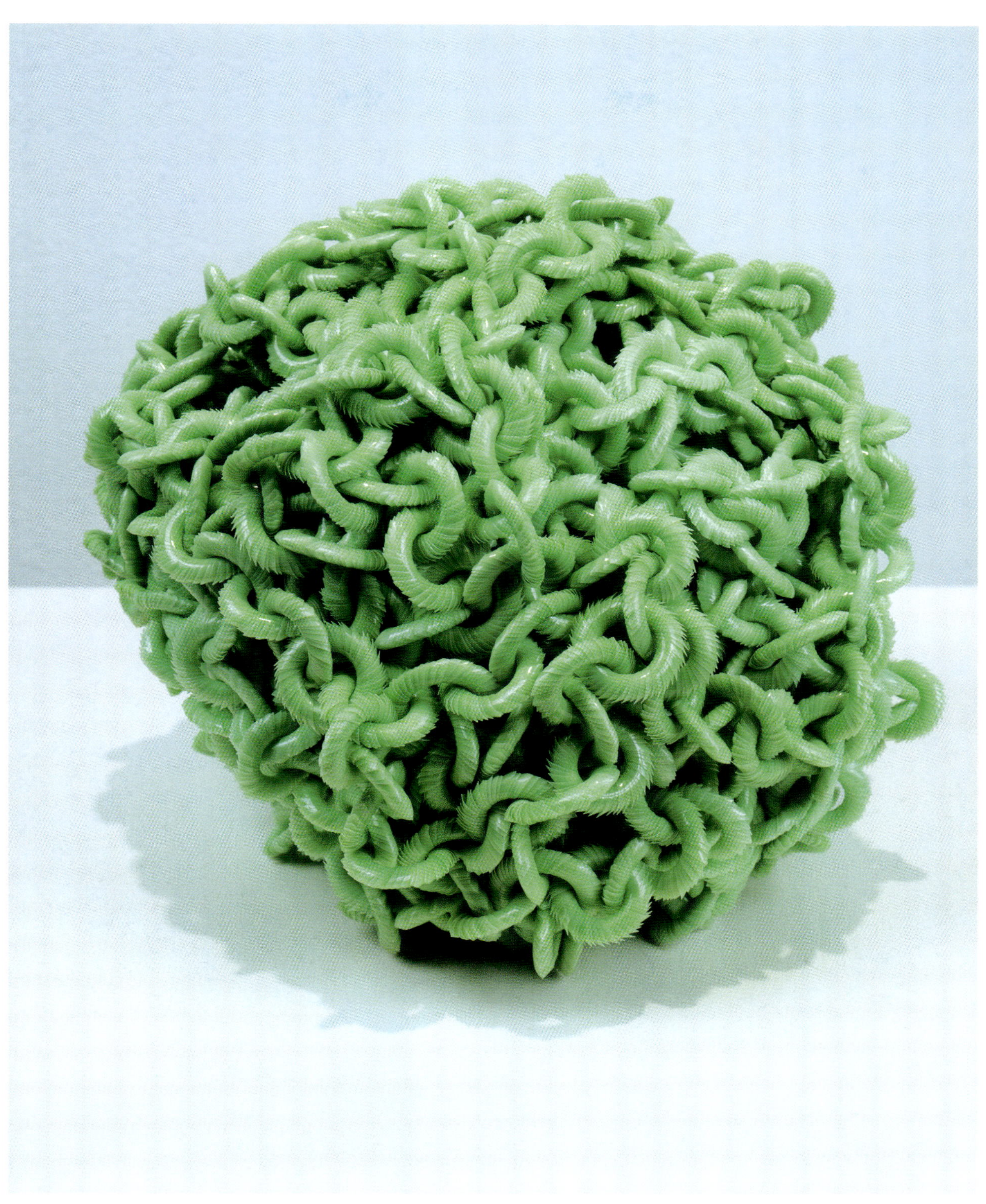

Geraldine Lau

Information Retrieval #63, 2001 (with detail)
Vinyl and tape on wall
Dimesions variable
Wall: 16 x 14 feet

Born 1970 in Singapore
Lives in New York, N.Y.

Education

1997 MFA, School of Visual Arts, New York, N.Y.
1994 BA, RMIT University, Australia/Singapore

Selected Group Exhibitions

2003 *Transgressing Boundaries*, Paint Gallery, Brooklyn, N.Y.
2002 *Art on Paper 2002*, Weatherspoon Art Museum, Greensboro, N.C.
25th Anniversary Benefit Selections Exhibition, The Drawing Center, New York, N.Y.
Art New York, Kunstraume auf Zeit, Linz, Austria
The Allegorical City, Staub, Zurich, Switzerland

Awards

2002 The Puffin Foundation
New York Foundation for the Arts
2001 The Pollock-Krasner Foundation

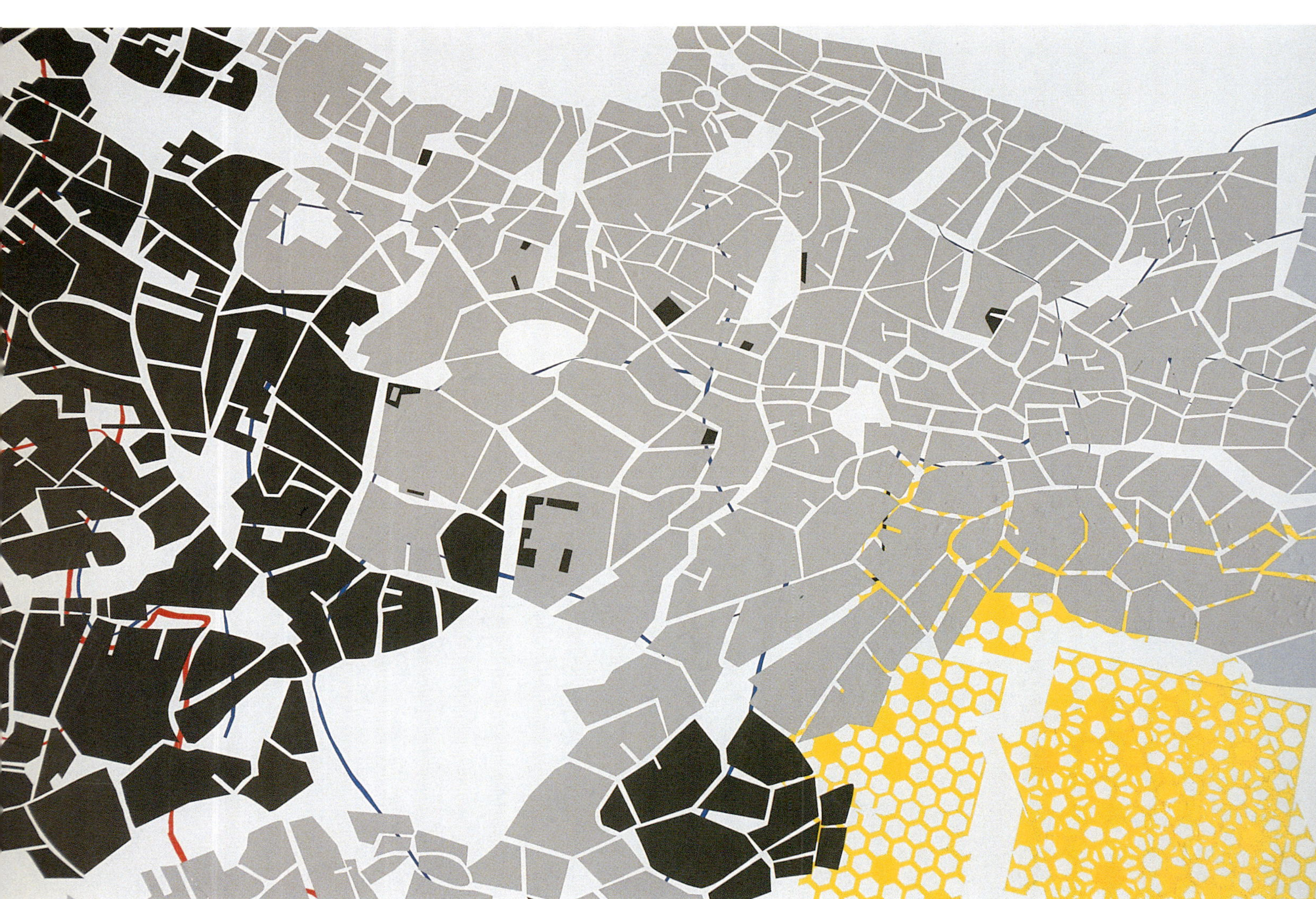

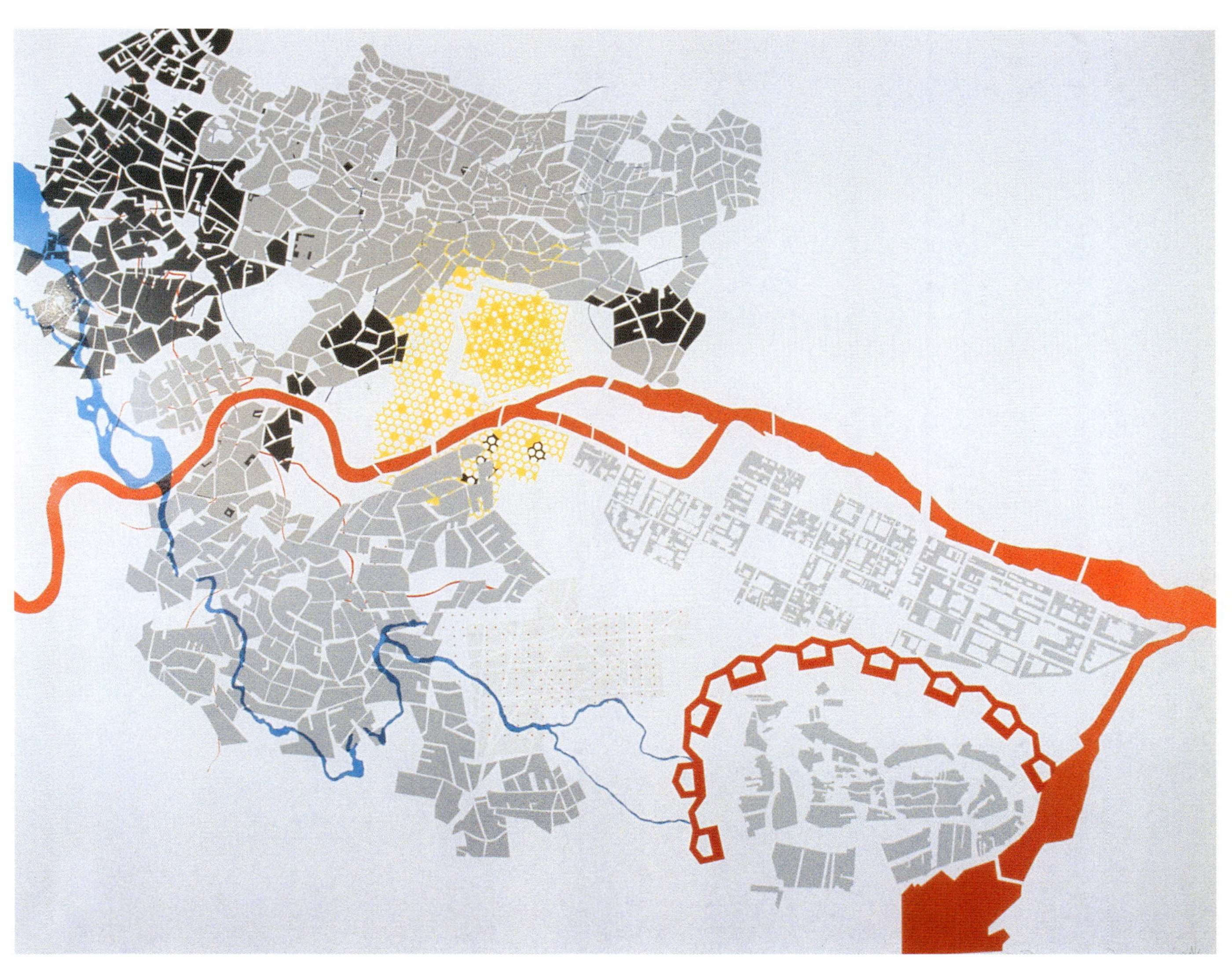

Vanessa Lawrence

Sunrise over Manhattan, 2002
Oil on linen
36 x 72 inches

Born 1975 in Manchester, U.K.
Lives and works in Scotland

Education

2001 The New York Studio School, N.Y.
2001 Exchange-Écoles des Beaux Artes, Marseille, France
1994 Lorenzo D'Medici School of Art, Florence, Italy

Selected Solo Exhibitions

2003 *Shapes of Things,* Kelly Cooper Bar, Glasgow, Scotland
Exhibition of Drawings & Paintings, The Dundas Street Gallery, Edinburgh, Scotland

Selected Group Exhibitions

2003 *115th Annual Exhibition*, Paisley Art Institute, Scotland
Winter Show, The High Street Gallery, Kirkudbright, Scotland
2002 *Re-imaging New York*, North Dakota Museum of Art, Grand Forks
2001 *Summer Show*, The Painting Center, New York, N.Y.
Tree Show, The Brooklyn Brewery, Brooklyn, N.Y.

My memories are as if it were yesterday; memories of mixed emotions. The happy and privileged two and a half months spent in the World Trade Center.

The buzz of walking through the city on my way to the studio, looking up through the buildings at the sky, excited to see how it would look from the ninety-first floor. Painting a clear view when light would bounce off surrounding buildings, then seeing nothing when clouds passed by, and watching rain dance in circles before falling on the streets below.

Early morning was special with only its empty lobby and lone security guards to greet, knowing that, in a few hours, the everyday hustle and bustle would funnel in.

The morning of September 11, I arrived as normal at 6:00 A.M. to continue working on my painting, Sunrise over Manhattan. *The light was beautiful and I was oblivious to the turmoil that would ensue only two hours later; being thrown across the corridor, walking down ninety-one flights of stairs, trying to hide from the cloud falling overhead.*

I am grateful for the experience of being part of the residency program. Those memories will forever remain unique.

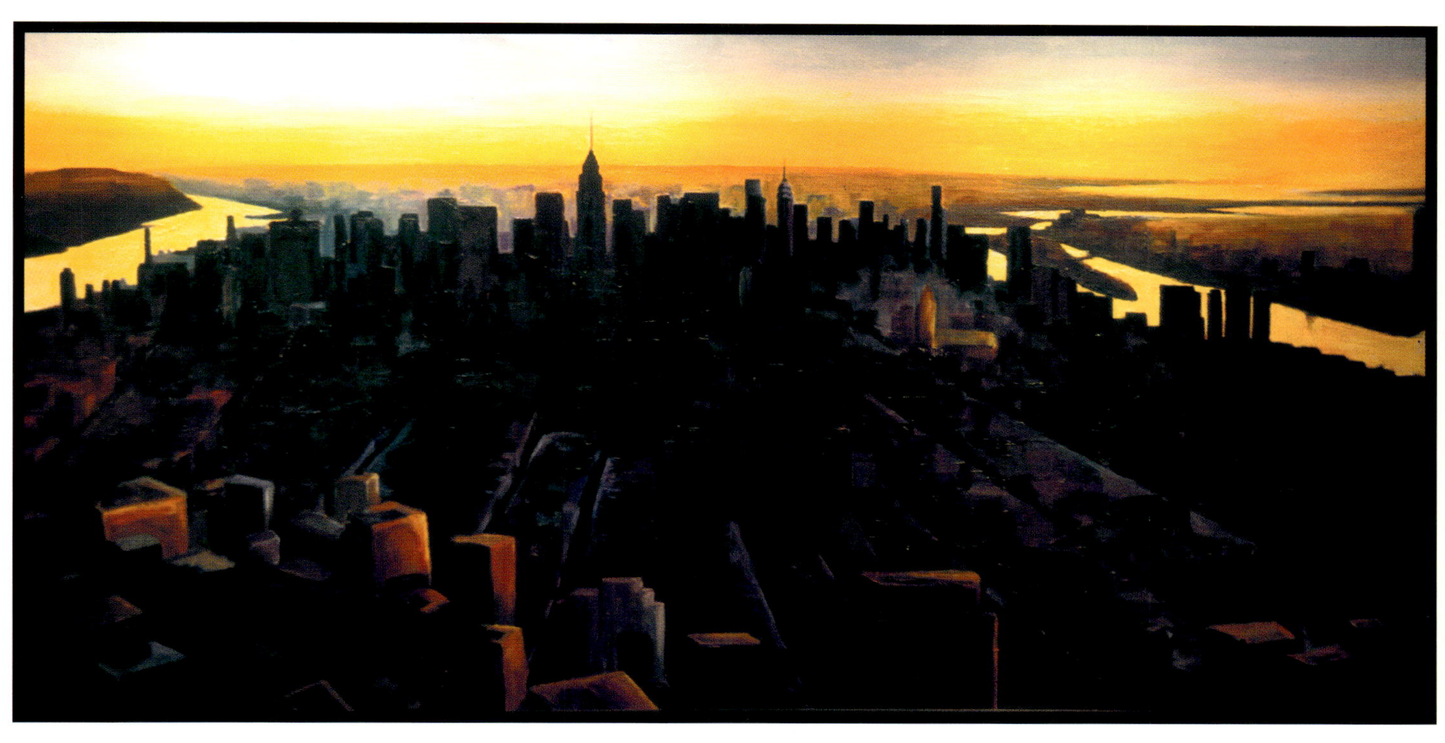

Nedra Newby

Study for WTC Views, 2001
Watercolor
20 x 20 inches
Photo: Adam Reich

Born 1949 in Spokane, Wash.
Lives in New York, N.Y.

Education

1979 The Central School of Art and Design, London, U.K.
1977 MFA, Georgia State University, Atlanta
1974 MA, State University of New York, Albany

Selected Group Exhibitions

2003 *Painting*, New Art Center, New York, N.Y.
2002 *Re-imagining New York,* North Dakota Museum of Art, Grand Forks
Microviews, Municipal Art Society, New York, N.Y.
Selections 24, The Drawing Center, New York, N.Y.
Living in the Shadows, The Bronx River Art Center, The Bronx, N.Y.

Residency

2002 Virginia Center for the Creative Arts, Sweet Briar

Awards

2002 The Pollock-Krasner Foundation, WTC Emergency Grant
1978 Fulbright Fellowship

Drawing: It is hard to describe the views from the World Trade Center. They seemed to be so massive and imposing. Thousands of geometric shapes changed and shifted as the sun's light moved overhead. You could get lost in the intricate geometric pattern created by the landscape of the city. When I don't know where to begin, I draw. I start my search with line. Something automatic happens then shapes start to emerge from the tangled lines. I use drawing to make sense of what I see.

Watercolor: I had to complete this watercolor study from photographs. As I worked from the photos taken from the ninety-first floor I remembered the walk into the building, the ride in the elevator and the faces of people who worked there.

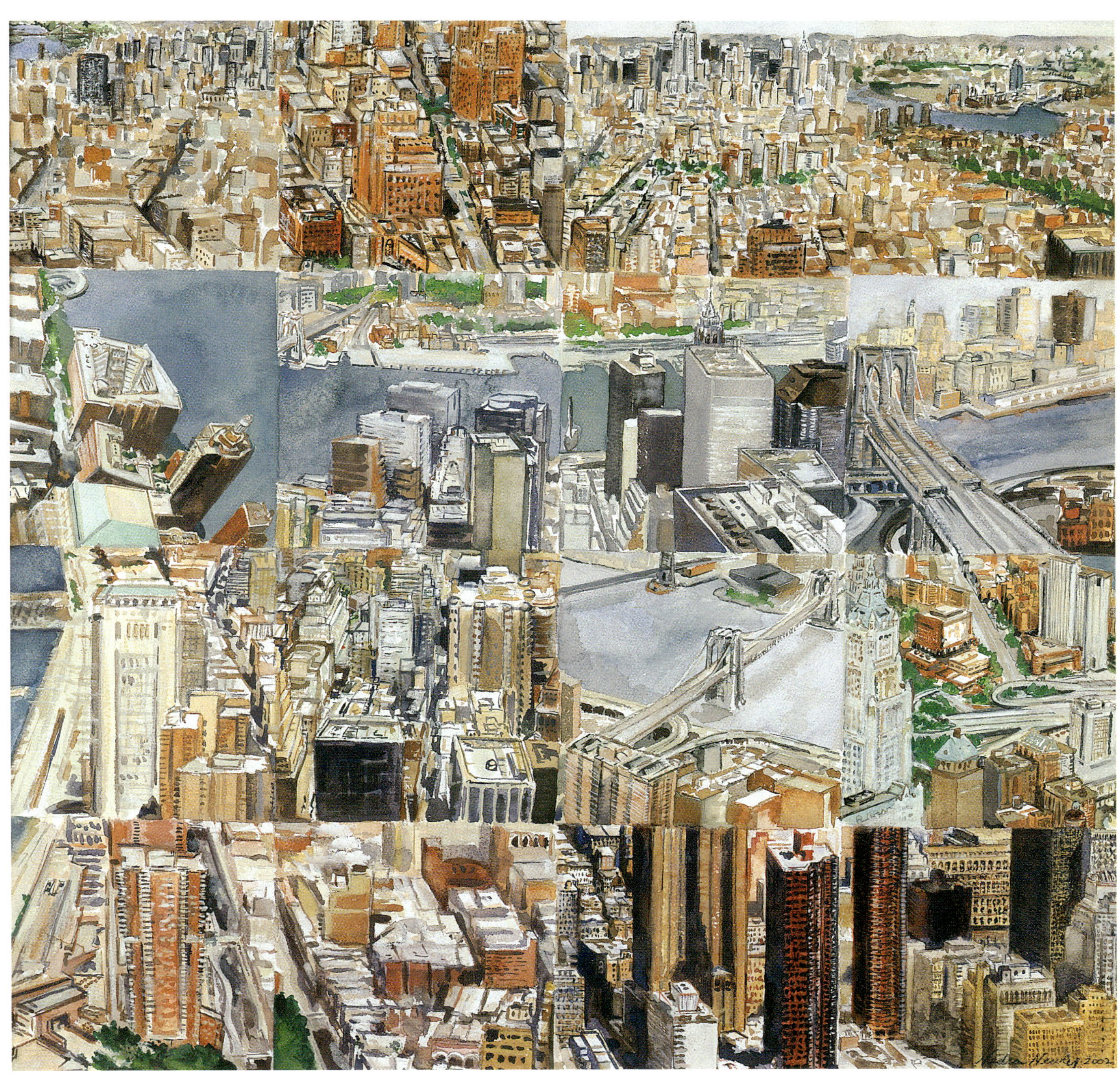

Ocean Earth

Ocean Earth Development Corporation
Documentation of research completed during residency

A generation ago artists in the New York area who were seeking a greater voice in the world began tackling the need of their home city to coexist with nature. This led to campaigns for reviving the coastal marshes, for restoring the flow of nutrients from waste treatment schemes and for bringing back precolonial levels of wild animals. In their way, however, stood an industrial system based on the extraction of minerals from faraway places. In the early '80s, a group of artists formed a business corporation, Ocean Earth, that enacted plans for coexistence with nature based on artistic paradigms; on the works of artists like Dennis Oppenheim, Robert Smithson and Carolee Schneemann. The company focused on repopulating birds and fish in the coastal marshes adjacent to New York—Jamaica Bay, Raritan Meadows and Barnegat Bay, together known as the New York Bight. The LMCC residency enabled Ocean Earth to headquarter their office temporarily in the World Trade Center, where the Port Authority of New York and New Jersey and the Tri-State Regional Planning Commission were located.

Incorporated 1980, New York, N.Y.

Active members:
George Chaikin
Peter Fend, founder and president*
Colleen Fitzgibbon
Ingo Günther
Sara Peschel
Sante Scardillo
Wolfgang Staehle
Taro Suzuki
Eve Vaterlaus
Joan Waltemath

*in residence at WTC

Selected Public Projects & Press Conferences

2004 *Independence from Big Oil: A Renewable Energy Campaign,* Dublin City Council and Fingal County Council, Ireland
2002 *Giant Algae System: At-Sea Harvesting,* Stroom, The Hague, The Netherlands
1991 *Regarding Earthworks under Kuwait Action Plan* (sponsored by Turkish Press Corps), United Nations Correspondents Association, New York, N.Y.
1987 *Regarding Iran-Iraq War UN Scandal* (sponsored by Voice of America and TASS), United Nations Correspondents Association, New York, N.Y.

Selected Exhibitions

2003 Medialab, Madrid, Spain
Zentrum fuer Kunst und Medientechnologie, Karlsruhe, Germany
Palais de Tokyo, Paris, France
1993 *Ocean Earth: For a World Which Works,* Neue Galerie am Landesmuseum Joanneum, Graz, Austria

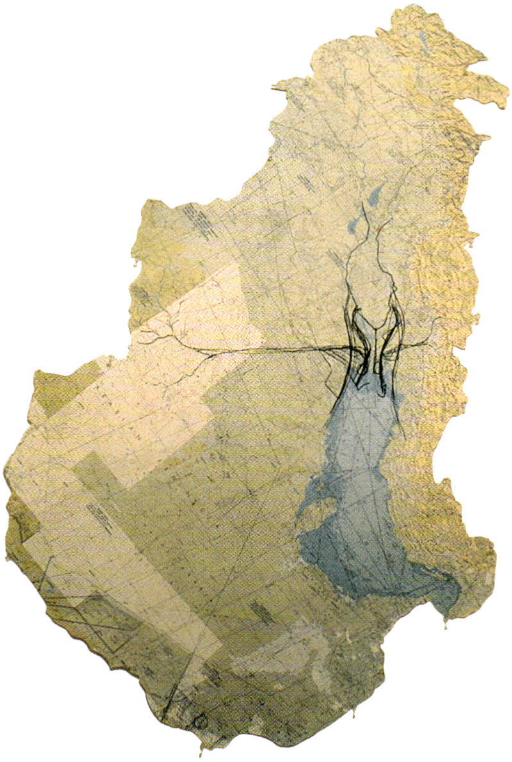

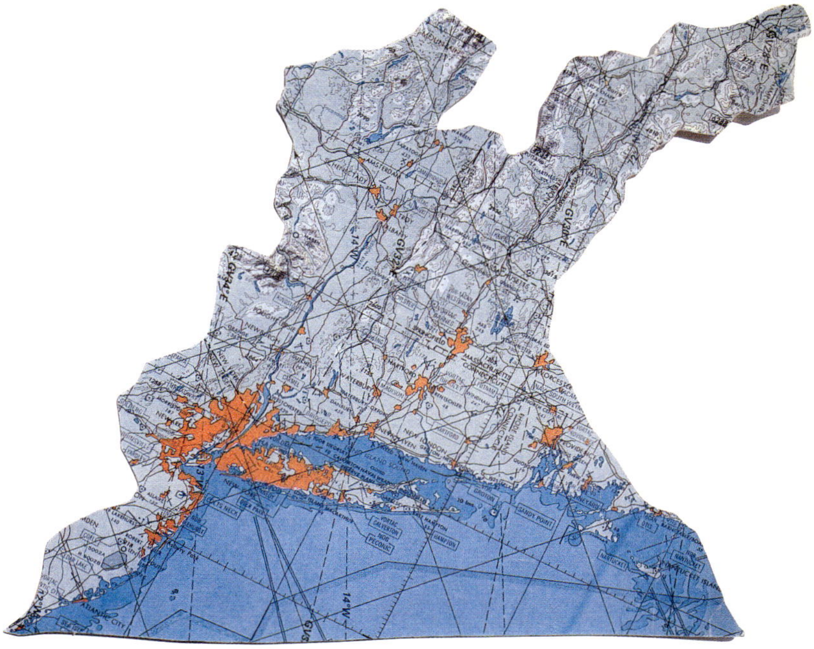

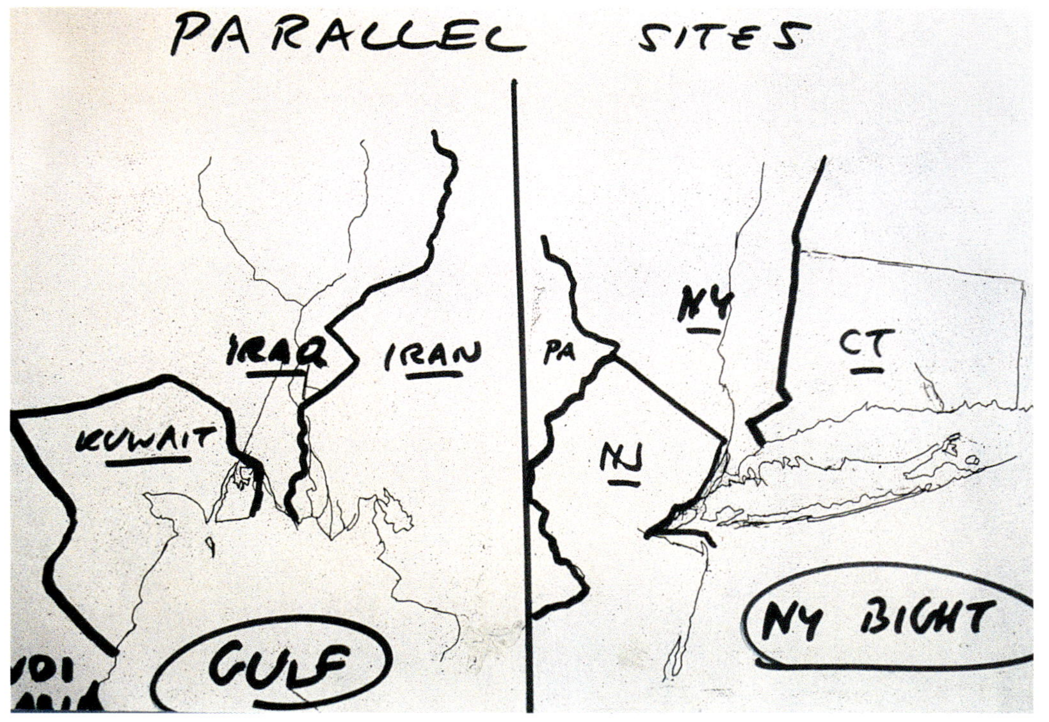
PARALLEL SITES
IRAQ
IRAN
KUWAIT
GULF
PA
NY
CT
NJ
NY BIGHT

Michael Richards

Are You Down?, 2000
Fiberglass, bronze, bonded resin, concrete, Black Beauty sand
3 x 22½ x 22½ feet
Courtesy Franconia Sculpture Park, Shafer, Minn.

Born 1963 in New York, N.Y.
Died 2001 in New York, N.Y.

Education

1992–93 Whitney Museum of American Art Independent Study Program, New York, N.Y.
1991 MA, New York University, N.Y.
1986 BA, Queens College, Flushing, N.Y.

Selected Solo Exhibitions

2000 Ambrosino Gallery, Miami, Fla.
1997 *Recent Work* (two-person show), The Bronx Museum of the Arts, The Bronx, N.Y.

Selected Group Exhibitions

2000 Corcoran Gallery of Art, Washington, D.C.
Passages: Contemporary Art in Transition, The Studio Museum in Harlem, New York, N.Y. (tour)
1998 *Postcards from Black America*, De Beyerd Center for Contemporary Art, Breda, The Netherlands. (tour)
1996 *No Doubt*, The Aldrich Museum, Ridgefield, Conn.

Awards

2000 Franconia Sculpture Park/Jerome Fellowship
1997 National Foundation for Advancement in the Arts Fellowship

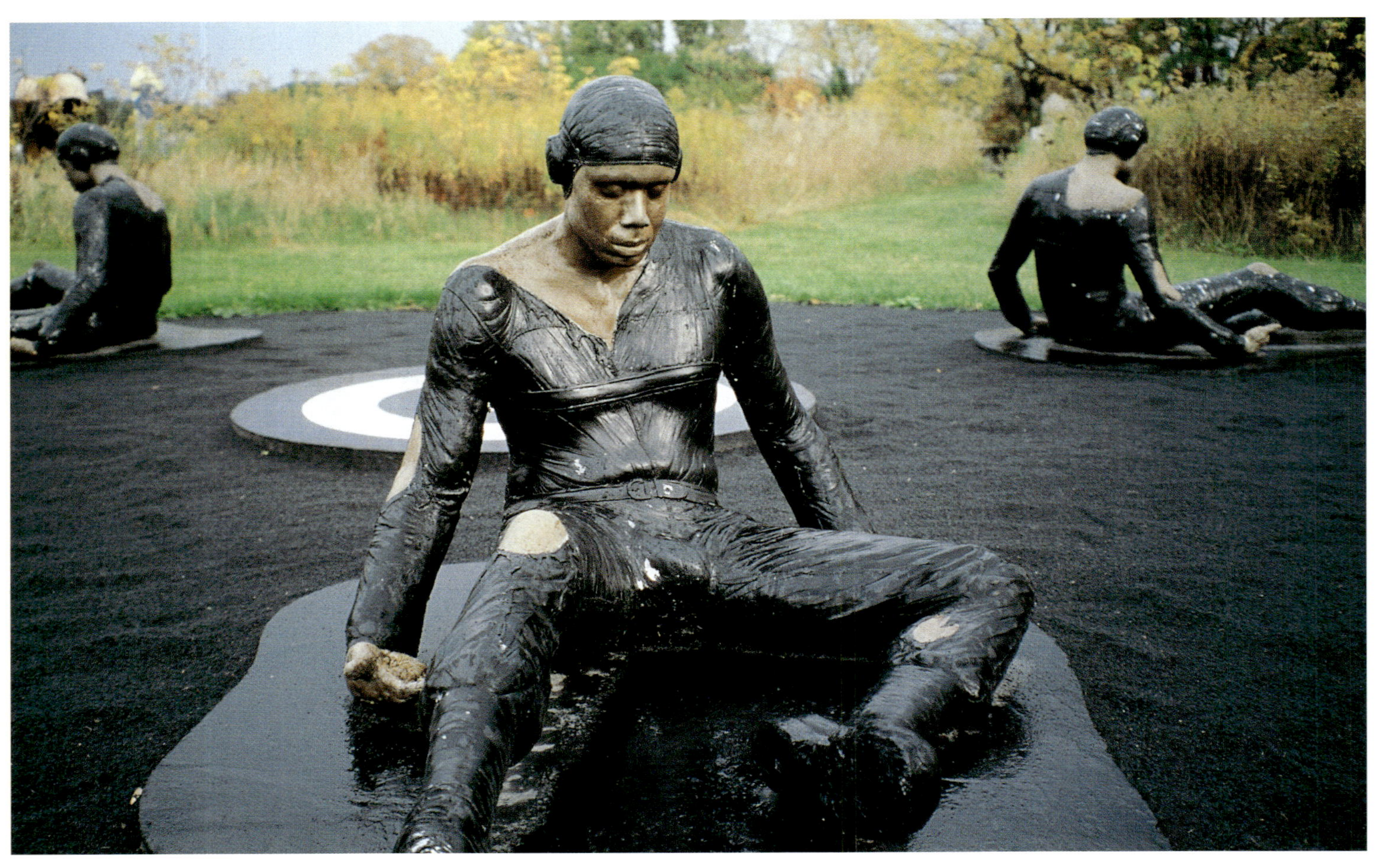

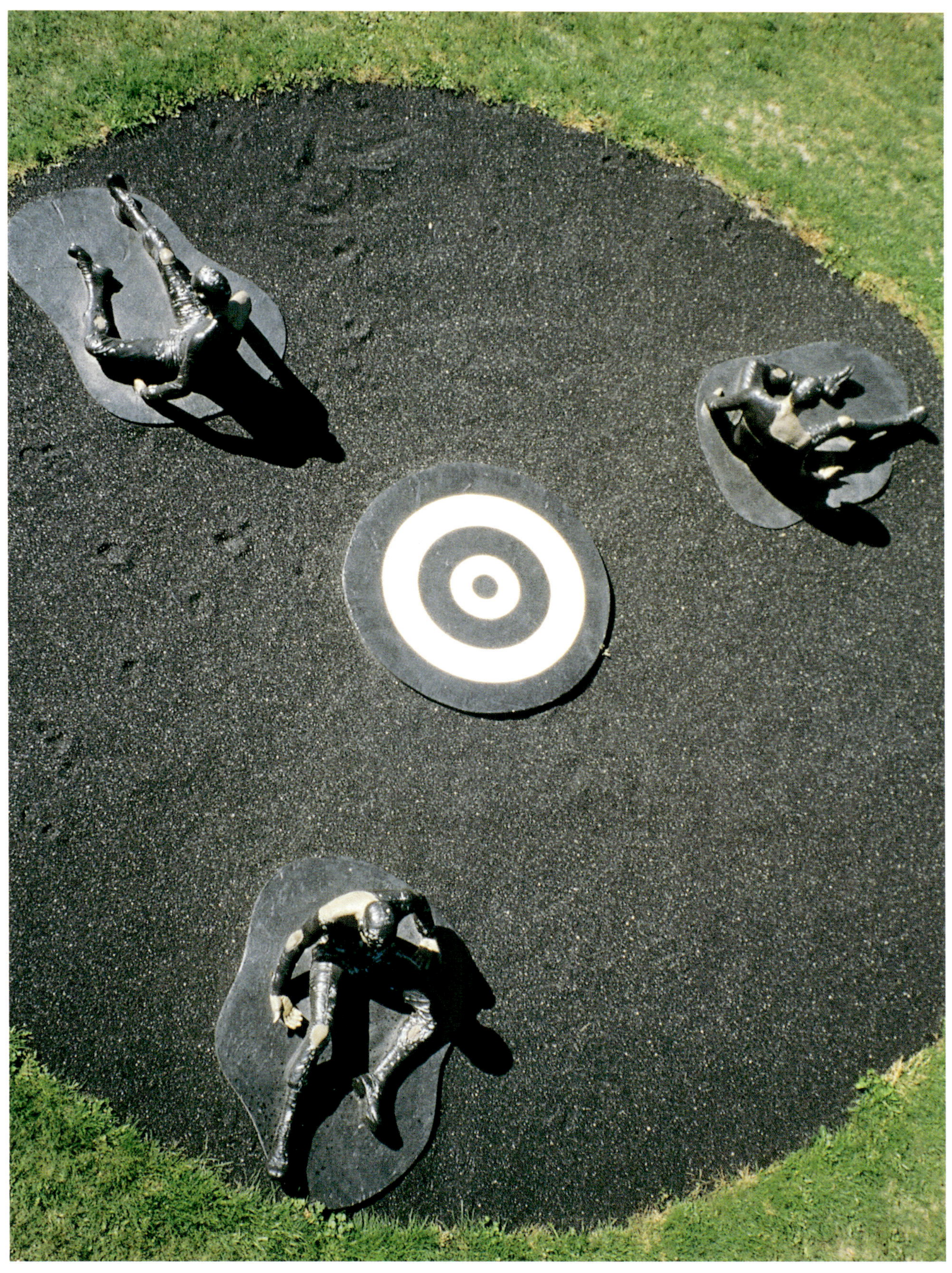

Hyungsub Shin

Silence, 2001
Lens, lightbulb, screen
Dimensions variable

Smash!, 2001
Plastic, metal
12 x 18 inches

Born 1969 in Seoul, Korea
Lives in New York, N.Y.

Education

2000 MFA, School of Visual Arts, New York, N.Y.
1996 BFA, Hong-Ik University, Seoul, Korea

Selected Solo Exhibitions

2002 *INSECTOPHOBIA*, im n il Gallery, Brooklyn, N.Y.
2001 Me Tamorphosis, Washington Square Windows, New York, N.Y.
1996 BODA Gallery, Seoul, Korea

Selected Group Exhibitions

2003 *PASS. AGE. NOW*, Gallery International, Baltimore, Md.
2002 Next*Next Visual Art*, Brooklyn Academy of Music, Brooklyn, N.Y.
SF(Soul of the Future), Seoul Animation Center, Korea
2001 *Spunky*, Exit Art, New York, N.Y.
Bug!, Anchorage Museum of History & Art, Alaska

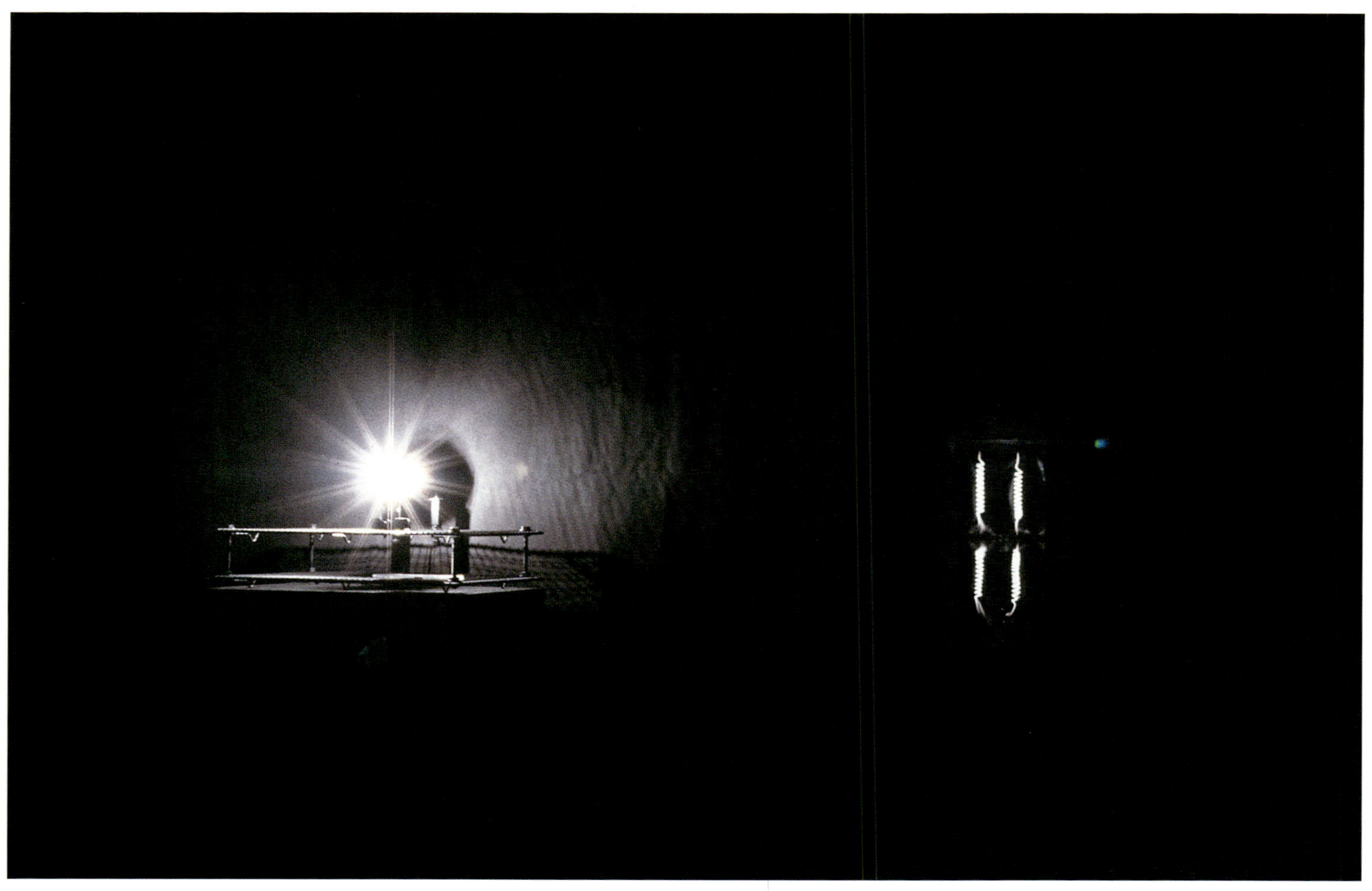

To me, the residency in the World Trade Center does not seem finished yet, and I guess may never. My memories of the building are still clear. I saw a metal thing moving up and down outside cleaning the windows, so many buttons (maybe over a hundred) in a freight elevator, the empty office space where we found broken computers still blinking. I made a low-tech projector with the computer junk. It was ready for Open Studios but the day didn't come.
I still wonder if the window-cleaning machine was automatic or if there was a person with Windex and wipers, and whether the broken computers were working on something.

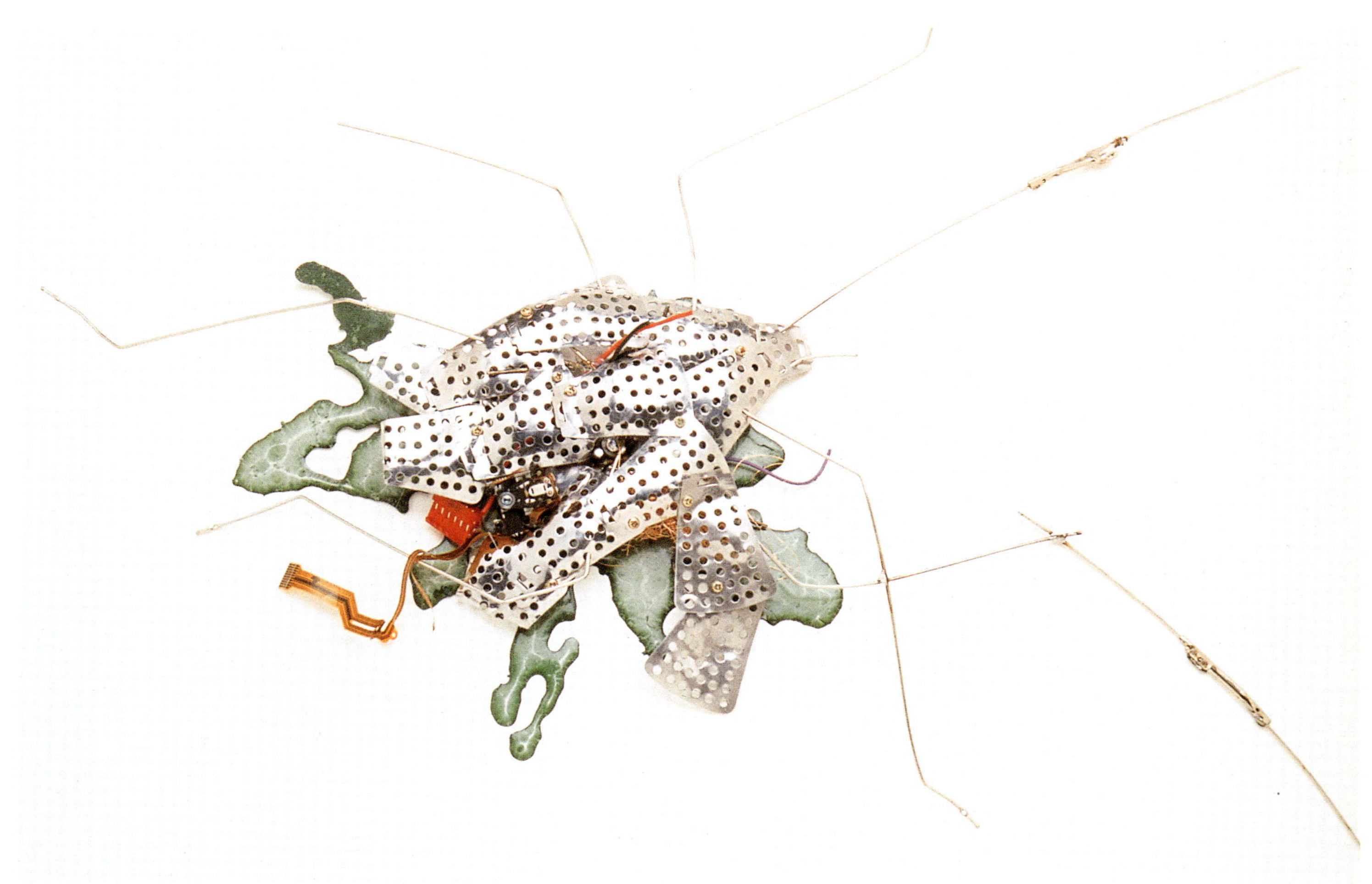

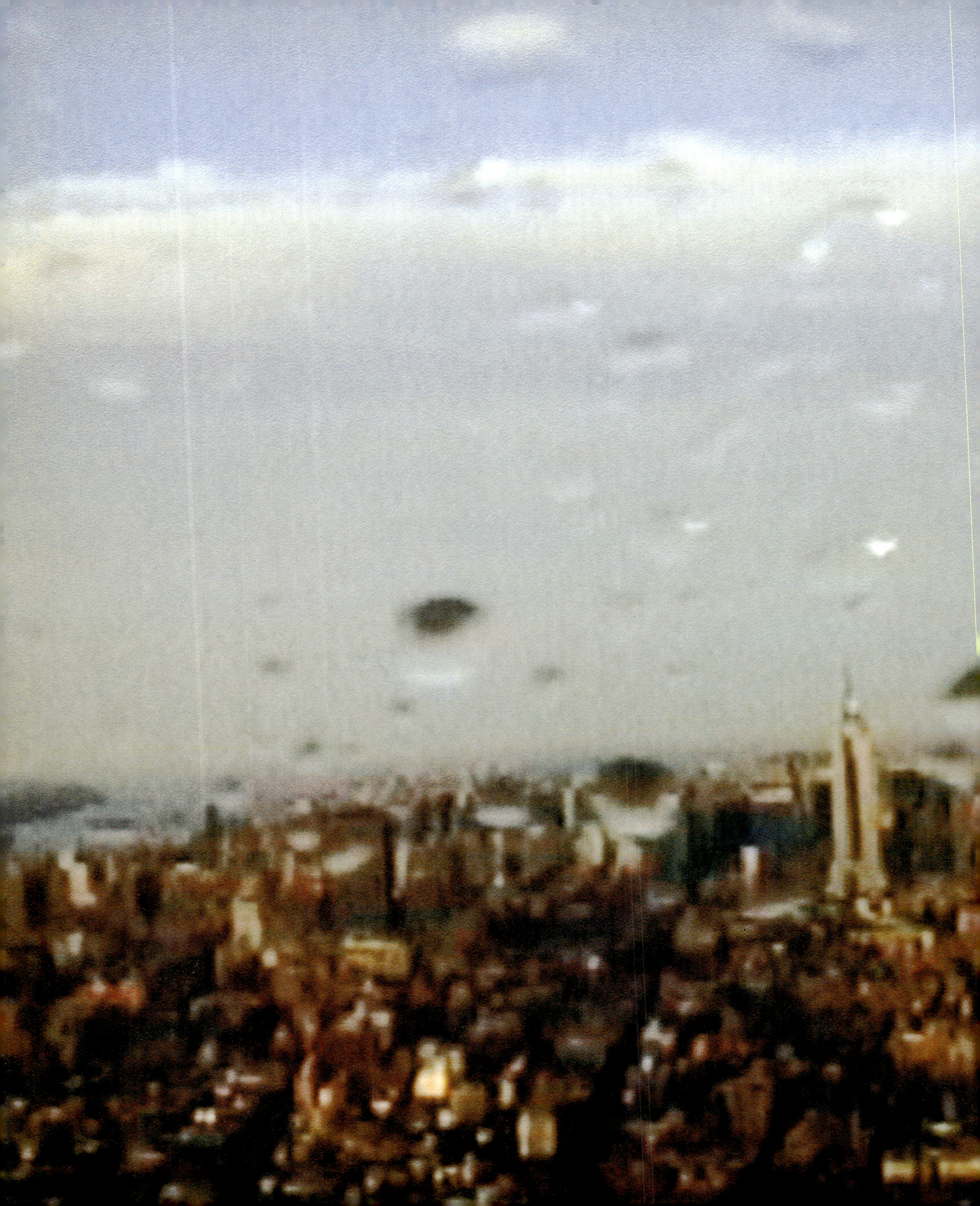

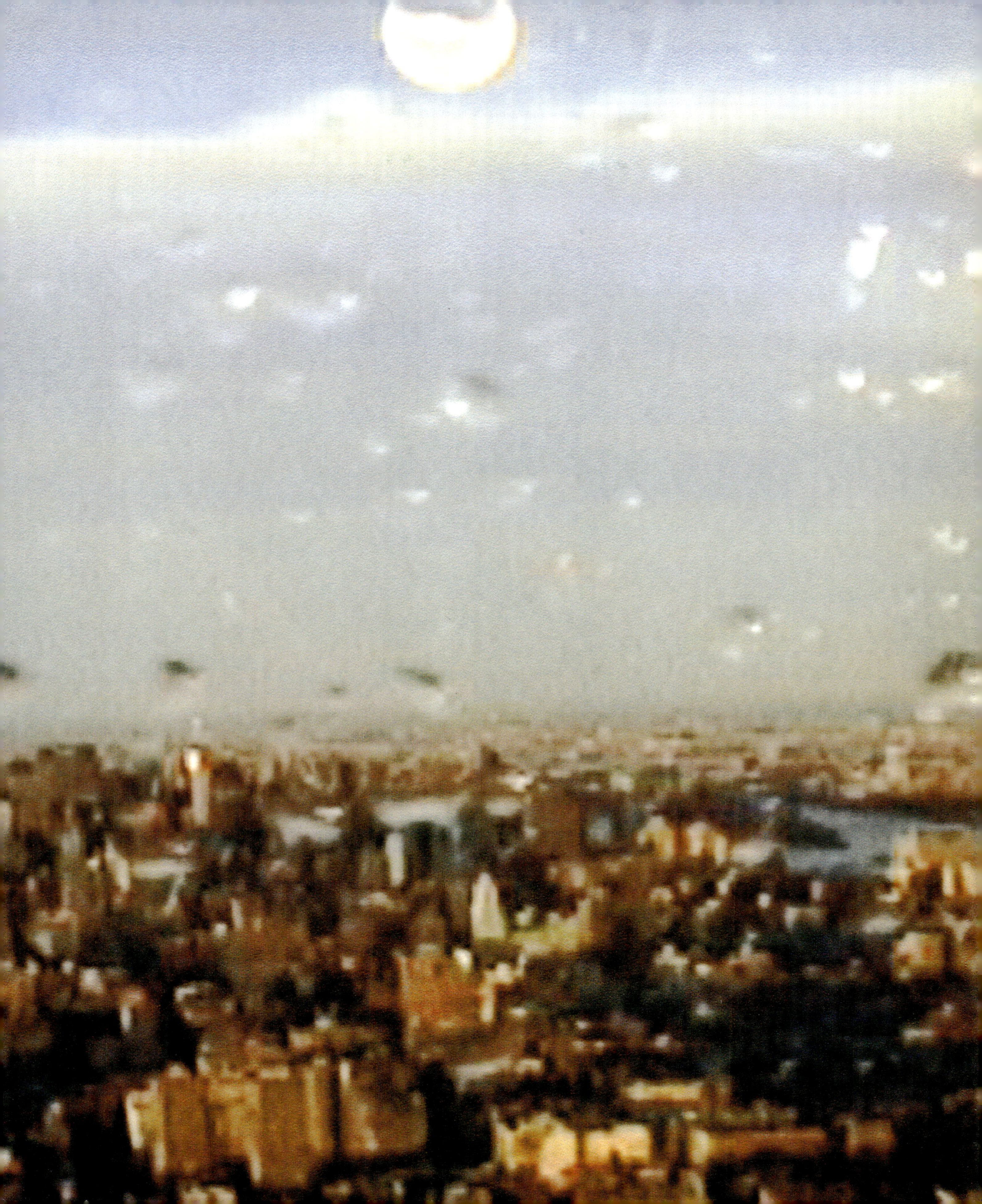

About the Authors

Erin Donnelly is associate director of programs at the Lower Manhattan Cultural Council.

Moukhtar Kocache was the director of visual and media arts initiatives at the Lower Manhattan Cultural Council from 1998 to 2003. He is currently program officer for media, arts and culture, Middle East and North Africa, at the Ford Foundation in Cairo.

Olu Oguibe is associate professor of art, art history and African–American studies at the University of Connecticut. He is a writer, curator and critic, and a former LMCC artist-in-residence at the World Trade Center.

Liz Thompson was executive director of the Lower Manhattan Cultural Council from 1997 to 2003.

Anthony Vidler is dean and professor of architecture at the Irwin S. Chanin School of Architecture, The Cooper Union, New York. His most recent books are *The Architectural Uncanny* and *Warped Space*, both from MIT Press.

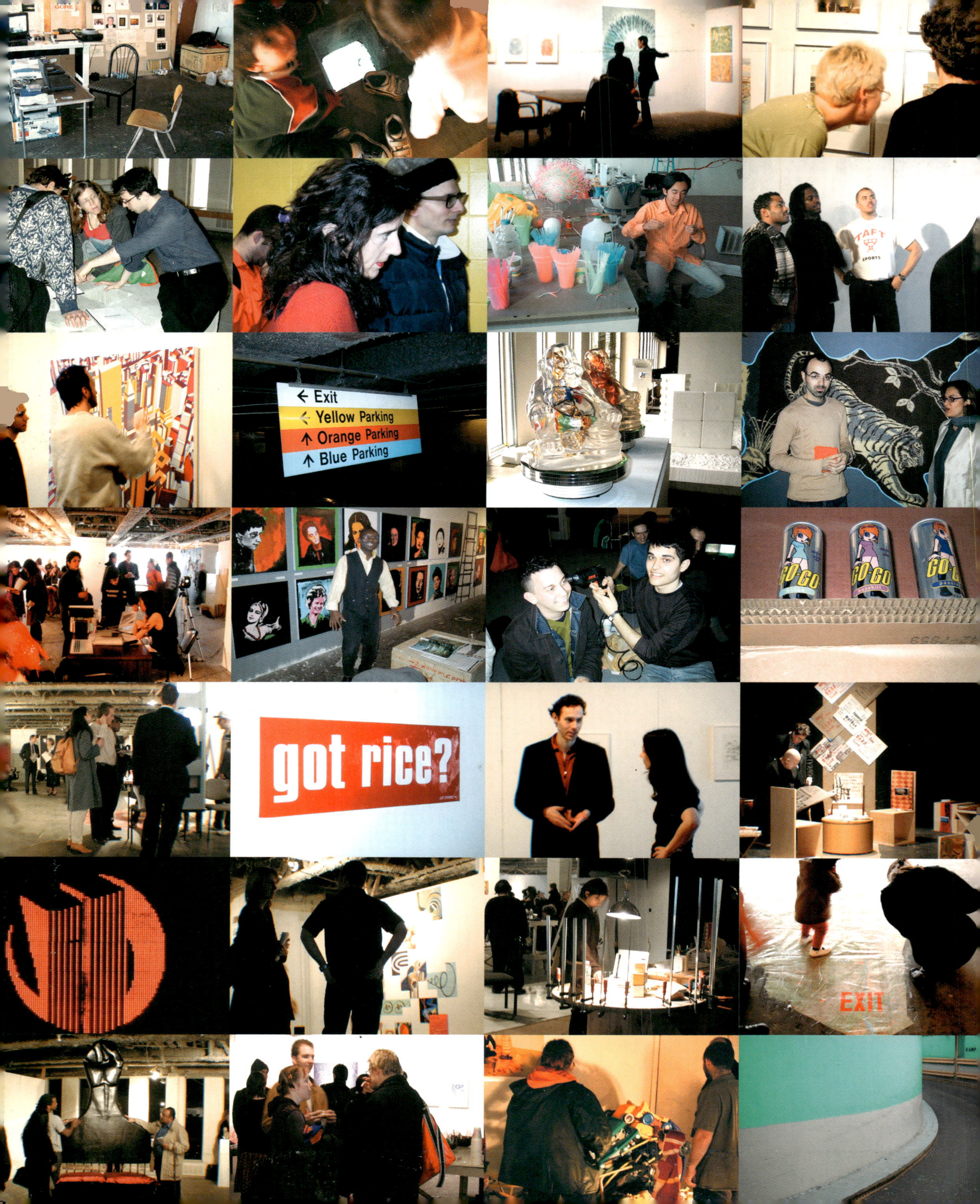
← Exit
← Yellow Parking
↑ Orange Parking
↑ Blue Parking
got rice?
TAFT
SPORTS
GO-GO
GO-GO
EXIT